Fluent
Windows® 8.1
App Development

Rebecca M. Riordan

ASSOCIATE PUBLISHER
Greg Wiegard

EXECUTIVE EDITOR
Loretta Yates

MANAGING EDITOR
Kristy Hart

PROJECT EDITOR
Andy Beaster

INDEXER
Cheryl Lenser

COPY EDITOR
Gill Editorial Services

TECHNICAL EDITOR
James Bodie

PUBLISHING COORDINATOR
Cindy Teeters

COVER DESIGNER
Chuti Prasertsith

COMPOSITION
Rebecca M. Riordan

FLUENT WINDOWS 8.1® APP DEVELOPMENT
Copyright © 2014 by Rebecca M. Riordan

All rights reserved. No part of this book shall be reproduced, stored in a retrieval system, or transmitted by any means, electronic, mechanical, photocopying, recording, or otherwise, without written permission from the publisher. No patent liability is assumed with respect to the use of the information contained herein. Although every precaution has been taken in the preparation of this book, the publisher and author assume no responsibility for errors or omissions. Nor is any liability assumed for damages resulting from the use of the information contained herein.

ISBN-13: 978-0-672-33616-4

ISBN-10: 0-672-33616-2

Library of Congress Control Number: 2014933265

Printed in the United States of America

First Printing July 2014

TRADEMARKS
All terms mentioned in this book that are known to be trademarks or service marks have been appropriately capitalized. Sams Publishing cannot attest to the accuracy of this information. Use of a term in this book should not be regarded as affecting the validity of any trademark or service mark.

The Windlass Lowercase and Brandywine fonts are copyrights of the Scriptorium foundry, www.fontcraft.com.

WARNING AND DISCLAIMER
Every effort has been made to make this book as complete and as accurate as possible, but no warranty or fitness is implied. The information provided is on an "as is" basis. The author and the publisher shall have neither liability nor responsibility to any person or entity with respect to any loss or damages arising from the information contained in this book.

SPECIAL SALES
For information about buying this title in bulk quantities, or for special sales opportunities (which may include electronic versions; custom cover designs; and content particular to your business, training goals, marketing focus, or branding interests), please contact our corporate sales department at corpsales@pearsoned.com or (800) 382-3419.

For government sales inquiries, please contact governmentsales@pearsoned.com.

For questions about sales outside the U.S., please contact international@pearsoned.com.

CONTENTS

Find out how the book works and what you need to use it, and then take a whirlwind tour of Windows 8 development.

GETTING STARTED

- ⓪ Introduction 1
- ① Welcome to Windows 8.1 . 9
- ② The Deep End 43

XAML BASICS

- ③ XAML 83
- ④ Building Blocks 113
- ⑤ XAML Controls, Part I ... 151
- ⑥ XAML Controls, Part II ... 199

Learn how to use XAML to build your UI declaratively.

XAML IN DETAIL

- ⑦ Dependency Properties 239
- ⑧ Events & Input 279
- ⑨ Commanding 309
- ⑩ Text & Graphics 343
- ⑪ Resources, Styles & Templates ... 387
- ⑫ XAML Binding 433

Explore the bits and pieces that really make XAML sing.

WORKING WITH WINDOWS 8

- ⑬ Displaying Your App 477
- ⑭ The Application Lifecycle . . . 529
- ⑮ Tiles & Notifications 555
- ⑯ Files & Capabilities 595
- ⑰ App Contracts 641
- ⑱ Search 677

Learn how to integrate your app with the Windows 8 operating system.

FINAL PROJECT

- ⑲ On Your Own 713
  - Determine the requirements
  - Design the UX
  - Design the Data Structures
  - Create the Graphics Assets
  - Implement the System

Put all you've learned to good use by building a complete application.

WE WANT TO HEAR FROM YOU!

As the reader of this book, you are our most important critic and commentator. We value your opinion and want to know what we're doing right, what we could do better, what areas you'd like to see us publish in, and any other words of wisdom you're willing to pass our way.

We welcome your comments. You can email or write to let us know what you did or didn't like about this book, as well as what we can do to make our books better.

Please note that we cannot help you with technical problems related to the topic of this book.

When you write, please be sure to include this book's title and author as well as your name and email address. We will carefully review your comments and share them with the author and editors who worked on the book.

Email: consumer@samspublishing.com

Mail: Sams Publishing
         ATTN: Reader Feedback
         800 East 96th Street
         Indianapolis, IN 46240 USA

READER SERVICES

Visit our website and register this book at informit.com/register for convenient access to any updates, downloads, or errata that might be available for this book.

Welcome! I'm so glad you stopped by.

This book doesn't look much like other technical tutorials, does it? Well, for once, looks aren't deceiving, because Fluent Learning books aren't much like other technical tutorials. **We don't want to teach you things. We want to help you learn things.** We've done a lot of research into how people learn, and it turns out that talk, talk, talking at you (like most books do) isn't wrong, exactly, but it makes learning harder than it needs to be.

Did you learn to speak your native language by reading a book? Of course not; that's not how people learn. You heard people speaking, tried it for yourself, and then corrected yourself when other people pointed out your mistakes. Sure, you studied grammar and learned new words in school, but the basics ("More milk, Mommy") **you learned by yourself**. Now, barring accident and illness (or one-too-many mojitos), you're not likely to forget it, are you? And you don't have to think about the mechanics of speech, just what you want to say.

That's really how we learn everything. We gather some initial information, practice, correct our mistakes, and then add to our basic knowledge. That's not what happens in most tutorials, but that's how Fluent Learning works. I'll give you enough information to get started, give you some exercises to figure out how to do something, and then elaborate on what you've learned. Simple, natural, and **if you do the work, you will learn.** Soon you'll be able to concentrate on what you want to do, not how to do it, just like when you learned to speak. (But it won't take as long as learning to speak well.)

1

FLUENT LEARNING BECAUSE...

WE WANT TO LEARN, NOT LISTEN

Our minds like to learn anything the way we learned our native language: by trial & error. Instead of reading a lot of words, you'll do a lot of exercises. Real exercises, that make you think, not walkthroughs that tell you what to type. (But we'll have a few of those, too.)

PUT ON YOUR THINKING HAT

Can you write the code to set a Color named MyColor to each of the following colors?

A pure blue at 50% transparency

A purple with R=127, G=68 and B=182, fully opaque

The color named CadetBlue in the Colors class, which has R=95, G=158, and B=160, with 75% transparency

WE WANT TO WORK, NOT PASS TESTS

You want to be able to apply what you learn in the real world, not just pass a test on the subject. To help you do that, the On Your Own exercises invite you to make those connections as part of the learning process.

ON YOUR OWN

Can you think of situations in which each of the panels might be useful as a layout root?

WE'RE ARTISTS, NOT FREIGHT TRAINS

Our minds don't chug along from point A to point B on a single track. Like any artist, we start with a sketch and then fill in the details. Rather than presenting all the information about a topic at one time, we'll start simply and add the details as you have more context. That way they'll stick.

WE THINK IN PATTERNS, NOT STRAIGHT LINES

Our minds work best with patterns, not individual facts. We'll always present new ideas in context to help you understand how all the pieces fit together.

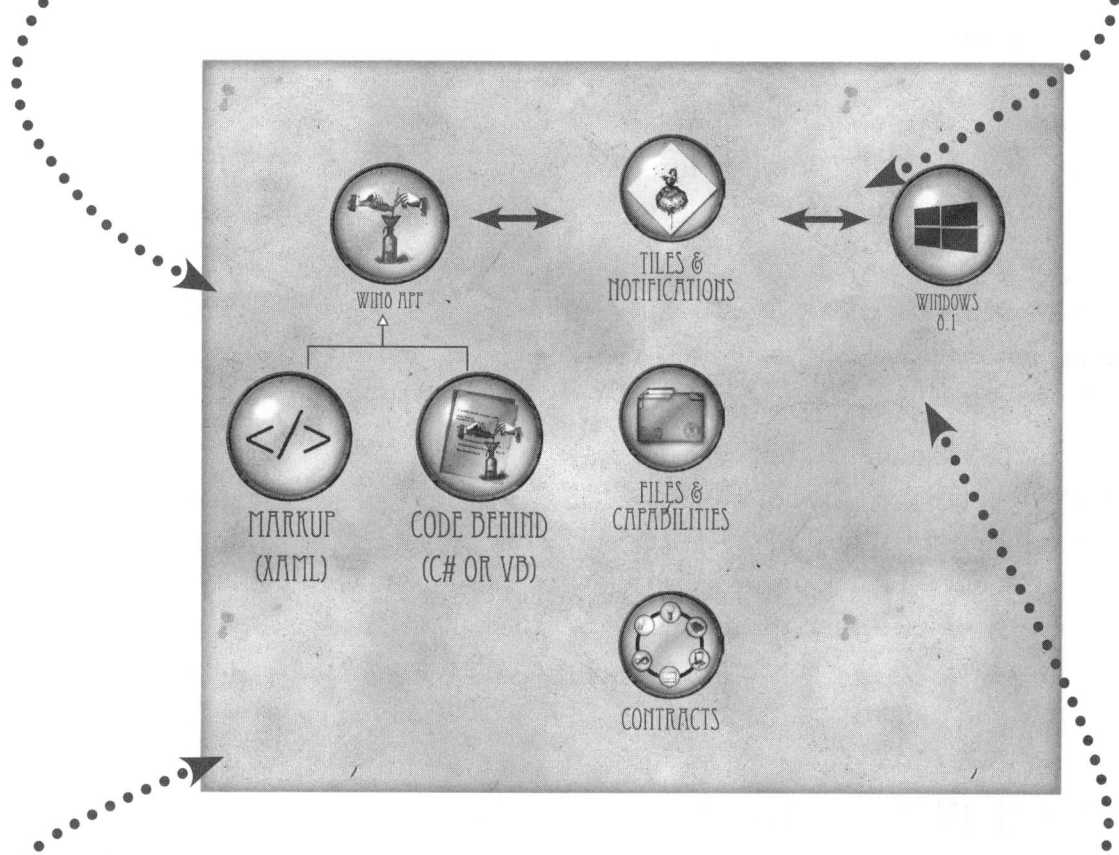

WE DON'T LIVE IN A WORLD OF WORDS

Our minds absorb information through all our senses, not just speech. We'll use graphics, context, and rhythmic language to appeal to sight, touch, and sound.

WE WANT A MAP, NOT A MYSTERY

Our minds are constantly evaluating progress, but that's not possible unless we know where we're going. We'll use lots of signposts so you always know where you are and where you're headed.

THIS BOOK ISN'T FOR EVERYONE

I really hate it when technical books announce that they're for "everyone", don't you? It can't possibly be true, and saying that it is doesn't sell any more books in the long run. It just irritates people who get confused (because the book's too advanced for them) or bored (because the book's too basic). I don't want to irritate or bore you, so I'll say it plainly: This book isn't for everyone.

THIS BOOK IS FOR YOU IF:

- You want to learn how to develop for Microsoft's new Windows 8.1 platform, and...

- You've done at least a little .NET programming, even if you've never used WPF or Silverlight, and...

- You want to program in C# or Visual Basic. (To keep the book size manageable, many of the examples are only in C#, but I'll tell you when Visual Basic is very different, and the sample code downloads are available in both languages.)

THIS BOOK PROBABLY ISN'T FOR YOU IF:

- You've never worked with .NET at all. .NET programming is big and complex, so you'll probably want to start with a basic tutorial. (There are two in the Fluent series...hint, hint, nudge, nudge...)

- You want to develop using JavaScript. I'll only be talking about development using C# and Visual Basic.

- You're going to be writing desktop applications. This book concentrates on the new Windows 8.1 Store applications, and the two platforms are still pretty distinct.

THIS BOOK MIGHT BE FOR YOU IF:

- You're a WPF or Silverlight wizard and just looking for the differences between those platforms and developing Windows Store applications. You'll find that information here, but you might find yourself a bit bored looking for it.

- You want to write the next Adobe Photoshop. This book will give you the basic information you'll need about the XAML part of an app like that, but to do something that low level effectively, you'll need to work in DirectX too, and we won't be talking about that toolkit.

WHAT YOU'LL LEARN

You and I both know that you won't be an expert Windows 8.1 developer after reading one book, no matter how good it might be. You won't be an expert after reading two books, or three, or a dozen. Of course, a good book can help, but the only way to build real expertise is to write a bunch of applications, make a bunch of mistakes, and fix them. It takes time and experience, and I can't give you that. But I can get you started.

AFTER YOU FINISH THIS BOOK YOU WILL:

- Be able to create a user interface for a Windows 8.1 store app declaratively using XAML
- Be familiar with the WinRT XAML UI widgets and how to control and customize them
- Understand the Windows 8 touch language
- Know how to provide live updates to your users via Tiles and Notifications
- Cooperate with other Metro applications via contracts and extensions

BUT YOU WON'T:

- Be an expert in XAML programming (unless you already are one)
- Be a graphic designer—although we'll be discussing some design issues, this book isn't a substitute for art school
- Know everything you need to know to sell your applications in the Windows Store. In fact, we won't be talking about selling your apps through the Store at all, because it's both pretty straightforward and a moving target.

WHAT YOU'LL NEED

You don't need much to get started. This book, of course. (You did buy this copy, didn't you?) And a copy of Visual Studio Express 2013 for Windows. You'll also need something to write with, because not all of the exercises are done at the computer, and you might want a notebook of some kind if you don't like writing in books.

You'll also need a machine running Windows 8.1. It doesn't have to have touch capability (although that's very cool, of course).

GETTING VISUAL STUDIO 2013

There are several different levels of Visual Studio. If you've already bought and installed a copy, you're good to go. If you haven't, you can use the free Visual Studio Express 2013 for Windows, which you can download from the Microsoft Web site. Here's what you need to do on the day I'm writing this, but Microsoft has been known to move things around, so be forewarned: You may have to hunt around a bit.

1. From the main Microsoft Web site (www.microsoft.com), choose Visual Studio from the Products menu.

2. Click the "download" link that will be somewhere on the page. (They change this landing page a lot, so you may have to hunt for it.)

3. Choose Visual Studio Express 2013 for Windows. Just follow the instructions on the page to download. When you install Visual Studio, you'll also get the Expression Blend design tool. We'll be talking about Blend a little bit in Chapter 10.

4. The first time you launch the product, you'll be asked to register it (once you register online you'll be given a product key) and to get a developer license. The developer license is free, but you'll need to renew it periodically. (If you want to pubish an app in the Store, you'll need a developer account that does cost money. The exact amount varies depending on your type of account, so check the Microsoft site for details if that's what you want to do.)

GETTING THE SOURCE CODE

You won't need to download the source code in order to do the exercises in this book, but it's available on the Web at informit.com/title/9780672336164

HOW IT WORKS

If you've read this far, you already know that you're not going to be able to just sit back and listen to me talk at you. The core of this book is the exercises, and if you're going to learn, you'll need to work through them. Really do them. You can't just think about the answers. You need to sit down at the computer or pick up your pencil and do the work. Here's a taste of some of the things you'll be doing:

THE THINKING HAT

Most of the exercises in the book tell you to Put on Your Thinking Hat. I'll give you answers to these exercises, but it's really important to understand that you won't always get the answers completely right, and **that's okay**. It doesn't mean you're not "getting it". It means that I don't always play fair, because you learn as much (or more) from your mistakes.

ON YOUR OWN

Some exercises ask you to do things on your own, and I won't give you the answers. Sometimes there really aren't answers; they're just things you need to think about. It might be tempting to put these aside for "later", but it's best if you don't. They're part of the learning process.

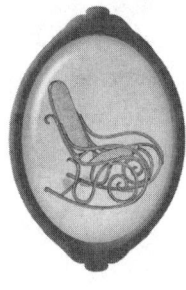

TAKE A BREAK

From time to time I'll suggest that you take a break before you move on to the next section. Of course you can take breaks whenever you like, but these suggestions aren't because I think you might be getting tired. I make these suggestions because learning research tells us that if you stop for 15 minutes or so before you review, you're much more likely to transfer information to long-term memory. (In other words, you'll actually learn it.)

WELCOME TO WINDOWS 8.1

On the first of June, 2011, Microsoft posted a "First Look" video on YouTube in which Jensen Harris, Director of Product Management for the Windows User Experience, implied that applications for the new Windows 8 platform (codenamed "Metro") could only be written in HTML and JavaScript. Microsoft, for reasons known only to itself, refused to comment.

To say that the video set off a firestorm is something of an understatement. Developers all over the world canceled new XAML projects and started reconsidering their career choices. (Can you imagine how frustrating that must have been for the WinRT XAML team inside Microsoft?) Even when the Developer Preview reassured all of us that our existing XAML and .NET skills would translate to the new environment, well, let's just say that the response wasn't (and still isn't) uniformly enthusiastic. Some people have decided that the Windows 8 Start Screen is inappropriate for non-touch systems (it took about 2.3 milliseconds for someone to post a registry hack that allows you to boot Windows 8 directly to the desktop), and others believe that the platform is only suitable for toy applications on tablets.

Perhaps they're right. Or perhaps as developers and application designers, we just need to think differently about how we structure our applications. But one thing is certain—Microsoft is a major player, and that makes Windows 8 too big to ignore. But since you're reading this, you know that. I hope this book will help you make up your own mind.

In this chapter, we'll start by taking a look at the Windows 8.1 platform. We'll try to assign some tangible meaning to those marketing terms Microsoft is using to describe its "re-imagined Windows", and we'll look at some of the functionality that Windows 8.1 gives you for free.

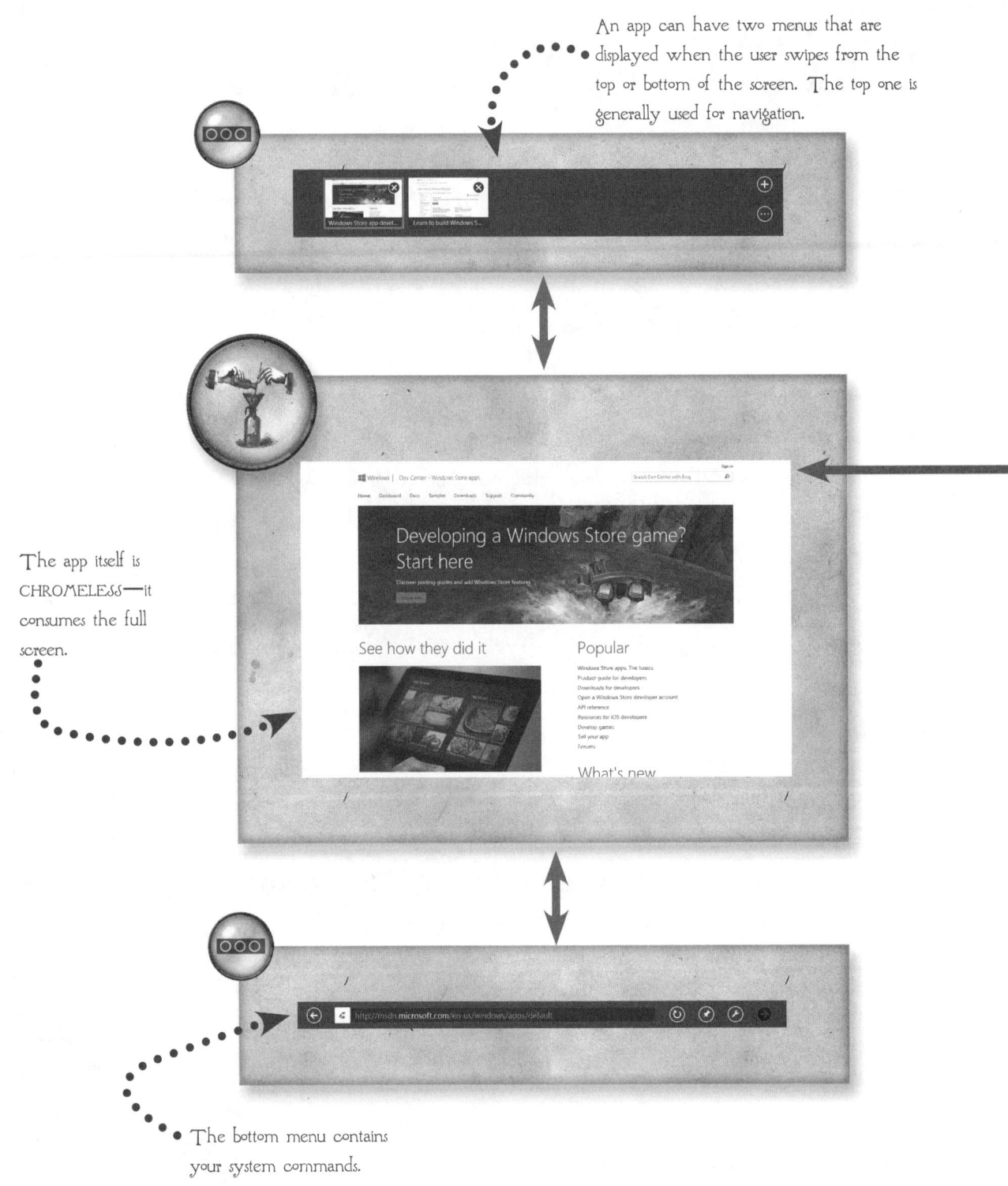

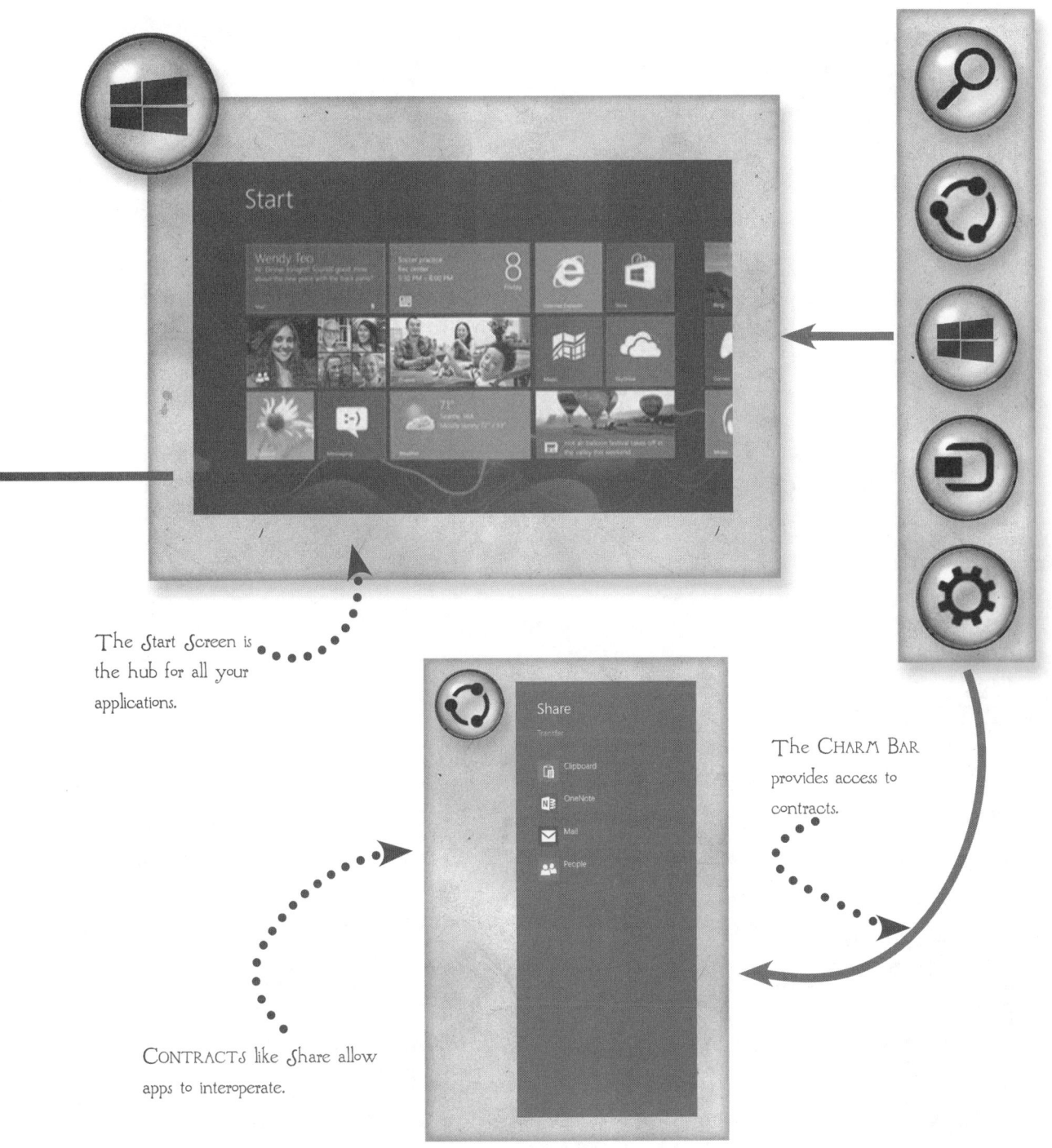

The Start Screen is the hub for all your applications.

The CHARM BAR provides access to contracts.

CONTRACTS like Share allow apps to interoperate.

ON YOUR OWN

Before we get started, why don't you take a few minutes to list some applications you'd like to develop (or port) as a Windows 8.1 app? We'll come back to this list at various points in the book, but for right now, just describe them briefly, and spend a little time thinking about why they're appropriate for this environment.

-
-
-

WORDS FOR THE WISE

Until just a few months before its release, the two styles of Windows 8 applications were called "Metro" and "Desktop". With release, the UI-Platform-Formerly-Known-As-Metro is now officially called "Windows 8 Store-Style". Doesn't exactly roll off the tongue, does it? I'm just going to call them "Win8 apps" and refer to the other style as a "desktop application".

TASK LIST

In this chapter we'll take a first look at the Windows 8.1 interface so that we'll know what we're getting into when we start exploring the development process in the next chapter.

A QUICK TOUR

We'll start by taking a quick tour of the Windows 8.1 operating system. You've probably already given yourself a tour, but you might have missed some things, or you might not know what they're called, so we'll run through it again so we have a common vocabulary when we start development.

THE CHARACTERISTICS OF A WIN8 APP

Of course, Win8 apps *look* different, but it's a little more complicated than that. So after we've seen how Win8 apps fit into Windows 8.1, we'll take a look at what makes them different from desktop applications. (It isn't just the lack of chrome!)

WHAT YOU GET FOR FREE

Learning a new platform or technology always requires climbing (yet another) learning curve. Even if you're coming from another XAML platform, you'll need to learn the Win8 environment and get your head around the limitations that Win8 places on your development. And if you're new to XAML, you'll need to learn that, too. Is it worth it? At the end of the chapter, we'll take a look at what you get in exchange. You might be surprised to see how many tedious development tasks Win8 takes off your shoulders.

A QUICK TOUR

You might think that Windows 8.1 doesn't add a whole lot of brand new functionality. After all, we've always had a way to log on, some way to start an application, and Windows has always provided common dialogs for things like opening a file.

As we'll see when we get into the details of Win8 app development in the rest of the book, you can ignore a lot of the differences. You can treat the live tile that represents your application on the Start Screen just like a shortcut. You can design the application app bar the same way you design menu bars in a desktop application. But I don't recommend it.

You've probably had the experience of using an application that was obviously ported from a different environment. Even if it complies with the "letter of the law" for the Windows UI, if it doesn't comply with the spirit, it just doesn't feel right. And if you're like me, you only use it until something more comfortable comes along.

I'm sure you don't want that to happen to your applications, so you can think of this chapter as the first step in understanding what's required to build a Win8 app that *feels* like a Win8 app. One that takes advantage of the unique functionality that Windows 8.1 provides. We'll start here with a tour of the operating system. We'll come back to the subject throughout the rest of the book, so you can also think of this chapter as a preview of coming attractions. Just remember...

As always, the devil's in the details...

14

ON YOUR OWN

Before we start our tour, can you name the Windows 8.1 equivalents of these Window 7 components and identify the differences and benefits of the Windows 8.1 version?

What is the Windows 8.1 equivalent of the login screen?

Does the Windows 8.1 version provide any additional functionality?

Windows 8.1 still provides a desktop, but does the Start Screen provide equivalents to the circled items?

If so, do they provide any additional functionality?

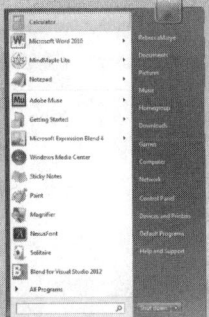

What is the Windows 8.1 equivalent of the Start Menu?

Does the Windows 8.1 version provide any additional functionality?

15

THE LOCK SCREEN

The Windows 8.1 version of the login screen is called the LOCK SCREEN. In addition to providing three different ways to log on to the computer, it also provides live updates from applications the user chooses. When the user signs in with a Microsoft ID, Windows 8.1 provides synchronization between all their devices.

Users can choose to display updates from applications on the lock screen.

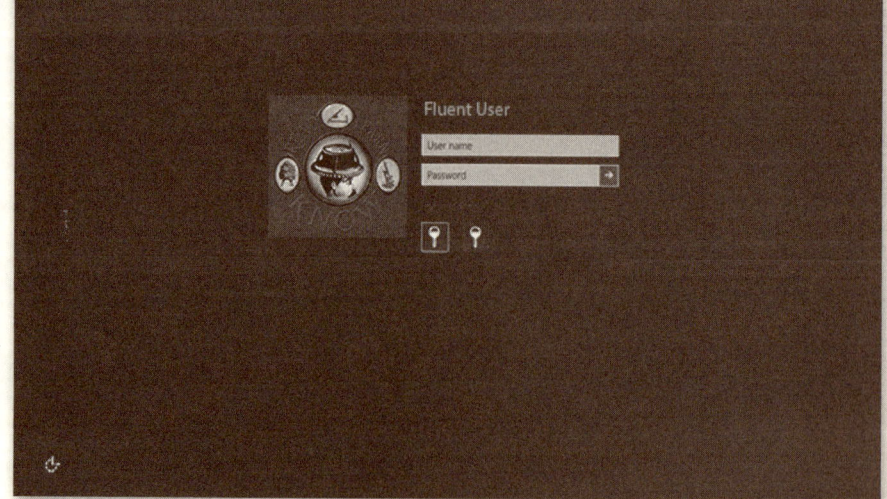

The user can log in with a PIN, a password, or gestures on a picture.

THE START SCREEN

Like a shortcut on the Windows 7 desktop or an item in the Windows 7 start menu, the Windows 8.1 START SCREEN provides a way for users to run an application, but unlike a shortcuts Windows 8.1 LIVE TILES aren't static: We'll explore live tiles in Chapter 15.

Visual Studio provides templates for creating small, medium, and large tiles.

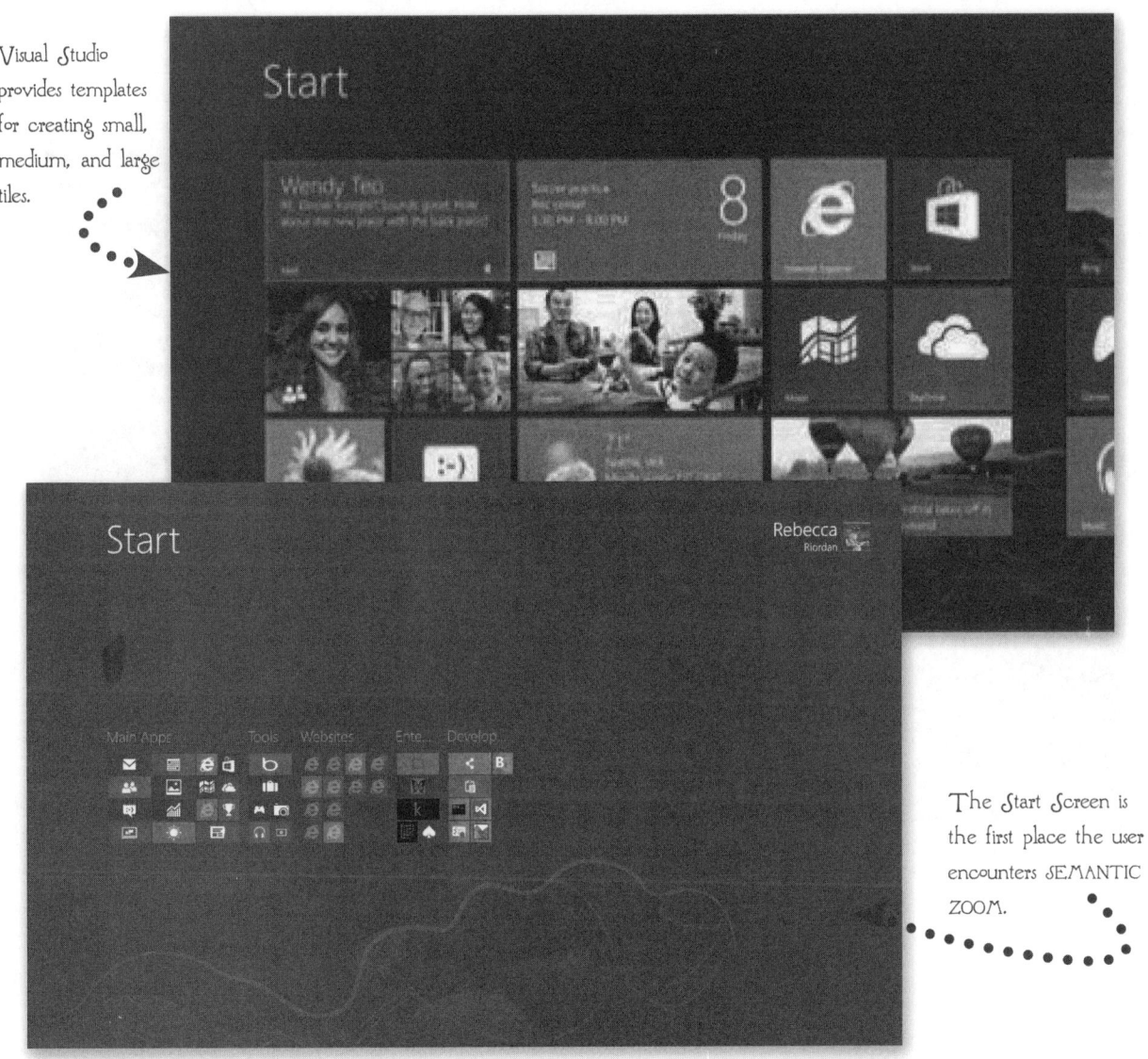

The Start Screen is the first place the user encounters SEMANTIC ZOOM.

17

SEMANTIC ZOOM

Windows 8.1 is, of course, a touch-first operating system, and the widget that exemplifies that focus is the `SemanticZoom` control.

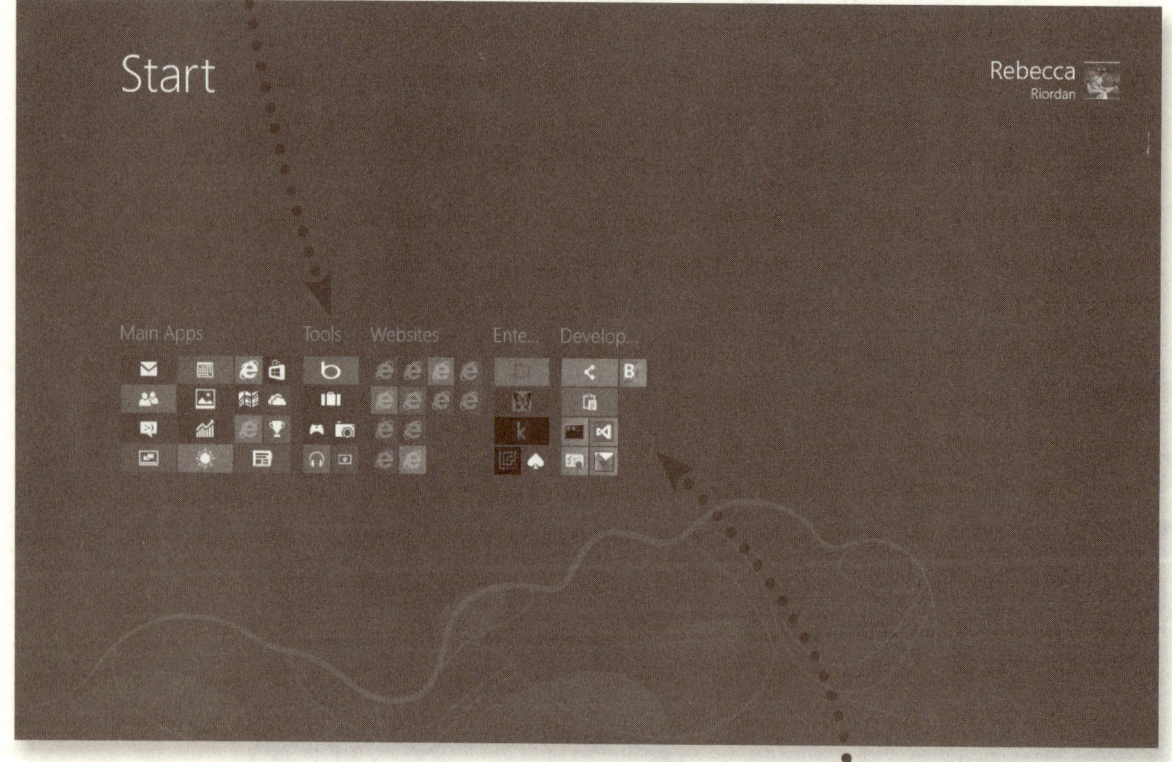

Semantic zoom doesn't just make things smaller; it allows users to think at a different (semantic) level.

The zoomed-out level of a `SemanticZoom` control allows users to quickly navigate to the item they're looking for.

CHARMS

To my mind, one of the most exciting—and challenging—things about Win8 apps is the way that they interoperate, making it possible to share data and functionality in whole new ways. The key to that is the CHARM BAR that is displayed when the user swipes from the side of the screen. We'll be exploring the charm bar and how your app can work with it in Chapter 17.

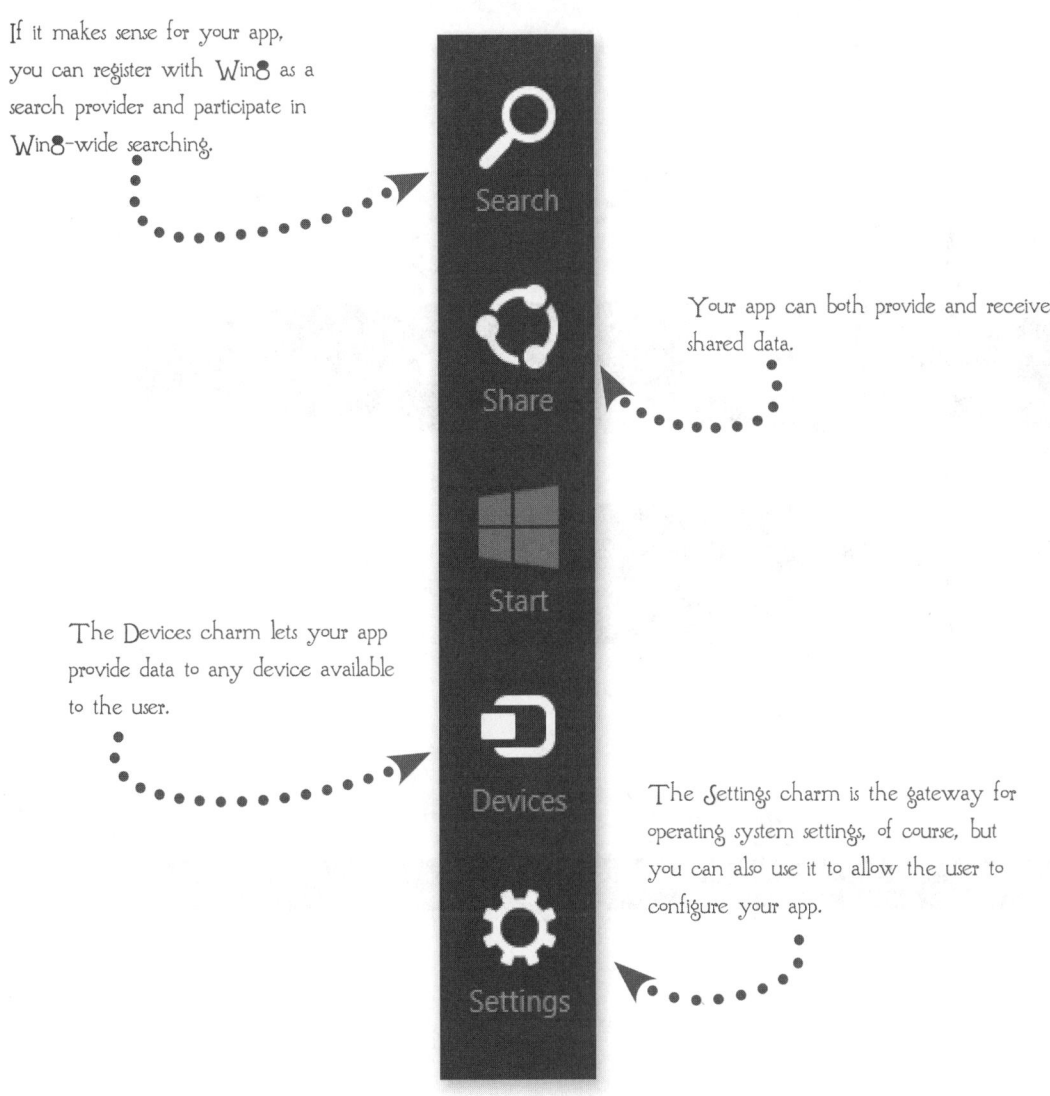

If it makes sense for your app, you can register with Win8 as a search provider and participate in Win8-wide searching.

Your app can both provide and receive shared data.

The Devices charm lets your app provide data to any device available to the user.

The Settings charm is the gateway for operating system settings, of course, but you can also use it to allow the user to configure your app.

APP SURFACES

Whether you're a one-person operation doing it all or part of a large development team with a dedicated UX designer, you can bet that *somebody* has spent a lot of time worrying about the UI of every successful development project you've worked on. The good news is that (unlike early versions of WPF) Win8 XAML widgets provide good default visual styles, as we'll see in Chapters 5 and 6. The bad news is that because Win8 apps are chromeless, and the orientation and view can be changed at any time, handling screen real estate is more complicated, as we'll see in Chapter 13.

A first step in handling the complexity is to understand the SURFACES you have to work with:

You have two "menu bars" (technically COMMAND BARS) to work with. They're displayed when the user swipes from the top or bottom or presses Windows Logo Key + Z.

The top command bar is typically used for navigation.

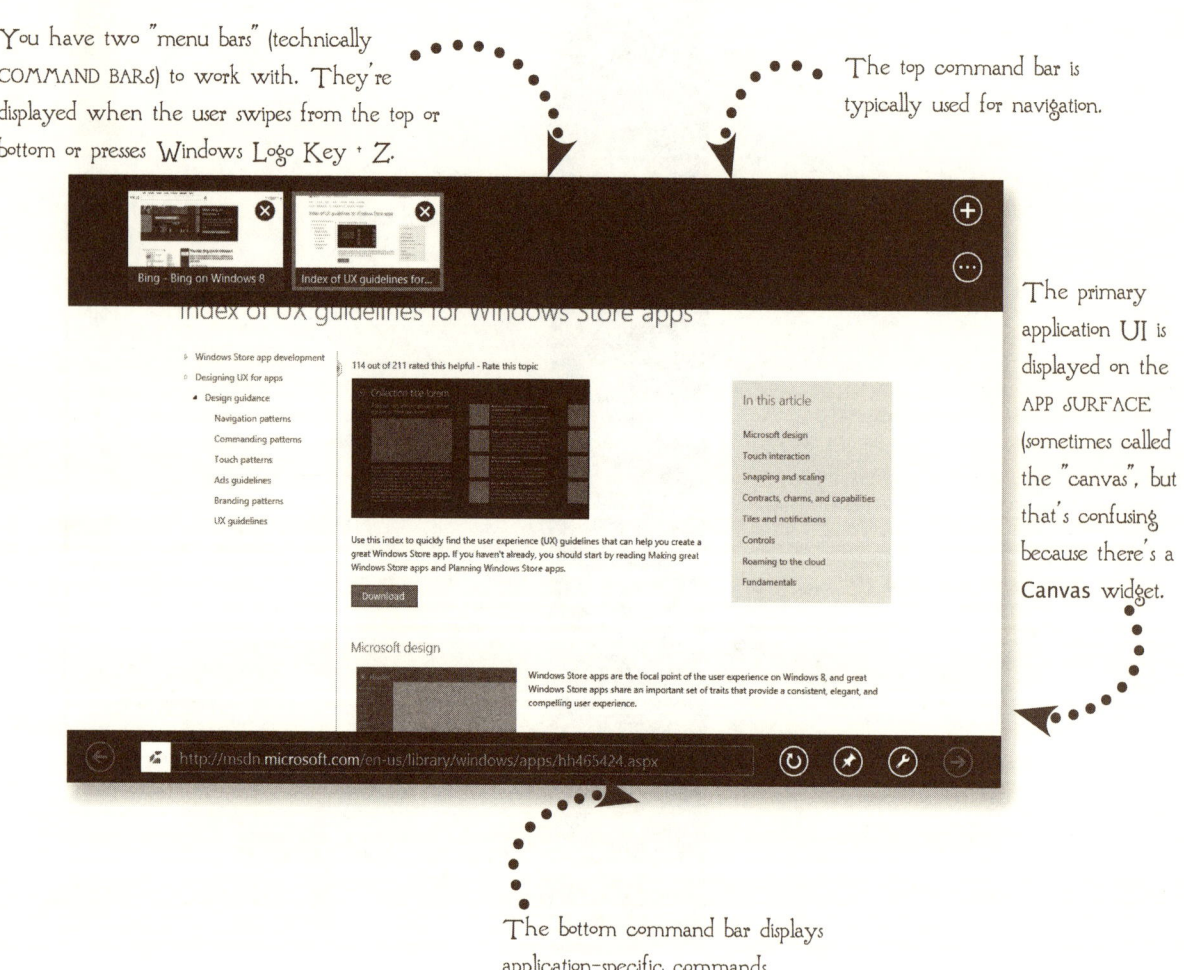

The primary application UI is displayed on the APP SURFACE (sometimes called the "canvas", but that's confusing because there's a Canvas widget.

The bottom command bar displays application-specific commands.

VIEW STATES

Another reason designing the UX of a Win8 app is complicated is that you need to support different widths, something that will almost certainly require changing your UI:

In full-screen view, your app controls the entire screen.

A user can reduce the width of your app to 500 or (with the app's permission) 320 pixels.

Or anything in between....

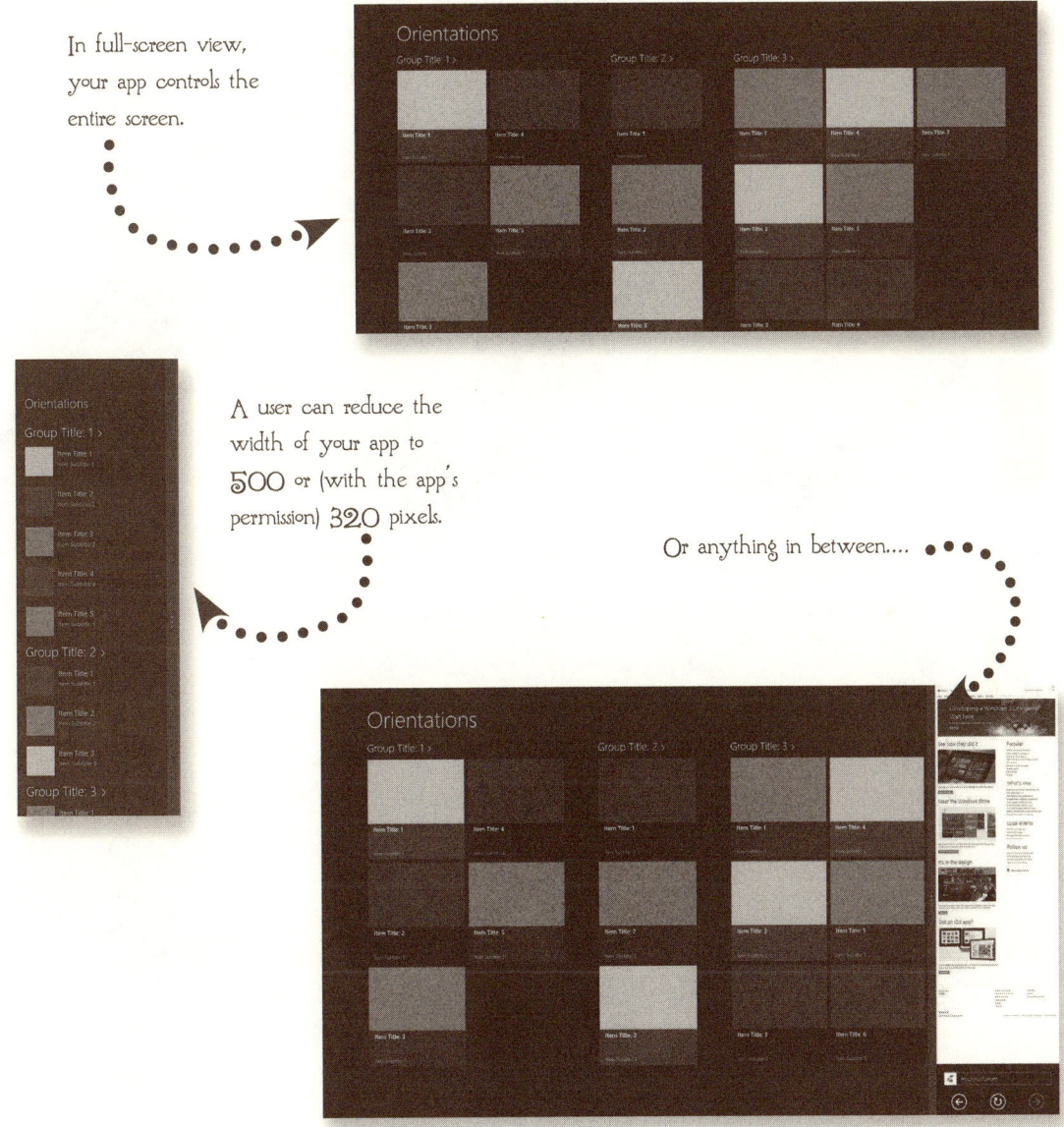

THE TOUCH LANGUAGE

Microsoft performed an impressive amount of research in developing their touch language. Not only did they perform usability studies (we'd expect that), but they researched the anthropomorphics of the human hand. They arrived at a language that's made up of only four core gestures: touch, slide, swipe, and pinch. Your apps need to comply with how those gestures are interpreted in the Windows 8.1 environment:

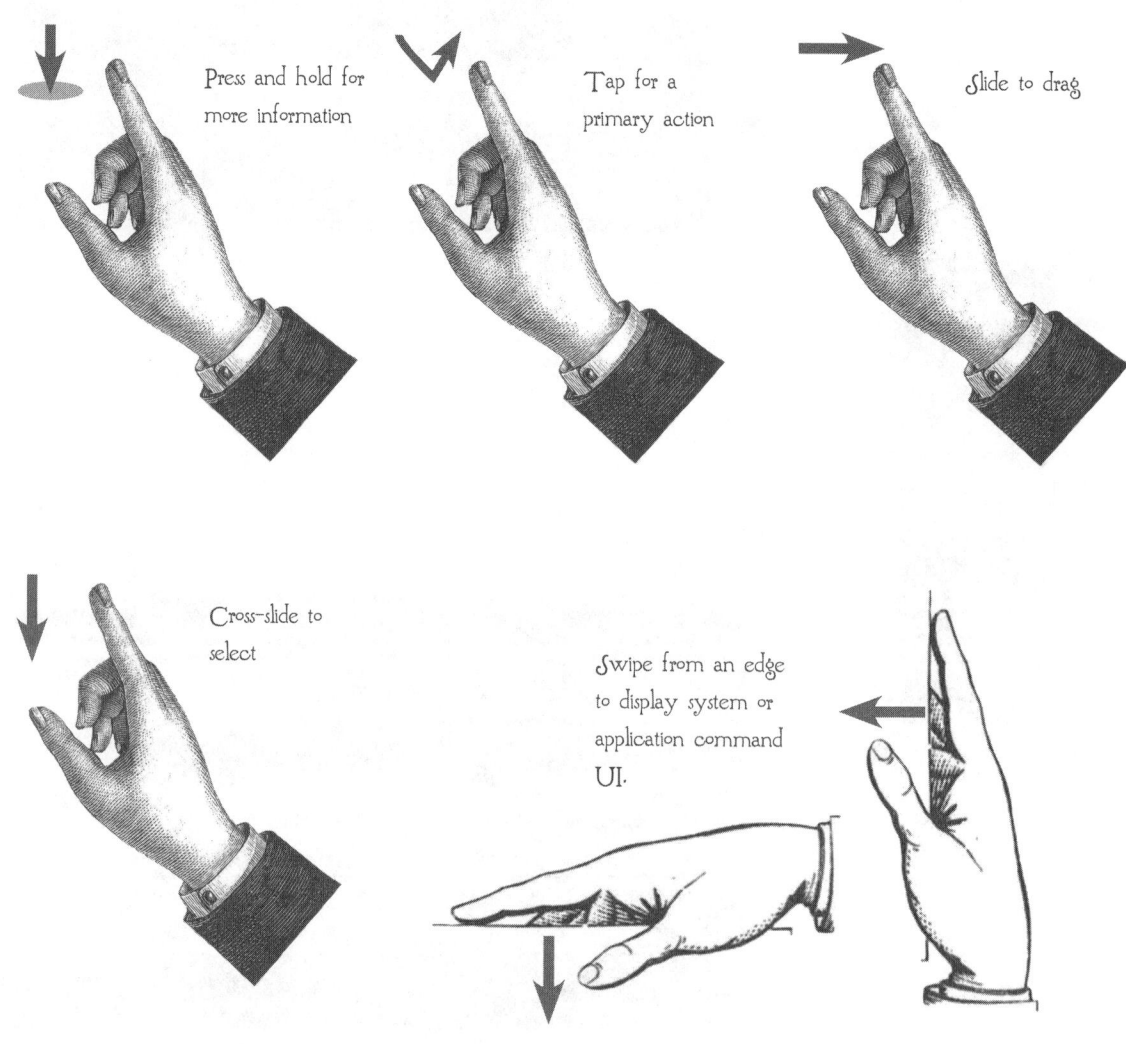

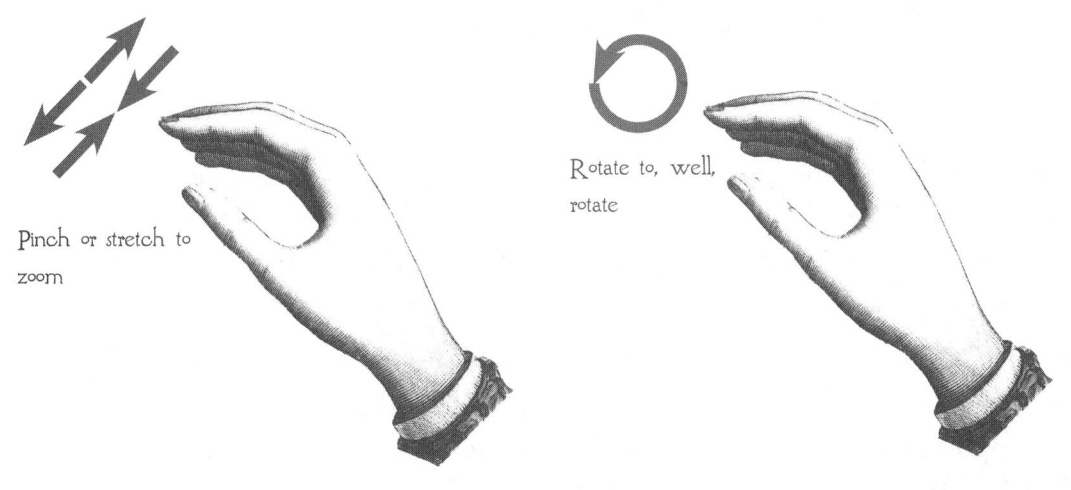

Pinch or stretch to zoom

Rotate to, well, rotate

ACTION	TOUCH	MOUSE	KEYBOARD
Move focus			Arrow keys, Tab
Start or activate	Tap	Click	Enter
Select	Cross-slide	Right-click	Space
Rearrange or drag-and-drop	Cross-slide past distance threshold	Drag	
Place input caret	Tap	Click	Arrow keys and modified arrow keys
Scroll	Slide	Scroll bar or mouse wheel	Page Up or Page Down
Zoom	Pinch	Mouse wheel	Ctrl+Plus and Ctrl+Minus
Rotate	Rotate		
More information (all require a time threshold)	Press and hold	Hover	Focus
Context menu	Press and hold	Right-click	Context menu key

THE BACK STACK

In Windows 8.1, applications that are running but not visible on the screen are in the BACK STACK, and the user can return to them at any time by simply swiping.

If you're old enough to remember the late Cretaceous period, you may remember that one of the exciting things about the first version of Windows wasn't just that it had a pretty GUI, but that you could actually run more than one application at a time. Wow! And a Clipboard for transferring data between applications! Groovy!

Of course that's all pretty boring now, and in fact the Windows 8.1 Share charm makes the Clipboard look a little lame, but as a developer the Windows 8.1 BACK STACK does have some implications you'll need to pay attention to. (But the Clipboard is still there, and still useful.) We'll be discussing them in detail in Chapter 13, but here's a taste:

- You need to handle every possible view state, and (usually) both landscape and portrait orientations.

- You need to maintain the user's context when your application is restored from the back stack—they'll expect to be exactly where they were the last time they looked at you.

- You'll be notified when your app is suspended, but not when it is closed (which could happen at any time).

TAKE A BREAK

That's it for our whirlwind tour of Windows 8.1. Was there anything you didn't already know?

Why don't you take a break before we move examine the characteristics of Win8 apps in more detail?

ON YOUR OWN

Going back to the list of Win8 apps you made on page 12, do you have any new ideas? Did our tour give you some more ideas for new apps, or some new ideas about why your app ideas are well-suited to Windows 8.1? Jot your ideas down here...

Characteristics of a Win8 App

Win8 apps are immersive!

They're alive!

They're responsive!

MY VIEW
While I'm not generally going to be hesitant about expressing my opinion, in this section I'm going to ask you to make your own decisions about what, if anything, these marketing terms mean. Not because I think they're meaningless (although I do think they're vague), but because it's going to be your job to make them tangible, and you might as well start now...

MY VIEW, AGAIN

Okay, I lied. I do have an opinion to express: I detest the phrase "authentically digital". Microsoft seems to be using it to mean non-skeuomorphic graphic design. (And I can certainly understand why they wouldn't want to use "non-skeuomorphic"!) But I would like to refer whoever thought up the term to the films of James Cameron. Does Avatar strike any of you as *inauthentically* digital?

And as someone who started her life as an art historian, you *really* don't want to get me stated on the meaning of "modern"... but relax; we'll discuss Microsoft's UI guidelines in some detail, but I promise I won't be talking about aesthetic issues in this book. (Much.)

They're authentically digital!

We'll create a web of apps!

IMMERSIVE

There are three fundamental characteristics that every Win8 app shares: they're chromeless, they display a single "screen" or "canvas" at a time, and they are touch-first. Do they correspond to "immersiveness"?

Win8 apps are CHROMELESS: They don't live inside a window, they don't have toolbars or status bars, and the application menu is only displayed on demand.

With a few very limited exceptions, Win8 apps can only display a single screen of information at a time.

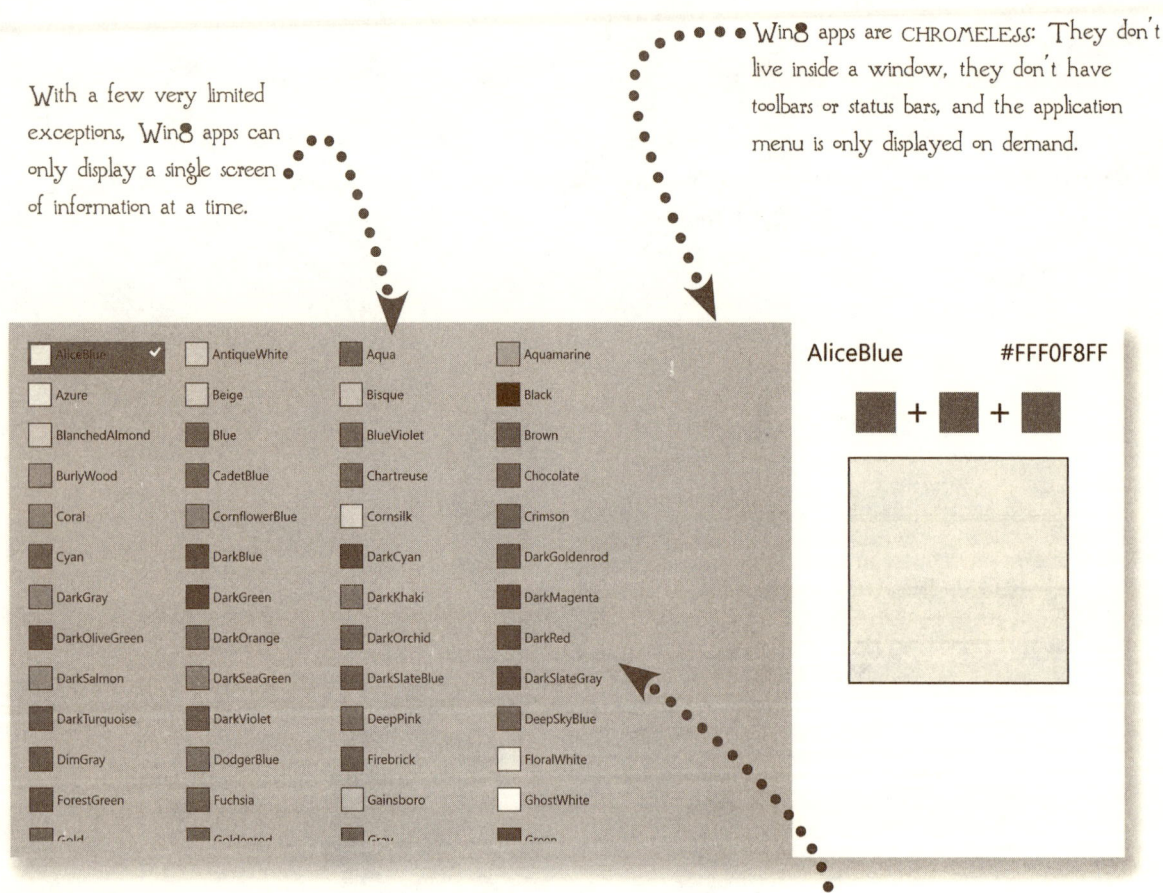

Win8 apps are touch-first. Of course, they need to support mouse, keyboard, and stylus as well, but they are designed for touch, and as we'll see, that has some important implications for your UI design.

 ## ON YOUR OWN

Do you think the absence of chrome and a touch-first orientation help make Win8 apps "immersive"?

What other characteristics do you think might contribute to the user's ability to lose themselves in their task? (Or do you think "immersive" means something else entirely, and if so, what?)

RESPONSIVE

Every Win8 app needs to support different screen resolutions and different views. Does that make them "responsive"?

FULL SCREEN IN LANDSCAPE AND PORTRAIT

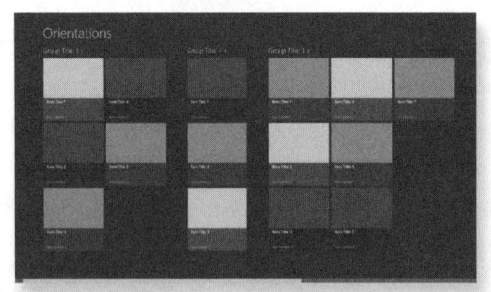

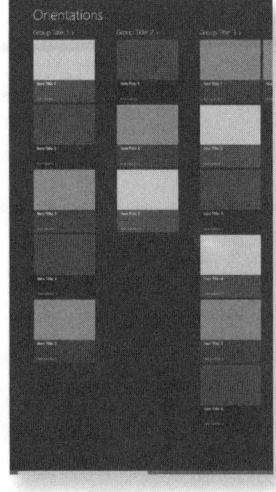

FILLED is a Windows 8 term, too, but like snapped, it's convenient, so I'll use it for anything between snapped and full screen.

SNAPPED

In Windows 8, the narrower, vertical layout of an app was always 320 pixels wide, and called SNAPPED VIEW. That's no longer true in 8.1, but it's still a convenient way to talk about this layout.

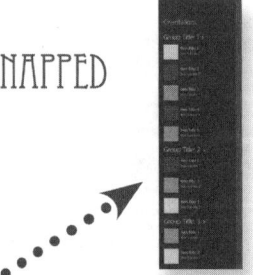

FILLED

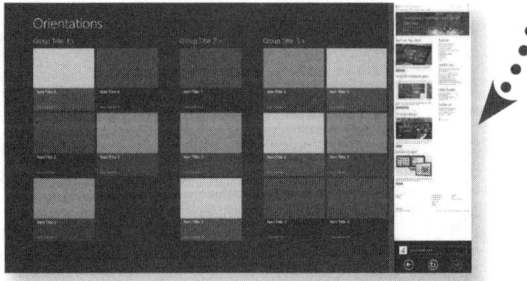

MAKE A NOTE
There's another characteristic of Win8 apps that I can't show you but is probably more important for making an application responsive than any other: animation. We'll explore the Win8 UI animations in detail in Chapter 11.

# ON YOUR OWN

Do you think responsiveness is important to an application? If so, why?

Do you think that responding to view state and tablet orientation are important examples of responsiveness? Why or why not?

What about animation? Is that important? If so, why?

ALIVE

Your app is represented by a tile on the Start Screen. Tiles can be static, animated, or you can update them. You can also send notifications that will be displayed even if your app isn't running. We'll explore tiles and notifications in Chapter 15.

Static tiles display a single image.

Live tiles can cycle through images or be updated with new information.

At your user's discretion, your app can display notifications even when it's not running.

 ## ON YOUR OWN

Unfortunate Frankenstein jokes not withstanding, I think most of us tend to anthropomorphize our computers. I'm pretty sure that's not what Microsoft is talking about, though. What do you think they mean by "alive"?

Do you think live tiles contribute to the sense of (perhaps a better word) "liveliness"? Is that enough, do you think?

What other characteristics do you think might contribute to this sense?

A WEB OF APPS

By way of contracts like Settings and Share, which we'll explore in Chapter 17, and extensions, which we'll look at in Chapter 16, your app can collaborate with other Win8 apps and with the operating system.

Even the operating system participates in the Search charm.

A **GridView** like this is common, but your app can display search results any way that makes sense.

ON YOUR OWN

In what way do you think that charms create a "web of apps"?

Do you think this is a case of the whole being more than the sum of its parts, or just more marketing hype?

TAKE A BREAK

In this section I asked you to form your own opinion about what those suspiciously marketing-department-sounding Win8 app characteristics mean. Have you changed your mind about any of them?

Why don't you take a break now before you complete the review and we explore some of the goodies that you get for free when you build a Win8 app?

REVIEW

Can you answer these questions based on what you've learned about the characteristics of Win8 apps?

We've examined four characteristics of Win8 apps (and I vented about a fifth). Can you list them, and describe some of the ways that these characteristics are manifested in tangible application or operating system functionality?

①

②

③

④

⑤

Re-visiting the list of Win8 apps you'd like to develop, can you think of any ways that they can be made to conform more closely to the characteristics described in this chapter?

Jot your ideas down here:

WHAT YOU GET FOR FREE

With every release of Windows and .NET, more and more of the functionality that developers had previously needed to write themselves (or users had to do without) is provided by the operating system or included in the development environment. Windows 8.1 is, of course, no exception. We'll be looking at some of the enhanced functionality provided by Win8 widgets as we go along, but are a few of the services the operating system now provides to your apps:

MULTI-TOUCH SUPPORT
No surprises here, unless, of course, you've ever had to roll your own.

SYSTEM-WIDE SPELL-CHECKING
The last few versions of .NET have provided some basic spell-checking, but Windows 8.1 now provides access to the operating system dictionary from within your app simply by setting a property or two.

THE TOUCH KEYBOARD
The Windows 8.1 touch keyboard provides support for input prediction.

FUNCTIONAL TEMPLATES
The Visual Studio templates for Win8 app development provide an immediate working skeleton for your app.

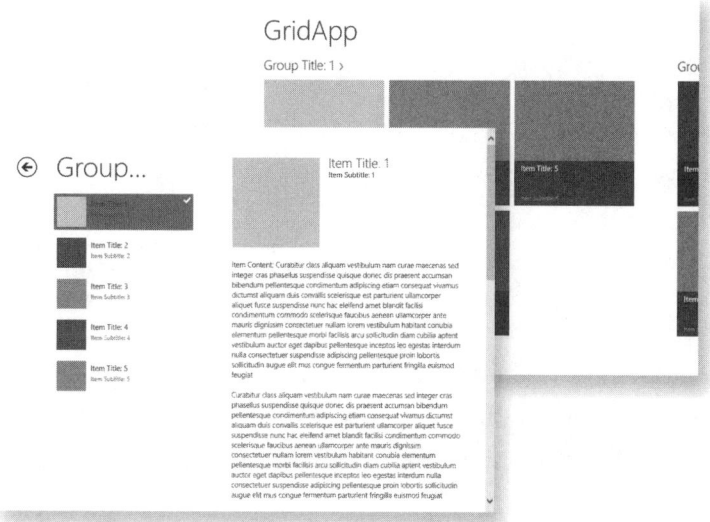

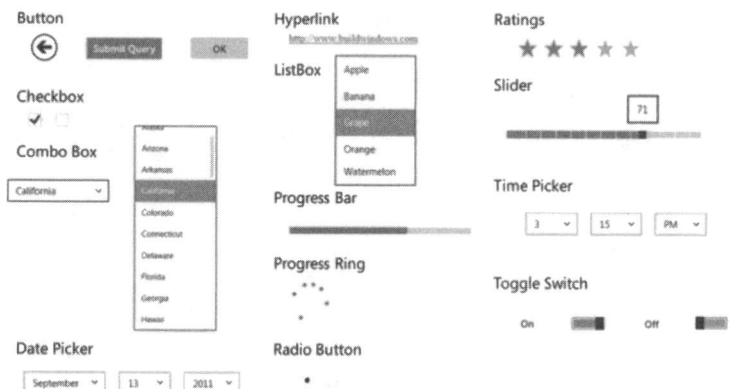

A RICH CONTROL SET
The control widget set has gotten richer, and both the behavior and appearance are usable out of the box.

REVIEW

What distinguishes a live tile from a Windows 7 (or earlier) shortcut?

Can you name three things that will make managing your app surface complicated?

What gestures comprise the Microsoft touch language?

Do you think the absence of chrome makes an app more immersive? What other characteristics might contribute to the user's ability to concentrate on the task at hand without distraction (at least, without distraction from the application)?

There are two charms that are directly involved in the interoperability of Win8 apps ("the web of apps"). What are they?

Congratulations! You've finished the chapter. Take a minute to think about what you've accomplished before you move on to the next one...

List three things you learned in this chapter:

①

②

③

Why do you think you need to know these things in order to develop Win8 apps?

Is there anything in this chapter that you think you need to understand in more detail? If so, what are you going to do about that?

THE DEEP END

In the last chapter we took a quick tour of the Win8 UI and explored some of the benefits it provides to your application. Starting with the next chapter, we'll spend the next several hundred pages studying Win8 app development in detail.

But first, let's take another tour. In this chapter, we'll jump in at the deep end and build a complete Win8 app so that when we do start working on the details, you'll know where and how they fit.

We'll start by quickly building the project using one of the project templates provided with Visual Studio and then explore some of the new components of Visual Studio for Win8 app development. Then we'll add a couple of items that allow your app to interface with Windows 8.1: a contract and a tile. Finally, we'll run through the Windows Certification process that you'll need to deploy your app, whether through the store or directly to users.

After we've taken the new app for a test run, we'll back up and examine some of the details that are unique to the Win8 app development process.

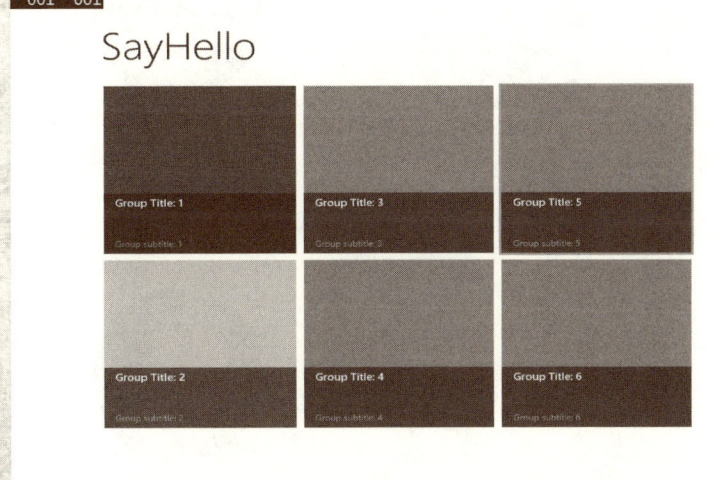

FITTING IT IN

Here's a very high-level view of a minimal Win8 app. In this chapter we'll be looking at most of these components, and we'll come back to the diagram in each chapter so that you'll know where things fit.

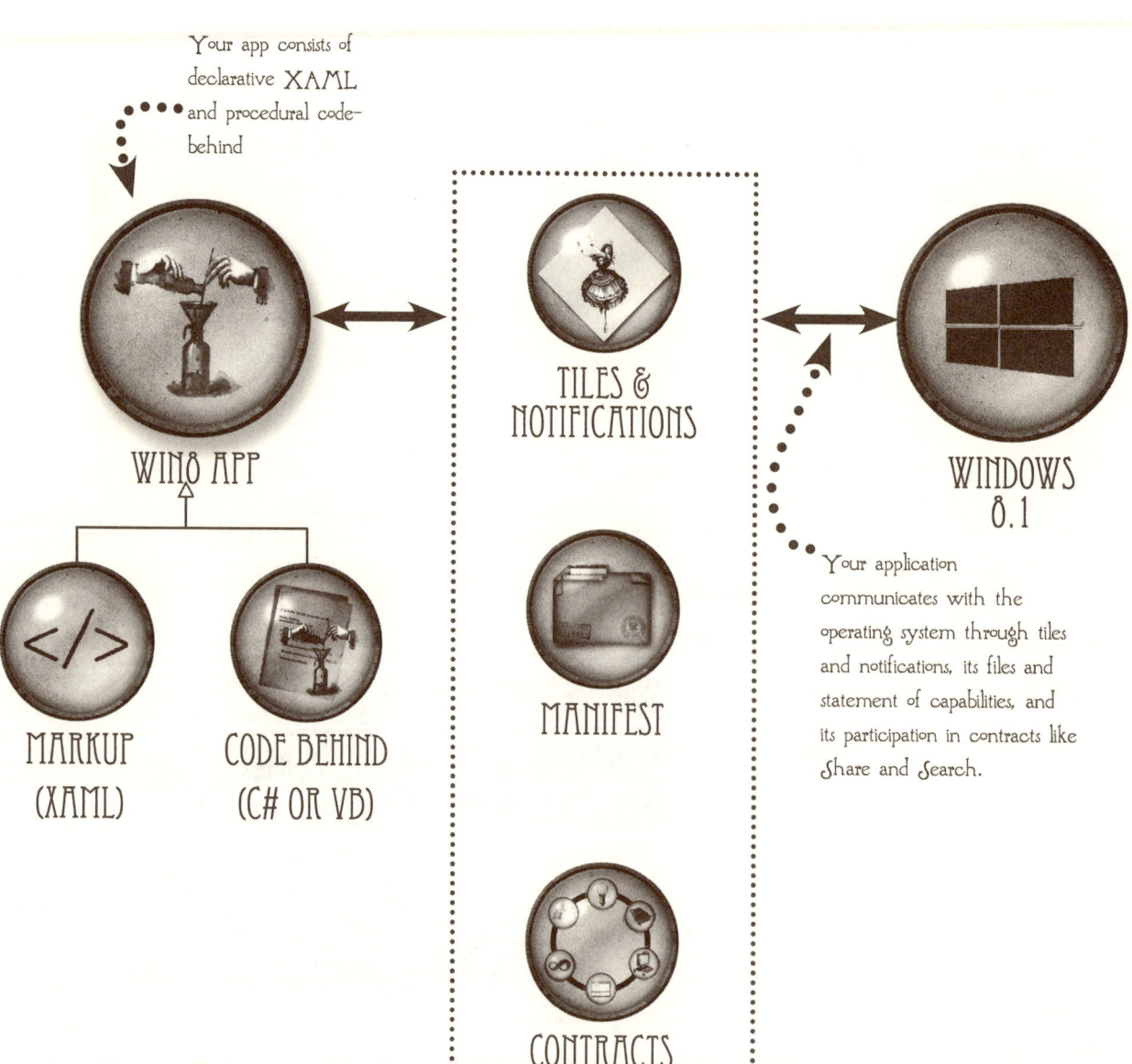

Your app consists of declarative XAML and procedural code-behind

Your application communicates with the operating system through tiles and notifications, its files and statement of capabilities, and its participation in contracts like Share and Search.

TASK LIST

In this chapter we'll create a very simple app based on one of the Visual Studio templates.

SAY HELLO

We'll start the chapter with a walk-through. You'll create a complete (albeit very simple) Win8 app based on a Visual Studio template.

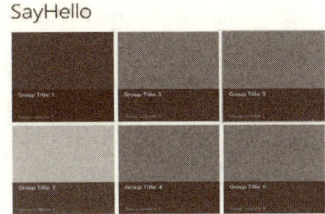

SAY WHAT?

Of course, you're not reading this book just to learn how to follow directions, so after saying hello to Win8, we'll back up a little and examine what we've just done. It's important to understand the process, because you'll do more or less the same thing for every Win8 app you build.

THE DEVELOPMENT PROCESS IN A NUTSHELL

Even if you're an experienced developer, there may be a few steps that will be new to you when you start developing Win8 apps. Here they are in a nutshell:

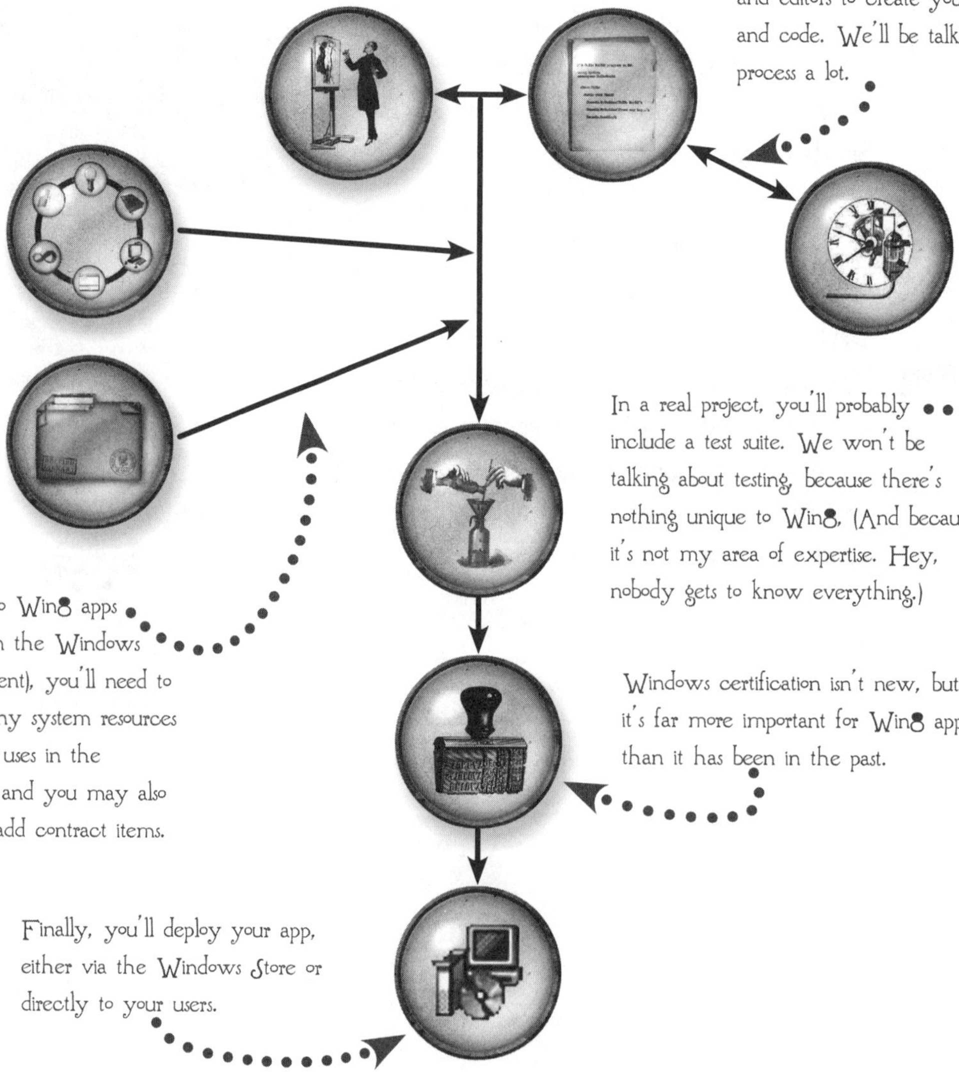

You'll use the Visual Studio designers and editors to create your XAML and code. We'll be talking about this process a lot.

In a real project, you'll probably include a test suite. We won't be talking about testing, because there's nothing unique to Win8. (And because it's not my area of expertise. Hey, nobody gets to know everything.)

Unique to Win8 apps (at least in the Windows environment), you'll need to declare any system resources your app uses in the manifest, and you may also want to add contract items.

Windows certification isn't new, but it's far more important for Win8 apps than it has been in the past.

Finally, you'll deploy your app, either via the Windows Store or directly to your users.

46

SAY HELLO

Ready to get started? Of course you are. In this section we'll build a very simple, but relatively complete, Win8 app. Here's what we'll do:

① **CREATE A NEW PROJECT**
We'll use the SplitApp template, one of the project templates provided by Visual Studio.

② **RUN THE APP IN THE SIMULATOR**
Visual Studio 2013 Express for Windows provides a wonderful tool called the Simulator that lets you test your UI in different states, resolutions, and orientations. We'll play with that next.

③ **SET SOME XAML PROPERTIES**
Next we'll change our UI a little bit by setting some properties in the XAML designer and directly in the XAML.

④ **ADD A CONTRACT**
You've seen that contracts are an important part of Windows 8.1, and we'll get a taste of how that works by adding a Settings contract to our app.

⑤ **ADD A TILE**
What would a Win8 app be without a cool tile? We'll add that next.

⑥ **CERTIFY YOUR APP**
Finally, we'll run the Windows App Certification Kit to ensure that our app complies with the requirements for deployment to the Windows Store.

① CREATE A NEW PROJECT

Okay, time to get coding.

Start Visual Studio and choose the New Project option from the Start Screen. Navigate to the Windows Store category for Visual C# or Visual Basic and choose the Split App template.

I'm using C# here, but feel free to use Visual Basic if you'd prefer. (JavaScript and C++, however, use entirely different APIs.)

We'll be using the Split App (XAML) template.

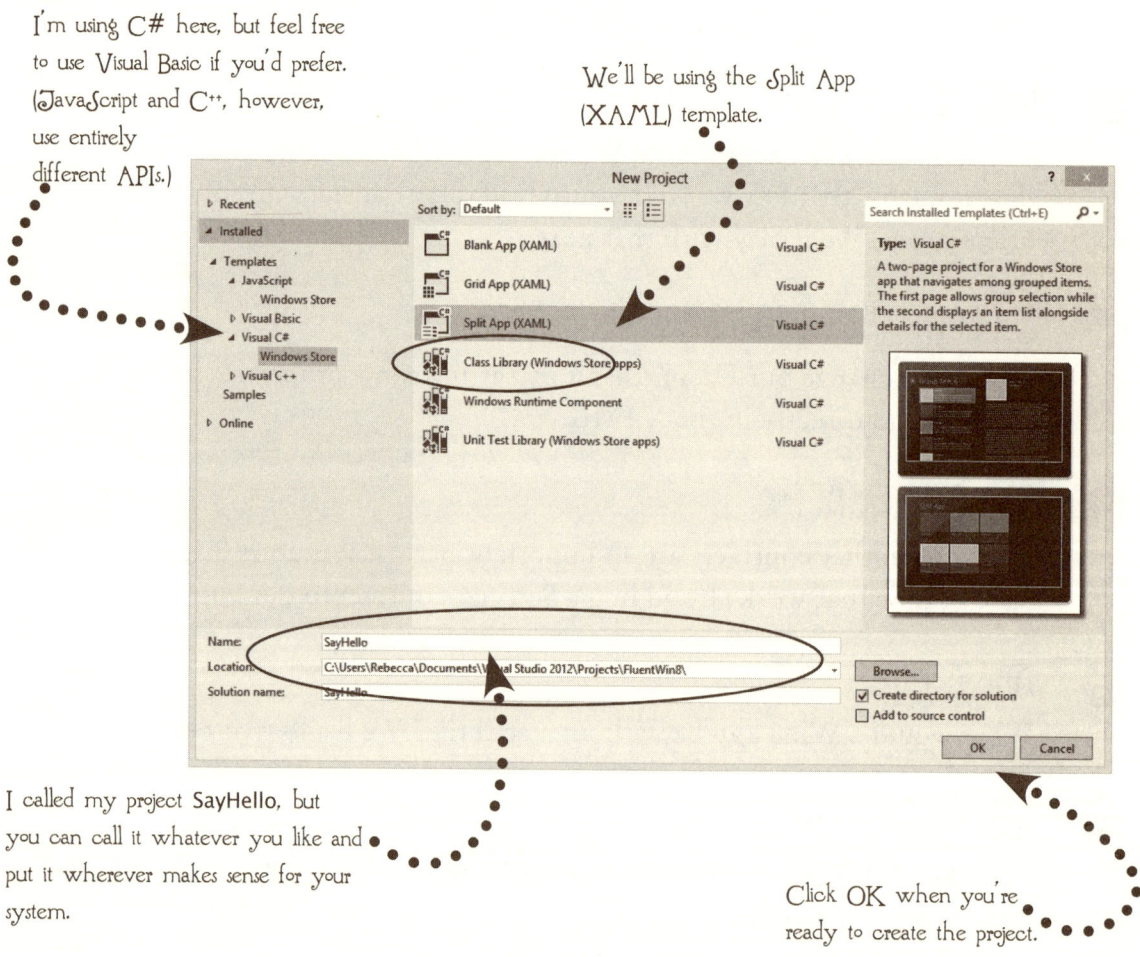

I called my project **SayHello**, but you can call it whatever you like and put it wherever makes sense for your system.

Click OK when you're ready to create the project.

2 RUN IN THE SIMULATOR

As I've said, the Visual Studio Win8 app templates are far more complete than the application templates for other environments. Let's give this one a whirl in the Simulator:

● SET THE DEVELOPMENT ENVIRONMENT TO RUN IN THE SIMULATOR

You can do this from the Visual Studio toolbar. Just select Simulator instead of Local Machine:

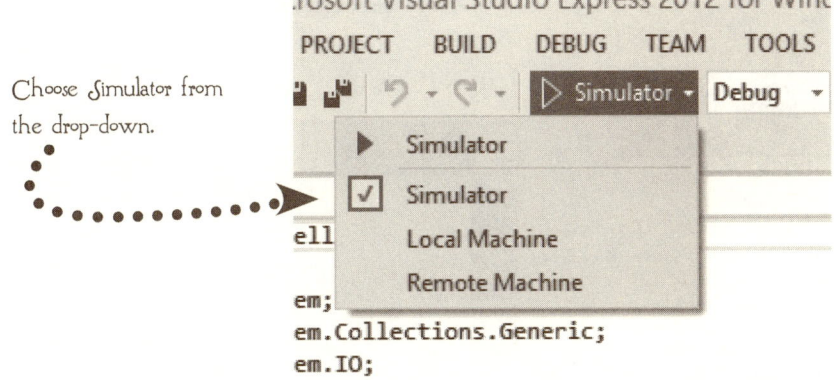

Choose Simulator from the drop-down.

● BUILD AND RUN THE APPLICATION

You can click the green arrow next to Simulator on the toolbar, choose Start Debugging from the Debug menu, or just press F5.

After a moment or two (or more—sometimes it takes awhile), your app will open in the Simulator, as shown on the next page.

MAKE A NOTE
There are dozens of studies establishing that white-on-black text is much, much more difficult to read than black-on-white. You can change Visual Studio's default by choosing Options from the Tools menu if, like me, you wonder what they were thinking.

 These numbers are for profiling when you're running in Debug mode.

The first screen displayed by the template shows a list of groups on the home page. (Your screen will have a black background. I changed mine to make it more legitble.

When you select one of the groups, a master/detail page replaces the home page. You can select items from the list on the left, and their details are displayed on the right.

ON YOUR OWN

Take a few minutes to just play with the app. Not bad for out-of-the-box functionality, is it?

Microsoft recommends this project template, which displays groups of items on the home page, and a master/detail view on the secondary pages, for applications like news readers. Do any of your list of apps fit this paradigm?

SET SOME XAML PROPERTIES

Now that we've seen what Visual Studio gives us to start with, let's make some changes.

STOP THE APPLICATION

You can either click the red(ish) stop button on the Visual Studio toolbar or press Ctrl+F5. (Notice that the Simulator doesn't close. If you check, you'll see that it's displaying your Start Screen. You can close it from the toolbar, if you wish.)

OPEN ITEMSPAGE.XAML IN THE DESIGNER

Just double-click it in the Solution Explorer (be sure you open ItemsPage.xaml, not ItemsPage.xaml.cs or ItemsPage.xaml.vb). You can close App.xaml.cs if you wish (but you don't need to).

You can arrange the panes and tabs in Visual Studio any way you want—that hasn't changed. This is the layout I use on my tablet, but your default view will probably be different.

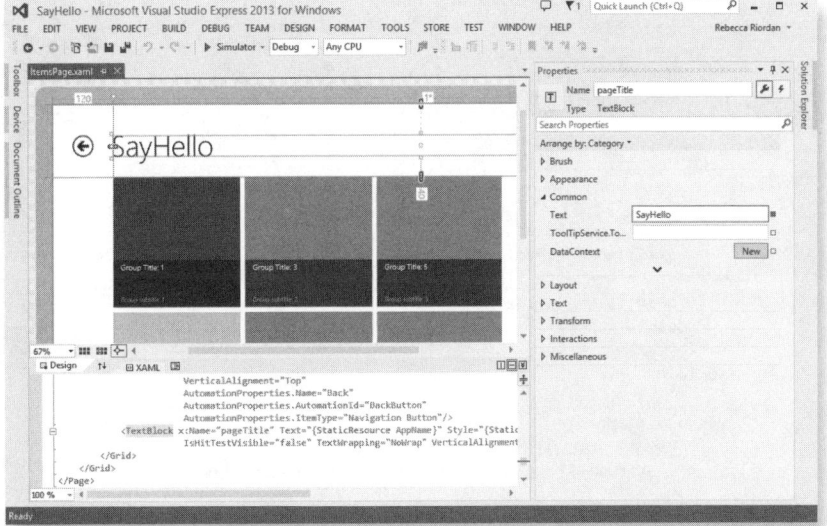

There are two ways to set the properties of your XAML widgets in Visual Studio XAML designer: by typing in the XAML directly or by setting properties in the properties window. We'll be exploring XAML in detail in the next chapter, but here's a taste:

 ### NAVIGATE TO THE TEXTBLOCK NAMED PAGETITLE

You can either just scroll through the XAML in the bottom pane of the designer or use the Document Outline pane (docked to the left side of the window by default) to go directly to the element:

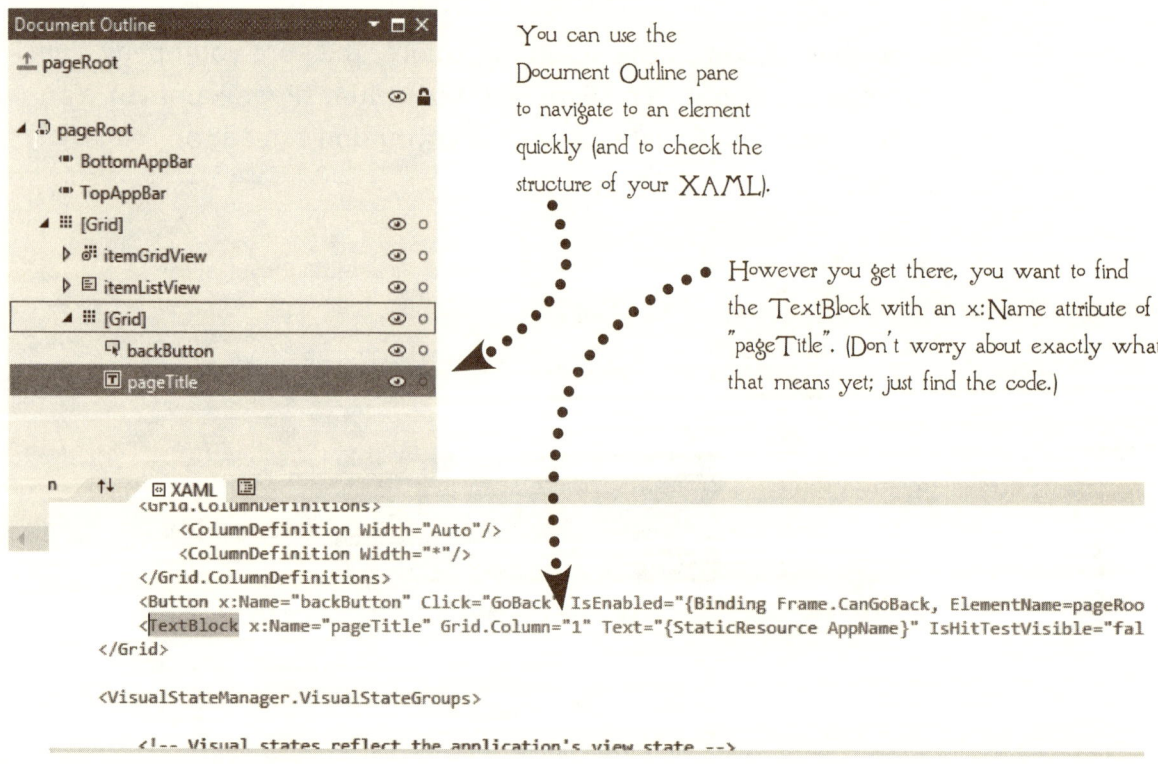

You can use the Document Outline pane to navigate to an element quickly (and to check the structure of your XAML).

However you get there, you want to find the TextBlock with an x:Name attribute of "pageTitle". (Don't worry about exactly what that means yet; just find the code.)

CHANGE THE XAML

Unlike, say, WPF, where the widgets are pretty ordinary-looking by default, the designers at Microsoft have very carefully honed the appearance of the Win8 widgets and apps and they really, really don't want us to mess about with them. Oh, well. Let's do it anyway:

● CHANGE THE FONT FAMILY

Place your cursor after x:Name="pageTitle" and press space, then type FontFamily="Tahoma". (IntelliSense will help you with the attribute name and the quote marks.)

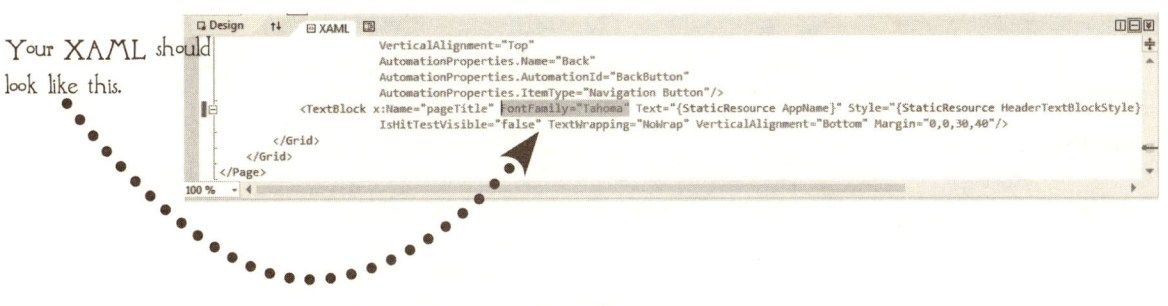

Your XAML should look like this.

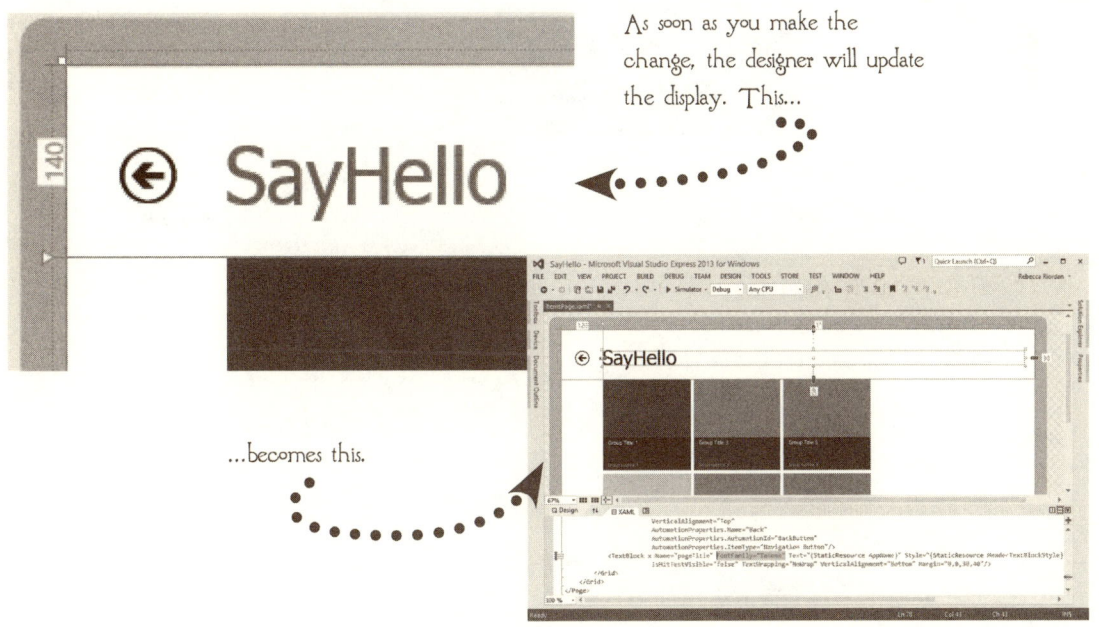

As soon as you make the change, the designer will update the display. This...

...becomes this.

53

USE THE PROPERTY WINDOW

A second way to change the attributes of your widgets in the XAML designer is using the property window. Let's give that a whirl, too:

 ### CHANGE THE TEXT COLOR

Make sure that **pageTitle** is still selected, expand the Brush category, and click anywhere in the display to pick a new color:

Make sure **pageTitle** is still selected.

Expand the Brush category in the properties window by clicking on the little arrow-thingy (that's a technical term).

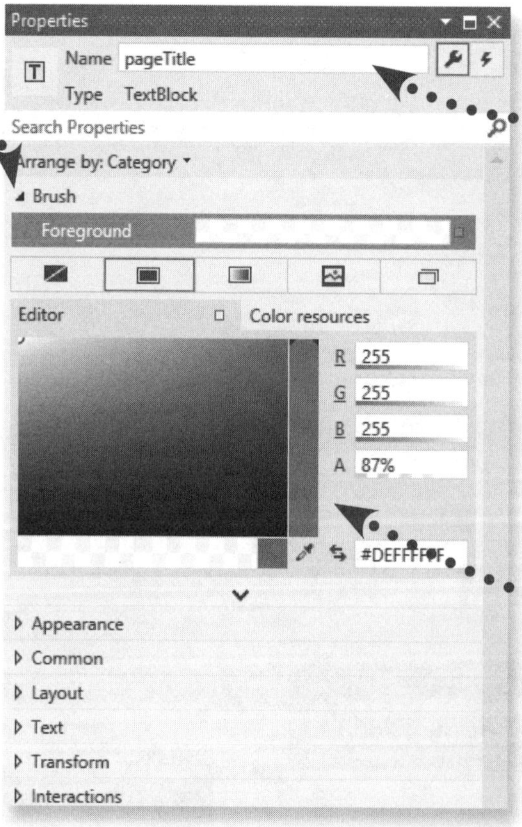

Click anywhere in the color gradient to change the text color. Or you could enter an RGBA value if you'd rather.

ADD A CONTRACT

In the last chapter we saw that Windows 8.1 provides new ways for applications to cooperate via charms and contracts. We'll explore them in detail in Chapter 14, but let's add a (semi-functional) settings contract to our app, just to get a taste for the process:

ADD A SETTINGS FLYOUT TO YOUR PROJECT

Choose Add New Item from the Project menu or the Solutions Explorer conteAdd xt menu, and choose the Settings Flyout item from the Add New Item dialog, and then click the Add button.

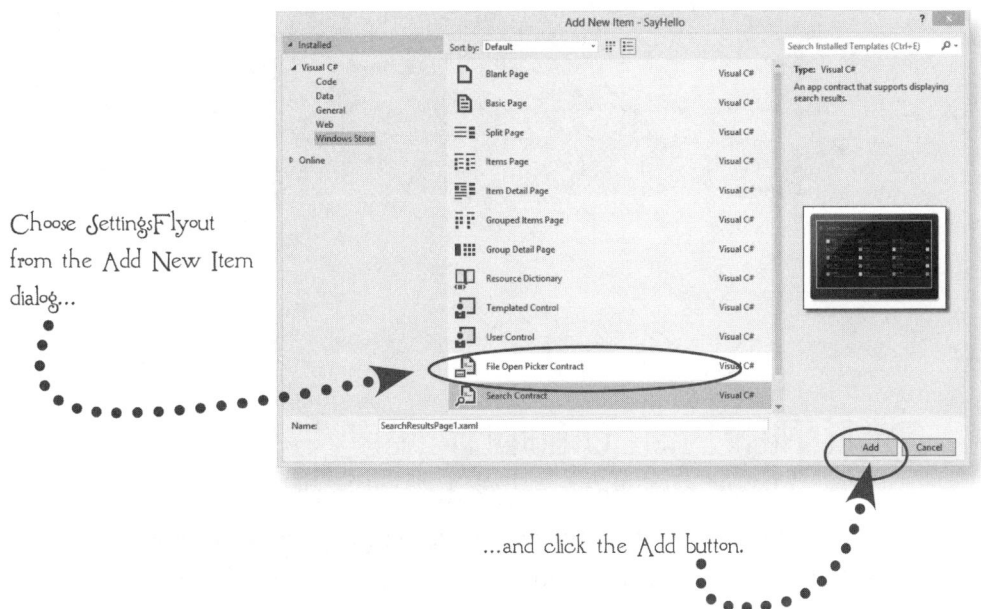

Choose SettingsFlyout from the Add New Item dialog…

…and click the Add button.

WIRE UP THE FLYOUT

When you add a new item to a project, Visual Studio does a lot of the work for you, but it can't do everything. In the case of the `SettingsFlyout`, we need to add code to the `App.Xaml.cs` or `App.Xaml.vb` file to hook the flyout we create to the Settings charm. Here's how:

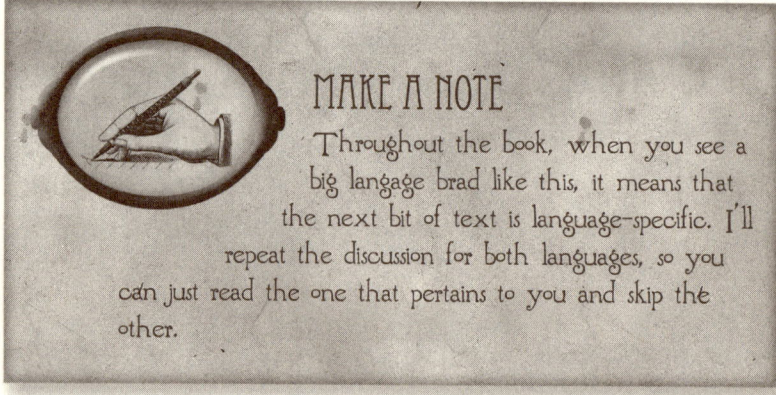

MAKE A NOTE

Throughout the book, when you see a big langage brad like this, it means that the next bit of text is language-specific. I'll repeat the discussion for both languages, so you can just read the one that pertains to you and skip the other.

- REFERENCE APPLICATIONSETTINGS

  The objects we'll be using are defined in the Windows.UI.ApplicationSettings namespace, so open up the App.Xaml code-behind file and add a using statement to the top of the file:

  ```
  using Windows.UI.ApplicationSettings;
  ```

REGISTER AN EVENT HANDLER

We want to display our custom settings flyout when the user opens the Settings charm, so the first thing we need to do is register an event handler to the **CommandsRequested** event of the **SettingsPane**.

Don't worry too much about the details of how this works right now. We'll discuss contracts and the structure of the **App.Xaml.cs** file in detail in Chapter 17. Just scroll to the bottom of the file and add the **OnWindowCreated** function shown below. Notice that Visual Studio offers a conventional name for the event handler and then offers to create a skeleton function for us. Press Tab twice to save yourself some typing.

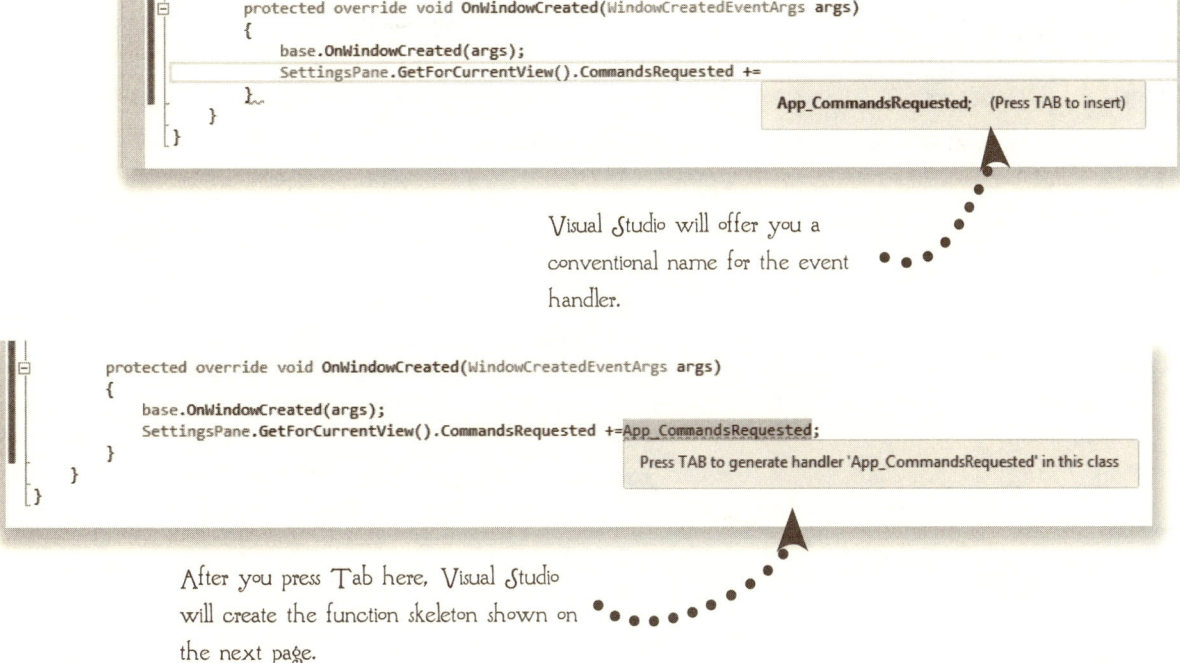

Visual Studio will offer you a conventional name for the event handler.

After you press Tab here, Visual Studio will create the function skeleton shown on the next page.

HANDLE THE EVENT

We could do everything inside the event handler Visual Studio created for us, but best practice dictates that we should separate responding to the event from opening the flyout, and that's what we'll do:

Here's the skeleton Visual Studio created.

```csharp
void App_CommandsRequested(SettingsPane sender, SettingsPaneCommandsRequestedEventArgs args)
{
    throw new NotImplementedException();
}
```

Replace the NotImplementedException with a call to the Add() method of the ApplicationCommands object.

```csharp
void App_CommandsRequested(SettingsPane sender, SettingsPaneCommandsRequestedEventArgs args)
{
    args.Request.ApplicationCommands.Add(new SettingsCommand(
        "Custom Setting", "Custom Setting", (handler) => ShowCustomSettingsFlyout()));
}
```

And then write the function to instantiate and show our custom Flyout.

```csharp
public void ShowCustomSettingsFlyout()
{
    SettingsFlyout1 CustomFlyout = new SettingsFlyout1();
    CustomFlyout.Show();
}
```

> **MAKE A NOTE**
> Just in case you missed it a few pages ago (in which case I apologize for the confusion), this big brad tells you that this page contains Visual Basic code examples. If you're using C#, you've already seen them and can skip to page 62.

REFERENCE APPLICATIONSETTINGS

The objects we'll be using are defined in the Windows.UI.ApplicationSettings and Windows.UI.Popups namespaces, so open up the App.xaml code-behind file and add a using statement to the top of the file:

```
Imports Windows.UI.ApplicationSettings
Imports Windows.UI.Popups
```

REGISTER AN EVENT HANDLER

We want to display our custom settings flyout when the user opens the Settings charm, so the first thing we need to do is register an event handler to the **CommandsRequested** event of the **SettingsPane**.

Don't worry too much about the details of how this works right now. We'll discuss contracts and the structure of the **App.Xaml.vb** file in detail in Chapter 17. Just scroll to the bottom of the file and add the **OnWindowCreated** function shown below. Because we haven't created the method yet, Visual Studio will display an error. If you click on the red button and choose "Generate method stub…", you'll save yourself some typing.

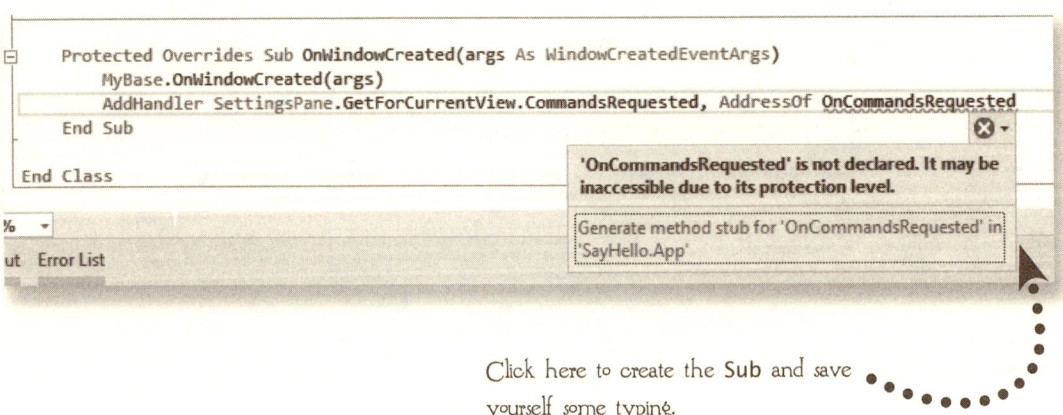

Click here to create the **Sub** and save yourself some typing.

HANDLE THE EVENT

We could do everything inside the event handler Visual Studio created for us, but best practice dictates that we should separate responding to the event from opening the Flyout, and that's what we'll do:

Here's the skeleton Visual Studio created.

```vb
Private Sub OnCommandsRequested(sender As SettingsPane, args As SettingsPaneCommandsRequestedEventArgs)
    Throw New NotImplementedException
End Sub
```

Replace the NotImplementedException with a call to the Add() method of the ApplicationCommands object.

```vb
Private Sub OnCommandsRequested(sender As SettingsPane, args As SettingsPaneCommandsRequestedEventArgs)
    Dim handler As New UICommandInvokedHandler(AddressOf ShowCustomSettingsFlyout)
    args.Request.ApplicationCommands.Add(New SettingsCommand("Custom Setting", "Custom Setting", handler))
End Sub
```

And then write the function to instantiate and show our custom Flyout.

```vb
Private Sub ShowCustomSettingsFlyout()
    Dim CustomFlyout As New SettingsContract1
    CustomFlyout.Show()
End Sub
```

RUN THE APPLICATION ON YOUR LOCAL MACHINE

You can't use the simulator to test how your application interacts with the operating system, so choose Local Machine from the toolbar, and then click the green arrow to run the app.

OPEN THE SETTINGS CHARM

Once the application loads, open the Charm Menu and choose the Settings charm.

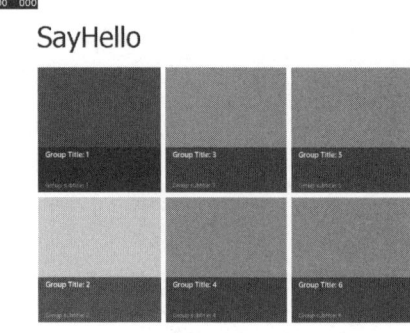

CHOOSE CUSTOM SETTING

Choose Custom Settings and (if you got all those event handlers right) our custom flyout will display. Not much there now, but don't worry, you'll learn how to expand its functionality in Chapter 17.

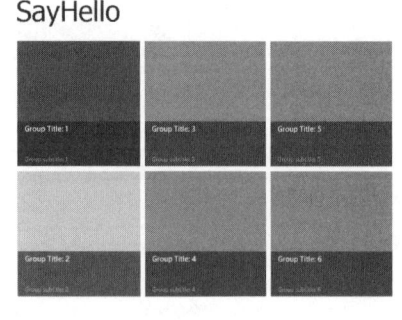

5 ADD A LIVE TILE

Let's add one more component to our app: a Live Tile that will represent it on the user's Start Screen.

● OPEN THE MANIFEST EDITOR

Close your application in Windows by swiping from the top of the screen, and then click the red square on the toolbar in Visual Studio to stop debugging. Once you're back in design mode, double-click the Package.appxmanifest file in the Solution Explorer.

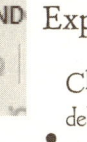

Click here to stop the debugger.

The application manifest is how your app tells Windows 8.1 what it wants to do about its resources, capabilities, and requirements to use system resources. We'll be working with it a lot in later chapters.

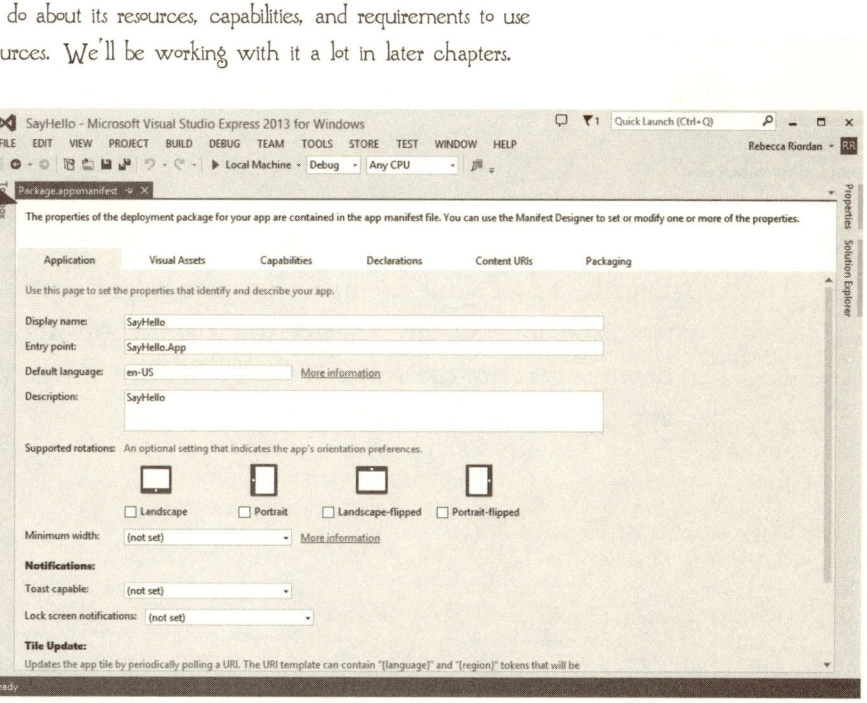

SPECIFY THE IMAGES

At a minimum, you'll need two images for your tiles: one that's 150 pixels square and one that's 30 pixels square. It's probably a good idea to add a third image, 310x150 pixels, to support wide tiles, because you can't change that once the app is deployed.

To tell Windows 8.1 about your images, just navigate to them on the Visual Assets tab of the Manifest Editor. There are images included in the Assets folder of the sample application you can download from the site, or you can provide your own if you prefer:

You can use the sample images or provide your own.

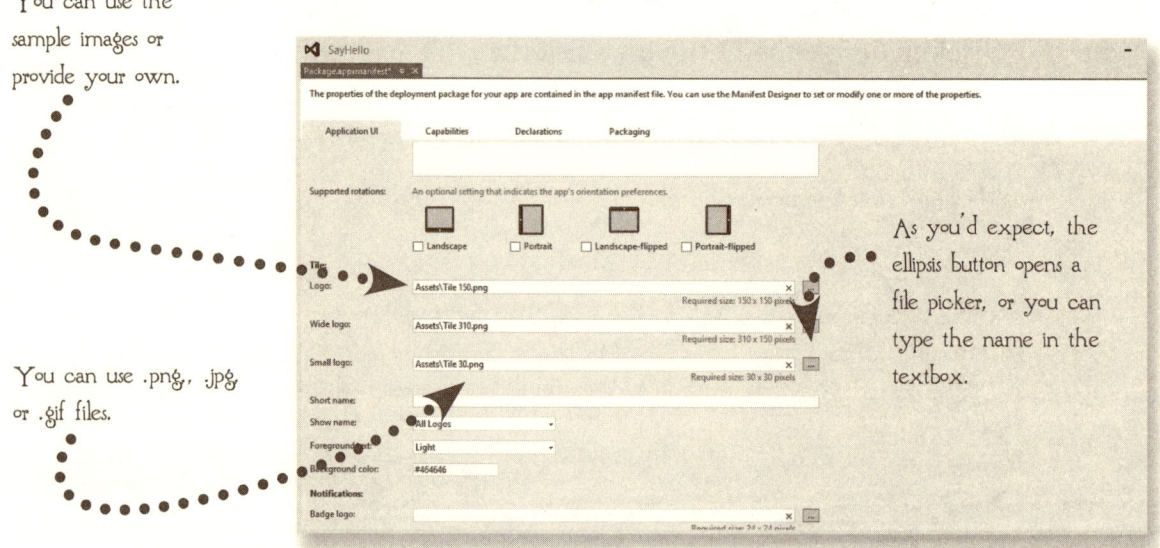

As you'd expect, the ellipsis button opens a file picker, or you can type the name in the textbox.

You can use .png, .jpg or .gif files.

In order to see your tile in action, you might need to uninstall the app from the Start Screen by selecting it and choosing Uninstall from the app menu. Then run the app and verify that the image you chose represents the application for the user.

6 CERTIFY YOUR APP

There's one last step before you're ready to deploy your app: certification testing. Of course, Windows has always had various certification tests, but for the first time it's a requirement for application development. The process is simple. Here's how:

● START THE WINDOWS APP CERTIFICATION KIT

The Windows App Certification Kit is a separate application, not part of Visual Studio. You'll find it on the Start Screen.

● CHOOSE VALIDATE WINDOWS STORE APP

Once you start the certification kit from the Start Menu, you'll probably get a UAC warning. You need to grant the application permission to make changes, and then it will display a menu asking what you want done. Select the first option.

You want to certify a Windows Store app. (You knew that, right?)

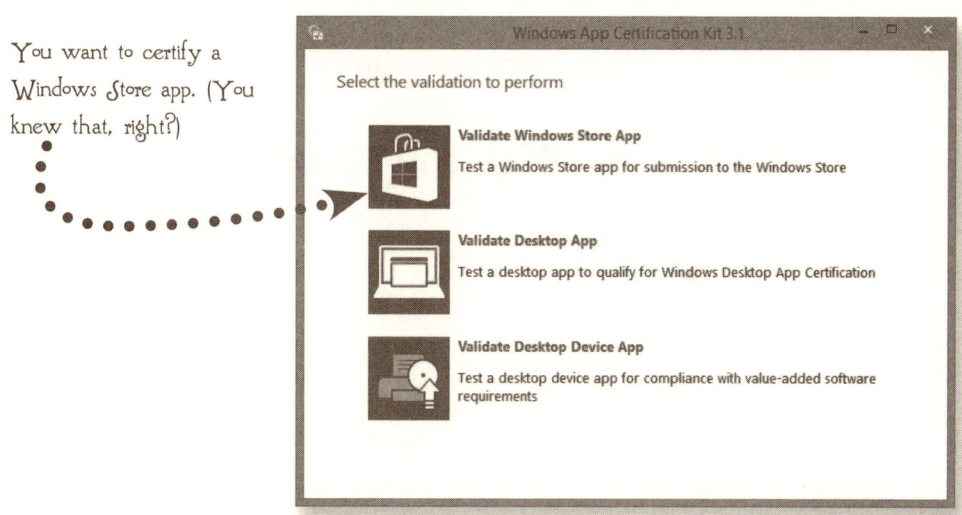

SELECT OUR SAMPLE APP

Once you select the type of test to perform, the application will display a progress screen and then present you with a list of installed Win8 apps. Scroll down to our sample app, select it, and click Next.

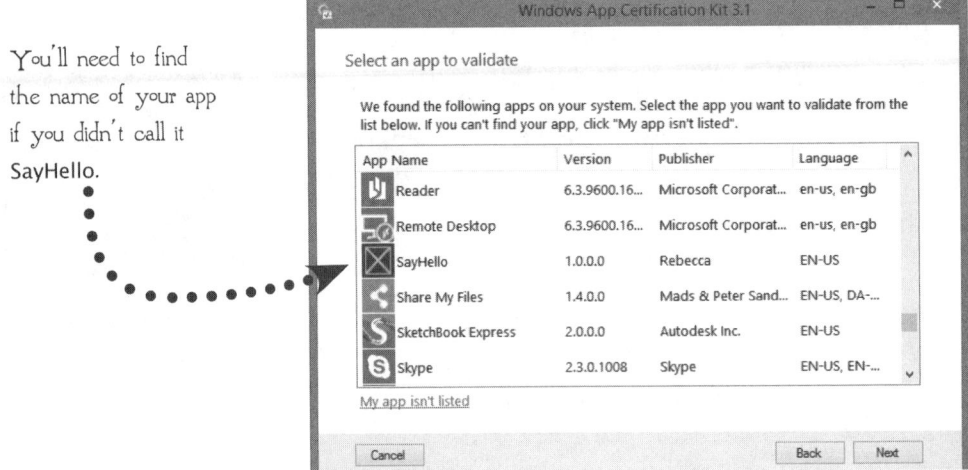

You'll need to find the name of your app if you didn't call it SayHello.

CHOOSE THE TESTS

You really should run all the tests before you submit to the Store, but you have the option of running them one at a time. We'll run the whole suite this time, so choose Next. (You might want to go get some fresh coffee at this point, because certification takes some time.)

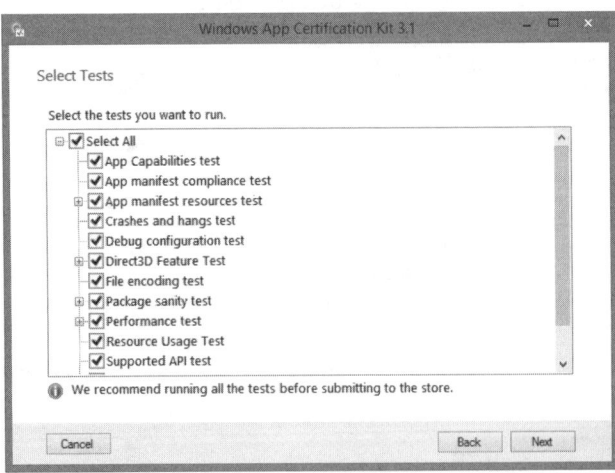

⬤ SAVE THE FILE

Eventually the certification kit will ask you for a name and location for the XML file it generates. I usually put it in the project directory, but you can put it wherever you like:

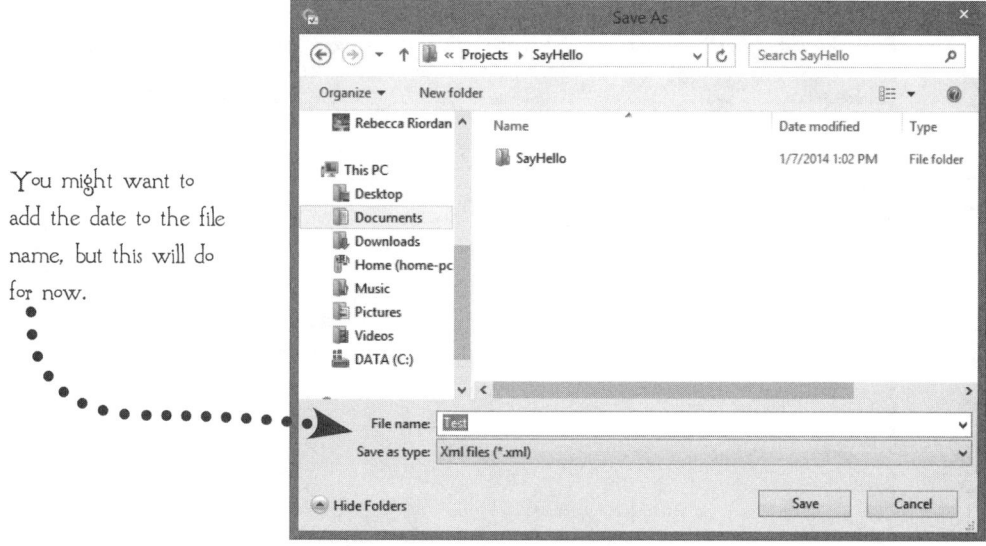

You might want to add the date to the file name, but this will do for now.

⬤ GET THE VERDICT

Once you select a file name and location, the certification kit will generate the report and give you the results:

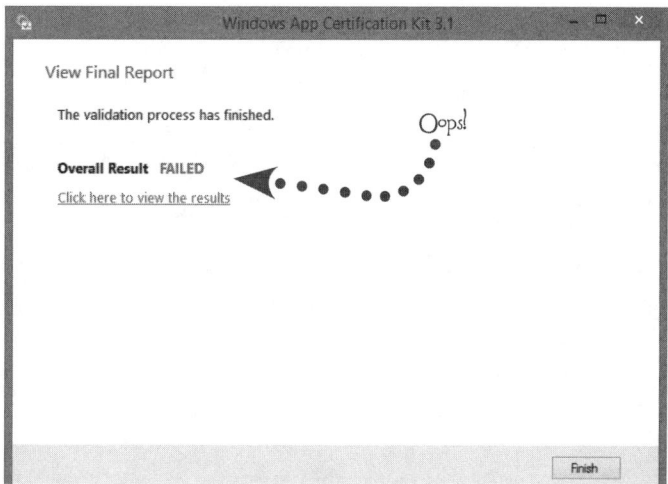

Oops!

VIEW THE RESULTS

When you click on the hyperlink, the certification kit will give you the option of what tool to use to view the xml report. You'll probably want to choose Internet Explorer. (Visual Studio will display the raw XML, which isn't as easy to read.) Here's our result:

If you scroll down through the file, you'll see that we failed certification because, among other things we're still in debug mode. That's easy to fix.

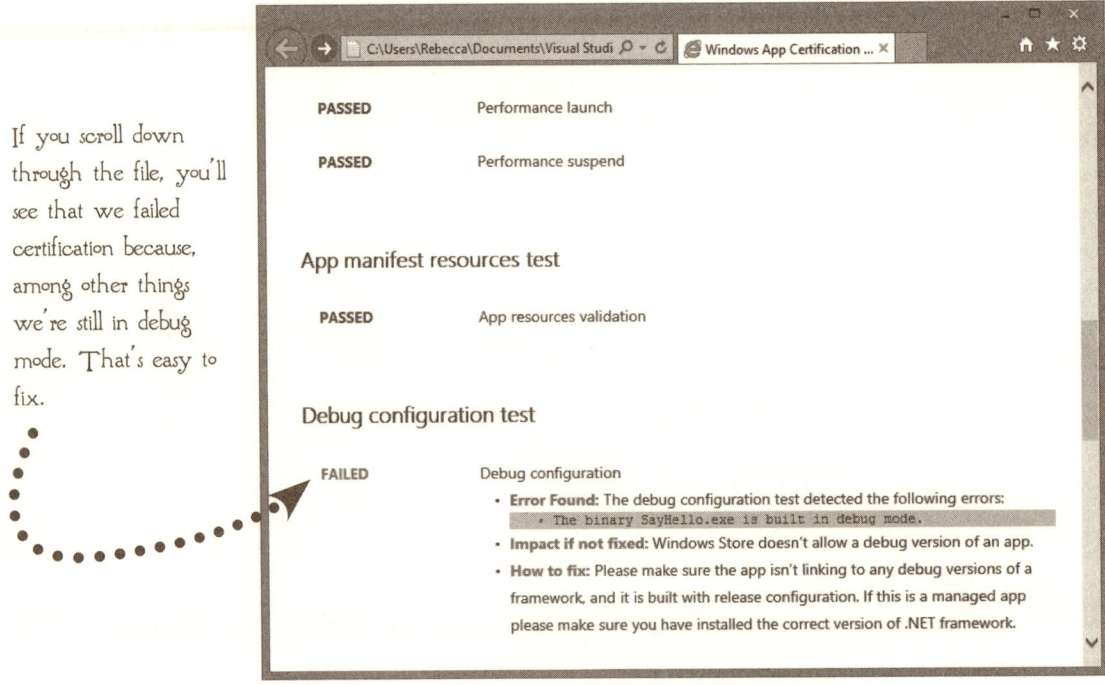

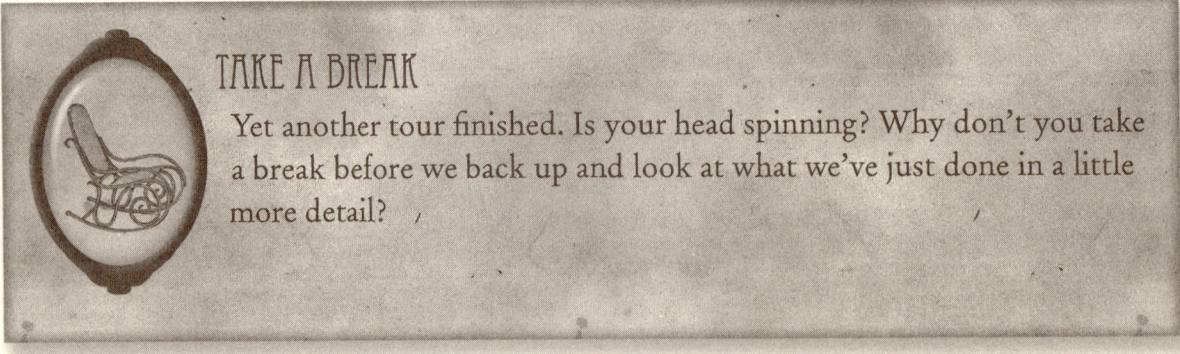

TAKE A BREAK

Yet another tour finished. Is your head spinning? Why don't you take a break before we back up and look at what we've just done in a little more detail?

SAY WHAT?

Let's start our more detailed examination with re-visiting that development process diagram, and then we'll look at some of the steps in more detail.

① CREATE THE PROJECT
We used one of the Visual Studio templates to create our project.

② USE THE DESIGNER
We used the XAML deisgner to change a few properties.

② WRITE THE CODE
We haven't written any code yet, but of course that's part of this step as well.

③ ADD CONTRACT ITEMS
We added a Settings contract to our sample app.

The goal of those steps is, of course, a Win8 app.

④ DEFINE THE MANIFEST
We only needed to add a few images to the manifest. You'll often need to do more. You'll almost always need to do something.

Of course, you'll also have to *create* the resources.

DEPLOY THE APP
Whether you're selling your app in the Windows Store or distributing directly to clients, the last step is to deploy it.

⑤ TEST CERTIFICATION
This process is so simple that we won't be doing it again, but it should be part of every development project.

VISUAL STUDIO TEMPLATES

I've said before that the Win8 app project templates are more complete than you're probably used to, and in addition to the app templates that we're talking about here, there are also templates for some individual project items. We'll be using some of those in later chapters. They're certainly more complete than the desktop project templates in earlier versions of Visual Studio. Let's take a look at what that means. Here are the solution items in our sample app:

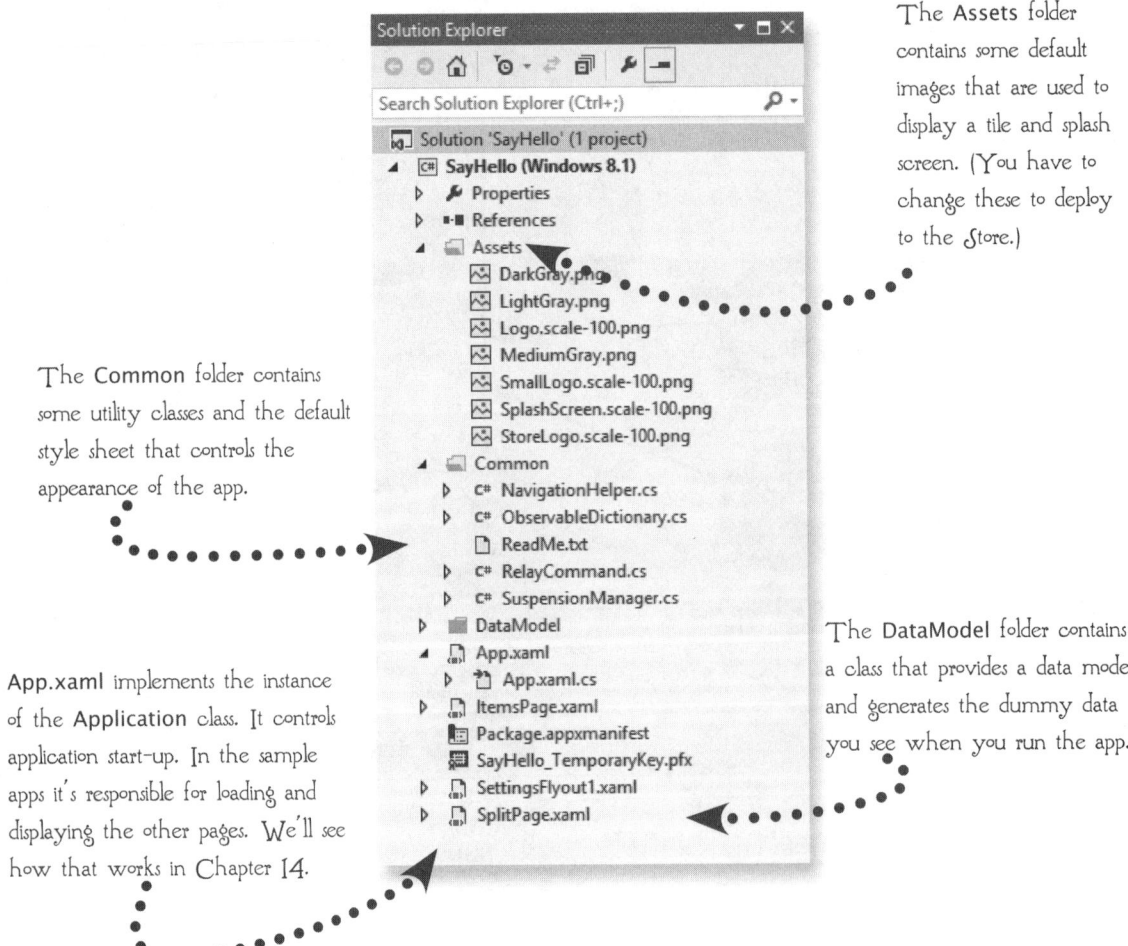

The Assets folder contains some default images that are used to display a tile and splash screen. (You have to change these to deploy to the Store.)

The Common folder contains some utility classes and the default style sheet that controls the appearance of the app.

The DataModel folder contains a class that provides a data model and generates the dummy data you see when you run the app.

App.xaml implements the instance of the Application class. It controls application start-up. In the sample apps it's responsible for loading and displaying the other pages. We'll see how that works in Chapter 14.

COMMON FILES

The files in the Common folder aren't included in a project created from the Blank App template, but there's some useful stuff here. We'll be discussing all of these and the issues they address in later chapters, but here's a preview of coming attractions:

- ## NAVIGATION HELPER
  Most of the Visual Studio templates, including the Hub app we just created, include the ability to navigate forward and backward through you app's pages. The NavigationHelper provides support for this functionality, which we'll explore in detail in Chapter 13.

- ## OBSERVABLEDICTIONARY
  The ObservableDictionary is a standard dictionary object (that is, it has keys defined as Strings and entries defined as Objects) that supports data binding. ObservableDictionary is the default type of the ViewModel implemented by the Visual Studio templates. We'll discuss MVVM and ViewModels (briefly) on the next page, and data binding in Chapter 12.

- ## RELAYCOMMAND
  Relay commands are a common method of implementing commanding across app levels when using the MVVM design pattern. You can use the RelayCommand class implemented by the templates in your own code, and it's also used by the NavigationHelper class.

- ## SUSPENSIONMANAGER
  The SuspensionManager class handles saving and restoring state information when a user switches to another app. We'll discuss suspension in Chapter 14.

Under the Microscope: Model-View-ViewModel

The Visual Studio templates implement the Model-View-ViewModel design pattern (among others).

If you've worked with WPF, you've almost certainly heard of the MVVM design patern. (You've probably used it.) But if you're new to this environment, terms like VIEWMODEL might need a bit of explanation. At it's most basic, the MVVM design pattern divides an application into three layers:

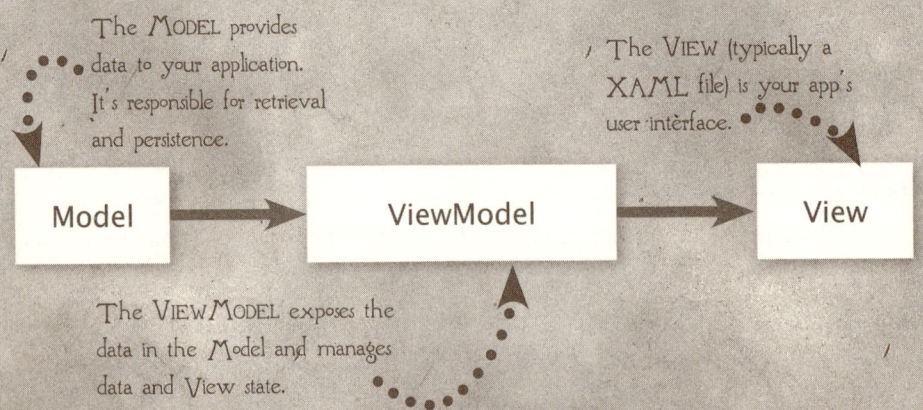

The MODEL provides data to your application. It's responsible for retrieval and persistence.

The VIEW (typically a XAML file) is your app's user interface.

The VIEWMODEL exposes the data in the Model and manages data and View state.

The XAML binding infrastructure that we'll examine in Chapter 12 makes MVVM very clean and relatively simple to implement. The pattern has been widely adopted by the development community, and it is implicit in the structure of the Visual Studio project templates.

If you're interested in learning more about the MVVM pattern, Josh Smith's article "WPF Apps With The Model-View-ViewModel Design Pattern", available on MSDN, is a good place to start. You might also want to look at the MVVM Light toolkit, available on CodePlex.

VISUAL STUDIO 2013 EXPRESS

You won't find much that's new in the basic Visual Studio IDE—although you need to allow for the fact that this is an Express version—but there are a few things worth pointing out:

You now have targeting options. We targeted the Simulator and the local machine in our walk-through.

You can search for a file, class, or member directly in the Solution Explorer. Files found in this or any search function will be opened in Preview mode.

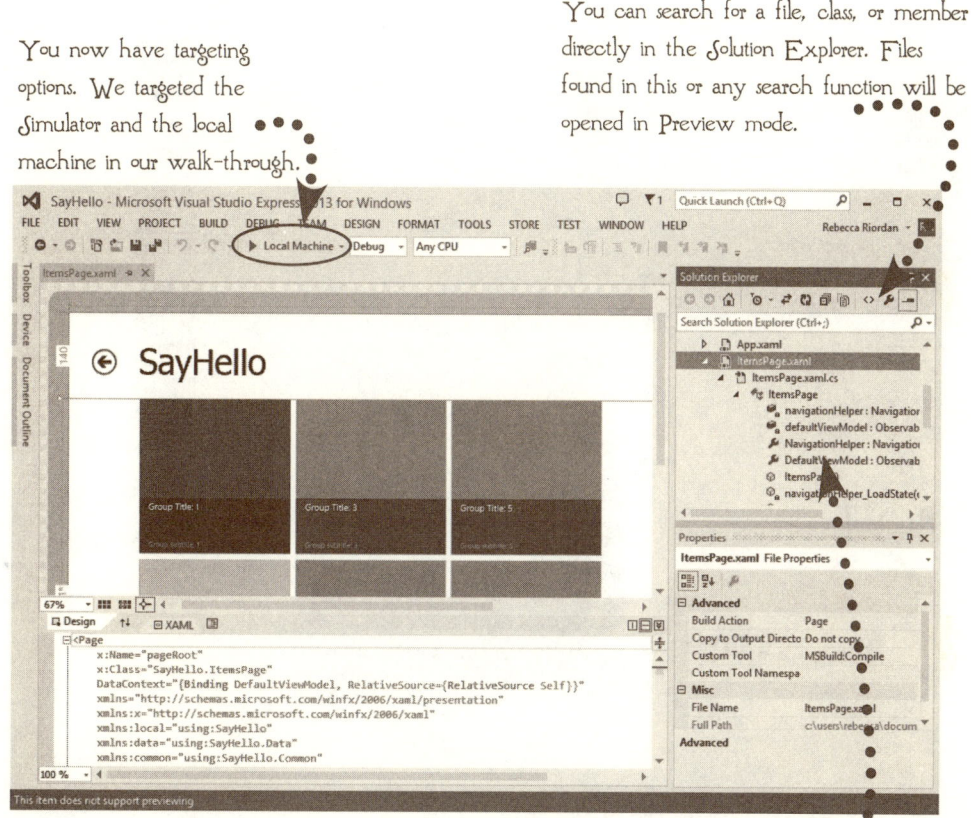

The Solution Explorer now shows class declarations. This is particularly useful for visual thinkers (like me), because the Express versions of Visual Studio don't support class diagrams.

USING THE SIMULATOR

The Visual Studio Simulator lets you test the runtime behavior of your apps at various resolutions and orientations. It also provides a means to test touch behavior if you're not working on a machine that supports touch. It even lets you simulate a geographic location.

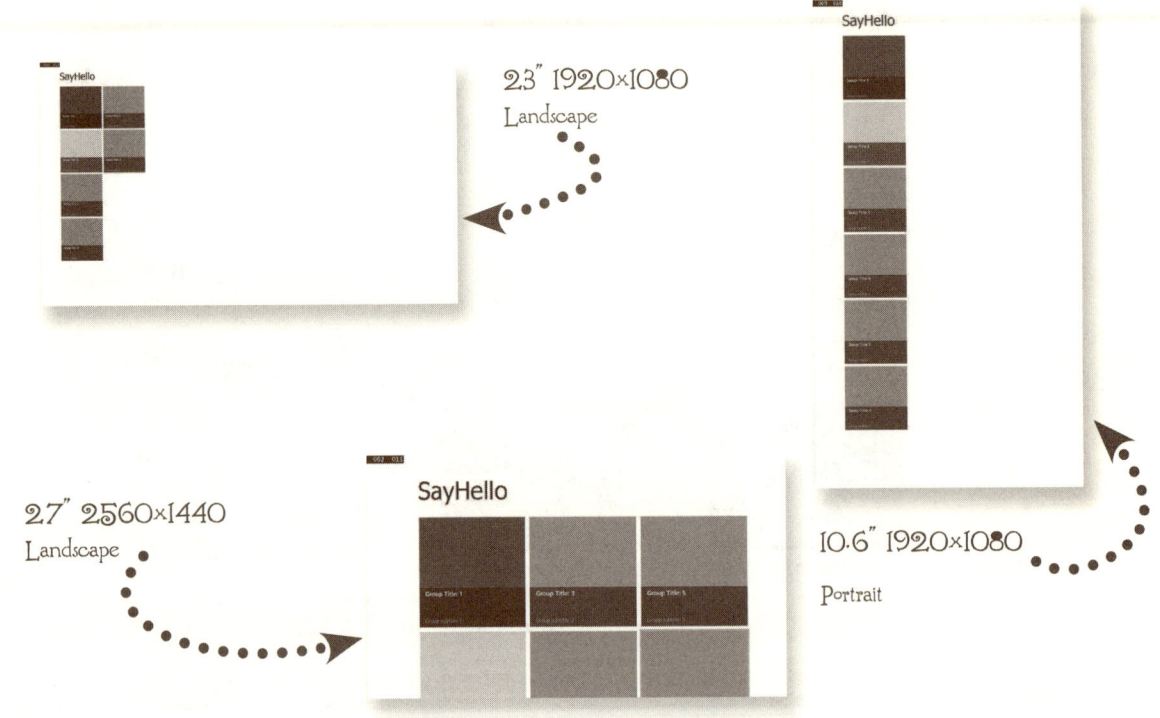

23" 1920×1080 Landscape

27" 2560×1440 Landscape

10.6" 1920×1080 Portrait

MAKE A NOTE

The Simulator is flexible, but one thing it doesn't do is let you run your apps in snapped or filled view. As we'll see in Chapter 13, Visual Studio provides design-time support for view states via the Devices panel, but to check run-time behavior you'll have to actually run the app, either on your local machine or a remote one. (You can control this via the same drop-down you used to choose the simulator.)

PUT ON YOUR THINKING HAT

The tool panel displayed on the right side of the Simulator is shown below. What does each tool do?

_____
_____
_____
_____
_____
_____
_____
_____
_____
_____
_____
_____
_____

HOW'D YOU DO?

This button minimizes the Simulator.

This set of buttons toggles the interaction mode. The top button uses mouse gestures, and the second uses single finger touch (tap with the left button and slide by dragging). The third button simulates pinch and zoom (use the mouse wheel and the left button). The final button simulates the rotate gesture (again, use the mouse wheel and the left button to initiate the gesture).

This button toggles the "Always on top" state.

This set of buttons rotate the display between portrait and landscape.

This button allows you to select a screen resolution.

This button lets you simulate a location by setting a latitude, longitutde, and altitude.

These buttons let you take screen shots of the simulated view.

This button takes you to online help for the Simulator.

THE XAML DESIGNER

We'll be working with the XAML designer a lot, and we'll explore many of its details as we go along. Let's start by getting the basic lay of the land:

The design surface supports drag-and-drop.

The toolbox works with the drag-and-drop design surface.

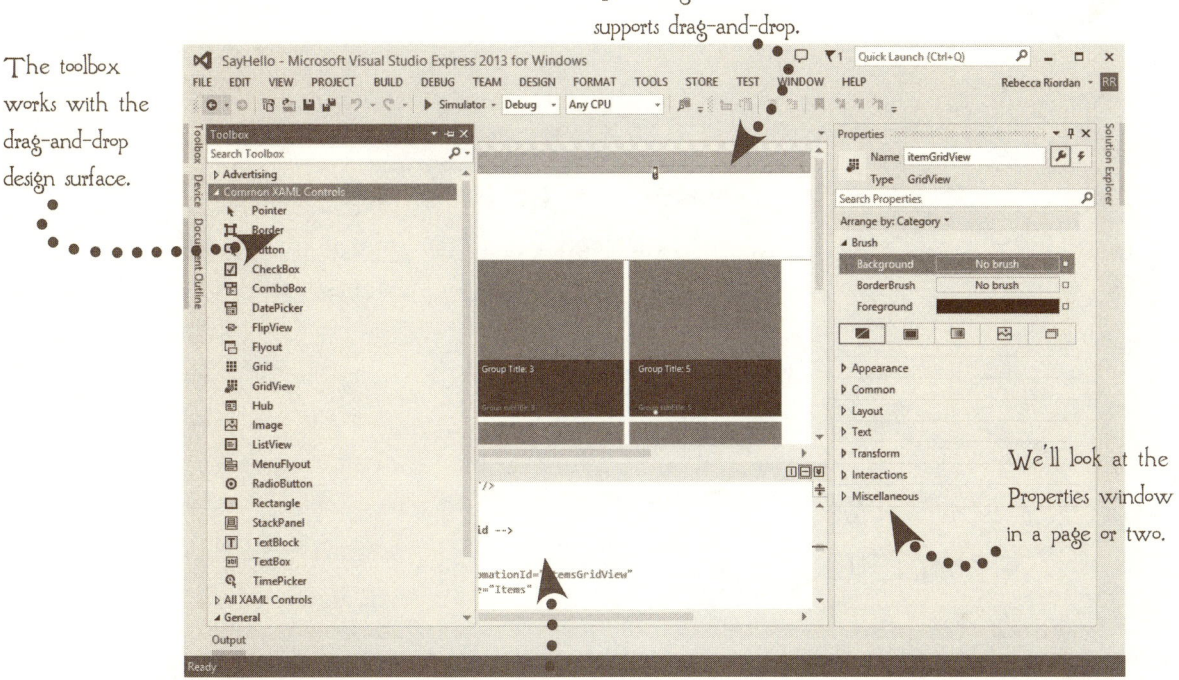

We'll look at the Properties window in a page or two.

The XAML pane lets you edit (or just examine) the XAML. Visual Studio keeps it synched with the design surface.

PUT ON YOUR THINKING HAT

There are two sets of widgets between the design surface and the XAML pane. What does each widget do?

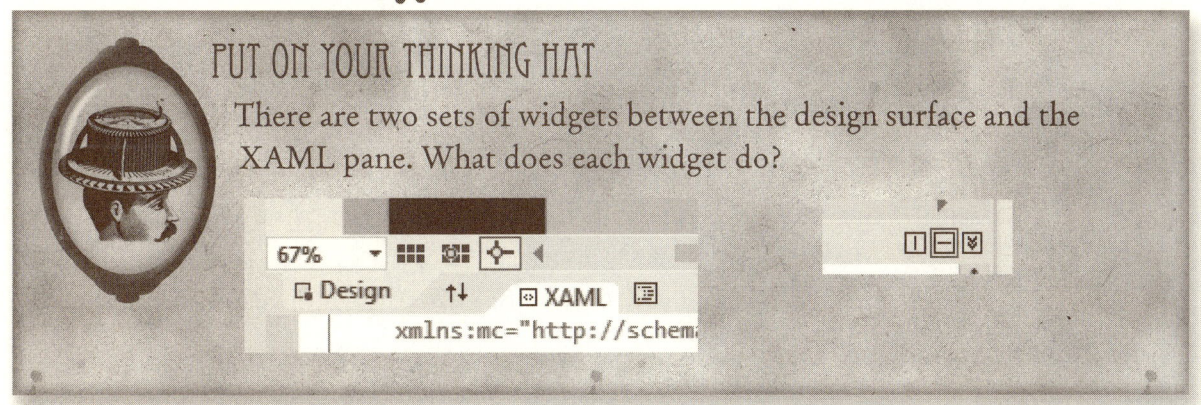

77

HOW'D YOU DO?

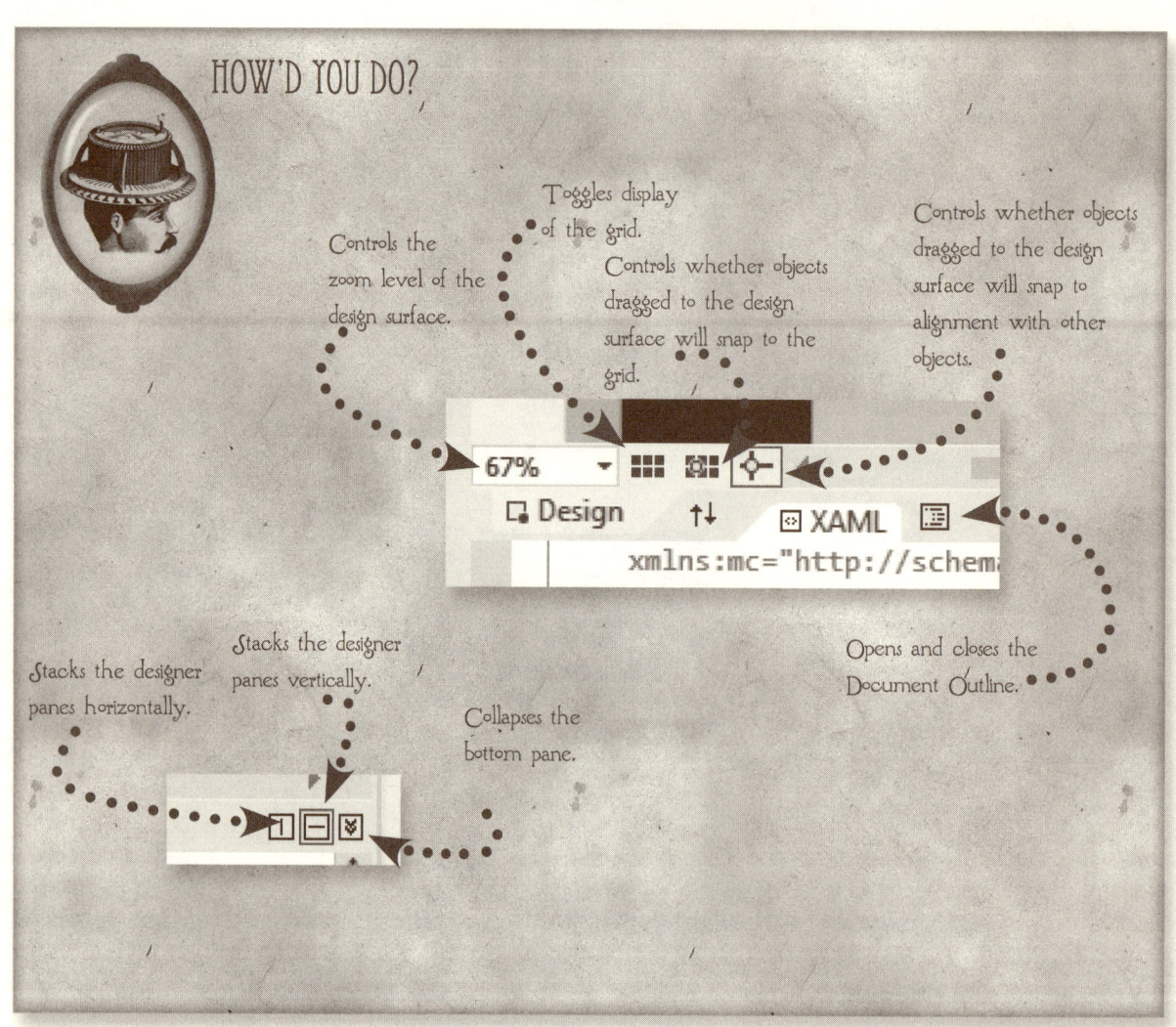

Controls the zoom level of the design surface.

Toggles display of the grid.

Controls whether objects dragged to the design surface will snap to the grid.

Controls whether objects dragged to the design surface will snap to alignment with other objects.

Stacks the designer panes horizontally.

Stacks the designer panes vertically.

Collapses the bottom pane.

Opens and closes the Document Outline.

ON YOUR OWN
Why don't you spend a little time getting used to controlling the XAML designer IDE? You can't save a window layout in Visual Studio Express, but it is "sticky", so your layout will remain the same even if you open or close the application.

BLEND INTEGRATION

Expression Blend has been around for several years now, and it has always played nice with Visual Studio. That's been enhanced in Visual Studio 2013, which includes a copy of Expression Blend. Not only can you still open your XAML files in Blend (either directly or via Visual Studio), but the two applications share the same code base. This is perhaps most evident in the Properties window.

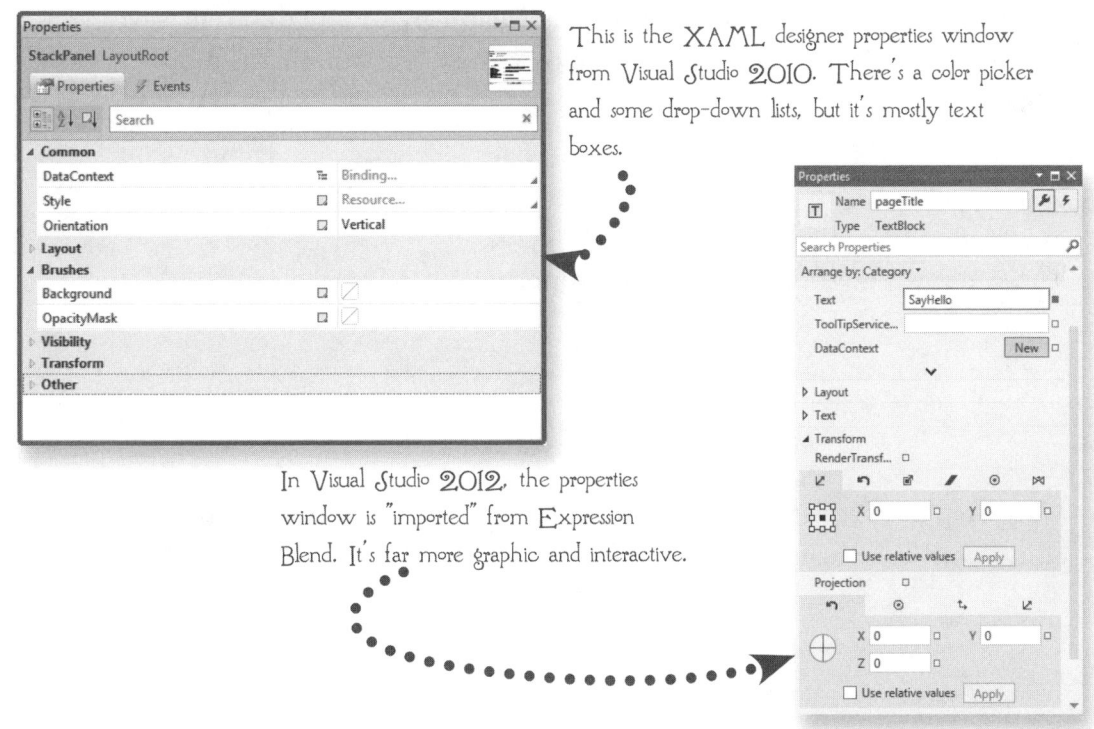

This is the XAML designer properties window from Visual Studio 2010. There's a color picker and some drop-down lists, but it's mostly text boxes.

In Visual Studio 2012, the properties window is "imported" from Expression Blend. It's far more graphic and interactive.

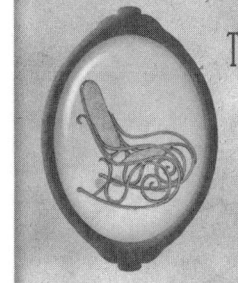

TAKE A BREAK

That's it for our tour of Win8 app development. Why don't you take a break before you complete the Review and we move on to our detailed study of the topic, with an exploration of the XAML language?

REVIEW

Can you answer these questions based on what you've learned about Win8 app development so far? (Checking the text or Visual Studio isn't considerd cheating.)

Most of the steps involved in developing an app aren't any different when you're working with Win8, but there are two new ones, and one that is more important. What are they?

There are two ways to set a XAML property. What are they?

Why does the property window in the XAML designer look different in this edition of Visual Studio?

What are the four types of project templates?

Congratulations! You've finished the chapter. Take a minute to think about what you've accomplished before you move on to the next one...

List three things you learned in this chapter:

①

②

③

Why do you think you need to know these things in order to develop Win8 apps?

Is there anything in this chapter that you think you need to understand in more detail? If so, what are you going to do about that?

XAML

3

Is your head spinning after that whirlwind tour of Win8 XAML development? It's okay. You can take a deep breath and relax now. In the rest of the book we'll slow down and look at each area in some detail. We'll start in this chapter with the XAML language that you'll use to define the UI of your application declaratively. If you've worked with WPF or Silverlight, there won't be much here that's new to you—by and large, XAML is XAML. What changes are the namespaces, the widgets, and the way the XAML interacts with the code-behind in a running application.

But don't panic if you come from a WinForms or WebForms background. You've probably used XML (it's hard to do much development these days without bumping into—or tripping over—some XML), and XAML is just a form of XML. Even if you haven't used XML, there's a reason it's become ubiquitous: its syntax is simple. Really, really simple.

FITTING IT IN

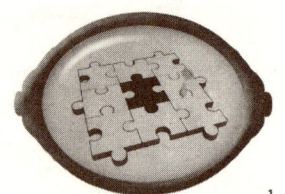

In this chapter we'll be concentrating on the details of the XAML markup language. Here's how it fits in the development process:

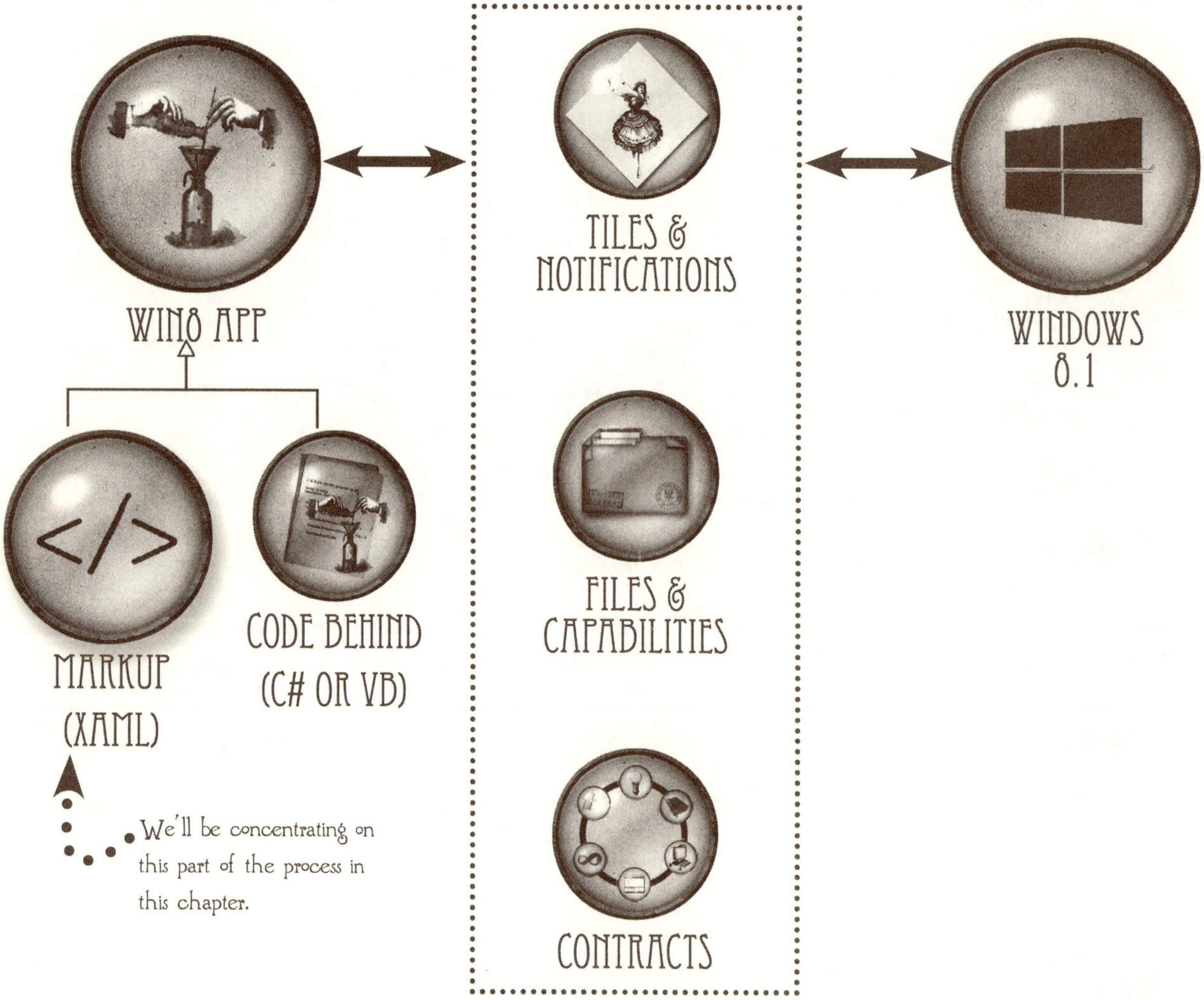

WIN8 APP

MARKUP (XAML)

CODE BEHIND (C# OR VB)

We'll be concentrating on this part of the process in this chapter.

TILES & NOTIFICATIONS

FILES & CAPABILITIES

CONTRACTS

WINDOWS 8.1

84

WHAT?? ANOTHER LANGUAGE?

You might be one of the developers who was mightily relieved to discover that Win8 apps didn't require JavaScript. (I was.) But if you're coming from a WinForms background, you'll still have to learn another language: XAML (which stands for e**X**tensible **A**pplication **M**arkup **L**anguage).

Why another language?

I'm glad you asked. Just as a well-educated English speaker is expected to know at least a few common phrases in Latin, a programmer, whatever language or type of application you specialize in, needs to know the basics of XML (which is trivially easy). XAML, which is based on XML, is becoming a pervasive part of .NET Framework programming.

To be fair, I need to say that it's perfectly possible to write a Win8 app without writing a single line of XAML. But splitting the behavior and the code into two separate files has several advantages, and we'll see some of them later in this chapter.

TASK LIST

In this chapter we'll explore the declarative XAML language that you'll use to define the user interface of your Win8 app.

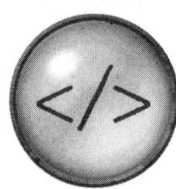

XAML FUNDAMENTALS

XAML is a specialized form of XML, and the rules of its syntax conform to XML rules. We'll start by looking at exactly what those rules are and how to use them to make your XAML code as readable as possible.

XAML NAMESPACES

Roughly equivalent to a C# **using** or Visual Basic **Imports** statement, the XAML elements and attributes that are available to you are defined by the NAMESPACES you declare in your file. We'll examine those next and see how XAML markup extensions are used to link your UI declarations to code-behind.

LOGICAL & VISUAL TREES

XAML, like XML, is intrinsically hierarchical. We'll end the chapter by exploring the two different hierarchies you'll work with in Win8 apps: the OBJECT TREE (often called the LOGICAL TREE) that you build in your XAML markup and the VISUAL TREE that represents how elements are displayed to the user.

XAML FUNDAMENTALS

Let's start our examination of XAML by comparing XAML markup to something you're already familiar with: C#. (The Visual Basic code is almost identical; just leave out the semicolons and capitalize the keywords.) The following code snippets produce the same window:

```xml
<Page x:Class="sayHello.MainPage" x:Name="MyPage">

  <Grid x:Name="layoutRoot">
    <!-- The button is inside the grid -->
    <Button x:Name="FirstButton" Height="74"
      Width="229">
      Click Me, Please
    </Button>
  </Grid>

</Page>
```

```csharp
Page MyPage = new Page();

Grid LayoutRoot = new Grid();
MyPage.Content = LayoutRoot;

// The button is inside the grid
Button FirstButton = new Button();
FirstButton.Height = 74;
FirstButton.Width = 229;
FirstButton.Content = "Click Me, Please";

LayoutRoot.Children.Add(FirstButton);
```

PUT ON YOUR THINKING HAT

If C# or Visual Basic can do everything XAML can do, and a lot more besides, can you think of some reasons why using both languages in the application development process is a good idea?

87

HOW'D YOU DO?

Did you think of some reasons? Were you convinced by them? Here's a list of a few you might not have thought of:

XAML IS OFTEN MORE CONCISE

If you compare the snippets on the previous page, you'll see that the XAML version of the window is much less verbose. (But that's not always true.)

XAML IS DECLARATIVE

"Declarative" doesn't necessarily mean better, but it's often easier to understand (and write). Imagine the difference between saying, "I want an electrical outlet on that wall" and actually wiring it.

XAML CLEARLY EXPRESSES THE WIN8 APP COMPOSITION MODEL

As we'll see when we explore logical and visual trees, Win8 app interfaces are composed. Things don't just float around on their own; a String is contained in a Button that's contained in a Grid that's contained in a Window. The hierarchical structure of XAML makes that much, much clearer than procedural code.

XAML IS TOOLABLE

The boffins at Microsoft talk about XAML being "toolable". What they mean is that because XAML is plain old XML, it can be easily parsed and manipulated by any application. A great example of that is Microsoft's Expression Blend, a designing and prototyping tool aimed at designers rather than developers, for which read, "it will feel familiar to people used to working in Adobe Photoshop". Well, at least more familiar than Visual Studio.

XAML SUPPORTS SEPARATE WORKFLOWS

Programmers, as a class of people, aren't known for their graphic design skills; it's a different profession. But once you have separate tools for designing the graphics and implementing the behavior, it becomes trivially simple to let different people perform the tasks they're trained to do. Doesn't it make sense to let the graphic designers design and the programmers program? XAML makes that easy. And because many graphic designers are familiar with another XML-based language, HTML, many of them find working directly in XAML quite comfortable.

SYNTAX BASICS

If you're familiar with XML or HTML, the syntax of XAML will already be familiar, but it adds some extensions to basic XML and uses some special vocabulary. If you're not familiar with XML, don't worry. It's really, really easy. (I think I've mentioned that, haven't I?)

OBJECT ELEMENTS

The basic unit of a procedural language like C# or Visual Basic is a statement. The basic unit of XAML is an OBJECT ELEMENT. Just as in your procedural language you can write single- or multi-line statements, you can write single- and multi-line object element declarations:

This syntax is used for elements that don't contain any other elements. It's roughly equivalent to a single-line C# statement.

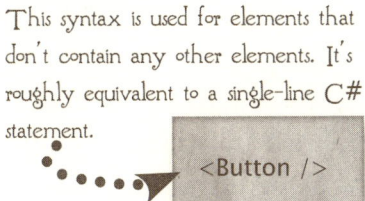

This syntax is used when other elements are nested inside the object. It's roughly equivalent to a C# statement block surrounded by braces or a Visual Basic something...end something block.

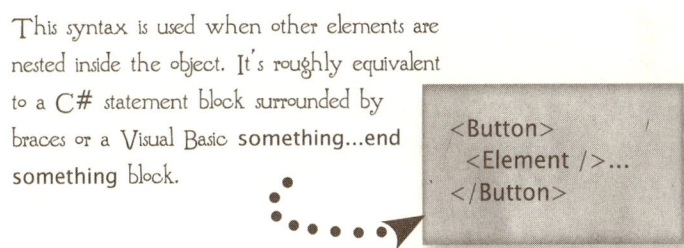

ATTRIBUTES AND PROPERTIES

In a procedural language you assign a value to the property of an object using syntax like **Object.Property = value**. In XAML, you have two options. You can either set the property as an attribute that's declared in the opening tag, or you can define the property as a separate nested element:

This is ATTRIBUTE SYNTAX. Attributes are contained in quotation marks, and multiple attributes are separated by white space.

This is called PROPERTY ELEMENT SYNTAX. For some complex attributes, it's a lot easier to write and understand than attribute syntax.

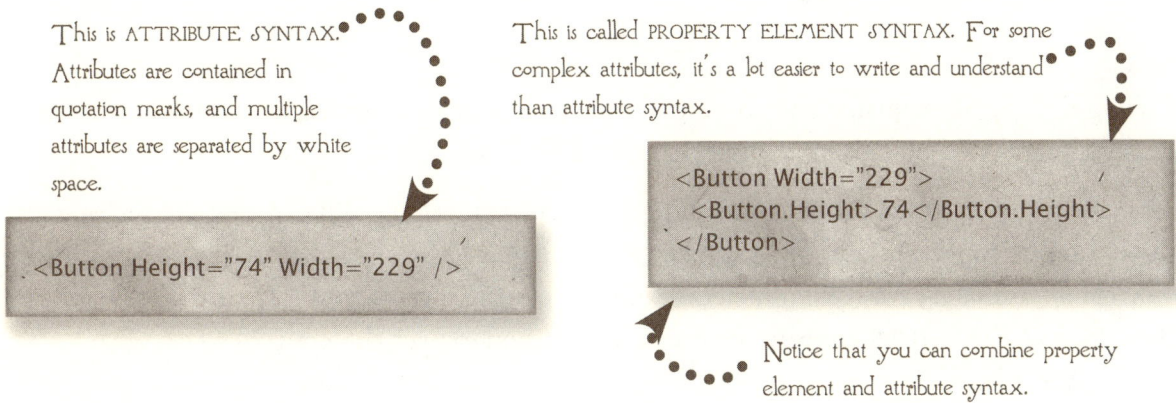

Notice that you can combine property element and attribute syntax.

89

CONTENT PROPERTIES

Did you notice that in the Button property element example, we had to specify the Height property as Button.Height?

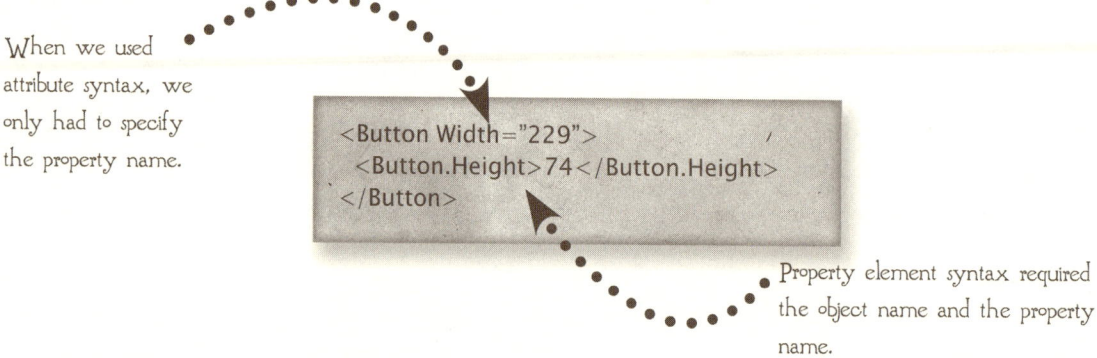

When we used attribute syntax, we only had to specify the property name.

Property element syntax required the object name and the property name.

Repeating the object name like that makes it clear that you're referring to a property, not some other element named "Height". But every XAML element can define a single property, called **Content**, that can simply be placed between the opening and closing tags of the object. For the Button, the content property is whatever's displayed inside the Button, usually a string:

The content property doesn't need to be enclosed in tags (although you can), and some elements, like the Button, can even interpret strings directly without enclosing them in quotes.

The cool thing about using the content property is that it's defined as an **Object**. It can be anything. We'll be talking a lot about that a bit later.

The tricky thing about using the content property is knowing what it means. Technically, the content property is any object that will be displayed by the **ContentPresenter** of the control's template. (We'll examine control templates in Chapter 11.) It's usually intuitive, though, like the Button. I mean, what else would you expect the control to do with "Click Me, Please" but display it?

PUT ON YOUR THINKING HAT

Time to get your feet wet. Can you translate the code snippet below into XAML, and the XAML code into C# (or Visual Basic, if you'd rather)? (Don't worry about what all the elements are. We'll be examining them in later chapters.)

```
Page MainPage = new Page();

Grid layoutRoot = new Grid();

AppBar mainMenu = new AppBar();
StackPanel menuStack = new StackPanel();
Button menuButton = new Button();

menuStack.Children.Add(menuButton);
mainMenu.Content = menuStack;
MainPage.BottomAppBar = mainMenu;
```

Notice that you add the button to the Children collection of the StackPanel but set the Content of the AppBar. We'll find out why when we examine Panels in the next chapter.

The Visual Basic version of the code is identical. Just leave off the semicolons at the end of the statements and capitalize the keywords like New.

```
<Page x:Class="SayHello.MainPage">
 <Grid name="LayoutRoot">
  <Button Height="50" Width="75">
   Cancel
  </Button>
 </Grid>
</Page>
```

91

HOW'D YOU DO?

Remember, there are different ways to express the same thing in both code-behind and in XAML so don't worry if your code is a little different than mine, so long as the syntax is correct.

```csharp
Page MainPage = new Page();

Grid layoutRoot = new Grid();

AppBar mainMenu = new AppBar();
StackPanel menuStack = new StackPanel();
Button menuButton = new Button();

menuStack.Children.Add(menuButton);
mainMenu.Content = menuStack;
MainPage.BottomAppBar = mainMenu;
```

```xml
<Page x:Name="MainPage">
  <Page.BottomAppBar>
    <AppBar>
      <StackPanel>
        <Button/>
      </StackPanel>
    </AppBar>
  </Page.BottomAppBar>
  <Grid x:Name="layoutRoot" />
</Page>
```

This one was a little tricky. Did you get it right? You don't explicitly need to add elements because it's implicit in the nesting.

Did you have a problem figuring out what to call the variables here? Unlike C# or VB variables, XAML elements don't have to have names unless you're going to reference them in code, but it's a good idea to give them one using the name attribute.

```xml
<Page x:Class="SayHello.MainPage">
  <Grid name="LayoutRoot">
    <Button Height="50" Width="75">
    Cancel
    </Button>
  </Grid>
</Page>
```

```csharp
Page MyPage = new Page();
Grid LayoutRoot = new Grid();
Button MyButton = new Button();

MyButton.Height = 50;
MyButton.Width = 75;
MyButton.Content = "Cancel";

LayoutRoot.Children.Add(MyButton);
MyPage.Content = LayoutRoot;
```

REVIEW

Can you answer the following questions about XAML syntax?

Can you re-write the following XAML using attribute syntax?

```
<Button>
    <Button.Height>30</Button.Height>
</Button>
```

What's wrong with the following XAML element?

```
<Page x:Name=MyPage />
```

What about this one?

```
<Page>
    "MyPage"
</Page>
```

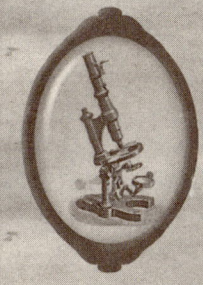

UNDER THE MICROSOCOPE: CONVERTERS

We talked about how text content properties don't need to be enclosed in quotation marks, but have you noticed that XAML is really smart about interpreting value types? In a procedural language, you have to be really careful about using 1.0 to specify a Double rather than an Integer.

XAML COLLECTIONS

In the last exercise we saw that XAML makes it unnecessary to explicitly add elements to the elements that contain them because the ownership hierarchy is implicit in the way the element tags are nested. XAML even makes it easy to add all the items of a collection using a very similar syntax:

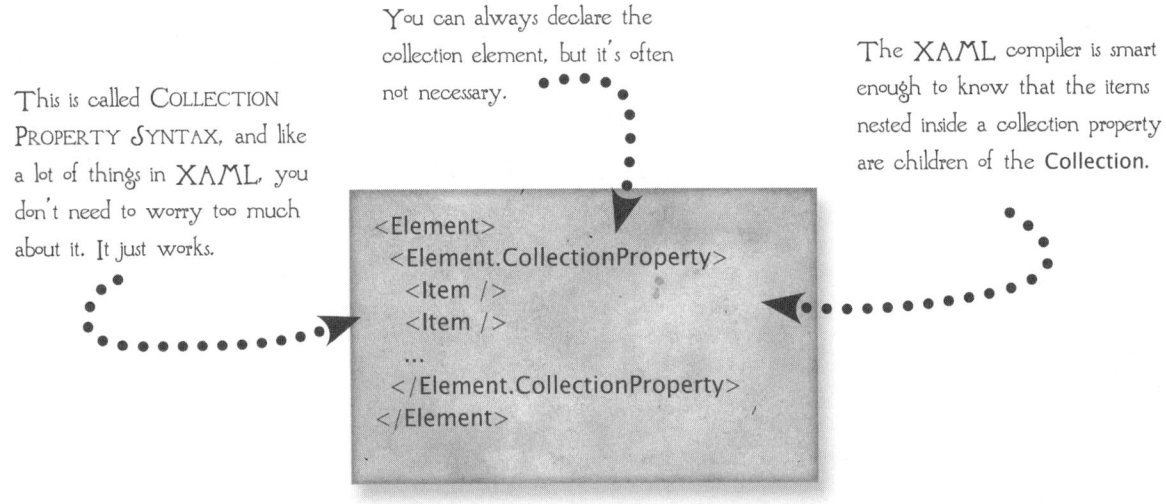

This is called COLLECTION PROPERTY SYNTAX, and like a lot of things in XAML, you don't need to worry too much about it. It just works.

You can always declare the collection element, but it's often not necessary.

The XAML compiler is smart enough to know that the items nested inside a collection property are children of the Collection.

```
<Element>
  <Element.CollectionProperty>
    <Item />
    <Item />
    ...
  </Element.CollectionProperty>
</Element>
```

PUT ON YOUR THINKING HAT

One of the Win8 app elements that has collection properties is the Grid layout panel. (We'll look at layout panels in detail in the next chapter.) Like other panel controls, the Grid can contain multiple children, and it organizes those children into rows and columns. The rows are defined as <RowDefinition> elements in the <Grid.RowDefinitions> collection and columns are <ColumnDefinition> elements in the <Grid.ColumnDefinitions> collection.

Using collection property syntax, can you write the XAML that declares a <Grid> element with three rows and three columns? Don't worry about any other attributes or properties.

HOW'D YOU DO?

Be careful about how your elements are declared. RowDefinitions (plural) is a collection property. RowDefinition (singular) is a member of the collection.

`<Grid.RowDefinitions>` is the collection property. It's declared using standard XAML property element syntax.

Because we're not specifying any attributes, the single-tag syntax works fine for RowDefinition.

You need to be careful that nested elements are completely enclosed in their parent. IntelliSense will help you with this.

```
<Grid>
    <Grid.RowDefinitions>
        <RowDefinition />
        <RowDefinition />
        <RowDefinition />
    </Grid.RowDefinitions>
    <Grid.ColumnDefinitions>
        <ColumnDefinition />
        <ColumnDefinition />
        <ColumnDefinition />
    </Grid.ColumnDefinitions>
</Grid>
```

The `<RowDefinition>` elements are the members of the collection and use collection property syntax.

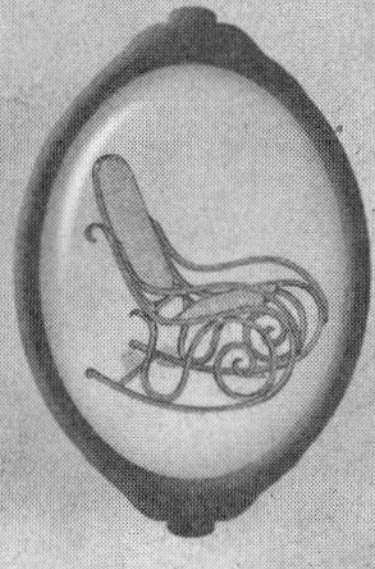

TAKE A BREAK

That's it for basic XAML syntax. Why don't you take a break before you complete the short Review on the next page and we move on to XAML namespaces?

XAML NAMESPACES

Just like the code you've written in C# or Visual Basic, the elements that are available to your XAML are defined by namespace declarations. Here's how they work:

You'll remember that XAML is based on XML. It uses the standard XML attribute **xmlns** to declare a namespace. The basic syntax is straightforward:

> xmlns:[id]="<namespace>"

- It isn't strictly required, but namespaces are almost always declared in the root element of your XAML file.

- The [id] value is used to prefix elements contained in that namespace. So, for example, if you use the id of **MyLib** to reference a namespace that contains the **Widget** class, you'd create **Widget** elements like this:

> <MyLib:Widget ... />

- One (and only one) namespace can omit the [id] value. It's called the DEFAULT NAMESPACE.

- The namespace can be specified as a URI or by using a special **using** keyword that references a library in your project. (We'll see how that works in a minute.)

STANDARD NAMESPACES

When you add a XAML file to your project, Visual Studio will define (at least) four namespaces for you:

```
xmlns="http://schemas.microsoft.com/winfx/2006/xaml/presentation"
xmlns:x="http://schemas.microsoft.com/winfx/2006/xaml"
xmlns:d="http://schemas.microsoft.com/expression/blend/2008"
xmlns:mc="http://schemas.openxmlformat.or/markup-compatibility/2006"
```

- The default namespace is assigned to the XAML namespace that is mapped by the compiler to the XAML elements defined for Win8 apps.

- The x prefix is mapped to the XAML language elements. We'll look at these in detail on the next page.

- The d prefix is mapped to a namespace that provides designer (specifically Expression Blend) support. Any attributes marked with the d prefix are used when the XAML is displayed in Expression Blend or the Visual Studio XAML designer but are ignored at runtime.

- The mc prefix is mapped to a markup compatibility namespace that has a single attribute, mc:Ignorable. Setting mc:Ignorable to the "d" prefix is the technique that allows design-time attributes to be ignored. (Visual Studio does this for you.)

> mc:Ignorable = "d"

MAKE A NOTE

If you're familiar with XML, you might think that the default XAML namespace defines a schema. It doesn't. The elements that are mapped to this namespace are defined by attributes in the WinRT libraries, and the actual mapping is performed by the XAML parser. This is how Microsoft is able to use the same namespace for multiple XAML platforms, including WPF and Silverlight, which is convenient if you're trying to write cross-platform code.

XAML LANGUAGE ATTRIBUTES

The XAML language namespace defined by the Visual Studio with the x prefix implements some important attributes:

- ## CLASS

    The **x:Class** attribute (used only in the root element declaration) links the XAML file to the code-behind file defined as a partial class with the specified name:

    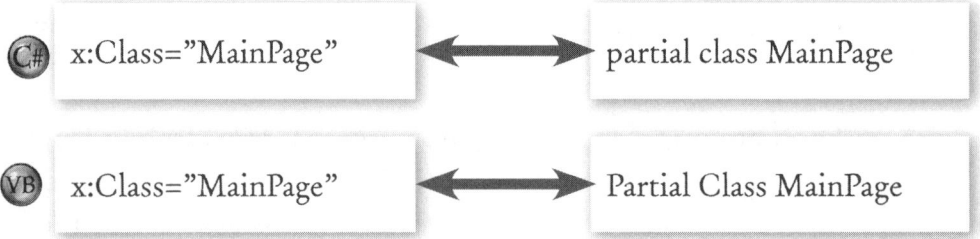

- ## KEY

    The **x:Key** attribute is used in a **ResourceDictionary** to uniquely identify an element. Resource dictionaries define resources such as a **Brush** that defines a color or a template that specifies how a widget looks. We'll see how all that works in Chapter 11.

- ## NAME

    The **x:Name** attribute provides a unique identifier that you can use to refer to the element in your code.

    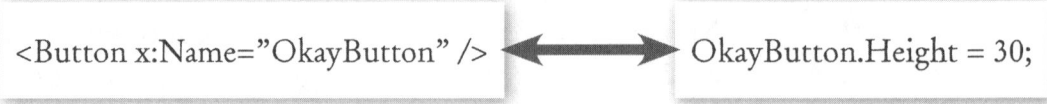

The same namespace defines some basic data types:

- **NULL**

  Used to specify a null value for a property:

  ```
  <Button Background="{x:Null}" />
  ```

  Those curly braces indicate a MARKUP EXTENSION. I'll explain those on the next page.

- **STRING**

  Used to declare a String element:

  ```
  <x:String>Some Text</x:String>
  ```

- **BOOLEAN**

  Used to declare a Boolean element:

  ```
  <x:Boolean>true</x:Boolean>
  ```

- **DOUBLE**

  Used to declare a Double element:

  ```
  <x:Double>3.56</x:Double>
  ```

- **INT32**

  Used to declare an Int32 element:

  ```
  <x:Int32>-143</x:Int32>
  ```

Markup Extensions

Actually, I cheated in that list of data types on the last page. In XAML terms, x:Null isn't a data type; it's a MARKUP EXTENSION. Markup extensions are a bit of XML sleight of hand that allow you to provide an object instead of a literal value. The XAML language namespace defines five:

 BINDING AND RELATIVESOURCE

The {Binding} extension allows you to defer the value of a property to runtime. The {RelativeSource} extension, used within a {Binding}, is used to refer to properties of the element or its parent. We'll discuss XAML binding in detail in Chapter 12.

```
<TextBox Text="{Binding RelativeSource={RelativeSource Self, Path=FontFamily}}" />
```

Markup extensions are always specified within curly braces.

Notice that you have to specify RelativeSource and then create an instance of a RelativeSource using another extension.

 STATICRESOURCE AND CUSTOMRESOURCE

The {StaticResource} extension allows you to set a property to a resource defined in a ResourceDictionary. The {CustomResource} extension is similar, but it allows you to write a custom loader that provides the resource. We'll discuss resources in detail in Chapter 11.

```
<TextBox Text="{StaticResource <key>}" />
```

TEMPLATEBINDING

The {TemplateBinding} extension is used inside a control template to refer to a property of the control. We'll explore control templates in detail in Chapter 11.

CUSTOM NAMESPACES

In addition to the two namespace declarations that are required in a XAML root element and the others that Visual Studio adds for you by default, you can reference the namespaces you create in your project or .NET namespaces. The syntax for referencing these namespaces is a little different:

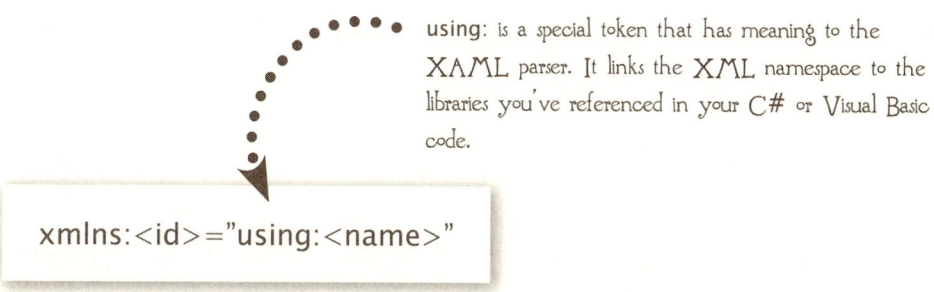

using: is a special token that has meaning to the XAML parser. It links the XML namespace to the libraries you've referenced in your C# or Visual Basic code.

xmlns:<id>="using:<name>"

Along with the other namespace declarations that Visual Studio adds by default, it will map the current project to the local prefix:

xmlns:local="using:SayHello"

The partial class that is linked to the XAML file using the x:Class attribute is considered to be in the CURRENT PAGE SCOPE and doesn't need to be mapped. That means, for example, that you can reference an event handler that you've defined in the code-behind without creating an xmlns definition (or using a mapping prefix).

TAKE A BREAK

There's lots more to learn about XAML, and we'll look at some refinements in later chapters, but now you've seen the basic syntax. It's certainly a lot easier than C# or Visual Basic, isn't it?

Why don't you take a break before you do one final review and we move on to XAML logical and visual trees?

REVIEW

Can you answer the following questions based on what you've learned about declaring XAML namespaces?

Of the namespaces that Visual Studio adds to your XAML file by default, there are two that are so critical that it would be difficult to work without them. What are they?

How many namespaces can be declared without a prefix? What is a namespace that doesn't include a prefix called?

What XAML language attribute is used to link a XAML file to the partial class definition in the code-behind?

What characters delimit a markup extension?

What token do you use to declare a namespace that you've defined in your project?

LOGICAL & VISUAL TREES

There's one last thing to examine before we move on to exploring the elements that are available to you in your Win8 apps: the trees that your XAML defines, and how to navigate them.

We've talked about how XAML elements are hierarchical. Programmers find it useful to think of hierarchies as trees, and in XAML there are two. The OBJECT TREE (sometimes called the LOGICAL TREE) is probably the simplest to understand: It represents the way elements are nested in the XAML markup (or in code).

The VISUAL TREE, on the other hand, contains all the elements that are displayed on the screen. Almost all of the XAML controls you'll work with are actually composed of multiple visual elements—the default **Button**, for example, usually includes a **Border**, a **ContentPresenter**, and a **TextBlock**. (As we'll see in Chapter 11 when we examine control templates, you have a lot of control over the elements that compose a XAML control, so this isn't an absolute.)

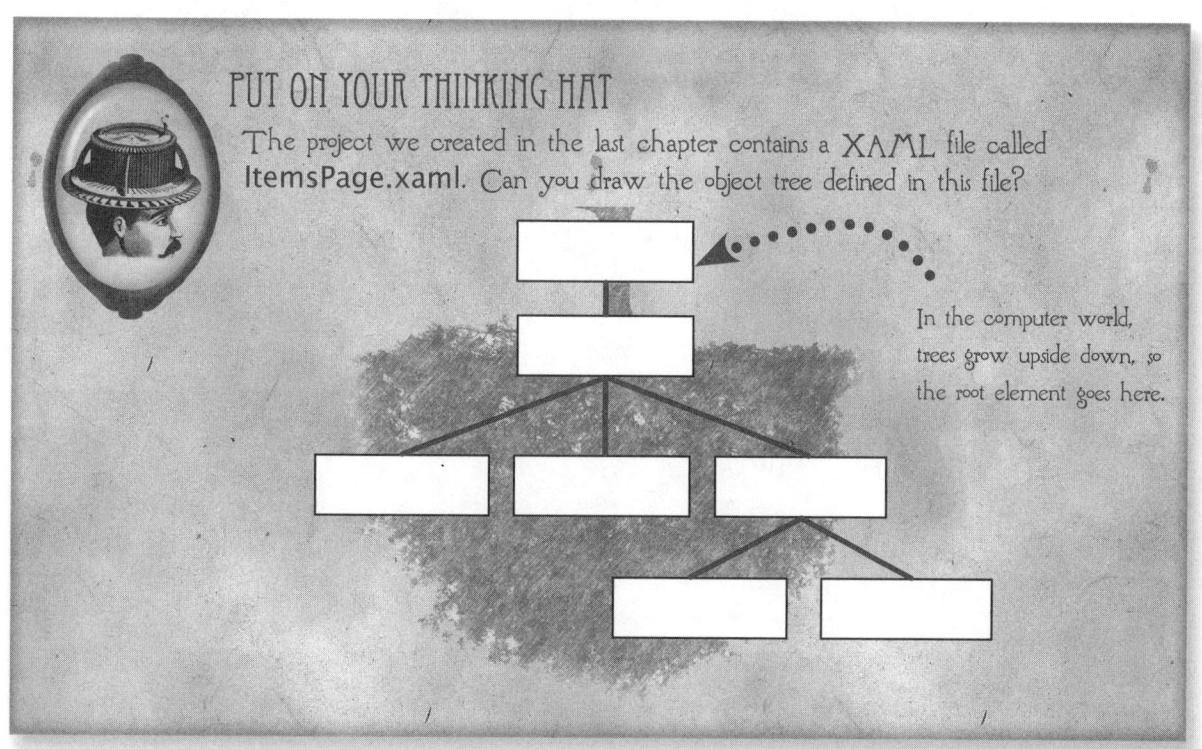

PUT ON YOUR THINKING HAT

The project we created in the last chapter contains a XAML file called **ItemsPage.xaml**. Can you draw the object tree defined in this file?

In the computer world, trees grow upside down, so the root element goes here.

103

HOW'D YOU DO?

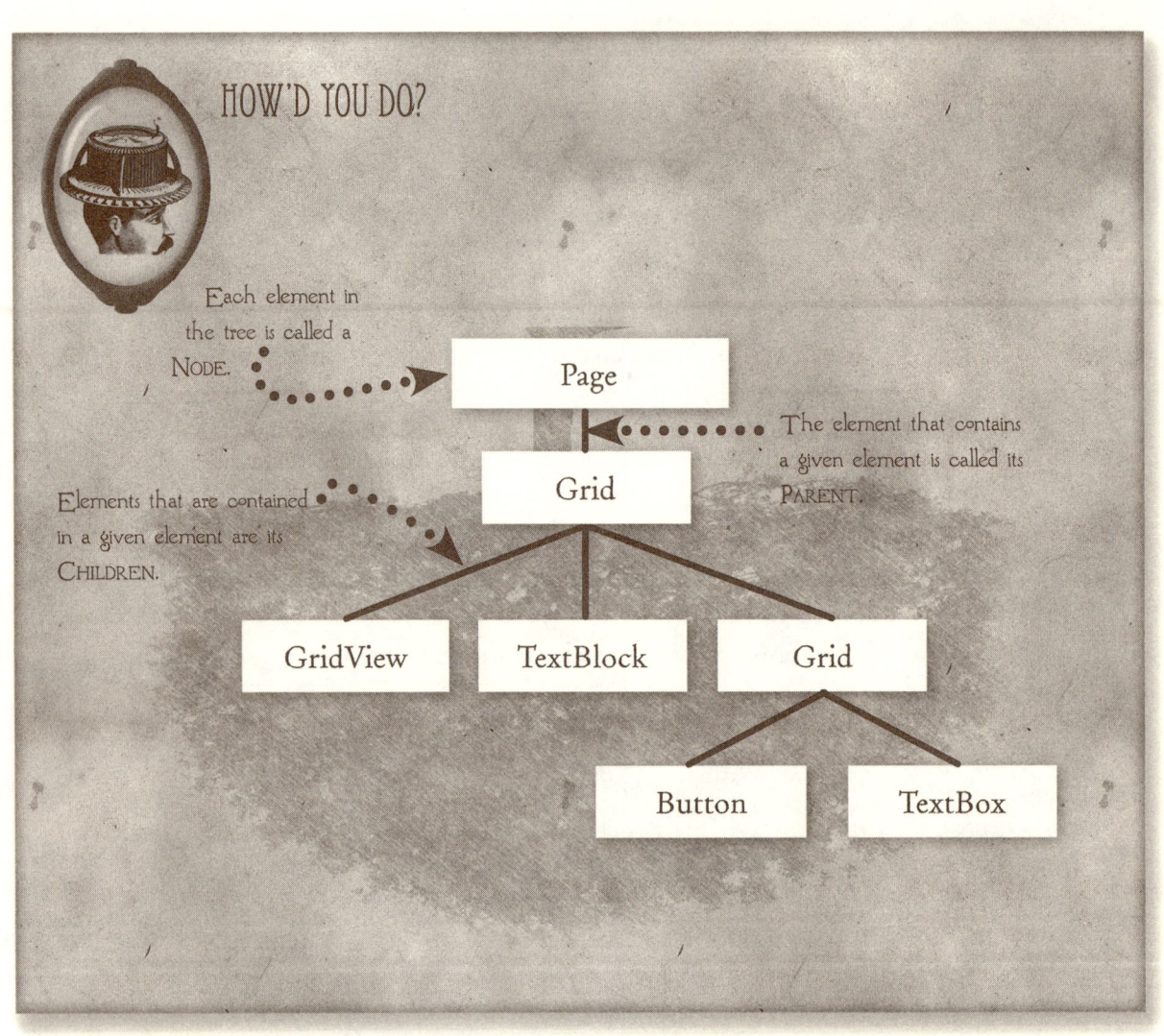

Each element in the tree is called a NODE.

The element that contains a given element is called its PARENT.

Elements that are contained in a given element are its CHILDREN.

MAKE A NOTE
We're discussing trees because you'll run across trees a fair bit in the Microsoft documentation, and I don't want you to be afraid of them. But in reality, you won't need to manipulate them very often unless you're manipulating your object tree in code or in a few special data-binding situations.

NAVIGATING THE OBJECT TREE

As I've said, you won't need to work with the XAML trees as often as, say, you need to use XPath with XML or navigate the HTML DOM, but if you should need to, it's fairly straightforward. Let's start with the object tree:

Going up the tree is easy. As we'll see in the next chapter when we examine the class library, almost all the elements you'll use to build a UI in XAML descend from a class called **FrameworkElement**. Conveniently, FrameworkElement exposes a **Parent** property that returns, well, the parent of an element. For example, given this XAML:

```
<Grid x:Name="MyGrid">
  <TextBlock x:Name="MyTB" />
</Grid>
```

the expression **MyTB.Parent** would return the **Grid** element named **MyGrid**.

Finding the children of a given element is a little trickier, only because the properties don't have a consistent name, so you can find yourself poking around the class library a little bit (and you can sometimes wind up with some odd conditional code if you're trying to walk the tree generically). In general:

- Panel elements like the **Grid** expose a property called **Children**,
- Items controls like a **ListBox** expose a property called **Items**, and
- Content controls like a **Button** contain a single child that they call **Content**

Then there are the odd controls like **TextBox** that call their child elements something else. In the case of a **TextBox**, the property is called (not suprisingly) **Text**.

By the way, don't worry too much about what a "panel" or "content control" is at this point. We'll look at those categories in the next couple of chapters. And don't worry too much about what the child/children property is called, either. The properties are always easy to find if you check the documentation.

Navigating the Visual Tree

In some ways, navigating a visual tree is simpler because you don't need to guess at propertie names, but it does require the use of a helper class called (wait for it...) VisualTreeHelper.

We haven't explored the Win8 XAML class library yet (we'll do that in the next chapter), so you'll have to take my word for it that the root class for the vast majority of the UI types used in Win8 apps is DependencyObject. Since all three of the VisualTreeHelper navigation methods accept an argument of that type, you can start with pretty much any UI object you happen to have on hand to navigate the tree.

All three methods are static (Shared in Visual Basic), so you don't need to instantiate the VisualTreeHelper in order to use them.

- GETPARENT

    The GetParent() method accepts a single DependencyObject and returns that object's parent in the visual tree.

- GETCHILDRENCOUNT

    The GetChildenCount() method also accepts a single DependencyObject and returns the number of visual children.

- GETCHILD

    The GetChild() method accepts a DependencyObject and an index into the collection of visual children. It returns a reference to the visual child at that position in the collection.

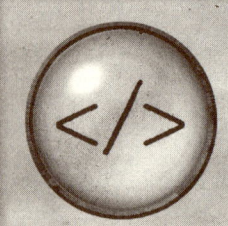

FOR XAML PROS
Windows 8 XAML doesn't have an equivalent to the LogicalTreeHelper class available in WPF.

PUT ON YOUR THINKING HAT

Can you write a function that displays all the visual children of an object in a ListBox? The signature of the routine should be:

 void ShowChildren(DependencyObject source, ListBox lb)

 Sub ShowChildren(source As DependencyObject, lb As ListBox)

Hint: You can add items to the ListBox using the following method:
    ListBox.Items.Add(object)

HOW'D YOU DO?

Don't worry if you structured your function a little bit differently; as long as you called the methods of the VisualTreeHelper correctly, you got the point.

```csharp
void ShowChildren(DependencyObject source, ListBox lb)
{
    for (int i = 0; i < VisualTreeHelper.GetChildrenCount(source), i++)
    {
        lb.Items.Add(VisualTreeHelper.GetChild(source, i).GetType());
    }
}
```

```vb
Function ShowChildren(source As DependencyObject, lb As Listbox)
    For i As Integer = 0 to VisualTreeHelper.GetChildrenCount(source)
        lb.Items.Add(VisualTreeHelper.GetChild(source, i).GetType())
    Next i
End Function
```

BY THE WAY...

The VisualTreeHelper class isn't restricted to navigation. It also exposes two other methods that are useful in special situations:

- **DISCONNECTING CHILDREN**
  The DisconnectChildrenRecursive(UIElement) method is intended for use by tools (like the Visual Studio XAML designer) that are hosting the tree.

- **FINDING ELEMENTS BY LOCATION**
  The four overloads of FindElementsInHostCoordinates() return the visual children in the point or rectangle provided. It's useful for advanced hit testing situations.

TAKE A BREAK

That's it for our exploration of XAML. I think I've mentioned once or twice that I think it's really, really simple. Do you agree?

Why don't you take a break now before you complete the Review and we dive into the building blocks of Win8 apps in the next chapter?

REVIEW

How do you specify a collection in XAML?

XAML is based on XML. What does the extra "A" stand for?

How do you specify a namespace in XAML (i.e., the equivalent of Imports in Visual Basic or using in C#)?

XAML supports two ways of specifying what would be a property in a procedural language. What are they?

Congratulations! You've finished the chapter. Take a minute to think about what you've accomplished before you move on to the next one...

List three things you learned in this chapter:

①

②

③

Why do you think you need to know these things in order to develop Win8 apps?

Is there anything in this chapter that you think you need to understand in more detail? If so, what are you going to do about that?

BUILDING BLOCKS 4

After the last chapter you should have a basic understanding of XAML syntax, the Win8 XAML namespaces, and navigating a XAML tree. If you're new to XAML you may not feel very confident about your skills yet, but don't worry too much. It's hard to learn a language's syntax—any language, whether it's XAML or Swahili—out of context, and you'll be getting lots of in-context XAML practice in the rest of the book.

So enough of this theoretical stuff; it's time to take those skills and models you've been developing and start putting them to work. We'll begin in this chapter by exploring the basic building blocks of a Win8 app.

We'll start with a quick look at the .NET and WinRT namespaces that define the APIs you'll be working with and the XAML class hierarchy that sheds some light on the functionality of the many widgets available to you.

From there we'll move on to the panels that define the basic architecture of your UI by laying out your widgets. We'll finish the chapter by examining the properties and methods that affect the layout of controls like padding and margins. (But we'll defer a discussion of transformations to Chapter 10 when we'll have a few more XAML graphic concepts under our belts.)

FITTING IT IN

In this chapter we'll start exploring the XAML widgets that are available for use in your Win8 apps.

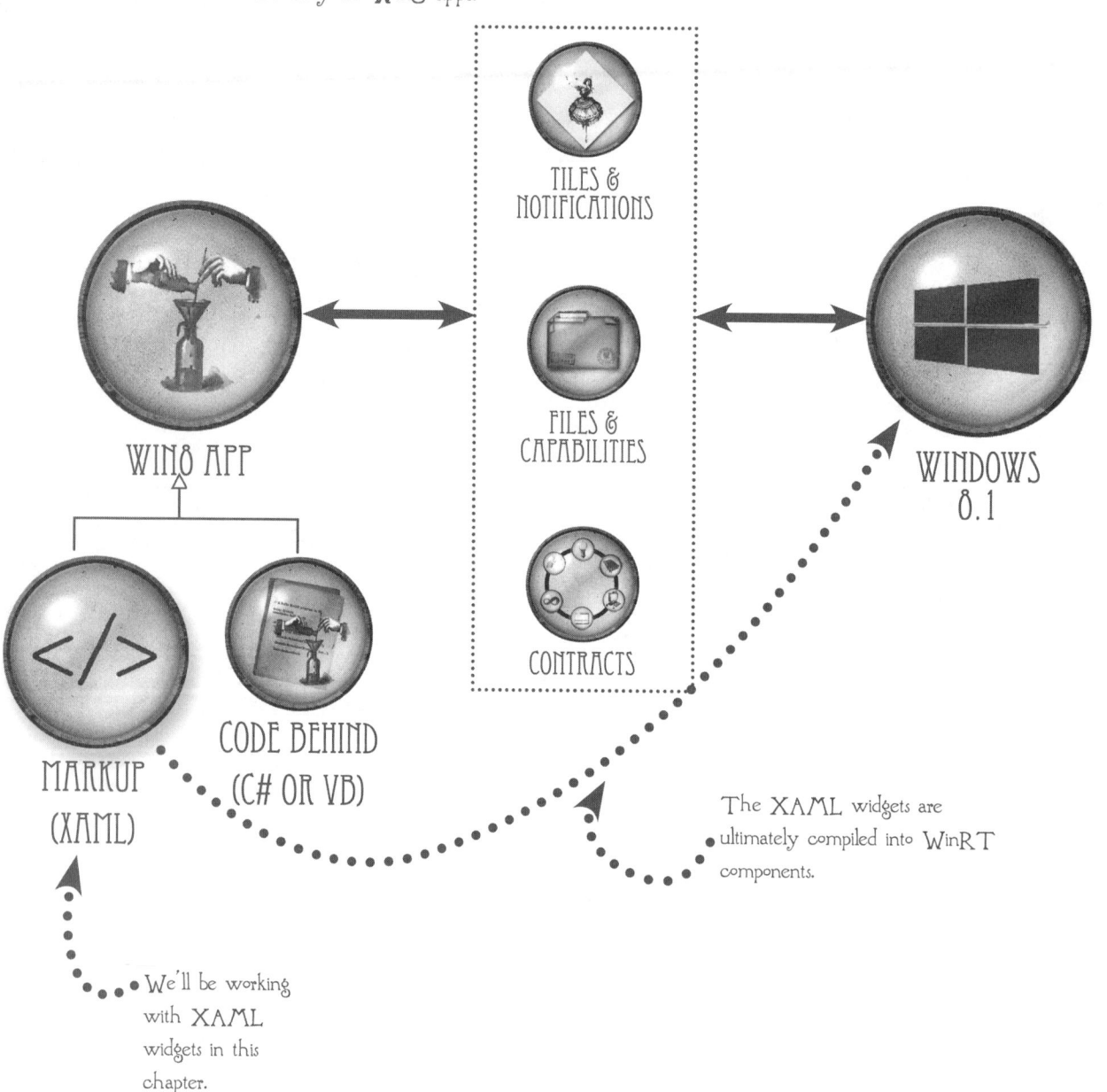

WIN8 APP

TILES & NOTIFICATIONS

FILES & CAPABILITIES

CONTRACTS

WINDOWS 8.1

MARKUP (XAML)

CODE BEHIND (C# OR VB)

We'll be working with XAML widgets in this chapter.

The XAML widgets are ultimately compiled into WinRT components.

TASK LIST

In this chapter we'll start our detailed exploration of Win8 app development by looking at WinRT class library, and then we'll start building Win8 app interfaces by exploring the panels and panel-like controls that let you arrange your interface and the layout and rendering properties that you can use to control that arrangement.

THE CLASS LIBRARY

If you've done any .NET development, you already know that the Framework Class Library is, well, huge. The WinRT library used for Win8 app development is only a little bit smaller. We'll start the chapter by getting a feel for the general structure that will help you find your way around.

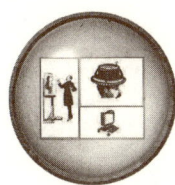

PANELS

If you're used to developing interfaces using a platform like WinForms, you may be surprised at the way XAML controls are laid out. Rather than specifying the exact position of a widget, you place them inside another control that knows how to arrange its children, and let it do all the work. It might take a little while to get used to—it's a different way of thinking about your UI—but it does save you work (a lot of work) in the long run.

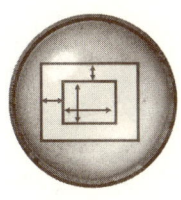

LAYOUT PROPERTIES

Of course, the panel controls can't know everything they need to know to display your interface. We'll end the chapter by examining the properties that control the relationships between widgets like alignment and margins.

THE CLASS LIBRARY

In the last chapter we looked at the XAML namespaces that control the XAML language itself, but there's another set of namespaces that are important in Win8 app development: the namespaces that comprise the WinRT runtime library. Let's start by looking at the small subset of standard .NET APIs that are available to your Win8 apps:

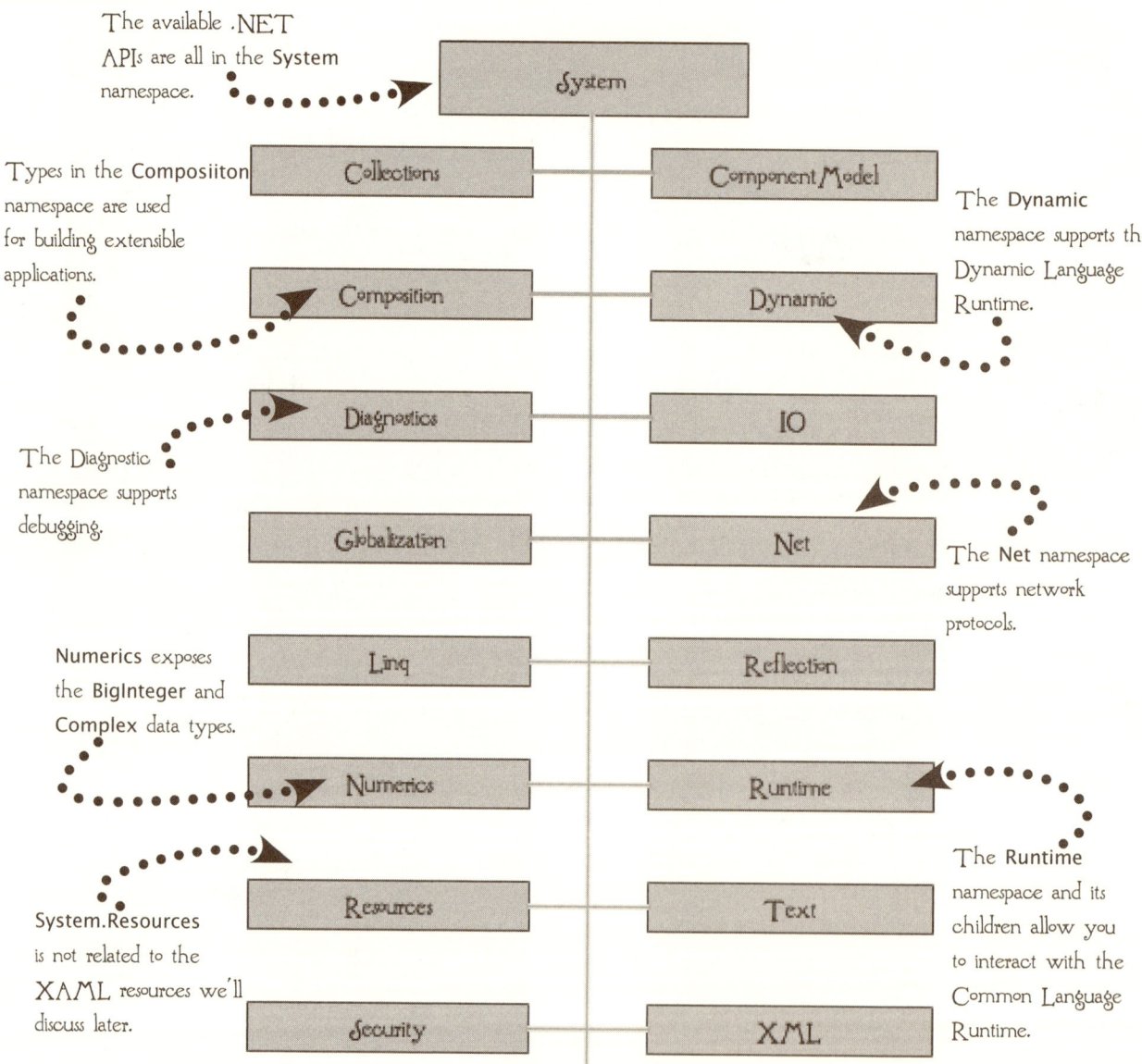

The available .NET APIs are all in the System namespace.

Types in the Composition namespace are used for building extensible applications.

The Diagnostic namespace supports debugging.

Numerics exposes the BigInteger and Complex data types.

System.Resources is not related to the XAML resources we'll discuss later.

The Dynamic namespace supports the Dynamic Language Runtime.

The Net namespace supports network protocols.

The Runtime namespace and its children allow you to interact with the Common Language Runtime.

116

MAKE A NOTE

Only a small subset of the .NET Framework Class Library is available to your Win8 apps. Some of the missing namespaces have been supplanted by other types that we'll explore in the next few pages, but others are just missing, either because they're inappropriate in this environment or haven't (yet) been implemented.

Even when the namespace is present, not all of the types are necessarily available. If and when you need more information, there are (some) details on MSDN and a lot of discussion about missing functionality on the Microsoft forums.

PUT ON YOUR THINKING HAT

Can you answer the following questions based on the .NET namespaces shown in the diagram?

Based on the available namespaces, would you expect generic collection types like List<T> to be available?

System.Linq and System.ComponentModel.DataAnnotations are both available, but there's one significant data-related API that's missing. Can you spot it?

The System.Deployment namespace isn't available to Win8 apps. Given what these apps are now called, does the omission seem reasonable to you?

HOW'D YOU DO?

Based on the available namespaces, would you expect generic collection types like List<T> to be available?

> You should. System.Collections and its child namespaces System.Collections.Concurrent, System.Collections.Generic, System.Collections.ObjectModel, and System.Collections.Specialized are all available.
>
> The Windows.Foundation.Collections namespace, part of WinRT, extends this functionality with support for the PropertySet class, observable maps, and observable vectors.

System.Linq and System.ComponentModel.DataAnnotations are both available, but there's one significant data-related API that's missing. Can you spot it?

> System.Data is missing. The Windows.Data namespace provides support for manipulating local data as HTML, Json or XML, but ADO.NET isn't available to Win8 apps. (But check CodePlex before you give up. There are some third-party data platforms like Sterling and SQL Lite that either are, or are expected to be, available for Win8 apps.)

The System.Deployment namespace isn't available to Win8 apps. Given what these apps are now called, do you know why?

> The System.Deployment namespace supports ClickOnce deployment. Although private deployment (Microsoft calls is SIDE-LOADING) is possible, they really want you to deploy your apps via the Windows Store.

WINRT NAMESPACES

The other side of the class library is the WinRT namespaces, all of which descend from the core Windows namespace and are available only to Win8 apps. We'll be looking at most of these in detail as we work through the book, but here's an overview of the main ones:

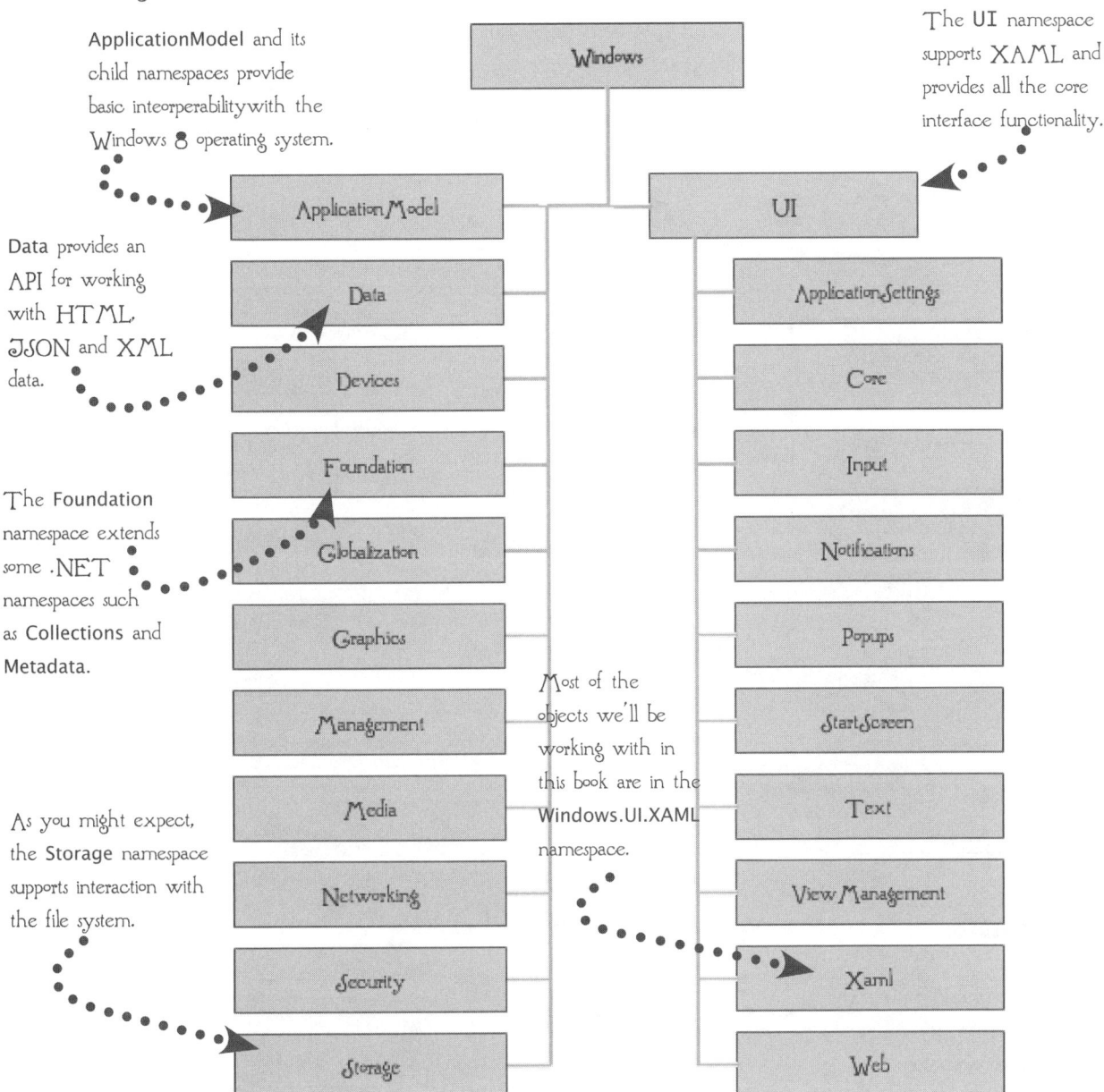

ApplicationModel and its child namespaces provide basic interoperability with the Windows 8 operating system.

The UI namespace supports XAML and provides all the core interface functionality.

Data provides an API for working with HTML, JSON and XML data.

The Foundation namespace extends some .NET namespaces such as Collections and Metadata.

Most of the objects we'll be working with in this book are in the Windows.UI.XAML namespace.

As you might expect, the Storage namespace supports interaction with the file system.

THE XAML CLASS HIERARCHY

A roadmap of the namespaces is helpful in getting your head around the class library, but it's also useful to know where in a class hierarchy objects live, because that tells you a great deal about what any given class can do.

The majority of XAML objects descend from the DependencyObject class (which, in turn, descends directly from Object). Here's a partial hierarchy:

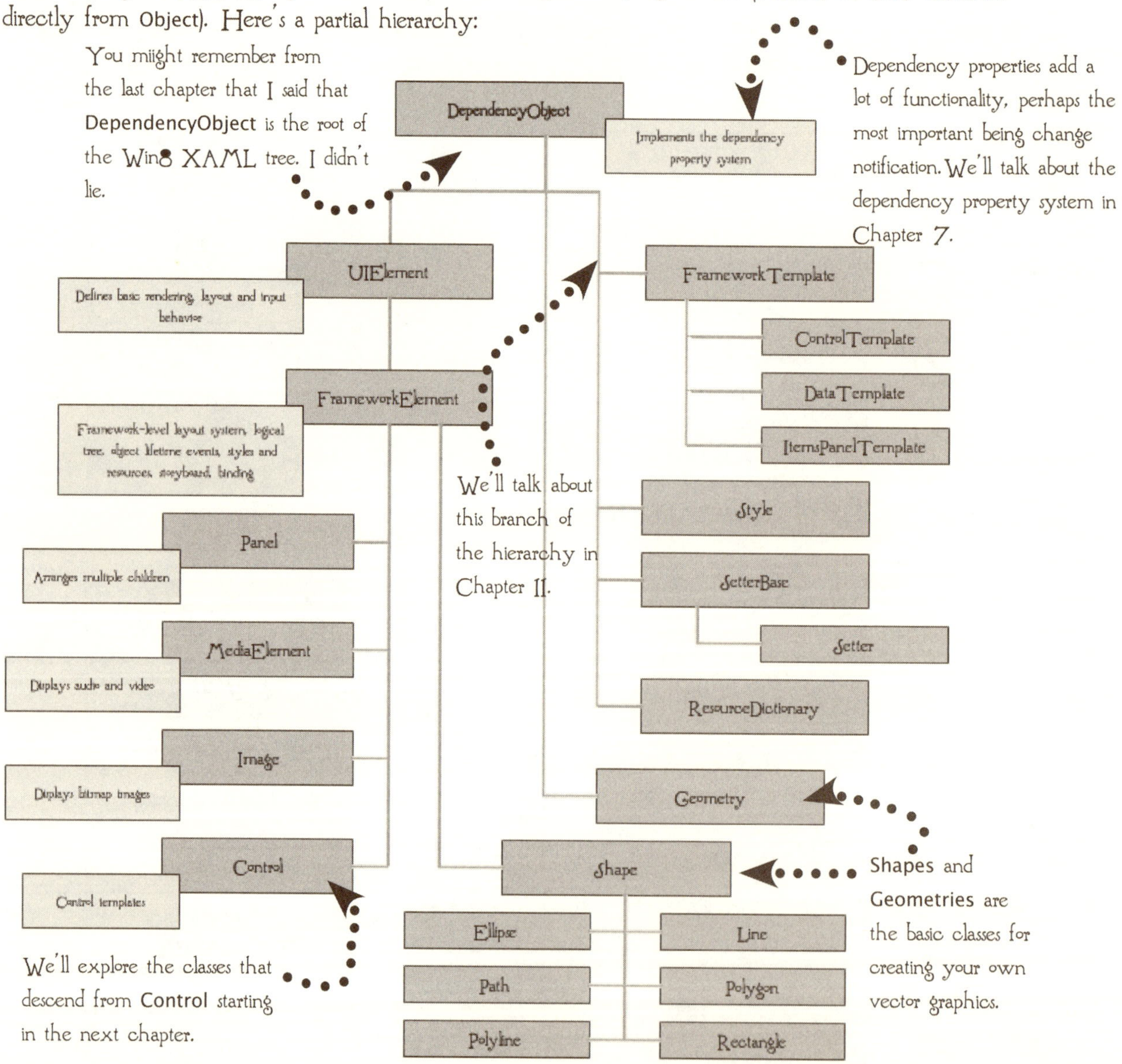

You might remember from the last chapter that I said that **DependencyObject** is the root of the Win8 XAML tree. I didn't lie.

DependencyObject — Implements the dependency property system

Dependency properties add a lot of functionality, perhaps the most important being change notification. We'll talk about the dependency property system in Chapter 7.

UIElement — Defines basic rendering, layout and input behavior

FrameworkElement — Framework-level layout system, logical tree, object lifetime events, styles and resources, storyboard, binding

Panel — Arranges multiple children

MediaElement — Displays audio and video

Image — Displays bitmap images

Control — Control templates

We'll explore the classes that descend from **Control** starting in the next chapter.

We'll talk about this branch of the hierarchy in Chapter 11.

FrameworkTemplate
- ControlTemplate
- DataTemplate
- ItemsPanelTemplate

Style

SetterBase
- Setter

ResourceDictionary

Geometry

Shape
- Ellipse
- Path
- Polyline
- Line
- Polygon
- Rectangle

Shapes and Geometries are the basic classes for creating your own vector graphics.

PUT ON YOUR THINKING HAT

Can you answer the following questions based on the diagrams in this section?

There are three classes in the XAML hierarchy (one of them has children) that are used for displaying graphics. What are they?

If a class descends directly from **DependencyObject**, would you expect to be able to display it?

If a class descends directly from **UIElement**, would you expect to be able to bind its properties?

Control templates, which we'll examine in detail in Chapter 11, define the visual tree of a control. Can you define a control template for a class that descends from **Panel**?

 ## HOW'D YOU DO?

There are three classes in the XAML hierarchy (one of them has children) that are used for displaying graphics. What are they?

> **Image** is used to display bitmapped images like JPEGs. **Geometry** is used to display an arbitrary vector (usually within a **Path**), and **Shapes** are used to display vector images. (Don't worry if you're not entirely sure about bitmapped and vector images. We'll discuss them in detail in Chapter 10.)

If a class descends directly from **DependencyObject**, would you expect to be able to display it?

> No. The **UIElement** class, which descends from **DependencyObject**, knows how to display itself, but **DependencyObject** doesn't.

If a class descends directly from **UIElement**, would you expect to be able to bind its properties?

> No. That's added by the **FrameworkElement** class that descends from **UIElement**.

Control templates, which we'll examine in detail in Chapter 11, define the visual tree of a control. Can you define a control template for a class that descends from **Panel**?

> No. Control templates are only supported by classes that descend from **Control**. If you need to change the way a **Panel** displays its children, you'll need to build your own. (That's not as scary as it sounds, but we won't be doing it in this book.)

PANELS

Panels aren't the only controls that can have more than one element nested inside them. They're not even the only ones that can lay out their children in interesting ways—because of the way XAML works, any element that can contain multiple children can do that—but they're the ones that you'll use to create the skeleton on which you'll build your UX. There are four types of panels available to your Win8 apps:

The Grid organizes its contents in rows and columns.

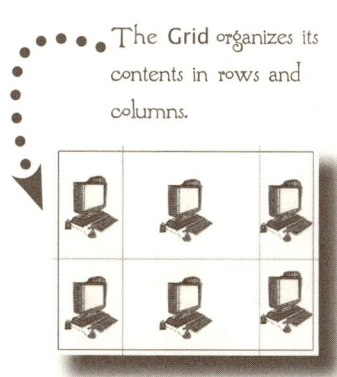

The StackPanel stacks its contents, either horizontally or vertically.

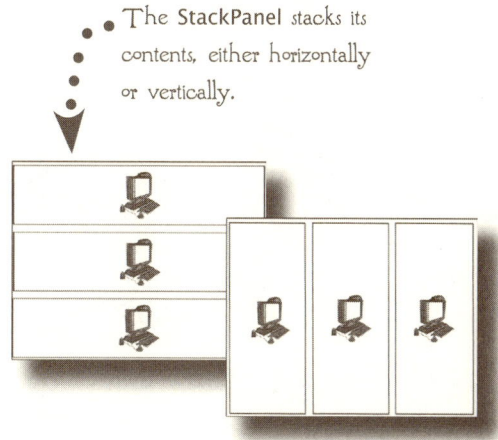

The Canvas places its elements at specified coordinates relative to the edges of the panel.

The VariableSizedWrapGrid organizes its contents either horizontally or vertically and wraps them from one line to another.

ON YOUR OWN

Can you think of situations in which each of the panels might be useful as a layout root?

123

ATTACHED PROPERTIES

I've mentioned dependency properties a few times and told you that XAML adds a lot of functionality to the basic concept of a property. We'll examine dependency properties in detail in the next chapter, but there's one aspect of the dependency property that's important for (among other things) working with panels.

ATTACHED PROPERTIES are a special kind of dependency property that are defined in one class but can be treated as though they belong to another. In other words, they're defined in class x and *attached* to class y. The theory behind attached properties is a little complex, and frankly, not all that important for our purposes. In practice, they're easy to use:

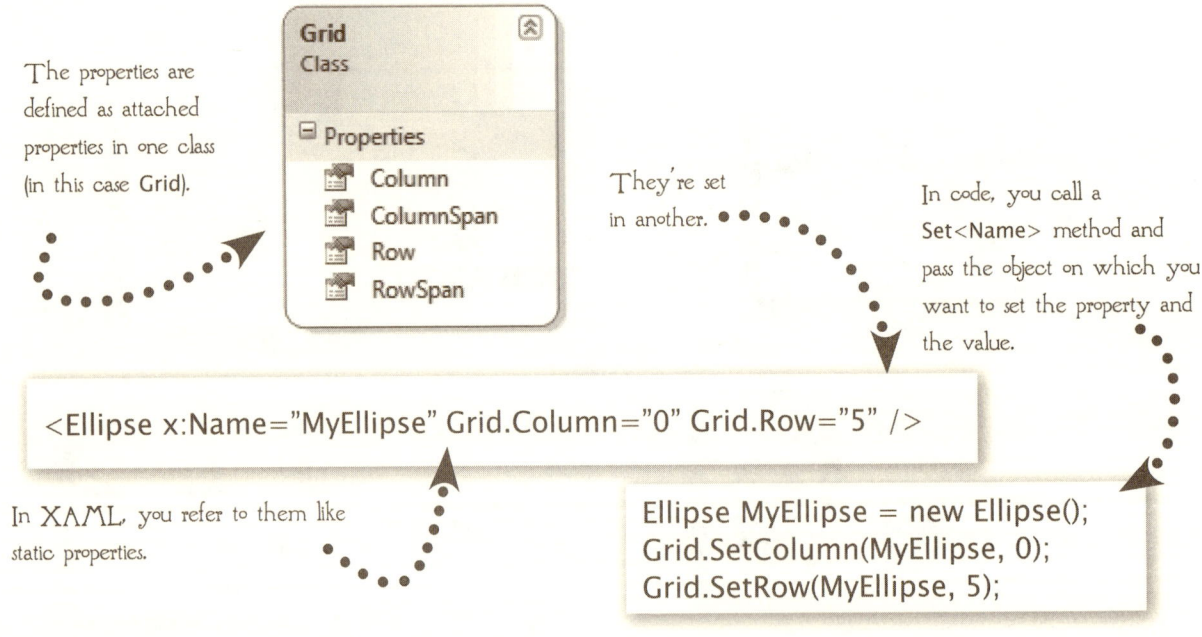

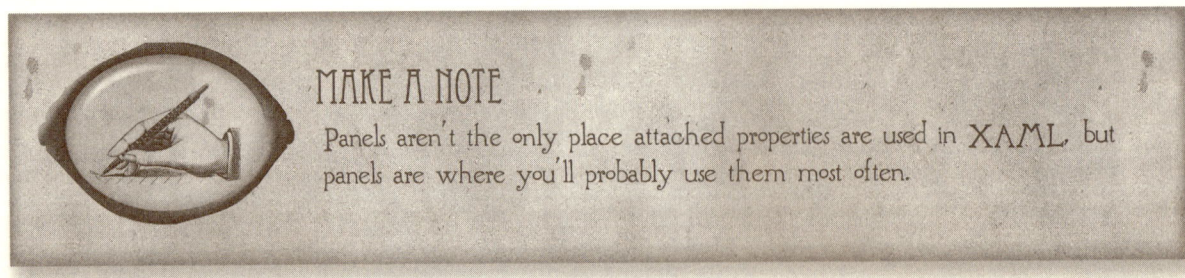

MAKE A NOTE
Panels aren't the only place attached properties are used in XAML, but panels are where you'll probably use them most often.

PUT ON YOUR THINKING HAT

In many ways, the Canvas is the simplest of the panels to understand. You specify a position relative to the left and top of the panel, and that's where the elements sit. End of discussion. Well, except that the children of the Canvas can actually be outside it — it doesn't clip its contents.

For right now, just write the code below without creating a Visual Studio project.

The Ellipse is 30 from the left, 30 from the top, has a Height of 100, a Width of 200, and a Fill of White.

The Button is 100 from the left, 100 from the top, 100 high and 250 wide. Its Background property is set to Gray.

The Rectangle is 300 from the left, 150 from the top, 100 high, and 200 wide. Its Fill is White.

The other objects are arranged on a Canvas.

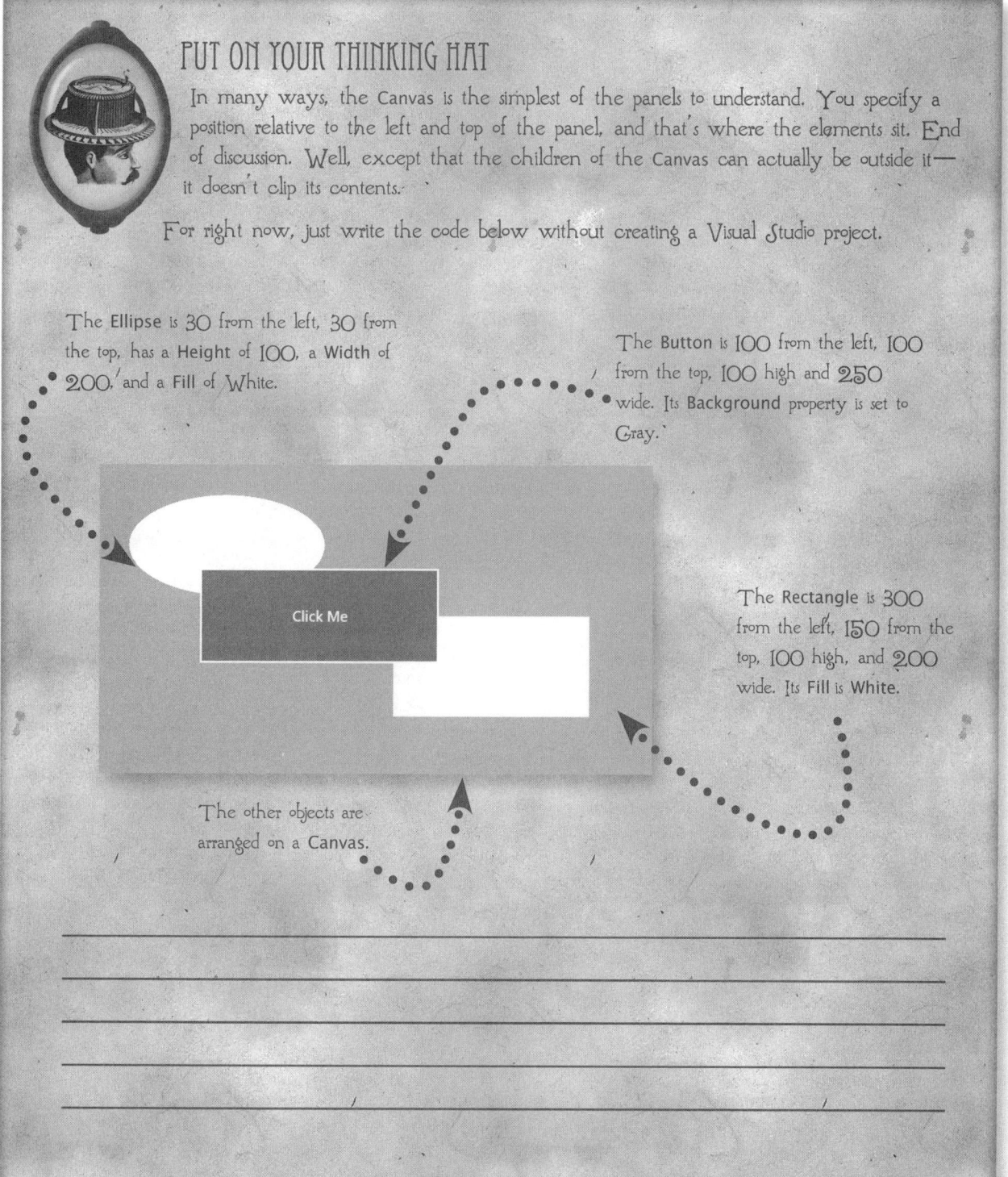

HOW'D YOU DO?

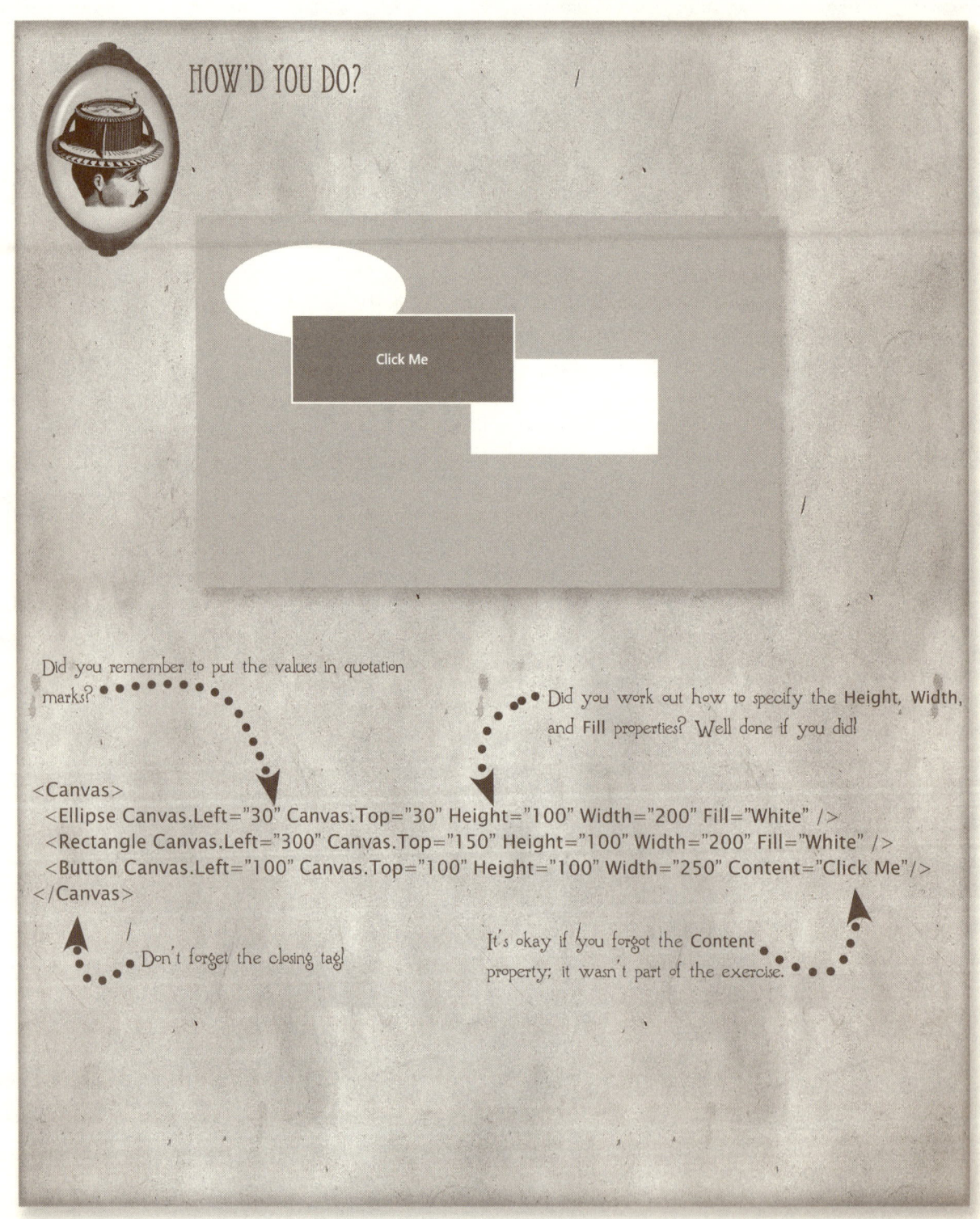

Did you remember to put the values in quotation marks?

Did you work out how to specify the **Height**, **Width**, and **Fill** properties? Well done if you did!

```
<Canvas>
    <Ellipse Canvas.Left="30" Canvas.Top="30" Height="100" Width="200" Fill="White" />
    <Rectangle Canvas.Left="300" Canvas.Top="150" Height="100" Width="200" Fill="White" />
    <Button Canvas.Left="100" Canvas.Top="100" Height="100" Width="250" Content="Click Me"/>
</Canvas>
```

Don't forget the closing tag!

It's okay if you forgot the **Content** property; it wasn't part of the exercise.

ON YOUR OWN

Create a blank project in Visual Studio, and add the Canvas and other elements from the last exercise.

The Button appears on top of the Ellipse and the Rectangle. What happens if you change the order of the elements inside the Canvas? (You might find it easier to see the difference if you set the Grid.Background property to Gray.)

In the Properties window, the Button shows a property called ZIndex (in the Layout section) that takes a numeric value. Try setting that value. What object defines ZIndex? (Hint: Look at the XAML.)

Try playing around with the ZIndex values of the various objects. How does ZIndex work?

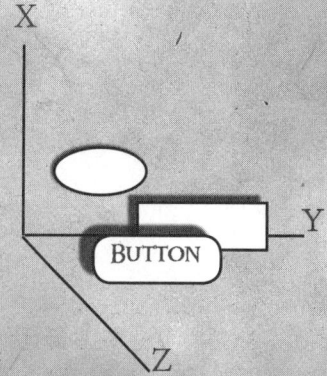

Try running the application in the Simulator and changing the screen resolution and orientation. What happens? Does the app behave the way you think Win8 apps should behave?

What does this tell you about using a Canvas panel for basic layout?

THE GRID

The Canvas is simple to use, and if you come from a WinForms background, it probably feels very comfortable to you. But elements in a Canvas are always positioned relative to the top-left corner of the screen, and that means you're looking at a lot of work if you want to use the real estate provided by different screens effectively, much less respond to the changes in orientation and width required by Win8. Let's look at some other panels that will save you all that bother.

We'll start with the Grid, which is the default layout root when you create a Page in Visual Studio. Like a spreadsheet, the Grid divides the available space into rows and columns:

When you work with a Grid, you specify the number and size of rows and columns.

The elements inside the Grid can span multiple columns...

...or multiple rows.

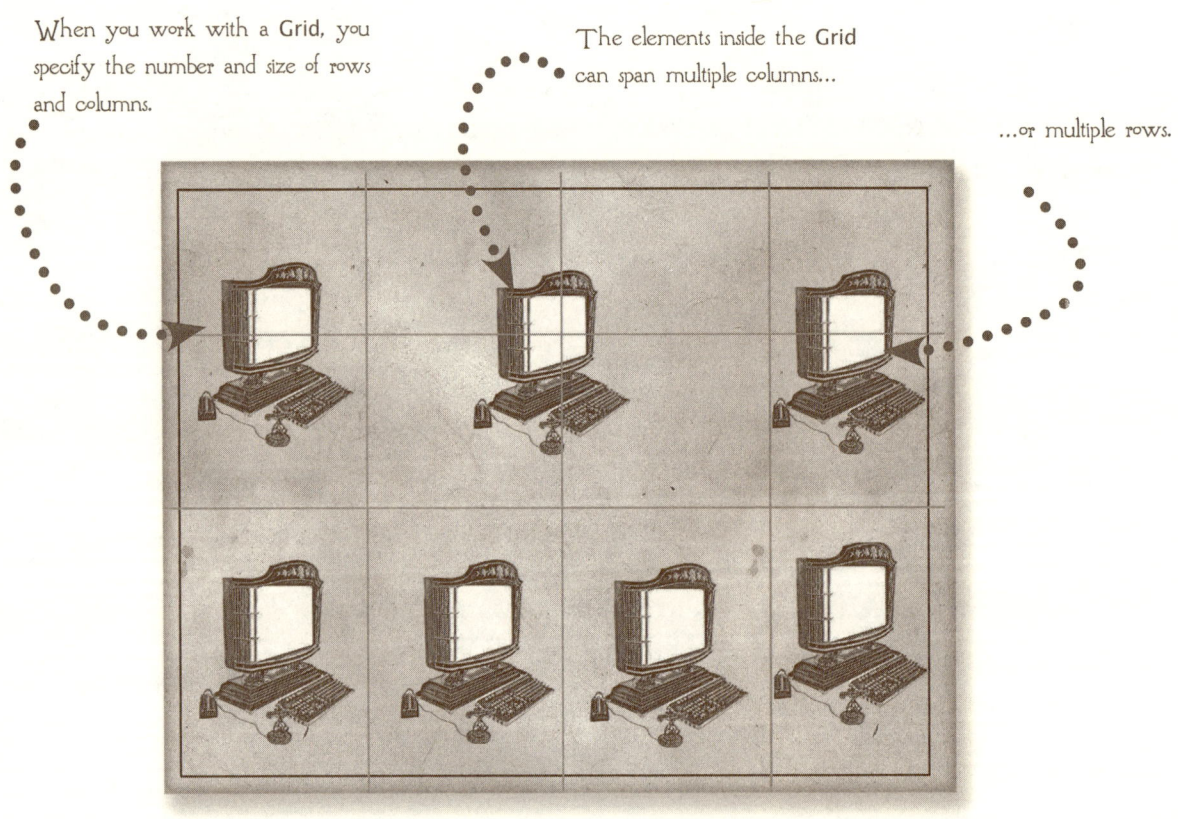

The Grid panel exposes two collection properties, **RowDefinitions** and **ColumnDefinitions**, that you'll use to define the basic structure of your **Grid**. To add a row, you add a **RowDefinition** to the **RowDefinitions** collection and (optionally) define its height. To add a column, you add a **ColumnDefinition** to the **ColumnDefinitions** collection and (optionally) define its width:

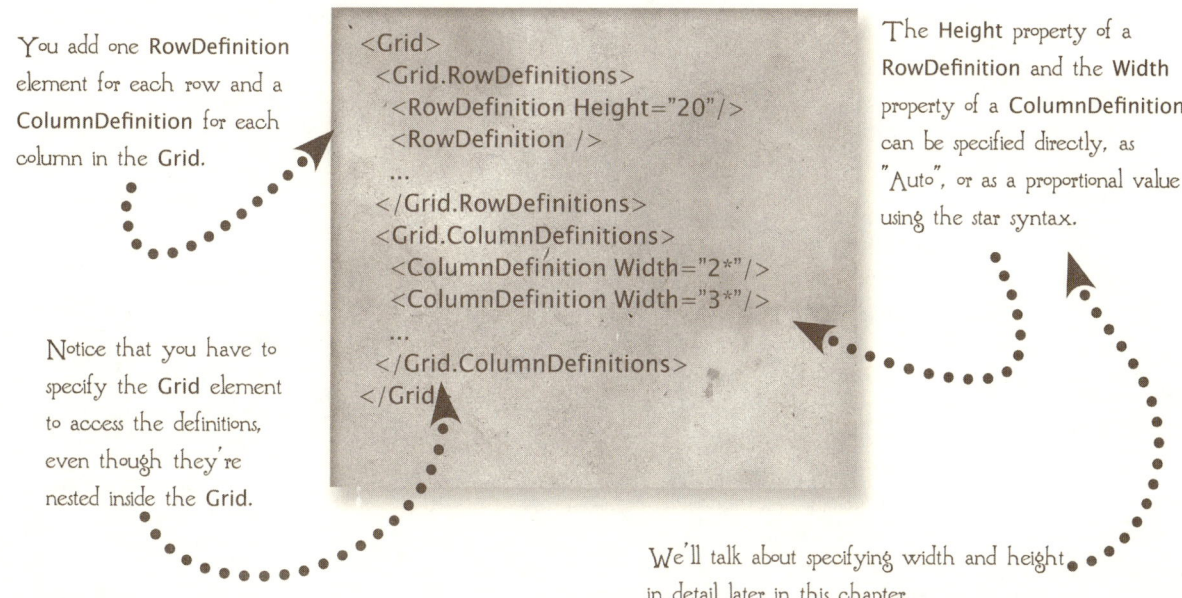

You add one RowDefinition element for each row and a ColumnDefinition for each column in the Grid.

```
<Grid>
  <Grid.RowDefinitions>
    <RowDefinition Height="20"/>
    <RowDefinition />
    ...
  </Grid.RowDefinitions>
  <Grid.ColumnDefinitions>
    <ColumnDefinition Width="2*"/>
    <ColumnDefinition Width="3*"/>
    ...
  </Grid.ColumnDefinitions>
</Grid>
```

The **Height** property of a RowDefinition and the **Width** property of a ColumnDefinition can be specified directly, as "Auto", or as a proportional value using the star syntax.

Notice that you have to specify the Grid element to access the definitions, even though they're nested inside the Grid.

We'll talk about specifying width and height in detail later in this chapter.

PUT ON YOUR THINKING HAT

The Grid panel defines **Row** and **Column** attached properties that allow you to assign a child element to a specific cell. In addition, it defines **RowSpan** and **ColumnSpan** attached properties that allow an element to stretch across more than one cell.

Can you re-create the diagram on page 128 using a Grid? Don't worry about specifying width or height at this point; just create the columns and rows. You can either use rectangles as the Grid's children or add images, using this syntax (which assumes the image file is in your Assets folder) as a model:

`<Image Source="Assets/MyImage.png" .... />`

Just be sure to specify the row and column and span values. (Hint: Like most things in the .NET world, the rows and columns in a Grid start at zero.)

HOW'D YOU DO?

Here's my version of the Grid definition:

```
<Grid ...>
  <Grid.RowDefinitions>
    <RowDefinition />
    <RowDefinition />
  </Grid.RowDefinitions>
  <Grid.ColumnDefinitions>
    <ColumnDefinition />
    <ColumnDefinition />
    <ColumnDefinition />
    <ColumnDefinition />
  </Grid.ColumnDefinitions>

  <Image Grid.Column="0" Grid.Row="0" Source="..." />
  <Image Grid.Column="1" Grid.ColumnSpan="2" Grid.Row="0" Source="..." />
  <Image Grid.Column="3" Grid.Row="0" Grid.RowSpan="2" Source="..." />
  <Image Grid.Column="0" Grid.Row="1" Source="..." />
  <Image Grid.Column="1" Grid.Row="1" Source="..." />
  <Image Grid.Column="2" Grid.Row="1" Source="..." />
</Grid>
```

The example has two rows and four columns.

You'd specify your own image file here.

Did you get the ColumnSpan and RowSpan definitions right? I get so used to counting from zero that I sometimes get them off by one the first time.

THE VARIABLESIZEDWRAPGRID

Unless you tell it otherwise (we'll see how to do that in a bit), the Grid panel will take all the available space and divide it equally between the rows and columns you define. Because "all the available space" automatically adjusts to the app width and screen orientation, that makes it a lot more flexible than the Canvas.

But the Grid works best if you know in advance how many rows and columns your layout requires. What if you don't? You can add row and column definitions to the Grid at runtime, but it's extraordinarily tedious (and yes, dear readers, that's the voice of experience). Or you can use a VariableSizedWrapGrid, which will add them for you, as necessary:

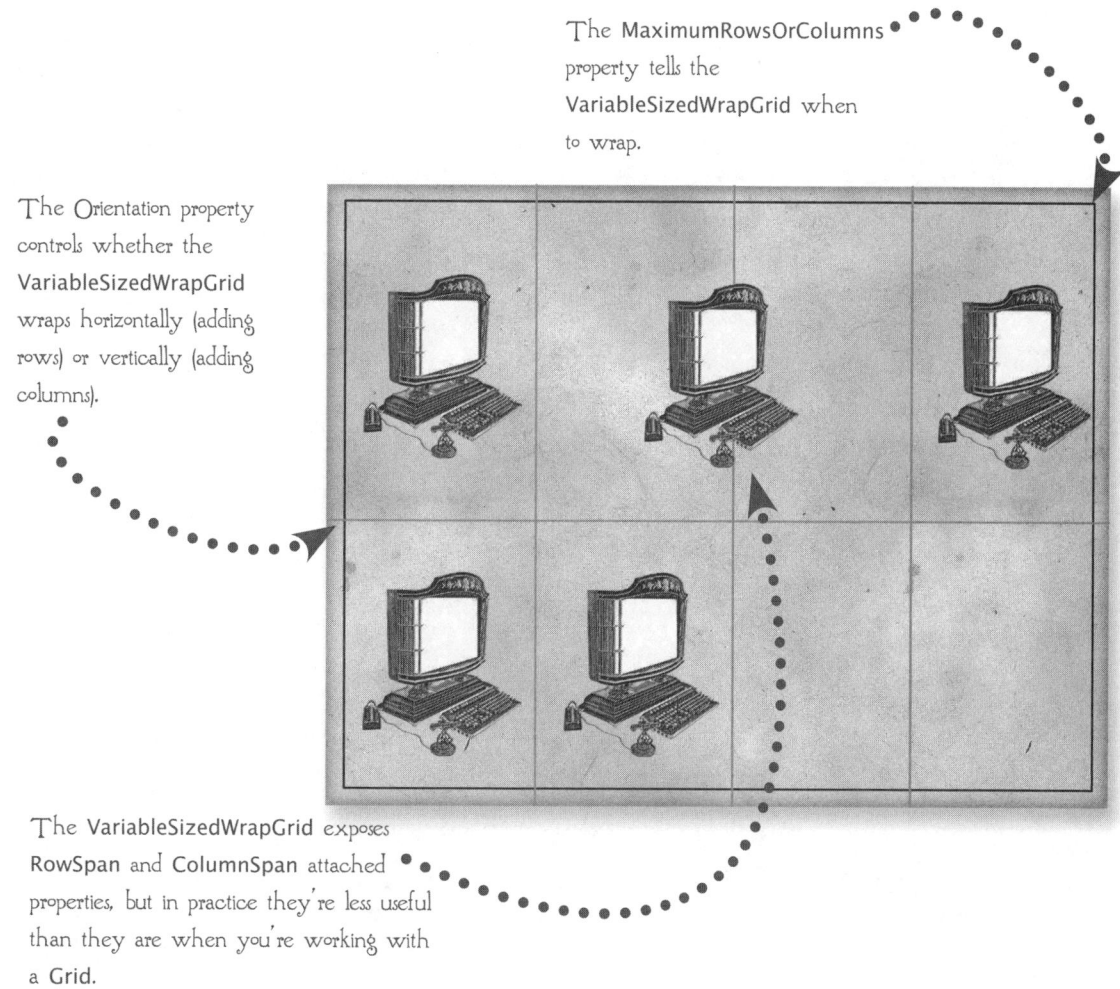

The MaximumRowsOrColumns property tells the VariableSizedWrapGrid when to wrap.

The Orientation property controls whether the VariableSizedWrapGrid wraps horizontally (adding rows) or vertically (adding columns).

The VariableSizedWrapGrid exposes RowSpan and ColumnSpan attached properties, but in practice they're less useful than they are when you're working with a Grid.

MAKE A NOTE

If you poke around in MSDN, you'll see that Grid and VariableSizedWrapGrid aren't the only grids in the library. The GridView also lays out children in rows and columns.

What's the difference? The GridView isn't a panel; it's an items control. Technically, that means widgets like Grid and VariableSizedWrapGrid descend from the Panel class, which descends directly from FrameworkElement. GridView (and its siblings ListView, ListBox, and so on) descends from ItemsControl, which descends from FrameworkElement via the Control class.

Panels arrange their children. That's really their sole purpose in life. Controls, on the other hand, are first-class UI elements. They can receive focus, be enabled or disabled, and (perhaps most importantly in the context of XAML), you can completely re-define their visual appearance and to some extent their behavior using templates. We'll talk about templating in Chapter 11. (You're going to love it.)

There are a few panels that we won't be discussing here. Classes that descend from the VirtualizingPanel class (which descends from Panel) are typically used inside of items controls. Not surprisingly, the difference is that they virtualize their items, which usually results in better performance.

ON YOUR OWN

Both the Grid and the VariableSizedWrapGrid arrange their children in rows and columns, but the VariableSizedWrapGrid is usually the best choice when you don't know how many rows or columns you're going to need. Returning to your list of the Win8 applications you'd like to develop, are there any that are going to require one or the other?

PUT ON YOUR THINKING HAT

Time to give the VariableSizedWrapGrid a whirl...

- Create a new project using the Blank App template, and add a VariableSizedWrapGrid to the MainPage XAML. (You can either replace the Grid that Visual Studio adds as a default, or add the VariableSizedWrapGrid as the Grid's only child.)

- Set the MaximumRowsOrColumns property of the VariableSizedWrapGrid to 4 and add 10 or so Rectangle elements with a Height of 100, a Width of 100 and a Background of White. Give them a Margin of 10 to separate them. (We'll discuss the Margin property later in this chapter.)

- Run the application. Since you haven't explicitly set the Orientation property, the VariableSizedWrapGrid will use the default value. What is it?

- Change the Width of the second Rectangle element to 200 and run the application again. Is the display any different?

- Change the Width of the first Rectangle element to 200 and run the application. Now what happens?

- Set the ItemWidth property of the VariableSizedWrapGrid to 50. Now what happens?

- How do you think the VariableSizedWrapGrid decides how tall or wide to make the items it displays? Test your theory. Were you right?

HOW'D YOU DO?

- Here's the basic XAML. (The Rectangle element gets repeated.)

    ```
    <VariableSizedWrapGrid MaximumRowsOrColumns="4" >
       <Rectangle Width="100" Height="100" Fill="White" Margin="10"/>
       ...
    </VariableSizedWrapGrid>
    ```

- Run the application. Since you haven't explicitly set the **Orientation** property, the VariableSizedWrapGrid will use the default value. What is it?

    The default **Orientation** is **Vertical**.

- Change the **Width** of the second **Rectangle** element to 200 and run the application again. Is the display any different?

    No.

- Change the **Width** of the first **Rectangle** element to 200 and run the application. Now what happens?

    All of the rectangles are displayed in a space 200 pixels wide.

- Set the **ItemWidth** property of the **VariableSizedWrapGrid** to 50. Now what happens?

    All of the rectangles are displayed in a space 50 pixels wide.

- How do you think the **VariableSizedWrapGrid** decides how tall or wide to make the items it displays? Test your theory. Were you right?

    If you explicitly set the **ItemWidth** or **ItemHeight** properties, the **VariableSizedWrapGrid** will use those values for all items. Otherwise, it uses the size of the first item in the collection.

THE STACKPANEL

The StackPanel is like the VariableSizedWrapGrid in that it makes it easy to add items at runtime, but it won't wrap and it doesn't attempt to control the size of the items it displays.

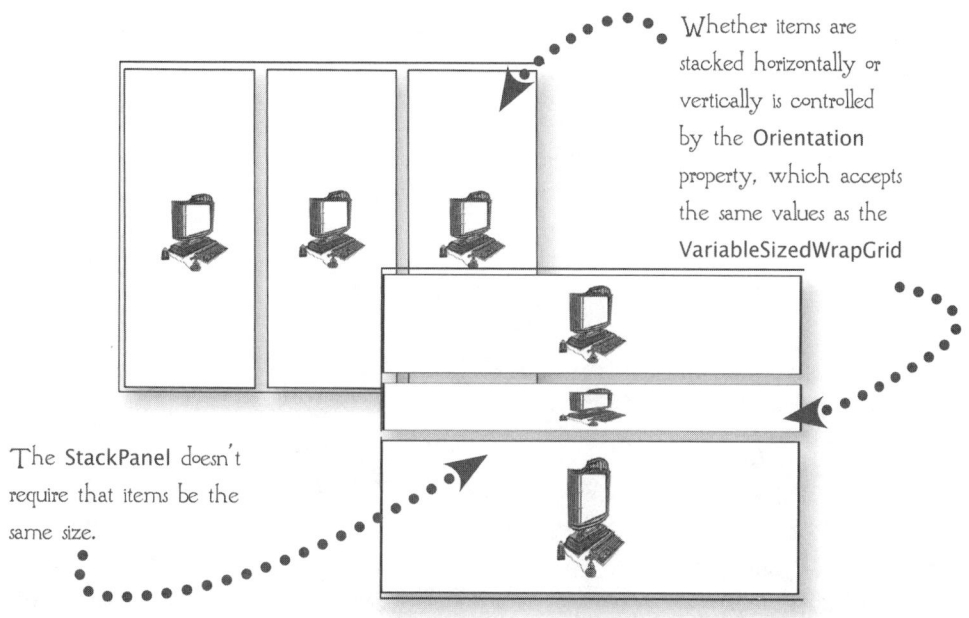

Whether items are stacked horizontally or vertically is controlled by the Orientation property, which accepts the same values as the VariableSizedWrapGrid

The StackPanel doesn't require that items be the same size.

PUT ON YOUR THINKING HAT

Let's try it out:

Replace the VariableSizedWrapGrid in your project with a StackPanel with a Vertical orientation. Change the Height property of one of the Rectangle elements to 50. What happens?

There should be 10 Rectangle elements declared in your code. How many are displayed if you set the resolution in the Simulator to, say, 1920x1080? Is it what you'd expect to happen? Is it what you'd want to have happen?

HOW'D YOU DO?

Here's the basic XAML:

```
<StackPanel Orientation="Vertical">
   <Rectangle Width="100" Height="100" Fill="White" Margin="10"/>
   <Rectangle Width="100" Height="50" Fill="White" Margin="10"/>
   ...
</StackPanel>
```

If there isn't enough screen real estate (as is the case in our example with the resolution set to 1920x1080), the StackPanel displays what it can and ignores the rest. This isn't typically the behavior you'd want. In Chapter 11, we'll see how to wrap the contents of the StackPanel in a ScrollViewer that will fix the problem.

NESTING PANELS

You've seen that the panels are responsible (and only responsible) for displaying a collection of child elements. But has it occurred to you that those child elements can, in turn, be panels? Here's a pretty typical Win8 app page. It's actually comprised of four top-level panels, and each item is a panel, as well.

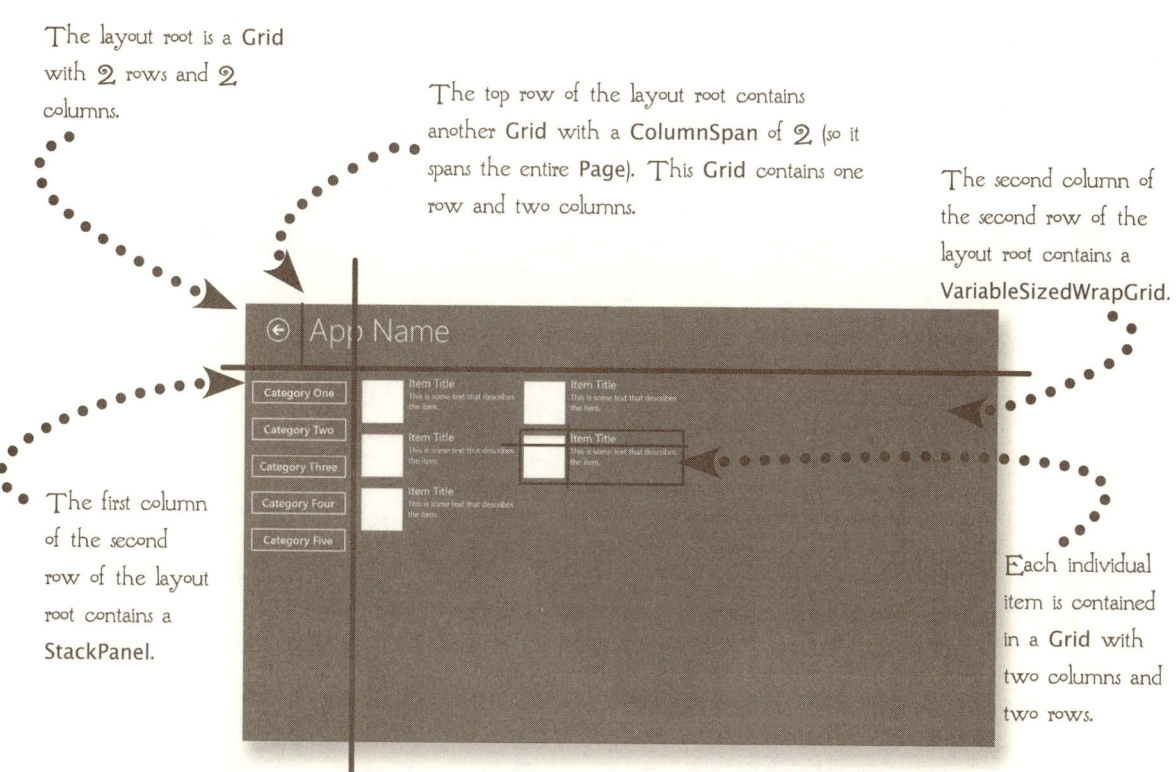

The layout root is a **Grid** with 2 rows and 2 columns.

The top row of the layout root contains another **Grid** with a **ColumnSpan** of 2 (so it spans the entire **Page**). This **Grid** contains one row and two columns.

The second column of the second row of the layout root contains a **VariableSizedWrapGrid**.

The first column of the second row of the layout root contains a **StackPanel**.

Each individual item is contained in a **Grid** with two columns and two rows.

TAKE A BREAK

That's it for the first section. Panels can get complicated, as you can see from this example, but by and large they're just complex, not difficult. In fact, they're really easy to use, and you'll get lots of practice as we move through the rest of the book. For now, why don't you take a break before you complete the review and we move on to the XAML layout properties?

REVIEW

Based on what you've learned about how panels work in Win8 apps, can you identify the panels being described below?

This panel exposes a **MaximumRowsOrColumns** property to determine when to wrap.

This panel doesn't adapt to screen size, format, or resolution, but it does give you absolute control over positioning.

These two panels both have an **Orientation** property that specifies whether they should lay out their children in columns or rows.

You define the number of rows and columns in this panel using collections.

This panel doesn't impose a specific size on the children it lays out in a single row or column.

This panel allows you to easily add items at runtime, but they'll all be the same size.

LAYOUT PROPERTIES

There are three ways to control where and how an element is rendered inside its parent. You can specify the size of the element, how the element is positioned relative to the space available, and how much space is maintained within and around the element. Let's start with the simplest: size.

PUT ON YOUR THINKING HAT

The properties that control an item's size are defined by the FrameworkElement class, and there are eight (!) of them. Can you work out what each pair of properties does?

The Height and Width properties tell the element's container:

The MaxHeight and MaxWidth properties tell the element's container:

The MinHeight and MinWidth properties tell the element's container:

The ActualHeight and ActualWidth properties are:

HOW'D YOU DO?

The names of the properties are a pretty good indication of what they do, but there are a few quirks:

The Height and Width properties tell the element's container:

> These properties indicate the size the element would like to be. As we saw when we were working with the VariableSizedWrapGrid, these values are only a suggestion. The element's parent isn't required to abide by them.

The MaxHeight and MaxWidth properties tell the element's container:

> These properties indicate the maximum size at which the element should be displayed. Again, they're only suggestions to the parent. If the Height and Width properties conflict with MaxHeight and MaxWidth, these properties will take precedence.

The MinHeight and MinWidth properties tell the element's container:

> These two properties indicate the minimum size at which the element should be displayed. Like the others, they are only a suggestion to the parent. These properties take precedence over both MaxHeight/MaxWidth and Height/Width in the event of conflict.

The ActualHeight and ActualWidth properties are:

> These read-only properties indicate the actual height and width at which the parent is displaying the element.

SPECIFYING SIZES

You have two options when you're specifying most of the size properties. (Grid has another option, which we'll discuss in a minute.)

- **IN PIXELS**

  If you simply provide a number in XAML or code, the values will be interpreted as pixels (i.e., 1/96th of an inch). This is the only option available for the MaxHeight/MaxWidth and MinHeight/MinWidth properties.

- **AS AUTO**

  The Height and Width properties also accept a special value: "Auto" in XAML or Double.NaN in code. Exactly what happens when you specify Auto sizing (or don't specify a size at all, since Auto is the default for most size properties) depends on the element and the value of the Alignment property, but it basically tells XAML to figure out the value for you. In most cases, the element will either be sized to fit its content or expand to the size of the parent.

> **MAKE A NOTE**
>
> If you're coming to Win8 apps from other XAML environments like WPF or Windows Phone, you may be surprised to see that QualifiedDouble is not an option. The only option for specifying size properties for Win8 apps is pixels. While qualifiers like "in" and "em" are available for some classes (mostly relating to typography) you can't use them for the basic properties defined by FrameworkElement.

GRID LENGTHS

The RowDefinition and ColumnDefinition classes that are used to define the rows and columns of a Grid panel don't descend from FrameworkElement, but they do expose the same sizing properties. There's a difference, though: The Height and Width properties aren't defined as Double values, but as instances of the GridLength structure. You have three options when specifying a GridLength:

- **IN PIXELS**

    Just as with the FrameworkElement versions of these properties, if you simply provide a number in XAML or code, the values will be interpreted as pixels.

- **AS AUTO**

    The GridLength structure also supports an auto value. It's specified as "Auto" in XAML, and using the GridLength.Auto static property (rather than Double.NaN) in code:

    ```
    MyRow.Height = GridLength.Auto
    ```

- **STAR SIZING**

    The final option for specifying a GridLength is STAR SIZING, which makes it possible for you to allocate the available space among your rows or columns proportionally. Star sizing can be combined with other methods of specifying size, so for example, the following snippet makes the first row 300 pixels high and divides the remaining space between the other two rows, giving 1/4 of the available space to the second row and 3/4 to the third:

    ```xml
    <Grid.RowDefintions>
      <RowDefinition Height="300" />
      <RowDefinition Height="1*" />
      <RowDefinition Height="3*" />
    </Grid.RowDefinitions>
    ```

PUT ON YOUR THINKING HAT

Can you answer the following questions, based on what you've learned about sizing elements?

How would you specify that a **Rectangle** can't be any wider than 300 pixels?

What property would you use to determine how tall an element is?

If you don't explicitly specify the **Width** property of a **Grid**, how wide will it be?

Write the XAML to define five columns for a Grid, specifying that the first column should be as wide as necessary to display its children, the second column should be 400 pixels wide, and the remaining space should be divided equally among the remaining three columns:

HOW'D YOU DO?

How would you specify that a **Rectangle** can't be any wider than 300 pixels?

    `<Rectangle MaxWidth="300" ... />`

What property would you use to determine how tall an element is?

    ActualHeight

If you don't explicitly specify the **Width** property of a **Grid**, how wide will it be?

> The value of the **Width** property defaults to "Auto", so the Grid will take all the space that its parent allocates to it.

Write the XAML to define five columns for a **Grid**, specifying that the first column should be as wide as necessary to display its children, the second column should be 400 pixels wide, and the remaining space should be divided equally among the remaining three columns:

```
<Grid.ColumnDefinitions>
    <ColumnDefinition Width="Auto" />
    <ColumnDefinition Width="400" />
    <ColumnDefinition Width="*" />
    <ColumnDefinition Width="*" />
    <ColumnDefinition Width="*" />
</Grid.ColumnDefinitions>
```

You're not incorrect if you used the numeral 1 here as well as the star.

RELATIVE POSITIONING

In addition to the properties like Width and Height that relate to the size of an element, there are two properties that control the relationship between the layout of objects: Margin and Padding. They're probably easiest to understand using a picture:

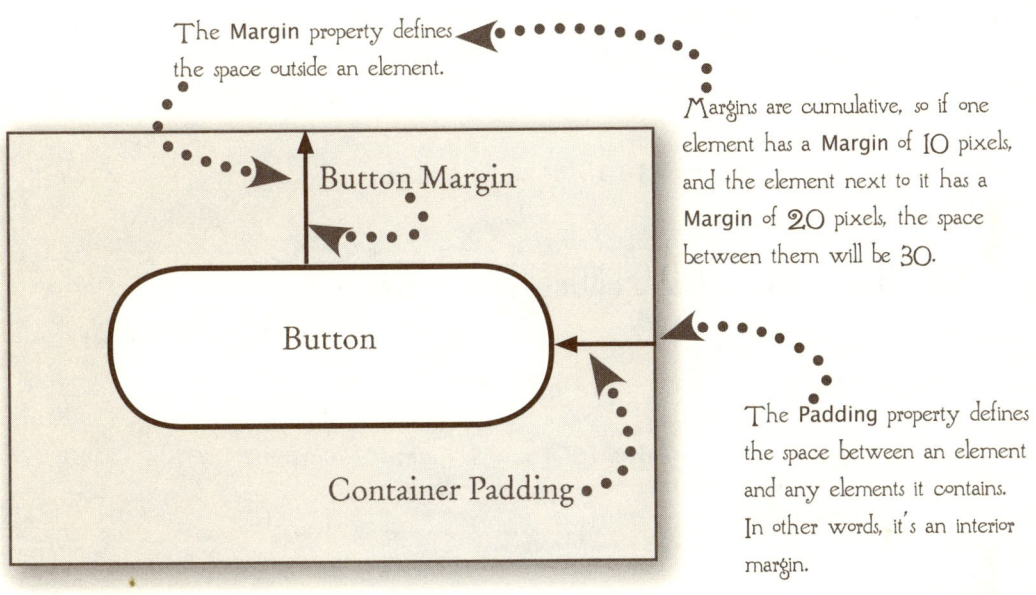

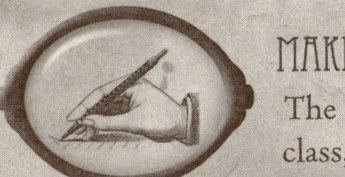

MAKE A NOTE
The Padding property isn't defined by the FrameworkElement class, only on some of its descendants, and it may not be available when you expect it to be.

The Control class defines it, for example, but Panel doesn't, so you can define the Padding of a Button (as in the example) or a TextBox, but not on a Grid.

SPECIFYING MARGINS & PADDING

The Margin and Padding properties are defined as instances of the Thickness structure. Thickness has four properties: Left, Right, Top, and Bottom, but when you're working in XAML you don't necessarily have to specify all four values. (In code, you always have to set the properties individually.)

- ## INDIVIDUAL VALUES USING ATTRIBUTE SYNTAX

    If you specify four values separated by commas, they'll be interpreted as the Left, Top, Right, and Bottom values, in that order. (I remember that by thinking "Left to right and clockwise, the way I read and tell time.")

    ```
    <Element Margin="10,5,7,3" ... />
    ```

- ## INDIVIDUAL VALUES USING PROPERTY SYNTAX

    If you want to be really explicit, you can use property syntax to set each value individually.

    ```
    <Element>
      <Element.Margin>
        <Thickness Left="10" Top="5" Right="7" Bottom="3" />
      </Element.Margin>
    </Element>
    ```

- ## SYMETRICALLY

    If you specify two values using attribute syntax, they will be interpreted as the Left/Right and Top/Bottom values, respectively.

    ```
    <Element Margin="10,5" ... />
    ```

- ## UNIFORMLY

    If you specify a single value using attribute syntax, all four properties of the Thickness will be set to that value.

    ```
    <Element Margin="10" ... />
    ```

ALIGNMENT

There are two final properties that control how an element is positioned relative to its container: VerticalAlignment and HorizontalAlignment. I think they're the easiest to understand:

VERTICALALIGNMENT

The **VerticalAlignment** property accepts an enumeration whose values are:

- Top
- Center
- Bottom
- Stretch (default)

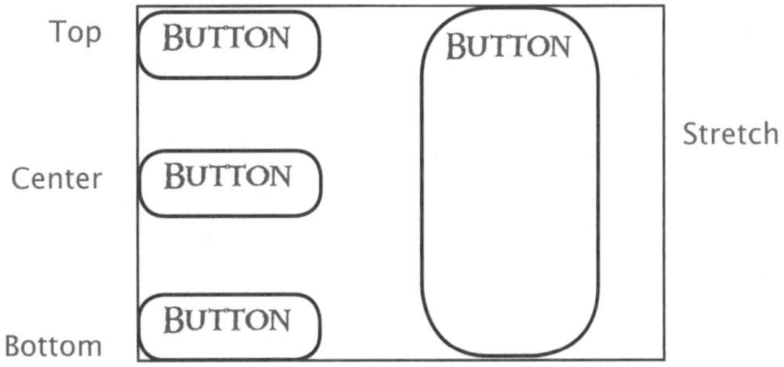

HORIZONTALALIGNMENT

The **HorizontalAlignment** property accepts an enumeration whose values are:

- Left
- Center
- Right
- Stretch (default)

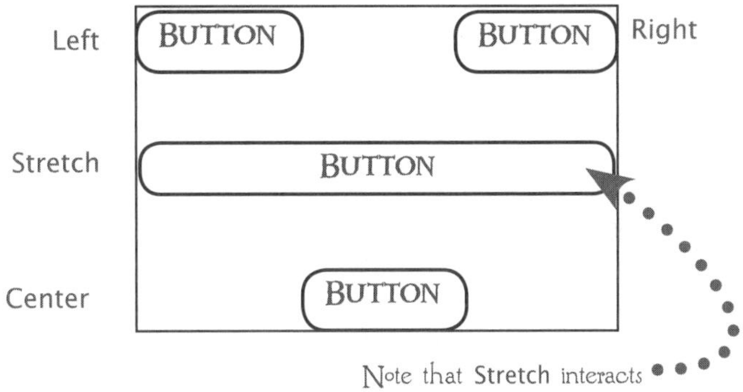

Note that **Stretch** interacts with the various height and width properties.

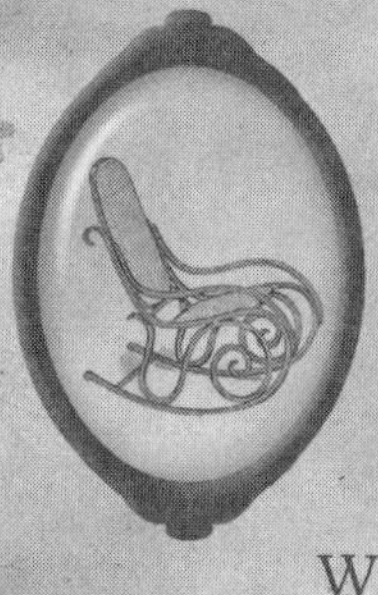

TAKE A BREAK

In this chapter we've explored the basic building blocks of your XAML code: the structure of the class library, the panel classes that are the basic tools for laying out your UX, and the properties that you can use to define how elements are laid out.

Why don't you take a break now, before you complete the Review and we start looking at the widgets that are available to your applications in the next chapter?

REVIEW

There are two primary top-level namespaces that you'll use in your application. What are they, and what kind of classes does each namespace hierarchy contain?

There are two primary differences between how a VariableSizedWrapGrid and a StackPanel lay out their children. What are they?

When would using property syntax be useful for specifying the Margin or Padding of an element?

Why is it best to leave most sizing properties to their default value? (Hint: Think about how they're specified and the different amount of real estate your app might have available.)

Congratulations! You've finished the chapter. Take a minute to think about what you've accomplished before you move on to the next one...

List three things you learned in this chapter:

①

②

③

Why do you think you need to know these things in order to develop Win8 apps?

Is there anything in this chapter that you think you need to understand in more detail? If so, what are you going to do about that?

XAML Controls, Part 1: Basic Widgets

Now that you know how to use panels to arrange the UI widgets in your application and how to control the layout of those widgets, it's time to explore the widgets that those panels arrange. Most—but not all—of these widgets are XAML controls (in the technical sense of "classes that descend from the Control class".) Controls and control-like widgets are the subject of this chapter and the next.

We'll start in this chapter by examining the Control class itself and the hierarchy of classes that descend from it, because knowing where a given widget sits in the class hierarchy tells you a lot about how it works and how to use it. Then we'll move on to exploring the basic controls that are available to your Win8 apps: widgets like buttons and textboxes that you'll almost certainly be familiar with from other UI platforms. In the next chapter we'll explore the more complex controls that display multiple items and those that provide special functionality for displaying other widgets.

WinRT provides most of the control types you would expect in a modern UI toolkit (although there are some surprising omissions), and the standard controls provide some very sophisticated functionality, like the touch-first orientation that's a hallmark of Win8 apps, and system-wide spell-checking. We'll get started using them in this chapter.

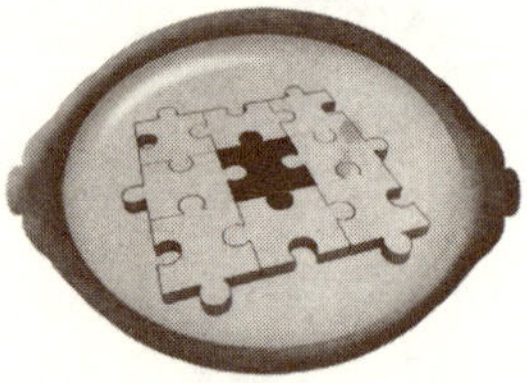

FITTING IT IN

Here's how this chapter fits in to the book as a whole...

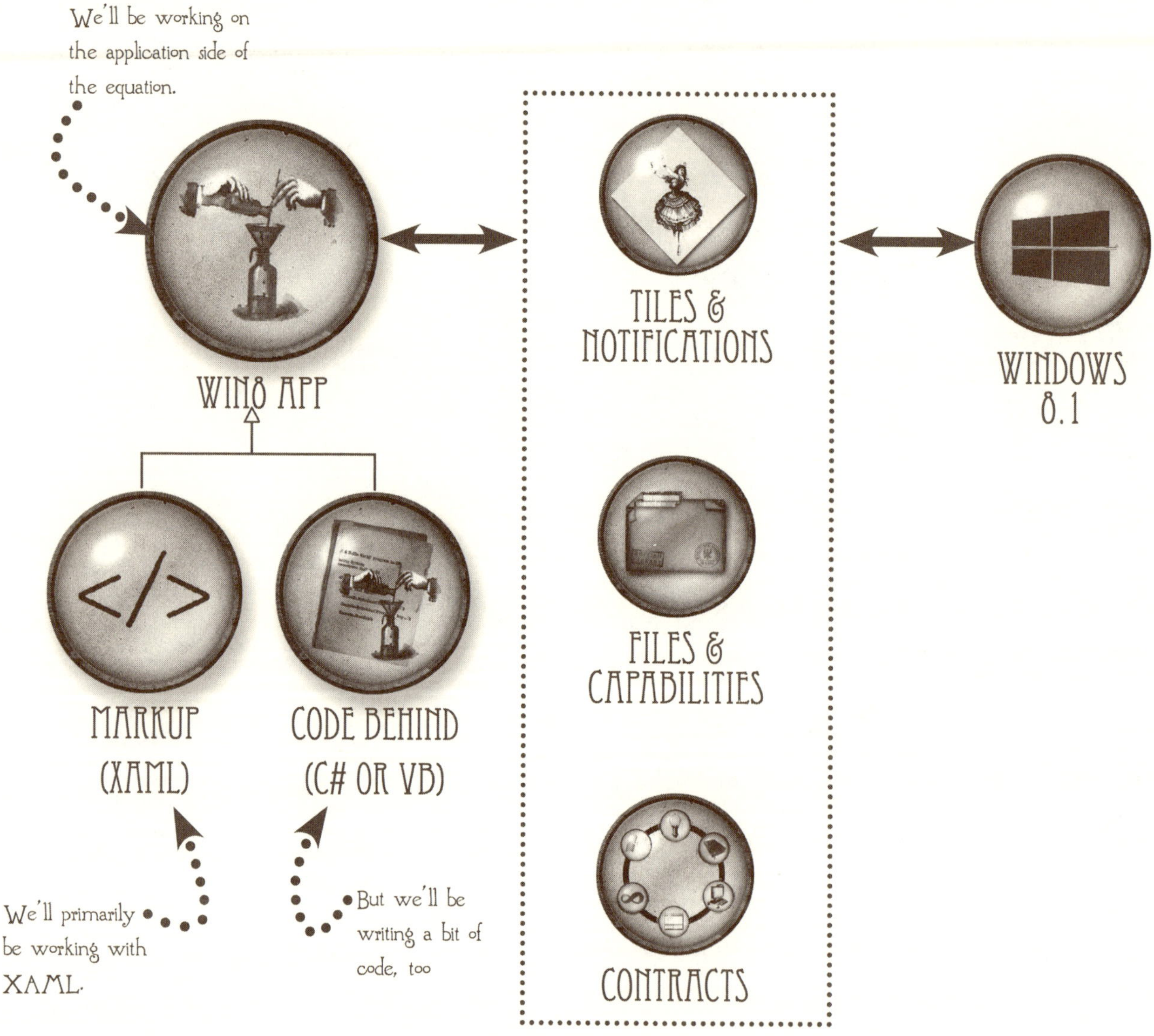

We'll be working on the application side of the equation.

WIN8 APP

MARKUP (XAML)

CODE BEHIND (C# OR VB)

We'll primarily be working with XAML.

But we'll be writing a bit of code, too

TILES & NOTIFICATIONS

FILES & CAPABILITIES

CONTRACTS

WINDOWS 8.1

152

TASK LIST

In this chapter we'll start by exploring how UI widgets fit into the class hierarchy, and then we'll start working with the basic widgets that provide the UI for making choices, displaying and editing text, and displaying progress.

THE CONTROL FAMILY

We'll start by exploring where the control and control-like widgets fit in the Win8 app class hierarchy and what that means for how you can use them.

CONTROLS FOR DISPLAYING PROGRESS

We'll start our exploration of the widget library with a couple of relatively simple controls: the **ProgressRing** and **ProgressBar**. From a programming standpoint, both of these controls are quite simple to use, but they'll give you a taste of how the Microsoft usability guidelines will impact your system designs.

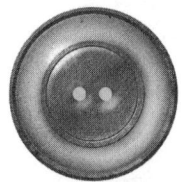

CONTROLS FOR ACTIONS & CHOICES

Next we'll explore the most basic of basic controls: the buttons and switches that let users initiate actions and make choices. They'll give us a good sense of how interactive Win8 app controls work in general.

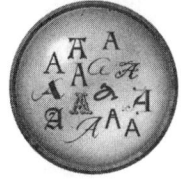

TEXT & DATE CONTROLS

Once we have the basics down, we'll finish the chapter by working with the Win8 app widgets for editing and displaying text: the text controls that allow users to edit text values, and the text blocks (which aren't controls because they descend directly from **FrameworkElement**) that display them. We'll also explore the date controls that were added to the XAML framework in Windows 8.1.

THE CONTROL FAMILY

Remember when I said that most of the widgets you'll use to build your applications will descend from Control? Here's a partial hierarchy. I've left out some command and display controls like the MessageDialog and the AppBar, both of which we'll talk about later, and some very basic components like the Border that you use when you build control templates. We'll talk about those later, too. But I promise I haven't left out any of the basic UI widgets.

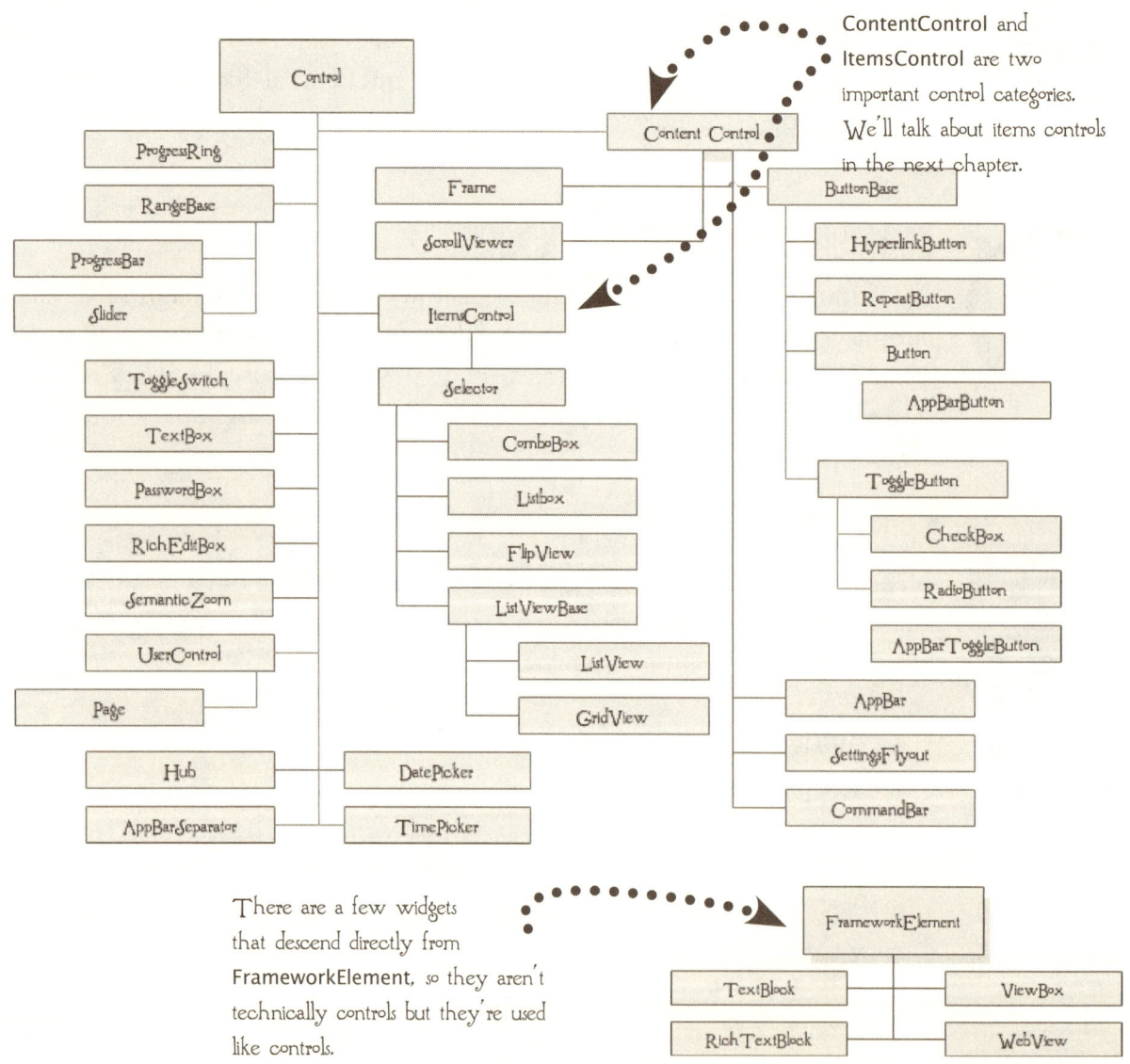

ContentControl and ItemsControl are two important control categories. We'll talk about items controls in the next chapter.

There are a few widgets that descend directly from FrameworkElement, so they aren't technically controls but they're used like controls.

PUT ON YOUR THINKING HAT

Knowing the basic capabilities provided by FrameworkElement and Control gives you a head start on learning to use any of the Win8 app controls. Based on the diagram, can you answer the following questions?

(Note: These questions are just intended to get you thinking. Don't spend a lot of time trying to figure out the "right" answer.)

The Control class descends from FrameworkElement. I've mentioned two bits of functionality that Control adds. Do you remember what they are?

Why do you think the widgets that descend from FrameworkElement don't need this functionality?

What functionality would you guess ContentControl brings to the control hierarchy?

How about ItemsControl? What functionality would you guess it provides?

While the diagram is missing some primitive controls and some that are used for commanding, all the basic high-level UI widgets are shown. Are there controls that you would have expected to find that aren't there?

HOW'D YOU DO?

The Control class descends from FrameworkElement. I've mentioned a few bits of functionality that Control adds. Do you remember what they are?

> The Control class adds formatting properties like Padding, properties that support focus, and a Template property that lets you completely re-define the visual tree of the control. (We'll see how templating works in Chapter 11.)

Why do you think the widgets that descend from FrameworkElement don't need this functionality?

> These four widgets display their content in specific, specialized ways. Rather than using templates, they expose the properties to control that display directly.

What functionality would you guess ContentControl brings to the control hierarchy?

> It exposes a Content property that contains a single element (but that element can be arbitrarily complex—panels that contain other panels, whatever you need).

How about ItemsControl? What functionality would you guess it provides?

> It displays a collection of items in its Items property. (By the way, all of the items controls in the Win8 app library descend from Selector, so they all support a single selected item. That isn't true of other XAML libraries.)

While the diagram is missing some primitive controls and some that are used for commanding, all the basic high-level UI widgets are shown. Are there controls that you would have expected to find that aren't there?

> I can't know what you expected, of course, but you might have noticed that there's no TreeView (or any other widget to display hierarchical data). Tabs are missing too, but that might be expected given the very different UI paradigm of Win8 apps.

ON YOUR OWN

Here's a partial class diagram of Control, showing the properties it adds to FrameworkElement (and UIElement, from which FrameworkElement descends). They fall into three categories: formatting, templating, and focus control. Can you identify which members fall into which category?

FOCUS

We'll be exploring formatting and templating in detail later in the book, but before we move on to specific control groups, lets take a minute to look at how focus works in Win8 apps, starting with how the TAB key works:.

TAB ORDER

Win8 apps support the standard Tab and Shift+Tab keyboard navigation. By default, the **IsTabStop** property, which determines whether the control can receive focus is **true**. (But the control must also be visible and enabled, that is, the **Visibility** property must be set to **Visible** and the **IsEnabled** property must be set to **true**.)

By default, the **TabIndex** of controls inside a container is the order in which the XAML elements are declared, but as you'd expect, you can change this value if necessary. (Sometimes it's convenient to declare elements in the XAML in an order other than the desired tab order.)

The **Control** class also exposes a **TabNavigation** property that gives you finer control over how tabbing works. The **TabNavigation** property takes an instance of the **KeyboardNavigationMode** enumeration. Here's what MSDN says about the values of the **KeyboardNavigationMode**:

Value	Meaning
Local	Tab indexes are considered on the local subtree only inside this container.
Cycle	Focus returns to the first or the last keyboard navigation stop inside of a container when the first or last keyboard navigation stop is reached.
Once	The container and all of its child elements as a whole receive focus only once.

PUT ON YOUR THINKING HAT

If the MSDN description of the KeyboardNavigationMode doesn't make much sense to you, don't feel stupid. It doesn't make much sense to a lot of people. So let's do a little exercise to try and figure out what these options actually do:

○ Create a project using the Blank app template. (I called mine BasicWidgets01.) Open the MainPage.xaml file, add three rows to the default Grid, and set their Height property to "Auto". Put a Button in the first row, a ListBox containing three or four TextBox elements in the second row, and another Button in the third row. I'm betting you can figure out how to do this without my help, but the XAML is on the next page if you're unsure about anything.

○ MSDN says the default value for TabNavigation is Local, but that's not true for all controls. You can see the default in the Common section of the Properties window. (You may have to expand it.) Which element type has a different default? What is it?

○ Run the app and press the Tab key to cycle around the controls. What happens?

○ Change the TabNavigation property of the ListBox to Local and re-run the app. Now what happens?

○ Now try changing the TabNavigation property of the ListBox to Cycle and re-running the app. What happens now?

HOW'D YOU DO?

```xml
<Grid ... >
  <Grid.RowDefinitions>
    <RowDefinition Height="Auto" />
    <RowDefinition Height="Auto" />
    <RowDefinition Height="Auto" />
  </Grid.RowDefinitions>
  <Button Grid.Row="0">First Button</Button>
  <ListBox Grid.Row="1">
    <TextBox Width="200" Text="Item One" />
    <TextBox Width="200" Text="Item Two" />
    <TextBox Width="200" Text="Item Three" />
  </ListBox>
  <Button Grid.Row="2">Second Button</Button>
</Grid>
```

- MSDN says the default value for **TabNavigation** is **Local**, but that's not true for all controls. You can see the default in the Common section of the Properties window. Which element type has a different default? What is it?

    The ListBox has a default **TabNavigation** value of **Once**.

- Run the app and press the Tab key to cycle around the controls. What happens?

    Focus moves to, but not into the **ListBox**. When you hit the TAB key a third time, focus moves to the third button.

- Change the **TabNavigation** property of the **ListBox** to **Local** and re-run the app. Now what happens?

    Focus moves into the **ListBox** and then through the items. After the last item, the Tab key moves to the third button.

- Now try changing the **TabNavigation** property of the **ListBox** to **Cycle** and re-running the app. What happens now?

    Focus moves into the **ListBox** and then cycles through the items. Once you enter the **ListBox**, you can't reach the third button using the TAB key

ON YOUR OWN

Now that you've performed your experiment, how would you describe the function of each of the TabNavigation options?

Once:

Local:

Cycle:

EXTRA CREDIT:

The Blank project template provides basic styling that's consistent with the general Win8 app look and feel, but our page is still pretty ugly.

Using the layout properties you learned about in the last chapter, can you make the page slightly less ugly?

FOCUS STATE

The `Control` class inherits two events that will help you respond to focus changes: `GotFocus` and `LostFocus`. `GotFocus` and `LostFocus` are actually ROUTED EVENTS. Routed events are an extension to the standard .NET event pattern that we'll talk about in Chapter 8. Basically, a routed event adds the ability to bubble up the logical tree.

In addition to the focus events, the `Control` class defines a `FocusState` property that returns a member of the `FocusState` enumeration, and a `Focus()` method that accepts a `FocusState` and returns a Boolean value indicating whether focus was set to the control.

The `FocusState` enumeration has the following values:

Value	Meaning
Unfocused	Indicates that the control doesn't currently have focus.
Pointer	Indicates that the control obtained focus through a Pointer action. (We haven't talked about the `Pointer` class yet. It represents touch, mouse, and pen interactions in a single API.)
Keyboard	Indicates that the control obtained focus through a keyboard action like the Tab navigation we just explored.
Programmatic	Indicates that the control obtained focus through code (generally by a call to the Focus() method).

> **MAKE A NOTE**
> The `Control.FocusState` property is read-only, and it isn't possible to remove focus from an element by calling `Focus(FocusState.Unfocused)`. The only way to remove focus from an element is to set focus to something else.

FOCUSMANAGER

One last thing before we leave the subject of focus in Win8 apps: It's often useful to know which element has focus. The `FocusManager` class, defined in the `Windows.UI.Xaml.Input` namespace, lets you do just that using its static `GetFocusedElement()` method:

The `GetFocusedElement()` method is static, so you don't need to instantiate `FocusManager` before using it.

C#: `Object CurrentWidget = FocusManager.GetFocusedElement();`

VB: `Dim CurrentWidget As Object = FocusManager.GetFocusedElement()`

`GetFocusedElement()` returns an `Object`, so you'll probably have to cast it before you can do anything useful.

TAKE A BREAK

Whew! Does that seem like a lot of theory to you? Well, we'll have a little more in the next section, because I want you to know about the Microsoft Usability Guidelines, but you'll start doing some more coding, too.

But why don't you take a quick break before you complete the Review and we move on to progress controls?

REVIEW

Can you answer the following questions based on what you've learned about the control widget class hierarchy and the navigation properties that the Control class brings to the party?

In the class hierarchy, all of the controls that let the user select items from a list descend from Selector, which descends from ItemsControl. What functionality do you think ItemsControl and Selector add to the hierarchy?

If the IsTabStop property of a control is set to false, can the control receive focus in some other way?

All of the button-like controls (Button, ToggleButton, etc.) descend from the ButtonBase class, which descends from Control via ContentControl. What functionality do you think ButtonBase adds to the hierarchy?

What value would you pass to the Focus() method if you were setting focus to the control in code?

Name three categories of functionality that the Control class passes on to its descendants.

Controls for Displaying Progress

We all know that an app should never leave people wondering what's going on. (You do know that, right?) Progress controls are one of the tools at your disposal for avoiding that situation. There are two kinds of progress controls available to Win8 apps: the `ProgressBar`, which can be displayed in DETERMINATE or INDETERMINATE mode, and the `ProgressRing`, which is always used for indeterminate progress.

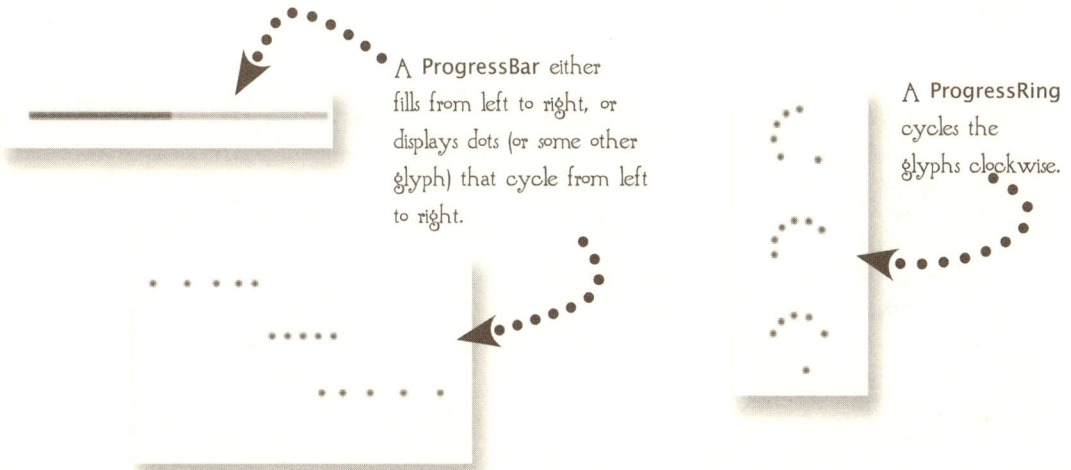

A `ProgressBar` either fills from left to right, or displays dots (or some other glyph) that cycle from left to right.

A `ProgressRing` cycles the glyphs clockwise.

Words for the Wise

Roughly speaking, DETERMINATE MODE means that you know exactly how many tasks you need to perform, and you can give the user a relatively accurate indication of how far along you are. For example, if you're downloading 100 files, and you have 50 of them, you know you're about 50% done.

INDETERMINATE MODE, on the other hand, means you know you have some work to do, but you can't provide a meaningful estimate of how long things will take. For example, you might be checking a user's credentials with a web service, and you can't predict the response time.

BUILD A PROGRESS EXERCISER

There are some rules about when and how to use the two progress controls, but before we get into more theory (we'll do that in a few pages), let's write a little app to exercise the properties of the two progress controls. Here's what we want to end up with:

These two grid cells contain **ProgressBar** controls. They both have a **Margin** of **100** and a **Height** of **50**.

There are three rows and two columns in the layout **Grid**.

This grid cell contains a **StackPanel** with a **Button** and three **RadioButtons**. They all have a **Margin** of **10**.

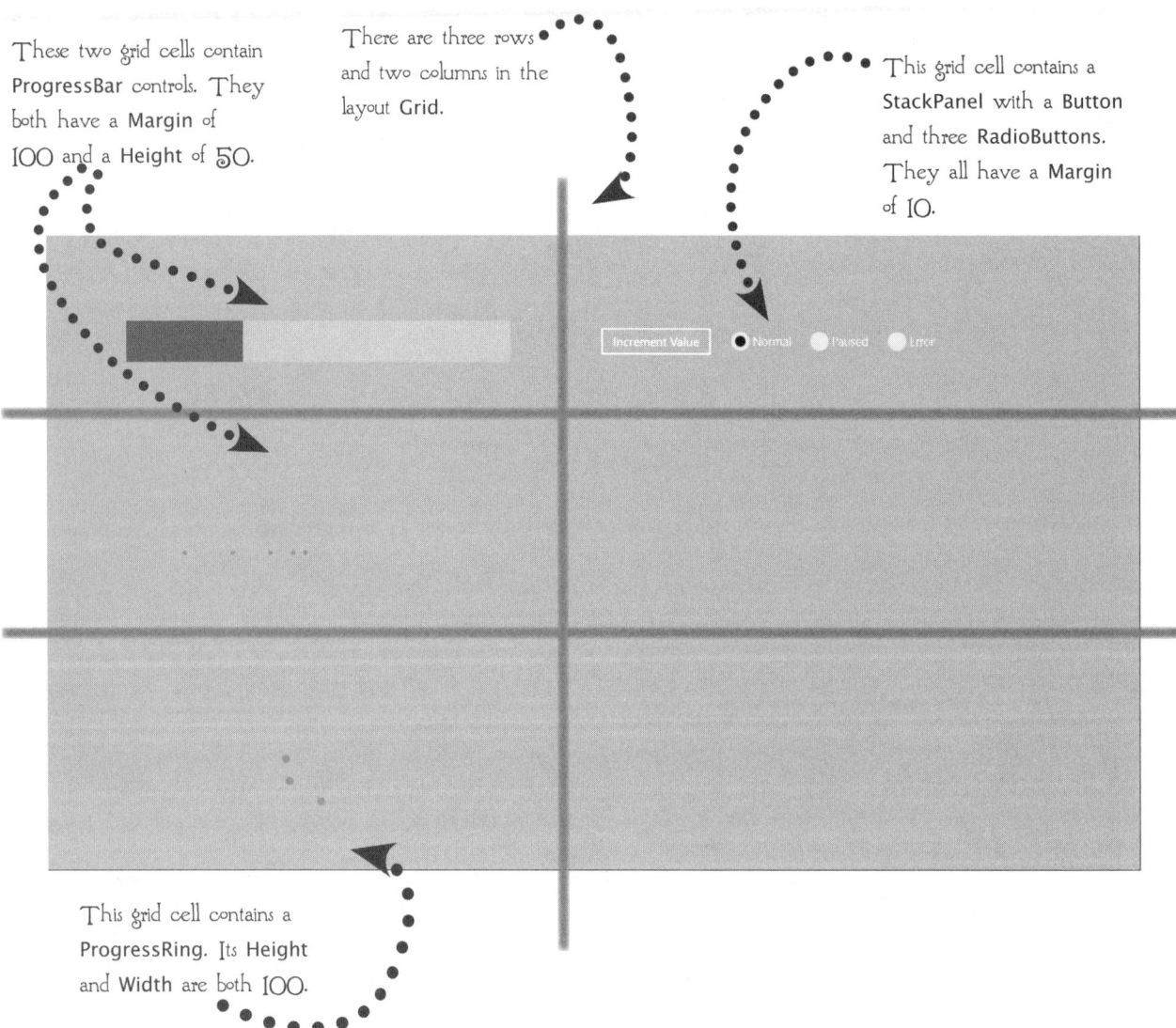

This grid cell contains a **ProgressRing**. Its **Height** and **Width** are both **100**.

PUT ON YOUR THINKING HAT

- Create a new app using the Blank Application template (mine is named BasicWidgets02), and create the screen shown on the previous page in MainPage.xaml. Be sure to give each of the items a Name.

  (If you can't quite figure out the syntax for the buttons, the XAML is on the next page, but try to figure it out on your own before you peek, okay?)

- Run the app. The buttons aren't wired up yet, and that's okay. But the progress widgets won't look like the sample, either. What's wrong with them?

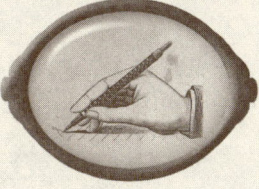

MAKE A NOTE

This is the first of several little apps I'm going to ask you to build that I call "exercisers" (as in exercising properties and methods). I think they're a good way to teach you about how widgets work—better than just blah blahing at you, anyway—but there are a few things you need to understand about them:

- They're not good apps. In fact, most of them are ridiculous. (Can you think of any good reason to have a progress ring just sitting there on your Page? I can't.)

- They don't necessarily represent good programming style. They're just silly little things to demonstrate some aspect of a class. Implementing Inversion of Control would just be distracting.

- Most of them violate the UX guidelines. Again, that's not the point.

So please, take these exercisers as they're intended: They'll teach you something, but that something isn't going to be good programming style!

HOW'D YOU DO?

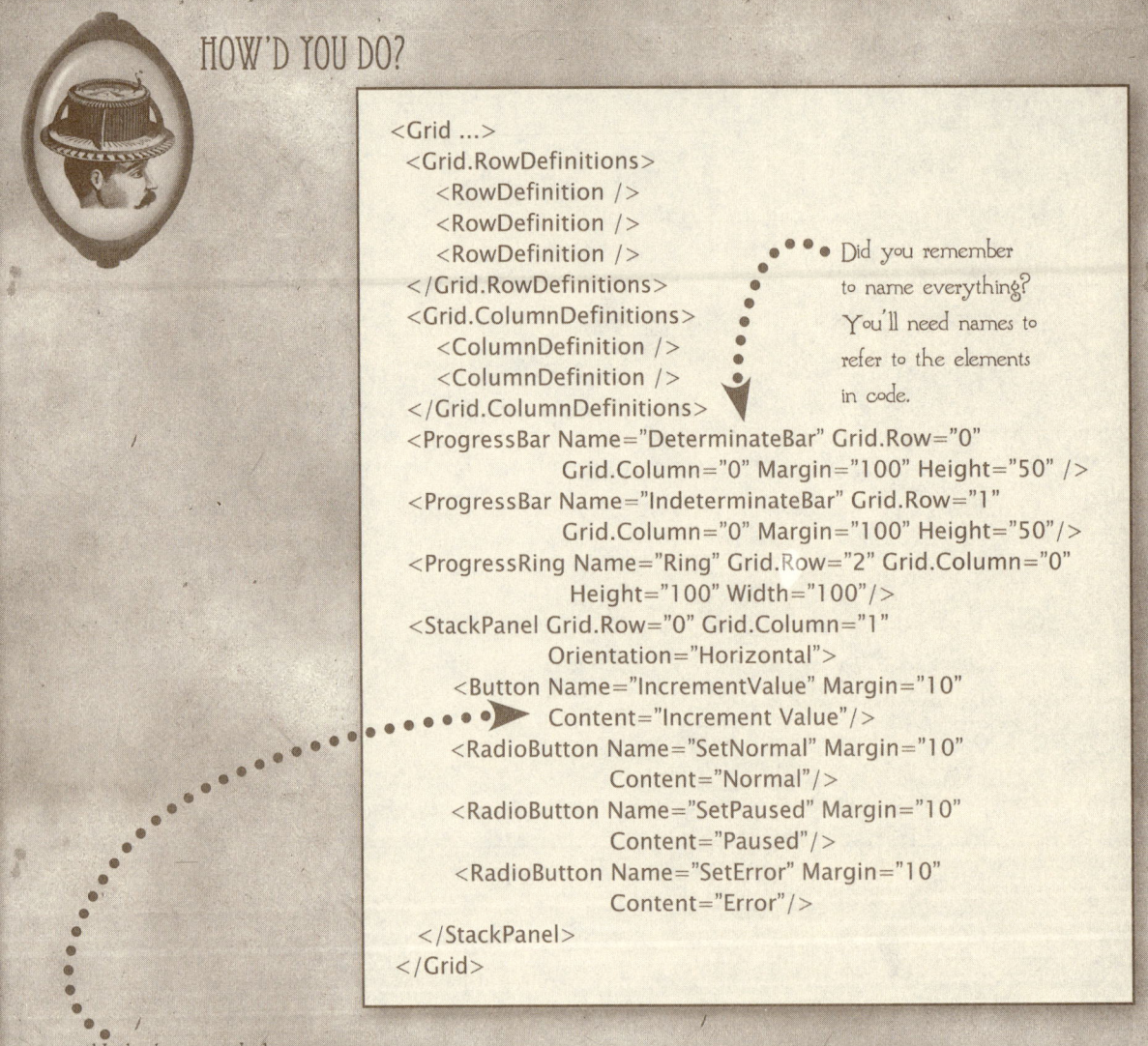

```
<Grid ...>
  <Grid.RowDefinitions>
    <RowDefinition />
    <RowDefinition />
    <RowDefinition />
  </Grid.RowDefinitions>
  <Grid.ColumnDefinitions>
    <ColumnDefinition />
    <ColumnDefinition />
  </Grid.ColumnDefinitions>
  <ProgressBar Name="DeterminateBar" Grid.Row="0"
            Grid.Column="0" Margin="100" Height="50" />
  <ProgressBar Name="IndeterminateBar" Grid.Row="1"
            Grid.Column="0" Margin="100" Height="50"/>
  <ProgressRing Name="Ring" Grid.Row="2" Grid.Column="0"
            Height="100" Width="100"/>
  <StackPanel Grid.Row="0" Grid.Column="1"
            Orientation="Horizontal">
    <Button Name="IncrementValue" Margin="10"
            Content="Increment Value"/>
    <RadioButton Name="SetNormal" Margin="10"
            Content="Normal"/>
    <RadioButton Name="SetPaused" Margin="10"
            Content="Paused"/>
    <RadioButton Name="SetError" Margin="10"
            Content="Error"/>
  </StackPanel>
</Grid>
```

Did you remember to name everything? You'll need names to refer to the elements in code.

You could also have used element syntax:
`<Button ...>Increment Value</Button>`

Did you spot the problems?

- The first `ProgressBar` doesn't show any sort of value.
- The second `ProgressBar` isn't showing up as indeterminate dots.
- The `ProgressRing` isn't showing up at all.

PROGRESS PROPERTIES

Fixing up the display of the progress controls is just a matter of setting the appropriate properties. Here are class diagrams of the ProgressBar and ProgressRing controls showing the properties they expose:

The ...Change, Minimum and Maximum properties are inherited from ProgressBar's parent, RangeBase.

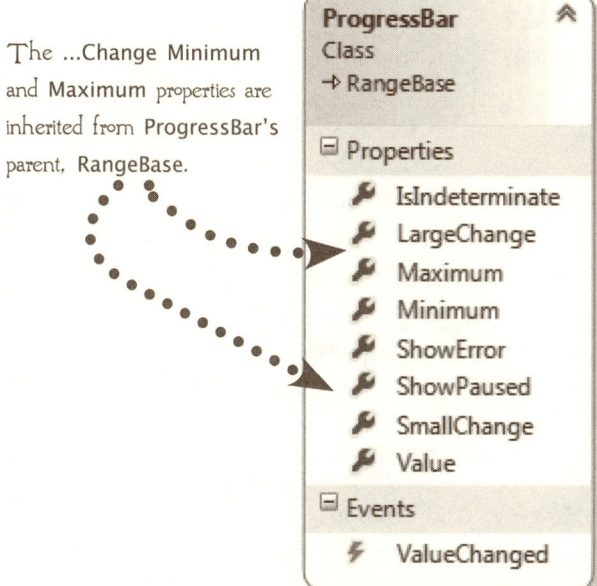
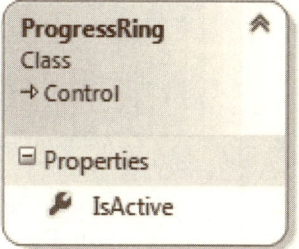

PUT ON YOUR THINKING HAT

Using the class diagrams, can you fix up the initial display of the app and wire up the event handlers so the buttons do what they should?

We'll talk about events in detail in Chapter 8, but for now, let Visual Studio handle the icky details for you. Just select the appropriate event in the Properties window (**Click** for the **Button** and **Checked** for the **RadioButton** elements), type the event handler name and press Enter. Visual Studio will create the code skeleton and take you right to it.

By the way, the convention for naming event handlers hasn't changed. It's still ObjectName_EventName.

PUT ON YOUR THINKING HAT

How'd you do?

It doesn't matter if you picked different initial values here.

```xml
<Grid ...>
  <Grid.RowDefinitions>
    <RowDefinition />
    <RowDefinition />
    <RowDefinition />
  </Grid.RowDefinitions>
  <Grid.ColumnDefinitions>
    <ColumnDefinition />
    <ColumnDefinition />
  </Grid.ColumnDefinitions>
  <ProgressBar Name="DeterminateBar" Grid.Row="0"
               Grid.Column="0" Margin="100" Height="50"
               Maximum="100" Value="30"/>
  <ProgressBar Name="IndeterminateBar" Grid.Row="1"
               Grid.Column="0" Margin="100" Height="50"
               IsIndeterminate="True"/>
  <ProgressRing Name="Ring" Grid.Row="2" Grid.Column="0"
                Height="100" Width="100"
                IsActive="True"/>
  <StackPanel Grid.Row="0" Grid.Column="1"
              Orientation="Horizontal">
    <Button Name="IncrementValue" Margin="10"
            Content="Increment Value"
            Click="IncrementValue_Click"/>
    <RadioButton Name="SetNormal" Margin="10"
                 Content="Normal"
                 Checked="SetNormal_Checked"/>
    <RadioButton Name="SetPaused" Margin="10"
                 Content="Paused"
                 Checked="SetPaused_Checked"/>
    <RadioButton Name="SetError" Margin="10"
                 Content="Error"
                 Checked="SetError_Checked"/>
  </StackPanel>
</Grid>
```

```vb
Private Sub IncrementValue_Click(sender As Object, e As RoutedEventArgs) _
            Handles IncrementValue.Click
    If DeterminateBar.Value < 100 Then
        DeterminateBar.Value += 10
    Else
        DeterminateBar.Value = 0
    End If
End Sub

Private Sub SetNormal_Checked(sender As Object, e As RoutedEventArgs) _
            Handles SetNormal.Checked
    DeterminateBar.ShowError = False
    DeterminateBar.ShowPaused = False
End Sub

Private Sub SetPaused_Checked(sender As Object, e As RoutedEventArgs) _
            Handles SetPaused.Checked
    DeterminateBar.ShowError = False
    DeterminateBar.ShowPaused = True
End Sub

Private Sub SetError_Checked(sender As Object, e As RoutedEventArgs) _
            Handles SetError.Checked
    DeterminateBar.ShowPaused = False
    DeterminateBar.ShowError = True
End Sub
```

Again, the specific values you chose don't matter.

Did you remember to "undo" the other settings?

Turn the page for the C# version of the event handlers...

```csharp
private void IncrementValue_Click(Object sender, RoutedEventArgs e)
{
    if (DeterminateBar.Value < 100)
    {
        DeterminateBar.Value += 10;
    }
    else
    {
        DeterminateBar.Value = 0;
    }
}

private void SetNormal_Checked(Object sender, RoutedEventArgs e)
{
    DeterminateBar.ShowError = false;
    DeterminateBar.ShowPaused = false;
}

private void SetPaused_Checked(Object sender, RoutedEventArgs e)
{
    DeterminateBar.ShowError = false;
    DeterminateBar.ShowPaused = true;
}

private void SetError_Checked(Object sender, RoutedEventArgs e)
{
    DeterminateBar.ShowError = true;
    DeterminateBar.ShowPaused = false;
}
```

UX GUIDELINES

Out of the box, the widgets that are available to your Win8 apps are fully functional, as you'd expect, and they look pretty good, which might come as a surprise to anybody who struggled with the early versions of the WPF platform. Of course, you have complete freedom to re-define how controls look (and as I keep saying, we'll find out how in Chapter 11), but you probably shouldn't change how they behave. At least not without a *really* compelling reason.

Part of that is not re-defining the core functionality, which doesn't usually make much sense anyway—what use is a button that can't be clicked?—but part of it is how the widgets behave in the context of your app, and that has to do with following the UX guidelines. This exercise should give you a taste of how that works:

PUT ON YOUR THINKING HAT

If you search for "progress guidelines" on MSDN, you'll find a page called "Guidelines and checklist for progress controls". Make sure you're looking at the one for VB/C#/C++ and XAML (it won't be the first to come up, but you'll find the link at the top of the text).

Can you answer the following questions based on the MSDN recommendations?

- Which control do you use in the following situations?

	Modal	Non-Modal
Determinate		
Indetermiante		

- What should you do when an operation starts out indeterminate but doesn't stay that way?

- Should you display progress as text as well as via the ProgressBar?

HOW'D YOU DO?

○ Which control do you use in the following situations?

	Modal	Non-Modal
Determinate	Determinate ProgressBar	Determinate ProgressBar
InDetermiante	ProgressRing	Indeterminate ProgressBar

○ What should you do when an operation starts out indeterminate but doesn't stay that way?

> Use a ProgressBar, but switch its state from indeterminate to determinate.

○ Should you display progress as text as well as via the ProgressBar?

> No. It duplicates the information the ProgressBar already provides.

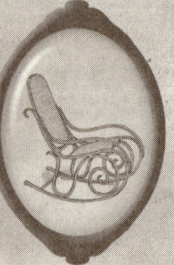

TAKE A BREAK

That's it for progress controls. Why don't you take a break before we move on to the controls that allow your users to initate actions and make choices (otherwise known as "buttons and switches").

CONTROLS FOR ACTIONS & CHOICES

I'd be prepared to bet cash money that if you've done any programming at all, you've worked with buttons, and if you've worked with them in any other UI platform, you know most of what you need to know to work with them in Win8 apps. But there are a few things that are unique to the XAML environment, and we'll explore those aspects of buttons in this section. We'll also take a look at a couple of other controls (the ToggleSwitch and Slider) that aren't actually buttons, but are used in similar ways.

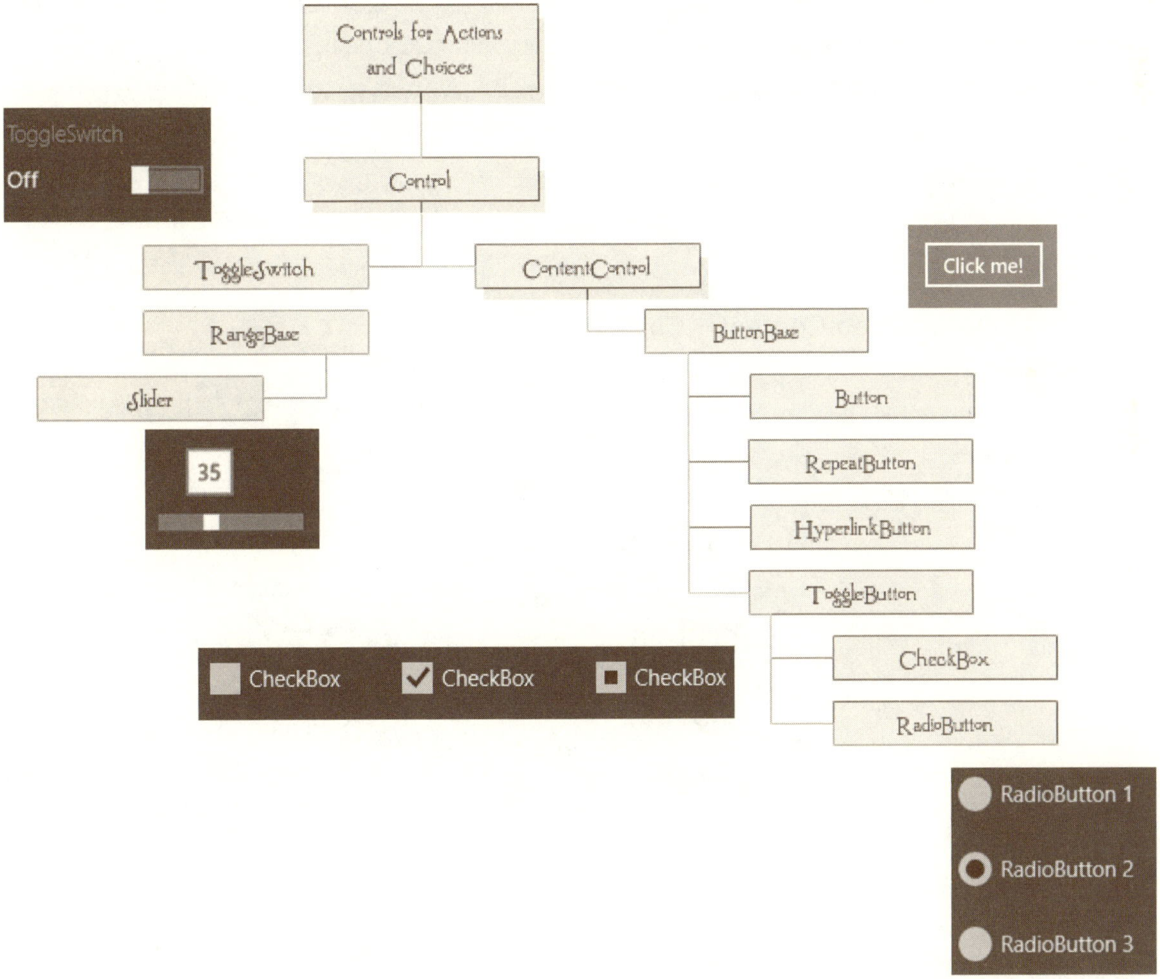

175

CONTENT CONTROLS

On of the interesting things about XAML buttons, unlike buttons in other platforms, is that because they descend from `ContentControl`, you can do things that are far more exciting than just changing the text that's displayed inside a button.

The `ContentControl` class adds a cluster of properties that allow it to contain a single `Object`, and that content can be arbitrarily complex—you can use panels and other content controls that themselves contain panels that contain panels that...well, you get the idea.

Like any property of a XAML element, you can assign the **Content** property using either attribute or element syntax (technically, CONTENT SYNTAX, because you're setting the **Content** property and you don't need to specify the property explicitly):

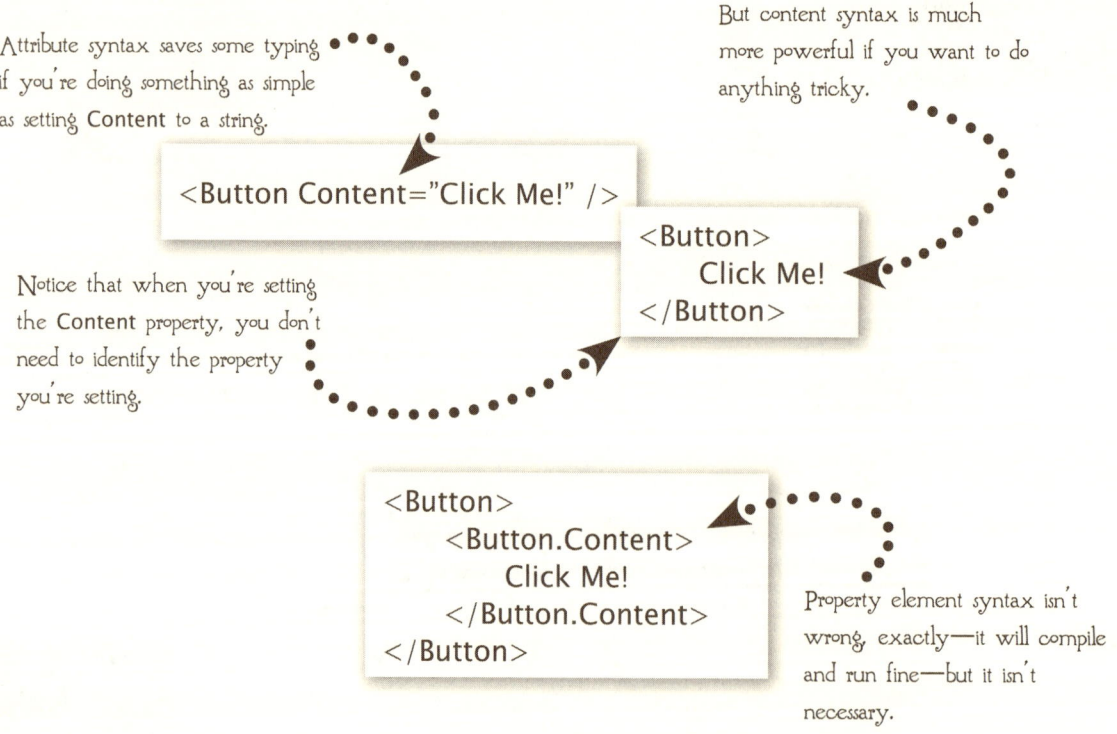

When you use content syntax, you can do some pretty complex things as easily as you set a label. Here's a simple example:

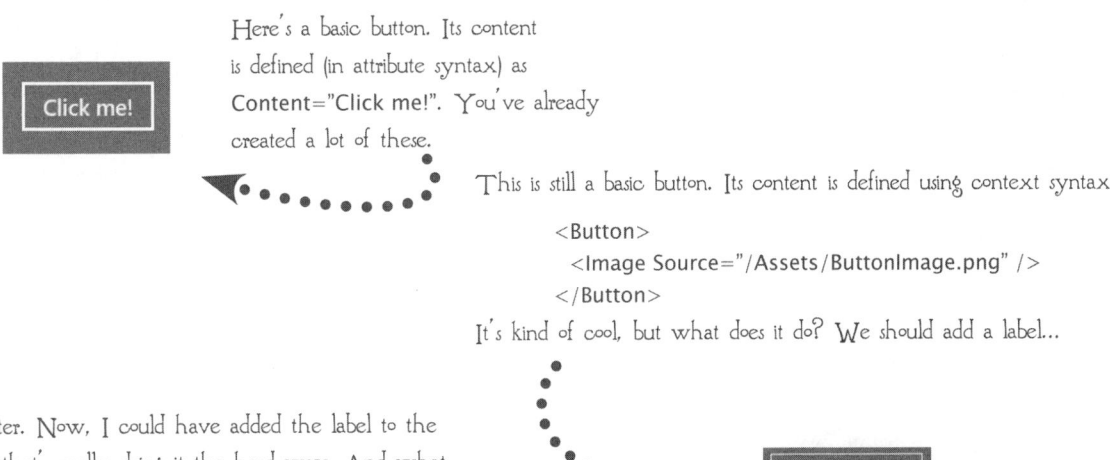

Here's a basic button. Its content is defined (in attribute syntax) as Content="Click me!". You've already created a lot of these.

This is still a basic button. Its content is defined using context syntax:

```
<Button>
  <Image Source="/Assets/ButtonImage.png" />
</Button>
```

It's kind of cool, but what does it do? We should add a label…

That's better. Now, I could have added the label to the image, but that's really doing it the hard way. And what if you want to re-use the image with different labels? Instead, the direct content of the Button is a StackPanel that contains the Image and the Label:

```
<Button>
  <StackPanel>
    <Image Source="Binoculars.png" />
    <TextBlock>More Details</TextBlock>
  </StackPanel>
</Button>
```

PUT ON YOUR THINKING HAT

Build yourself a button exerciser. Create a new project based on the Blank Application template (I called mine BasicWidgets03), and add one of each type of button (Button, RepeatButton, HyperlinkButton, ToggleButton, CheckBox and a set of RadioButton elements) to MainPage.xaml. You can lay out the controls any way that appeals to you.

Once you've got the basic app running, add a Button that contains an Image and a TextBlock inside a panel of some sort. (I used a StackPanel in the example, but Grid is a common choice as well.)

HOW'D YOU DO?

Here's my version. Yours will be different in detail, but as long as you got the button types to display, you're fine.

```xml
<Grid ...>
   <Grid.RowDefinitions>
      <RowDefinition Height="Auto"/>
      <RowDefinition Height="Auto"/>
      <RowDefinition Height="Auto"/>
      <RowDefinition Height="Auto"/>
   </Grid.RowDefinitions>
   <Grid.ColumnDefinitions>
      <ColumnDefinition Width="Auto"/>
      <ColumnDefinition />
   </Grid.ColumnDefinitions>
   <Button Name="StandardButton" Grid.Row="0" Margin="10">Click me!</Button>
   <RepeatButton Name="Repeater" Grid.Row="1" Margin="10">Hold me!</RepeatButton>
   <HyperlinkButton Name="Link" Grid.Row="2" Margin="10">
        Let's go somewhere!
   </HyperlinkButton>
   <ToggleButton Name="Toggle" Grid.Row="0" Grid.Column="1" Margin="10">
        Turn me on and off!
   </ToggleButton>
   <CheckBox Name="Check" Grid.Row="1" Grid.Column="1" Margin="10">
       Check me out!
   </CheckBox>
   <StackPanel Grid.Row="2" Grid.Column="1" Orientation="Horizontal" Margin="10">
     <RadioButton Name="R1" GroupName="RadioGroup">Pick me!</RadioButton>
     <RadioButton Name="R2" GroupName="RadioGroup" Margin="10" >No, me!</RadioButton>
     <RadioButton Name="R3" GroupName="RadioGroup" Margin="10">Me, me!</RadioButton>
   </StackPanel>
   <Button Name="ContentButton" Margin="10" Grid.Row="3" >
      <StackPanel>
         <Image Margin="10" Height="250" Width="250" Source="/Assets/Button.png" />
         <TextBlock HorizontalAlignment="Center">
             Show me some computer stuff
         </TextBlock>
      </StackPanel>
   </Button>
</Grid>
```

ON YOUR OWN

Changing the Content of one of the button widgets (or any other control that descends from ContentControl) can accomplish a lot, but it doesn't change the VISUAL BEHAVIOR of a control, things like when its background changes colors. For that you'll need to change the template, and for that you'll need to wait for Chapter 11. (Are you tired of me saying that yet?)

But let's start by figuring out what the visual behavior of each type of button widget is by default. Run your exerciser app again, and answer the following questions:

How does the ToggleButton indicate its state?

When you first run the application, is there anything to distinguish the Button, RepeatButton, and ToggleButton controls?

Does the RepeatButton indicate to the user that the click event is being issued as long as they hold it down?

I personally don't think the default styles for the various button controls distinguish themselves sufficiently. Do you agree or disagree? What, if anything, would you change?

THE TOGGLESWITCH

The `ToggleSwitch` control is closely related to both the `ToggleButton` and the `CheckBox`: it's used to indicate state. Unlike those two controls, however, the `ToggleSwitch` doesn't have a third, indeterminate state. And the `ToggleSwitch` is used differently in the UI.

Unlike the `ToggleButton` and `Checkbox` (or, for that matter, the `RadioButton`) that can represent any arbitrary values or settings, according to the Microsoft UI guidelines the `ToggleSwitch` should only be used when changing the setting has an immediate effect, just like turning a power switch on or off.

There isn't anything tricky about implementing a `ToggleSwitch`. It has a `Header` property that functions as its label and two content properties: `OnContent` and `OffContent`. The content properties accept an `Object`, and you can replace them using the same techniques you used to replace the contents of a `Button`, with the exception that `ToggleSwitch` isn't a content control (it descends directly from the `Control` class), so you have to use element syntax, not content syntax, to set their values. Here's a partial class diagram:

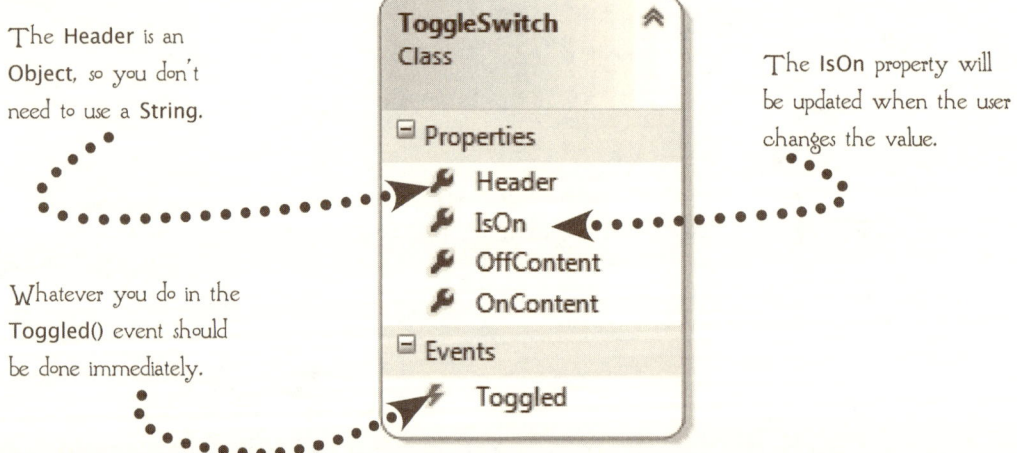

The `Header` is an `Object`, so you don't need to use a `String`.

The `IsOn` property will be updated when the user changes the value.

Whatever you do in the `Toggled()` event should be done immediately.

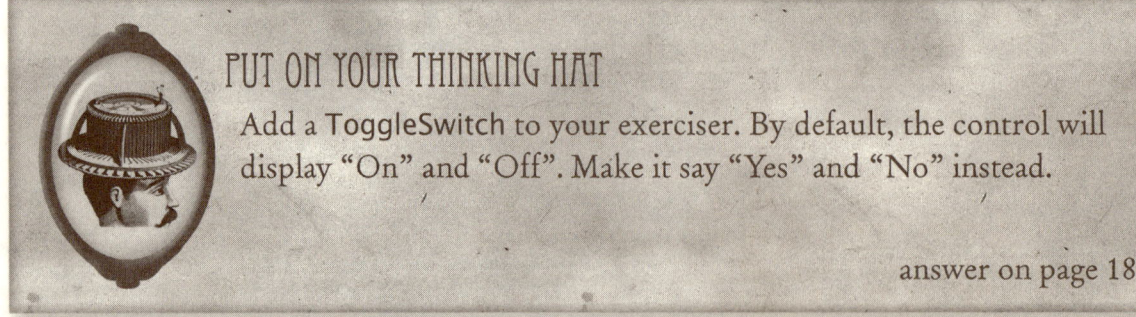

PUT ON YOUR THINKING HAT

Add a `ToggleSwitch` to your exerciser. By default, the control will display "On" and "Off". Make it say "Yes" and "No" instead.

answer on page 182

THE SLIDER

There's one more button-like control available when you want your users to make a choice. The `Slider` control is useful when users need to select a value that they think of as (roughly) "more or less". The classic example is volume: we think "louder" or "softer", not "35" or "10".

The Win8 XAML slider works very much like other slider widgets you'll have worked with in other platforms. Here's a partial class diagram:

Slider — Class

Properties
- Header
- IntermediateValue
- IsDirectionReversed
- LargeChange
- Maximum
- Minimum
- Orientation
- SmallChange
- SnapsTo
- StepFrequency
- TickFrequency
- TickPlacement

Events
- ValueChanged

The `Slider` inherits these properties from RangeBase. → Maximum, Minimum, SmallChange

The TickPlacement enumerations accept the values None (the default), TopLeft, BottomRight, Outside, and Inline. → TickPlacement

---

PUT ON YOUR THINKING HAT

Add a Slider to your exerciser. Set the Maximum to 100 and have it increment by 10 units at a time. The ticks should be displayed within the Slider bar.

answer on page 183

181

PUT ON YOUR THINKING HAT (FROM PAGE 180)

How'd you do? Here's my version:

I added some formatting properties here.

The Header property defines the label for the control.

```
<ToggleSwitch Name="Switch" ...
              Header="Toggle Me!" >
    <ToggleSwitch.OnContent>
      On
    </ToggleSwitch.OnContent>
    <ToggleSwitch.OffContent>
      Off
    </ToggleSwitch.OffContent>
</ToggleSwitch>
```

You can't use Content Syntax to specify the On and Off content (how would the compiler know which one you meant?) but you don't need to wrap the text in quotation marks.

The Microsoft guidelines imply that the content should always be text and recommend that it be no more than 3 or 4 characters. But you could use an image (or anything else that makes sense for your situation).

PUT ON YOUR THINKING HAT (FROM PAGE 181)

How'd you do? Here's my version:

Again, my example has some formatting properties. They're not relevant to our discussion right now.

```
<Slider Name="Slide" ...
        Orientation="Horizontal" Minimum="0" Maximum="100"
        Value="20" StepFrequency="10"
        TickFrequency="10" TickPlacement="Inline" />
```

Slider isn't a content control, so I was able to use attribute syntax to define it, but you could have used element syntax for any of these properties.

Remember that you have complete control over how the ticks will look via the control template.

REVIEW

Can you answer the following questions based on what you've learned about the widgets for making choices or taking action?

Why can't you use content syntax with the TogglesSwitch?

What criteria would you use to choose between a ToggleSwitch and a ToggleButton or CheckBox?

What do the terms determinate and indeterminate mean in the context of progress widgets?

What widget do the Microsoft guidelines say you should always use to represent a determinate state?

What event should you respond to when the user changes the state of a ToggleSwitch?

TEXT & DATE CONTROLS

The last group of basic widgets we'll discuss in this chapter are the controls for displaying and editing text and dates. There are several in the Win8 XAML toolkit:

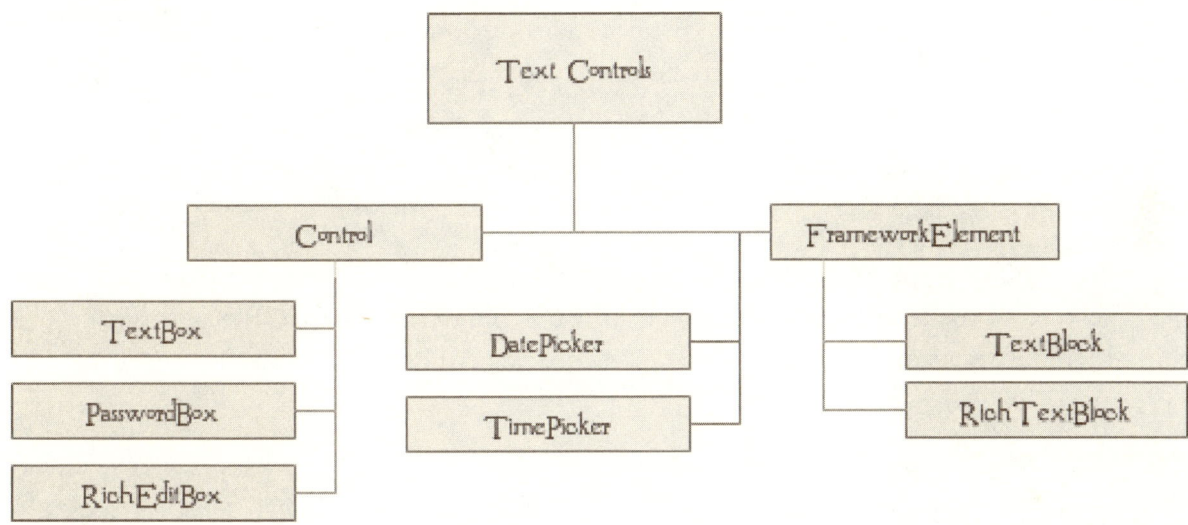

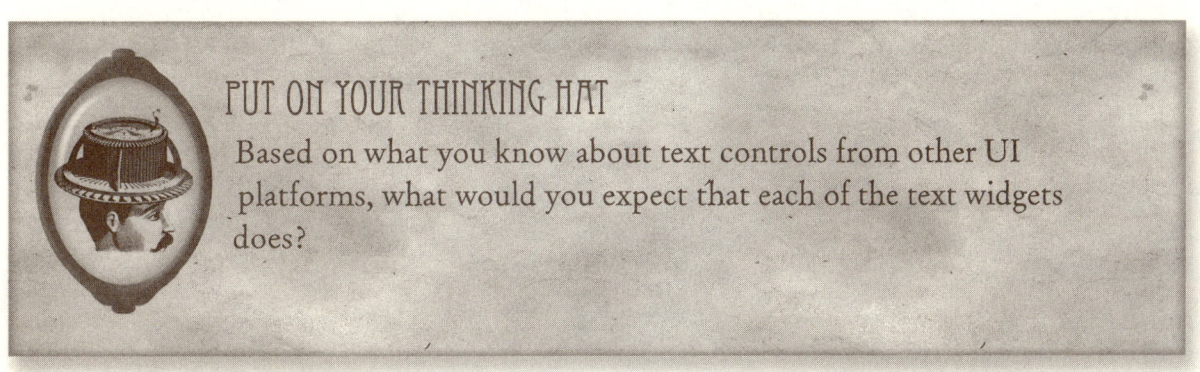

PUT ON YOUR THINKING HAT

Based on what you know about text controls from other UI platforms, what would you expect that each of the text widgets does?

185

HOW'D YOU DO?

TextBox

The TextBox control is used to display and input one or more lines of text. When you're using the TextBox, all of the characters must have the same format. So, for example, you can't italicize a single word.

PasswordBox

The PasswordBox is used for entering passwords. It displays a specified character instead of the actual characters the user types. The Win8 XAML PasswordBox includes functionality to show the password (which can be disabled).

RichEditBox

The RichEditBox is used for entering formatted text. We'll discuss text formatting and XAML typography in Chapter 10.

TextBlock

The TextBlock is used for displaying small amounts of text that cannot be edited. It's roughly equivalent to a label in other platforms (but without the navigation capabilities).

RichTextBlock

The RichTextBlock is used for displaying larger amounts of text that cannot be edited. It supports text overflow.

TEXTBOXES

Like the other basic Win8 XAML widgets that appear in multiple platforms, the `TextBox` (and its relative, the `RichEditBox`) behaves the way you'd expect it to. It inherits font properties from the `Control` class and exposes properties and methods for setting and selecting text. But it does have a few properties that may be new to you: `InputScope` (which also exists in Silverlight and Windows Phone 7, `IsSpellCheckEnabled`, and `IsTextPredictionEnabled`. Here's a partial class diagram:

The properties that control basic font characteristics are inherited by all the classes that descend from `Control`.

We'll examine these properties in detail when we explore XAML typography in Chapter 10.

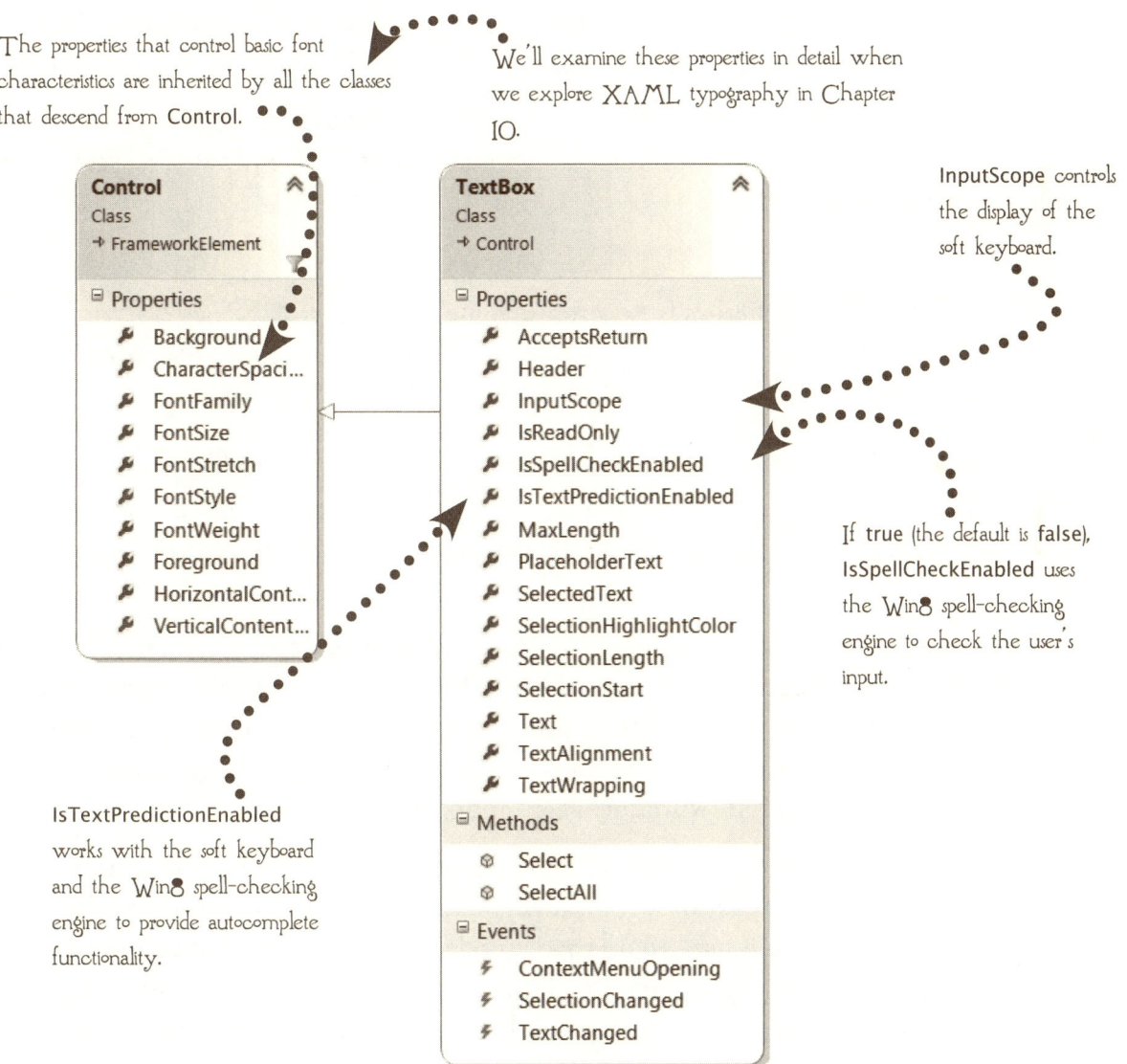

`InputScope` controls the display of the soft keyboard.

If true (the default is false), `IsSpellCheckEnabled` uses the Win8 spell-checking engine to check the user's input.

`IsTextPredictionEnabled` works with the soft keyboard and the Win8 spell-checking engine to provide autocomplete functionality.

187

WIN8 PROPERTIES

As I've said, there are three properties of the Win8 XAML `TextBox` and `RichEditBox` that might be new to you. Let's look at them in a little more detail.

SPELL-CHECKING

The Win8 XAML text controls can participate in the system-wide spell-checking system by simply setting the `IsSpellCheckingEnabled` property to `true`. Spell-checking isn't always appropriate, of course, but it is handy.

Notice that I said "system-wide spell-checking". You can't build your own application-specific dictionaries using this property. (That's possible, but it's very low-level stuff, and way outside our scope.)

TEXT PREDICTION

Like spell-checking, text prediction is easy to implement (just set `IsTextPredictionEnabled` to `true`), but again, it's not appropriate in every situation. This functionality has another limitation: it only works with the soft keyboard.

INPUT SCOPE

The final XAML property, `InputScope`, is also available for Windows Phone (and there are more options available in that platform). It controls the way the soft keyboard is displayed.

`InputScope` actually accepts a collection of `InputScopeName` objects, each of which has its `NameValue` property set to a member of the `InputScopeNameValue` enumeration. In practice, you'll only use multiple `InputScopeName` elements if you need to specify both the type of input and the character set. In most situations, you'll set a single value to `Default`, `Url`, `EmailSmtpAddress`, `Number`, `TelephoneNumber`, or `Search`.

It's important to understand that `InputScope` only controls the initial display of the soft keyboard. It doesn't work with a physical keyboard, and it doesn't constrain the user's input in any way. (You'll need to do that in code.) So, for example, if you set the `InputScope` to `Number`, the soft keyboard will initially be displayed on the numeric "page", but the user can easily switch back to alphanumeric input, and the `TextBox` will accept those values.

PUT ON YOUR THINKING HAT

Time to build another exerciser. (Yep, I called mine BasicWidgets04.) Create a new Blank App and add 8 TextBox controls. (My version of the XAML is on the next page.)

- The first TextBox should use the default values for the special properties.

- The second TextBox should be integrated with the spell-checking system.

- The third TextBox should support text prediction.

- The remaining TextBox controls should have the InputScope set to each of the commonly used values: Email, Number, Search, TelephoneNumber, and Url. (Those aren't the necessarily the names of the enumeration values. You'll have to figure that out for yourself. Not that it's difficult to do using IntelliSense.)

When you run the app, how does the behavior of each TextBox differ? (You can test the soft keyboard in the Simulator if you don't have a touch screen.)

PUT ON YOUR THINKING HAT

How'd you do? Here's my XAML:

As always, I've elided the irrelevant formatting.

```xml
<Grid...>
    <Grid.RowDefinitions>
        <RowDefinition Height="Auto" />
        ...
    </Grid.RowDefinitions>
    <Grid.ColumnDefinitions>
        <ColumnDefinition Width="Auto"/>
        <ColumnDefinition />
    </Grid.ColumnDefinitions>
    <TextBox ... PlaceholderText="Default TextBox" />
    <TextBox ... PlaceholderText="Spellchecked" IsSpellCheckEnabled="True" />
    <TextBox ... PlaceholderText="Predicted" IsTextPredictionEnabled="True"/>
    <TextBox ... PlaceholderText="Email" InputScope="EmailSmtpAddress"/>
    <TextBox ... PlaceholderText="Number" InputScope="Number"/>
    <TextBox ... PlaceholderText="Search" InputScope="Search"/>
    <TextBox ... PlaceholderText="Telephone" InputScope="TelephoneNumber"/>
    <TextBox ... PlaceholderText="Url" InputScope="Url"/>
</Grid>
```

There are eight identical RowDefinition elements in my version.

And how did each TextBox behave? Here's how I'd describe it:

DEFAULT:
The soft keyboard displayed in its standard alphanumeric layout.

SPELL-CHECKING ON:
The soft keyboard displayed in its standard alphanumeric layout, but the Caps key was set, and misspellings were indicated with red squiggles.

TEXT PREDICTION ON:
The soft keyboard displayed in its standard alphanumeric layout, but suggestions were displayed along with an Insert key as you typeed.

EMAIL SCOPE:
The soft keyboard displayed in alphanumeric layout with @ and .com keys.

NUMBER SCOPE:
The soft keyboard displayed in numeric layout (but could be changed).

SEARCH SCOPE:
The soft keyboard displayed in alphanumeric layout with a Search key.

TELEPHONE NUMBER SCOPE:
The soft keyboard displayed in numeric layout.

URL SCOPE:
The soft keyboard displayed in alphanumeric layout with an emoticon link, a forward slash, and a .com key.

DATE & TIME CONTROLS

Date and time pickers were absent from the Windows 8.0 XAML toolkit, but fortunately they're included in the latest version. (Rolling your own is painful, and yes, that's the voice of experience.) With the exception of date formatting, which we'll talk about on the next page, the basic properties and events are pretty self-explanatory.

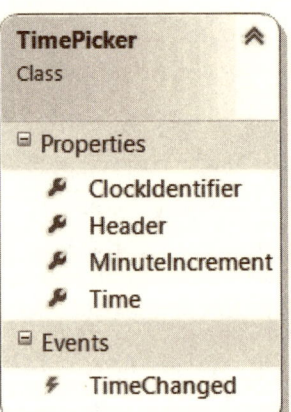

FORMATTING DATES

The display of the date in a `DatePicker` control is determined first by the `CalendarIdentifier` and second by the formats specified by the `DayFormat`, `MonthFormat`, and `YearFormat` properties.

Behind the scenes, the `DatePicker` uses the strings you provide to the `DayFormat`, `MonthFormat`, and `YearFormat` properties to create instances of the `DateTimeFormatter` class, which it uses to format each `ComboBox` in the control. (You can create instances of `DateTimeFormatter` in code if, for example, you want to format a date to display as a string, but when you're working with the `DatePicker`, you have to use the individual properties.)

In code, the `DateTimeFormatter` accepts either a FORMAT TEMPLATE or a FORMAT PATTERN. When you're working with the `DatePicker` control, templates, which always specify a whole format (day of week, day, month, year, for example) don't make sense. IntelliSense will offer you format patterns instead (and limit its list to those that make sense—the compiler will accept patterns, like ones that specify time formats, that don't make sense, and the result will not make you happy).

> ### PUT ON YOUR THINKING HAT
> Let's add a couple DatePicker and TimePicker controls to the second column of your exerciser.
>
> - Add a DatePicker that uses the default values.
>
> - Add a DatePicker that uses a two-digit number for the month.
>
> - Add a TimePicker that uses the default values.
>
> - Add a TimePicker that uses a 24-hour clock.

HOW'D YOU DO?

Aren't you glad you can rely on IntelliSense to format this?

```
<Grid ... >
   ...
   <DatePicker ... />
   <DatePicker ... MonthFormat="{}{month.integer(2)}"/>
   <TimePicker ... />
   <TimePicker ... ClockIdentifier="24HourClock" />
</Grid>
```

There's really not much you can do with a TimePicker, is there?

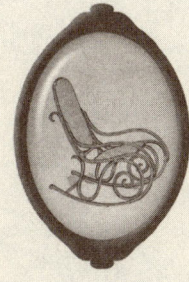

TAKE A BREAK
Well, that's it for our exploration of basic Win8 app XAML widgets. Why don't you take a break before you complete the Review and we move on to more complex widgets in the next chapter?

REVIEW

Can a widget receive focus if its IsTabStop property is set to false?

What widget should you use to show non-modal indeterminate progress?

Which of the three Win8 XAML text properties that we discussed works with both the physical and the soft keyboard?

What property distinguishes content controls? What does it do?

What helper class do you use to determine which element has focus?

Can you use content syntax when declaring a ToggleSwitch? Why or why not?

Congratulations!

You've finished the chapter. Take a minute to think about what you've accomplished before you move on to the next one...

List three things you learned in this chapter:

③

Why do you think you need to know these things in order to develop Win8 apps?

Is there anything in this chapter that you think you need to understand in more detail? If so, what are you going to do about that?

XAML Controls, Part 2: Complex Widgets

In the last chapter we explored the basic scalar Win8 XAML widgets. If you have some XAML experience, you'll probably have noticed that there are a couple that are new, and some of our old friends expose some new functionality. But you probably didn't have any big surprises. (Well, unless you were surprised at some of the widgets that are still missing in this release...)

In this chapter we'll explore two kinds of more complex widgets: the LAYOUT WIDGETS (not to be confused with Panels) that manipulate the display of their content and the ITEMS CONTROLS whose content is a collection rather than a single item.

Again, a lot of these controls are going to be familiar. ListBox might seem like an old friend. (But if you're new to XAML, you might change your mind when you see the syntax.) Some of them, like the SemanticZoom, are new. None of them are really any more difficult to use than the basic widgets we examined in the last chapter, at least not once you get the hang of them.

MAKE A NOTE

There's one other complex widget in the XAML toolkit, the Hub control, that provides an immersive entry point to your apps. If you've used the "Search Everywhere" functionality in Windows 8.1, you've see the Hub control (or a Hub-like control) in action. The Hub control requires data templates, which you haven't seen yet. We'll look at them in Chapter 12.

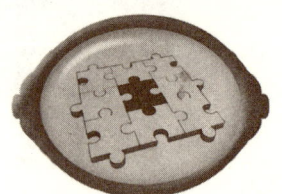

FITTING IT IN

Here's how this chapter fits in to the book as a whole...

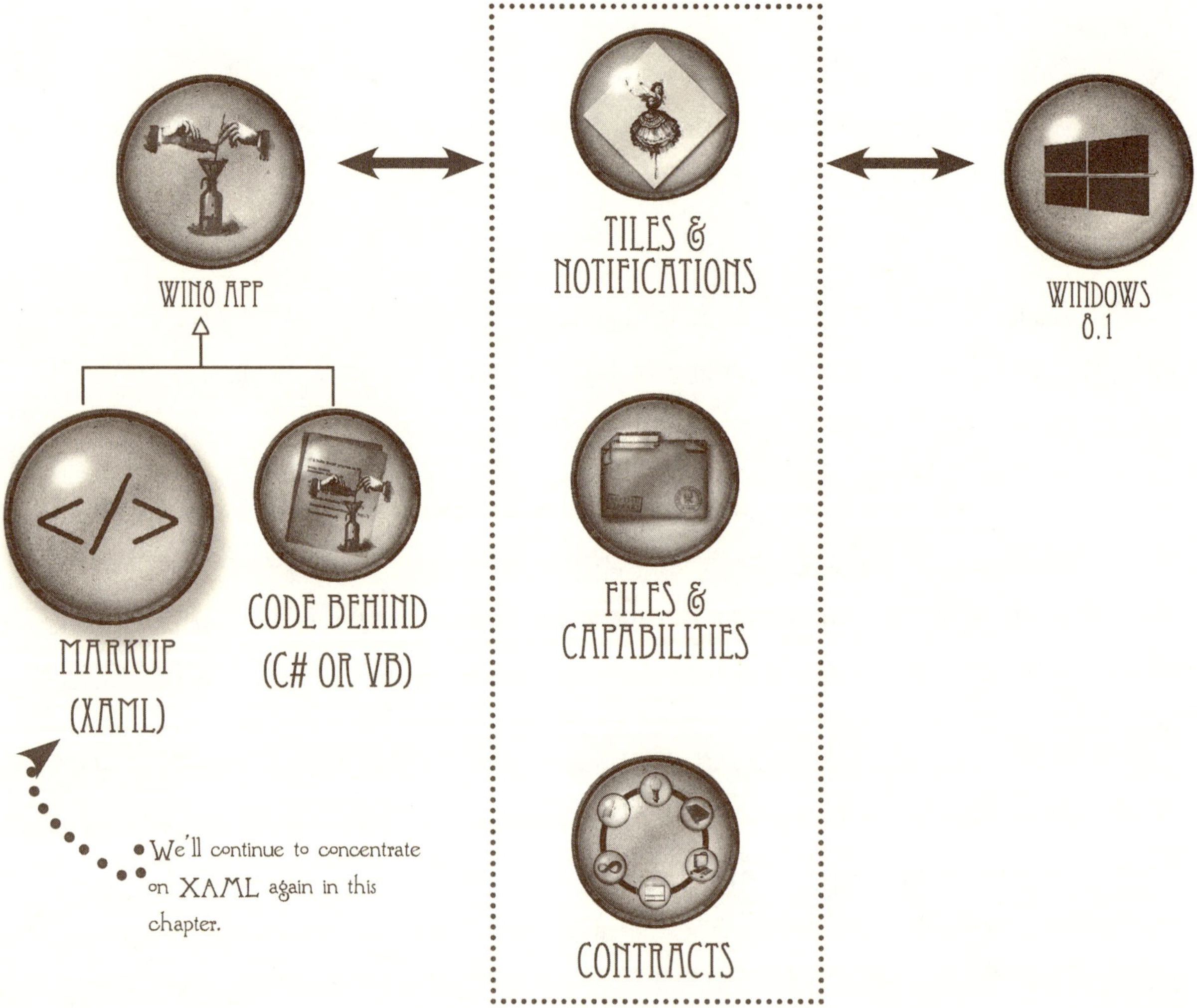

- WINRT APP
  - MARKUP (XAML)
  - CODE BEHIND (C# OR VB)
- TILES & NOTIFICATIONS
- FILES & CAPABILITIES
- CONTRACTS
- WINDOWS 8.1

We'll continue to concentrate on XAML again in this chapter.

200

TASK LIST

In this chapter we'll explore some of the more complex widgets that are included in the Win8 XAML toolkit.

SIMPLE LAYOUT WIDGETS

We'll start by exploring two of the four layout controls that let you control how your content is displayed. The **ScrollViewer**, as you'd expect, adds scrollbars to its content when there isn't enough room, while **ViewBox**, used primarily (but not exclusively) for images, can scale and stretch its content to fit the available space.

ITEM CONTROLS

In the last chapter I said that there were two important categories of controls: content controls and items controls. We explored content controls in the last chapter. In this chapter we'll look at their companions: the **ItemsControl** and its descendants.

SEMANTICZOOM

At the end of the chapter, we'll return to the subject of layout controls and examine one of the quintessential Windows 8.1 controls: the **SemanticZoom** control that displays its items at two distinct logical levels.

201

SIMPLE LAYOUT WIDGETS

There are four widgets in the Win8 app XAML toolkit that exist only to control how their contents are displayed. We'll start this chapter by examining the two simplest: the Viewbox that can stretch and scale a single UIElement child (but of course, a UIElement can be arbitrarily complex), and the ScrollViewer that supports scrolling and optical zooming. At the end of the chapter we'll explore the other important layout widget: the SemanticZoom control that supports logical zooming.

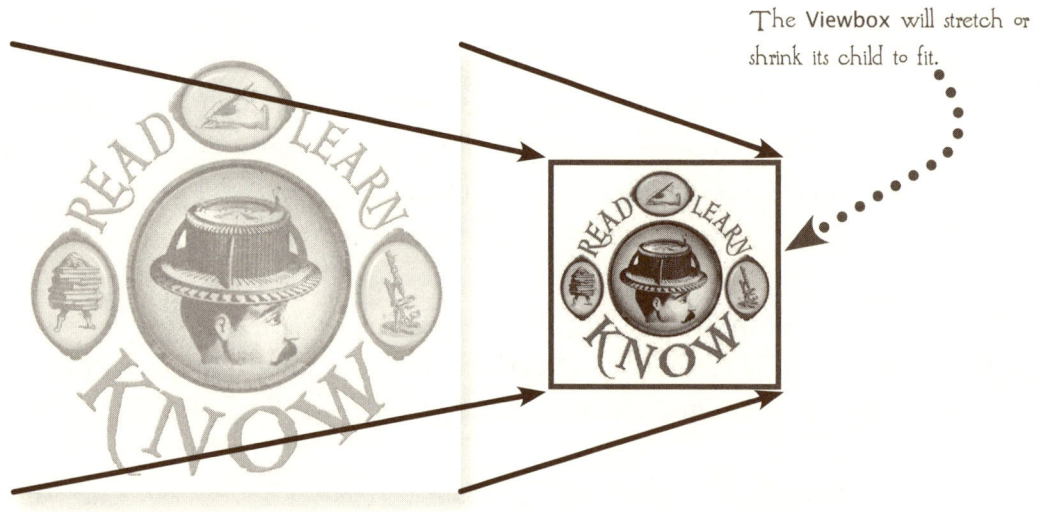

The Viewbox will stretch or shrink its child to fit.

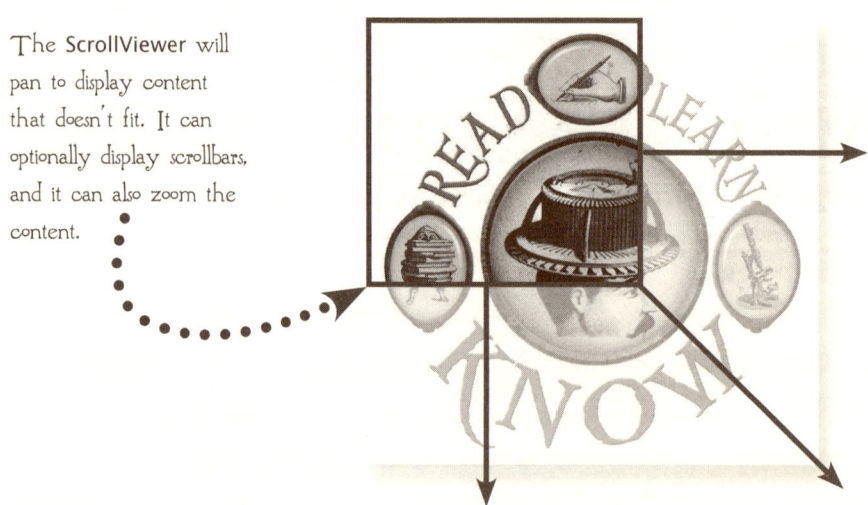

The ScrollViewer will pan to display content that doesn't fit. It can optionally display scrollbars, and it can also zoom the content.

PUT ON YOUR THINKING HAT

Of the two simple layout widgets, the ViewBox (which descends directly from FrameworkElement) has the fewest moving parts, so let's start with it. There are only two properties to worry about: Stretch, which determines how its Child is manipulated to fill the space, and StretchDirection, which determines, well, the direction in which its Child is stretched (or shrunk).

To get a sense of how it how ViewBox works, build a little exerciser based on the Blank template (I named mine ComplexWidgets01) to change the properties. Here's my version:

Be sure to give the ViewBox a name (so you can reference it in code-behind) and an explicit Width and Height.

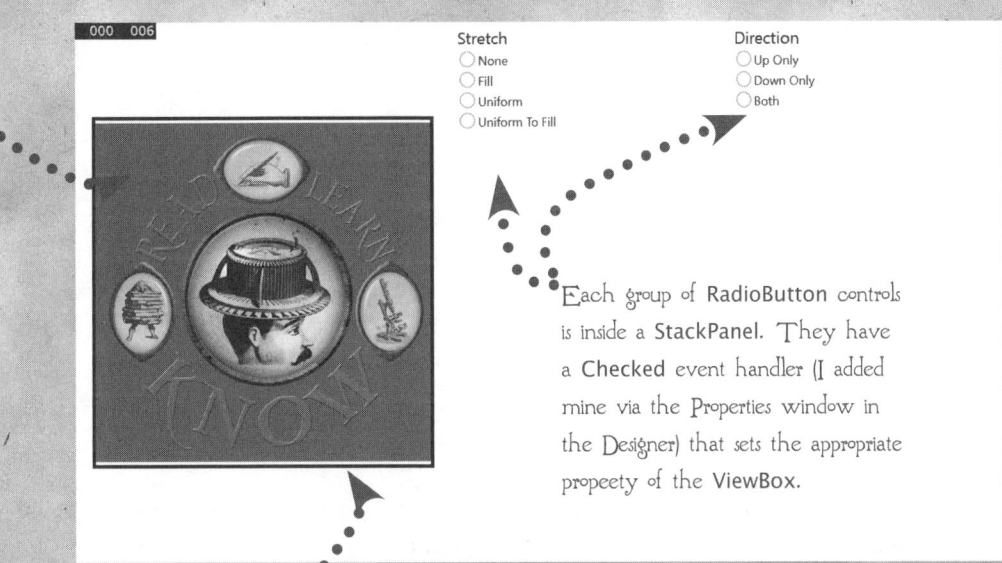

Each group of RadioButton controls is inside a StackPanel. They have a Checked event handler (I added mine via the Properties window in the Designer) that sets the appropriate propeety of the ViewBox.

I wrapped the ViewBox in a Border widget just to make the size of the ViewBox itself clear.

203

PUT ON YOUR THINKING HAT

How'd you do? Here's my version of the XAML. It doesn't matter if yours is a bit different, as long as it works. As usual, I've elided the (irrelevant) formatting like **FontSize** and **Foreground** color.

```xml
<Grid ...>
    <Grid.ColumnDefinitions>
        <ColumnDefinition Width="550"/>
        <ColumnDefinition />
        <ColumnDefinition />
    </Grid.ColumnDefinitions>
    <Border BorderBrush="Black" BorderThickness="5" Width="500" Height="500"
            Grid.Column="0">
        <Viewbox Name="TestViewer" Width="500" Height="500">
            <Image Source="/Assets/FluentLogo.png" />
        </Viewbox>
    </Border>

    <StackPanel Orientation="Vertical" Grid.Column="1" Margin="10" >
        <TextBlock Text="Stretch" FontSize="24" />
        <RadioButton ame="StretchNone" Content="None" Checked="StretchNone_Checked" ... />
        <RadioButton Name="StretchFill" Content="Fill" Checked="StretchFill_Checked" ... />
        <RadioButton Name="StretchUniform" Content="Uniform" Checked="StretchUniform_Checked" .../>
        <RadioButton Name="StretchUniformToFill" Content="UniformToFill"
                Checked="StretchUniformToFill_Checked" ... />
    </StackPanel>

    <StackPanel Orientation="Vertical" Grid.Column="2" Margin="10">
        <TextBlock Text="Direction" FontSize="24" />
        <RadioButton Name="DirectionUpOnly" Content="Up Only" Checked="DirectionUpOnly_Checked" .../>
        <RadioButton Name="DirectionDownOnly" Content="Down Only"
                Checked="DirectionDownOnly_Checked" ... />
        <RadioButton Name="DirectionBoth" Content="Both" Checked="DirectionBoth_Checked" .../>
    </StackPanel>
</Grid>
```

The **Border** just draws a box around its content. It doesn't matter if you didn't include one.

```csharp
private void StretchNone_Checked(object sender, RoutedEventArgs e)
{
        TestViewer.Stretch = Stretch.None;
}
private void StretchFill_Checked(object sender, RoutedEventArgs e)
{
        TestViewer.Stretch = Stretch.Fill;
}
private void StretchUniform_Checked(object sender, RoutedEventArgs e)
{
        TestViewer.Stretch = Stretch.Uniform;
}
private void StretchUniformToFill_Checked(object sender, RoutedEventArgs e)
{
        TestViewer.Stretch = Stretch.UniformToFill;
}
private void DirectionUpOnly_Checked(object sender, RoutedEventArgs e)
{
        TestViewer.StretchDirection = StretchDirection.UpOnly;
}
private void DirectionDownOnly_Checked(object sender, RoutedEventArgs e)
{
        TestViewer.StretchDirection = StretchDirection.DownOnly;
}
private void DirectionBoth_Checked(object sender, RoutedEventArgs e)
{
        TestViewer.StretchDirection = StretchDirection.Both;
}
```

THE SCROLLVIEWER

You've probably worked with a widget like the Win8 ScrollViewer before. Most UI platforms have some way of panning content. But like all Win8 app widgets, the ScrollViewer is optimized for touch interactions, and that means it has some functionality (and a few quirks) that may be new to you. We'll concentrate on those capabilities and quirks in this section.

RAILS

Touch interactions are immediate and (largely) intuitive, which is cool, but compared to a mouse pointer, a fingertip is big, clumsy, and likely to shake. You've probably noticed it in the Win8 version of Internet Explorer: instead of scrolling down a page, you're likely to go a bit sideways. (I know that's not just because I drink too much coffee.)

The Win8 app ScrollViewer supports horizontal and vertical RAILS, controlled by the IsHorizontalRailEnabled and IsVerticalRailEnabled properties, that "lock" horizontal and vertical scrolling, while still allowing the user to scroll in any (wobbly) direction.

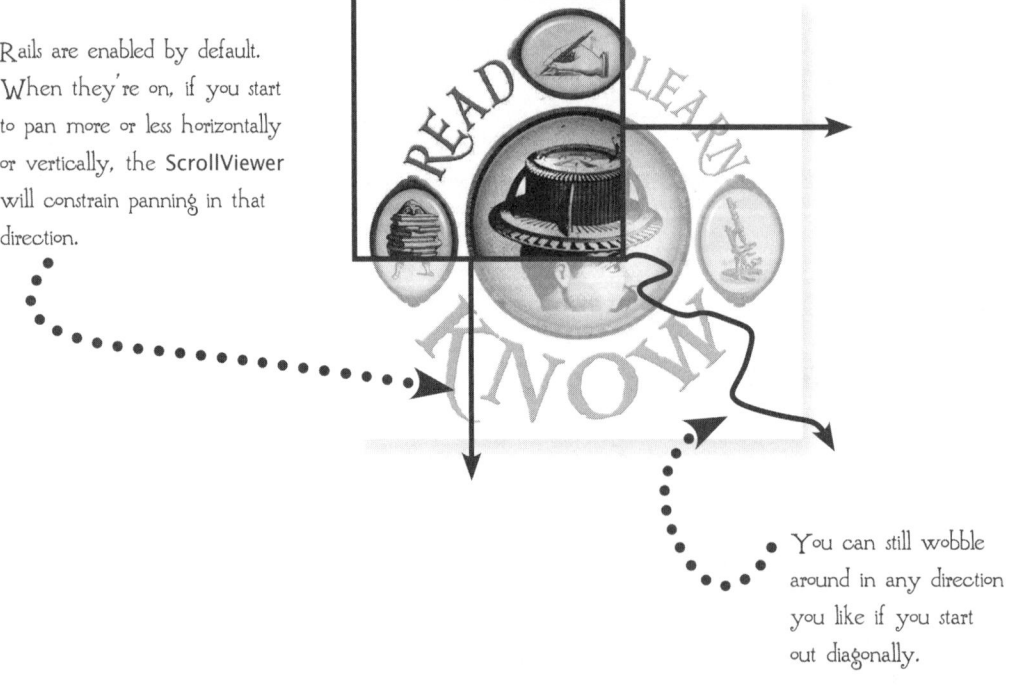

Rails are enabled by default. When they're on, if you start to pan more or less horizontally or vertically, the ScrollViewer will constrain panning in that direction.

You can still wobble around in any direction you like if you start out diagonally.

OPTICAL ZOOM

Although the ViewBox can zoom its content, it would be tedious to make it work interactively, particularly since the ScrollViewer provides optical zoom functionality out of the box. You can control the minimum or maximum zoom factors using the MinZoomFactor and MaxZoomFactor properties, and constrain the zoom factors by adding values to the ZoomSnapPoints collection.

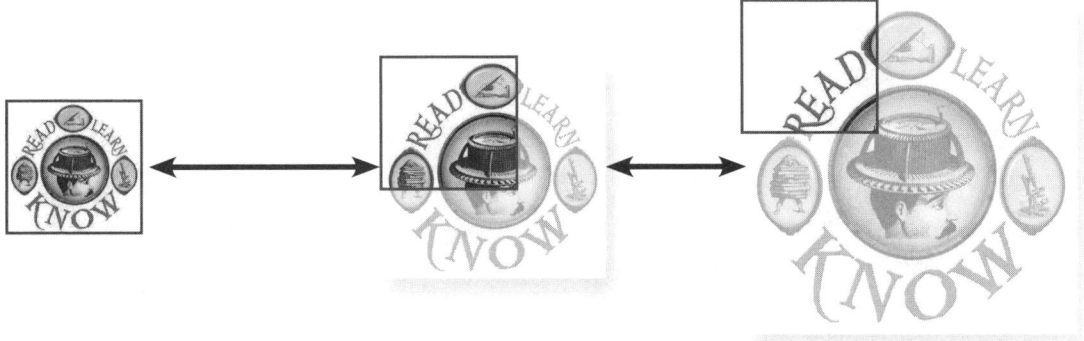

SNAP POINTS

Those big shaky fingertips of ours can make precise positioning a little tricky. If your ScrollViewer is displaying multiple items, you can use the VerticalSnapPointsType and VerticalSnapPointsAlignment properties (and their Horizontal... companions) to always snap an item to an edge or the center of the ScrollViewer.

Using the ScrollViewer

Now that you have a sense of what the `ScrollViewer` is capable of, I think it's time to kick the tires. We won't build an exerciser this time; we'll just fiddle around with the properties directly in the XAML. Start by building a page that contains a 3-column, 3-row Grid inside a `ScrollViewer`. (Again, I put a `Border` around mine so we can see what we're doing.) You'll need to put something inside each cell of the Grid. I just used a `Rectangle`, but you could use images or text if you'd rather. Here's what mine looks like, (Not very exciting, is it?)

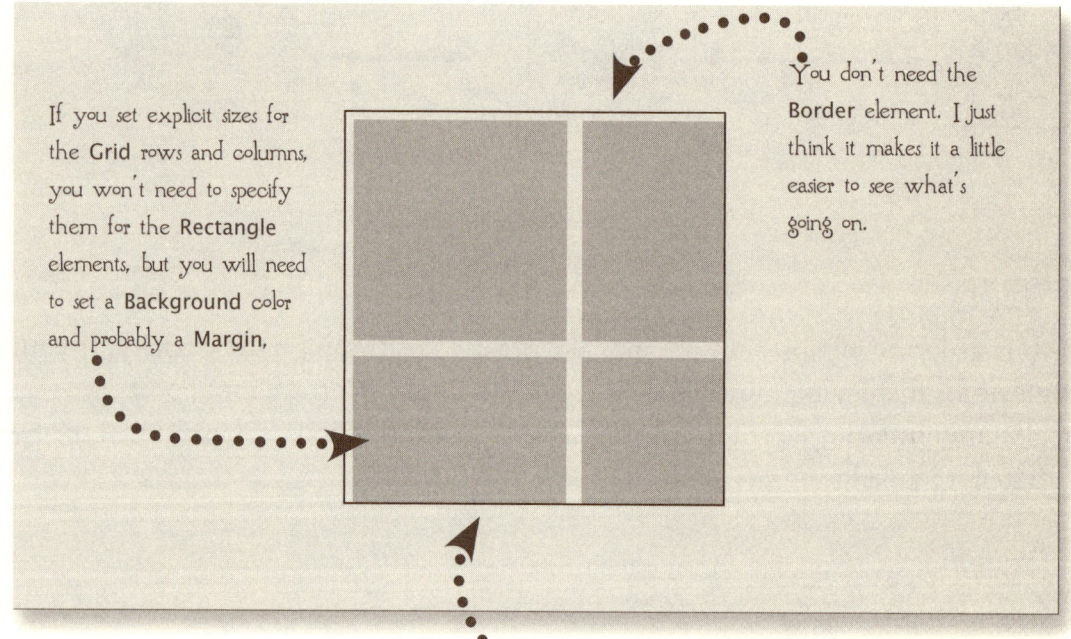

If you set explicit sizes for the Grid rows and columns, you won't need to specify them for the Rectangle elements, but you will need to set a Background color and probably a Margin.

You don't need the Border element. I just think it makes it a little easier to see what's going on.

Make sure that the Grid is big enough not to fit inside the ScrollViewer. I made the ScrollViewer 500x500, and each Grid row and column 300, but the exact values don't matter.

PUT ON YOUR THINKING HAT
Get coding! I called my project **ComplexWidget**.

BUILD THE PROJECT
You can use my notes to guide you, and my version of the XAML is on the next page. You'll need to set the **Width** and **Height** properties of the **ScrollViewer** but leave all the other properties at their default values.

RUN IT
Once you have the basic layout built, run the app and do a little experimenting:

Can you pan in both directions?

What happens when you reach the bottom edge of the grid?

Can you zoom? (Use the mouse wheel or Ctrl+Plus if you don't have a touch-enabled system.)

Is the display correct when you zoom out?

HOW'D YOU DO?

Here's my version of the XAML and the results of the experiments:

```
<Grid ...>
    <Border BorderBrush="Black" BorderThickness="2"
        Width="500" Height="500">
        <ScrollViewer Name="ViewerTest" Width="500" Height="500" >
            <Grid>
                <Grid.ColumnDefinitions>
                    <ColumnDefinition Width="300"/>
                    <ColumnDefinition Width="300"/>
                    <ColumnDefinition Width="300"/>
                </Grid.ColumnDefinitions>
                <Grid.RowDefinitions>
                    <RowDefinition Height="300"/>
                    <RowDefinition Height="300"/>
                    <RowDefinition Height="300"/>
                </Grid.RowDefinitions>
                <Rectangle Grid.Row="0" Grid.Column="0" Margin="10" Fill="BurlyWood" />
                ...
            </Grid>
        </ScrollViewer>
    </Border>
</Grid>
```

There's a **Rectangle** in every cell of the **Grid**.

Can you pan in both directions?

> No, only vertically.

What happens when you reach the bottom edge of the grid?

> There's a nice little animated "bounce".

Can you zoom? (Use the mouse wheel or Ctrl+Plus if you don't have a touch-enabled system.)

> Yes.

Is the display correct when you zoom out?

> No. The right side of the **Grid** is never displayed.

SCROLLBAR DEFAULTS

Did it surprise you that you can't pan the **Grid** horizontally? It did me the first time I tried it. The problem is with the default values for the scrollbar properties.

SCROLLBAR VISIBILITY

The ScrollViewer exposes two properties, **HorizontalScrollBarVisibility** and **VerticalScrollBarVisibility**, that control whether and when a scrollbar is displayed. Each of these properties takes an instance of the **ScrollBarVisibility** enumeration:

Member	Meaning
Disabled	The scrollbar does not appear, and scrolling is disabled.
Auto	The scrollbar only appears when scrolling is possible (and the user has their finger on the content in touch mode).
Hidden	Scrolling is enabled, but the scrollbar isn't displayed.
Visible	The scrollbar always appears.

By default, the **VerticalScrollBarVisibility** property is **Visible**, but the **HorizontalScrollBarVisibility** property is **Disabled**. That means that, by default, you can only scroll vertically.

SCROLL MODE

The **ScrollViewer** also exposes **HorizontalScrollMode** and **VerticalScrollMode** properties that can be set to **Disabled**, **Enabled**, and **Auto**. Both are set to **Enabled** by the default style of the **ScrollViewer**, but in reality, you can control its behavior using the scrollbar visibility and rails properties, so you have no reason to fiddle with this one.

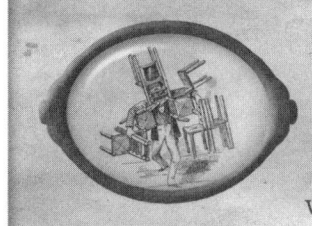

ON YOUR OWN
Set the **HorizontalScrollBarVisibility** property to **Auto** and re-run the app to confirm that horizontal scrolling and zoom work as expected.

OPTICAL ZOOM

To my knowledge, the Win8 app ScrollViewer is the only scroll widget that also supports zooming. The logic of that appeals to me—you can move "in and out" as well as "from side to side". (Yes, that's imprecise. It's an analogy. What do you expect?)

Zooming is controlled by the ZoomMode property and enabled on the ScrollViewer by default, and it works pretty well out of the box. The control also exposes a set of properties (and one method) that provide a fine level of control should you need it.

ZOOM MODE

The **ZoomMode** property controls whether zooming is possible at all. It accepts a member of the **ZoomMode** enumeration that has only two members: **Enabled** and **Disabled**.

MINIMUM AND MAXIMUM ZOOM LEVELS

The **MinZoomFactor** and **MaxZoomFactor** properties allow you to set the minimum and maximum zoom levels. Like all zoom factors, the properties accept a single-precision floating point value (**Single** in Visual Basic, **float** in C#) that represents the percentage the content is zoomed. So, for example, a zoom factor of 0.50 would display the content at 50%, while a factor of 2.0 would display it at 200%.

CHANGEVIEW()

The **ChangeView()** method accepts three arguments: **HorizontalOffset**, **VerticalOffset**, and **ZoomFactor** that do exactly what you'd expect them to do:

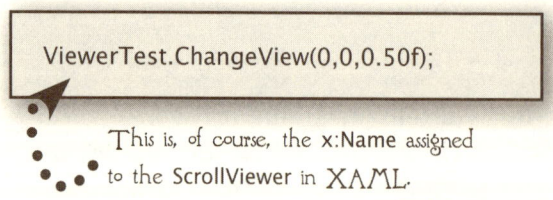

This is, of course, the x:Name assigned to the ScrollViewer in XAML.

Zoom Snap Points

Two properties, **ZoomSnapPoints** and **ZoomSnapPointsType**, control the available zoom factors. **ZoomSnapPoints** is defined as an **IList<Single>** of zoom factors and can only be set in code:

```
ViewerTest.ZoomSnapPoints.Add(0.25f);
```

The **ZoomSnapPointsType** property controls how the zoom snap points are handled. It accepts an instance of the **SnapPointsType** enumeration, whose members are:

Member	Meaning
None	Zoom snap points are ignored.
Optional	Zoom levels will snap if the user is close, but any zoom factor is possible.
Mandatory	The content can only be displayed at the specified zoom levels.
OptionalSingle	Zoom snap points are optional, but they cannot be skipped.
MandatorySingle	The content can only be displayed at the specified zoom levels, and they cannot be skipped.

> **Put On Your Thinking Hat**
>
> Take control of zooming in your sample app.
>
> - Set the ZoomSnapPointsType to Mandatory in the XAML.
> - Add code to the constructor (after the call to InitializeComponent) that only allows the content to be displayed at 50%, 100%, 150%, and 200%.
> - Set the initial zoom factor to 50%.

HOW'D YOU DO?

Here's my version.

```xml
<ScrollViewer x:Name="ViewerTest" Width="500" Height="500"
       HorizontalScrollBarVisibility="Auto"
       ZoomSnapPointsType="Mandatory" >
```

The ZoomSnapPointType is set like any other property.

```csharp
public MainPage()
{
    this.InitializeComponent;
    ViewerTest.ZoomSnapPoints.Add(0.5f);
    ViewerTest.ZoomSnapPoints.Add(1.0f);
    ViewerTest.ZoomSnapPoints.Add(1.5f);
    ViewerTest.ZoomSnapPoints.Add(2.0f);
    ViewerTest.ChangeView(0,0,0.5f);
}
```

```vb
Sub New()
    InitializeComponent;
    ViewerTest.ZoomSnapPoints.Add(0.5F)
    ViewerTest.ZoomSnapPoints.Add(1.0F)
    ViewerTest.ZoomSnapPoints.Add(1.5F)
    ViewerTest.ZoomSnapPoints.Add(2.0F)
    ViewerTest.ChangeView(0,0,0.5F)
```

SNAPPING

As I've said, snap points are intended to help compensate for our big shaky fingertips. You've seen how zoom snap points work, and there are equivalent properties for use in panning.

The HorizontalSnapPointsType and VerticalSnapPointsType properties take an instance of the same SnapPointsType enumeration that the ZoomSnapPointType property does. The HorizontalSnapPointAlignment and VerticalSnapPointAlignment properties take an instance of the SnapPointsAlignment enumerations whose members, Near, Center, and Far, determine whether the snapped item appears centered in the ScrollViewer or aligned to one edge.

Okay, that all sounds pretty straightforward, right? Well, it is, but there's a problem. In order for snapping to work, the immediate child of the ScrollViewer must implement the IScrollSnapPointsInfo interface, and not many classes do. It's implemented by some low-level classes like the CarouselPanel and the WrapGrid that are only supported as items panels. (We'll talk about items controls in the next section.) It's implemented by the ItemsPresenter that's used in control templates. (We'll discuss those in Chapter 11.) And it's implemented by the StackPanel. (Yes, that's right. The StackPanel is the only high-level widget that supports snapping inside a ScrollViewer.)

So what does this mean in real terms for ScrollViewer snapping? Either sub-class whatever widget you want to use and implement IScrollSnapPointsInfo yourself—I have it on good authority that it's not too tedious to do—or use a StackPanel.

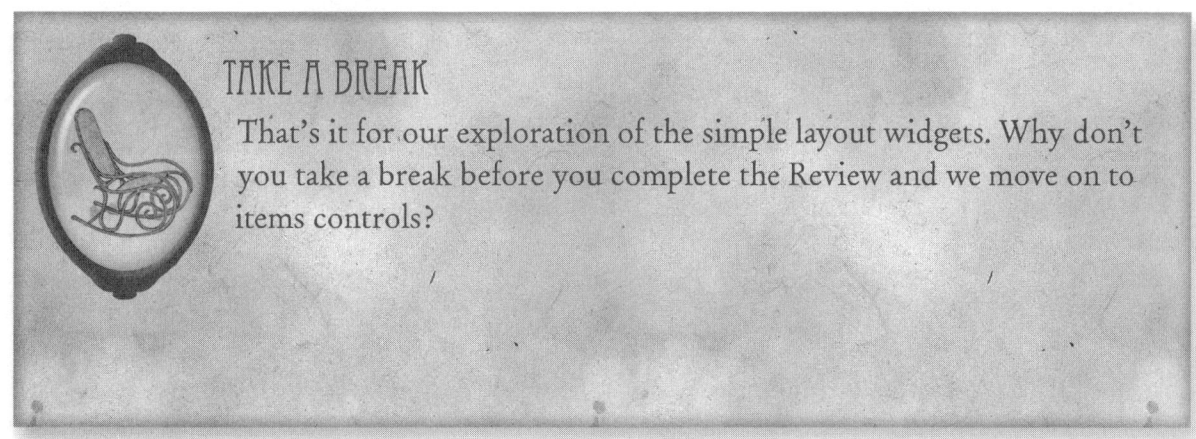

TAKE A BREAK

That's it for our exploration of the simple layout widgets. Why don't you take a break before you complete the Review and we move on to items controls?

REVIEW

Can you answer the following questions based on what you've learned?

Re-work the ScrollViewer sample application to use nested StackPanel controls and set the appropriate properties on the ScrollViewer so that the Rectangle elements snap.

When working with the ViewBox, which of the Stretch property values maintain the content's aspect ratio? (ASPECT RATIO is the relative proportions of the image.)

What object type do you use to specify a zoom factor?

How would you set a minimum zoom of 100%?

When setting up a ScrollViewer, there are two things you can't do in XAML. What are they?

ITEMS CONTROLS

You've seen the "simple" controls like the TextBox and ToggleSwitch that provide functionality directly, and the content controls that provide some functionality for a single piece of content (which can be arbitrarily complex). The final group of widgets that descend from the Control class are the items controls. Instead of a Content property that accepts a single Object, the ItemsControl exposes a property (called, not surprisingly, Items) that accepts a collection of FrameworkElement objects.

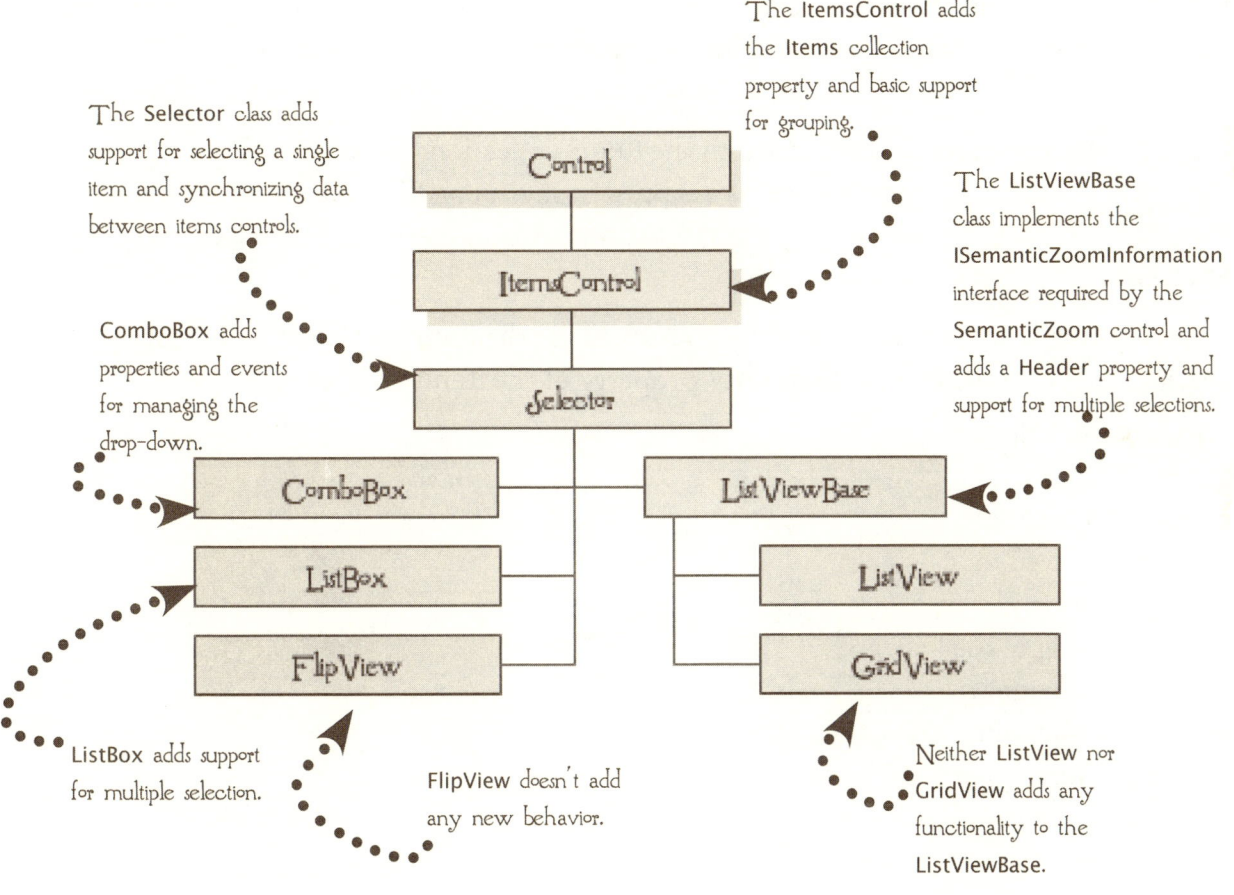

The Selector class adds support for selecting a single item and synchronizing data between items controls.

The ItemsControl adds the Items collection property and basic support for grouping.

The ListViewBase class implements the ISemanticZoomInformation interface required by the SemanticZoom control and adds a Header property and support for multiple selections.

ComboBox adds properties and events for managing the drop-down.

ListBox adds support for multiple selection.

FlipView doesn't add any new behavior.

Neither ListView nor GridView adds any functionality to the ListViewBase.

217

ITEMS MAGIC

There are two ways to add items to an items control: You can add them directly by using collection syntax in XAML or the Add() method of the Items collection property, or you can assign the ItemsSource property to a collection using binding or a resource (we'll discuss both of those in later chapters). Either way, there's some useful magic that goes on behind the scenes.

If you check the documentation, it will tell you that the **ItemsControl.Items** property is defined as an **ItemCollection** and that the **ItemCollection** accepts elements of type **FrameworkElement**. But many of the **ItemControl** examples use types that *don't* descend from **FrameworkElement**—the **ListView** example uses <x:String>—and if you play around a bit you'll see that you can add any **Object** to the collection. So what's going on?

Behind the scenes, every object added to the **Items** collection (either directly or indirectly through the **ItemsSource**) is wrapped in the appropriate class that descends from **SelectorItem**. **SelectorItem** is a **ContentControl** (and therefore descends from **FrameworkElement**).

The wrapping is actually performed by an instance of the **ItemContainerGenerator** class specifed in the **ItemContainerGenerator** property of the **ItemsControl** class.

Fortunately, unless you're writing your own **ItemsControl** class or you need to do some low-level pre-processing of the items, you can ignore the details. But you do need to know that it happens, and you'll find the items types useful when you're formatting the items in a style or template.

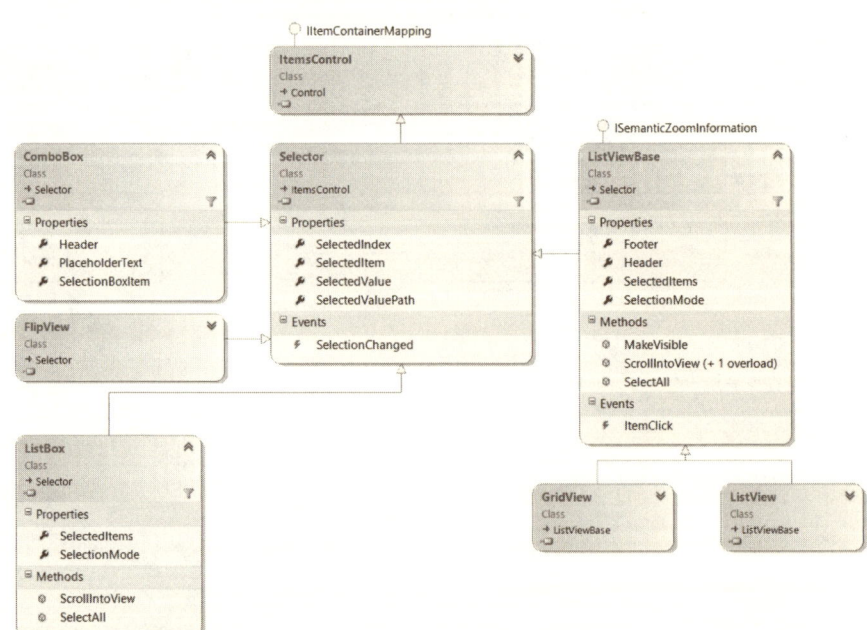

PUT ON YOUR THINKING HAT

To my mind, there are two things that make XAML items controls fun and exciting: the items can be any kind of "thing", and you have complete control over the appearance and visual behavior of the widgets. We'll look at the visual stuff in Chapter 11, but let's have a little fun with the thing-ness of the Items collection:

- Create a new project and add two columns and two rows to the basic Grid. (Mine is ComplexWidgets03.)

- Add a StackPanel to the first column with a RowSpan of 2.

- Add one of each of the basics items controls to the StackPanel:

  - The ListBox items should be StackPanels, each containing an Image and a TextBlock.

  - The ComboBox items should be 10 dpi high Rectangles. (Note: when you run the app, the Rectangles won't display properly in the drop-down. Just ignore that for right now; it's a problem with the template.)

  - The FlipView items should be TextBlocks.

MAKE A NOTE

You might have noticed that there's one common items control that's missing from the Win8 XAML class library: the TreeView that's typically used for displaying hierarchical data. I'm not sure that I agree with the decision, but as I understand it, the problem is that Win8 is touch-first, and the library designers decided that fingertips are just too big and clumsy to manipulate a TreeView. The SemanticZoom control and grouped items controls are probably the best replacement, but I'll warn you: If your application requires hieararchies that are more complex than master-child, you're going to have a lot of re-designing (dare I say "re-imagining"?) to do.

HOW'D YOU DO?

Here's my version. I've included several items in each items control, but since they're more or less identical (colors and text vary), I've only shown the first one below.

```xml
<Grid ...>
  <Grid.ColumnDefinitions>
    <ColumnDefinition Width="500"/>
    <ColumnDefinition />
  </Grid.ColumnDefinitions>
  <Grid.RowDefinitions>
    <RowDefinition />
    <RowDefinition />
  </Grid.RowDefinitions>

  <StackPanel Grid.Row="0" Grid.Column="0" Orientation="Vertical" Grid.RowSpan="2">
    <ListBox Margin="10" Height="250">
      <StackPanel Orientation="Horizontal">
        <Image Source="/Assets/FluentLogo.png" Width="100" Height="100"/>
        <TextBlock Text="First ListBoxItem" VerticalAlignment="Center" Margin="10"/>
      </StackPanel>
      ....
    </ListBox>
    <ComboBox>
      <Rectangle Fill="Aqua" Height="20"/>
      ....
    </ComboBox>
    <FlipView Width="350" Height="150" Background="White">
      <TextBlock FontSize="24" Foreground="Black" VerticalAlignment="Center"
                 HorizontalAlignment="Center">First FlipView Item</TextBlock>
      ...
    </FlipView>
  </StackPanel>
</Grid>
```

Each item is repeated several times.

THE LISTVIEWBASE

Both the `ListView` and the `GridView` items controls descend directly from the `ListViewBase` class, and neither adds any functionality to the class. But the `ListViewBase` class does add some significant functionality to these items controls:

SEMANTIC ZOOM SUPPORT
The `ListViewBase` class implements the `ISemanticZoomInformation` interface, so the classes that descend from it can be used inside the `SemanticZoom` control that we'll discuss later in this chapter.

HEADERS
The `ListViewBase` adds a `Header` property, defined as an `Object`, that represents the list header.

ADVANCED INTERACTIONS
Any class that descends from `UIElement` can support low-level interactions like drag, drop, and hold (we'll explore these interactions in Chapter 8), but the `ListViewBase` adds high-level properties and methods to make the most common interactions simple to implement. We'll explore them in this section.

> ## PUT ON YOUR THINKING HAT
> Let's get started. Add a `ListView` and a `GridView` to the second column of the `Grid` in your items control project.
>
> Add a `Header` to the `ListView`. You can use attribute syntax if you just want to use a `String`, but you'll probably want to use element syntax so you can format a `TextBlock`.
>
> Add some `TextBlock` items to the `ListView` and some `Rectangle` items to the `GridView`.

221

HOW'D YOU DO?

Here's my version. It doesn't matter if you formatted your app differently, as long as it works.

The Grid row and column definitions haven't changed from the last exercise.

The contents of the StackPanel are the same, too.

```xml
<Grid ...>
   ...
   
   <StackPanel Grid.Row="0" Grid.Column="0" Orientation="Vertical" Grid.RowSpan="2">
      ...
   </StackPanel>
   
   <ListView Grid.Row="0" Grid.Column="1" Margin="20">
      <ListView.Header>
         <TextBlock Text="This is my ListView" FontSize="18" Foreground="Red" />
      </ListView.Header>
      <TextBlock Text="One" />
      <TextBlock Text="Two" />
      <TextBlock Text="Three" />
   </ListView>
   
   <GridView Grid.Row="1" Grid.Column="1" Margin="20">
      <Rectangle Width="100" Height="200" Fill="Beige" />
      <Rectangle Width="100" Height="200" Fill="Coral" />
      <Rectangle Width="100" Height="200" Fill="Violet" />
   </GridView>
</Grid>
```

You add items to these controls the same way you did to one of the basic items controls (and, like them, in practice you're more likely to bind to the ItemsSource property).

ON YOUR OWN

No matter what UI platform you're used to working in, you've probably used a couple of items controls that are missing from the Win8 XAML suite: the `TabControl` and the `TreeView`. Here are some questions to ponder:

Why do you think the designers of Win8 decided that those two controls aren't really appropriate in a touch-first environment?

The `TreeView` is used to represent hierarchical data. Given what you've seen of the Win8 environment, how might you handle the same data in an immersive environment? Would you look to substitute a single control or control set, or would you re-think how the pages of your app are structured and related?

Tab controls are typically used to break up information into manageable chunks or to maximize the screen footprint of the app. How would you handle those two tasks in the Win8 XAML environment? The `FlipView` is frequently recommended as a replacement for a tab control. Do you think that's a good recommendation? Is there some other way you think might work?

LISTVIEWBASE DRAG & CLICK

By default, you can select a single item in a `ListViewBase`. The class also supports multiple selection, and we'll talk about that in a minute. But first let's look at two kinds of interactions that the `ListViewBase` makes very straightforward: re-ordering items, and enabling item click.

TO ALLOW ITEM REORDERING

Users can drag items within the `ListViewBase` control to reorder them if you set three properties to `True` (all of them default to `False`): `CanDragItems`, `CanReorderItems`, and `AllowDrop` (which the `ListViewBase` inherits from `UIElement`).

TO ALLOW ITEM CLICK

Sometimes you want the items in the `ListViewBase` control to act like buttons. In other words, rather than being selected when the user clicks or taps them, you want some action to occur. Again, it's just a matter of setting some properties: `SelectionMode` should be set to `None`, `IsItemClickEnabled` to `True`, and `IsSwipeEnabled` to `False`.

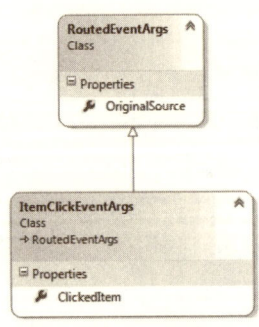

Once you've set the properties, clicking or tapping an item will generate an `ItemClick` routed event. We'll discuss routed events in detail in Chapter 8, but for now you only need to know that the item that initiated the handler receives an instance of the `ItemClickEventArgs` class, which exposes a `ClickedItem` property. Your event handler will look like this:

 `void Element_ItemClick(object sender, ItemClickEventArgs e)`

 `Sub Element_ItemClick(sender As Object, ItemClickEventArgs as e)`

PUT ON YOUR THINKING HAT

Give it a try. This exercise involves some principles that you haven't seen yet, so don't feel bad if you can't quite work out how to write the event handler. (But give yourself a gold star if you do!)

 Set up the ListView in the sample app so that it allows items to be reordered, and the GridView so that the items are clickable.

 Add an ItemClicked event handler (via the Properties window) to the GridView that turns the item cyan. This is a little trickier in code than in XAML. Here's what you need to do:

- Add references to the Windows.UI and Windows.UI.Xaml.Shapes namespaces to the top of the code-behind file.

- Cast the ClickedItem property of the ItemClickEventArgs to a Rectangle.

- Set the Fill property of the Rectangle to a new SolidColorBrush. (We'll discuss brushes and colors in Chapter 10.) You can pass Colors.Cyan to the constructor:

    new SolidColorBrush(Colors.Cyan)

MAKE A NOTE

All items controls support grouped data, but it's particularly important when you're working with the GridView. Grouping is surprisingly easy to implement, but it only works when you bind the ItemsSource property to a CollectionViewSource. We'll see how that works in Chapter 12.

PUT ON YOUR THINKING HAT

How'd you do? Here's the whole XAML file (but with only one item of each type shown).

```xml
<Grid Background="AntiqueWhite">
    <Grid.ColumnDefinitions>
        <ColumnDefinition Width="500"/>
        <ColumnDefinition />
    </Grid.ColumnDefinitions>
    <Grid.RowDefinitions>
        <RowDefinition />
        <RowDefinition />
    </Grid.RowDefinitions>
    <StackPanel Grid.Row="0" Grid.Column="0" Orientation="Vertical" Grid.RowSpan="2">
        <ListBox Margin="10" Height="250">
            <StackPanel Orientation="Horizontal">
                <Image Source="/Assets/HatBrad.png" Width="100" Height="100"/>
                <TextBlock Text="First ListBoxItem" VerticalAlignment="Center" Margin="10"/>
            </StackPanel>
            ...
        </ListBox>
        <ComboBox Margin="10" Padding="10" SelectedIndex="0">
            <Rectangle Fill="#FFBAF3F3" Height="20" Width="400"/>
            ...
        </ComboBox>
        <FlipView Width="350" Height="150" Background="White">
            <TextBlock FontSize="24" Foreground="Black" VerticalAlignment="Center"
                       HorizontalAlignment="Center">First FlipView Item</TextBlock>
            ...
        </FlipView>
    </StackPanel>
    <ListView Grid.Row="0" Grid.Column="1" Margin="20"
              CanDragItems="True" CanReorderItems="True" AllowDrop="True">
        <ListView.Header >
            <TextBlock Text=" This is my Listview" FontSize="18" Foreground="Red" />
        </ListView.Header>
        <TextBlock Text="One" Foreground="Black"/>
        ...
    </ListView>
    <GridView Grid.Row="1" Grid.Column="1" Margin="20"
              SelectionMode="None" IsItemClickEnabled="True"
              IsSwipeEnabled="False" ItemClick="GridView_ItemClick" >
        <Rectangle Width="100" Height="200" Fill="#FFBAF3F3" />
        ...
    </GridView>
</Grid>
```

```csharp
private void GridView_ItemClick(object sender, ItemClickEventArgs e)
{
  Rectangle theRect = (Rectangle)e.ClickedItem;
  theRect.Fill = new SolidColorBrush(Colors.Cyan);
}
```

```vb
Private Sub GridView_ItemClick(sender As Object, e As ItemClickEventArgs)
  Dim theRect As Rectangle = e.ClickedItem
  theRect.Fill = New SolidColorBrush(Colors.Cyan)
}
```

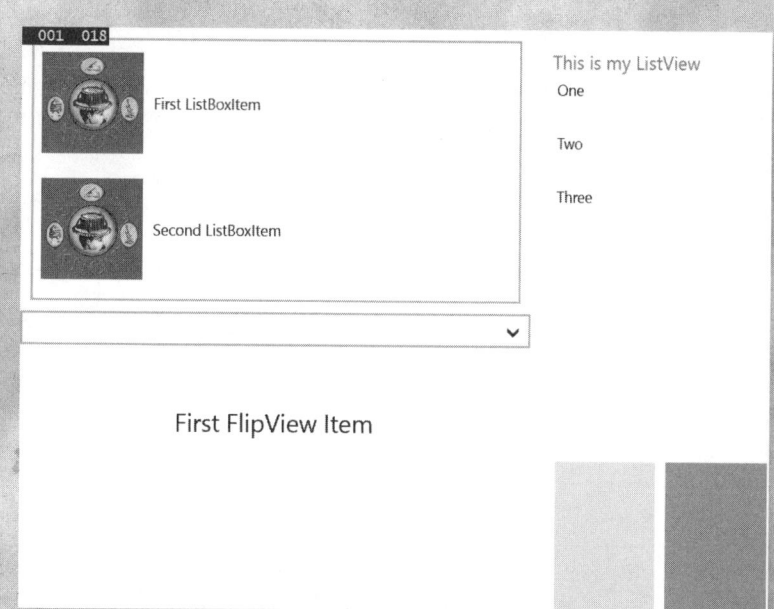

SELECTION PROPERTIES

The class hierarchy is different, but the basic properties, events, and methods for working with selected items in a Win8 XAML items control should look familiar to you from other .NET UI platforms. Here's the class hierarchy showing the selection members. (Remember, the class diagrams throughout the book aren't complete. They only show the members that are pertinent to what we're doing.)

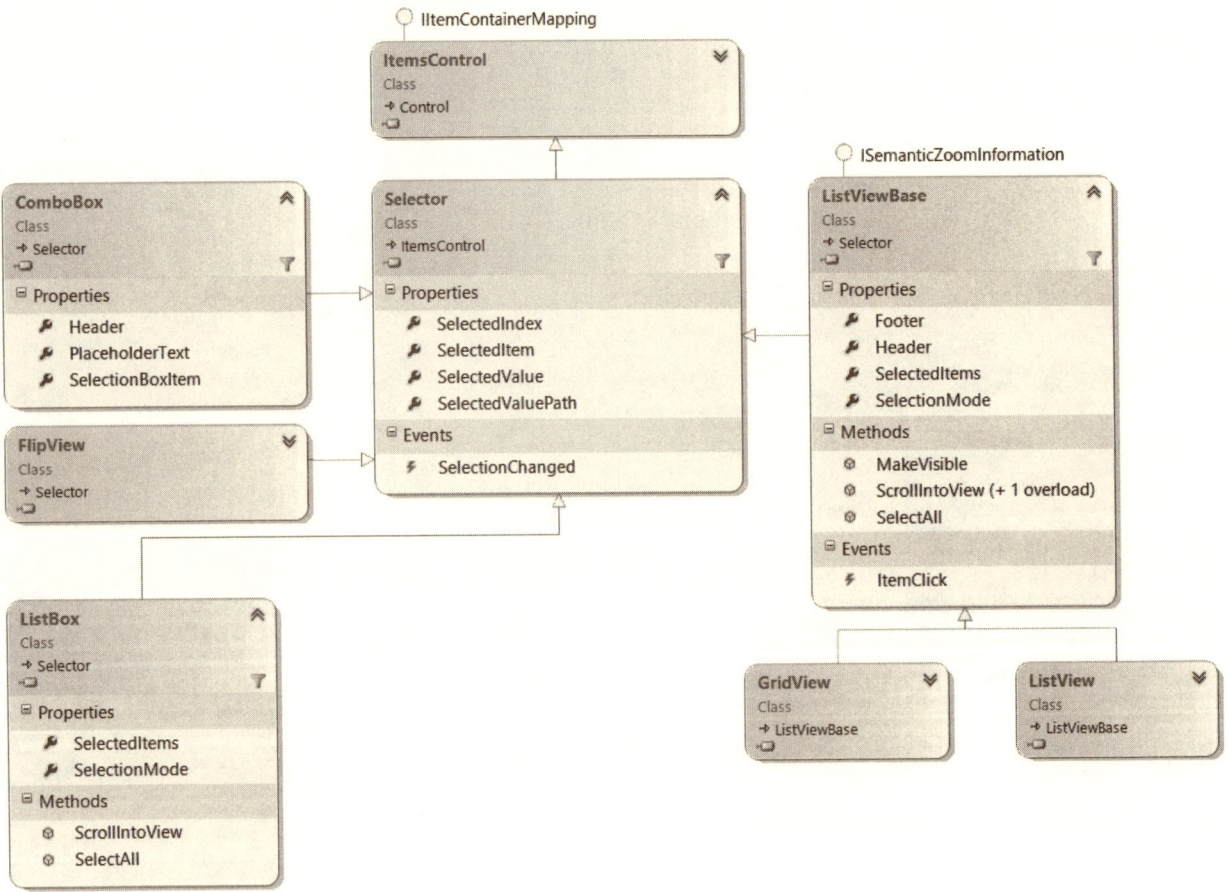

PUT ON YOUR THINKING HAT

Can you answer the following questions based on the class diagram on page 228?

Does the ComboBox support multiple selection?

Both the ListBox and the ListViewBase expose a SelectionMode property, but they're instances of different enumerations. What is the implication of None being a member of ListViewSelectionMode but not of SelectionMode?

In addition to the selection properties it inherits from the Selector class, the ComboBox exposes a SelectionBoxItem property. How do you think this differs from, say, SelectedItem?

What's the difference between SelectedIndex and SelectedItem?

How would you take some action when the user selects a different item (or items) in an items control?

HOW'D YOU DO?

Does the ComboBox support multiple selection?

> No. Only the ListBox and the classes that descend from ListViewBase expose a SelectedItems collection.

Both the ListBox and the ListViewBase expose a SelectionMode property, but they're instances of different enumerations. What is the implication of None being a member of ListViewSelectionMode but not of SelectionMode?

> The user can always make a selection in a ListBox, but the ListViewBase class can be configured so that no selection is possible.

In addition to the selection properties it inherits from the Selector class, the ComboBox exposes a SelectionBoxItem property. How do you think this differs from, say, SelectedItem?

> The SelectionBoxItem is the item that's displayed in the ComboBox when the drop-down is closed. It may or may not be selected.

What's the difference between SelectedIndex and SelectedItem?

> SelectedIndex is the position of the selected item in the Items collection. The SelectedItem is the item itself.

How would you take some action when the user selects a different item (or items) in an items control?

> You would respond to the SelectionChanged event.

TAKE A BREAK
Why don't you take a break before you complete the Review and we move on to the SemanticZoom control?

REVIEW

Can you answer the following questions based on what you've learned about items controls?

The **ListViewBase** class adds three primary kinds of functionality to the items control. What are they?

What happens behind the scenes when you add an item to an items control?

There are two ways to add items to an items control. What are they?

Are there any items controls that aren't **Selectors**?

What controls can you use if you want the items to act like buttons?

Semantic Zoom

I think the `SemanticZoom` control might be the coolest of all the cool new things in Win8. It's a powerful navigation mechanism—the Windows 8 Start Screen is an exmaple of that—and it has the potential to help your users understand the underlying structure of complex data.

The `SemanticZoom` control is conceptually sophisticated, but functionally quite simple. It lets users swap between two views of a given set of data:

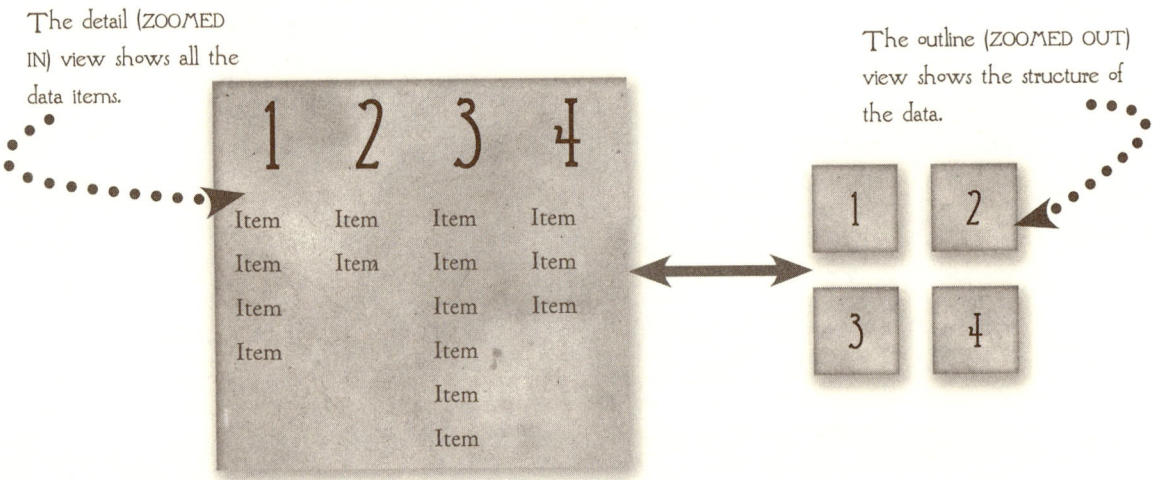

The detail (ZOOMED IN) view shows all the data items.

The outline (ZOOMED OUT) view shows the structure of the data.

MAKE A NOTE

You might be tempted to add additional semantic levels to your UI by nesting `SemanticZoom` controls. Aside from the fact that it's not technically possible with the control out of the box—the children of a SemanticZoom control must implement ISemanticZoomInformation, and SemanticZoom itself doesn't—you're more likely to confuse your users than help them. That said, of course, it's only a matter of time before an innovative UX designer proves me wrong...

IMPLEMENTING SEMANTICZOOM

Unfortunately, most of the SemanticZoom examples you'll see have a lot of moving parts: data bindings and resources and templates and styles (and lions and tigers, and bears, oh my!) While it's true that SemanticZoom works best when its contents are bound to grouped data, that isn't strictly necessary. The basic structure is quite simple:

The SemanticZoom has two bits of content: the ZoomedInView and the ZoomedOutView.

```
<SemanticZoom>
  <ZoomedInView>
    <! ISemanticZoomInformation instance />
  </ZoomedInView>
  <ZoomedOutView>
    <! ISemanticZoomInformation instance />
  </ZoomedOutView>
</SemanticZoom>
```

The views must implement ISemanticZoomInformation. Out of the box, only the ListViewBase does, which means you have to use a ListView or a GridView.

PUT ON YOUR THINKING HAT

To prove how simple the SemanticZoom really is, let's build a simple example. A really, really simple example. Okay, a ridiculous example. (But it proves the point.)

- Create a new project and add a SemanticZoom control to the LayoutRoot of the main page of a new Blank project. (I called mine ComplexWidgets01).
- Use a ListView as the ZoomedInView and a GridView as the ZoomedOutView.
- Add some TextBlock elements to the ListView. (I used a list of cats and bears.)
- In the GridView, add an element to represent each kind of thing in your list. (I formatted mine as a TextBlock inside a Border, but you can do whatever appeals to you.)

HOW'D YOU DO?

Here's my version of the XAML. As always, I've left out some of the formatting properties.

```xml
<Grid ... >
    <SemanticZoom>
        <SemanticZoom.ZoomedInView>
            <ListView ..>
                <TextBlock ...>Lions</TextBlock>
                <TextBlock ...>Tigers</TextBlock>
                <TextBlock ...>Cheetahs</TextBlock>
                <TextBlock ...>Panther</TextBlock>
                <TextBlock ...>Black Bears</TextBlock>
                <TextBlock ...>Brown Bears</TextBlock>
                <TextBlock ...>Polar Bears</TextBlock>
            </ListView>
        </SemanticZoom.ZoomedInView>
        <SemanticZoom.ZoomedOutView>
            <GridView ....>
                <Border ...>
                    <TextBlock ...>Kitty</TextBlock>
                </Border>
                <Border ...>
                    <TextBlock ...>Teddy</TextBlock>
                </Border>
            </GridView>
        </SemanticZoom.ZoomedOutView>
    </SemanticZoom>
</Grid>
```

SEMANTICZOOM CLASSES

Were you surprised at how easy the `SemanticZoom` control is to implement? It gets more complex when you start binding it to grouped data and creating styles and templates to define how the data appears, but all that isn't really part of the control itself, which is quite simple:

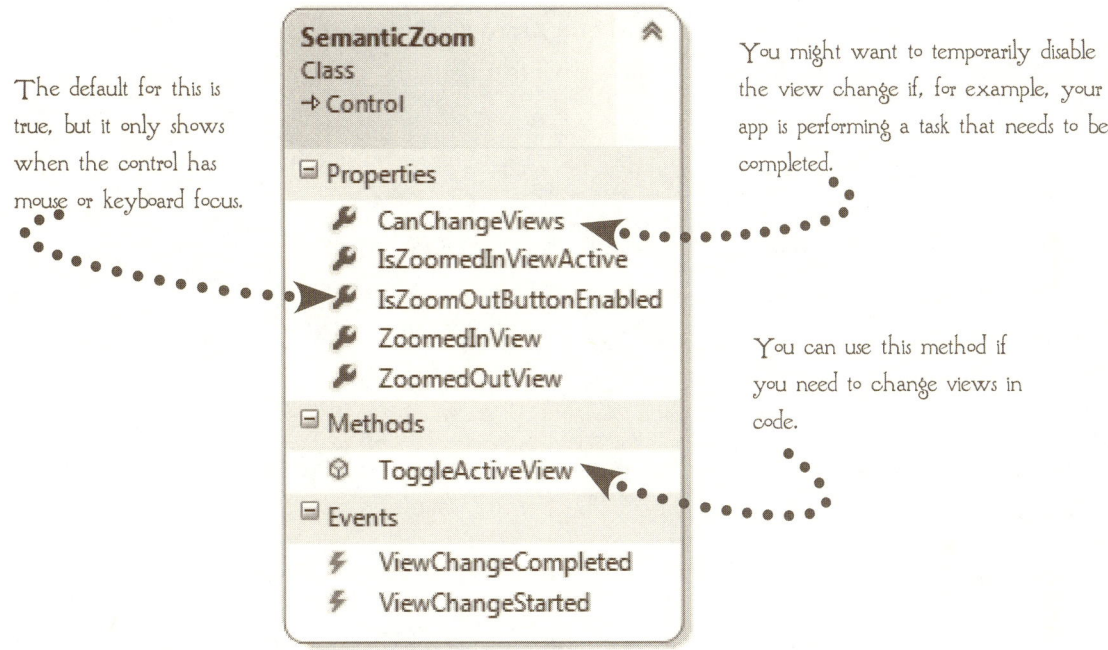

The default for this is true, but it only shows when the control has mouse or keyboard focus.

You might want to temporarily disable the view change if, for example, your app is performing a task that needs to be completed.

You can use this method if you need to change views in code.

TAKE A BREAK

We'll be working with XAML controls throughout most of the rest of the book, and in particular we'll come back to the `SemanticZoom` when we look at data binding in Chapter 12, but we're through with our overview. Why don't you take a break before you complete the Review and we move on to dependency properties in the next chapter?

REVIEW

All of the items controls in the Win8 XAML control class hierarchy descend from Selector. What functionality does that class provide?

What interface does ListViewBase implement that makes it important for use of the SemanticZoom control?

What happens behind the scenes to objects that you add to an items control?

The ViewBox and ScrollViewer both control the display of their content. Which one can change the size of the object it displays?

What standard control do you need to use inside a ScrollViewer for snapping to work? Why?

Congratulations! You've finished the chapter. Take a minute to think about what you've accomplished before you move on to the next one...

List three things you learned in this chapter:

Why do you think you need to know these things in order to develop Win8 apps?

Is there anything in this chapter that you think you need to understand in more detail? If so, what are you going to do about that?

DEPENDENCY PROPERTIES 7

Back in Chapter 4 you saw that **DependencyObject** is the top of the WinRT XAML class hierarchy, and I told you that it's the base class for objects that participate in the dependency property system. Yeah, okay, fine. What's a dependency property system, and why do you care? You'll find out in this chapter.

As we'll see, dependency properties (known as "DPs" to their friends) work with standard .NET properties to provide several important functions: they calculate their values, they provide change tracking and notification, they can be the target of data binding and animation, and they use a sparse storage model that's the basis for the attached properties like the ones we used to place an element in a **Grid** (check page 124 if you've forgotten how that works).

But that's still a little techie and vague, isn't it? How about this: In order for a property to be the target of data binding, for its appearance to be controlled via styles and templates, or for its value to be animated, the property must be a dependency property.

For existing classes, all you really need to know is whether a given property is or isn't a dependency property, but if you want access to all that XAML goodness in the classes you write, you need to know a bit more about how dependency properties work and how to create them. That's what this chapter is about.

> ### MAKE A NOTE
> We all know that it's a bad thing to make your app code more complex than it needs to be, right? Dependency properties add complexity to your code—not a lot, but some—and they're not always necessary. Don't assume that every property (or even most properties) of every class you write needs to be a DP.

FITTING IT IN

You know that .NET Framework types have four kinds of members: fields, properties, methods, and events. Dependency properties don't change that. Just like regular .NET properties, dependency properties are implemented using fields and properties. The magic happens when you register the property with the dependency property system, and use `GetValue()` and `SetValue()` methods to change the value of the field instead of setting its value directly.

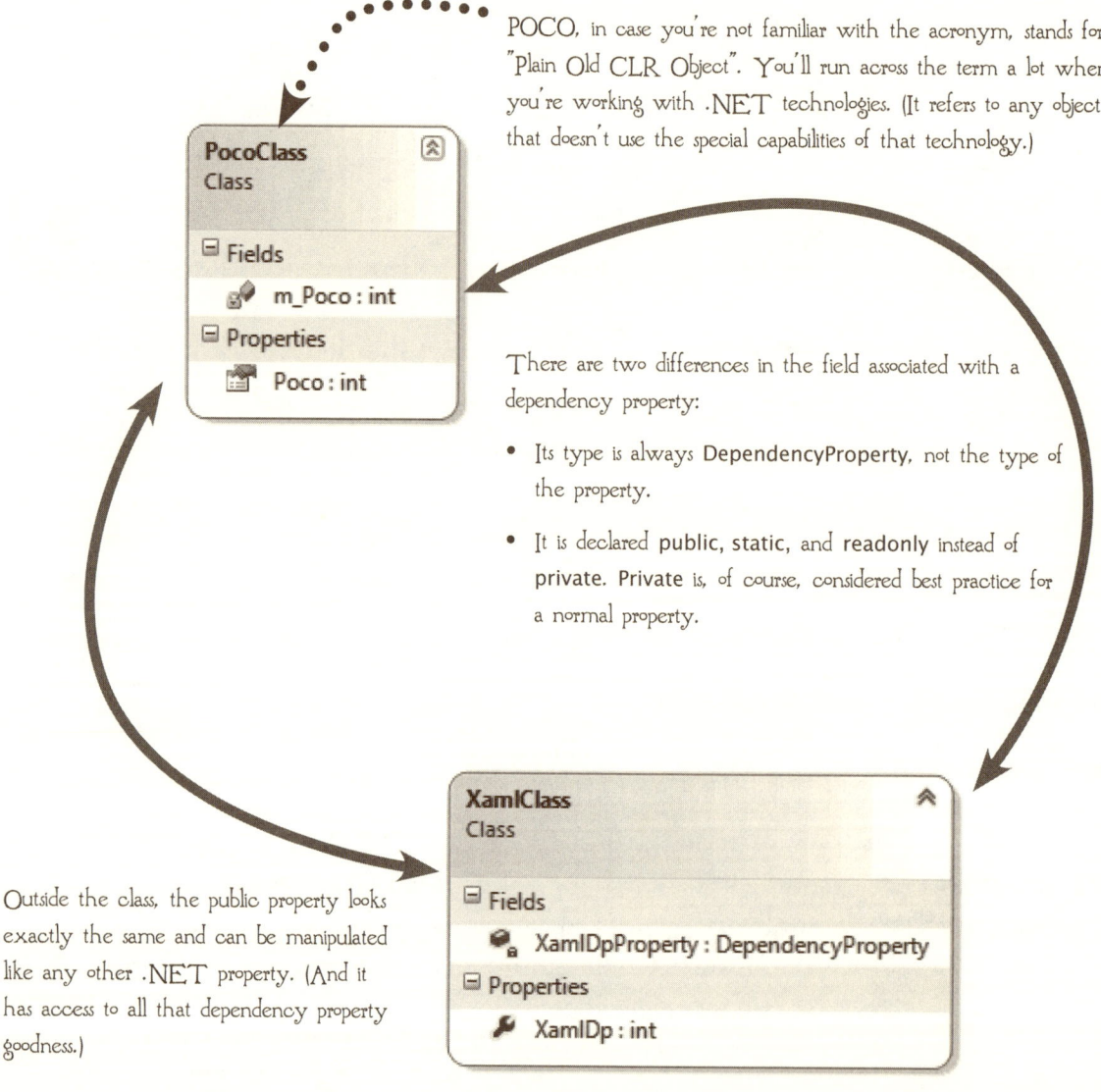

POCO, in case you're not familiar with the acronym, stands for "Plain Old CLR Object". You'll run across the term a lot when you're working with .NET technologies. (It refers to any object that doesn't use the special capabilities of that technology.)

There are two differences in the field associated with a dependency property:

- Its type is always **DependencyProperty**, not the type of the property.

- It is declared **public, static,** and **readonly** instead of **private**. Private is, of course, considered best practice for a normal property.

Outside the class, the public property looks exactly the same and can be manipulated like any other .NET property. (And it has access to all that dependency property goodness.)

A Comparison

Here are some samples of POCO and dependency property declarations:

```csharp
public class PocoClass
{
    private int m_Poco;

    public int Poco
    {
        get { return m_Poco; }
        set { m_Poco = value; }
    }
}
```

```csharp
public class XamlClass : DependencyObject
{
    public int XamlDp
    {
        get { return (int) Getvalue(XamlDpProperty); }
        set { SetValue(XamlDpProperty, value); }
    }

    public static readonly DependencyProperty XamlDpProperty =
        DependencyProperty.Register(...);
}
```
(C#)

You have to call the **GetValue()** and **SetValue()** methods inside the standard **get** and **set** accessors of a dependency property in order to keep it synchronized with the dependency property system.

```vb
Public Class PocoClass
    Dim m_Poco As Integer
    Property Poco() As Integer
        Get
            Return m_Poco
        End Get
        Set(ByVal Value As Integer)
            m_Poco = Value
        End Set
End Class
```

```vb
Public Class XamlClass Inherits DependencyObject
    Public Property XamlDp() As Integer
        Get
            Return DirectCase(GetValue(XamlDpProperty), Integer)
        End Get
        Set
            SetValue(XamlDpProperty, value)
        End Set
    End Property

    Public Shared ReadOnly XamlDpProperty As DependencyProperty = _
        DependencyProperty.Register(...)
End Class
```
(VB)

Dependency properties must be registered with the dependency property system by calling the **Register()** method.

TASK LIST

In this chapter we'll explore the ways in which XAML extends the way that .NET objects can communicate and interact with the dependency property system.

CALCULATING DEPENDENCY PROPERTY VALUES

As we'll see, dependency properties can do a lot of cool things, but the one you'll rely on most often is their ability to calculate their values, so we'll begin by exploring exactly how that happens.

DEPENDENCY PROPERTY CLASSES

Like any set of .NET objects, the class hierarchy defines how dependency properties function and interact, so after we've explored how they arrive at their final values, we'll take a quick look at the class hierarchy that defines them.

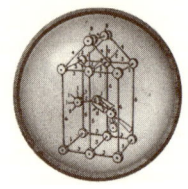

CREATING DEPENDENCY PROPERTIES

There are several steps to creating a dependency property in the classes you define, and, frankly, the syntax is pretty complex. Fortunately, Visual Studio includes a code snippet that does (almost) all the heavy lifting. We'll see how that works in the next section of the chapter.

DEPENDENCY PROPERTY CALLBACKS

At the end of the chapter, we'll come full circle when we explore how you can control the calculated value of a dependency property using callback methods. A CALLBACK is rather like an event handler—it's a method that's called at specific points during processing. Dependency properties support two callbacks, and we'll finish the chapter by examining them.

DEPENDENCY PROPERTIES

Dependency properties "extend the functionality of CLR properties". Fine. What does that mean, exactly? Do they do things that you can't do with a CLR property? No, not really. It's just that dependency properties encapsulate a bunch of useful functionality that can be tedious to implement using CLR properties, and because they're part of the WinRT infrastructure, other components of WinRT know how to work with them. So, for example, you can bind a dependency property value to another object (we'll see how to do that in Chapter 12) or animate its value using a Storyboard. (We'll take a quick look at animation in Chapter 10.)

```
                    ┌─────────────────┐
                    │  CLR PROPERTY   │
                    └─────────────────┘
                             ▲
                             │
                    ┌─────────────────┐
                    │ DEPENDENCY PROPERTY │
                    └─────────────────┘
                             ▲
           ┌─────────────────┼─────────────────┐
           │                 │                 │
┌───────────────────┐ ┌───────────────┐ ┌───────────────────┐
│ VALUE CALCULATION │ │ SPARSE STORAGE│ │  CHANGE TRACKING  │
└───────────────────┘ └───────────────┘ └───────────────────┘
```

VALUE CALCULATION — This is arguably the most important capability of dependency properties from a programming perspective. It lets you inherit values, animate them, and ensure that they're always valid.

SPARSE STORAGE — This means that a dependency property only takes up space if it's being used. It's particularly important for attached properties (which are a form of dependency property), but it's true of all dependency properties. And you don't have to do a thing.

CHANGE TRACKING — A lot of applications need to react when the value of a property changes. That can be bothersome with POCO properties, because they don't automatically generate change events, but support for change notification is built into the dependency property system.

CALCULATING DP VALUES

Dependency properties go through an entire sequence of processes to calculate their final value. In most cases, this is one of those XAML things that usually "just works", but here's the process in outline, so you'll understand what happens when you run across something weird:

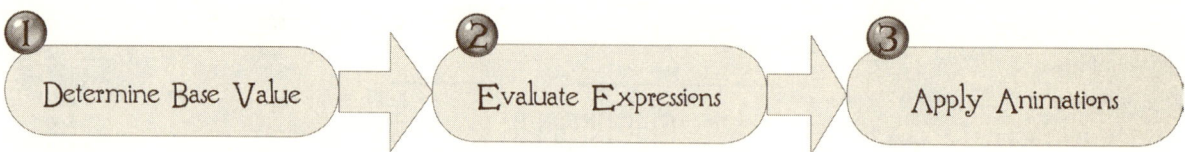

① The process begins by determining a base value for the property. The base property itself is calculated from a series of sources. (Keep reading.)

② The value of a property can be based on an expression, like the value of a field in a data source. (We'll talk about that in Chapter 12.) An expression takes precedence over the base value.

③ When a value is ANIMATED, its value will change over time. (We'll talk about animations in Chapter 11.) The animation is applied to the result of Step 2, so it takes precedence over the expression and the base value.

DETERMINING THE BASE VALUE

The first step a dependency property performs in calculating its final value is to determine its base value. Like a standard .NET property, the process starts with a default value, but a dependency property has a whole bunch more steps (most of which we won't talk about for a chapter or two. Sorry.)

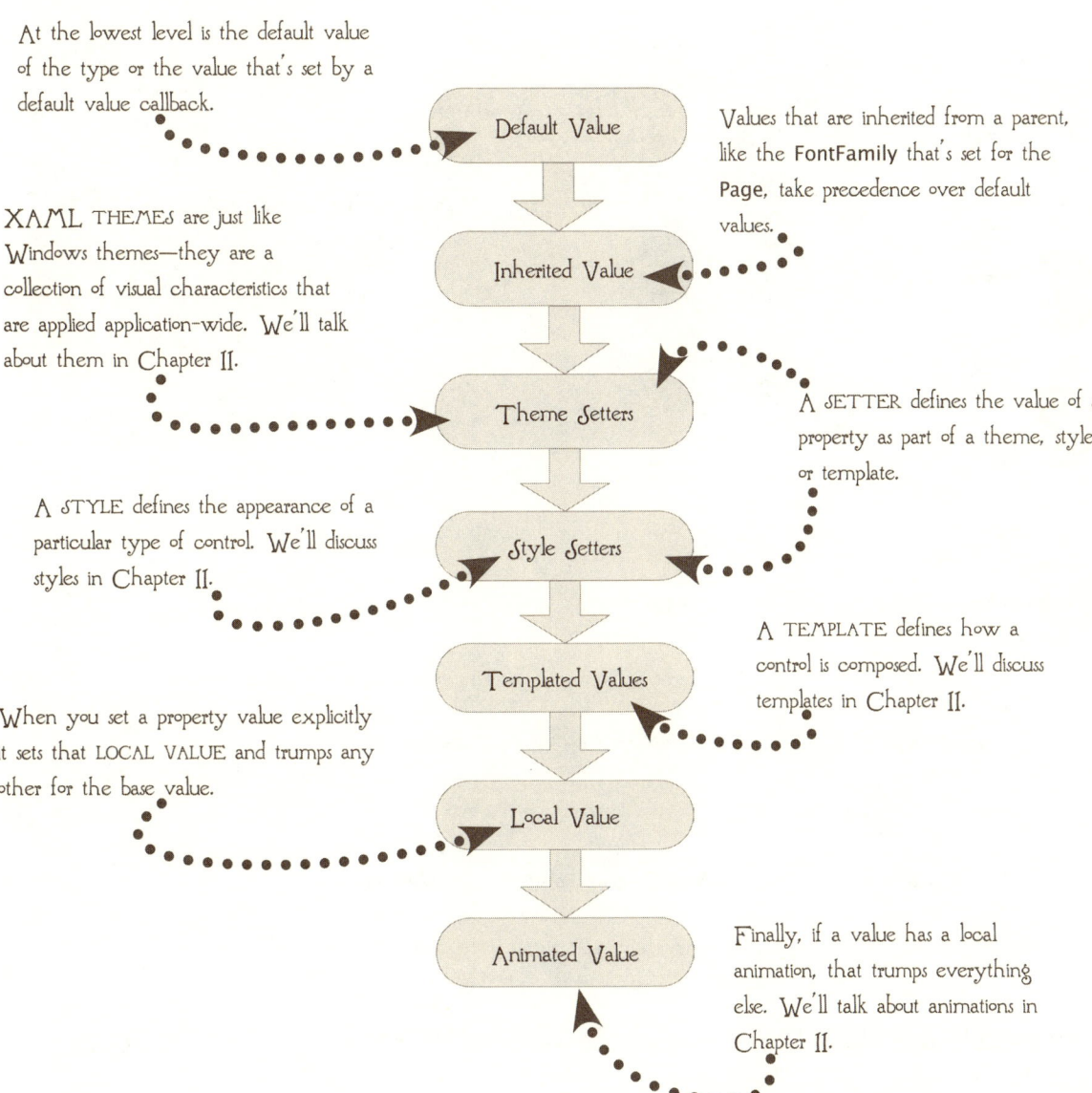

At the lowest level is the default value of the type or the value that's set by a default value callback.

Values that are inherited from a parent, like the FontFamily that's set for the Page, take precedence over default values.

XAML THEMES are just like Windows themes—they are a collection of visual characteristics that are applied application-wide. We'll talk about them in Chapter II.

A SETTER defines the value of a property as part of a theme, style or template.

A STYLE defines the appearance of a particular type of control. We'll discuss styles in Chapter II.

A TEMPLATE defines how a control is composed. We'll discuss templates in Chapter II.

When you set a property value explicitly it sets that LOCAL VALUE and trumps any other for the base value.

Finally, if a value has a local animation, that trumps everything else. We'll talk about animations in Chapter II.

245

AN EXAMPLE

This all seems really complicated, doesn't it? Relax. In practice, figuring out the value of a dependency property is pretty simple. Let's look at an example (assume that there aren't any resources like styles or templates that are affecting the element in the background).

Don't worry about how this **Style** is defined. We'll look at how styles work in Chapter 11. (I think I may have mentioned that...)

```
<Page ...
    FontStretch="Expanded">
<StackPanel>
    <TextBlock FontStretch="Medium">
    <TextBlock.Style>
        <Style TargetType="TextBlock">
            <Setter Property="FontStretch" Value="Condensed" />
        </Style>
    </TextBlock.Style>
    Hello, Dependency!
    </TextBlock>
</StackPanel>
</Page>
```

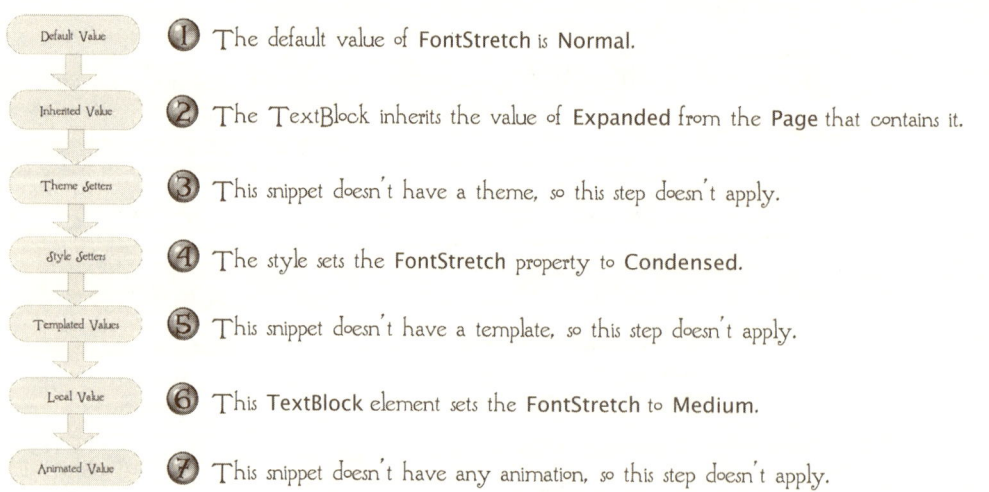

① The default value of **FontStretch** is **Normal**.

② The **TextBlock** inherits the value of **Expanded** from the **Page** that contains it.

③ This snippet doesn't have a theme, so this step doesn't apply.

④ The style sets the **FontStretch** property to **Condensed**.

⑤ This snippet doesn't have a template, so this step doesn't apply.

⑥ This **TextBlock** element sets the **FontStretch** to **Medium**.

⑦ This snippet doesn't have any animation, so this step doesn't apply.

And the final value of the **Label.FontStretch** property? It's **Medium**, the local value, which always trumps any other source.

PUT ON YOUR THINKING HAT

Let's try a little dependency property experiment.

By default, when you create a new XAML Page, the FontFamily attribute will be set to the default system font, Segoe UI (which, by the way, is pronounced "see-go"), the FontSize to 11pt, and the Background to Black.

These aren't bad choices. But they're not the only ones, and they may not be the most appropriate for your application. So, suppose you want your text to display in Times New Roman at 14 point in dark brown on a pale yellow background. Because dependency properties inherit their values, you should be able to set the font properties for the window, right? Here's a simple example:

```
<Page ... >
  <Grid Background="{StaticResource ApplicationBackgroundThemeBrush}">
    <ListView
        FontFamily="Times New Roman" FontSize="14"
        Foreground="SaddleBrown" Background="Cornsilk"
        Margin="50" Padding="20">
      <TextBlock>Now is the time</TextBlock>
      <TextBox Text="For all good men" Width="300" />
      <CheckBox>To come to the aid of their countries</CheckBox>
    </ListView>
  </Grid>
</Page>
```

Before you create the application, take a minute to think about what you expect to have happen:

What text and color values do you think will be displayed in the Properties window for the Label and TextBlock controls? How do you expect them to display? Will they use the values set for the Page, or the default properties? Will both controls behave the same?

Okay, now create a new app (mine is called DPs01), and see what really happens.

HOW'D YOU DO?

Okay, so dependency property value calculations don't *always* work the way we expect them to. What happened and why?

Foreground, Background, FontFamily, and FontSize are all dependency properties, so in theory they should have inherited their values from the ListView, but while the TextBlock inherited the Foreground color, the TextBox and CheckBox didn't, and none of the controls inherited the Background, FontFamily, or FontSize.

The reason for the inconsistent behavior is that all of the standard XAML controls have implicit default styles set by an application theme that lives somewhere in the bowels of WinRT, and if you look back at the way base values are calculated, you'll see that theme values take precedence over inherited values.

Even once we've explored styles in Chapter 11, you'll occasionally be surprised by this kind of thing. (And yes, once more, that's the voice of experience.) So what's a poor programmer to do? Take control. Either define your own control styles (probably the best solution in the long run), or set the value explicitly.

(And if you come from a WPF background, as I do, and are used to setting properties on your Window or UserControl as a quicky style test, as I am, just accept that you're not going to be able to depend on value inheritance the way you're used to. Oh, well.)

TAKE A BREAK

The final value of a dependency property can be determined by a lot of things, and as we've just seen, sometimes that final value won't be what you were expecting, if what you were expecting was inheritance. But now that you've seen the pipeline, you know how to address them. So for now, why don't you take a break before completing the Review and we take a look at the dependency property classes?

REVIEW

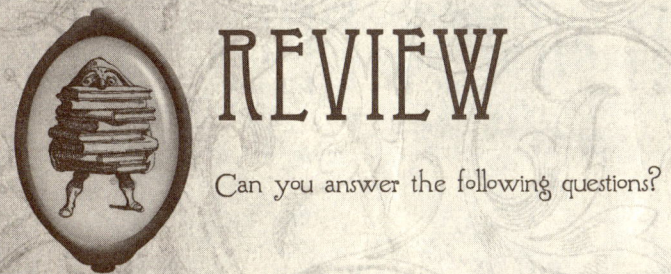

Can you answer the following questions?

What does POCO stand for?

What does it mean to say that a dependency propery "wraps" a POCO property?

What value always trumps the base value calculation?

What are the values of the FontFamily properties for the two labels in the following snippet (ignore the issue of default themes for this now)?

```xml
<ListView FontFamily="Times New Roman">
    <TextBlock Name="Label1">Hello</TextBlock>
    <TextBlock Name="Label2" FontFamily="Tahoma">World</TextBlock>
</ListView>
```

DEPENDENCY PROPERTY CLASSES

The keys to the dependency property system are the DependencyProperty and PropertyMetadata classes that encapsulate all the functionality required to extend the behavior of a POCO property. The classes are straightforward, although the method creating callbacks is inconsistent, and that adds a little complexity that we'll explore in a few pages.

UnsetValue is used rather than null (Nothing in Visual Basic) to indicate that the value exists but doesn't have a value.

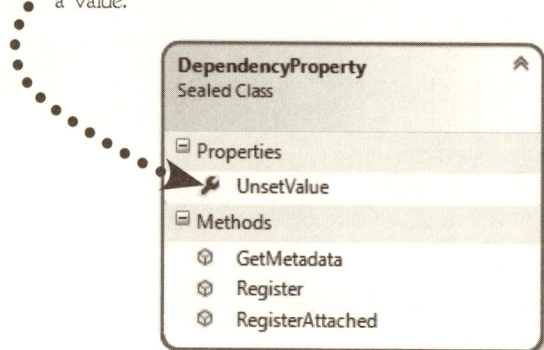

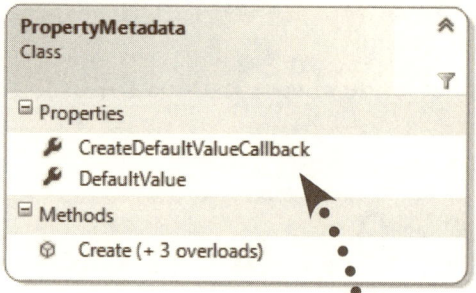

WinB dependency properties actually support two callbacks: a CreateDefaultValueCallback and a PropertyChangedCallback. (There's no way—at least no way that I've found—to retrieve a reference to the PropertyChangedCallback method once the dependency property is created.

MORE CLASSES

Did you notice something odd about the DependencyProperty and PropertyMetadata classes? They descend directly from Object, not one of the XAML classes like FrameworkElement. I think of them as sitting outside the system in order to manipulate it. (I'm sure the architects of Win8 would have a more elegant description.)

But most XAML classes descend, more or less directly, from FrameworkElement, and one of the ancestors of FrameworkElement, the DependencyObject, provides some important functions for creating and working with dependency properties. In fact, DependencyObject, which as you can see sits quite high in the XAML class hierarchy, specifically encapsulates the functionality of objects that participate in the dependency property system.

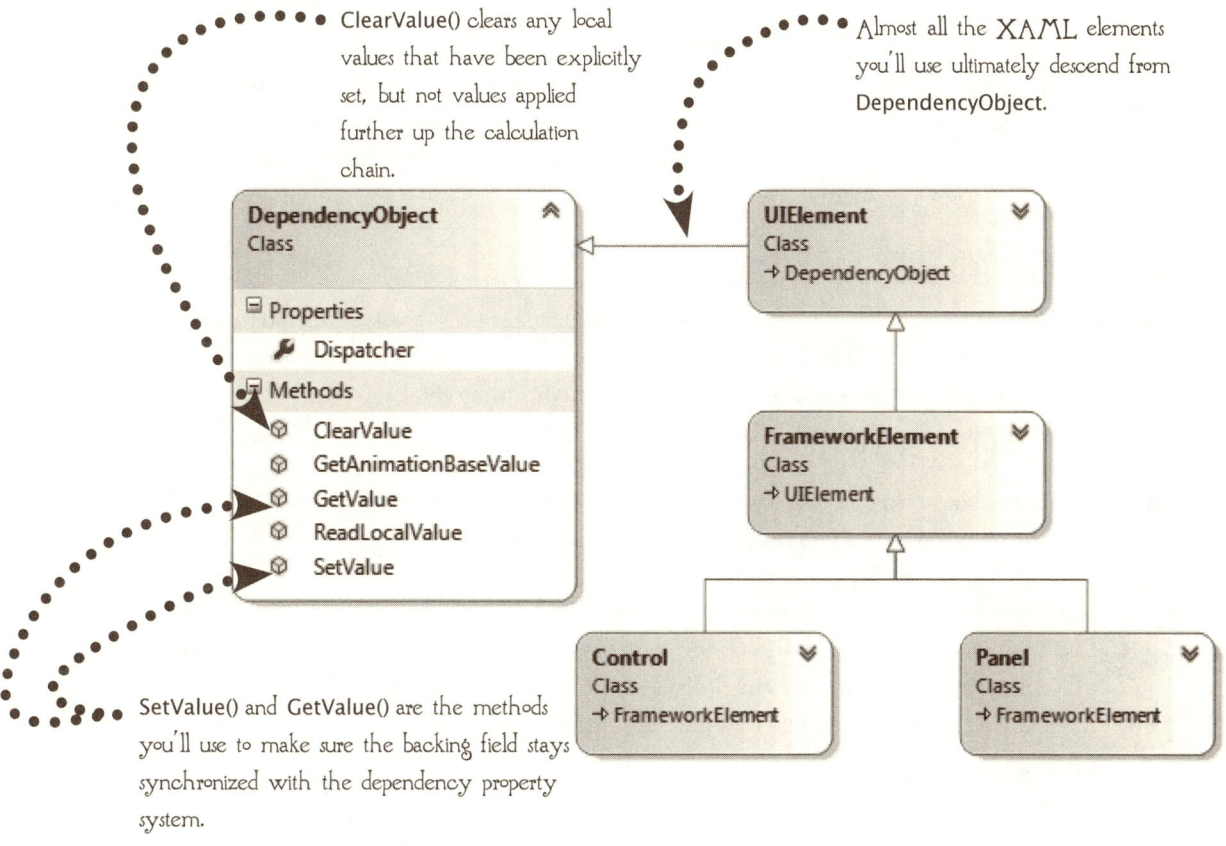

ClearValue() clears any local values that have been explicitly set, but not values applied further up the calculation chain.

Almost all the XAML elements you'll use ultimately descend from DependencyObject.

SetValue() and GetValue() are the methods you'll use to make sure the backing field stays synchronized with the dependency property system.

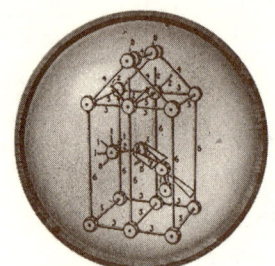

Creating Dependency Properties

You don't have to define the properties of your classes as dependency properties. Plain old .NET properties work just fine, but they don't take advantage of the things that make XAML such a joy to work with. So don't assume that a property needs to be a DP, but if it does, don't be shy.

It's really not that difficult to make the magic happen. There are only four steps, and two of them are optional:

Create the POCO Property

This is just a basic POCO property, but you must use GetValue() and SetValue() within the get and set accessors to make sure the property works within the dependency property system. (Your class must descend from DependencyObject in order for GetValue() and SetValue() to be available.)

Create the Callbacks

This one's optional, but if you need to define callbacks to provide a default value or execute some code when the property value changes, you'll need to create the callback methods. We'll see how callbacks work at the end of this chapter.

Create the Metadata

In practice, you'll do this right inside the call to the Register() function (in Step 4) unless you're providing a CreateDefaultValueCallback.

Register the Property

The final step is to call one of the static Register...() methods of the DependencyProperty class. There are two versions: Register() for creating a standard dependency property, and RegisterAttached() for creating attached properties.

When you register the dependency property, the name you specify should be the name of the POCO property plus the word "Property". There's nothing that enforces this convention, but if you don't follow it, your app can break in surprising and apparently unrelated places. (Just trust me on that, okay? The reasons are complex and irrelevant. Until it happens to you, of course.)

WALK-THROUGH

The four steps to creating a dependency property are pretty standard, so it will probably come as no surprise that Visual Studio IntelliSense can stub out the code for you. Let's walk through the process using Visual Studio to define a basic dependency property. (This version is in C#. If you're using Visual Basic, skip to page 258.)

ADD A DEPENDENCY PROPERTY SNIPPET TO MAINPAGE.XAML.CS

Inside the class declaration, but outside the **MainPage**() constructor, either right-click and select Insert Snippet...or press Ctrl-K, X to open the IntelliSense menu. Select NETFX30 and press Enter, and then select Define a Dependency Property and press Enter. Visual Studio will insert the stub for you:

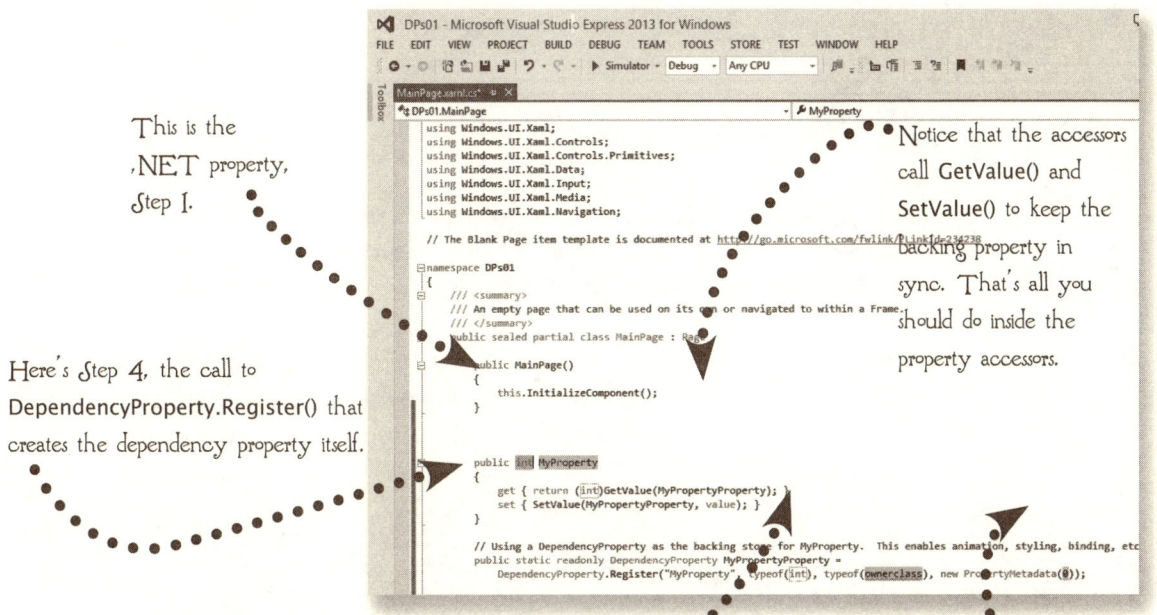

This is the .NET property, Step 1.

Here's Step 4, the call to **DependencyProperty.Register**() that creates the dependency property itself.

Notice that the accessors call **GetValue**() and **SetValue**() to keep the backing property in sync. That's all you should do inside the property accessors.

The dependency property has the same name as the POCO property with the word "Property" appended to it.

The metadata, Step 3, is created inside the **Register**...() method call. This is common practice.

253

 CHANGE THE PROPERTY TYPE TO STRING

The IntelliSense stub defaults to an **int**, so we'll need to change that. Change "int" to "String" and move the cursor off the line. As soon as you do, Visual Studio will update the get accessor and the call to **Register()**.

SetValue() returns an **Object** that must be cast. Visual Studio updates the **get** accessor for you when you change the declaration.

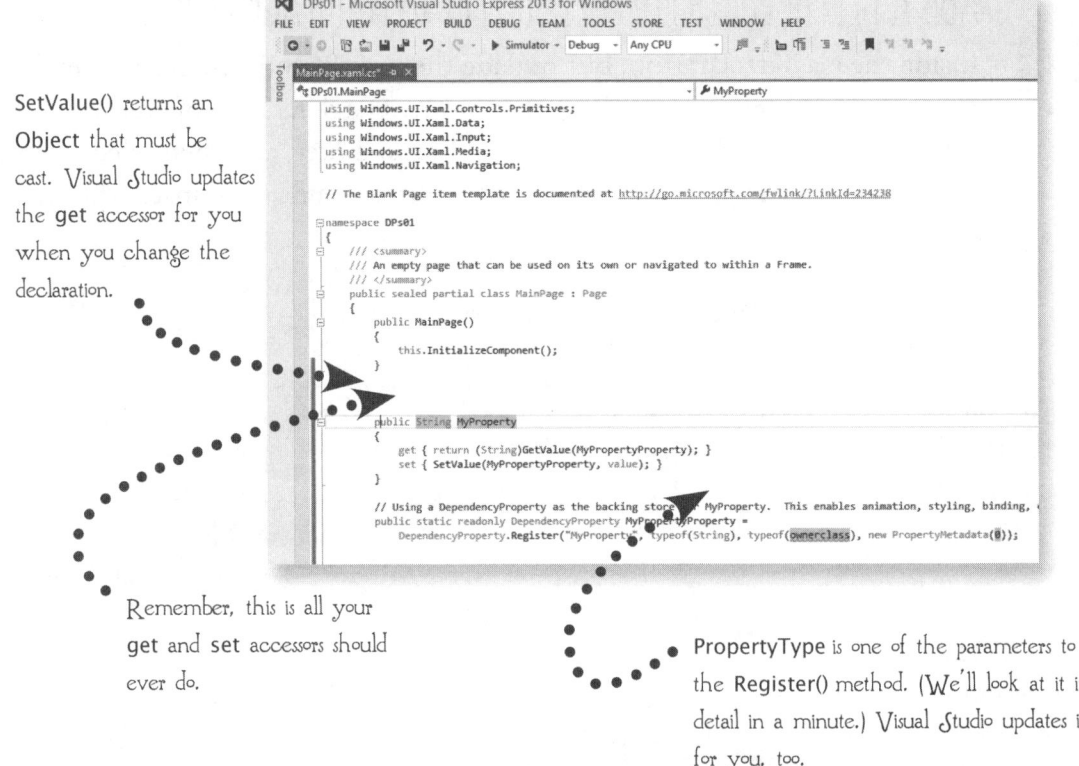

Remember, this is all your **get** and **set** accessors should ever do.

PropertyType is one of the parameters to the **Register()** method. (We'll look at it in detail in a minute.) Visual Studio updates it for you, too.

MAKE A NOTE
Don't do anything other than call **GetValue()** and **SetValue()** inside the POCO property definition, because it's not guaranteed to be called. If you set the value in XAML, for example, the XAML parser will call **SetValue()** directly, without calling your accessor.

CHANGE THE PROPERTY NAME

You can name your property with any valid C# identifier. I've used TestDP in this example. Visual Studio will update the stub for you once you leave the line, just as it did when you changed the property type.

• Visual Studio updates the name of the dependency property to match the POCO property name plus "Property". You should always follow this convention.

SPECIFY THE OWNER CLASS

Now we need to tell the dependency property system about the class that owns the property. This will almost always be the class in which you're declaring the property. (In fact, I haven't ever seen a situation that required anything else.)

Change this value to the name of the class that owns the dependency property, **MainPage** in this case.

CHANGE THE DEFAULT VALUE

The stub that Visual Studio adds for a dependency property creates the metadata inside the call to the **Register**() method, and it uses the version of the constructor that accepts a default value for the property. Because the default property type is int, the default value is 0. That's not valid for a string, of course, so you'll need to manually update the default value. (It's easy to omit this step, and very hard to find if you do, so be careful here.)

I've used an empty string here, but of course you can use any valid value for the underlying type.

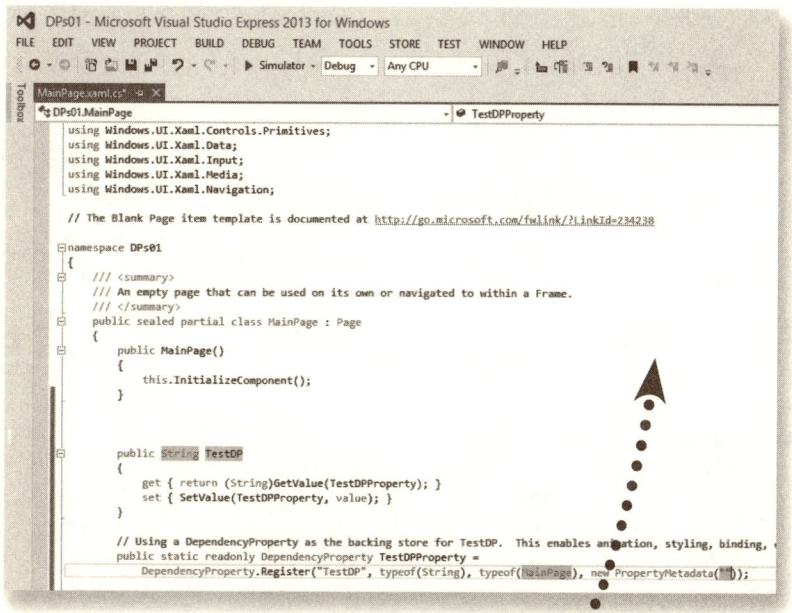

There are other versions of the **PropertyMetadata** constructor. We'll look at them later in the chapter.

257

WALK-THROUGH

The four steps to creating a dependency property are pretty standard, so it will probably come as no surprise that Visual Studio IntelliSense can stub out the code for you. Let's walk though the process using Visual Studio to define a basic dependency property. (This version is in Visual Basic. If you're using C#, go back to page 255.)

 **ADD A DEPENDENCY PROPERTY SNIPPET TO MAINPAGE.XAML.VB**

Inside the class declaration, either right-click and select Insert Snippet...or press Ctrl-K, X to open the IntelliSense menu. Select WPF and press Enter, and then select Add a Dependency Property Registration and press Enter. Visual Studio will insert the stub for you:

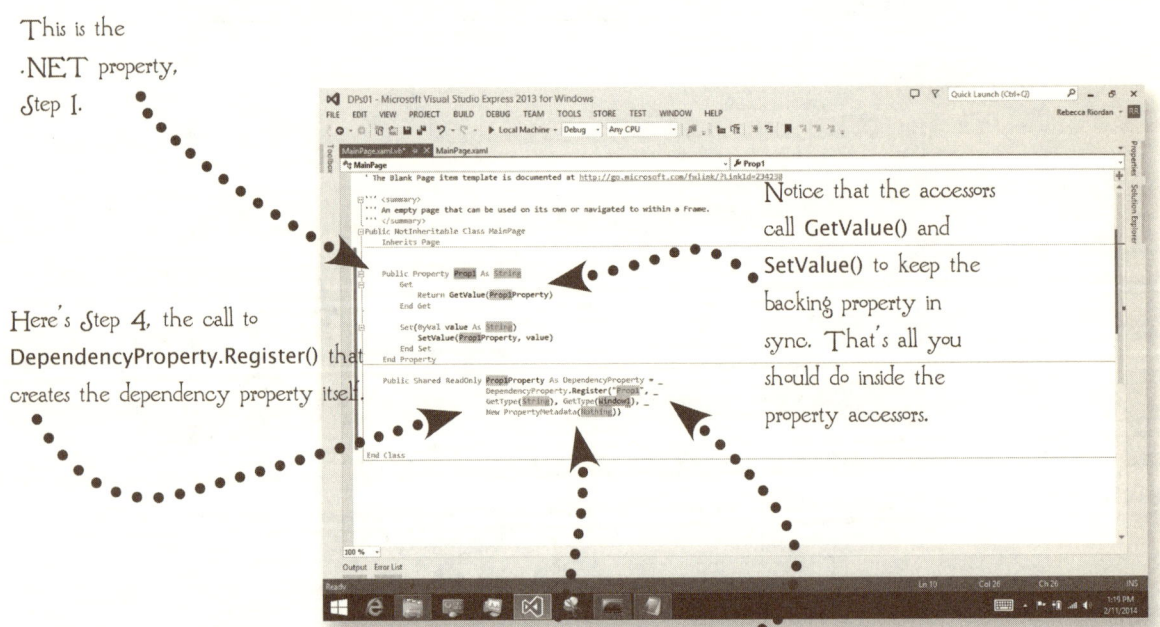

This is the .NET property, Step 1.

Here's Step 4, the call to **DependencyProperty.Register()** that creates the dependency property itself.

Notice that the accessors call **GetValue()** and **SetValue()** to keep the backing property in sync. That's all you should do inside the property accessors.

The dependency property has the same name as the POCO property with the word "Property" appended to it.

The metadata, Step 3, is created inside the Register...() method call. This is common practice.

258

CHANGE THE PROPERTY NAME

You can name your property with any valid VB identifier. I've used **TestDP** in this example. As soon as you do, Visual Studio will update the **get** accessor and the call to **Register()**.

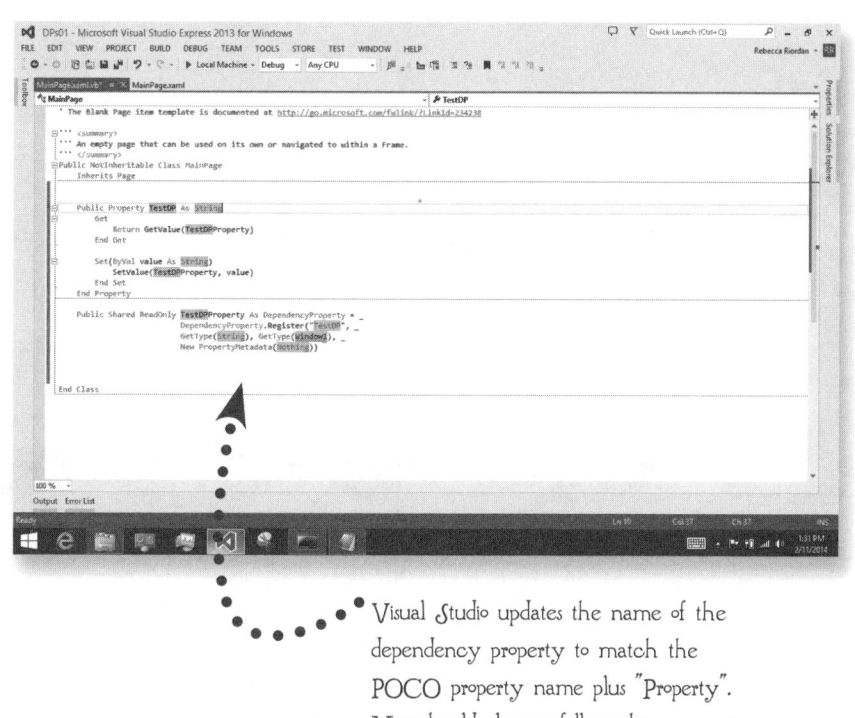

Visual Studio updates the name of the dependency property to match the POCO property name plus "Property". You should always follow this convention.

CHANGE THE PROPERTY TYPE TO INTEGER

The IntelliSense stub defaults to a string, so we'll need to change that. Change "String" to "Integer" and move the cursor off the line. Visual Studio will update the stub for you once you leave the line, just as it did when you changed the property name.

SetValue() returns an Object that must be cast. Visual Studio updates the get accessor for you when you change the declaration.

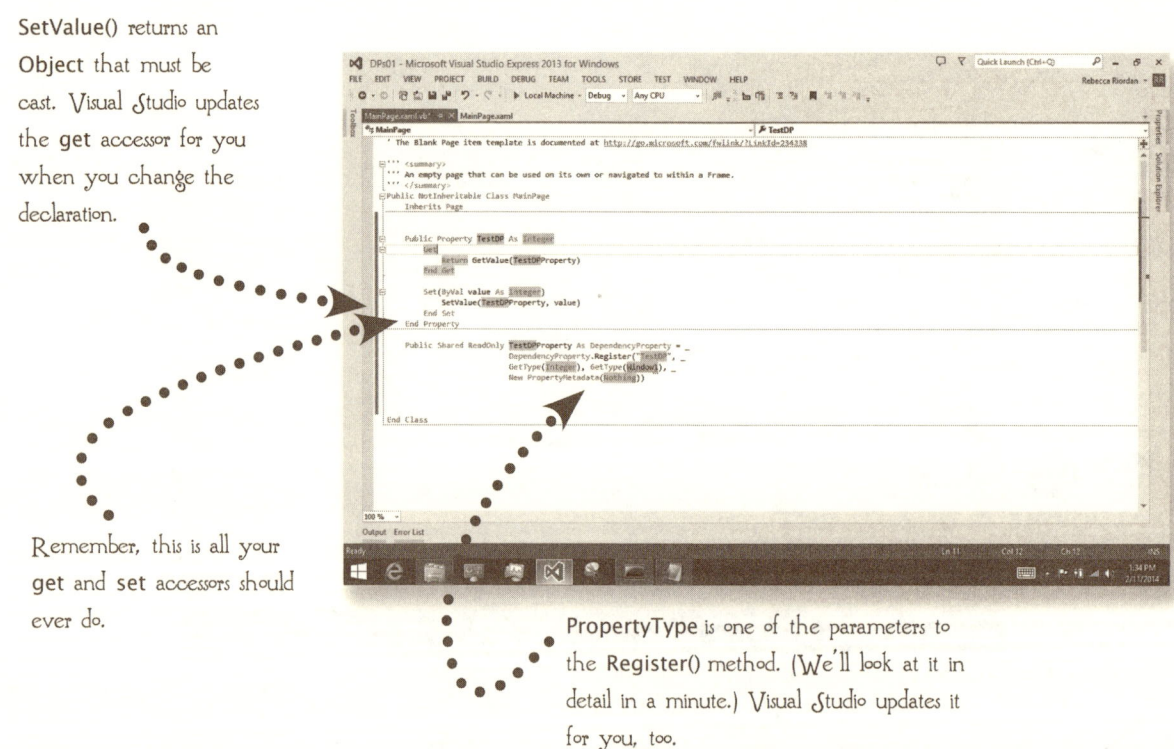

Remember, this is all your get and set accessors should ever do.

PropertyType is one of the parameters to the Register() method. (We'll look at it in detail in a minute.) Visual Studio updates it for you, too.

MAKE A NOTE
Don't do anything other than call GetValue() and SetValue() inside the .NET property definition, because it's not guaranteed to be called. If you set the value in XAML, for example, the XAML parser will call SetValue() directly, without calling your accessor.

SPECIFY THE OWNER CLASS

Now we need to tell the dependency property system about the class that owns the property. This will almost always be the class in which you're declaring the property. (In fact, I haven't ever seen a situation that required anything else.)

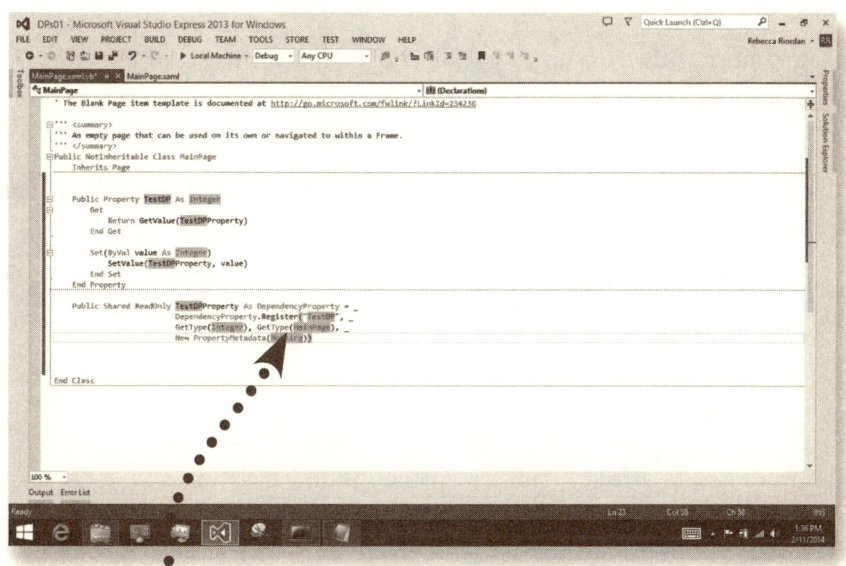

••• Change this value to the name of the class that owns the dependency property, MainPage in this case.

CHANGE THE DEFAULT VALUE

The stub that Visual Studio adds for a dependency property creates the metadata inside the call to the **Register()** method, and it uses the version of the constructor that accepts a default value for the property. Because the default property type is **String**, the default value is **Nothing**. That's not valid for a string, of course, so you'll need to manually update the default value. (It's easy to omit this step, and very hard to find if you do, so be careful here.)

I've used 0 here, but of course you can use any valid value for the underlying type.

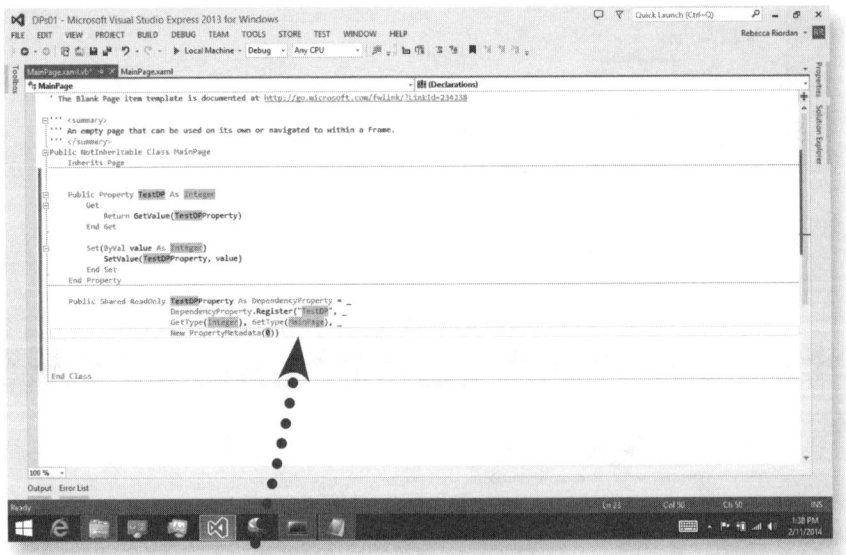

There are other versions of the **PropertyMetadata** constructor. We'll look at them later in the chapter.

ATTACHED PROPERTIES

Attached properties are a special kind of dependency property that, in essence, let you set a property value on a class that doesn't define that property. Attached properties are used most often to position elements in panel controls, and we've done that in assigning `Grid.Row` and `Grid.Column`, both attached properties, to XAML elements inside the `Grid` panel.

Although you can create a POCO wrapper that calls `GetValue()` and `SetValue()` for an attached property, it isn't common to do so. Instead, you create two methods, `Get<PropertyName>()` and `Set<PropertyName>()`, that call the appropriate methods instead:

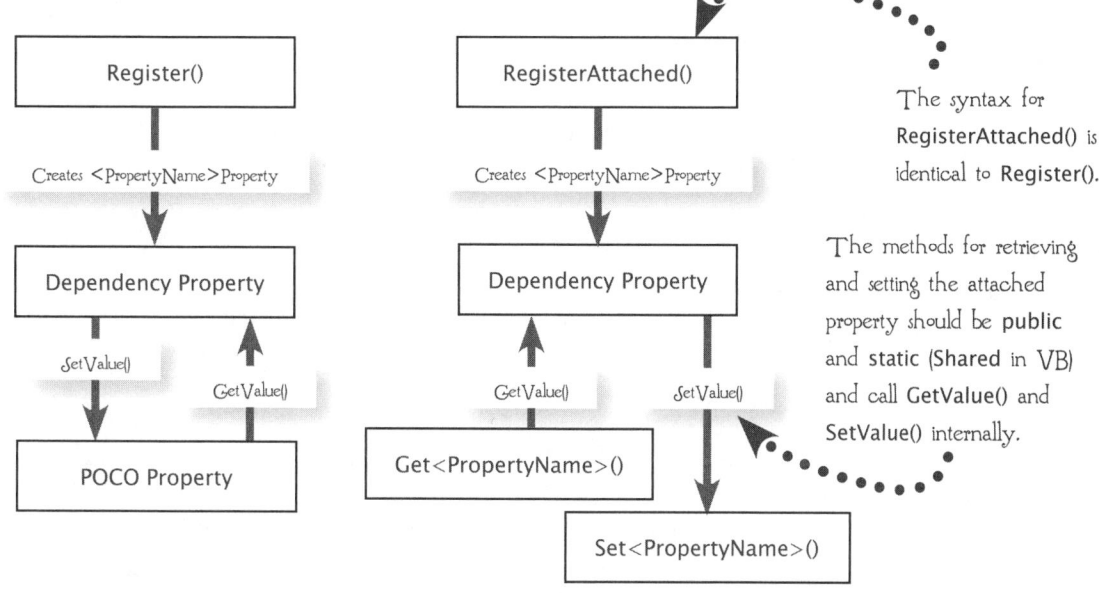

The syntax for RegisterAttached() is identical to Register().

The methods for retrieving and setting the attached property should be **public** and **static** (**Shared** in VB) and call GetValue() and SetValue() internally.

PUT ON YOUR THINKING HAT

In reality, you're unlikely to be creating many attached properties, but based on what you know about the **Register()** method (the syntax for **RegisterAttached()** is identical), can you do it? It's okay to look at the code you created for a standard dependency property, but don't use the insert attached property snippet yet. (Yes, there is one, and you access it the same way.)

263

HOW'D YOU DO?

It doesn't matter if you chose a different name or data type for your property, as long as you got the basic syntax right.

```csharp
public static int GetMyAP(DependencyObject obj))
{
    return (int)obj.GetValue(MyAPProperty);
}

public static void SetMyAP(DependencyObject obj, int value)
{
    obj.SetValue(MyAPProperty, value);
}

public static readonly DependencyProperty MyAPProperty =
    DependencyProperty.RegisterAttached("MyAP", typeof(int), typeof(MainPage),
        new PropertyMetadata(0));
```

```vb
Public Shared Function GetMyAP(ByVal element as DependencyObject) As Integer
    Return element.GetValue(MyAPProperty)
End Function

Public Shared Sub SetMyAP(ByVal element as DependencyObject, _
                         ByVal value as Integer)
    element.SetValue(MyAPProperty, value)
End Sub

Public Shared ReadOnly MyAPProperty As _
                DependencyProperty = DependencyProperty.RebisterAttached("MyAP", _
                GetType(Integer), GetType(MainPage), _
                New PropertyMetaData(0))
```

SETTING ATTACHED PROPERTIES

You already know how to set attached properties in XAML. You refer to it like a static property with the name of the defining class and the property name: `Grid.Row = "0"`. That won't work in code. The property isn't defined on the object you're setting it on, so the compiler won't know what to do with it.

Instead, you can either call the `get` and `set` methods defined for the attached property, or you can call `SetValue()` or `GetValue()` directly:

TO SET AN ATTACHED PROPERTY IN CODE:

You pass the name of the object on which you're setting the property to the method.

`SomeElement.SetValue(MyClass.MyAPProperty)` OR `MyClass.SetMyAP(SomeElement, 3)`

Pass the owning type and property name (remember the "Property" bit) to SetValue().

TO RETRIEVE THE VALUE OF AN ATTACHED PROPERTY IN CODE:

The syntax is the same; just replace "Set" with "Get".

`SomeElement.GetValue(MyClass.MyAPProperty)` OR `MyClass.GetMyAP(SomeElement, 3)`

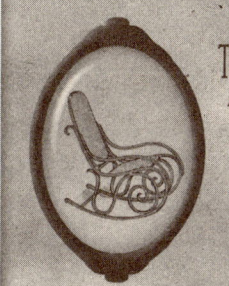

TAKE A BREAK

There's still a little more to learn about dependency properties, but we've covered a lot, so why don't you take a quick break before we move on to callbacks and adding owners?

REVIEW

Can you answer the following questions based on what you've learned about dependency properties?

Add an attached property to your project. (It isn't cheating to use the code snippet.)

What is a "wrapping property"?

What two methods should you call inside the POCO property method associated with a dependency property?

Should you do anything else inside the POCO get and set accessors? Why or why not?

Can you define a wrapper for an attached property?

What's the keyboard shortcut to insert a code snippet?

DEPENDENCY PROPERTY CALLBACKS

By and large the dependency property system takes care of itself. You create the property using either `Register()` or `RegisterAttached()`, and you're good to go. But sometimes you need a little more control, and there are two ways you can hook into the system via callbacks. If you're familiar with registering callback methods, there probably won't be any surprises here, but the syntax is slightly different depending on what you're doing. We'll explore both callback methods in this section.

RESPOND TO PROPERTY VALUE CHANGES

Change notification is a fundamental part of the dependency property system (and crucial for data binding), and you don't need to do anything for your custom dependency properties to participate. But sometimes you need to take additional actions when a property changes. You might need to change the value of some other property of the object, for example, or coerce the new value to a specified range.

In situations like this, you can register a property changed callback method with the dependency property.

CONTROL THE DEFAULT VALUE

You've seen that you can pass a simple default value to the `PropertyMetadata` constructor inside the `Register()` or `RegisterAttached()` method, but sometimes you'll want to do something a little more sophisticated, particularly when you're dealing with complex reference types.

The `CreateDefaultValueCallback` can be used in these situations, but you can't pass it to the `PropertyMetadata` constructor; you have to call the `Create()` factory method instead. We'll see how in a few pages.

PROPERTYCHANGEDCALLBACK

You'll use the `PropertyChangedCallback` whenever you want to respond to property value changes. The syntax is what you'd expect from a .NET delegate:

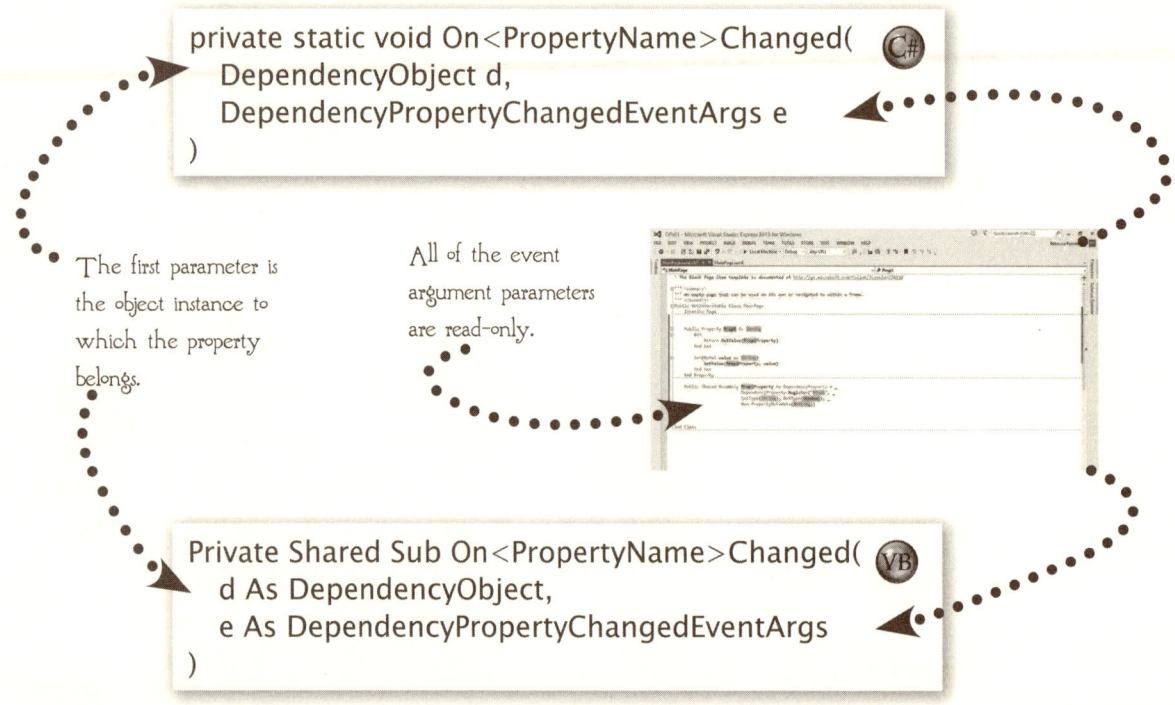

```
private static void On<PropertyName>Changed(
    DependencyObject d,
    DependencyPropertyChangedEventArgs e
)
```
C#

The first parameter is the object instance to which the property belongs.

All of the event argument parameters are read-only.

```
Private Shared Sub On<PropertyName>Changed(
    d As DependencyObject,
    e As DependencyPropertyChangedEventArgs
)
```
VB

MAKE A NOTE

Even though the **OldValue** and **NewValue** properties of the event argument are read-only, it's possible to adjust the value of the changed property by accessing it through the object passed to the callback.

Be very, very careful about doing this. Changing the property will trigger another loop through the property calculation pipeline (and another visit to the callback). That could mean a performance hit, and potentially you could get lost in an endless loop.

CREATEDEFAULTVALUECALLBACK

We've seen that you can pass a default value for your dependency property to the PropertyMetadata constructor, and that works well for value types. If you want to set default values for a reference type, you'll need to use the CreateDefaultValueCallback. The syntax is even simpler than a PropertyChangedCallback:

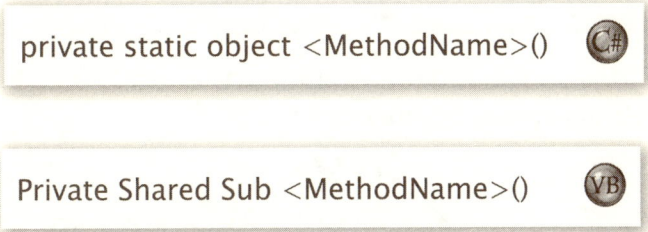

```
private static object <MethodName>()
```

```
Private Shared Sub <MethodName>()
```

Again, be careful about what you do in a CreateDefaultValueCallback. Typically you'll just instantiate the object, set whatever properties need to be changed from the defaults set by the constructor, and then return the object. Anything trickier than that and you'll need to start worrying about which UI thread you're working on. (Personally, I work very hard to avoid code that requires that kind of consideration.)

PUT ON YOUR THINKING HAT

Imagine you're defining a TextBox dependency property. (Yes, it's an odd thing to do. But it's perfectly legal.)

Write a CreateDefaultValueCallback() method called CreateTB() that sets the initial TextBox.Text property to "Type something here" and a PropertyChangedCallback() called OnTextChanged() that sets the TextBox.FontStyle to FontStyle.Italic if the text has been changed.

(We'll discuss XAML typography and the FontStyle enumeration in detail Chapter 10. For now, just accept that it does what you expect it to do: It makes the text italic.)

HOW'D YOU DO?

It doesn't matter if your syntax is a little more concise than mine (it could hardly be less), as long as the basic functionality is the same.

```csharp
public static void OnTextChanged(DependencyObject d,
    DependencyPropertyChangedEventArgs e)
{
    TextBox tb = d as TextBox;
    if (tb != null)
    {
        if (e.OldValue != e.NewValue)
        {
            tb.FontStyle = Windows.UI.Text.FontStyle.Italic;
        }
    {
}
```

It's always best to check that the value actually has changed. In this case, the user might have typed the same text into the TextBox.

```csharp
public static TextBox CreateTB()
{
    TextBox tb = new TextBox();
    tb.Text = "Type something here";
    return tb;
}
```

Nothing at all tricky going on here...

It's always best to check that the value actually has changed. In this case, the user might have typed the same text into the TextBox.

```vb
Public Shared Sub OnTextChanged(d As DependencyObject, _
     e As DependencyPropertyChangedEventArgs)
   Dim tb As TextBox = d As TextBox
   If (tb <> Null Then
      if (e.OldValue <> e.NewValue Then
         tb.FontStyle = Windows.UI.Text.FontStyle.Italic
End Sub
```

```vb
Public Shared Sub TextBox CreateTB()
   Dim tb As TextBox = New TextBox()
   tb.Text = "Type something here"
   Return tb;
End Sub
```

Nothing at all tricky going on here…

REGISTERING CALLBACKS

There's nothing at all unusual in the syntax for creating dependency property callbacks. They're standard .NET delegates. Registering them, however, is a little odd. The PropertyMetadata class provides two overrides to its constructor, and a Create() factory method with four overrides. Which one you use depends on what you need to do.

PROPERTYMETADATA CONSTRUCTORS

The PropertyMetadata class provides two constructors:

1. PropertyMetadata(Object)
   This is the one we've been using inside the Register() methods. It accepts a single Object that will be the default value of the property.

2. PropertyMetadata(Object, PropertyChangedCallback)
   The second version accepts both the default value and a reference to your PropertyChangedCallback() method.

CREATE() METHODS

1. Create(Object)
   Like the first version of the constructor, this version of the Create() method accepts a single Object that will be the default value of the property.

2. Create(Object, PropertyChangedCallback)
   This version is identical to the second version of the constructor. It accepts the default value and the PropertyChangedCallback() method.

3. Create(CreateDefaultValueCallback)
   This is the version you'll use if you only want to register a default value callback, not a property changed callback.

4. Create(CreateDefaultValueCallback, PropertyChangedCallback)
   This last version is what you need if you want to register both callbacks.

PUT ON YOUR THINKING HAT

For each of the following situations, pick a method for creating an instance of PropertyMetadata and write a snippet of code. Assume the simple defaul value is 10, the property changed callback is named DpChanged() and the create default value callback is named DbCreate().

You want to set a simple default value:

You want to set a simple default value and a property changed callback:

You want to set a default value callback:

You want to set a default value callback and a property changed callback:

HOW'D YOU DO?

You want to set a simple default value:

You can use the first constructor, or the first version of the Create() method:

    PropertyMetadata pm = new PropertyMetadata(10);

or

    PropertyMetadata pm = PropertyMetadata.Create(10);

You want to set a simple default value and a property changed callback:

You can use the second version of the constructor or the Create() method:

    PropertyMetadata pm = new PropertyMetadata(10, DpChanged);

or

    PropertyMetadata pm = PropertyMetadata.Create(10, DpChanged);

You want to set a default value callback:

You have to use the Create() method to set a default value callback:

    PropertyMetadata pm = PropertyMetadata.Create(DpCreate);

You want to set a default value callback and a property changed callback:

Again, you need to use the Create() method:

    PropertyMetadata pm = PropertyMetadata.Create(DpCreate, DpChanged);

You want to set a simple default value:

> You can use the first constructor, or the first version of the Create() method:

> pm As PropertyMetadata = new PropertyMetadata(10)

or

> pm As PropertyMetadata = PropertyMetadata.Create(10)

You want to set a simple default value and a property changed callback:

> You can use the second version of the constructor or the Create() method:

> pm As PropertyMetadata = new PropertyMetadata(10, DpChanged)

or

> pm As PropertyMetadata = PropertyMetadata.Create(10, DpChanged)

You want to set a default value callback:

> You have to use the Create() method to set a default value callback:

> pm As PropertyMetadata = PropertyMetadata.Create(DpCreate)

You want to set a default value callback and a property changed callback:

> Again, you need to use the Create() method:

> pm As PropertyMetadata = PropertyMetadata.Create(DpCreate, DpChanged)

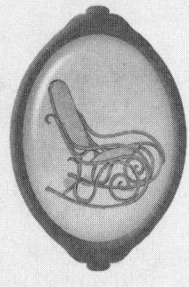

TAKE A BREAK

There's always more to know, but we've finished with dependency properties for the time being. (We'll look at them again, of course.) Why don't you take a break before you complete the Review and we start looking at events?

REVIEW

Why should you only use GetValue() and SetValue() when working with dependency properties?

What two callbacks are available to hook into the dependency property system?

What main functionality do dependency properties add to POCO properties?

If a dependency property has both an inherited and a local value, which one will take precedence in calculating its final value?

You can always use PropertyMetadata.Create() to create an instance of the PropertyMetadata class. When must you do so?

Congratulations! You've finished the chapter. Take a minute to think about what you've accomplished before you move on to the next one...

List three things you learned in this chapter:

①

②

③

Why do you think you need to know these things in order to develop Win8 apps?

Is there anything in this chapter that you think you need to understand in more detail? If so, what are you going to do about that?

Events & Input

8

In the last chapter we saw that dependency properties add functionality to POCO properties in order to make certain tasks (particularly binding) much easier. Routed events, although **conceptually much simpler** than dependency properties, also extend their POCO equivalents, and they make certain tasks easier. Well, one task. They solve the problem of handling input events when UI widgets are composible, which you'll remember most XAML widgets are. As we'll see, **routed events bubble** up the logical tree, allowing an event to be handled by the widget that is interested in it. It's more convenient to create an event handler for a ComboBox, for example, instead of the individual TextBox controls that it contains.

In Win8 XAML, routed events are defined by the UIElement class, and **they are all input events**. As you might expect in a touch-first environment, the input model is a little different from what we've grown used to in a mouse-first system. But different in a good way. As we'll see, the unified WinRT Pointer API insulates you from the tool the user chooses to initiate an action, whether finger, mouse, or stylus. You can simply respond to their intent.

We'll start the chapter by examining routed events in the abstract. You'll find the process familiar after your work with dependency properties. Then we'll explore the events exposed by the UIElement class and how they map to the gestures and semantics of application interaction. At the end of the chapter, we'll take a quick look at some of the lower-level classes and the support that WinRT provides for touch and gesture recognition.

FITTING IT IN

Here's how this chapter fits in to the book as a whole...

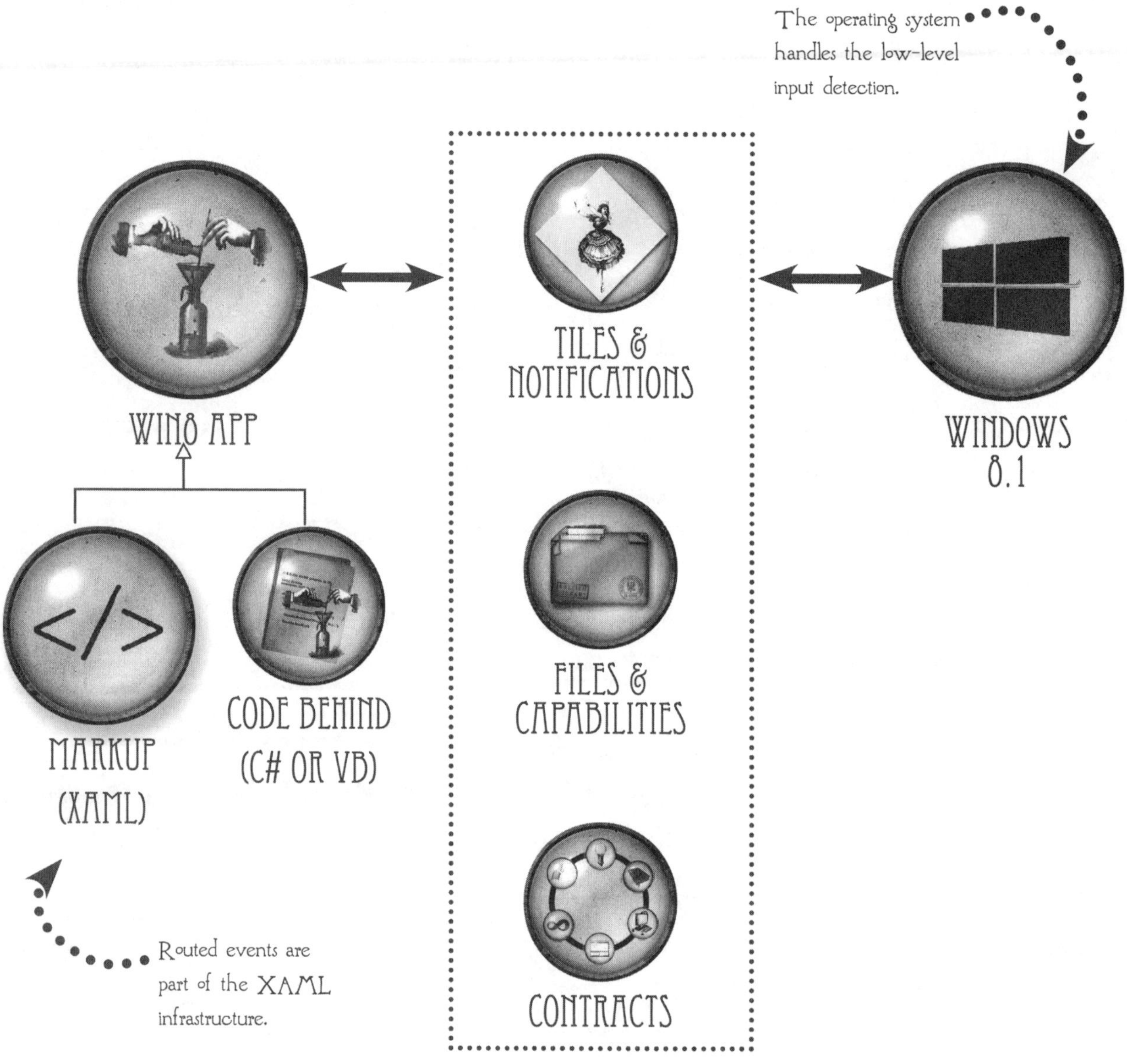

The operating system handles the low-level input detection.

WIN8 APP ↔ TILES & NOTIFICATIONS ↔ WINDOWS 8.1

MARKUP (XAML)

CODE BEHIND (C# OR VB)

FILES & CAPABILITIES

CONTRACTS

Routed events are part of the XAML infrastructure.

TASK LIST

In this chapter we'll explore Win8 app events, specifically the routed events that extend their POCO equivalents, and the gesture support that's specific to a touch-first environment.

ROUTED EVENTS

Routed events extend standard POCO events in much the same way that dependency properties extend POCO properties. But there's one major exception: you cannot define your own.

INPUT EVENTS

Next we'll explore the input events that UIElement exposes, and the pointer API that simplifies development when touch, mouse, stylus, and keyboard all have equal status.

THE INPUT API

At the end of the chapter we'll take a (very quick) look at the API that Win8 XAML exposes for input events.

ROUTED EVENTS...

Most applications are event-driven, and the POCO event system works pretty well. But compare it to this real-world situation in a restaurant:

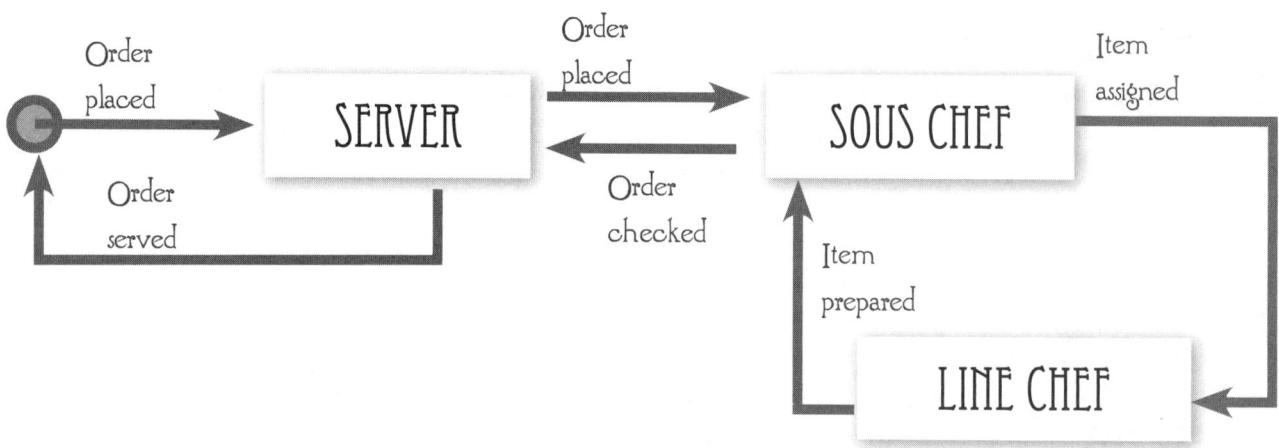

From a customer's point of view, eating at a restaurant is pretty simple. You choose what you want, tell the waiter, and get the dish. But in reality there are a few (sometimes a lot more) steps.

In a traditional kitchen, the sous chef (pronounced "sue chef") checks orders before they are assigned to line chefs to be prepared and then checks the dishes before they are served to customers.

If we were modelling this process, both the **OrderPlaced**, and **ItemPrepared** events would be sent first to the **SousChef** class, which would have to raise additional events for the next step in the process.

Every **LineChef** would have to register a handler for the **ItemAssigned** event, and the **SousChef** class would have to register a handler for the **ItemPrepared** event of every **LineChef** (which means the **SousChef** would have to know about every instance of **LineChef**, which raises issues of its own).

Starting to look pretty complicated, isn't it?

...ADDRESS A PROBLEM

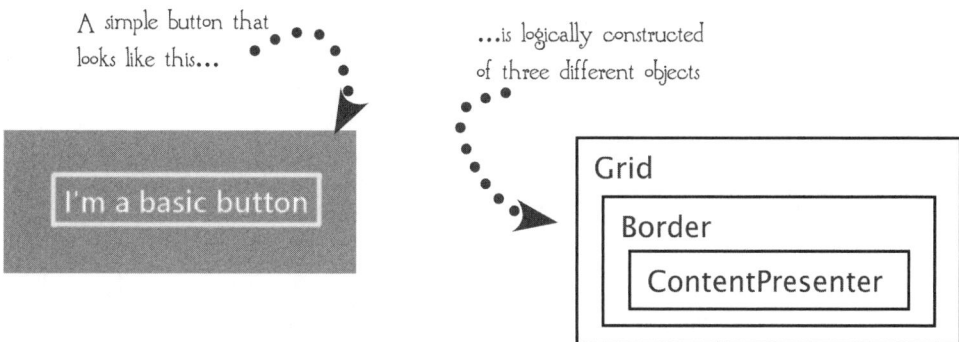

Now imagine the same situation applied to a Win8 app.

Remember that XAML controls are composed of other XAML elements. The default structure of a XAML **Button** consists of a **Grid** that contains a **Border**, that in turn contains a **ContentPresenter**. (We'll talk about the **ContentPresenter** when we explore templates in Chapter 11. It's just a placeholder element that displays whatever you've defined as the **Content** of your **Button**.)

When a user clicks the button, the mouse might actually be over any of these objects. So who raises the event? Do you *really* want to register the same event handler for the **Button**, the **Grid**, the **Border**, and the **ContentPresenter**? And as we'll see when we explore control templates, there's no guarantee that those are the elements that comprise the button, so you'd have to query that, and....No, I didn't think so.

And what if the **Button.Content** is set to a **ListBox** that by default is made up of a **Grid**, a **Border**, a **ScrollViewer**, and a **StackPanel** with all their individual components? And then there are the elements that make up the individual items the **ListBox** displays. Just how many times do you want to register that handler?

Of course, the architects of XAML thought of this problem, and they have a clean solution: routed events. A ROUTED EVENT can travel up the element tree, and it can be handled at the most appropriate level. Let the **Button** raise the **Click** event. That's sensible, efficient, and separates the logical action (the button was clicked) from the ugly details (the mouse was over a **ListItem** inside a **StackPanel** inside a **ScrollViewer** inside a...)

EVENT BUBBLING

Win8 XAML has its share of direct events that are triggered on the element that receives the input, but the routed events that are exposed by `UIElement` (and its descendants) will bubble up the element tree until they find an element that handles them (or they run out of elements).

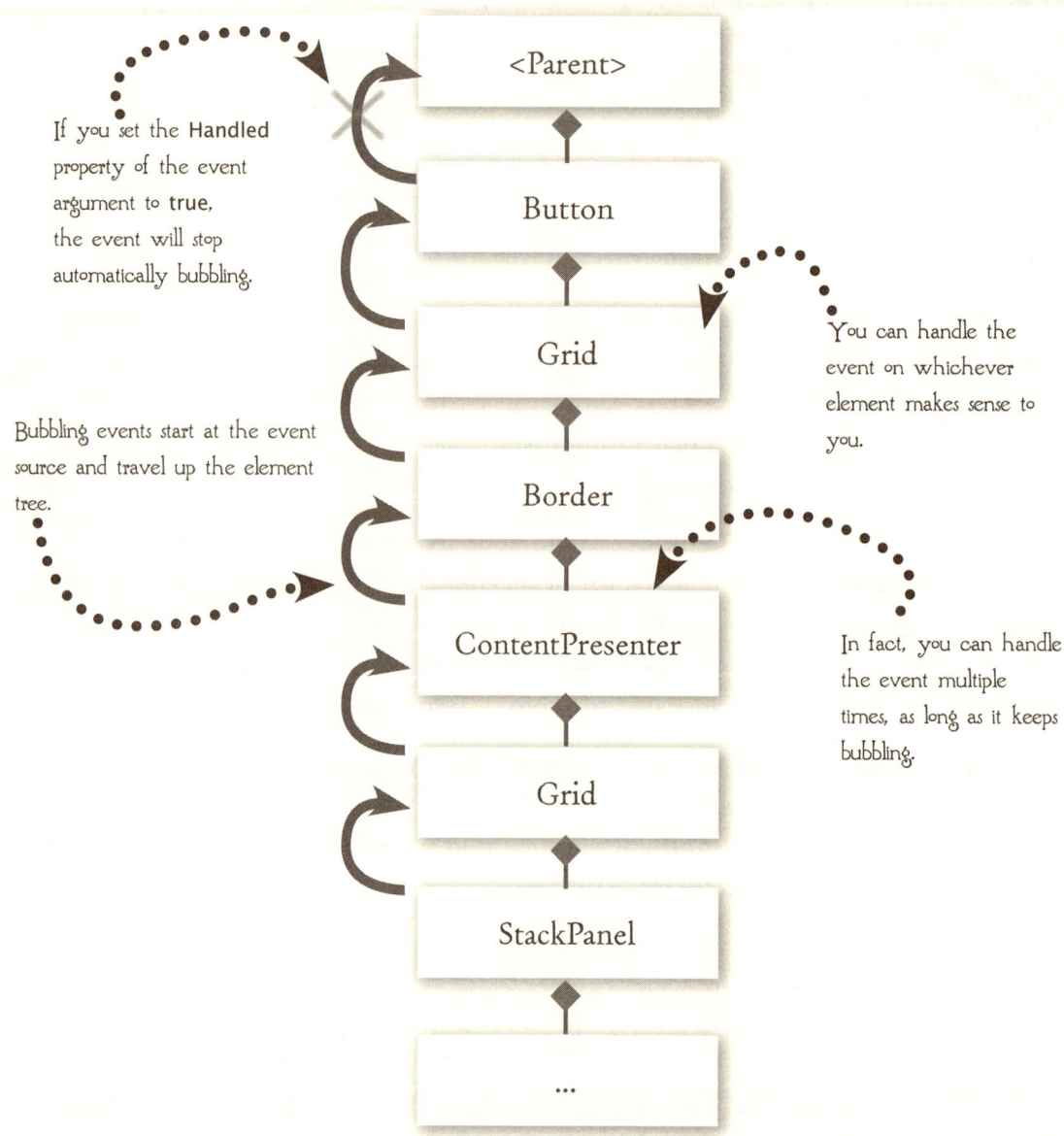

ROUTED EVENT HANDLERS

I think this might come as good news: You can't create routed events in WinS XAML, and the basics of handling them are no different than you're used to with standard POCO events. (In other words, there's very little you need to learn here.)

The event handlers for routed events look a whole lot like handlers for standard .NET events. They must match the delegate defined for the event, and all the delegates have the the same basic pattern, so all the event handlers have the same basic pattern:

Event handlers don't have to be private, but it's considered best practice.

InstanceName_Event is the convention for naming event handlers throughout .NET, but it isn't mandatory.

```
private void InstanceName_Event(object sender, <eventArgs> e)
```
C#

```
Private Sub InstanceName_Event(sender As Object, e As <eventArgs>)
```
VB

The event arguments class for a standard .NET event is an instance of **EventArgs** or a class that descends from it. The equivalent for routed events is **RoutedEventArgs** or a class that descends from it.

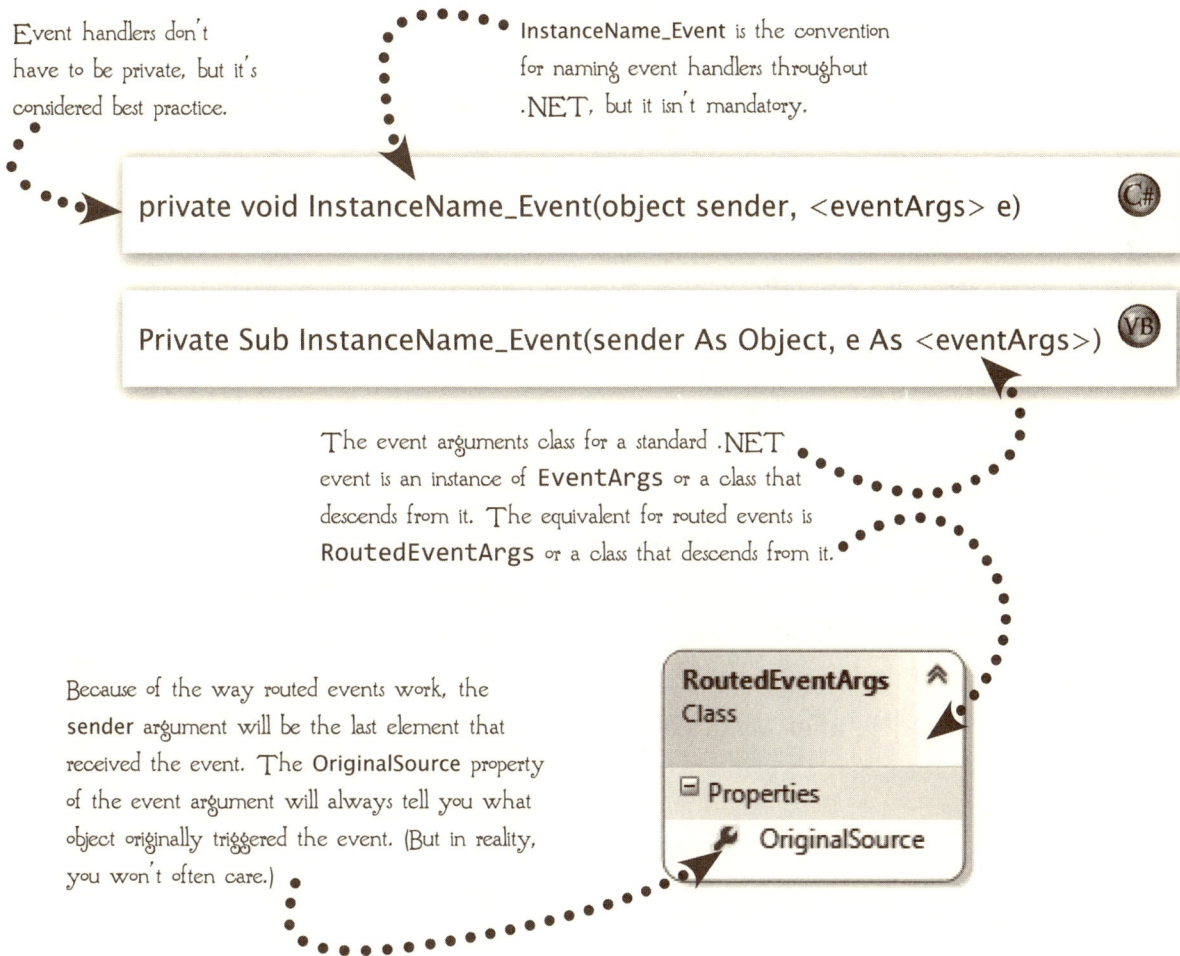

Because of the way routed events work, the **sender** argument will be the last element that received the event. The **OriginalSource** property of the event argument will always tell you what object originally triggered the event. (But in reality, you won't often care.)

REGISTERING HANDLERS, PART 1

Just like the event handler itself, the syntax for registering event handlers is identical for routed events and .NET events.

XAML

In XAML, you treat the event like a property and use attribute syntax to register the event. Intellisense will help you create a handler if you type the event name in the markup, or you can double-click the event in the Properties Window. (We've been using that last method.)

```
<MyElement x:Name="MyEl" SomeEvent="MyEl_SomeEvent" />
```

C#

C# uses the standard += operator:

```
MyEl.SomeEvent += MyEl_SomeEvent;
```

VISUAL BASIC

You can use the **Handles** keyword to register the event handler in Visual Basic, but the **AddHandler** method is recommended because it better supports the Designer/Developer workflow:

```
AddHandler MyEl.SomeEvent, AddressOf MyEl_SomeEvent
```

KINDA SORTA ROUTED EVENTS

From time to time I've talked about features of the XAML Framework that "just work"—they do what you'd expect them to do in the way you'd expect them to do it. Unfortunately, routed events aren't one of those features. You won't always get the events you're expecting.

To get a sense of how this does (and doesn't) work, let's look at a simple event: clicking a button.

We all know that conceptually buttons get clicked, and as you'd expect, the XAML **Button** class exposes a **Click** event. But at the physical level, there are actually four independent things that happen:

THE POINTER ENTERS THE BUTTON
The first thing that happens is that the pointer (in XAML, the mouse, stylus, and finger are all considered pointers) enters the bounds of the **Button**. That's represented by a `PointerEntered` event.

THE POINTER PRESSES THE BUTTON
Assuming the user doesn't change their mind, the next thing that happens is that the button gets pressed. That's represented by a `PointerPressed` event. (There might be some moving and holding going on, but let's ignore that for the time being.)

THE POINTER RELEASES THE BUTTON
As long as the user doesn't move the pointer outside the bounds of the **Button** before they let go, the next event will be `PointerReleased`.

THE POINTER LEAVES THE BUTTON
And finally, the pointer will move off the **Button**, which is represented by a `PointerExited` event.

TESTING EVENTS

Okay, you already know that what should happen in theory isn't going to happen in practice, because if it did I wouldn't be talking about it. But I don't want you to take my word for it, so let's build a little routed event exerciser. Start with the basics:

CREATE A PROJECT AND LAY OUT THE PAGE

Start by creating a new blank application (I called mine **RoutedEvents**) and adding some elements to the **MainPage.xaml**. Be sure to give the **Grid** and the **Listbox** names so we can refer to them in code.

Add two column definitions to the layout **Grid**. It doesn't really matter how you divide up the space.

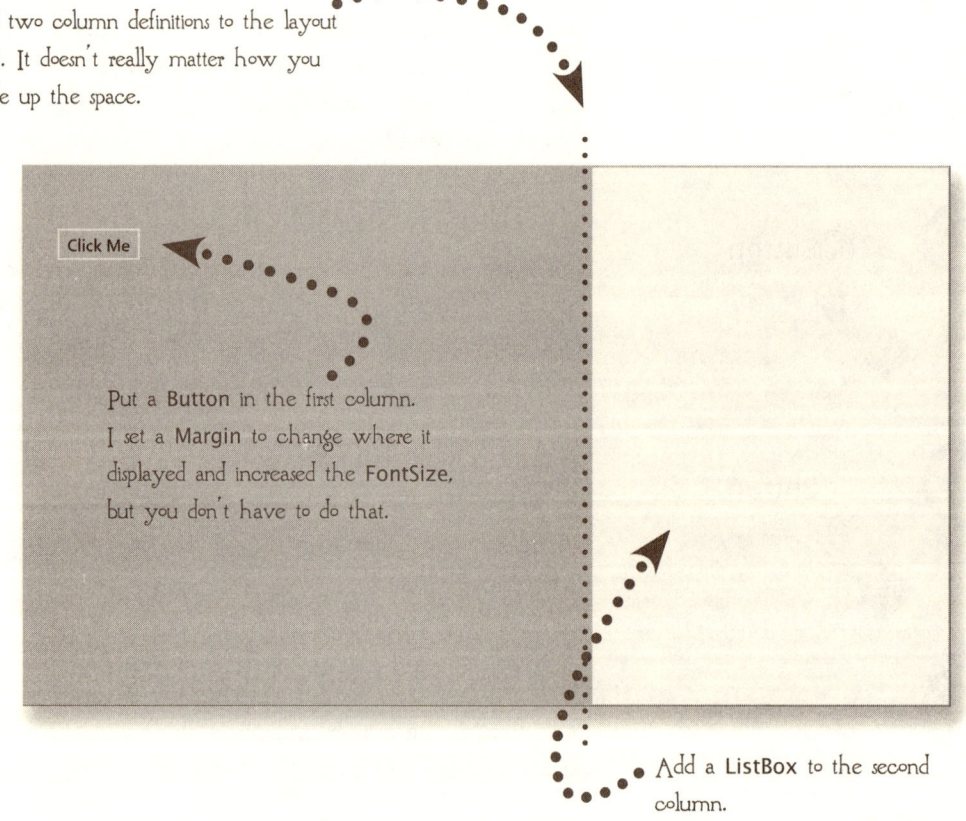

Put a **Button** in the first column. I set a **Margin** to change where it displayed and increased the **FontSize**, but you don't have to do that.

Add a **ListBox** to the second column.

② Now we need to add some event handlers to add the events and the object that triggered them to the ListBox. Each handler will execute the same basic code:

> <ListBoxName>.Items.Add(sender.ToString() + " <event name>")

Because we'll be invoking the handler from more than one element, the normal Instance_Event naming convention isn't appropriate. I named each of my handlers <EventName>Test, but of course you can pick any name you like.

You want to assign event handlers to the Grid and the Button for each of the following events: PointerEntered, PointerPressed, PointerReleased, and PointerExited. You'll also want to add a handler for the Click event of the Button. (The Grid doesn't have a Click event.)

The easiest way to do that is to create them in the Properties window of the XAML Designer. Just type the name of the handler and press Enter, and Visual Studio will create the correct method signature for you and take you right to it in the Code Editor. Once the handler is created on one of the objects, you can add it to the other using XAML attribute syntax.

PUT ON YOUR THINKING HAT

Go ahead and create the project. (I called mine RoutedEvents.) Lay out the XAML, and then create the handlers for all five events. Make sure that the pointer event handlers are assigned to the appropriate events for both the Grid and the Button. (Only the Button gets the Click handler.)

When you run it, click on the Grid (outside of the Button) and then click the Button. What events does the ListBox report?

HOW'D YOU DO?

Here's my XAML. I've left out the irrelevant formatting, and I haven't included the event handlers, because Visual Studio will do most of the work for you, but of course you can check the sample project if you have any trouble.

```xml
<Grid x:Name="REGrid" ...
      PointerEntered="PointerEnteredTest"
      PointerExited="PointerExitedTest"
      PointerPressed="PointerPressedTest"
      PointerReleased="PointerReleasedTest">
  <Grid.ColumnDefinitions>
    ...
  </Grid.ColumnDefinitions>
  <Button ...
      PointerEntered="PointerEnteredTest"
      PointerExited="PointerExitedTest"
      PointerPressed="PointerPressedTest"
      PointerReleased="PointerReleasedTest"
      Click="ClickTest">
    Click Me
  </Button>
  <ListBox x:Name="REList" ...
      Grid.Row="0" Grid.Column="1" FontSize="24"/>
</Grid>
```

MOMMY, THE BAD BUTTON ATE MY EVENTS...

Well, you knew it wasn't going to work, and it didn't. Here are the events that were reported on my system when I clicked in the Grid and then clicked in the Button:

1. Grid — Pointer Entered
2. Grid — Pointer Pressed
3. Grid — Pointer Released
4. Button — Pointer Entered
5. Button — Clicked
6. Button — Pointer Exited
7. Grid — Pointer Exited

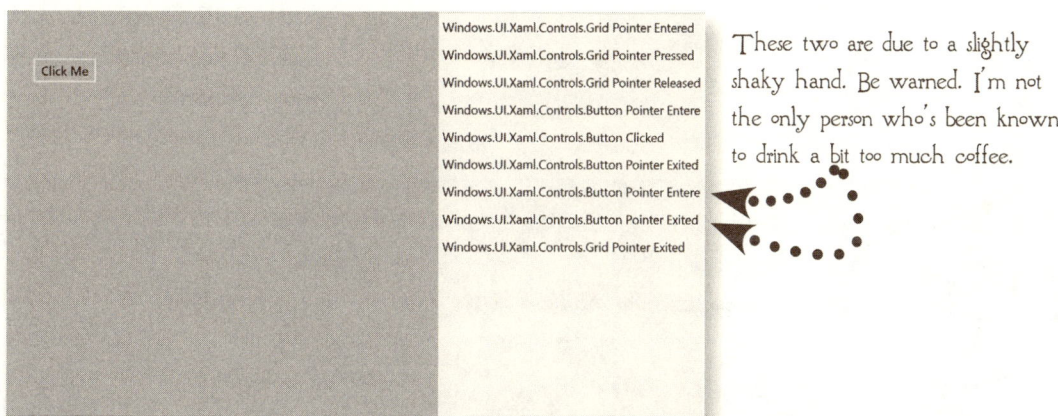

These two are due to a slightly shaky hand. Be warned. I'm not the only person who's been known to drink a bit too much coffee.

As you can see, the Button element didn't report the physical PointerPressed or PointerReleased events; it turned them into the conceptual Click event instead. This happens a lot in the Framework, and as with the Button, it almost always makes your life easier.

Almost always. Sometimes you need those physical events. And sometimes you'll want to stop events from bubbling any further. Don't panic. All is not lost. Keep reading...

291

HANDLED EVENTS

It's not declared on the base `RoutedEventArgs` class, but most of the classes that descend from it, like the `PointerRoutedEventArgs` that's used by all the `Pointer` events, declare a `Boolean` property named `Handled`, and you can use it in your own code.

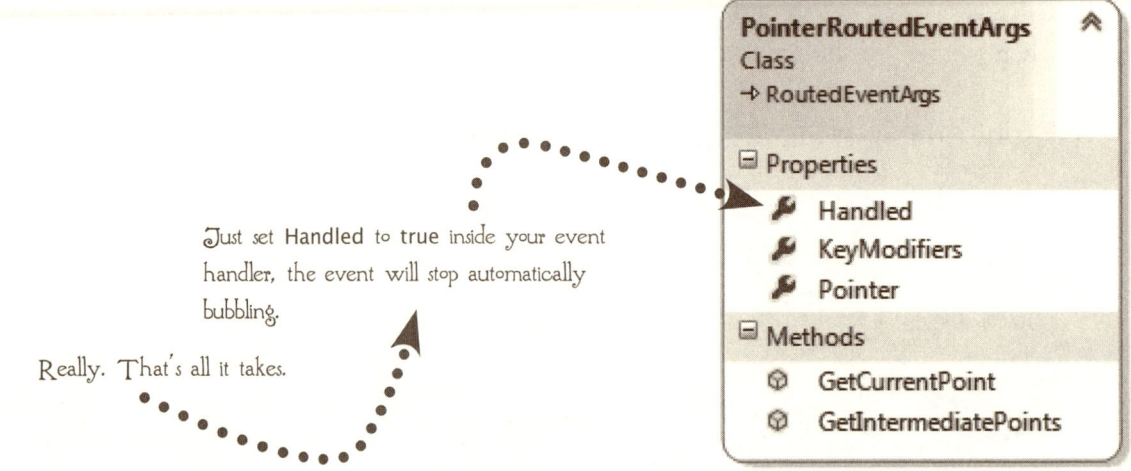

Just set `Handled` to true inside your event handler, the event will stop automatically bubbling.

Really. That's all it takes.

IN MY OPINION

The routed event system as it's implemented in Win8 XAML is not a shining example of class design.

The `AddHandler()` method can be used to attach an event handler to any event with an event identifier. `AddHandler()` knows about the `Handled` property, but not all routed events do. The event identifiers required to use `AddHandler()` are only declared for `UIElement` routed events, despite the fact that events like `ButtonBase.Click` have routed event handlers, which would lead one to believe that they're routed internally.

The base `RoutedEventArgs` class doesn't expose a `Handled` property, and some events like `GetFocus()` use `RoutedEventArgs` directly. That means that the whole "set `Handled` and trigger a conceptually higher event" pattern might, or might not, work for you.

But then, you can't create custom routed events in Win8 XAML, so the pattern isn't particularly useful anyway. (And I'm still waiting for an explanation for *that* constraint that actually explains the constraint and doesn't include irrelevant references to Silverlight workarounds.)

REGISTERING HANDLERS, PART 2

When a control consumes a `UIElement` routed event, like the `PointerPressed` and `PointerReleased` events that the `Button` changes to a `Click` or the `KeyDown` and `KeyUp` events that the `TextBox` handles, you can still get access to the events by registering your event handler using the `UIElement.AddHandler()` method.

```
public void AddHandler(RoutedEvent routedEvent,
                       object handler,
                       bool handledEventsToo)
```

The routed event identifier works like a dependency property identifier: It's the name of the event with the word Event appended to it, e.g., `PointerPressedEvent`.

```
Public Sub AddHandler(routedEvent as RoutedEvent,
                      handler As Object,
                      handledEventsToo As Boolean)
```

If you set `handledEventsToo` to true, your element will catch the `UIElement` events that have been consumed by their children.

Here are some examples:

```
MyElement.AddHandler(KeyDownEvent,
                     new KeyEventHandler(myHandler),
                     true)
```

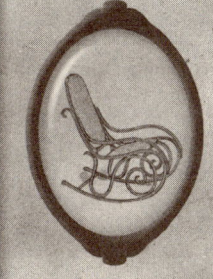

TAKE A BREAK

That's it for our overview of routed events. Why don't you take a break before you complete the Review and we move on to the semantics of Win8 gestures?

293

REVIEW

Can you answer the following questions based on what you've learned about routed events in Win8 XAML?

Change the routed events project so that the Grid receives PointerPressed events generated on the Button. (But make sure it only receives them once.)

Which way do routed events travel?

What property controls whether a routed event continues to travel?

What's the easiest way to determine the syntax of a routed event handler? How else might you do it?

Does the syntax for adding a routed event handler in code differ from adding a handler for a standard .NET event? If so, how?

What class declares the input routed events and the AddHandler() method?

INPUT EVENTS

Before we start exploring input events in detail, we need to be very clear about how gestures map to actions in order to avoid surprising (or worse, confusing) users. We took a quick look at gestures Chapter 1, but just to remind you, here's the basic vocabulary of the Windows 8.1 touch language:

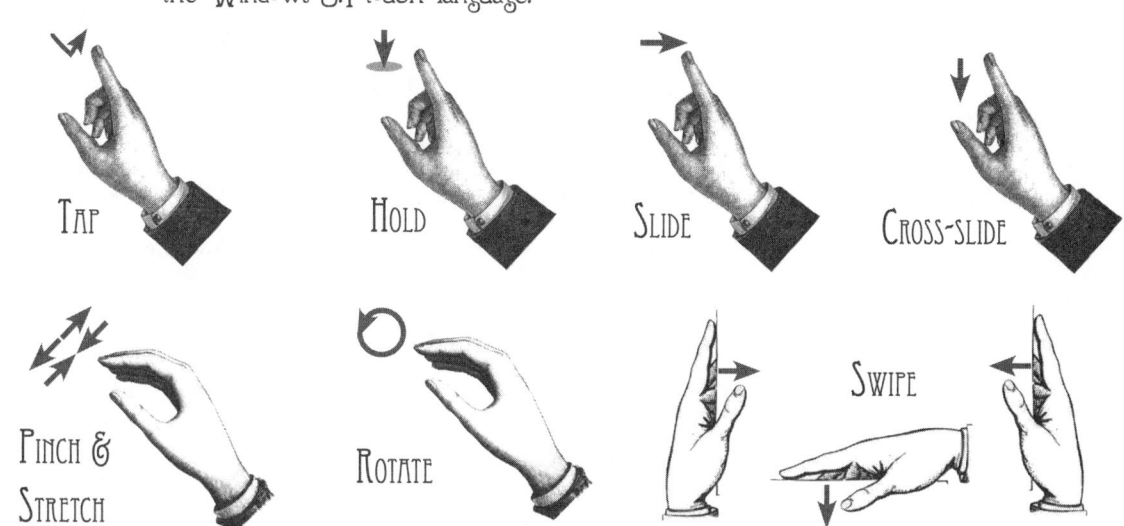

TOUCH	MOUSE & STYLUS	KEYBOARD
Tap	Double-click	Enter
Hold	Right-click	Menu key
Slide	Drag	Arrow keys, Page Up or Page Down
Cross-Slide	Left-click	Spacebar
Pinch & Stretch	Mouse Wheel	Ctrl+Plus and Ctrl+Minus
Rotate	Ctrl+Shift+Mouse Wheel	UI Command
Swipe from left	Hover in upper-left corner	Windows Logo Key+Tab
Swipe from top or bottom	Right-click (not on an item)	Windows Logo Key+Z
Swipe from right	Hover in either right corner	Windows Logo Key+C
Swip from top to bottom	Drag from top to bottom	Alt+F4

UIELEMENT EVENTS

The physical UI events that comprise the Windows 8.1 gesture language are all exposed on the `UIElement` class, and they're all routed events. We've used a few of them already, but here's the full list:

- DoubleTapped
- DragEnter
- DragLeave
- DragOver
- Drop
- GotFocus
- Holding
- KeyDown
- KeyUp
- LostFocus
- ManipulationCompleted
- ManipulationDelta
- ManipulationIntertiaStarting
- ManipulationStarted
- ManipulationStarting
- PointerCanceled
- PointerCaptureLost
- PointerEntered
- PointerExited
- PointerMoved
- PointerPressed
- PointerReleased
- PointerWheelChanged
- RightTapped
- Tapped

With the exception of the Manipulation... events, the list probably looks pretty familiar to you from other development environments. But it doesn't map very well to the gesture language defined on the previous page. There's a **Tapped** event, and **Holding** is there, but nothing resembling a swipe or a pinch. How do you deal with that?

Well, the good news is that you'll hardly ever need to. The XAML control set already handles all the basic gestures, and handles them well. Where it's appropriate, the controls raise semantic-level events like **Button.Click()** or **Selector.SelectionChanged()** that are simpler to work with.

When you do need to hook into the user input, it's normally to extend the behavior of a control within the context of your application, and the **UIElement** events almost always provide enough information and flexibility for that. (Once you get your head around them.)

When all else fails, WinRT provides very sophsticated support for input outside the XAML framework. (We'll take a quick look at how that works at the end of this chapter.)

SORTING EVENTS

Any given physical event will generate multiple UIElement events. As a general rule, you want to work at the highest level of abstraction that will allow you to do what you need to do. The events exposed by UIElement actually exist at several levels, and sorting them out is a useful step in deciding which one to use in any given situation.

SEMANTIC EVENTS

Events like **Tapped**, or the control events like **TextBox.TextChanged**, are SEMANTIC EVENTS. They describe what the input meant rather than what physically happened. UIElement doesn't expose semantic events.

GESTURE EVENTS

At the next level down are what Microsoft calls GESTURE EVENTS. They're the events, like **Tapped**, that correspond to the gestures of the touch language. Not all touch language gestures are available as UIElement events, and the ones that are exposed are all single-point interactions (so no pinch or zoom).

INTERACTION EVENTS

INTERACTION EVENTS represent (relatively) simple physical interactions. They include things like **KeyDown** and **PointerPressed**.

MANIPULATION EVENTS

At the lowest, most complete, and most complex level are the MANIPULATION EVENTS. They're the ones you'll need if you want to respond to multi-touch input or accomodate things like velocity.

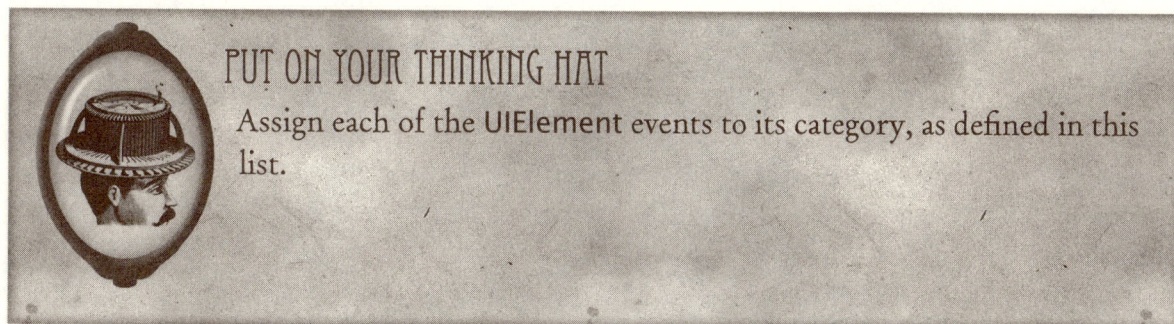

PUT ON YOUR THINKING HAT
Assign each of the UIElement events to its category, as defined in this list.

HOW'D YOU DO?

Most of these were pretty obvious, but did you make a different decision about **GetFocus** and **LostFocus**? I consider them gestures, but you might have decided they were interactions. That's fine. What's important is that you develop a useful model, not that your model exactly matches mine (or anybody else's, for that matter).

SEMANTIC EVENTS

UIElement doesn't expose any semantic events; they're exposed by controls.

GESTURE EVENTS

- DoubleTapped
- GotFocus
- Holding
- LostFocus
- RightTapped
- Tapped

INTERACTION EVENTS

- DragEnter
- DragLeave
- DragOver
- Drop
- KeyDown
- KeyUp
- PointerCanceled
- PointerCaptureLost
- PointerEntered
- PointerExited
- PointerMoved
- PointerPressed
- PointerReleased
- PointerWheelChanged

MANIPULATION EVENTS

- ManipulationCompleted
- ManipulationDelta
- ManipulationIntertiaStarting
- ManipulationStarted
- ManipulationStarting

THE INPUT APIS

WinRT supports some very sophisticated input handling. Let's start with pointers. `PointerPressed` seems like such a simple event, doesn't it? You don't even have to worry about whether the "pointer" in question was a finger, a mouse, or a stylus. And you can treat it very simply, if that suits your needs. But look at how rich the object graph is (and the diagram isn't complete, of course!):

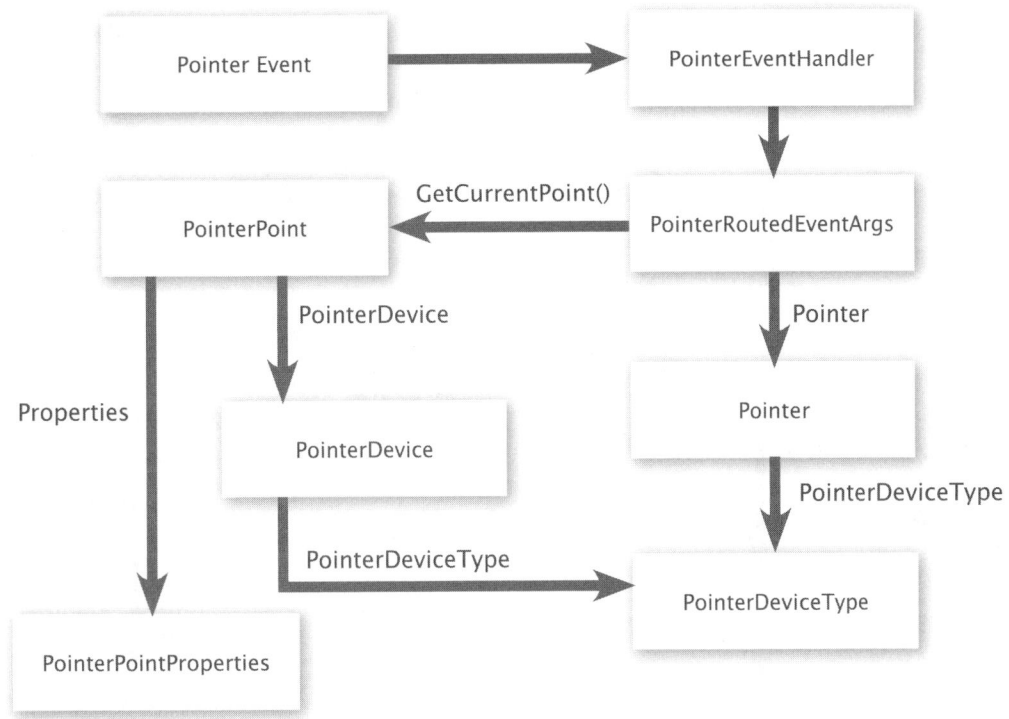

MAKE A NOTE

There's a lot of theory and very little coding in the rest of this chapter. I've tried to avoid that, but in this case, while I want you to know that the functionality is available and where to look for it should you need it, the reality is that you won't need it very often. There are plenty of simple examples available on Microsoft's Web sites and a non-trivial example would be way beyond scope of our discussion.

DOWN THE RABBIT HOLE

Your first step down the rabbit hole of the Pointer API is the instance of `PointerRoutedEventArgs` that all of the `UIElement` pointer events receive.

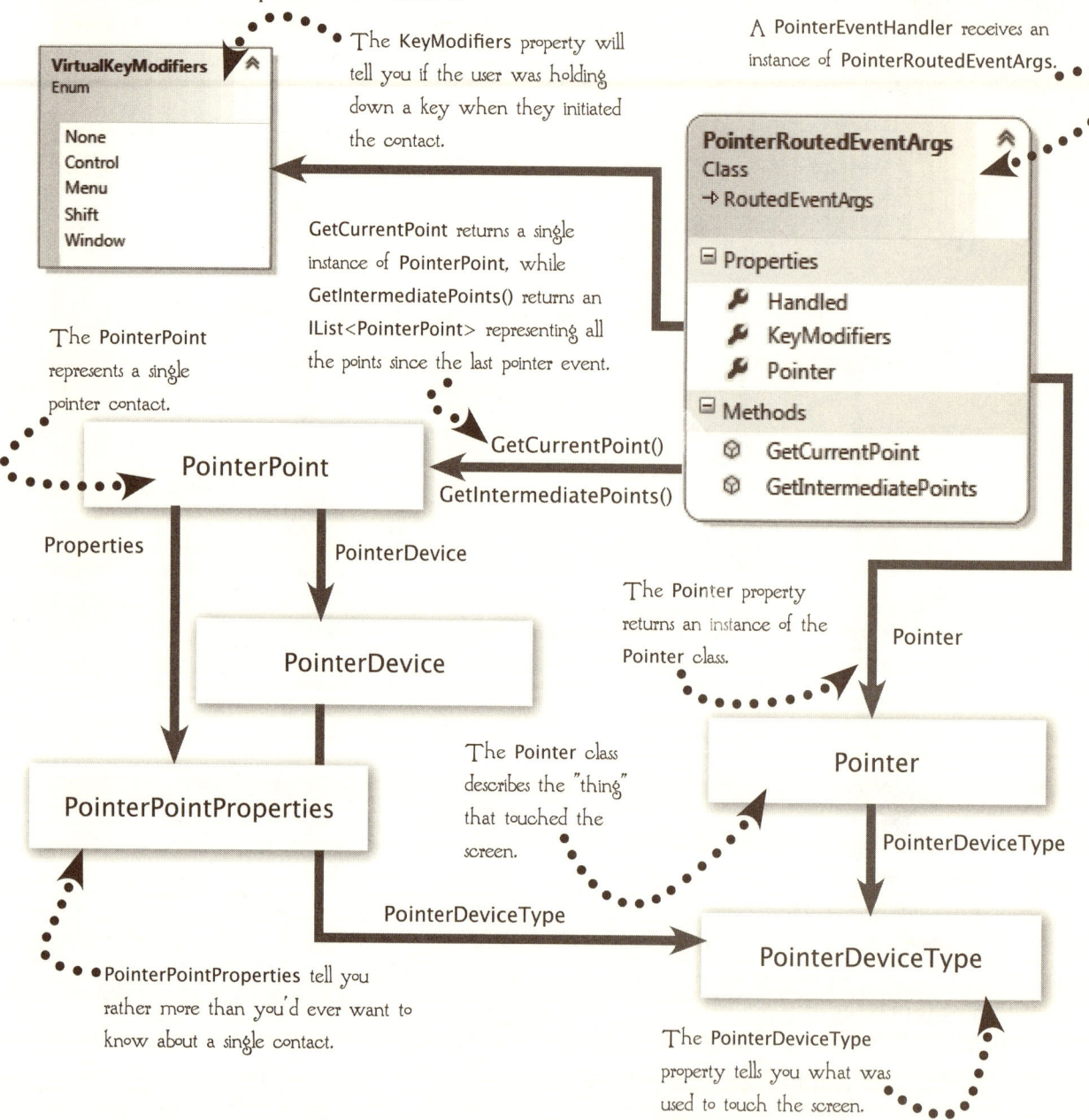

ON YOUR OWN

Can you answer the following questions based on the object graph? NOTE: This is going to require some guessing, so please promise me that you won't fret about it, and don't feel like you need to go off exploring on MSDN. The point here is just to think about how the object graph is structured.

The PointerDeviceType enumeration will tell you whether the "pointer" in question was a finger, a stylus, or the mouse. There are two ways to get to it. What are they, and which do you think would be easiest to use?

Where would you look to figure out the exact point that was touched by the user?

How would you figure out whether the user was holding down the Ctrl key when they touched the screen?

One class will tell you things like how much pressure was applied to a stylus or how far the mouse wheel was moved. In which class would you expect that kind of low-level detail?

THE POINTER

The Pointer property of the PointerRoutedEventArgs class returns an instance of the Pointer class, which exposes read-only properties that represent the "thing" that was used to touch the screen. Of all the classes involved in the Pointer API, Pointer might be the simplest. (I'm not sure why, but I find that rather ironic.)

You'll probably access the Pointer class most often to examine the PointerDeviceType. In theory you shouldn't care how the user initiated the pointer event, but in reality you'll sometimes need to handle the event slightly differently depending on the device.

But whatever happens behind the scenes, make sure the interaction always looks and feels the same to the user, no matter how they initiated it!

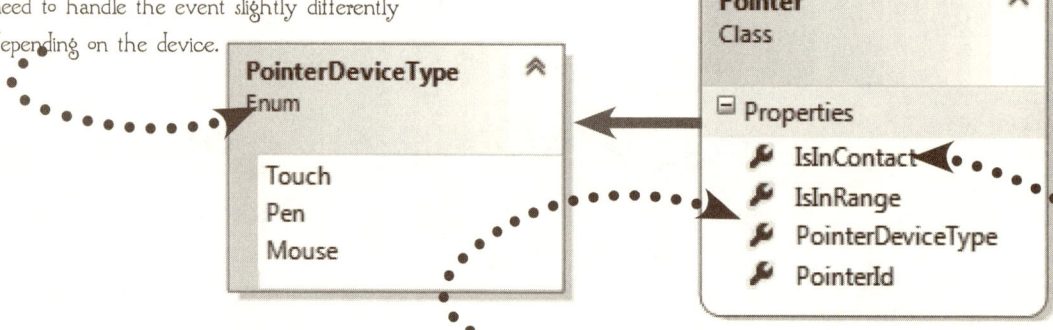

The PointerID is an unsigned integer that uniquely identifies this particular device. It's assigned by the operating system.

The name of the IsInContact property is a little misleading. It aqctually indicates whether the pointer was in contact with a sensor or digitizer at the time the pointer event was raised.

 **MAKE A NOTE**

Maybe it's just me, but when I was learning the Pointer API, it took me a while to find the PointerDevice class that provides information about the physical capabilities of a given device.

Interestingly, you can't access this information via the Pointer class. It's available through the PointerDevice property of the PointerPoint class. (Just because I don't know why that is, it doesn't follow that there isn't a good reason.)

THE POINTERPOINT

When you're developing control-based applications, you generally only need to know that a control has been touched. You don't need to know exactly where. But if you do, `PointerRoutedEventArgs` gives you access to that information via the `GetCurrentPoint()` method, which returns the `PointerPoint` that triggered the event, and the `GetIntermediatePoints()` method, which returns a `List<PointerPoint>` representing all the contact points since the last pointer event.

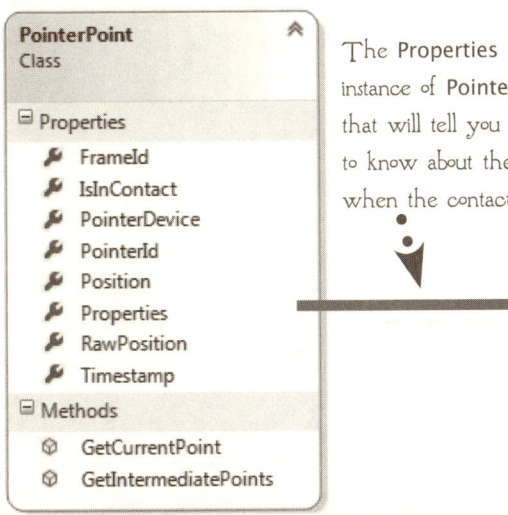

The Properties property returns an instance of `PointerPointProperties` that will tell you everything there is to know about the state of the pointer when the contact was made.

MAKE A NOTE

Instances of `PointerPoint` are usually fed to a `GestureRecognizer`, which is a set of WinRT classes that provide additional support for interpreting manipulation data. We won't be discussing gesture recognizers here (they're complicated and not generally necessary for XAML applications), but you'll need to learn about them if you're going to write the next Adobe Photoshop.

THE KEYBOARD API

Compared to pointer events, the keyboard events are quite simple. There are only two: `KeyDown()` and `KeyUp()`, both declared as instances of the `KeyEventHandler` delegate, which accepts an instance of the `KeyRoutedEventArgs`.

The XAML text controls and the Windows 8.1 soft keyboard all handle key input without your assistance when they have focus, including support for standard Ctrl-key editing combinations.

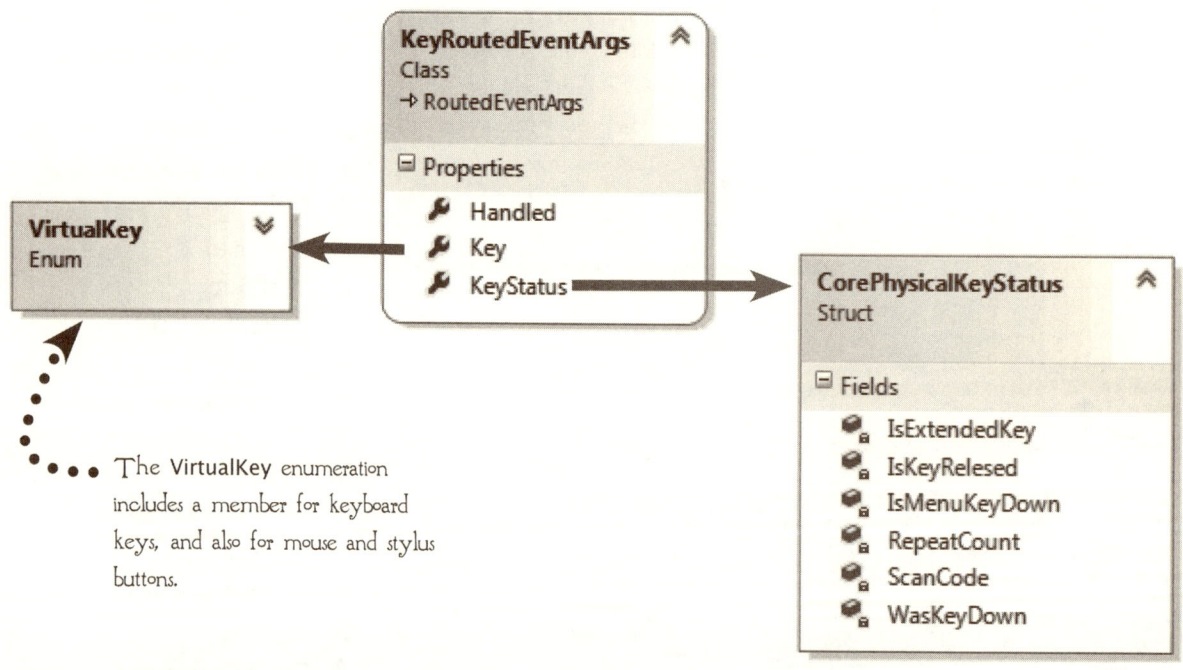

The VirtualKey enumeration includes a member for keyboard keys, and also for mouse and stylus buttons.

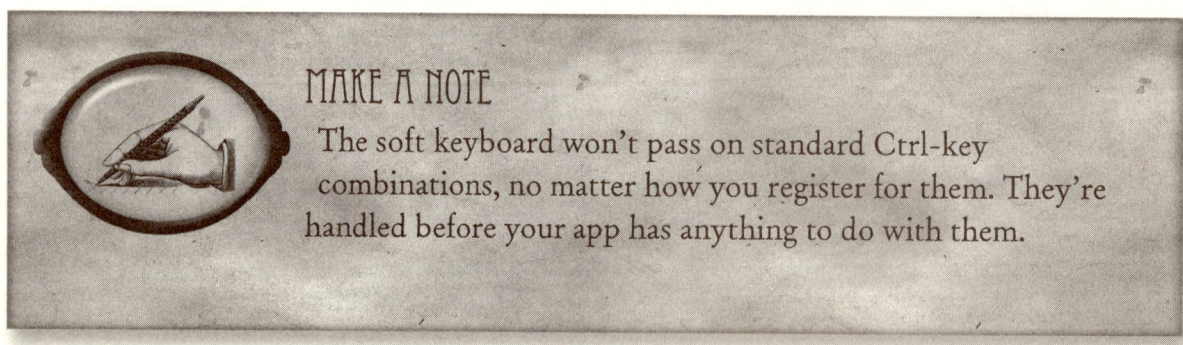

MAKE A NOTE
The soft keyboard won't pass on standard Ctrl-key combinations, no matter how you register for them. They're handled before your app has anything to do with them.

THE MANIPULATION API

The lowest level of UIElement events are the manipulation events that give you access to the nitty-gritty of pointer interactions. We're going to examine these events in even less detail than the rest of the Input API, because you're even less likely need them. But I do want you to understand the order of events, because they're not exactly intuitive.

As soon as the contact is made, the ManipulationStarting event is raised. This event is raised only once per interaction.

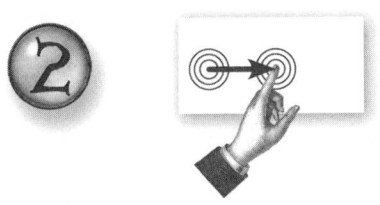

Once the user starts to move the pointer, the ManipulationStarted event is raised (once), followed by ManipulationDelta events that report on the change.

Once the user removes the pointer from the surface, the ManipulationInertiaStarting event is fired. ManipulationDelta events continue to be fired for the duration of inertial movement.

When interial movement is complete, the ManipulationComplete method is fired.

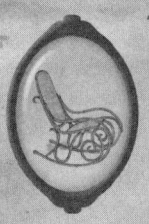

TAKE A BREAK

Did that whirlwind tour of the Input API leave you panting? Why don't you take a break before you complete the Review and we move on to commanding in the next chapter?

REVIEW

How do you register for an event when a control sets the Handled property to true?

Why is it unusual to need to inspect PointerPoint in a control-based app?

What class would you inspect to determine how far a stylus was tilted when contact was made?

When are ManipulationDelta events raised?

What enumeration would you reference inside a KeyDown event handler to determine which key was pressed?

What problem do routed events solve?

Congratulations! You've finished the chapter. Take a minute to think about what you've accomplished before you move on to the next one...

List three things you learned in this chapter:

①

②

③

Why do you think you need to know these things in order to develop Win8 apps?

Is there anything in this chapter that you think you need to understand in more detail? If so, what are you going to do about that?

COMMANDING 9

In an environment like Windows 8.1, the touch language gestures that we examined in the last chapter are a command language. But trying to write a non-trivial application with only touch input would be a bit like writing War and Peace with eight verbs—probably possible, but it would require more time and ingenuity than are available to the average development project.

Fortunately, while Windows 8.1 is going to require that we re-think how we do a lot of UX patterns, we don't have to start completely from scratch. The basic commanding surfaces that we're used to—menus, popups and dialogs—are still available; they just work a little differently. That's the good news. The bad news is that some of these elements are part of WinRT and aren't surfaced in XAML. That means you won't be able to create them declaratively. (It also means that a lot of the examples in the MSDN documentation are only in JavaScript. Sigh.)

In this chapter, we'll explore the command widgets, like menus and message dialogs, and some widgets that are conceptually related to them, like tooltips. We'll start by exploring the command surfaces that are available, and then we'll explore the two command interfaces that you'll use for connecting functionality to your command widgets: ICommand in XAML and IUICommand when you're working with WinRT.

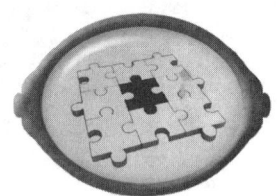

FITTING IT IN

Here's how this chapter fits in to the book as a whole...

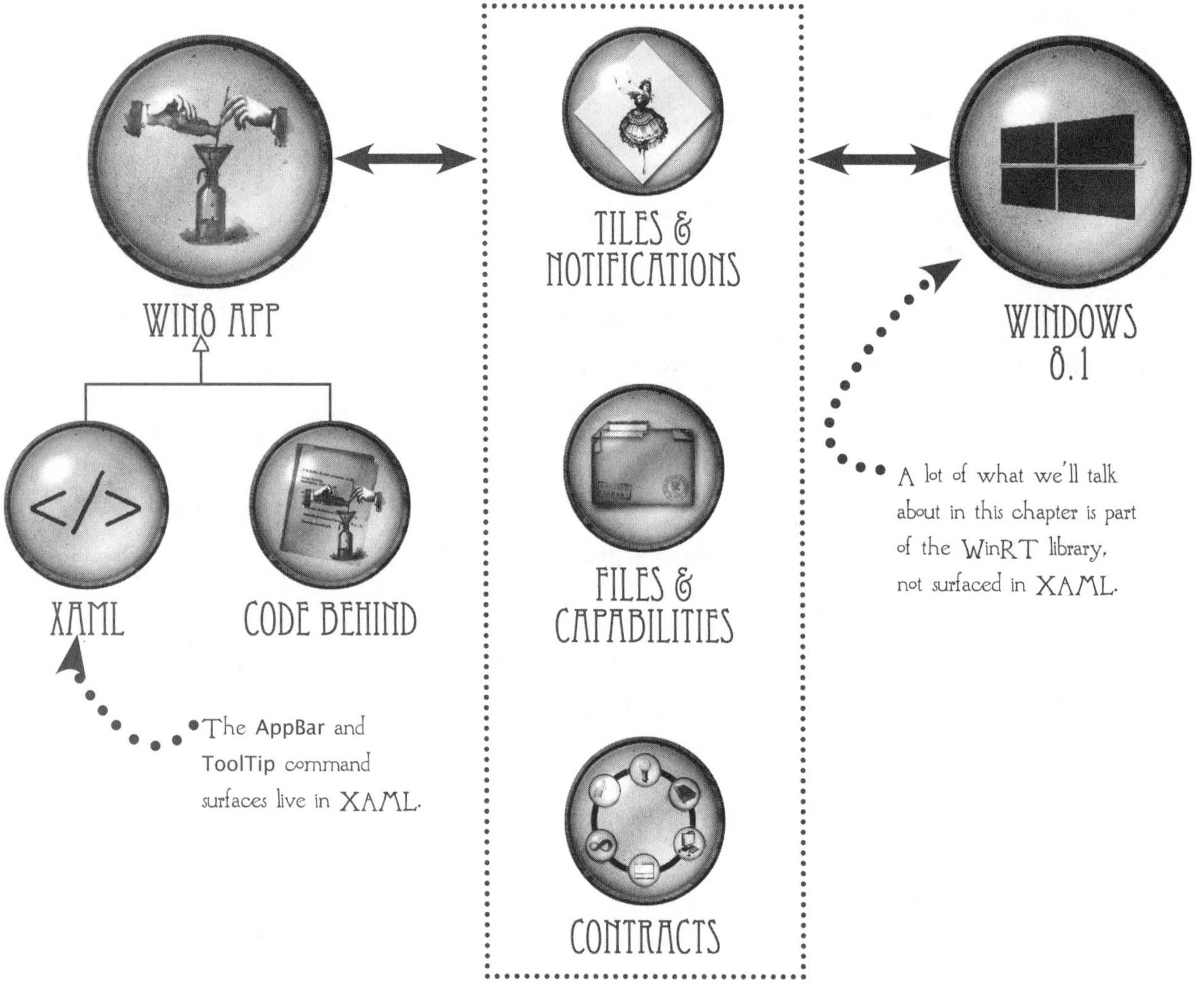

WIN8 APP

XAML

CODE BEHIND

TILES & NOTIFICATIONS

FILES & CAPABILITIES

CONTRACTS

WINDOWS 8.1

The AppBar and ToolTip command surfaces live in XAML.

A lot of what we'll talk about in this chapter is part of the WinRT library, not surfaced in XAML.

TASK LIST

In this chapter we'll explore the widgets and techniques for extending the command language implicit in the Win8 touch language.

COMMAND SURFACES

Because Win8 apps are chromeless, you simply don't have as much room or as many options for placing application commands in your UI. We'll start the chapter by exploring the options you do have and how you can use them.

COMMANDS

Writing event handlers in code-behind is fine in small apps (or silly ones, like our examples), but for non-trivial apps, best practice dictates that you separate the UI from the business code. We'll look at the two APIs that are available to you in Win8 apps: ICommand and IUICommand.

APPBARS & COMMANDBARS

AppBars are the primary command surface for our application, but in 8.1, you'll probably use their descendant, the CommandBar, most often. We'll look at the how and when of using them and the specialized widgets that they can contain next.

OTHER COMMAND SURFACES

Win8 XAML supports tooltips and two kinds of flyouts: the generic Flyout and the MenuFlyout. We'll examine those next.

MESSAGE DIALOGS

Finally, we'll explore the MessageDialog class that's the Win8 equivalent of a modal dialog.

COMMAND SURFACES

Let's start by looking at the different command surfaces that are available to you in a chromeless Win8 app:

The top **AppBar** is conventionally used for navigation or non-modal messages.

The top and bottom **AppBar** controls replace a conventional menu.

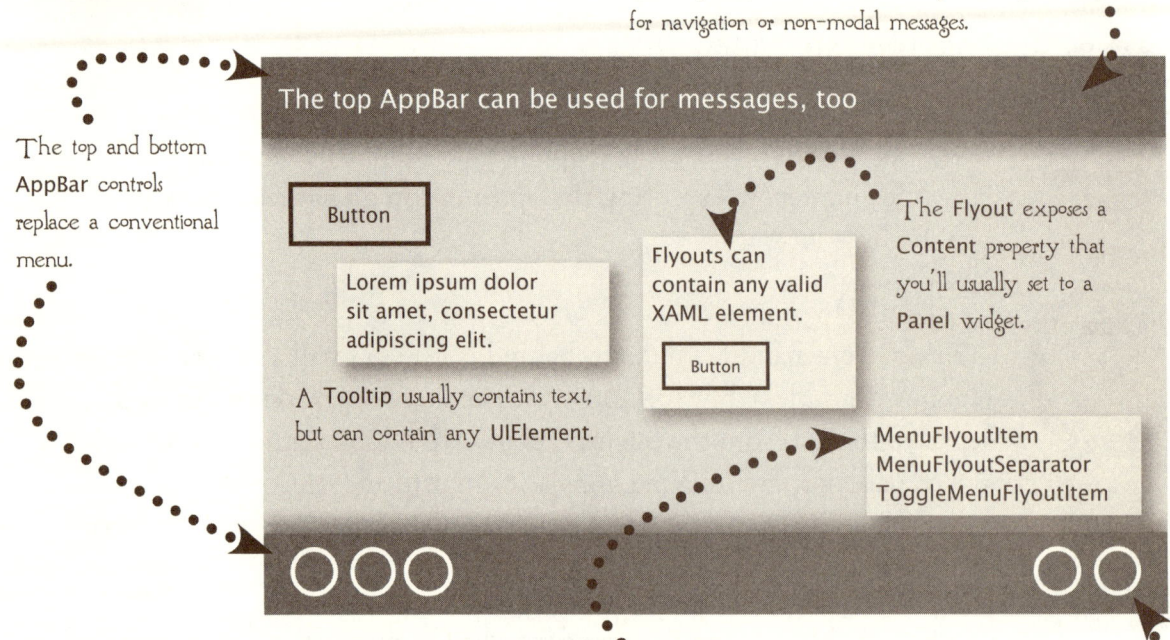

The **Flyout** exposes a **Content** property that you'll usually set to a **Panel** widget.

A **Tooltip** usually contains text, but can contain any **UIElement**.

The **FlyoutMenu** can contain commands and separators.

The commands on the bottom **AppBar** are divided into two groups: application-wide commands on the right, and context-specific commands on the left.

The **MessageDialog** is a heavy hitter. You should only use it when your app can't continue without user assistance.

PUT ON YOUR THINKING HAT

What command surface or widget would you use for each of these functions?

You need to tell the user that your app can't find an Internet connection and needs one to continue.

You want to display a command to close the application.

Your user has chosen to do something that can't be reversed, like delete files, and you want them to confirm the command.

Your app supports multiple open pages (and perhaps multiple instances of the same kind of page), and you want to provide a means to navigate between them.

You want to display a set of sub-commands that are grouped under a single AppBar button.

HOW'D YOU DO?

You need to tell the user that your app can't find an Internet connection and needs one to continue.

> This one justifies a MessageDialog since the user can't do anything else until the problem is resolved.

You want to display a command to close the application.

> Trick question. Don't even try to do this; you can't. The user can close the application by swiping from the top to the bottom of the screen.

Your user has chosen to do something that can't be reversed, like delete files, and you want them to confirm the command.

> The top AppBar is the conventional place to display this kind of message. It can just sit there until the user chooses to respond.

Your app supports multiple open pages (and perhaps multiple instances of the same kind of page), and you want to provide a means to navigate between them.

> Again, the top AppBar is the conventional place for this.

You want to display a set of sub-commands that are grouped under a single AppBar button.

> You'd use a PopupMenu that's displayed when the user clicks the button. We'll do just this later in the chapter.

COMMANDS

Well, I suppose that when when a company is simultaneously developing one new operating system, three application frameworks, and five languages simultaneously, perfect communication is too much to ask for. A "company" is just people, after all.

A slightly painful artifact of this less-than-perfect communication is that while the XAML team and the WinRT team both recognized the need to abstract functionality, they surfaced that ability differently, so as an app developer you'll need to deal with two different APIs, depending on whether you're working with a XAML element or a WinRT widget. Oh, well. If it was easy, everybody'd do it, right?

XAML COMMANDS

Like other XAML environments, commanding is abstracted in the Win8 XAML Framework via the ICommand interface. The methods of a class that implements the ICommand interface are bound to dependency properties on the element.

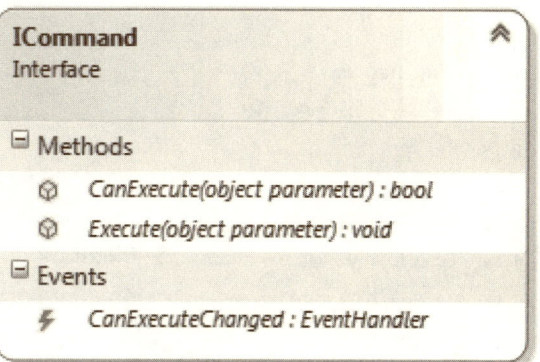

WINRT UICOMMANDS

When you're working with WinRT objects like the MessageDialog, you'll use a UICommand that implements the IUICommand interface.

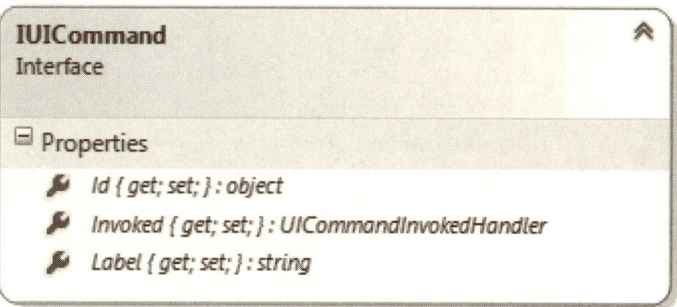

WORKING WITH COMMANDS

The XAML version of command abstraction is represented by the ICommand interface, which is implemented out of the box only by the ButtonBase and MenuFlyoutItem classes, but you can certainly add the functionality to classes you build.

DEFINE A COMMAND CLASS

The first step in implementing the XAML Command API is to define a class that implements the ICommand interface. Command classes are typically defined in the ViewModel, but the API doesn't require this: You can do it in the code-behind if you want to. (But I can't imagine why you would.)

The CanExecute() method returns a Boolean value indicating whether the command is available in the current state of the application. For example, a Cut command is only available if the user has something selected.

The Execute() method does whatever the command is supposed to do.

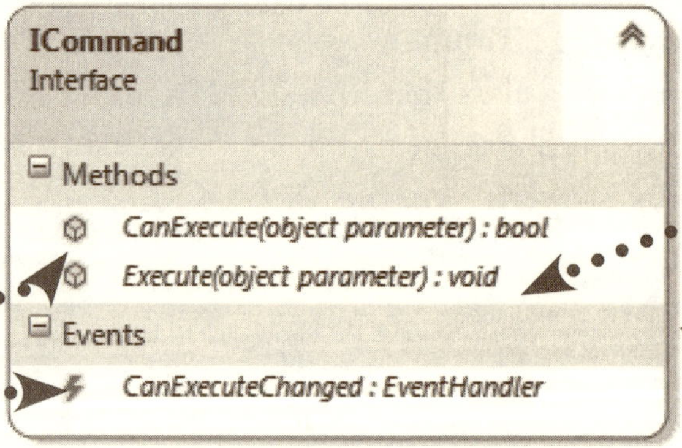

ICommand Interface

Methods
- CanExecute(object parameter) : bool
- Execute(object parameter) : void

Events
- CanExecuteChanged : EventHandler

You should raise the CanExecuteChanged event inside your CanExecute() method. Other objects can listen for the event to adjust the UI as appropriate.

Notice that both ICommand methods accept a single parameter, defined as an Object. (The same object is usually passed to both elements, but that depends on how the implementing class is designed.)

316

 ## CONNECT THE COMMAND TO AN OBJECT

Once the command class is defined, you need to instantiate it and connect it to the **Command** property of your element. Optionally, you can assign the **CommandParameter** property to any value that's within scope.

Because the properties are dependency properties, they can be data bound (which is very common in MVVM scenarios), and both can be assigned in XAML.

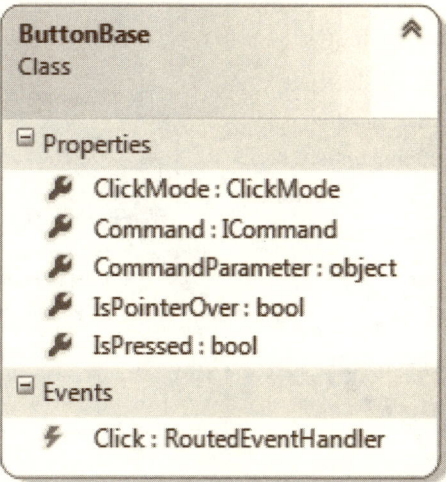

To implement XAML elements that support the Command API, you would need to define the **Command** and **CommandParameter** properties (which can, of course, be called something else) and then call the **CanExecute()** and **Execute** methods where appropriate.

CanExecute() is typically called by another object before the element is displayed. If the command isn't appropriate, you'll want to indicate that visually or not display it at all.

Execute(), on the other hand, is almost always (but not necessarily) called by the element itself in response to an input event.

WORKING WITH UICOMMANDS

The WinRT version of command abstraction uses the UICommand API, which involves more Framework classes, but it is actually simpler to use. (Of course, the price one almost always pays for simplicity is the lack of power and flexibility.) You'll use the UICommand API when you work with the MessageDialog class, which we'll explore later in this chapter.

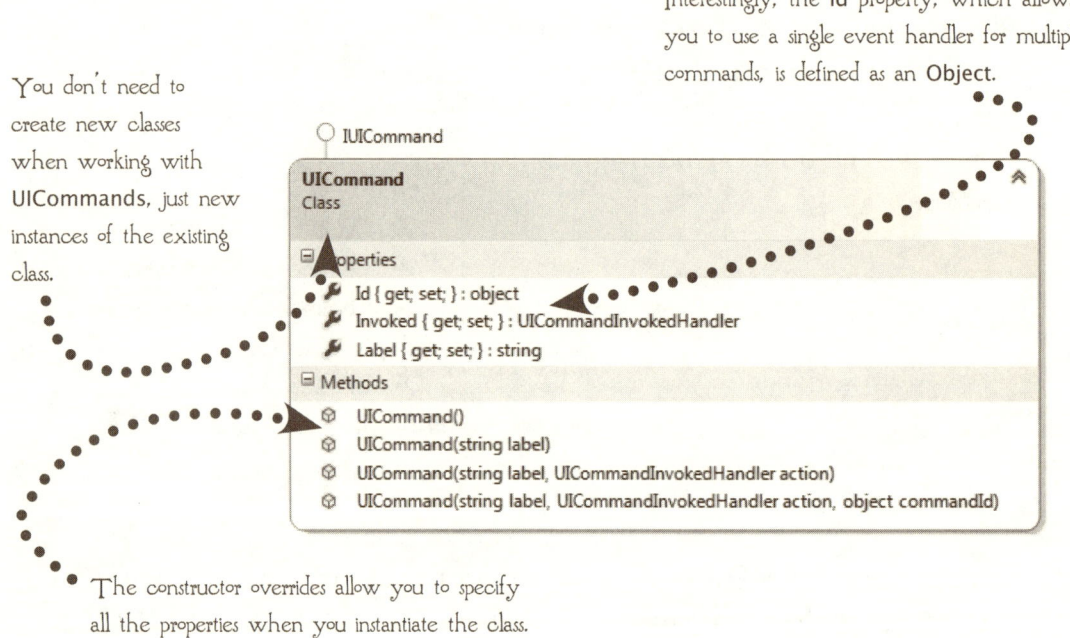

You don't need to create new classes when working with UICommands, just new instances of the existing class.

Interestingly, the Id property, which allows you to use a single event handler for multiple commands, is defined as an Object.

The constructor overrides allow you to specify all the properties when you instantiate the class.

Rather than overriding methods in a subclass, as you do when working with the XAML Command API, all of the funcitonality in a UICommand goes in the event handler, which has the following signature:

 void UICommandInvokedHandler(IUICommand command)

The WinRT objects that support the UICommand API expose a property named Commands that's defined as an IList<IUICommand>. Once you create your UICommandInvokedHandler, you can instantiate the class and add it to the Commands property using a very concise syntax:

```
void MyHandler(ICUICommand command)
{
  // do something
}

myPopup.Commands.Add(new UICommand("Command Text",
    new UICommandInvokedHandler(MyHandler),
    12);
```

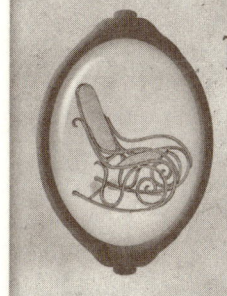

TAKE A BREAK

We're not through with the Command API; we'll build some examples later in the chapter. But why don't you take a quick break before we start actually building some command widgets?

AppBars & CommandBars

The **AppBar** is probably the most important of the command surfaces, and it's also one of the simplest to implement. (But for most purposes, the **CommandBar**, which we'll look at next, is even simpler.) The only functionality it exposes is the ability to show and hide itself. Everything else is handled by the widgets you put inside it.

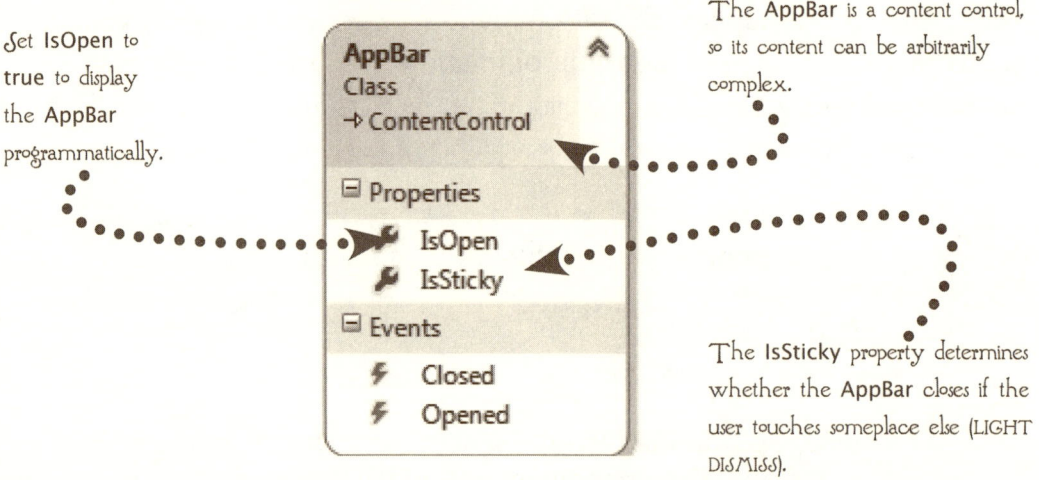

Set **IsOpen** to true to display the AppBar programmatically.

The **AppBar** is a content control, so its content can be arbitrarily complex.

The **IsSticky** property determines whether the **AppBar** closes if the user touches someplace else (LIGHT DISMISS).

The only thing you need to remember when working with **AppBar** controls is that **TopAppBar** and **BottomAppBar** are properties of the **Page**, so they go outside (typically above) the layout root (which you'll remember is really the **Content** property of the **Page**):

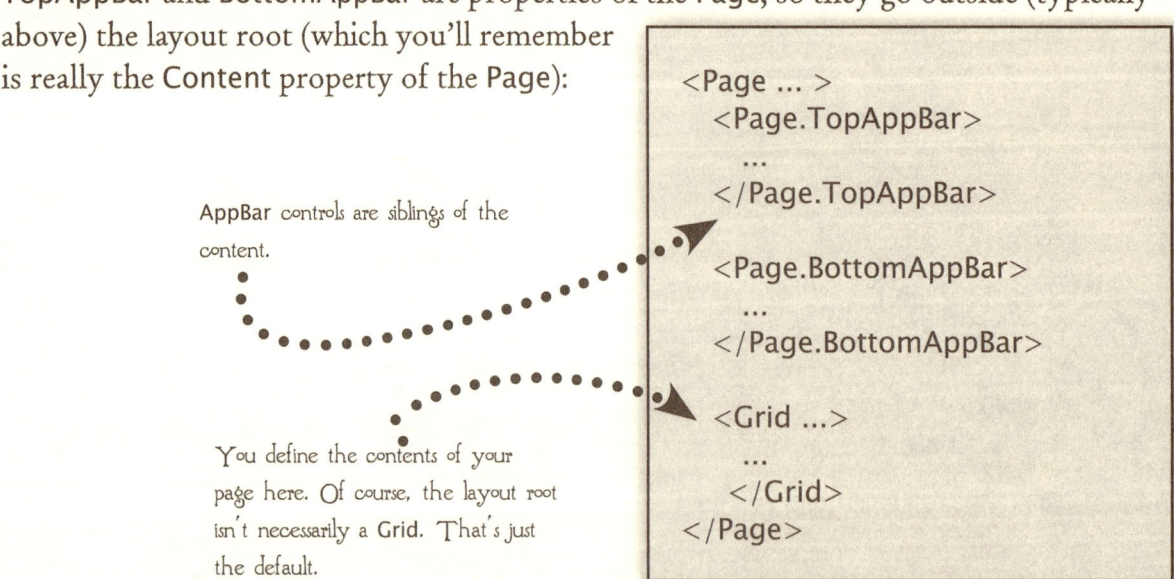

AppBar controls are siblings of the content.

You define the contents of your page here. Of course, the layout root isn't necessarily a Grid. That's just the default.

PUT ON YOUR THINKING HAT

I think that's more than enough theory to be going on with, don't you? Let's jump in and write some code. Create a new blank application (I called mine Commanding01) and add a couple of AppBar controls to it:

This AppBar contains a StackPanel, which in turn contains a TextBlock and two Buttons.

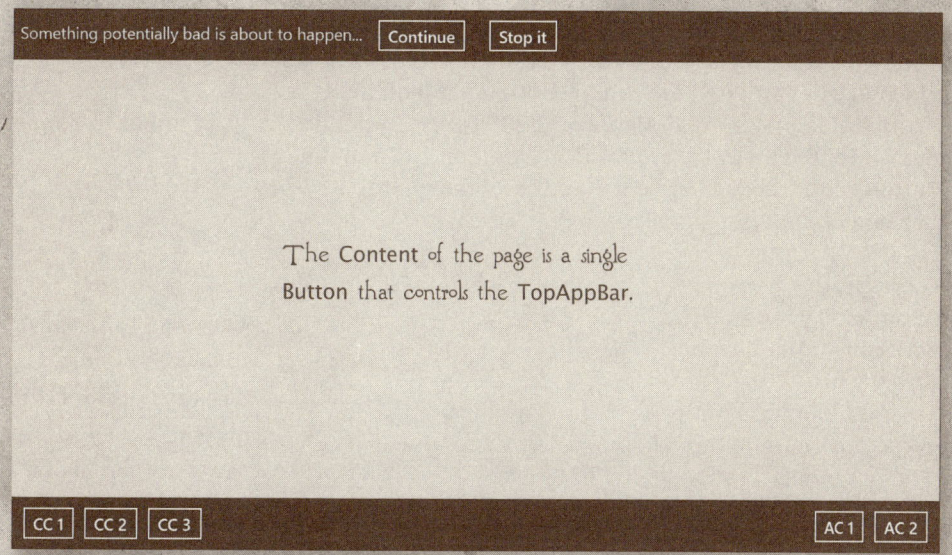

The Content of the page is a single Button that controls the TopAppBar.

A couple of things you'll need to figure out:

- The TopAppBar should be displayed when you click the Button, but not when you swipe from the top or bottom of the screen. The property that controls that is Visibility. Can you work out how to set it and where? You'll need to set some properties in the XAML and write a Button.Click event handler and an AppBar.Closed event handler.

- The BottomAppBar is a pretty standard configuration. Laying it out requires five Buttons, two StackPanels, and a two-column Grid. My version is on the next page, but you'll be doing it so often it would be good to figure it out on your own. (That way you'll remember how.)

PUT ON YOUR THINKING HAT
How'd you do?

You set a handler for the **Closed** event in exactly the same way that you set one for **Button.Click**.

You need to start with the **TopAppBar** collapsed so that it doesn't display when you swipe from the top or bottom.

```xml
<Page ...>
  <Page.TopAppBar>
    <AppBar Name="WarningBar" Closed="WarningBar_Closed" Visibility="Collapsed">
      <StackPanel Orientation="Horizontal" HorizontalAlignment="Left">
        <TextBlock FontSize="24" Margin="0,20" Text="Something scary is about to happen..." />
        <Button FontSize="24" Margin="20,0" Content="Continue" />
        <Button FontSize="24" Margin="10,0" Content="Stop it" />
      </StackPanel>
    </AppBar>
  </Page.TopAppBar>
  <Page.BottomAppBar>
    <AppBar Name="MenuBar">
      <Grid>
        <Grid.ColumnDefinitions>
          <ColumnDefinition Width="5*" />
          <ColumnDefinition Width="5*" />
        </Grid.ColumnDefinitions>
        <StackPanel Grid.Column="0" Orientation="Horizontal" HorizontalAlignment="Left">
          <Button Name="CC1" FontSize="24" Margin="5,10" Content="CC 1" />
          <Button Name="CC2" FontSize="24" Margin="5,10" Content="CC 2" />
          <Button Name="CC3" FontSize="24" Margin="5,10" Content="CC 3" />
        </StackPanel>
        <StackPanel Grid.Column="1" Orientation="Horizontal" HorizontalAlignment="Right">
          <Button Name="AC1" FontSize="24" Margin="5,10" Content="AC 1" />
          <Button Name="AC2" FontSize="24" Margin="5,10" Content="AC 2" />
        </StackPanel>
      </Grid>
    </AppBar>
  </Page.BottomAppBar>
  <Grid ...>
    <Button Name="Scary" FontSize="24" Foreground="Black" Margin="50"
        VerticalAlignment="Top" Content="Do Something Scary"
        Click="Scary_Click" />
  </Grid>
</Page>
```

This is the standard layout: two colums (which are equal here, but needn't be), and two **StackPanels** with their **HorizontalAlignment** property set to put the widgets to one side of the **AppBar** or the other.

We'll open the top **AppBar** here.

```csharp
private void WarningBar_Closed(object sender, object e)
{
    WarningBar.Visibility = Visibility.Collapsed;
}

private void Scary_Click(object sender, RoutedEventArgs e)
{
    WarningBar.Visibility = Visibility.Visible;
    WarningBar.IsOpen = true;
}
```

```vb
Private Sub WarningBar_Closed(sender As Object, e As Object)
    WarningBar.Visibility = Visibility.Collapsed;
End Sub

Private Sub Scary_Click(sender As Object, e As RoutedEventArgs)
    WarningBar.Visibility = Visibility.Visible
    WarningBar.IsOpen = True
End Sub
```

APPBAR WIDGETS

Creating an AppBar is pretty straightforward XAML programming, but the buttons in our little sample didn't exactly have the Windows 8 look and feel, did they? Of course, you can control that using styles and templates, and we'll see how in Chapter 11, but there's an easier way: Use the specialized AppBar widgets that were added in Windows 8.1.

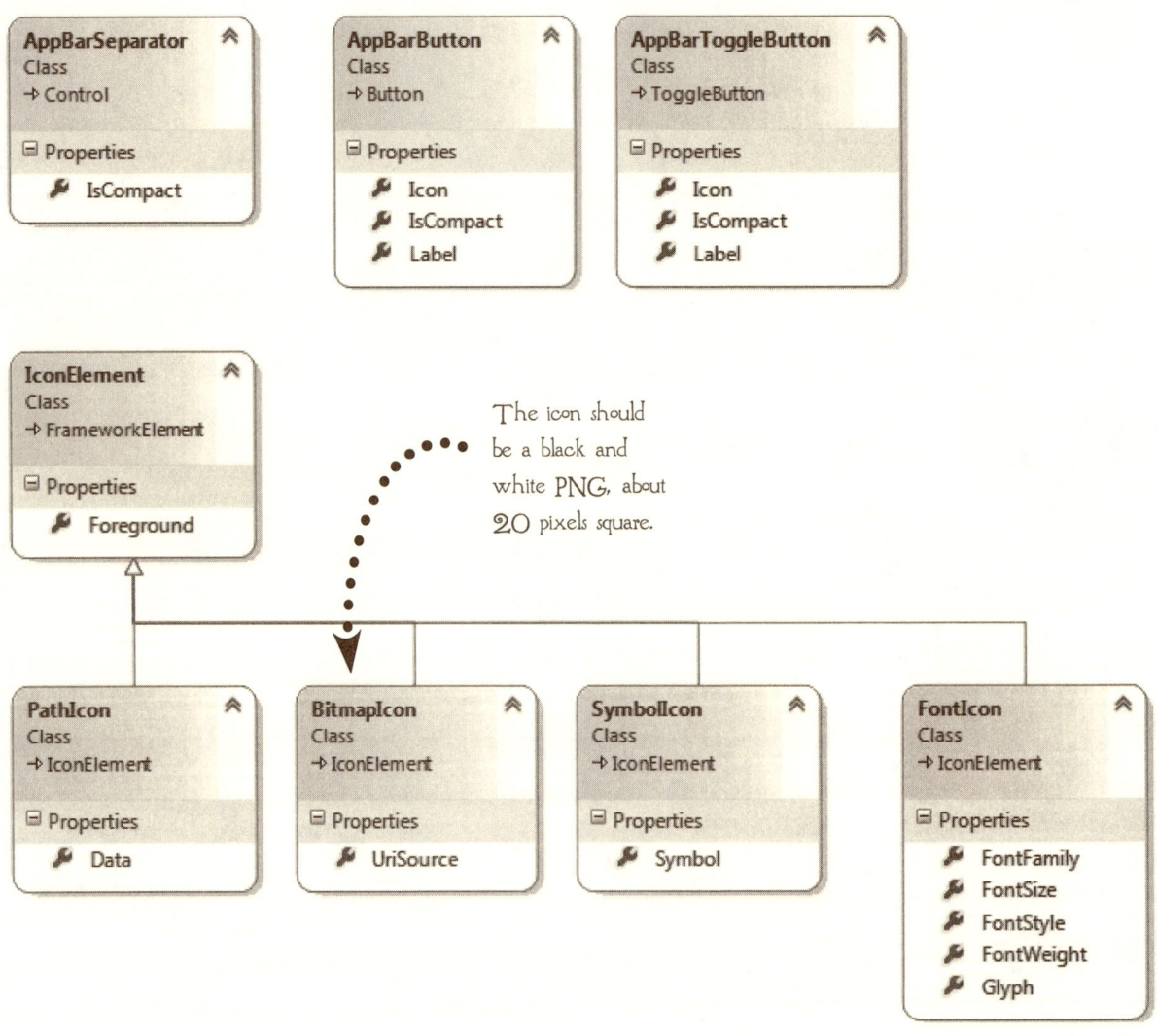

The icon should be a black and white PNG, about 20 pixels square.

PUT ON YOUR THINKING HAT

To get some experience with the AppBar widgets, let's update the bottom AppBar of our exerciser. Here's my updated version, but it doesn't matter if you choose different images or labels, as long as you get the widget declarations right:

Here's what you need to do:

- Replace the buttons on the left side of the AppBar with AppBarButton widgets. The Icon property for the first one is a bitmap, the second one is a symbol, and the third one is a font. You'll need to use the Uri syntax to specify the bitmap source: ms-appx:///Assets/filename.png.

- Replace the buttons on the right side of the AppBar with AppBarToggleButton widgets with an AppBarSeparator between them. Use the IsChecked property that AppBarToggleButton inherits from ToggleButton to enable the left-most button.

PUT ON YOUR THINKING HAT
How'd you do?

```xml
<Page.BottomAppBar>
  <AppBar Name="MenuBar">
    <Grid>
      <Grid.ColumnDefinitions>
        ...
      </Grid.ColumnDefinitions>
      <StackPanel Grid.Column="0" Orientation="Horizontal" HorizontalAlignment="Left">
        <AppBarButton Name="CC1" Label="Bitmap">
            <AppBarButton.Icon>
               <BitmapIcon UriSource="ms-appx:///Assets/flag.png"/>
            </AppBarButton.Icon>
        </AppBarButton>
        <AppBarButton Name="CC2" Label="Symbol" Icon="Edit"/>
        <AppBarButton Name="CC3" Label="Font">
            <AppBarButton.Icon>
               <FontIcon FontFamily="Webdings" Glyph="&#x00CD;" FontSize="30"/>
            </AppBarButton.Icon>
        </AppBarButton>
      </StackPanel>
      <StackPanel Grid.Column="1" Orientation="Horizontal" HorizontalAlignment="Right">
        <AppBarToggleButton Name="AC1" Icon="Globe" IsChecked="True"/>
        <AppBarSeparator/>
        <AppBarToggleButton Name="AC2" Icon="Account"/>
      </StackPanel>
    </Grid>
  </AppBar>
</Page.BottomAppBar>
```

COMMANDBARS

I'm prepared to bet that the majority of what you'll need to do in your menu bars can be handled by the AppBar widgets, and they certainly are a lot easier to configure. (And that IsCompressed property will come in very handy when we look at displaying your app in Chapter 13.) But our existing code still contains Grid and StackPanel elements that are going to have to be repeated for every menu bar. Who wants to do that? Fortunatelpry, Windows 8.1 introduced a new element, the CommandBar, that simplifies creating menus even more.

The PrimaryCommands and SecondaryCommands properties of the CommandBar are defined as an IObservableVector<ICommandBarElement>. In English, that means that you simply add any widget that implements the ICommandBarElement interface to your XAML using collection syntax.

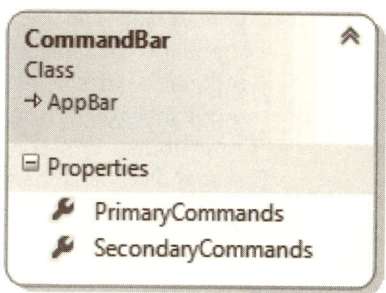

Out of the box, only the AppBar widgets we've been working with, the AppBarButton, AppBarToggleButton, and AppBarSeparator, implement ICommandBarElement, but the interface only implements a single Boolean property, IsCompact, so (at least in theory) creating your own widgets wouldn't be difficult.

PUT ON YOUR THINKING HAT

Swap the BottomAppBar in our example app for a CommandBar. (I created a new solution that I called Commanding02, but you can just change the code if you like.)

You'll need to pay attention to where the AppBar widgets go. Remember that PrimaryCommands are displayed on the right (for languages that read left-to-right.)

PUT ON YOUR THINKING HAT

How'd you do? Take a minute to compare this version of the code to the original version on page 322. It sure has gotten shorter, hasn't it?

```xml
<Page.BottomAppBar>
    <CommandBar Name="MenuBar">
        <CommandBar.PrimaryCommands>
            <AppBarToggleButton Name="AC1" Icon="Globe" IsChecked="True"/>
            <AppBarSeparator/>
            <AppBarToggleButton Name="AC2" Icon="Account"/>
        </CommandBar.PrimaryCommands>
        <CommandBar.SecondaryCommands>
            <AppBarButton Name="CC1" Label="Bitmap">
                <AppBarButton.Icon>
                    <BitmapIcon UriSource="ms-appx:///Assets/flag.png"/>
                </AppBarButton.Icon>
            </AppBarButton>
            <AppBarButton Name="CC2" Label="Symbol" Icon="Edit"/>
            <AppBarButton Name="CC3" Label="Font">
                <AppBarButton.Icon>
                    <FontIcon FontFamily="Webdings" Glyph="&#x00CD;" FontSize="30"/>
                </AppBarButton.Icon>
            </AppBarButton>
        </CommandBar.SecondaryCommands>
    </CommandBar>
</Page.BottomAppBar>
```

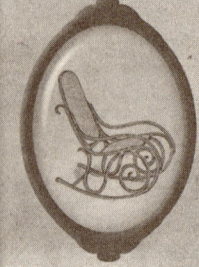

TAKE A BREAK

Why don't you take a quick break (or a long one, for that matter) before you complete the Review and we move on to **Popups** and **Flyouts** in the next section?

REVIEW

According to the Windows UI guidelines, how should the top and bottom menu bars be used?

What's the difference between a IUICommand and an ICommand? When do you use each? (For extra credit, what does the RoutedCommand class that's included in the Common solution folder do?)

What types of widgets can you use in a CommandBar?

How is the Icon property of an AppBarButton or AppBarToggleButton declared?

What classes descend from IconElement?

OTHER COMMAND SURFACES

I'm not entirely sure that I buy into the idea that eliminating window chrome makes an app more immersive, but I am sure that having the information needed by the user or application appear within the context of the app helps a lot. Popup widgets are the primary mechanism for achieving this kind of flow.

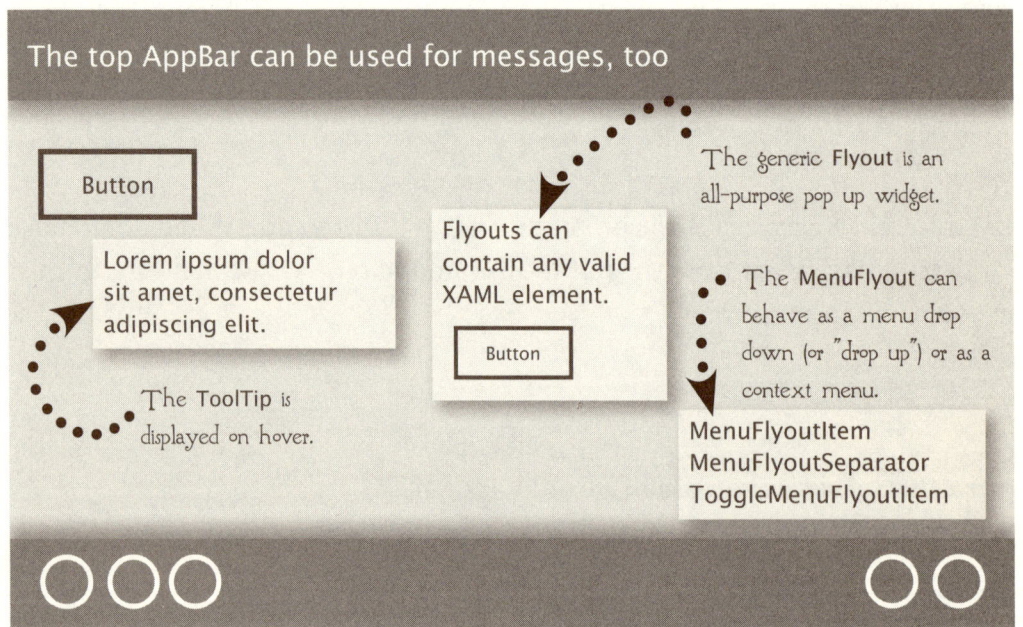

The top AppBar can be used for messages, too

Button

Lorem ipsum dolor sit amet, consectetur adipiscing elit.

The ToolTip is displayed on hover.

Flyouts can contain any valid XAML element.

Button

The generic Flyout is an all-purpose pop up widget.

The MenuFlyout can behave as a menu drop down (or "drop up") or as a context menu.

MenuFlyoutItem
MenuFlyoutSeparator
ToggleMenuFlyoutItem

MAKE A NOTE

There are two other widgets, the Popup and PopupMenu, that (more or less) duplicate the functionality of Flyout and MenuFlyout. But they're a lot more difficult to use. A lot.
Popup is officially deprecated, and while PopupMenu isn't, it doesn't do anything you can't achieve more easily with FlyoutMenu. We won't be examining either of them here.

TOOLTIPS

You're probably familiar with tooltips from other development platforms or just from using some version of Windows. The Win8 XAML version isn't that different from what you'd expect, but you use an intermediate class to attach them.

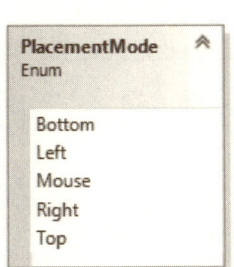
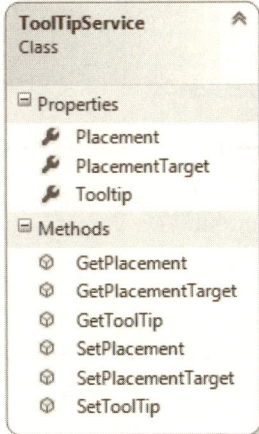
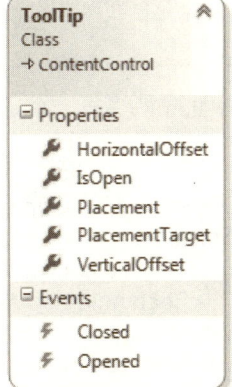

ToolTip is an attached property of the **ToolTipService**. Both **ToolTipService** and **ToolTip** expose some configuration properties, but at its simplest, all you need to do is assign a string to **ToolTipService.ToolTip**:

```
<MyElement ToolTipService.ToolTip="Tell me something" ... />
```

If you want to do something a little trickier, you can use element syntax:

```
<MyElement ... >
  <ToolTipService.ToolTip>
      ...
  </ToolTipService.ToolTip>
</MyElement>
```

PUT ON YOUR THINKING HAT
Add a **ToolTip** to the **Button** in the sample application. Set the **Content** of the **ToolTip** to a **StackPanel** that contains a **Textblock** and a **Rectangle**.

HOW'D YOU DO?

Here's my version. As always, it doesn't matter if you chose different text or formatting.

```xml
<Button x:Name="Scary" FontSize="24" Foreground="Black" Margin="50"
        VerticalAlignment="Top"  Content="Do Something Scary"
        Click="Scary_Click">
    <ToolTipService.ToolTip>
        <StackPanel>
            <TextBlock FontSize="18" Text="This is some text" />
            <Rectangle Fill="Black" Width="200" Height="50" />
        </StackPanel>
    </ToolTipService.ToolTip>
</Button>
```

MAKE A NOTE

ToolTip is a ContentControl, which is what allows us to do things like set the content to a StackPanel and include a Rectangle. But it doesn't support any interactive elements. If you add something like a Button, it won't be displayed when the ToolTip opens.

FLYOUTS

Windows 8.0 didn't have a XAML Flyout control. (JavaScript did.) There was (and still is, although its use is deprecated) a Popup widget, but it was, well, "painful" would be an understatement. Fortunately, Windows 8.1 remedies the situation with the Flyout widget, which can be created completely in XAML. The Flyout can be added directly to a Button via its Flyout property, or to any other element using the FlyoutBase.AttachedFlyout attached property (but that doesn't require a little bit of code to display it.

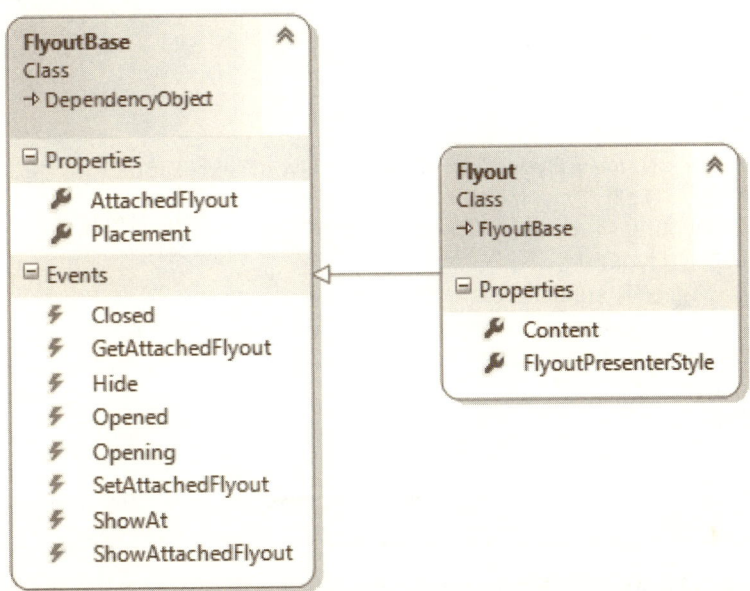

PUT ON YOUR THINKING HAT

Add a TextBlock to the main canvas of our exerciser (you'll need to change the existing Grid to a StackPanel). Add an AttachedFlyout that contains another TextBlock, and a Tapped event handler that calls FlyoutBase.ShowAttachedFlyout(). HINT: You'll need to cast the sender to a FrameworkElement.

I'm not giving you a whole lot to go on here, so don't feel too bad if you need to check the syntax on the next page. But give yourself a big gold star if you can figure it out on your own!

HOW'D YOU DO?

I haven't included the GetElementRect() function, because you've already seen that code a couple of times, and of course you'll have to link the event handler to the Click event, either in XAML or code.

```
<Page ... >
   ...
   <StackPanel>
      <Button ... />
      <TextBlock Name="FlyoutText" Tapped="FlyoutText_Tapped" .
            Text="Tap Me" ..>
         <FlyoutBase.AttachedFlyout>
            <Flyout>
               <TextBlock Text="Hi there!"/>
            </Flyout>
         </FlyoutBase.AttachedFlyout>
      </TextBlock>
   </StackPanel>
</Page>
```

```csharp
private void FlyoutText_Tapped(object sender, RoutedEventArgs e)
{
    FlyoutBase.ShowAttachedFlyout((FrameworkElement)sender);
}
```

```vb
Private Sub FlyoutText_Tapped(sender As object, e As RoutedEventArgs )
    FlyoutBase.ShowAttachedFlyout((CType(sender, FrameworkElement))
End Sub
```

MENUFLYOUTS

If the Popup is a pain (and it is), the Windows 8 PopupMenu was a beast, a code-only monster that required you to calculate its onscreen position and didn't use XAML ICommand objects. Unlike Popup, the PopupMenu hasn't been officially deprecated, but it has been largely replaced by the XAML-friendly FlyoutMenu. Using FlyoutMenu requires a few more classes than the AppBar, but it's wired up the same way, and the class pattern will be familiar to you after working with the AppBar widgets.

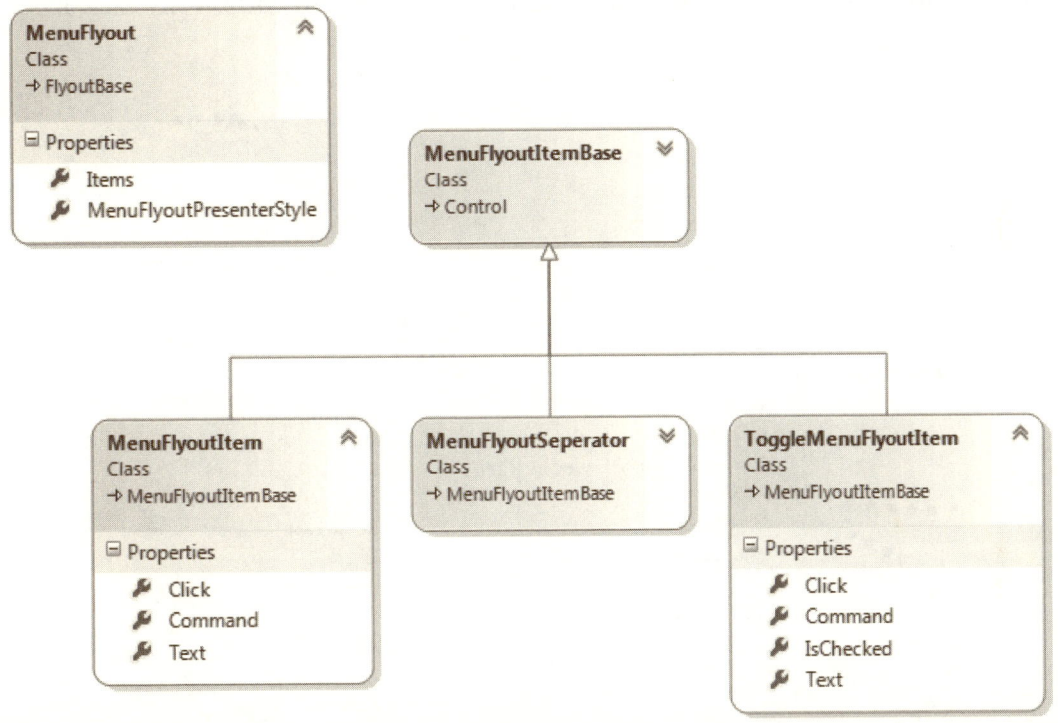

> ## ON YOUR OWN
>
> You know everything you need to know to add a MenuFlyout to an element. Why don't you add a simple Cut/Copy/Paste menu to one of the AppBarButton elements in our exerciser? Remember, the Button class exposes a Flyout property, so you don't need to use the AttachedFlyout, and you don't need any code. Just specify the menu right in the XAML

MESSAGE DIALOGS

The last of the command surfaces is something of a sledgehammer. The `MessageDialog` is roughly equivalent to a modal dialog, and you shouldn't use it unless your app absolutely can't continue to function until the user responds.

Like the `PopupMenu`, the `MessageDialog` belongs to WinRT, not the XAML Framework, so it can't be styled or data-bound, and you have to create it in code. That said, it's a fairly straightforward widget to implement.

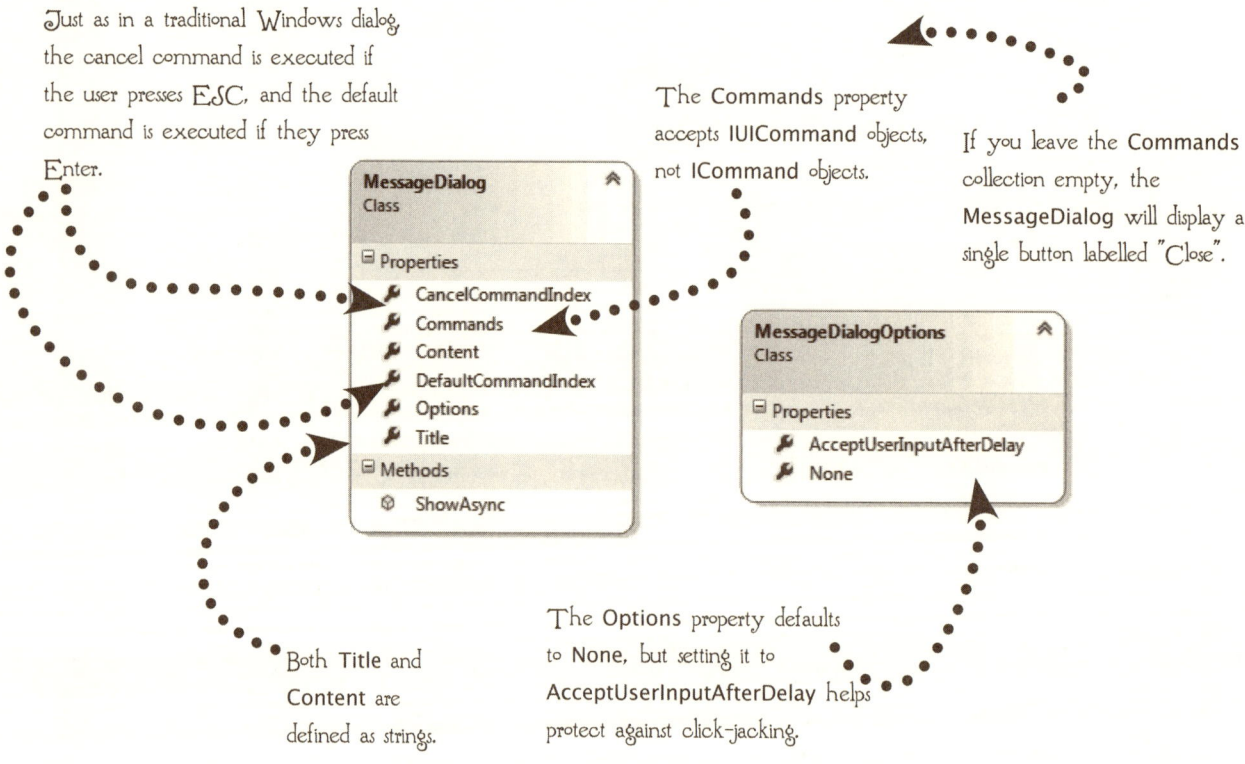

Just as in a traditional Windows dialog, the cancel command is executed if the user presses ESC, and the default command is executed if they press Enter.

The Commands property accepts IUICommand objects, not ICommand objects.

If you leave the Commands collection empty, the MessageDialog will display a single button labelled "Close".

Both Title and Content are defined as strings.

The Options property defaults to None, but setting it to AcceptUserInputAfterDelay helps protect against click-jacking.

The `MessageDialog` has two constructors: You can either pass it just a `Content` message, or you can pass the `Content` and `Title` (in that order).

PUT ON YOUR THINKING HAT

No surprises in our last exercise. Display a **MessageDialog** when the user clicks the Button labeled "CC1" on the **AppBar**.

![My First Dialog screenshot]

We've cheated a bit (well, quite a lot) with the exercises in this chapter. This time, use a pattern that more closely resembles what you'd do in code:

- Create a **UICommandInvokedCommandHandler** method: It can be empty (mine is), but it needs to conform to the delegate signature.

- You'll need two instances of the **UICommand**. You can create them inside the **Commands.Add()** method, but just for the practice, instantiate them separately.

- Set the default and cancel buttons of the **MessageDialog**.

- Use the constructor that accepts both a message and a title.

HOW'D YOU DO?

Here's mine. Did you decide to do something creative inside the event handler?

```csharp
private async void CC1_Click(object sender, RoutedEventArgs e)
{
    UICommand help = new UICommand("I'll help",
            new UICommandInvokedHandler(DialogCommandInvoked));
    UICommand goAway = new UICommand("Go away",
            new UICommandInvokedHandler(DialogCommandInvoked));
    MessageDialog md = new MessageDialog("I can't go on without your help...",
            "My First Dialog");
    md.Commands.Add(help);
    md.Commands.Add(goAway);
    md.DefaultCommandIndex = 0;
    md.CancelCommandIndex = 1;
    await md.ShowAsync();
}

private void DialogCommandInvoked(IUICommand command)
{ }
```

```vb
Private Async Sub CC1_Click(sender As object, e As RoutedEventArgs)
    Dim help As UICommand = New UICommand("I'll help", _
        New UICommandInvokedHandler(AddressOf DialogCommandInvoked))
    Dim goAway As UICommand = New UICommand("Go away", _
        New UICommandInvokedHandler(AddressOf DialogCommandInvoked))
    Dim md As MessageDialog = New MessageDialog("I can't go on without your help...", _
            "My First Dialog")
    md.Commands.Add(help)
    md.Commands.Add(goAway)
    md.DefaultCommandIndex = 0
    md.CancelCommandIndex = 1
    Await md.ShowAsync()
End Sub

Private Sub DialogCommandInvoked(IUICommand command)
End Sub
```

ON YOUR OWN

Other than providing the text for the title, message, and buttons, the `MessageDialog` provides essentially no styling. The only thing you can control is the color of the selected default `Button`. That's controlled by the background color that you set in the app manifest. We'll talk about the manifest in Chapter 15, but if you'd like, open it now and change the default button color. Exciting, isn't it?

TAKE A BREAK

That's it for our exploration of commands, command surfaces, and other popups in Win8 apps.

Why don't you take a break before you complete the Review and we move on to XAML graphics in the next chapter?

REVIEW

When would you need to use an AppBar instead of the more convenient CommandBar?

Congratulations! You've finished the chapter. Take a minute to think about what you've accomplished before you move on to the next one...

List three things you learned in this chapter:

①

②

③

Why do you think you need to know these things in order to develop Win8 apps?

Is there anything in this chapter that you think you need to understand in more detail? If so, what are you going to do about that?

TEXT & GRAPHICS   10

Okay, I'm going to tell you this right up front: When it comes to graphics, you can't do anything too tricky using Win8 XAML. There are no pixel shaders or layout transforms, and text display is pretty much limited to setting basic typeface properties. That isn't to say that you can't do those things in Win8, just not in XAML.

As you probably know, WinRT graphics rendering is built on DirectX, not the older (and slower) GDI. You can write DirectX Win8 applications in C++, and there is some interoperability between DirectX and XAML via the SurfaceImageSource, SwapChainBackgroundPanel and related classes. The Windows.UI.Text namespace provides pretty complete support for OpenType typography.

Or so I'm told. I've never had any reason to explore those APIs, because Win8 XAML does everything one needs to do in the kind of standard control-based application that's the focus of this book. Well, almost everything. I've struggled with a tile brush that doesn't tile, and I miss drop shadows. (And please promise me that you won't take the advice you'll see in the forums about substituting a rectangle offset from your element and filling it with low-opacity gray. That's not a shadow. That's a rectangle offset from your element and filled with low-opacity gray. Shadows have fuzzy edges.)

But it's not all bad news. The good news is that by reducing the feature set, the Win8 XAML architects have also reduced the complexity, making the simple things you're most likely to want to do really, really simple. And that's what this chapter is about: The kinds of XAML graphics you're likely to use on a daily basis. (Assuming, of course, that you're not building the next Photoshop.)

FITTING IT IN

You have a lot of control over the appearance of just about anything you'd want to display to the user in a Win8 app. (Complete control, if you're prepared to work with DirectX which, frankly, I'm usually not.)

This is just a standard TextBox, but its appearance has been modified (a lot!).

The text, background, and border of this TextBox are all painted with a Brush.

This is some Text

The TextBox has been skewed. Not something I'd recommend as a rule, but it can be useful in other situations. Skewing is a kind of TRANSFORMATION. We'll talk about those in the next chapter.

Typography can be extremely complex, but in Win8 XAML, the changes you're most likely to want to make are exposed as properties of the Control class.

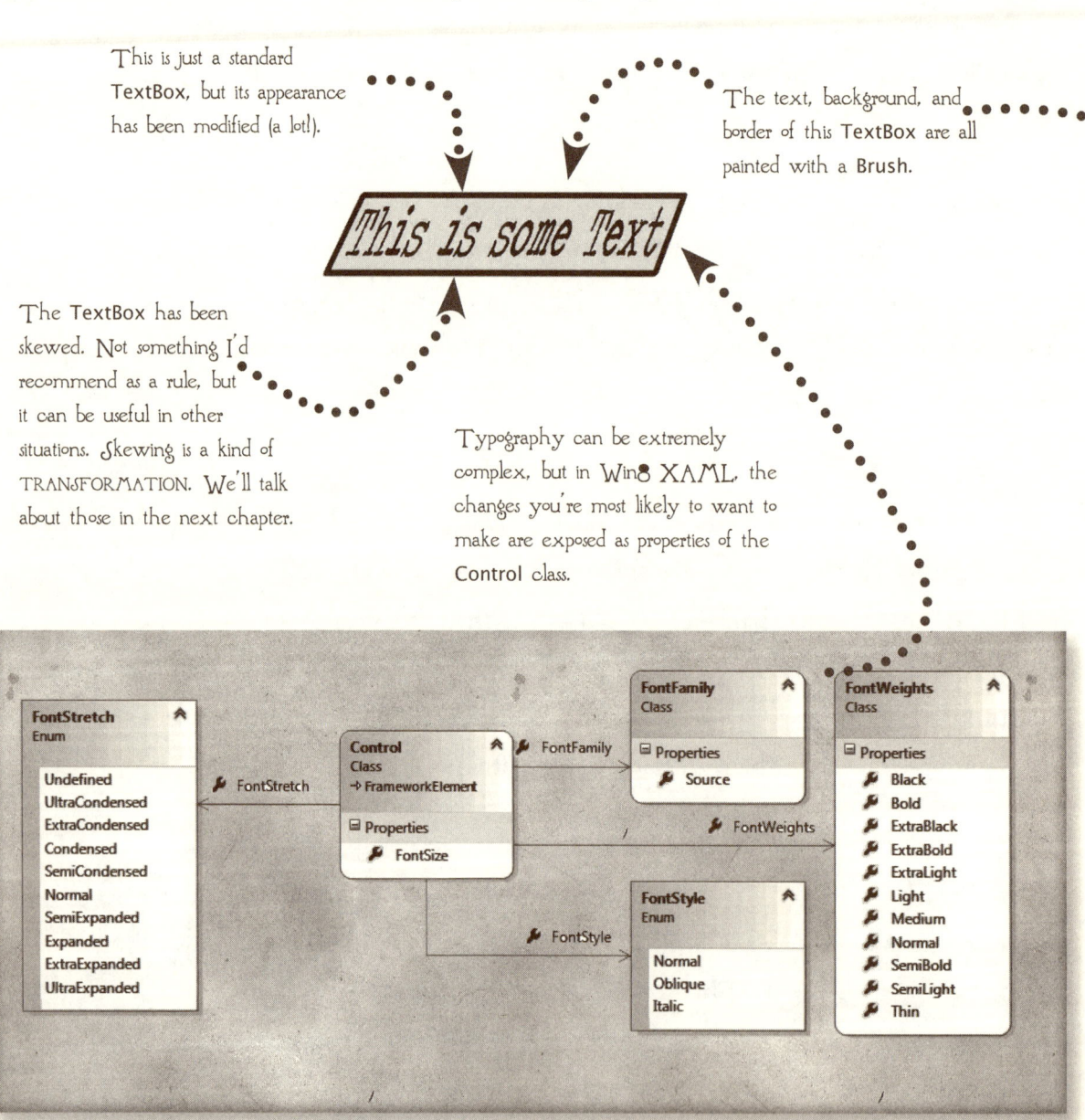

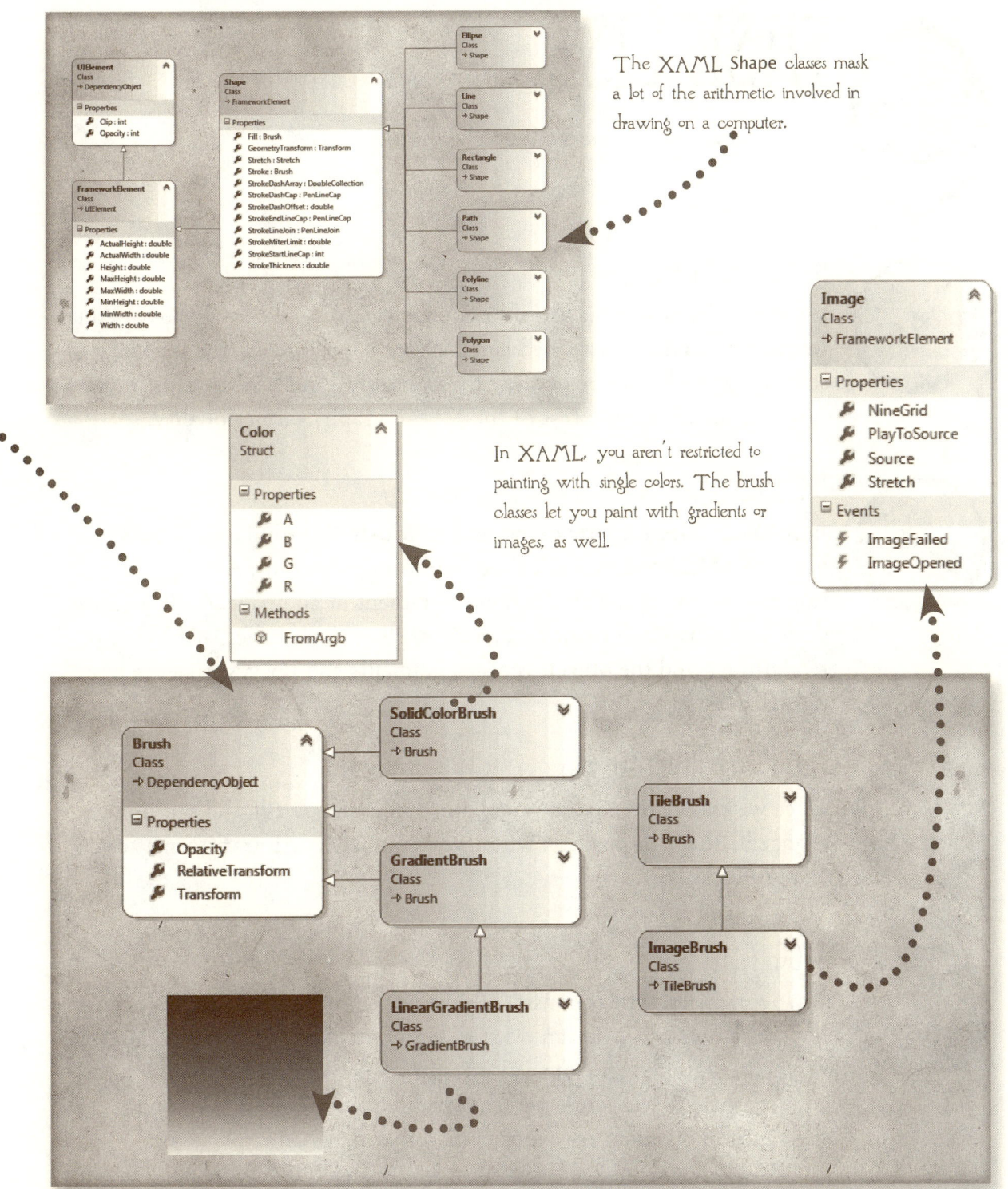

TASK LIST

In this chapter we'll explore the graphics capabilities of Win8 XAML.

DRAWING IN XAML

Win8 XAML provides a set of basic shape classes—we've already used the Rectangle—and sophisticated language for describing vector shapes. We'll start by exploring them, because they're useful, and because they're an easy way to explore the rest of the XAML graphics functionality.

BRUSHES

In XAML, objects are rendered using a **Brush**. But unlike an artist's brush, XAML brushes don't limit you to a single color. A brush can be a single color, but it can also contain a gradient or an image. After we have some basic shapes to work with, we'll explore the brushes we can use to render them and the objects (colors, gradients and images) that are our XAML paint.

TRANSFORMING OBJECTS

Once we know how to draw and paint something, we'll find out how to change its shape or position when we examine XAML transformations and projections.

TYPOGRAPHY

To typographers, type is considerably more complex than just specifying choosing a typeface. You can exert all the control you want over leading, kerning, and glyph sets from a Win8 app via DirectWrite, but we'll limit our discussion to the properties that you're likely to need in a control-based app, all of which are exposed directly on the **Control** class.

DRAWING IN XAML

I've already told you that Win8 XAML doesn't provide much in the way of graphics capabilities, but that doesn't mean you can't draw at all. The `Windows.UI.Xaml.Shapes` namespace provides a set of classes that you can use to generate all the basic geometries.

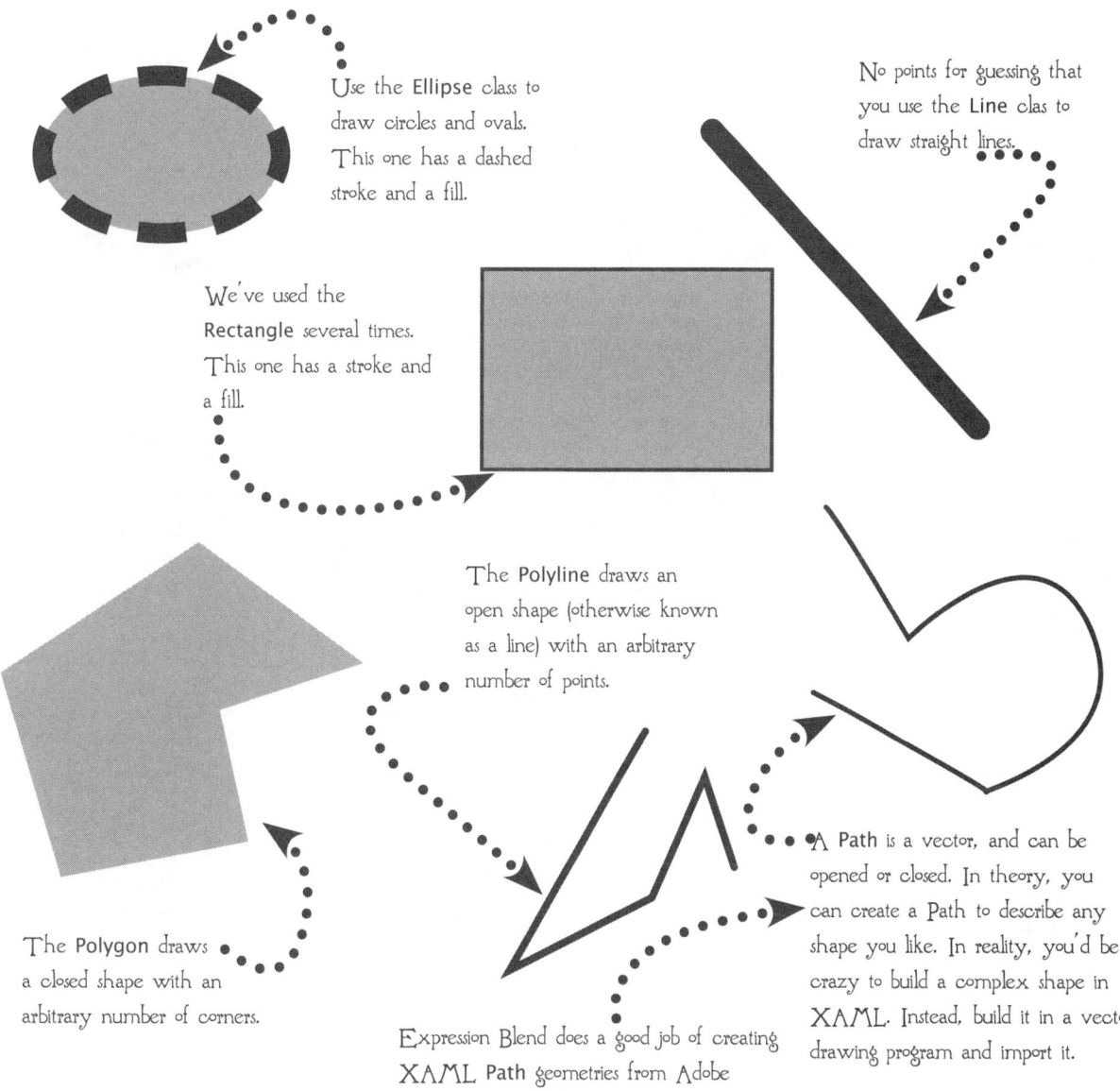

Use the **Ellipse** class to draw circles and ovals. This one has a dashed stroke and a fill.

No points for guessing that you use the **Line** class to draw straight lines.

We've used the **Rectangle** several times. This one has a stroke and a fill.

The **Polyline** draws an open shape (otherwise known as a line) with an arbitrary number of points.

The **Polygon** draws a closed shape with an arbitrary number of corners.

Expression Blend does a good job of creating XAML **Path** geometries from Adobe Illustrator and Encapsulated PostScript files.

A **Path** is a vector, and can be opened or closed. In theory, you can create a Path to describe any shape you like. In reality, you'd be crazy to build a complex shape in XAML. Instead, build it in a vector drawing program and import it.

BASIC SHAPES

Let's start with some basic shapes. Here's a class diagram. Notice that the shape classes themselves are quite simple, but they inherit some important display properties from **Shape** and its ancestors, **FrameworkElement** and **UIElement**.

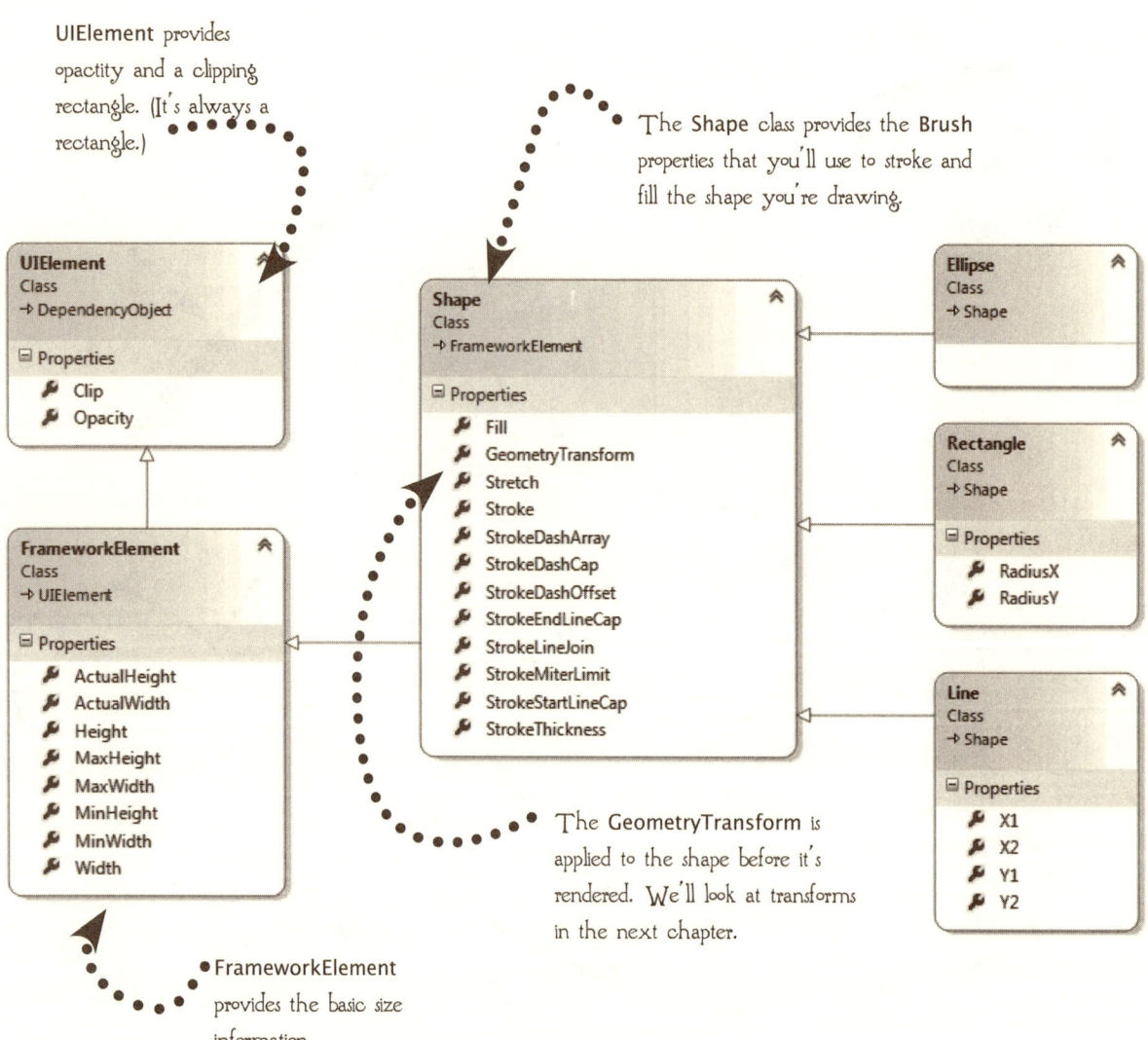

PUT ON YOUR THINKING HAT

Let's get going:

- Create a blank application (I called mine Shapes) and define three columns in the layout Grid. (We'll use the other two later.)
- Put a StackPanel in the first column.
- The label is (of course) contained in a TextBlock.
- The first shape is an Ellipse at 50% opacity, filled with Red.
- The second shapes is a Rectangle filled with Cadet Blue, with a corner radius of 70 in both directions.
- The line has a thickness of 10 and a Black stroke.

349

HOW'D YOU DO?

Here's my version. I gave you some specs for the shapes, but it's okay if you changed them, as long as you did it on purpose.

```xml
<Page ...>
  <Grid Background="AntiqueWhite">
    <Grid.ColumnDefinitions>
      <ColumnDefinition />
      <ColumnDefinition />
      <ColumnDefinition />
    </Grid.ColumnDefinitions>

    <StackPanel Grid.Column="0">
      <TextBlock Text="Basic Shapes" HorizontalAlignment="Center"
              FontSize="36" Foreground="Black" Margin="20"/>
      <Ellipse Fill="Red" Width="270" Height="175"
              Opacity="0.5" Margin="10" />
      <Rectangle Fill="CadetBlue" Width="270" Height="175"
              Margin="93,10,92,10"
              RadiusX="70" RadiusY="70"/>
      <Line X1="20" Y1="10" X2="440" Y2="75" Stroke="Black"
              StrokeThickness="10"/>
    </StackPanel>
  </Grid>
</Page>
```

Did you have trouble figuring out how to translate "50%" into "0.5"?

I'm sure there's a formula for determining corner radius, but in truth I do it by trial and error.

BOUNDING BOXES

When you set the various height and width properties of a shape, you're actually describing the BOUNDING BOX, which is the imaginary rectangle that the XAML layout engine wraps around any element it displays.

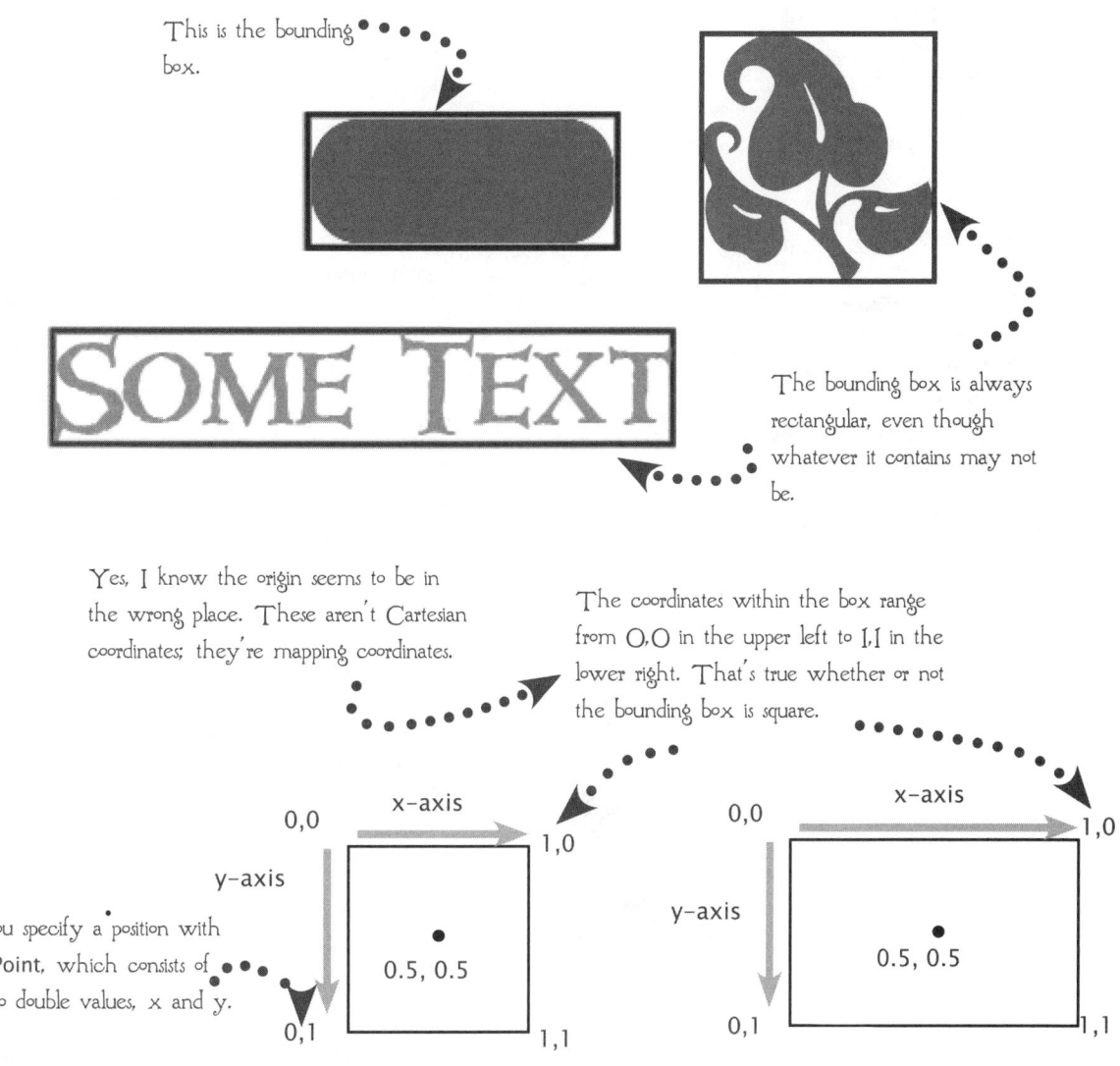

This is the bounding box.

The bounding box is always rectangular, even though whatever it contains may not be.

Yes, I know the origin seems to be in the wrong place. These aren't Cartesian coordinates; they're mapping coordinates.

The coordinates within the box range from 0,0 in the upper left to 1,1 in the lower right. That's true whether or not the bounding box is square.

You specify a position with a Point, which consists of two double values, x and y.

PEN PROPERTIES

In Win8 XAML, as in Silverlight, there isn't a separate Pen class. Instead, the properties of the Pen are exposed on the Shape class. And what a lot of properties there are!

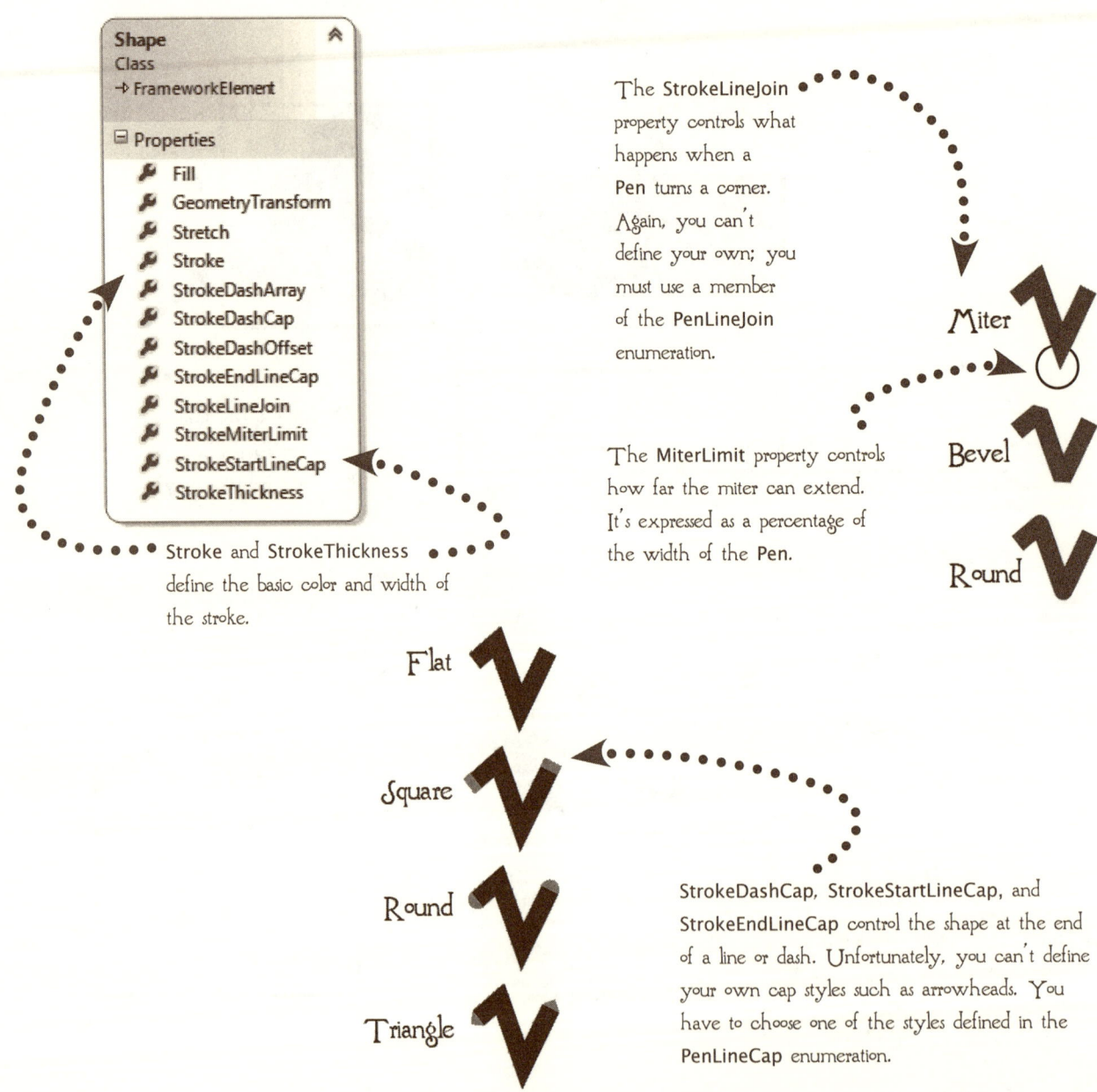

Stroke and StrokeThickness define the basic color and width of the stroke.

The StrokeLineJoin property controls what happens when a Pen turns a corner. Again, you can't define your own; you must use a member of the PenLineJoin enumeration.

The MiterLimit property controls how far the miter can extend. It's expressed as a percentage of the width of the Pen.

StrokeDashCap, StrokeStartLineCap, and StrokeEndLineCap control the shape at the end of a line or dash. Unfortunately, you can't define your own cap styles such as arrowheads. You have to choose one of the styles defined in the PenLineCap enumeration.

352

PUT ON YOUR THINKING HAT

Okay, let's add some strokes to our little exerciser. I haven't given you detailed descriptions this time. Can you figure out how to duplicate these images on your own?

You'll need to use collection syntax to define the stroke dashes:

`<Line.StrokeDashArray>`
...
`</Line.StrokeDashArray>`

- The first few elements are instances of the Line class. The remainder are instances of Rectangle with a fill. (Pick a color you like.)
- All of the new shapes are nested in a StackPanel in the second column of the layout Grid.

HOW'D YOU DO?

I've just shown my version of the second **StackPanel** below.

```xml
<StackPanel Grid.Column="1">
    <TextBlock .../>
        <Line X1="20" Y1="10" X2="440" Y2="10"
            Stroke="Black" StrokeThickness="30" />
        <Line X1="30" Y1="40" X2="430" Y2="40" Stroke="Black"
            StrokeThickness="30"
            StrokeStartLineCap="Triangle" StrokeEndLineCap="Round"/>
        <Line X1="30" Y1="40" X2="440" Y2="40" Stroke="Black"
            StrokeThickness="30">
            <Line.StrokeDashArray>
                0.75
                1
            </Line.StrokeDashArray>
        </Line>
        <Line X1="15" Y1="45" X2="440" Y2="45"
            Stroke="Black" StrokeThickness="30"
            StrokeDashCap="Round" StrokeDashOffset="0.5">
            <Line.StrokeDashArray>
                0
                1.5
            </Line.StrokeDashArray>
        </Line>
        <Rectangle Width="400" Height="100" Fill="Coral" Margin="20"
            Stroke="Black" StrokeThickness="30"
            StrokeLineJoin="Bevel"/>
        <Rectangle Width="400" Height="100" Fill="Coral" Margin="20"
            Stroke="Black" StrokeThickness="30"
            StrokeLineJoin="Miter"/>
        <Rectangle Width="400" Height="100" Fill="Coral" Margin="20"
            Stroke="Black" StrokeThickness="30"
            StrokeLineJoin="Round"/>
</StackPanel>
```

COMPLEX SHAPES

You've seen how to draw a basic shape like a circle or a square, and how to create some moderately cool outlines. The Shapes namespace also provides some slightly more complex shapes. Well, in the case of the Path, potentially much more complex shapes. Here are the basic classes:

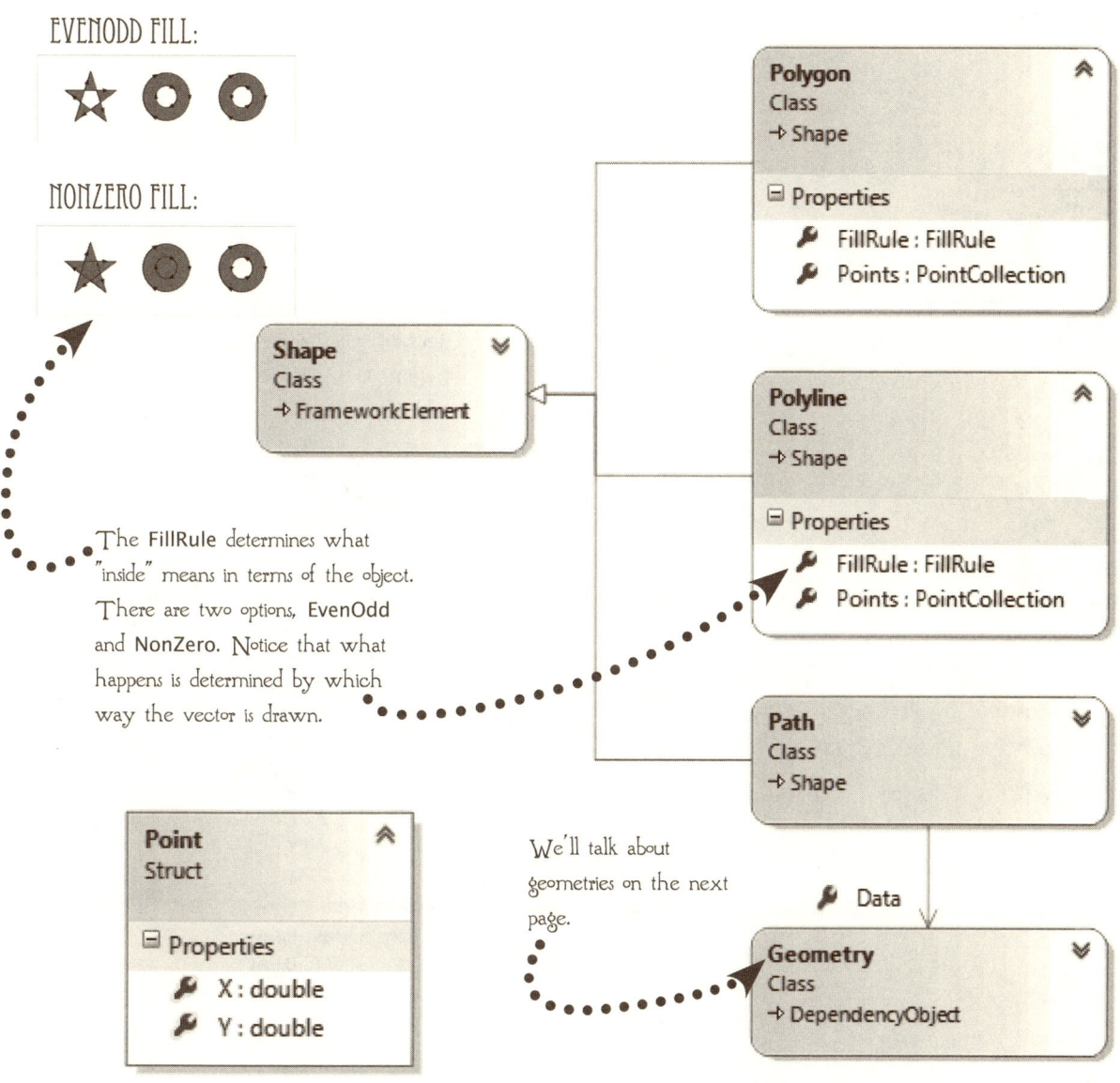

The FillRule determines what "inside" means in terms of the object. There are two options, EvenOdd and NonZero. Notice that what happens is determined by which way the vector is drawn.

We'll talk about geometries on the next page.

355

GEOMETRIES

The Path shape accepts an instance of a Geometry class rather than a set of points. You can think of a geometry as representing a set of vectors that make up the shape definition. Win8 XAML provides three geometry classes, known as CONCRETE GEOMETRIES, that correspond to the basic shapes, and a PathGeometry that lets you define an arbitrary set of vectors. We'll talk about that (and why you probably shouldn't try to create your own) in a few pages. Here are the basic classes:

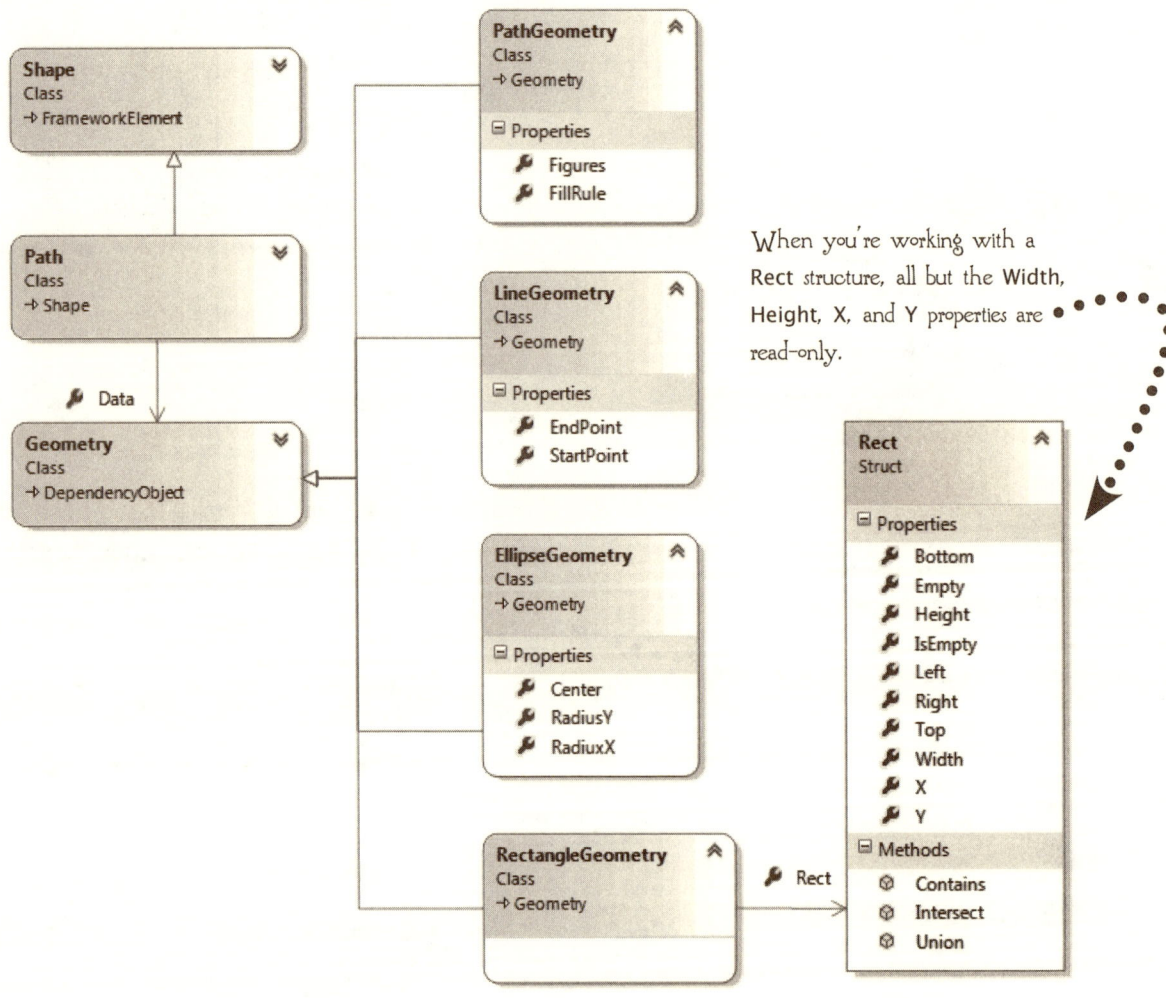

When you're working with a Rect structure, all but the Width, Height, X, and Y properties are read-only.

XAML POINT COLLECTIONS

When you're creating your shapes in XAML, there's a handy-dandy converter that lets you specify a collection of points as a string by (optionally) separating a pair of x and y values with a comma, and individual points by a space:

```
<Polyline Points="20,40 644,22 400,40" >
```

Is equivalent to:

```
MyPolyline.Points.Add(new Point(20,40));
MyPolyline.Points.Add(new Point(644,22));
MyPolyline.Points.Add(new Point(400,40));
```

PUT ON YOUR THINKING HAT

Let's add one more set of shapes to the exerciser. The StackPanel in the final column should include a Polygon shaped like an arrow, a zigzag LineGeometry, and instances of the EllipseGeometry and RectangleGeometry concrete classes. (You'll need to provide those to the Data property of a Path using element syntax.)

HOW'D YOU DO?

Here's my version. As long as yours looks more-or-less the same, don't worry about the details. (Again, I've only shown the code for the last StackPanel.)

Did you have trouble specifying the points? It seems intuitive to me, but I make no claims to normality...

```xml
<StackPanel Grid.Column="2">
   <Polygon Fill="CadetBlue"
         Points="20,10 75,75 20,150 400,75"/>
   <Polyline Stroke="Black" StrokeThickness="10"
            Points="2,40 100,100 200,40 300,100 400,40 300,40" />
   <Path Fill="Red" Opacity="0.5">
      <Path.Data>
         <EllipseGeometry Center="200,100" RadiusX="135" RadiusY="85" />
      </Path.Data>
   </Path>
   <Path Fill="CadetBlue">
      <Path.Data>
         <RectangleGeometry Rect="50,50,320,175" />
      </Path.Data>
   </Path>
</StackPanel>
```

How about the Path.Data syntax? Did that cause you any problems?

PATH GEOMETRIES

The remaining member of the Shape classes is the PathGeometry, which accepts a collection of PathFigure elements, which in turn contains a set of PathSegment elements of various mathematical types. We're not going to discuss how to create these segments because, frankly, you'd be crazy to code one from scratch. It would be like copying the Mona Lisa on an Etch-A-Sketch. Create them in a vector drawing program like Adobe Illustrator and then import them. Expression Blend 4 and 5 (but not the version of Expression Blend used for Win8 development) support the process. You can then copy and paste the path data.

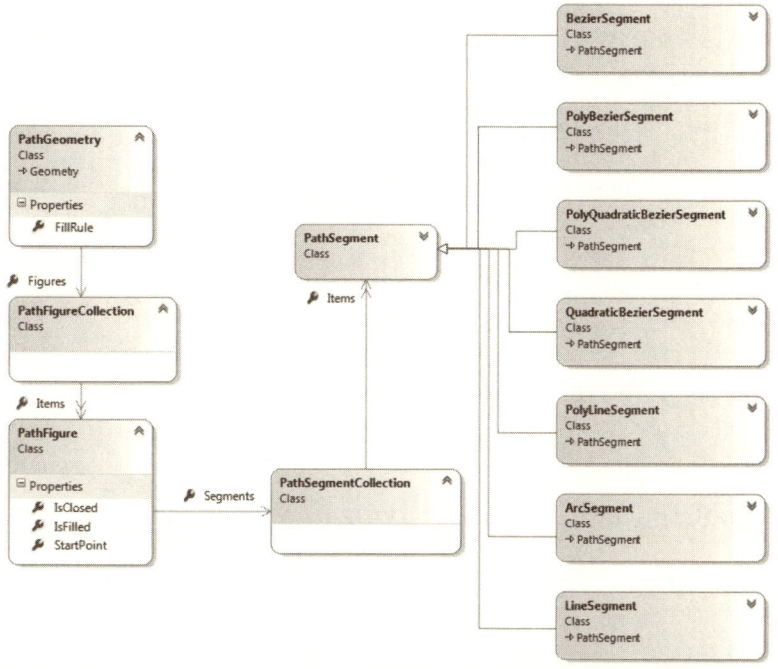

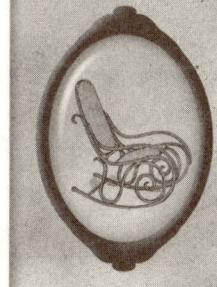

TAKE A BREAK

That's it for our discussion of shapes in Win8 XAML. Why don't you take a break before you complete the Review and we move on to the XAML Brush classes that actually render your images?

REVIEW

Can you answer the following questions based on what you've learned so far?

There are two primary ways to draw a rectangle. What are they?

Why do you think the MitreLimit property is important?

When you're specifying a point collection in XAML, what character separates the x and y values?

Where is the origin (0,0) when you're specifying points?

How do you specify the shape at the end of a line?

What syntax do you use to provide data to a Path in XAML?

BRUSHES

Painters these days don't necessarily use a brush to transfer paint from the palette to the canvas. (Come to think of it, they don't necessarily use a canvas, either.) But in XAML, if you're going to display a color, you need to load it into a Brush. On the other hand, XAML lets you paint with more than a single color. You can load a brush with multiple colors in a gradient or an image. So far, when we've specified a Fill or Background color in XAML, we've been using members of the static Colors class. Behind the scenes, those are actually instances of a SolidColorBrush, one of several brushes available in Win8 XAML.

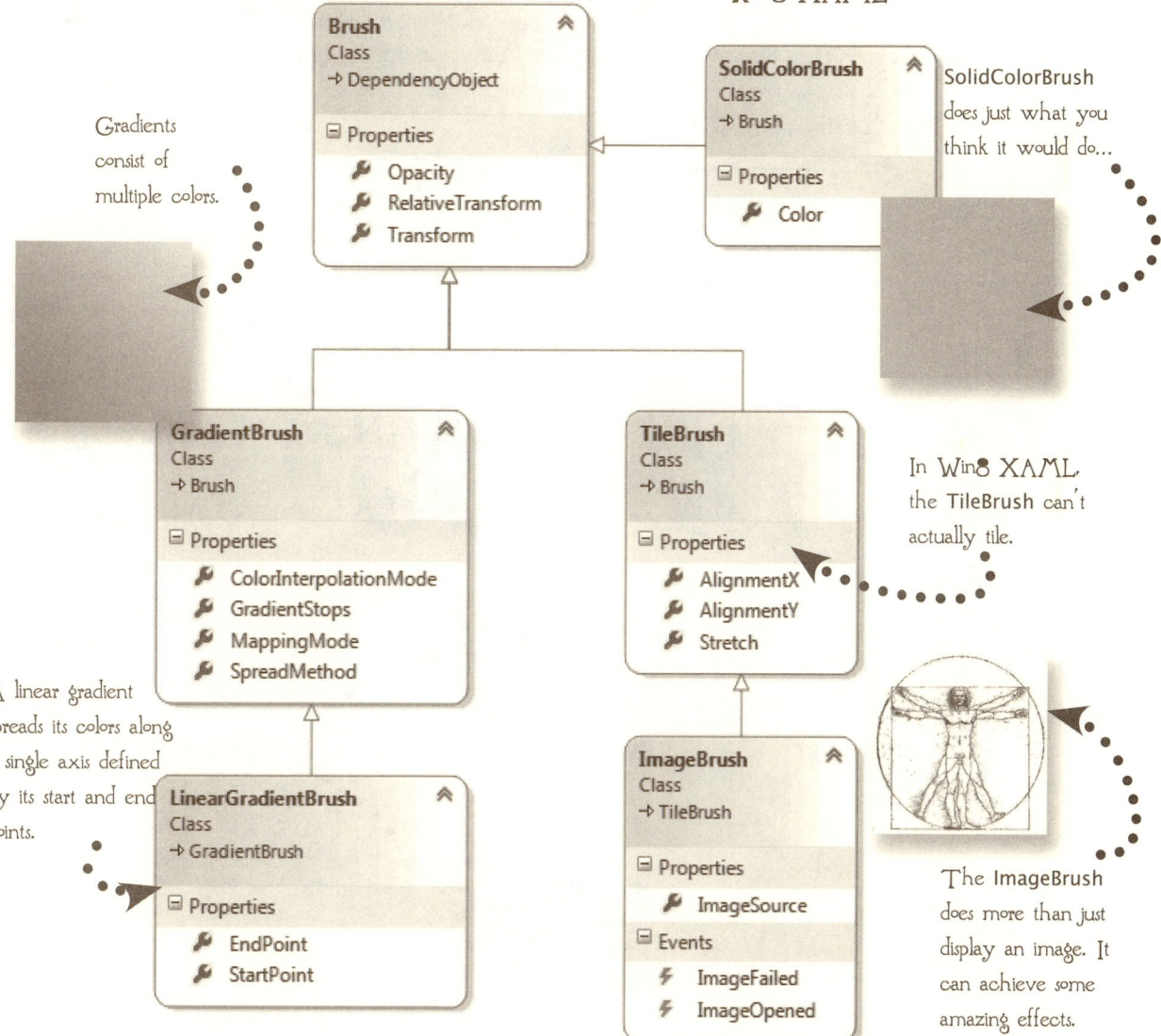

Gradients consist of multiple colors.

SolidColorBrush does just what you think it would do...

Brush
Class
→ DependencyObject
Properties
- Opacity
- RelativeTransform
- Transform

SolidColorBrush
Class
→ Brush
Properties
- Color

GradientBrush
Class
→ Brush
Properties
- ColorInterpolationMode
- GradientStops
- MappingMode
- SpreadMethod

TileBrush
Class
→ Brush
Properties
- AlignmentX
- AlignmentY
- Stretch

In Win8 XAML, the TileBrush can't actually tile.

A linear gradient spreads its colors along a single axis defined by its start and end points.

LinearGradientBrush
Class
→ GradientBrush
Properties
- EndPoint
- StartPoint

ImageBrush
Class
→ TileBrush
Properties
- ImageSource
Events
- ImageFailed
- ImageOpened

The ImageBrush does more than just display an image. It can achieve some amazing effects.

361

COLOR MODELS

Let's start with the simplest brush, the SolidColorBrush, which contains a single property, a Color.

In order to specify a color exactly, you need to use a color model, of which there are several. CMYK (Cyan, Magenta, Yellow, Black) is used by printers because those are the colors of ink from which all other colors are mixed. HSV (Hue, Saturation, Value) is used in many graphics programs because it's a fairly close match to how we perceive color and the way artists think about it.

Computer monitors and most programming languages, including XAML, C#, and Visual Basic, use some form of RGB (Red, Green, Blue). In the RGB model, the values for red, green and blue are specified as numbers, usually integer values between 0 and 255. Many versions of RGB, including the two supported by .NET, also support an alpha value, which determines the transparency of the color (and makes them ARGB rather than just RGB).

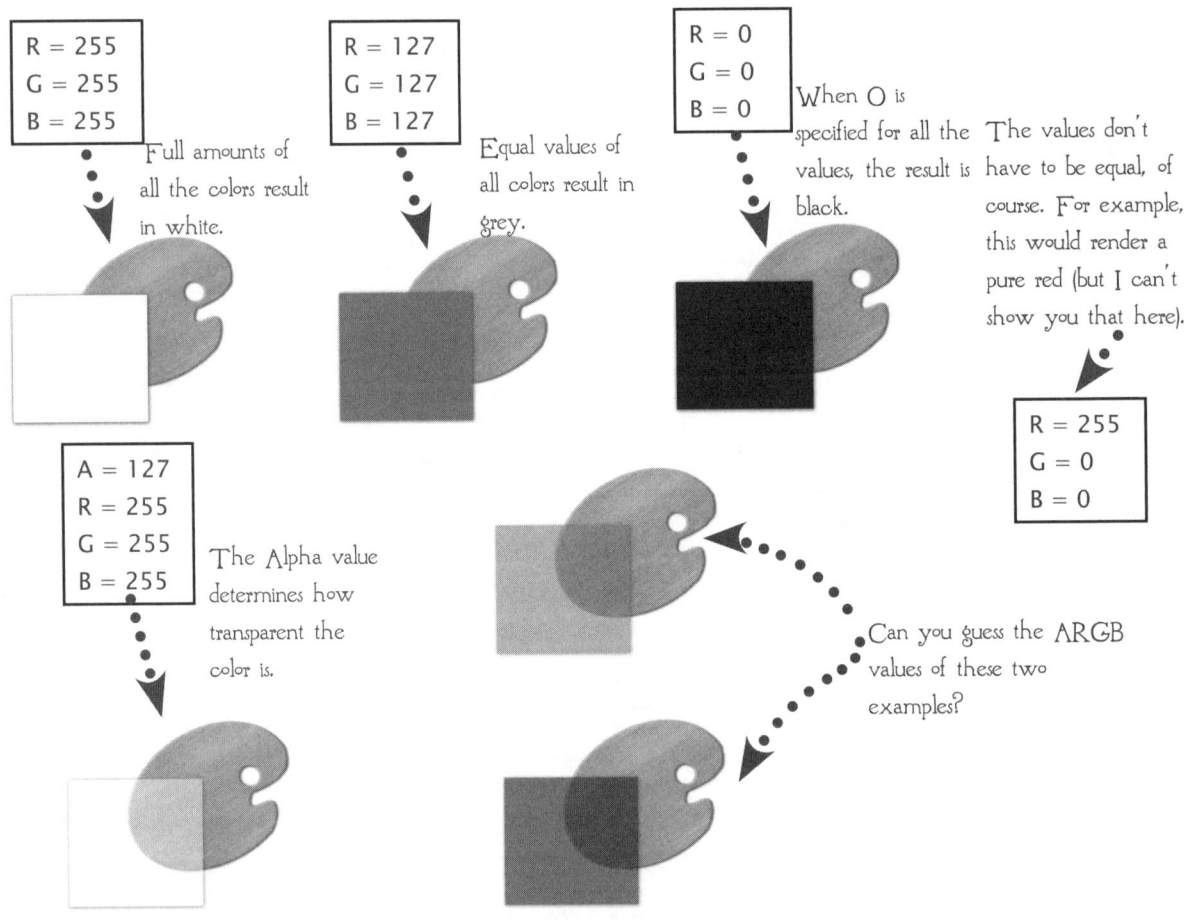

THE COLOR STRUCTURE

In Win8 XAML colors are represented by the `Color` structure, which simply exposes integer properties for the alpha, red, green, and blue values and a `FromArgb()` method that you'll mostly use to actually create an instance in code. There's also a `Colors` class defined in the `Windows.UI` namespace that provides the color names we've been using in XAML. (You can use them in code, too.)

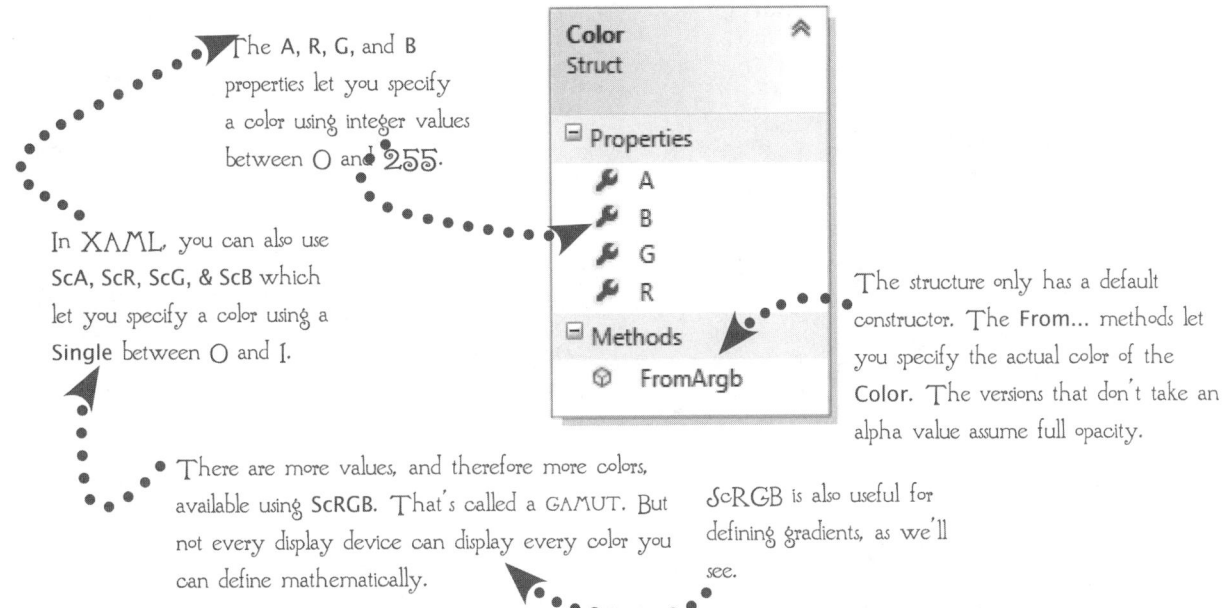

The A, R, G, and B properties let you specify a color using integer values between 0 and 255.

In XAML, you can also use ScA, ScR, ScG, & ScB which let you specify a color using a Single between 0 and 1.

The structure only has a default constructor. The From... methods let you specify the actual color of the Color. The versions that don't take an alpha value assume full opacity.

There are more values, and therefore more colors, available using ScRGB. That's called a GAMUT. But not every display device can display every color you can define mathematically.

ScRGB is also useful for defining gradients, as we'll see.

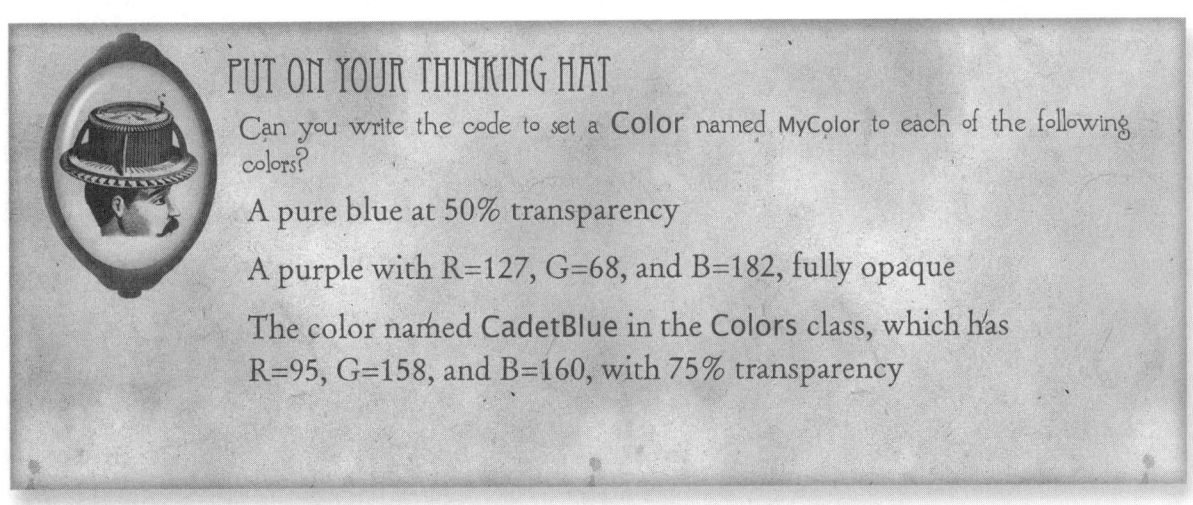

PUT ON YOUR THINKING HAT

Can you write the code to set a `Color` named MyColor to each of the following colors?

A pure blue at 50% transparency

A purple with R=127, G=68, and B=182, fully opaque

The color named CadetBlue in the Colors class, which has R=95, G=158, and B=160, with 75% transparency

HOW'D YOU DO?

A pure blue at 50% transparency

Color.FromArgb(255,127,0,0, 255)

A purple with R=127, G=68, and B=182, fully opaque

Color.FromArgb(127,68,182)

The color named **CadetBlue** in the **Colors** class, which has R=95, G=158, and B=160, with 75% transparency

Color.FromArgb(190,95,158,160)

Did you say 75 here? You need 75% of 255 (which is actually 191.25. I rounded.)

MOVING ON

You probably learned somewhere that the primary colors are red, yellow, and blue, and that you can mix any other color from those. That's only true for things that reflect light, like paint. When you're combining light, the primary colors are red, green, and blue, which is why monitor colors are specified that way. That's only one of the many complications when you're working with color. Printers and monitors display color differently, and they can display different colors (GAMUT). Different monitors or printers may display the same RGB values differently. (Monitors are notorious for not representing colors very well, and their colors shift over time.)

If you're interested in learning more about color theory, color models, gamuts, and profiles, *Real World Color Management* by Bruce Fraser is an excellent (if somewhat daunting) resource.

SPECIFYING COLORS

So far we've only specified colors in XAML, and only using the predefined colors that are defined as static properties of the `Windows.UI.Colors` class. That's easy and intuitive, but of course you don't want to be limited to that set of colors. Fortunately, you have lots of options:

USE THE COLORS CLASS

This is what we've been doing in XAML, and you can do it in code, too:

```
MyBrush.Color = Colors.AntiqueWhite;
```

USE FROMARGB()

In code, you'll call the static **FromArgb()** method of the **Color** structure and pass in (surprise!) the a, r, g, and b values in that order. You don't have to use hexidecimal, but it's conventional:

```
MyBrush.Color = Color.FromArgb(0xFF,0xFF,0,0);
```

USE STANDARD HEXADECIMAL IN XAML

In XAML, you can provide a standard hexadecimal color code in one of several formats: rgb, argb, rrggbb, or aarrggbb:

```
<Rectangle Fill="#FFFF0000" />
```

USE SCRGB IN XAML

An alternative to the standard ARGB model is the ScRGB model, which specifies colors as a value between 0 and 1. It's only supported in XAML and as a property of gradients:

```
<Rectangle Fill="sc# 1,1, 0, 0"/>
```

PUT ON YOUR THINKING HAT

There's a perfectly good color picker in the Properties Window of the XAML designer, but just in case you ever want to write one of your own, let's write a simple color exerciser. The layout isn't difficult, but it's a bit complex, and we'll actually have a sneak peek of binding to get it all to work. Here's the basic screen.

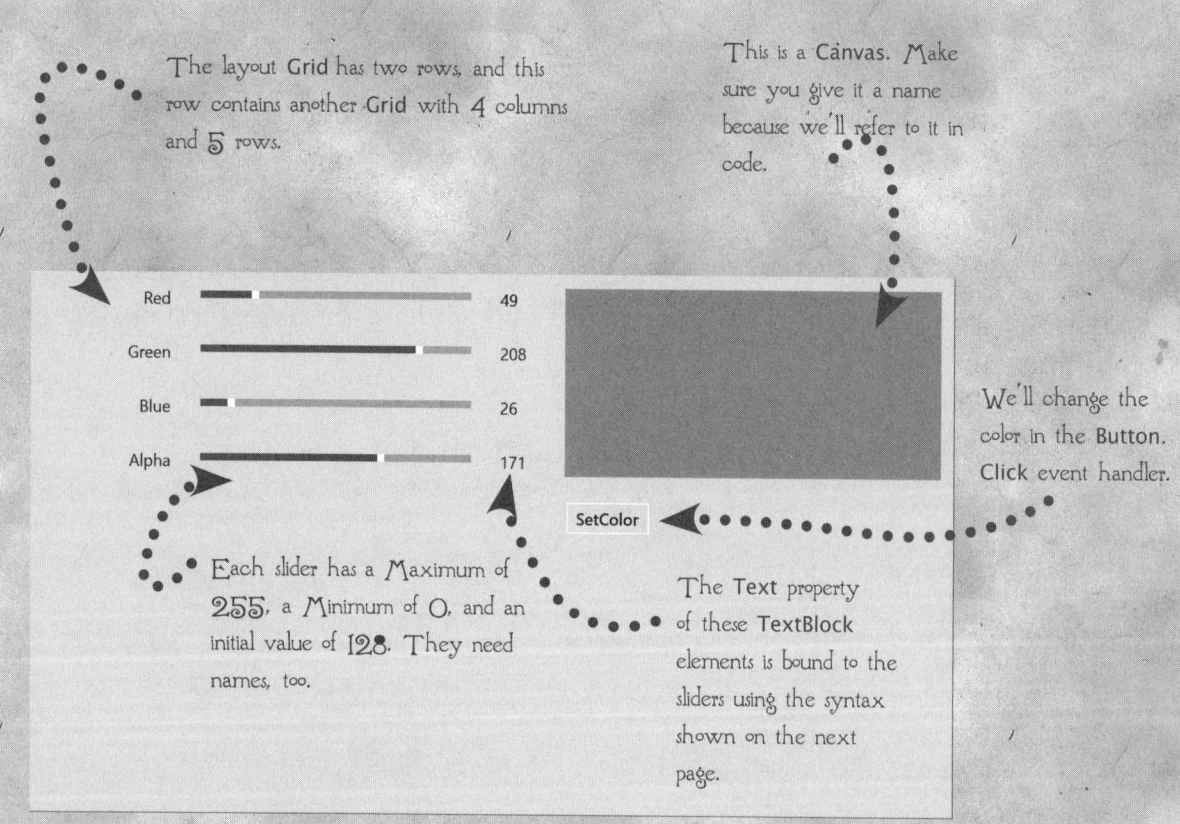

The layout Grid has two rows, and this row contains another Grid with 4 columns and 5 rows.

This is a Canvas. Make sure you give it a name because we'll refer to it in code.

We'll change the color in the Button.Click event handler.

Each slider has a Maximum of 255, a Minimum of 0, and an initial value of 128. They need names, too.

The Text property of these TextBlock elements is bound to the sliders using the syntax shown on the next page.

We'll use the rest of this space in the next exercise.

You'll learn how XAML binding works in Chapter 12. In a real application, you'd probably bind the Fill property of the Rectangle directly to the silders, but for our purposes, we'll just bind the TextBlock elements so you can see what you're doing. The syntax is a little odd-looking when you first see it, but you can just copy this sample and change the ElementName to whatever you name each slider:

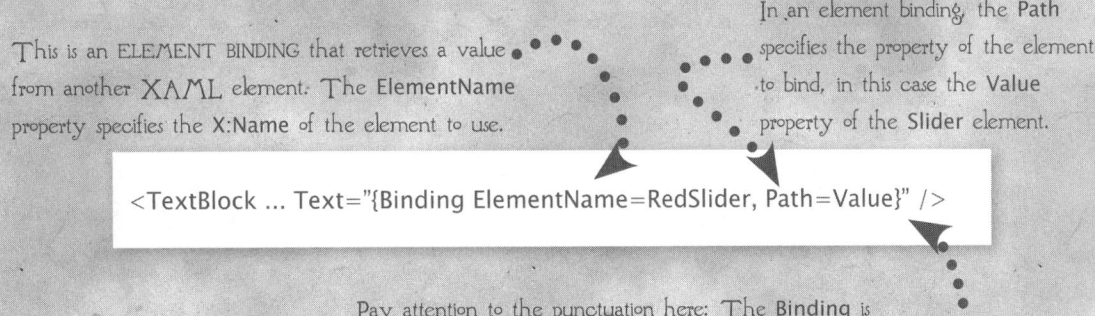

In the SetColor Button.Click event handler, you'll want to create a Color, passing in the Value property of each slider. (You'll need to cast them to bytes.) Then create a new SolidColorBrush passing the Color you created to the constructor. You haven't seen an example of that, but the constructor syntax shouldn't cause you any problems; it's just standard .NET programming. Finally, assign the Background property of the Canvas to the new Brush.

There's a lot going on here, and you haven't seen all of it. But don't let that scare you. Just take it one step at a time and you'll be fine, I promise. You can always peek at my solution if you get confused at any point.

PUT ON YOUR THINKING HAT

How'd you do? Here's my version. As always, I've left out basic formatting (margins and text formatting), and I've left out the row and column definitions. (I only have so much room to work with here...)

```xml
<Grid>
    <TextBlock Grid.Column="0" Grid.Row="0" Text="Red" ... />
    <TextBlock Grid.Column="0" Grid.Row="1" Text="Green" ... />
    <TextBlock Grid.Column="0" Grid.Row="2" Text="Blue" ... />
    <TextBlock Grid.Column="0" Grid.Row="3" Text="Alpha" ... />

    <Slider x:Name="RedSlider" Grid.Column="1" Grid.Row="0"
            Maximum="255" Value="128" ... />
    <Slider x:Name="GreenSlider" Grid.Column="1" Grid.Row="1"
            Maximum="255" Value="128" ... />
    <Slider x:Name="BlueSlider" Grid.Column="1" Grid.Row="2"
            Maximum="255" Value="128" ... />
    <Slider x:Name="AlphaSlider" Grid.Column="1" Grid.Row="3"
            Maximum="255" Value="128" ... />

    <TextBlock Grid.Column="2" Grid.Row="0"
               Text="{Binding ElementName=RedSlider, Path=Value}" ... />
    <TextBlock Grid.Column="2" Grid.Row="1"
               Text="{Binding ElementName=GreenSlider, Path=Value}" ... />
    <TextBlock Grid.Column="2" Grid.Row="2"
               Text="{Binding ElementName=BlueSlider, Path=Value}" ... />
    <TextBlock Grid.Column="2" Grid.Row="3"
               Text="{Binding ElementName=AlphaSlider, Path=Value}" .../>

    <Canvas x:Name="ColorDisplay" Grid.Row="0" Grid.Column="3" Grid.RowSpan="4"
            Background="Gray" Margin="20" />
    <Button x:Name="SetColor" Grid.Column="3" Grid.Row="4"
            Click="SetColor_Click" .../>
</Grid>
```

```csharp
private void SetColor_Click(object sender, RoutedEventArgs e)
{
  Color bkgdColor = Color.FromArgb(
        (byte)AlphaSlider.Value,
        (byte)RedSlider.Value,
        (byte)GreenSlider.Value,
        (byte)BlueSlider.Value);

  SolidColorBrush bkgdBrush = new SolidColorBrush(bkgdColor);
  ColorDisplay.Background = bkgdBrush;
}
```

```vb
Private Sub SetColor_Click(sender As Object, e As RoutedEventArgs )
    Dim bkgdColor As Color = Color.FromArgb(
        CType(AlphaSlider.Value, Byte),
        CType(RedSlider.Value, Byte),
        CType(GreenSlider.Value, Byte),
        CType(BlueSlider.Value) Byte)

    Dim bkgdBrush As SolidColorBrush = New SolidColorBrush(bkgdColor)
    ColorDisplay.Background = bkgdBrush
End Sub
```

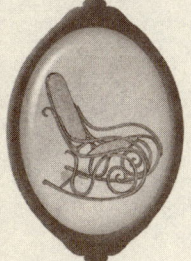

TAKE A BREAK

That exercise was quite a bit of work, wasn't it? Why don't you take a break before we move on to the Brush classes?

369

GRADIENT BRUSHES

The next type of brush to explore is the gradient brush which, in Win8 XAML, has a single concrete descendant, the `LinearGradientBrush`. A color gradient (you'll also see it called a color ramp) consists of a set of colors, called GRADIENT STOPS (or just STOPS), that are given a position along an axis. Colors between the stops are blended. The `GradientBrush` class in XAML defines the `GradientStops` collection and some properties that define how the gradient is created. `GradientBrush` is abstract, but the library defines the `LinearGradientBrush` that you can use in your apps. (Win8 XAML doesn't contain a radial gradient brush out of the box.)

The colors defined by the stops on a linear gradient are distributed perpendicularly to the gradient axis, like a window shade.

The axis can run in any direction.

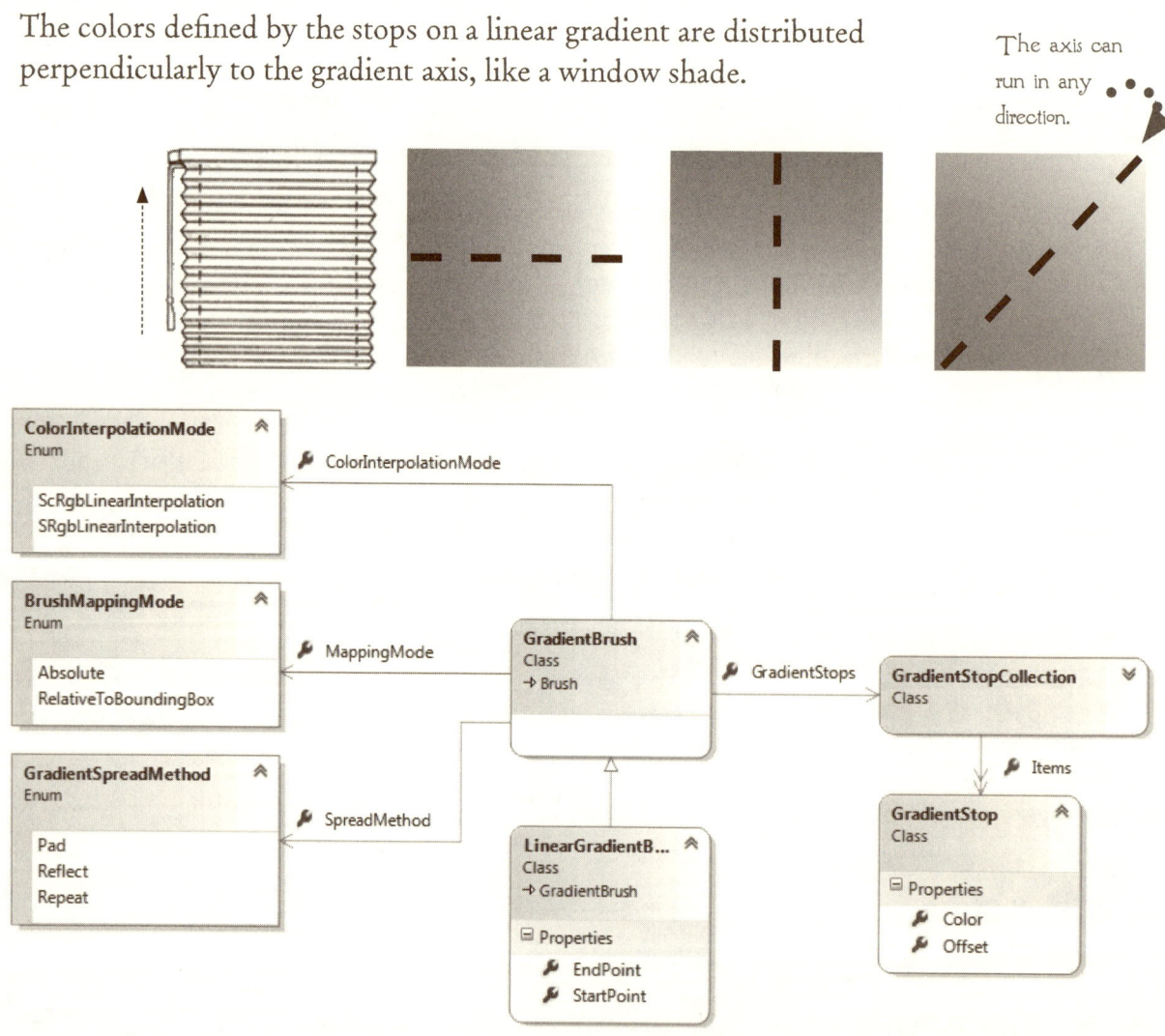

370

The axis of a LinearGradientBrush is defined by its starting and ending points relative to the bounding box. By default, the axis runs from 0,0 to 1,1, which is top left to lower right.

But you can specify any starting and ending point you like, including values outside the bounding box.

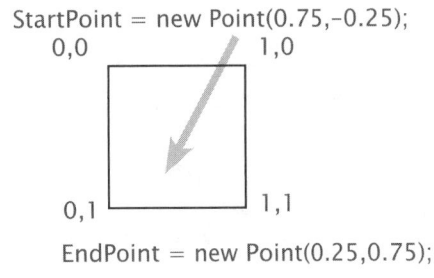

The position of a stop on an axis is defined relative to its origin as a double value. It doesn't matter which direction the axis points, or whether the gradient is radial or linear; stops are always expressed this way.

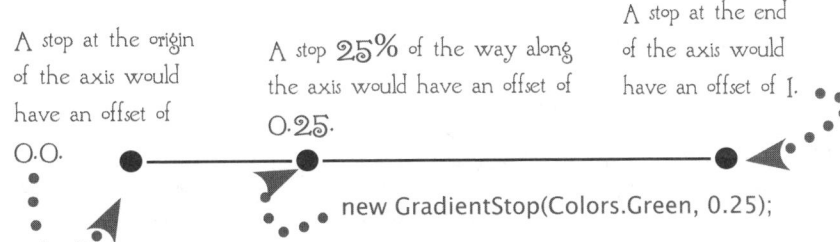

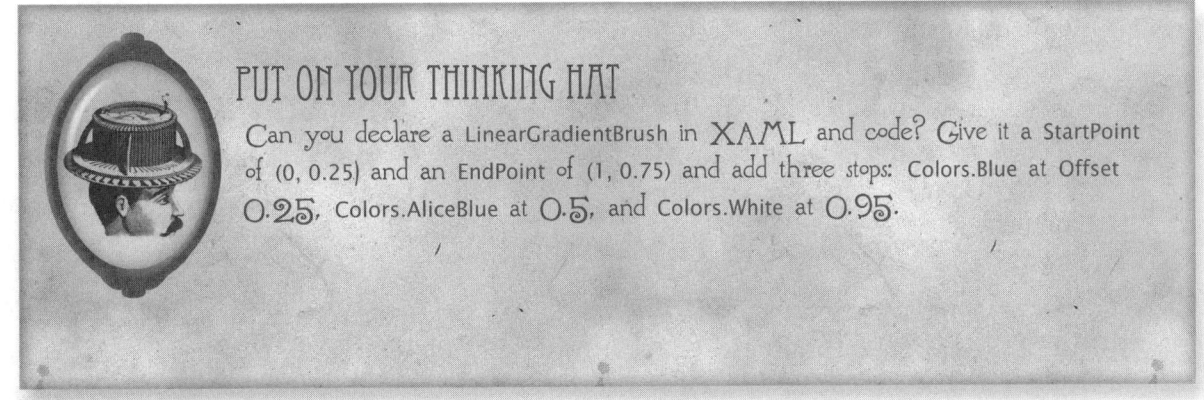

PUT ON YOUR THINKING HAT

Can you declare a LinearGradientBrush in XAML and code? Give it a StartPoint of (0, 0.25) and an EndPoint of (1, 0.75) and add three stops: Colors.Blue at Offset 0.25, Colors.AliceBlue at 0.5, and Colors.White at 0.95.

HOW'D YOU DO?
Here's my version:

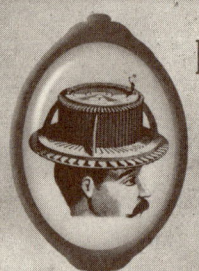

```xml
<LinearGradientBrush StartPoint="0,.25" EndPoint="1,.75">
  <GradientStop Color="Blue" Offset="0.25" />
  <GradientStop Color="AliceBlue" Offset="0.5" />
  <GradientStop Color="White" Offset="0.95" />
</LinearGradientBrush>
```

You can use collection syntax in XAML to declare the gradient stops.

```csharp
LinearGradientBrush lgb = new LinearGradientBrush();
lgb.StartPoint = new Point(0, 0.25);
lgb.EndPoint = new Point(1, 0.75);

lgb.GradientStops.Add(new GradientStop()
    {Color = Colors.Blue, Offset = 0.25});

...
```

But you need to call the Add() method on the GradientStops collection in code.

```vb
Dim lgb As LinearGradientBrush = New LinearGradientBrush()
lgb.StartPoint = New Point(0, 0.25)
lgb.EndPoint = New Point(1, 0.75)

Dim gs As New GradientStop
gs.Color = Colors.Blue
gs.Offset = 0.25
lgb.GradientStops.Add(gs)

...
```

PUT ON YOUR THINKING HAT

Time for another exerciser, this time with gradients.

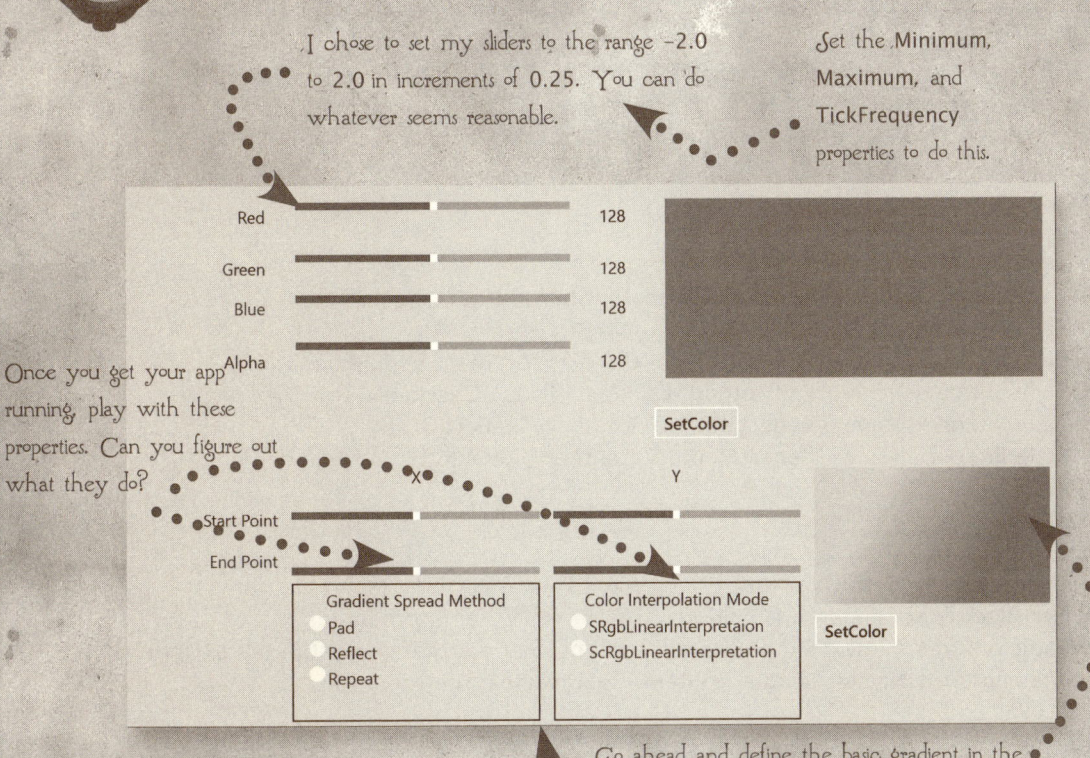

I chose to set my sliders to the range -2.0 to 2.0 in increments of 0.25. You can do whatever seems reasonable.

Set the Minimum, Maximum, and TickFrequency properties to do this.

Once you get your app running, play with these properties. Can you figure out what they do?

We haven't talked about these properties yet. In your code, you'll want to map the Spread Method group to the **SpreadMethod** property, which accepts a member of the GradientSpreadMethod enumeration, and the Color Interpretation group to the **ColorInterpretationMode** property, which accepts a member of the **ColorInterpretationMode** enumeration.

Go ahead and define the basic gradient in the XAML. I picked three stops—Bisque at 0.25, DarkSalmon at 0.5, and Chocolate at 0.75—but you can set it up any way you like.

Remember to name your brush so you can change its properties in the event handler for the button. I called mine LinearBrush.

```
<Canvas ...>
  <Canvas.Background>
    <LinearGradientBrush
      x:Name="LinearBrush" ... />
  ...
```

PUT ON YOUR THINKING HAT

How'd you do? Here's my version, and as always I've left out the bsic formatting.

```xml
<Grid>
    <TextBlock Grid.Column="1" Grid.Row="0" Text="X" ... />
    ... Repeat for remaining labels
    <Slider x:Name="StartXSlider" Grid.Column="1" Grid.Row="1" Maximum="1" Value="0.5"
        StepFrequency="0.1" ... />
    <Slider x:Name="StartYSlider" ... />
    <Slider x:Name="EndXSlider" ... />
    <Slider x:Name="EndYSlider" ... />
    <Border Grid.Row="3" Grid.Column="1" Grid.RowSpan="2" ... />
        <StackPanel Orientation="Vertical">
            <TextBlock Grid.Column="1" Grid.Row="0" Text="Gradient Spread Method" ... />
            <RadioButton x:Name="PadMethod" Content="Pad" IsChecked="True"/>
            <RadioButton x:Name="ReflectMethod" Content="Reflect" ... />
            <RadioButton x:Name="RepeatMethod" Content="Repeat" ... />
        </StackPanel>
    </Border>
    <Border Grid.Row="3" Grid.Column="2" ... >
        <StackPanel Orientation="Vertical">
            <TextBlock Grid.Column="1" Grid.Row="0" Text="Color Interpolation Mode" ... />
            <RadioButton x:Name="SRgb" Content="SRgbLinearInterpretaion" IsChecked="True"/>
            <RadioButton x:Name="ScRgb" Content="ScRgbLinearInterpretation" ... />
        </StackPanel>
    </Border>
    <Canvas x:Name="GradientDisplay" Grid.Column="3" Grid.Row="0" Grid.RowSpan="4" ... >
        <Canvas.Background>
            <LinearGradientBrush x:Name="LGBrush">
                <GradientStop Color="Bisque" Offset="0.25" />
                <GradientStop Color="DarkSalmon" Offset="0.5" />
                <GradientStop Color="Chocolate" Offset="0.75" />
            </LinearGradientBrush>
        </Canvas.Background>
    </Canvas>
    <Button x:Name="SetGradient" Grid.Column="3" Grid.Row="4"
            Content="Set Gradient" Click="SetGradient_Click"/>
</Grid>
```

```csharp
private void SetGradient_Click(object sender, RoutedEventArgs e)
{
  LGBrush.StartPoint = new Point(StartXSlider.Value, StartYSlider.Value);
  LGBrush.EndPoint = new Point(EndXSlider.Value, EndYSlider.Value);

  if (PadMethod.IsChecked == true)
      LGBrush.SpreadMethod = GradientSpreadMethod.Pad;
  else if (ReflectMethod.IsChecked == true)
      LGBrush.SpreadMethod = GradientSpreadMethod.Reflect;
  else
      LGBrush.SpreadMethod = GradientSpreadMethod.Repeat;

  if (SRgb.IsChecked == true)
      LGBrush.ColorInterpolationMode = ColorInterpolationMode.SRgbLinearInterpolation;
  else
      LGBrush.ColorInterpolationMode = ColorInterpolationMode.ScRgbLinearInterpolation;
}
```

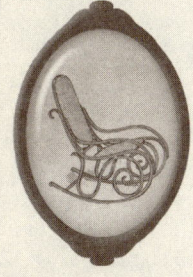

TAKE A BREAK

Another long exercise, but we're finished with brushes now, so why don't you take a break and then we'll take a quick look at transformations?

REVIEW

Can you answer the following questions based on what you've learned?

You can display three kinds of things with a brush. What are they?

How do you add a color to the gradient in a LinearGradientBrush?

What does the 'A' in Argb stand for?

What would the hexadecimal code for fully opaque black be?

Where does a gradient with a StartPoint property of 0.5, 0.5 originate?

What property do you set to load an image into an ImageBrush?

Transforming Objects

We've seen how to create basic shapes and how to apply strokes and fills to them to any UIElement. Now it's time to start really pushing them around. We'll start with transformations. They allow you to change the size, position, and and skew of an object, and there are four:

RotateTransform

The RotateTransform rotates an element the specified angles around the specified center point:

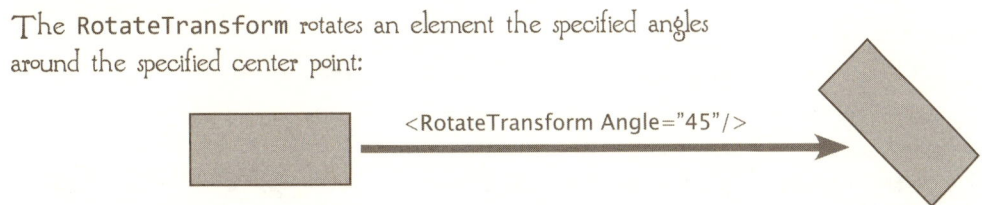

TranslateTransform

The TranslateTransform moves an element horizontally or vertically:

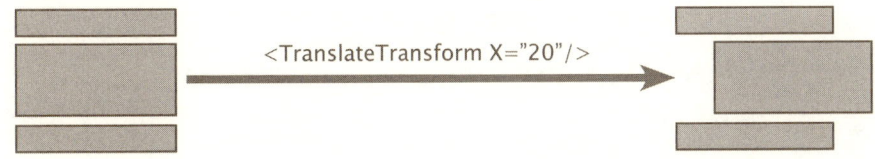

ScaleTransform

The ScaleTransform changes the horizontal or vertical size of an element by the percentage specified around the specified center:

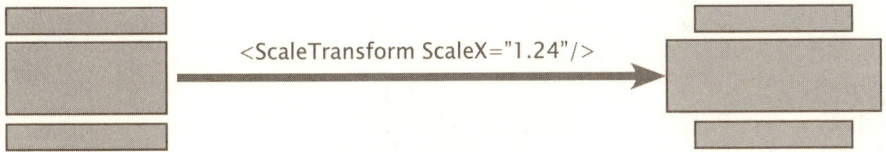

SkewTransform

Skews the element horizontally or vertically around a center point you can specify.

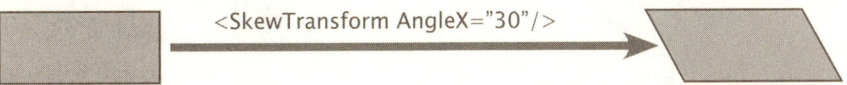

Applying Transforms

In Win8 XAML, a transform changes the size, shape, or position of an element. There are five concrete transform classes, plus a CompositeTransform class that allows you to combine them. (It basically exposes all the properties of each of the concrete transform classes.)

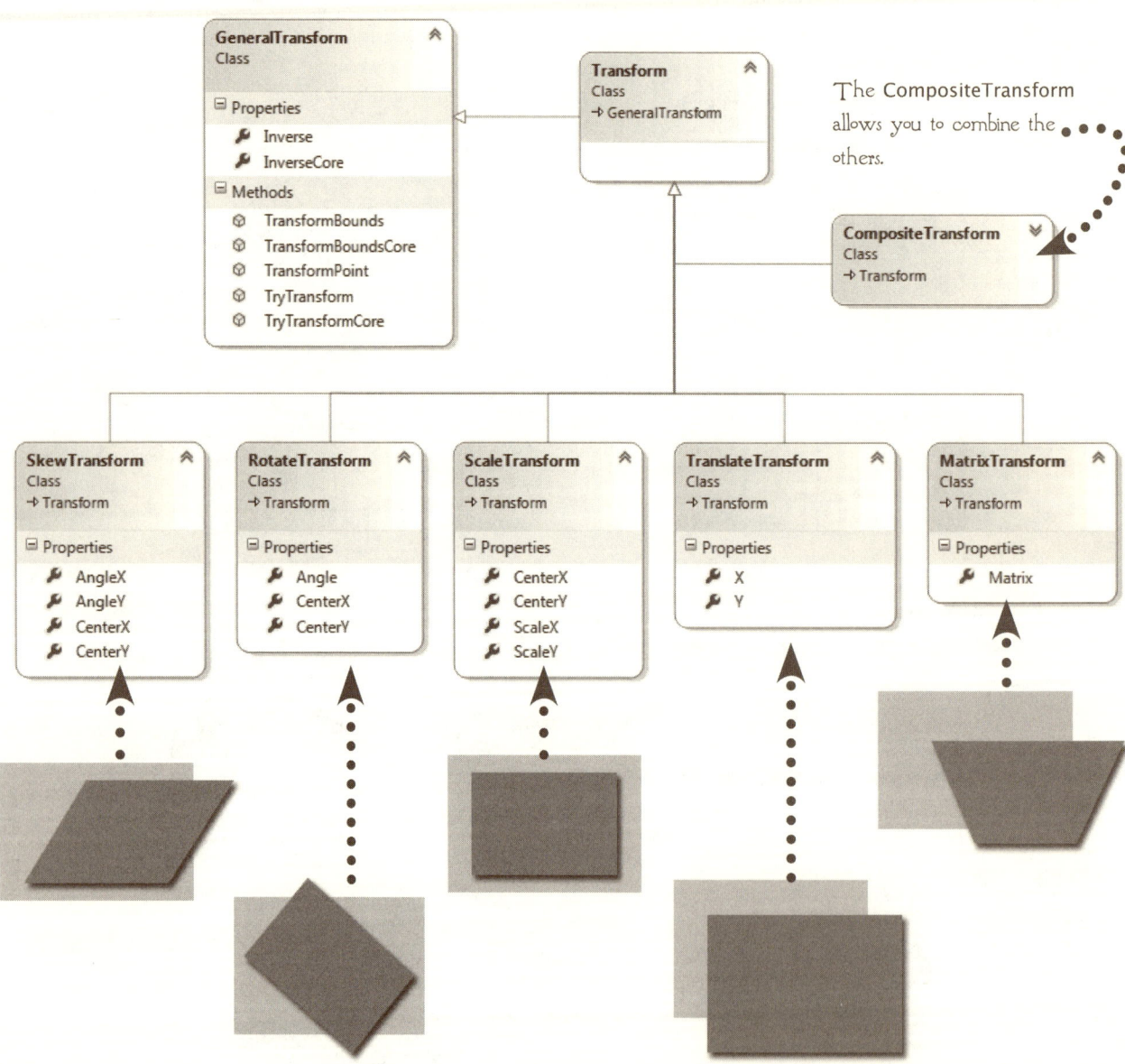

The UIElement class, from which most of the widgets you'll use on your pages descend, exposes a RenderTransform property that can accept a single instance of one of the concrete transform classes. You can create and apply transforms in code, but it's more common to declare them in the XAML, either directly, or via the Properties Window.

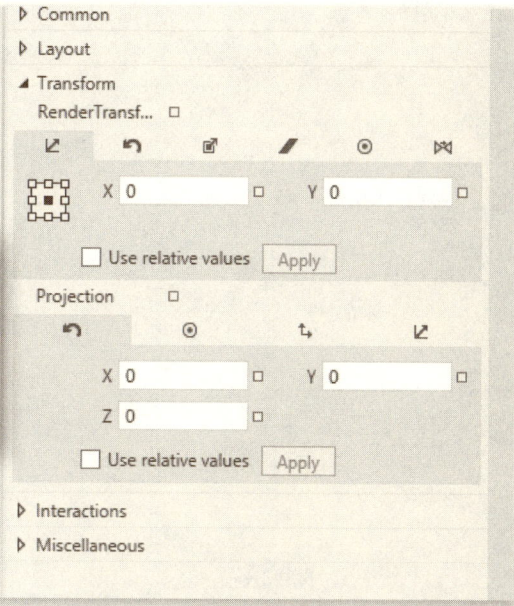

```
<Rectangle ... >
  <Rectangle.RenderTransform>
    <SkewTransform Angle="45" />
  </Rectangle.RenderTransform>
</Rectangle>
```

MAKE A NOTE

Win8 XAML transformations are RENDER TRANSFORMS, which means that they're applied after their parent container lays out all of its children. In other words, the element moves, not the bounding box. The GeneralTransform.TranslateBounds() method may help you out in these situations.

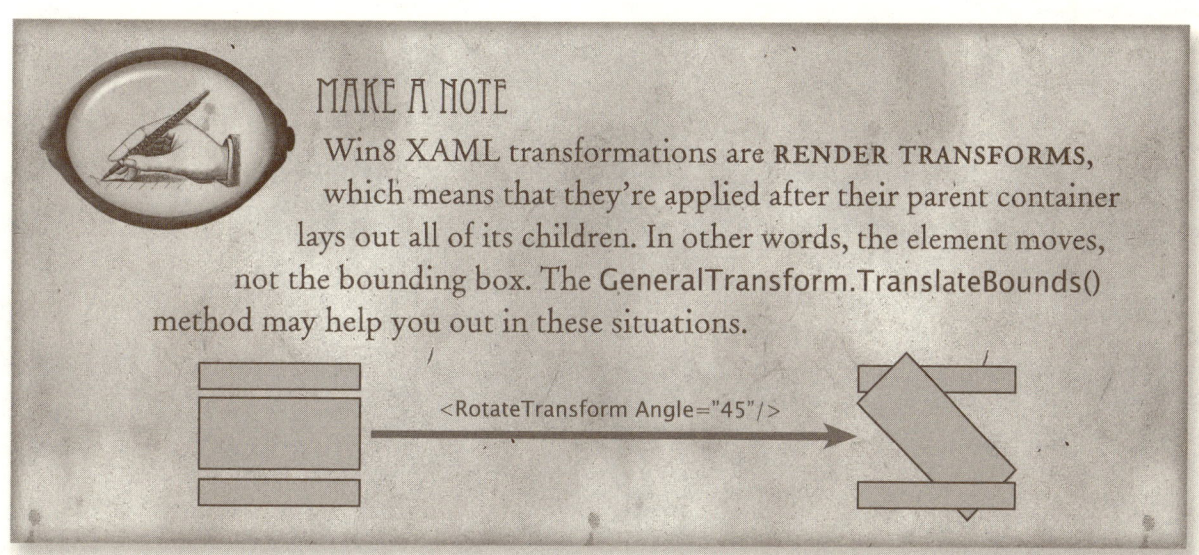

ON YOUR OWN

You're getting pretty good at this stuff, and the syntax of transforms is pretty easy. Can you duplicate this page without my help? Everything's done directly in the XAML (If you get stuck, it's included in the sample code for the book.)

Basic Rectangle

Skewed 45 degrees on the X axis

Scaled to 50% in each direction

Rotated 45 degrees from the center

Notice that the rotated version falls out of the page and overlaps another element.

XAML TYPOGRAPHY

Just about anything you want to do typographically is possible in WinRT. Swash capitals, ligatures, alternate glyphs...whatever you need, you can do. But this isn't a typography book; it's a book about building Win8 apps in XAML. So don't worry if you don't know what any of those things are; we're only going to explore the basic text characteristics that are exposed by the widgets you're likely to be using. And the good news is that XAML makes controlling these simple things simple.

Most of the complexity of typography in XAML is that you have two sets of concepts to juggle. First are the properties of the text itself, and second are the widgets that best suit your purpose. We'll take them one at a time.

WHAT DOES IT LOOK LIKE?

Normal or *Italic*

Times New Roman or Old Claude

Condensed or Expanded

Medium or **Bold**

Or *Some* of Each?

HOW IS IT BEING USED?

You've already used the TextBlock and TextBox.

If you need COMPLEX formatting, with different fonts, *styles* and **weights**, or you need to add decorations like underlining, you'll need a RichTextBlock.

If you need the text to be updatable, you'll use a RichEditBox.

TERMINOLOGY

Every technology that's been around for more than thirty minutes develops some jargon, and typography, one of the oldest, has more than its share. And be forewarned: The terminology is slippery. Calligraphers using steel nibs, letterpress artists using technology that would be familiar to Johannes Gutenberg, graphic designers concerned with ligatures and kerning, and XAML app developers concerned with building a beautiful, functional UX are all working with text, but they're using very different techologies and slightly different sets of terms. Here are the XAML basics:

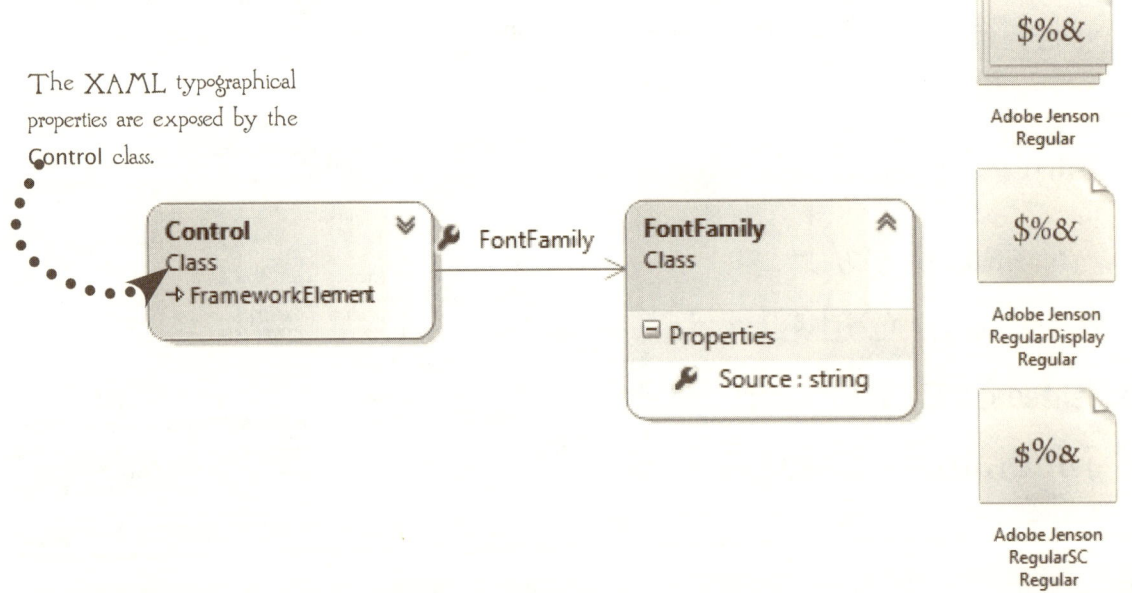

The XAML typographical properties are exposed by the Control class.

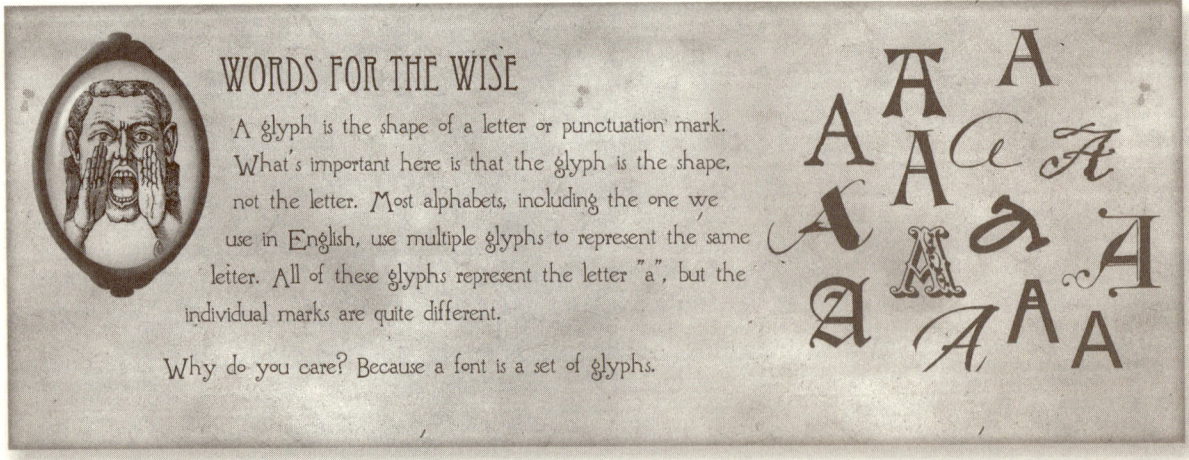

WORDS FOR THE WISE

A glyph is the shape of a letter or punctuation mark. What's important here is that the glyph is the shape, not the letter. Most alphabets, including the one we use in English, use multiple glyphs to represent the same letter. All of these glyphs represent the letter "a", but the individual marks are quite different.

Why do you care? Because a font is a set of glyphs.

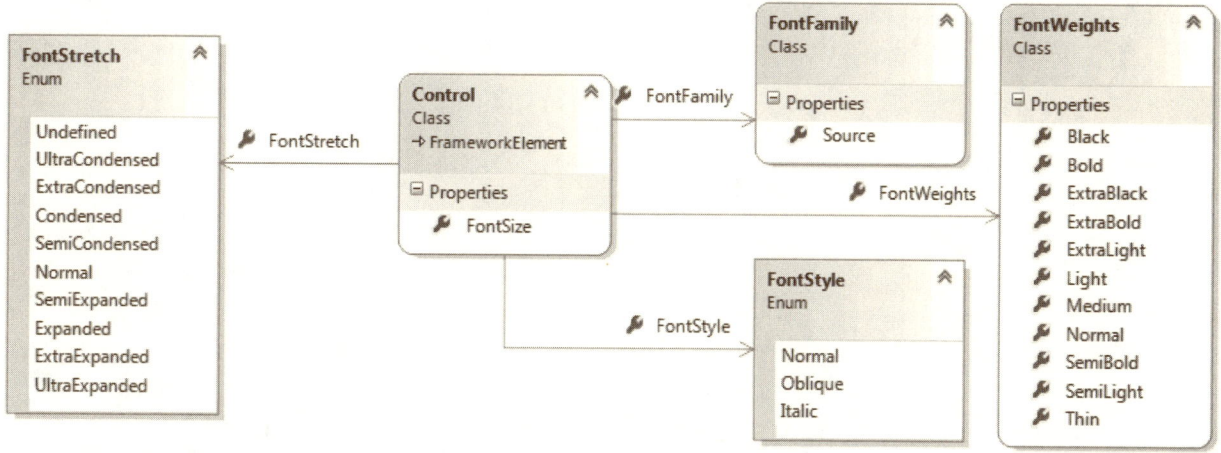

Most people don't make a distinction between oblique and italic, but they are quite different: The italic version of a font uses a different glyph.

a *a* *a*
Normal Oblique Italic

ON YOUR OWN

XAML typography is pretty straightforward, and we've built two rather complicated example apps in this chapter, so I'm not going to make you write another. Just have a play with the text properties of one of the TextBlock elements in an existing app to make sure you understand what's going on. Then finish the Review, and in the next chapter we'll (finally) start exploring the styles and templates I've been teasing you with.

REVIEW

How would you create a dotted line in XAML?

What class would you use to create an octagonal clickable shape in your app?

What shape is the bounding box of an ellipse?

How do you specify a collection of points in XAML?

What have I recommended that you do instead of coding a complex path geometry directly?

What does GradientSpreadMethod.Repeat do?

Congratulations! You've finished the chapter. Take a minute to think about what you've accomplished before you move on to the next one...

List three things you learned in this chapter:

①

②

③

Why do you think you need to know these things in order to develop Win8 apps?

Is there anything in this chapter that you think you need to understand in more detail? If so, what are you going to do about that?

RESOURCES, STYLES, AND TEMPLATES

Not long after WPF was released, I was hired by an antiques dealer to design a system for managing their appraisals. Because screen real estate was at a premium (isn't it always?) I wanted to use panels that opened and closed from the side of the screen—a simpler version of the Visual Studio toolbox, without docking. That wasn't part of the WinForms toolkit, and writing custom WinForms controls isn't for the faint of heart. The existing third-party controls seemed overkill, so a friend suggested I look at WPF. To say I was skeptical is something of an understatement. Like many of you, I had years invested in WinForms, and I wasn't at all sure that I wanted to tackle an entirely new platform for what was, after all, a relatively small contract.

But the idea of lookless controls seemed intriguing. I decided I'd devote a day or two playing around with WPF to see if creating a "sideways ComboBox" was feasible. It took less than an hour. I took an Expander (unfortunately, a WPF-only control not available in Win8 XAML), rotated it 90 degrees, transformed the content back, fiddled around a bit with some button widgets, and I was done. I poured myself a tall glass of Kool-Aid, and I've never looked back.

The magic that let me create my widget so quickly is the subject of this chapter. Styles let you completely define the way any FrameworkElement appears. Resources let you make objects (including styles) available for a single object or an entire application, and control templates let you replace the entire logical tree of a control with one that suits your purposes better. We'll explore all those things in this chapter. WinRT XAML isn't as powerful in this area as WPF (or at least, not in this release, but we live in hope), but it will support most scenarios (including turning a ComboBox on its side).

Fitting It In

You know that in OOP, objects have both state and behavior, and that good programmers try very hard not to duplicate either of them. Using resources, we can avoid duplicating state or behavior between instances of classes.

These are both instances of the class Button.

[Button]   [Button Too]

STATE:

I'm painted with a silver gradient. ⟷ I'm painted with a silver gradient.

I have a black border. ⟷ I have a black border.

My FontFamily is Segoe UI. ⟷ My FontFamily is Segoe UI.

BEHAVIOR:

I look different when I'm pressed. ⟷ I look different when I'm pressed.

I look different when I'm disabled. ⟷ I look different when I'm disabled.

I look different when I'm selected. ⟷ I look different when I'm selected.

All of this state and behavior (and a lot more besides) is defined at the instance level but shared by both instances. It's pretty common for you to want all (or at least most of) the buttons in your application to look the same, right?

You haven't been defining most of these characteristics in your applications and probably haven't thought a lot about how or where they're defined. They're actually being defined in default style sheets provided by XAML. Using what you learn in this chapter, you can take complete control over these characteristics (and more).

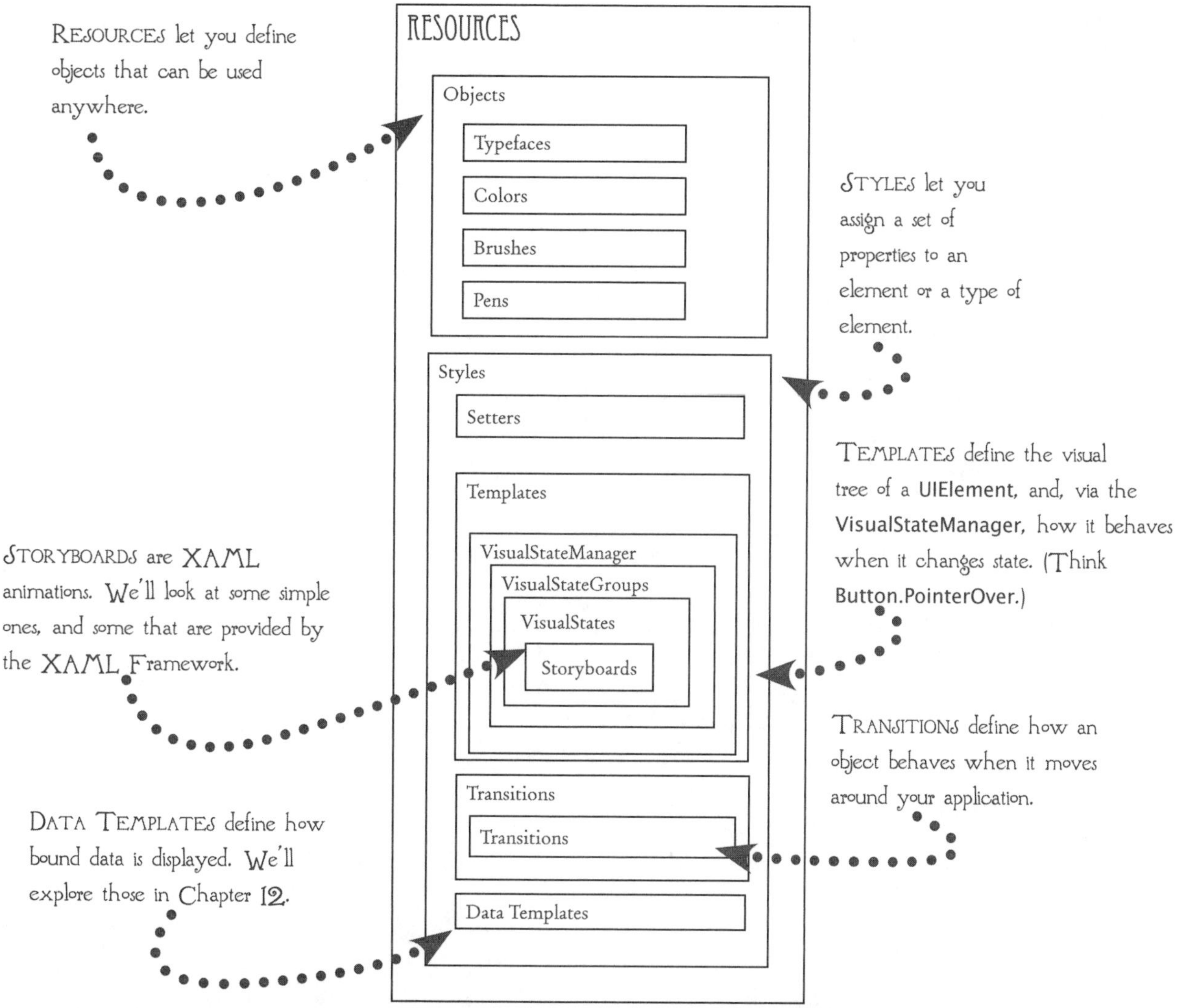

RESOURCES

Objects
- Typefaces
- Colors
- Brushes
- Pens

Styles
- Setters

Templates
- VisualStateManager
  - VisualStateGroups
    - VisualStates
      - Storyboards

Transitions
- Transitions

Data Templates

RESOURCES let you define objects that can be used anywhere.

STYLES let you assign a set of properties to an element or a type of element.

TEMPLATES define the visual tree of a **UIElement**, and, via the **VisualStateManager**, how it behaves when it changes state. (Think **Button.PointerOver**.)

STORYBOARDS are XAML animations. We'll look at some simple ones, and some that are provided by the XAML Framework.

TRANSITIONS define how an object behaves when it moves around your application.

DATA TEMPLATES define how bound data is displayed. We'll explore those in Chapter 12.

PUT ON YOUR THINKING HAT

Resources allow you to separate state and behavior in new and exciting ways. What benefits and drawbacks do you see to using this approach?

HOW'D YOU DO?
How many did you come up with? Did you think of some I haven't? Do you disagree with me about some of them?

BENEFITS

- Resources defined declaratively are easier to implement by non-programmers.

- Resources defined outside the element definition allow appearance and appearance-related behavior to be changed without re-compiling (if they're in a separate file).

- Resources defined outside the element allow different individuals or teams to work on code and appearance.

- Resources help enforce a consistent look and behavior throughout the application.

- Resources can improve performance by reducing the application's memory usage (but this is only true if resources are shared among multiple elements).

DRAWBACKS

- Multiple files can complicate managing and deploying the application.
- Property inheritance combined with resources can make tracking down display problems more complex (you have some extra places to look).

TASK LIST

In this chapter we'll explore the magic that is XAML styles and templates.

RESOURCES

Our first step, of course, is to figure out how resources are declared and how to use them once they are. There are several options, which probably comes as no surprise at this point, and we'll examine the most common.

STYLES & THEMES

While simply declaring an object as a resource so that it can be re-used is really useful, it's even better when you can combine a set of property declarations that will apply to all (or some) of the objects in your application. And when you can group styles and swap them in and out as needed, you're really on to something. (Or the architects of XAML are.)

TEMPLATES

Templates, usually defined as part of styles, let you completely re-define the element tree of your control. Control templates can get pretty complex pretty fast, but they don't need to be, and we'll re-design the **Button** as an example.

THE VISUALSTATEMANAGER

Think about a **Button**: It looks very different when it's pressed than when it isn't. These are Visual States, and the **VisualStateManager** gives you control over them.

THEME TRANSITIONS

We'll end the chapter by exploring the control transitions that provide behavior at the layout (as opposed to control) level.

RESOURCES

XAML Resources are simply elements that are defined independently of a visual tree. They can be defined as part of any `FrameworkElement`, or in separate files.

Resources are often defined inside the Application.xaml file to make them available throughout the application, but you can define them inside any element (often a container such as a Page or Grid) using the same syntax.

Remember the x:Key markup extension is like the x:Name extension in that it makes it possible to refer to the element elsewhere.

```
<Application ...>
  <Application.Resources>
    <SolidColorBrush x:Key="MyBlueBrush"
      Color="Blue" />
  </Application.Resources>
</Application>
```

There's nothing unusual about the way the properties of your resource element are declared.

You can define any element you want inside a resource dictionary, but of course not everything makes sense.

If the resources are defined in a separate file, as they often are, you include them in your application by setting the Source property of the ResourceDictionary.

```
<ResourceDictionary Source="dict.xaml" />
```

```
<ResourceDictionary>
...
</ResourceDictionary>
```

An external dictionary is just a XAML snippet that wraps everything in a ResourceDictionary element.

```
<Application.Resources>
  <ResourceDictionary>
    <ResourceDictionary.MergedDictionaries>
      <ResourceDictionary Source="First.xaml" />
      <ResourceDictionary Source="Second.xaml" />
      ...
    </ResourceDictionary.MergedDictionaries>
  </ResourceDictionary>
  <SolidColorBrush ... />
</Application.Resources>
```

If you have multiple external files, you can include them in the **MergedDictionaries** collection of the ResourceDictionary.

You can define other resources along with the merged dictionaries, but it isn't very common practice.

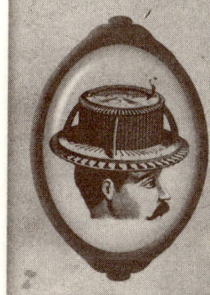

PUT ON YOUR THINKING HAT...

Add a Resource Dictionary called FluentDictionary to a new blank application. (It's available from the Add New Item dialog.)

Add a SolidColorBrush to FluentDictionary, any color you like. Give it the key SolidBackgroundBrush.

Add FluentDictionary to a MergedDictionary inside the project's `App.xaml` file.

HOW'D YOU DO?

Visual Studio adds some of the structure for you, but not all...

Here are the contents of FluentDictionary.xaml:

When you added the file to the project, Visual Studio created the **ResourceDictionary** tag for you. Good thing, too; who wants to type those namespaces?

I picked **DarkTurquoise**. You could have picked a different standard color or specified one using the hexadecimal values.

```
<ResourceDictionary ... >
  <SolidColorBrush x:Key="SolidBackgroundBrush"
      Color="DarkTurquoise" />
</ResourceDictionary>
```

```
<Application ... >
  <Application.Resources>
    <ResourceDictionary>
      <ResourceDictionary.MergedDictionaries>
        <ResourceDictionary Source="FluentDictionary.xaml" />
      </ResourceDictionary.MergedDictionaries>
    </ResourceDictionary>
  </Application.Resources>
</Application>
```

It always seems to me that there's one more ResourceDictionary than there should be in this syntax.

I'm wrong about that, of course. The **Resources** property is a collection, not a ResourceDictionary. The <ResourceDictionary> tag is an element in that collection, and the **MergedDictionaries** property contains another collection, with yet another **ResourceDictionary** contained in it.

```
Resources (collection)
  ResourceDictionary
    MergedDictionaries
    (Collection)
      ResourceDictionarySource
```

REFERENCING RESOURCES

As we'll see, it's possible to define a style that applies to all elements of a given type automatically, but most of the time you'll have to reference the ResourceKey directly using the StaticResource markup extension.

The syntax for using the StaticResource extension looks a lot like those bindings we keep tripping over and will explore in detail in the next chapter.

```
<property>="{StaticResource <key>}"
```

```
<Grid Background="{StaticResource SolidBackgroundBrush}" >
```

MAKE A NOTE
Win8 XAML does have one other way of referencing a resource the CustomResource extension that allows you define your own resource types by writing a class that derives from CustomXamlResourceLoader. Custom resources are very rare and very advanced, and now that you know the technology exists, we're finished with the subject...

PUT ON YOUR THINKING HAT

Change the Background property of the Grid in the MainPage.xaml of your application from the default reference to the ThemeResource to the resource you defined in FluentDictionary.xaml.

RESOURCES IN CODE

Most of the time resources are a XAML thing, not a code thing, but of course you can work with resource-related objects in your code. Here's the basic syntax:

THE RESOURCEDICTIONARY CLASS

There's nothing at all tricky about working with instances of a ResourceDictionary. It's just a .NET class that derives from DependencyObject and implements the IDictionary and IEnumerable interfaces.

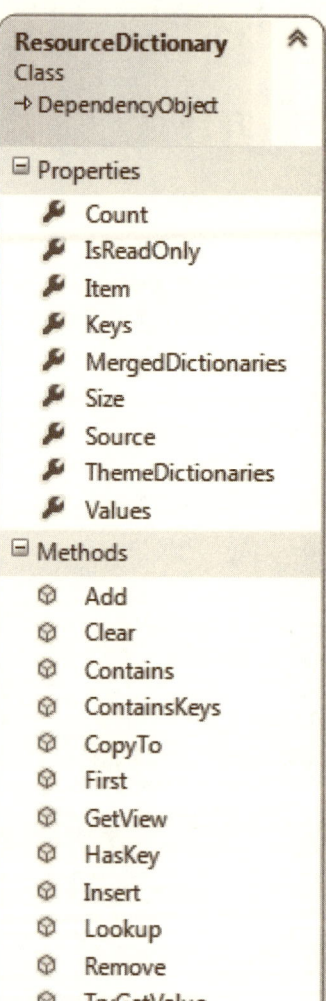

HOW'D YOU DO?

Except for that weird extension syntax (quote-brace-content-brace-quote), and you'll get used to that eventually, it's pretty straightforward.

```
<Grid ...
    Background="{StaticResource SolidBackgroundBrush}" >
```

TO ADD A RESOURCE TO A DICTIONARY

The only thing tricky about adding resources to a ResourceDictionary in code is remembering that the key has to be a String, even though it's defined as an Object.

```
<rd>.Add(<Key>,<Resource>);
```

```
MyDictionary.Add("BackgroundBrush", MySolidColorBrush)
```

TO ASSIGN A RESOURCE TO A PROPERTY

The ResourceDictionary exposes a TryGetValue() method that you can use to test for the existence of a resource with the specified key, and an Item property that you can use to reference it. Once you have the resource, you'll need to cast it to the appropriate type, then you can assign it using standard syntax. To get the resources that are currently defined for the app (as opposed to those you create in code), reference the Resource collection of the current application:

```
Application.Current.Resources["<key>"]
```

```
MyButton.Background = (Brush)Application.Current.Resources("MyBrush");
```

```
MyButton.Background = Application.Current.Resources("MyBrush") As Brush
```

TAKE A BREAK

Feel free to play with creating and referencing resources in code, but you really only need to remember that it's possible, because you're not going to do it often (if ever). For now, why don't you take a quick break before we tackle styles?

STYLES & THEMES

Resources are helpful, but defining individual resources for common properties can lead to some really verbose (not to mention tedious) code. The solution is to define a Style, which is, at its most basic, a resource that contains a collection of property values that will be applied all at once.

The x:Key works just like it does for any resource.

The TargetType identifies the type of widget the style applies to.

The Style contains a collection of Setter elements, each of which has a Property and a Value.

The Value property can be as complex as you need.

```xml
<ResourceDictionary>
    <Style x:Key="LabelStyle" TargetType="TextBox">
        <Setter Property="FontFamily" Value="Arial" />
        <Setter Property="Background">
            <Setter.Value>
                <LinearGradientBrush StartPoint="0,0.5" EndPoint="0,1">
                    <GradientStop Offset="0.0" Color="White"/>
                    <GradientStop Offset="0.5" Color="#f2f2f2"/>
                    <GradientStop Offset="0.75" Color="#eaeaea"/>
                </LinearGradientBrush>
            </Setter.Value>
        </Setter>
    </Style>
</ResourceDictionary>
```

```xml
<TextBox Style="{StaticResource LabelStyle}"
         Text="Hello!" .../>
```

IMPLICIT STYLES

If you declare a style's TargetType but don't give it a key, it will become the default style for elements of that type, called an IMPLICIT STYLE.

```xml
<ResourceDictionary>
    <Style TargetType="TextBlock">
        <Setter Property="FontFamily" Value="Arial" />
    </Style>
</ResourceDictionary>

<TextBlock>Hello!</TextBlock>
```

You don't need to explicitly apply an implicit style.

```xml
<TextBlock Text="Hello!"/>
```

STYLE HIERARCHIES

As with any code, it's best to avoid repetitive code in declaring styles and resources, not out of laziness, but in the service of maintainability. If a `LinearGradientBrush` is defined in 14 places and it changes, it's entirely too easy to miss one. Better to declare it as a resource and reference it where necessary. The `BasedOn` property of the `Style` class and its corresponding markup extension goes even further, by allowing you to base one `Style` on another and only change what needs changing. Think of it as stylish sub-classing.

INSTEAD OF:

```xml
<Style x:Key="BasicLabel" TargetType="TextBlock">
    <Setter Property="Margin" Value="5" />
    <Setter Property="HorizontalAlignment" Value="Right" />
    <Setter Property="VerticalAlignment" Value="Center" />
</Style>

<Style x:Key="RequiredLabel" TargetType="TextBlock">
    <Setter Property="Margin" Value="5" />
    <Setter Property="HorizontalAlignment" Value="Right" />
    <Setter Property="VerticalAlignment" Value="Center" />
    <Setter Property="FontWeight" Value="Black" />
    <Setter Property="Foreground" Value="Red" />
</Style>
```

BASEDON LETS US DO THIS:

Because the `StaticResource` markup extension requires a key, you can't use implicit styles with `BasedOn`.

```xml
<Style x:Key="BasicLabel" TargetType="TextBlock">
    <Setter Property="Margin" Value="5" />
    <Setter Property="HorizontalAlignment" Value="Right" />
    <Setter Property="VerticalAlignment" Value="Center" />
</Style>

<Style x:Key="RequiredLabel" BasedOn="{StaticResource BasicLabel}"
        TargetType="TextBlock">
    <Setter Property="FontWeight" Value="Black"/>
    <Setter Property="Foreground" Value="Red" />
</Style>
```

Styles in Visual Studio

The Style property is exposed by the FrameworkElement class, so it's available to most of the widgets you'll be working with in building a XAML app, and it's fully supported by the Visual Studio. Let's walk through how that works:

Create a Button Style

First add a style named **BigTextButton** to the FluentDictionary.xaml file we created in the last exercise. It should set four properties:

- The FontSize should be 24
- The Background should be White
- The Foreground should be Black
- The BorderBrush should be Black
- The BorderThickness should be 1

Create a Button

In MainPage.xaml, change the Grid.Background to AntiqueWhite and then add a big button to the upper-left corner:

 APPLY THE STYLE

The **Style** property lives in the Miscellaneous section of the Properties Window. With the **Button** selected, click the little box to the right of the property and then choose Local Resource. You'll see a list of available **Button** styles. Choose **BigTextButton**, and the **Button** will be updated in the Designer Window.

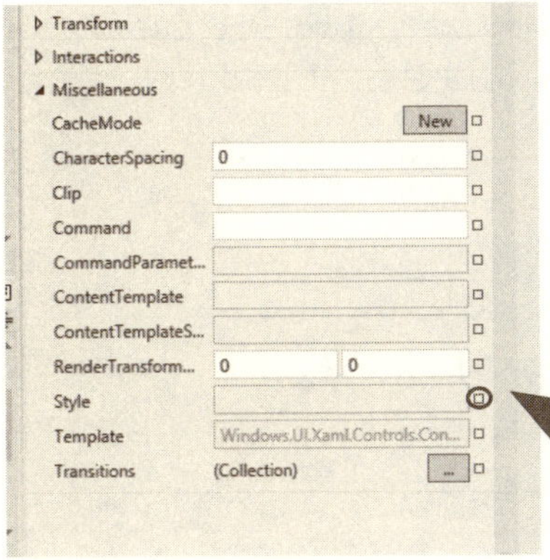

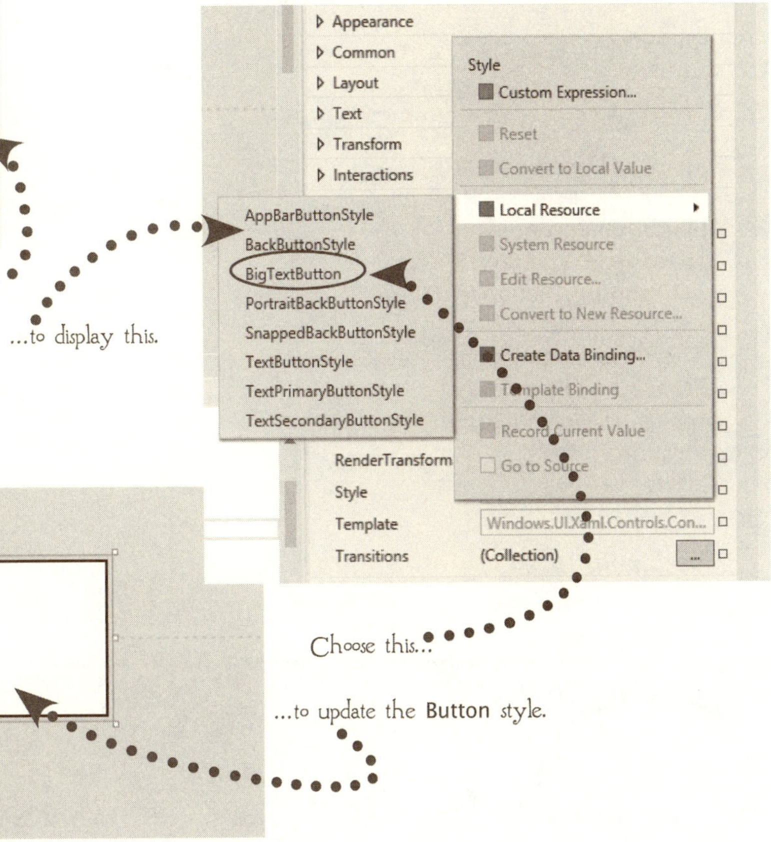

Click here... ...to display this.

Choose this... ...to update the **Button** style.

If you don't see your style listed on the menu, check to make sure that you've included the **ResourceDictionary** file in the **MergedDictionaries** defined in **App.xaml**.

401

WIN8 THEMES

In XAML a THEME is a set of resources and styles that are applied as a group. In other XAML platforms, you can create themes, and it's quite common to do so. Win8 XAML only supports three themes, Light, Dark, and HighContrast.

By default, your app will use the Dark theme. You can choose the Light theme at the app level by setting the RequestedTheme property of the Application element in App.xaml (I've done that for the sample apps in this book to make the screenshots more legible) or at an individual element level using the FrameworkElement.RequestedTheme property.

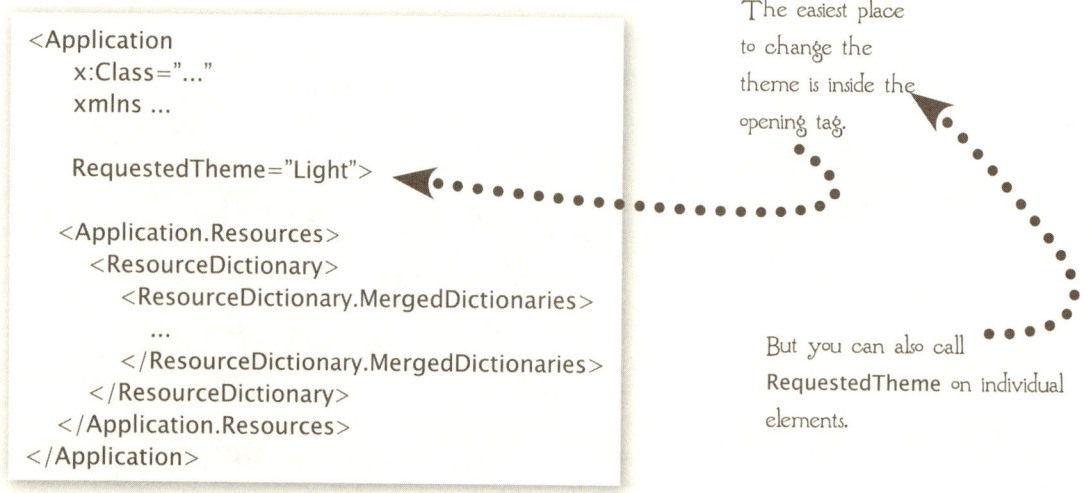

The easiest place to change the theme is inside the opening tag.

But you can also call RequestedTheme on individual elements.

`<Button RequestedTheme="Dark" ... />`

MAKE A NOTE

The user can choose the HighContrast theme via the Settings charm, and if they do so, that choice will trump any settings in your app.

SUPPORTING HIGH CONTRAST

Styling your app elements is very cool, and it's simple to do in XAML. But there is one little catch: If you want your app to have maximum reach (and you will, if you're selling it through the store), you really should support the `HighContrast` theme. It's pretty straightforward. Just define styles for black, white, and custom high contrast display along with your default (branded) theme styles, and declare them in the `ThemeDictionaries` collection of the `ResourceDictionary` instead of the `MergedDictionaries` collection with the appropriate keys.

```
<ResourceDictionary>
  <ResourceDictionary.ThemeDictionaries>
        <ResourceDictionary x:Key="Default" ... />
        <ResourceDictionary x:Key="HighContrastBlack" ... />
        <ResourceDictionary x:Key="HighContrastWhite" ... />
        <ResourceDictionary x:Key="HighContrastCustom" ... />
  </ResourceDictionary.ThemeDictionaries>
</ResourceDictionary>
```

To make things even easier, Visual Studio provides some useful resources for supporting high-contrast themes, and they're even surprisingly well documented. Just search MSDN for "XAML theme resource reference".

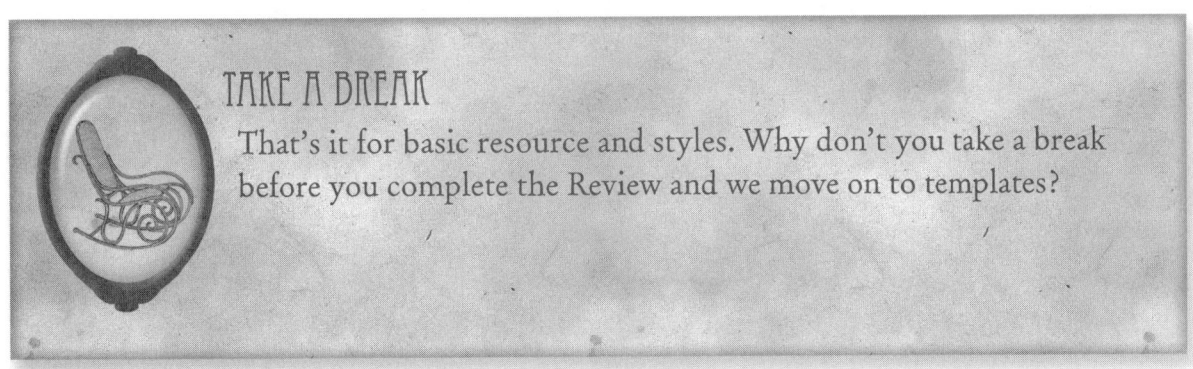

TAKE A BREAK
That's it for basic resource and styles. Why don't you take a break before you complete the Review and we move on to templates?

REVIEW

Can you answer the following questions based on what you've learned?

Where can you declare resources?

When is the theme assigned to an application?

What markup extension must be present in a resource?

What markup extension must be present in a style?

Where do you typically put MergedDictionaries so that they're available application-wide?

How do you define a style that applies to all instances of an element type by default?

TEMPLATES

As you know, when you add elements to a XAML Page, you're building the Visual Tree. At its most basic, the Template property, exposed by the Control class, allows you to do the same thing. There are some differences, of course. The ControlTemplate also provides access to the VisualStateManager, which allows you to change the appearance or the whole visual tree of the Control based on its state. (We'll discuss the VisualStateManager in the next section.) And ControlTemplates aren't the only kind of template in town. We'll look at DataTemplates, which define how bound values are displayed, in the next chapter.

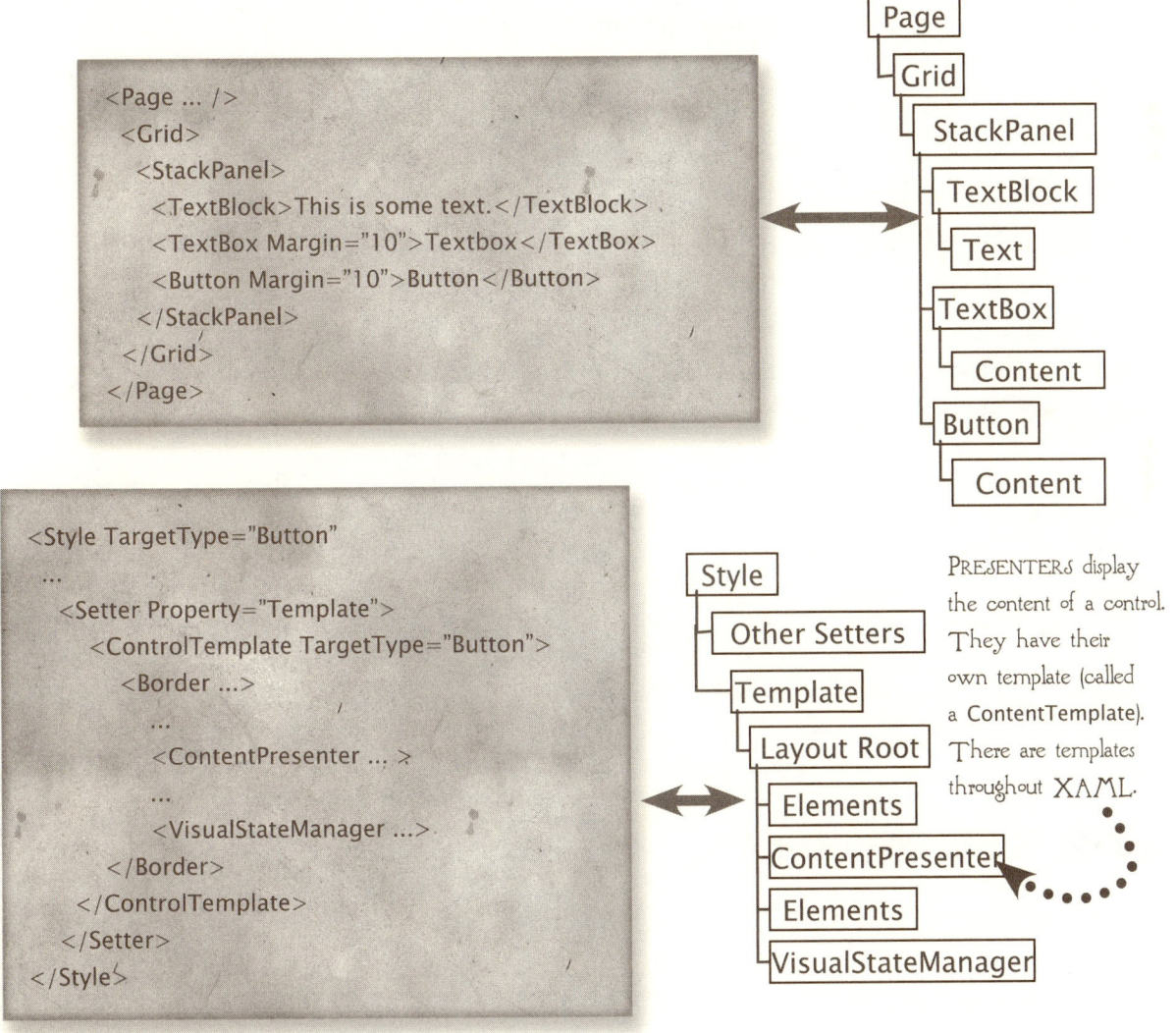

PRESENTERS display the content of a control. They have their own template (called a ContentTemplate). There are templates throughout XAML.

BUILDING TEMPLATES

Although the contents of a template can be quite complex, the structure of a `ControlTemplate` is quite straightforward:

 The **Template** property is defined as an instance of **ControlTemplate** by the **FrameworkElement** class. You can define it as part of an element tag (it's just a property), as a resource, or as part of a **Style**.

 A **ControlTemplate** has a **TargetType** property, just like a **Style**, and just like a **Style**, you must provide a value for this property (even when it would seem obvious).

 Like a **ContentControl**, the **ControlTemplate** can contain a single element, and just like a **ContentControl**, the contents of that element can be arbitrarily complex.

Visual Studio provides support for creating and applying templates from within the XAML Designer. Just right-click the element and choose either Edit Current (if you already have a template or style applied), Edit a Copy (if you want to start with the current style), or Create Empty. After you make a choice, you'll be presented with a dialog that lets you choose where you want the style or template to be created.

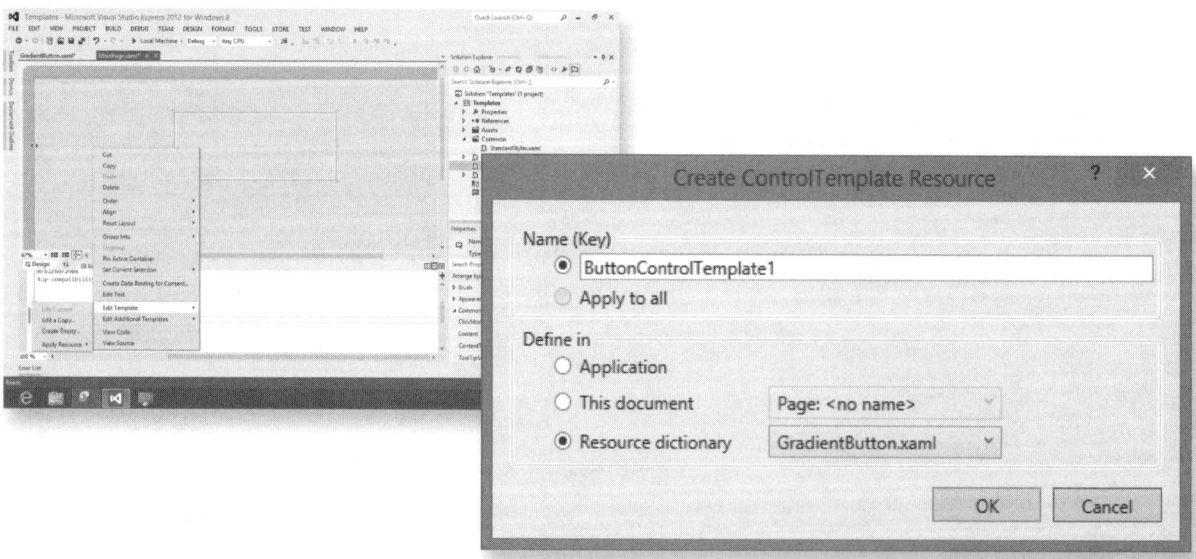

PUT ON YOUR THINKING HAT

Just for fun, let's create a very un-Wing looking Button template with a nice distinguishing gradient.

CREATE A PROJECT
Create a new blank application and add a Button to MainPage.xaml. (Make it big so you can work with it.)

ADD A RESOURCE DICTIONARY
Add a new ResourceDictionary file to the project to contain our template, and add a reference to it in the App.xaml MergedDictionaries collection.

CREATE AN EMPTY TEMPLATE
Right-click the Button on the Design Surface and choose Edit Template, Create Empty. Name the template GradientButtonTemplate, and place it in the resource dictionary you just created.

ADD SOME RESOURCES
You'll need to define three Color and one SolidColorBrush resources. The colors are LightGrey (#f2f2f2), MediumGray (#eaeaea), and DarkGray (#d6d6d6). The brush is a DarkGrayBrush that uses the DarkGray color. (Remember how to reference a static resource?)

DEFINE THE TEMPLATE
Visual Studio will have created a template skeleton for you. Ignore the VisualStateManager for now (we'll get to that in the next section), and add a Border inside the Grid. The Border should have a BorderThickness of 3, a CornerRadius of 30, and the BorderBrush you defined as a resource. The Background of the Border should be a LinearGradientBrush that moves from White at Offset 0.0, through LightGray at Offset 0.75, to MediumGray at Offset 1.

HOW'D YOU DO?

It doesn't matter if your button is a little different from mine, as long as it works and you're happy with it.

```xml
<ResourceDictionary ...>

    <Color x:Key="LightGray">#f2f2f2</Color>
    <Color x:Key="MediumGray">#eaeaea</Color>
    <Color x:Key="DarkGray">#d6d6d6</Color>
    <SolidColorBrush x:Key="DarkGrayBrush" Color="#d6d6d6"/>

    <ControlTemplate x:Key="GradientButtonTemplate" TargetType="Button">
        <Grid>
            <Border BorderThickness="3" BorderBrush="{StaticResource DarkGrayBrush}"
                CornerRadius="30" >
                <Border.Background>
                    <LinearGradientBrush StartPoint="0.5,0" EndPoint="0.5,1">
                        <GradientStop Color="White" Offset="0.0"/>
                        <GradientStop Color="{StaticResource LightGray}" Offset="0.75"/>
                        <GradientStop Color="{StaticResource MediumGray}" Offset="1"/>
                    </LinearGradientBrush>
                </Border.Background>
            </Border>
            <VisualStateManager.VisualStateGroups>
                <VisualStateGroup x:Name="CommonStates">
                    <VisualState x:Name="Pressed"/>
                    <VisualState x:Name="Disabled"/>
                    <VisualState x:Name="PointerOver"/>
                </VisualStateGroup>
                <VisualStateGroup x:Name="FocusStates">
                    <VisualState x:Name="Focused"/>
                    <VisualState x:Name="PointerFocused"/>
                </VisualStateGroup>
            </VisualStateManager.VisualStateGroups>
        </Grid>
    </ControlTemplate>

</ResourceDictionary>
```

TEMPLATE BINDINGS

As soon as you create the template for our sample Button, the XAML Designer will update its appearance. (It assigned the Template property for you.) But if you look at the Properties Window, you'll see that it doesn't reflect the templated values. That appears to be a limitation of the XAML Designer, and we'll live with it. What we shouldn't live with is that the Button isn't updated if we change those values. That, we can fix, by using a TemplateBinding markup extension:

The braces indicate a markup extension.

`<Property> ="{TemplateBinding <Property>}"`

The only parameter is the name of the public property that you want to use.

As long as the data types are compatible, you can bind any template property to any TemplateBinding property. If it makes sense in your application to bind the Background property of the widget to the BorderBrush property of one of the child controls in the template, go right ahead. Just be careful about confusing yourself at design time.

PUT ON YOUR THINKING HAT
Change the GradientButtonTemplate template so that the BorderThickness can be updated through the Properties Window. You'll probably have to use a fairly large change in order to see it in the Designer. Try 10.

HOW'D YOU DO?
There's only one simple change required.

```
<ControlTemplate x:Key="GradientButtonTemplate" TargetType="Button">
  <Grid>
    <Border BorderThickness="{TemplateBinding BorderThickness}"
        BorderBrush="{StaticResource DarkGrayBrush}"
        CornerRadius="30" >
      ...
  </Grid>
</ControlTemplate>
```

This is all you need to do to pull a property from the Properties Window.

ON YOUR OWN
With the exception of the Content property, which we'll discuss in a minute, what other properties of the Button do you think ought to be templated?

What about the gradient? Right now it's white-to-gray and doesn't reflect the design-time choice of Background color. Can you think of a way to fix that? (Hint: Think about opacity, and remember that you can have as many elements as you need inside your layout root.)

PRESENTING CONTENT

XAML has an entire set of classes called PRESENTERS that are like a `TemplateBinding`, but instead of presenting the value of a single property, they can display complex properties. For example, a `ContentPresenter` displays the `Content` property of a control, and that can get really complex. (Remember, the entire logical tree of a `Page` is contained in its `Content` property.) Presenters even have their own template properties (that might contain elements with their own template properties...it's never ending, really).

The `ContentPresenter`, like all presenters, inherits from `FrameworkElement`, so you have access to all the formatting properties like `FontFamily`, `HorizontalAlignment`, and `Height`, but you don't need to do anything special to include the actual content; the element handles that for you.

The contents of the control, as specified in the `Content` property, are inserted here.

PUT ON YOUR THINKING HAT

Add a `ContentPresenter` to the gradient button. Make the `Foreground` property the same as the border. (In a real application you'd probably want more design-time control, but that will do for our purposes.) Make sure the content is centered horizontally and vertically

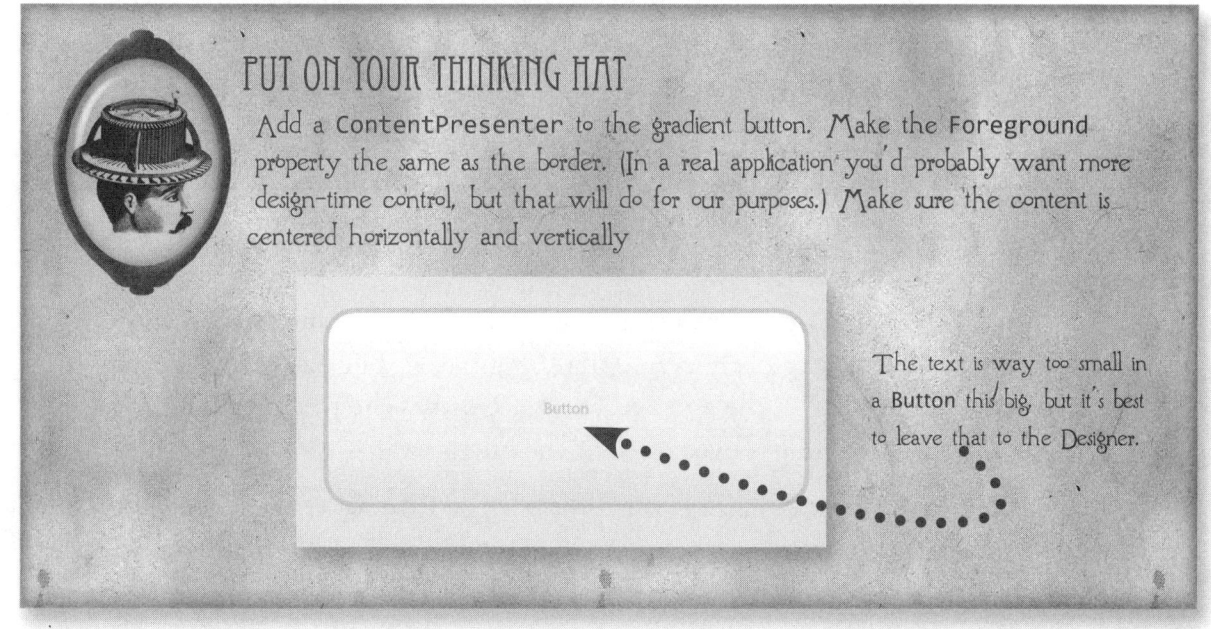

The text is way too small in a `Button` this big, but it's best to leave that to the Designer.

411

HOW'D YOU DO?

This exercise was a little more complicated than the last one. Did you figure out that you needed to put the `ContentPresenter` inside the `Border.Child`?

```xml
<ControlTemplate x:Key="GradientButtonTemplate" TargetType="Button">
   <Grid>
      <Border BorderThickness="{TemplateBinding BorderThickness}"
            BorderBrush="{StaticResource DarkGrayBrush}"
            CornerRadius="30" >
         <Border.Background ... />
         <Border.Child>
            <ContentPresenter Content="{TemplateBinding Content}"
                              Foreground="{StaticResource DarkGrayBrush}"
                              HorizontalAlignment="Center"
                              VerticalAlignment="Center" />
         </Border.Child>
      </Border>
   </Grid>
</ControlTemplate>
```

The `ContentPresenter` is the value of an existing property, in this case `Child`, but it will depend on exactly how your template is structured.

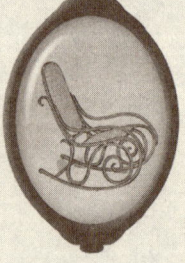

TAKE A BREAK

We'll find out more about control templates in the next section when we explore the `VisualStateManager`, but before we go, why don't you run the app and see if it behaves the way you want it to when you mouse over or click the button?

Then take a break before you complete the Review.

REVIEW

Can you answer the following questions based on what you've learned so far about control templates?

What kind of presenter do you use to display the Content property of a control?

Control templates are typically placed in one of two places. What are those places, and when would you use each?

What element do you use to make a control template reflect the public properties of an element?

What single property is exposed by the ControlTemplate class?

How many elements can be the direct children of a ControlTemplate?

THE VISUALSTATEMANAGER

I've made reference to the fact that a template lets you take control of both the visual tree and the visual behavior of a control. The VISUAL BEHAVIOR of a control effects only the UI, not the functionality of an app. It's probably easiest to understand by analogy: think "mouse over" as opposed to "mouse click". Or maybe by role: A graphic designer might define visual behavior, but if they start writing click handlers, they've become programmers. In Win8 XAML, visual behavior is controlled by the **VisualStateManager**.

At any given time, an element will be in one state from each **VisualStateGroup**.

A **VisualState** element contains a **Storyboard** that defines the new state.

The **Storyboard** contained in a **VisualTransition** will be activated when the element changes states.

The visual states within a **VisualStateGroup** are mutually exclusive.

An element can contain any number of visual state groups, and each group can contain any number of visual states.

XAML ANIMATIONS

In Win8 XAML, visual states and visual transitions are always defined as animations (even though they might be of zero duration). In XAML, the term "animation" doesn't have a lot to do with cranky hunters chasing wascally wabbits. A XAML animation changes the value of a dependency property over time, and unlike cartooning, this kind of animation can be really useful for making mainstream (and not-so-mainstream) interfaces responsive to the user. A few examples:

ANIMATION CAN CONTROL VISIBILITY

It's disconcerting to have things suddenly appear and disappear on the screen. By animating the opacity and size, you can fade things into and out of view smoothly and avoid startling people.

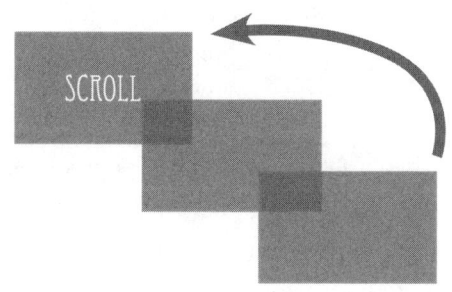

ANIMATION CAN MAKE MOVEMENT SEEM NATURAL

With the exception of slightly dubious experiments in quantum physics, things in the physical world don't get from one place to another without moving there. Things on a computer screen really shouldn't, either.

ANIMATION CAN SIMPLIFY PROGRAMMING

You can always change properties directly instead of animating them, but animations make some changes, particularly ones involving a change of size and position, much, much easier. Wouldn't you rather say "make this half-again as big" than write the code to calculate "how big am I times 1.5?" and maintain that state between calls? Yeah, me too.

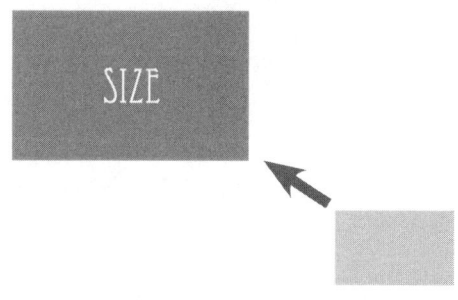

415

ELEMENTS OF AN ANIMATION

Like most things, you create a XAML animation declaratively, which is a real bonus for those of us who don't really enjoy linear algebra. (Personally, I'd rather clean the oven.) The catch is that there are quite a few objects involved. We'll take them one at a time.

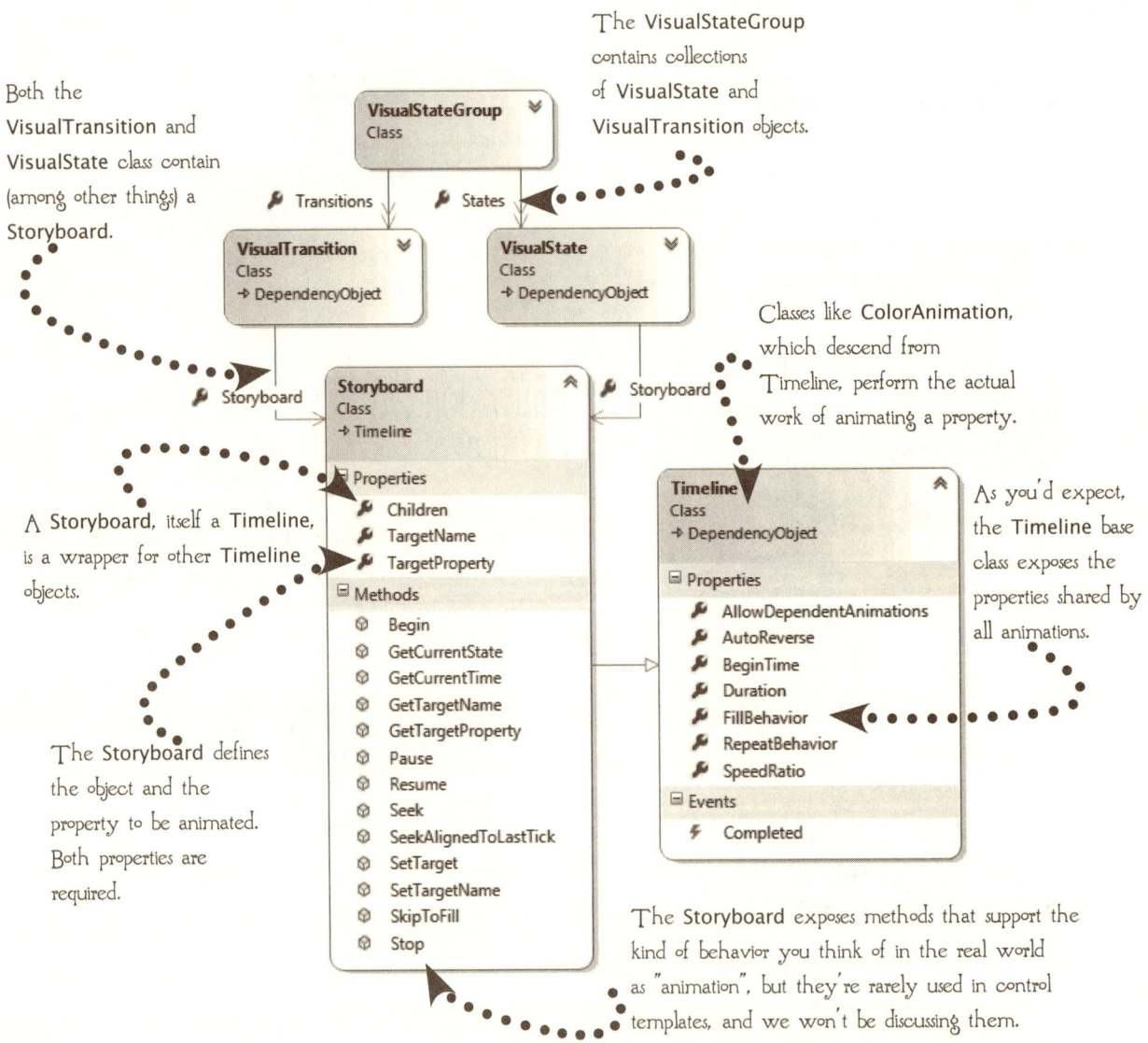

The VisualStateGroup contains collections of VisualState and VisualTransition objects.

Both the VisualTransition and VisualState class contain (among other things) a Storyboard.

Classes like ColorAnimation, which descend from Timeline, perform the actual work of animating a property.

A Storyboard, itself a Timeline, is a wrapper for other Timeline objects.

As you'd expect, the Timeline base class exposes the properties shared by all animations.

The Storyboard defines the object and the property to be animated. Both properties are required.

The Storyboard exposes methods that support the kind of behavior you think of in the real world as "animation", but they're rarely used in control templates, and we won't be discussing them.

416

STORYBOARDS

When you're defining the animations inside a `VisualStateManager`, you'll always access them via a `Storyboard`. The `Storyboard` identifies the element and property to be animated and also exposes the properties it inherits from `Timeline`, which can be set for the entire `Storyboard` or for the individual `Timeline` animations it contains.

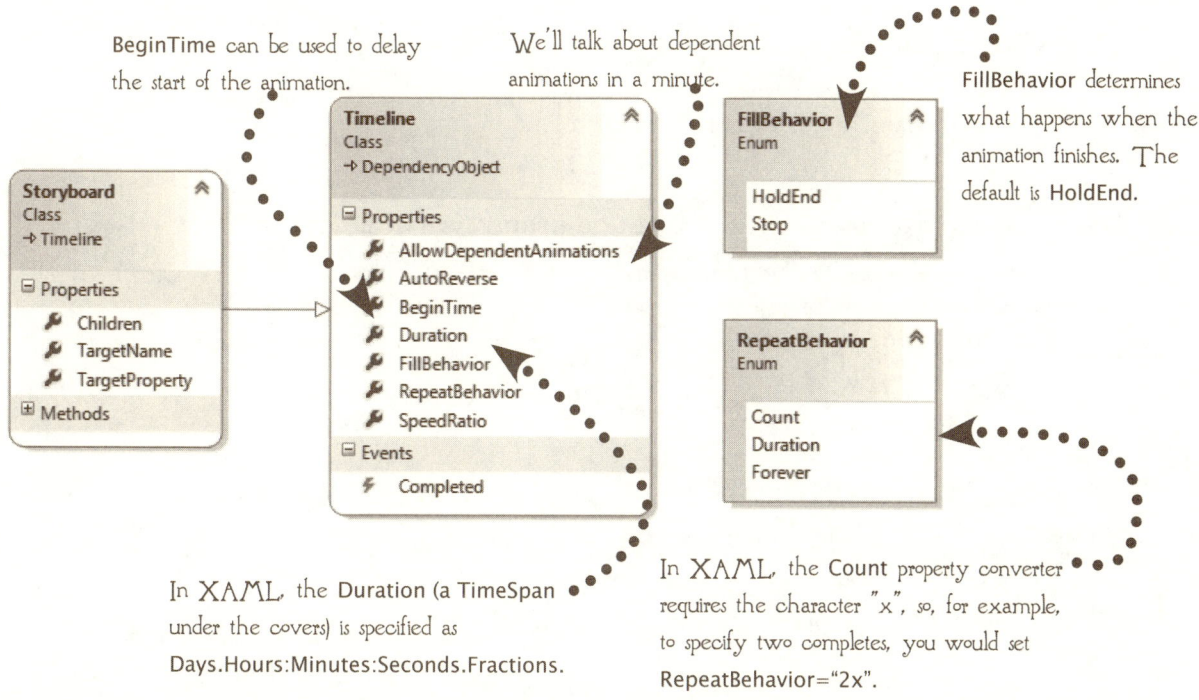

BeginTime can be used to delay the start of the animation.

We'll talk about dependent animations in a minute.

FillBehavior determines what happens when the animation finishes. The default is HoldEnd.

In XAML, the Duration (a TimeSpan under the covers) is specified as Days.Hours:Minutes:Seconds.Fractions.

In XAML, the Count property converter requires the character "x", so, for example, to specify two completes, you would set RepeatBehavior="2x".

PUT ON YOUR THINKING HAT

Can you write the following `Storyboard` declarations? Assume that in all cases the element is named `MyElement`. Don't worry about the actual animations yet, just the `Storyboard` declarations.

A `Storyboard` that targets the Background property.

A `Storyboard` that targets the Background property and repeats three times over 3.5 seconds.

A `Storyboard` that targets the Width property, lasts 0.5 seconds, and then returns to the original value.

417

HOW'D YOU DO?

I didn't give you much to go on this time, so don't worry if you got some of these wrong or not-quite-right.

A Storyboard that targets the Background property:

```
<Storyboard Storyboard.TargetName="MyElement"
    Storyboard.TargetProperty = "Background" />
```

This is just standard XAML, really.

A Storyboard that targets the Background property and repeats three times:

```
<Storyboard Storyboard.TargetName="MyElement"
    Storyboard.TargetProperty="Background"
    Storyboard.RepeatBehavior="3x">
```

Did you remember the "x"?

A Storyboard that targets the Width property of the element being styled, lasts 0.5 seconds, and then returns to the original value:

```
<Storyboard TargetName="MyElement"
    Storyboard.TargetProperty="Width"
    Storyboard.Duration="0:0:0.5"
    Storyboard.AutoReverse="True" >
```

Did you find AutoReverse? You might have thought you'd use FillBehavior to control this, but FillBehavior controls whether or not you can change the property after the animation ends. FillBehavior.HoldEnd (the default) keeps applying the end value. If you want to be able to change the value, set FillBehavior to Stop.

The format of the Duration specification can be tricky. Days is optional (and omitted here) and separated from the rest of the numbers by a period. The other numbers are separated by periods, and the FranctionalSeconds is optional as well:

[Days.]Hours:Minutes:Seconds.[FractionalSeconds]

DEPENDENT ANIMATIONS

The `Timeline` class exposes a Boolean property, `AllowDependentAnimations`, that determines whether animations can be performed on the UI thread. Why do you care? Because animations on the UI thread, called DEPENDENT ANIMATIONS, can make your app unresponsive. (That's why the default for the `AllowDependentAnimations` property is false.)

In reality, this isn't something you're going to have to worry about very often. But if you run across an animation that looks right but isn't running, this is one of the first things to check.

INDEPENDENT ANIMATIONS

The XAML Framework maintains a thread (called the COMPOSITION THREAD, but there's no particular reason for you to care about that) that's responsible for composing and animating the UI. It's distinct from the UI thread that runs your code. Animations that run on the composition thread are called INDEPENDENT ANIMATIONS. They'll always run, and they won't make your UI jittery or unresponsive.

That's the good news. The bad news is that only animations that don't effect layout (and can therefore be calculated from start to finish when they're created) can be run independently. Well, that's the general rule, but there are some exceptions. Aren't there always? Zero-duration animations are always independent, as are animations to the properties of a `RenderTransform` or `Projection`.

DEPENDENT ANIMATIONS

The flip side of independent animations is, of course, DEPENDENT ANIMATIONS that affect layout and must be run on the UI thread. Now, nobody's telling you you can't use dependent animations. Just be careful about them.

Since we all know that there are always a dozen different ways to achieve anything in programming, it's often possible to find an independent property that you can use to achieve the same result as a dependent animation. For example, instead of animating the `Width` of an element, you can create a `ScaleTransform` and animate that. (`RenderTransforms` are guaranteed to run independently, even though they kinda-sorta affect layout.)

TIMELINE CLASSES

A `Storyboard` lets you specify the dependency property to be animated, but you still need to specify how the property value will change. You do that using the descendants of `Timeline` in the `Windows.UI.XAMLMedia.Animation` namespace.

The animation classes let you specify discrete values over the animation, like the starting and ending values or positions along a path, and they'll calculate the intermediate values for you. The calculations can be tricky (did I mention linear algebra?), and they're unique to the type of value being calculated, so you'll need to use the appropriate class for the type of value.

XAML supports two kinds of animations, linear and key frame, and there are separate animation classes for each different data type: `Color`, `Double`, `Point`, and `Object`. (`Object` only supports key frame animations.) The key frame animations take a collection of key frame classes, and there are four types of those: linear, discrete, easing, and spline.

That makes for a lot of classes, but they're nicely hierarchical, so once you decide what type of value you're animating and whether you want a linear or key frame animation, the rest falls into place. Here's an example of the class hierarchy for animating a `Double` value:

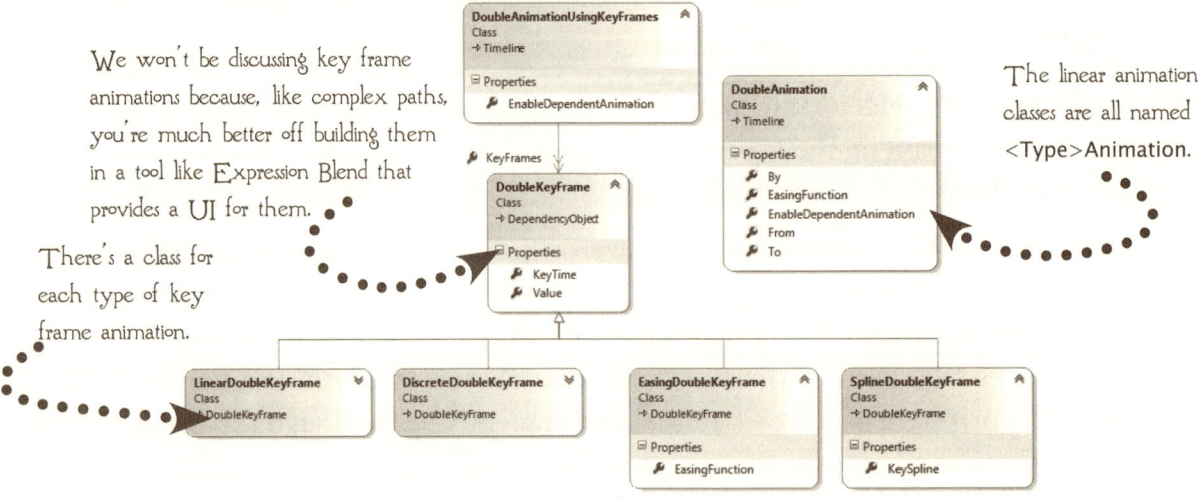

We won't be discussing key frame animations because, like complex paths, you're much better off building them in a tool like Expression Blend that provides a UI for them.

There's a class for each type of key frame animation.

The linear animation classes are all named `<Type>Animation`.

DOT-DOWN SYNTAX

There are a lot of animation classes in Win8 XAML, but they only support animating four different types. (By way of comparison, WPF exposes over 150 animation types.) And there are some obvious omissions. There are color animations, but most of the color properties actually take a Brush. Does that mean you can't change the Background or Foreground property in the VisualStateManager? No, of course not; that would be mean.

To animate a property that isn't directly supported by the Win8 XAML animation classes, you can (almost) always find a sub-property that is supported. For example, you can animate the Color of a SolidColorBrush (which is probably what you wanted to do anyway) by wrapping objects in parentheses using what's called DOT-DOWN SYNTAX:

> TargetProperty = (Button.Background).(SolidColorBrush.Color)

Pay attention to the parentheses here, one set around the control property, Button.Background in this example, and another around the sub-property, SolidColorBrush.Color. They're not always necessary, but like parentheses in a mathematical equation, they make things clearer.

PUT ON YOUR THINKING HAT

Once you figure out how to build an animation, sticking one inside a Storyboard inside a VisualState is pretty easy. Visual Studio has already built the skeleton of the VisualStateManager for our gradient button. Add an animation to the PointerOver VisualState that turns the border red over 1/10th of a second.

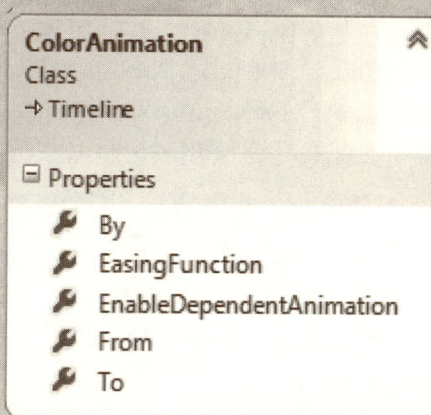

You'll need to set the x:Name property of the Border that's the layout root of the button (I called mine ButtonBorder), use dot-down syntax to specify the property, and set the To property of the ColorAnimation to specify the new value.

When you run the application, pay attention to what happens when you move the pointer off the button or press it. It won't be what we want. What do you think you need to do to fix that?

HOW'D YOU DO?

You probably had to fiddle around a little to get all the bits and pieces of syntax correct, but don't feel bad about that. It will get easier with practice.

```
<Border x:Name="ButtonBorder" ...>
   ...
   <VisualStateManager.VisualStateGroups>
     <VisualStateGroup x:Name="CommonStates">
       <VisualState x:Name="Pressed"/>
       <VisualState x:Name="Disabled"/>
       <VisualState x:Name="PointerOver">
          <Storyboard Storyboard.TargetName="ButtonBorder"
                  Storyboard.TargetProperty="(Button.BorderBrush).(SolidColorBrush.Color)">
             <ColorAnimation To="Red" Duration="0:0:1"/>
          </Storyboard>
       </VisualState>
     </VisualStateGroup>
       <VisualStateGroup x:Name="FocusStates">
       <VisualState x:Name="Focused"/>
       <VisualState x:Name="PointerFocused"/>
     </VisualStateGroup>
   </VisualStateManager.VisualStateGroups>
   ...
</Border>
```

As the code stands, once the Button enters the PointerOver state it stays there. Not a good thing. Ordinarily, the VisualStateManager transitions between states without requiring any further action on your part. (That's kind of the point.) But for reasons known only to the architects of Visual Studio, when you create an empty template, the VisualStateManager skeleton doesn't inclue the "default" states like Normal or Unfocused.

Since the default state is defined by the basic template, all you need to do to fix the problem is add an empty visual state:

```
<VisualState x:Name="Normal" />
```

THEME ANIMATIONS

We've had a little taste of how to write animations and use them in the VisualStateManager, but the Win8 XAML Framework also provides a set of pre-defined animations for common operations. We're not going to talk about them much, because they're well-documented (and there's a limit to how long this book can be), but here's a list of what's available:

DragItemThemeAnimation	Animates items being dragged
DragOverThemeAnimation	Animates elements underneath an element being dragged
DropTargetThemeAnimation	Animates potential drop targets
FadeInThemeAnimation	Animates the opacity of an element when it is first shown
FadeOutThemeAnimation	Animates the opacity of an element when it is being removed or hidden
PointerDownThemeAnimation	Animates an element when a user taps down on it
PointerUpThemeAnimation	Animates an element when a tap action is released
PopInThemeAnimation	Animates the opacity and position of a popup element when it is displayed
PopOutThemeAnimation	Animates the opacity and position of a popup element when it is being removed
RepositionThemeAnimation	Animates an object that is being repositioned
SplitOpenThemeAnimation	Splits open elements during repositioning
SplitCloseThemeAnimation	Closes split element after repositioning
SwipeBackThemeAnimation	Animates an element being returned to its position after a swipe
SwipeHintThemeAnimation	Indicates that a swipe gesture is possible

VISUAL TRANSITIONS

I've said that the `VisualStateManager` handles transitions between states without action on your part, and that's true. But the `VisualStateGroup` also exposes a `Transitions` collection that accepts instances of the `VisualTransition` class. As you'd expect, `VisualTransition` provides you with more control over how the transitions happen. The class is pretty simple:

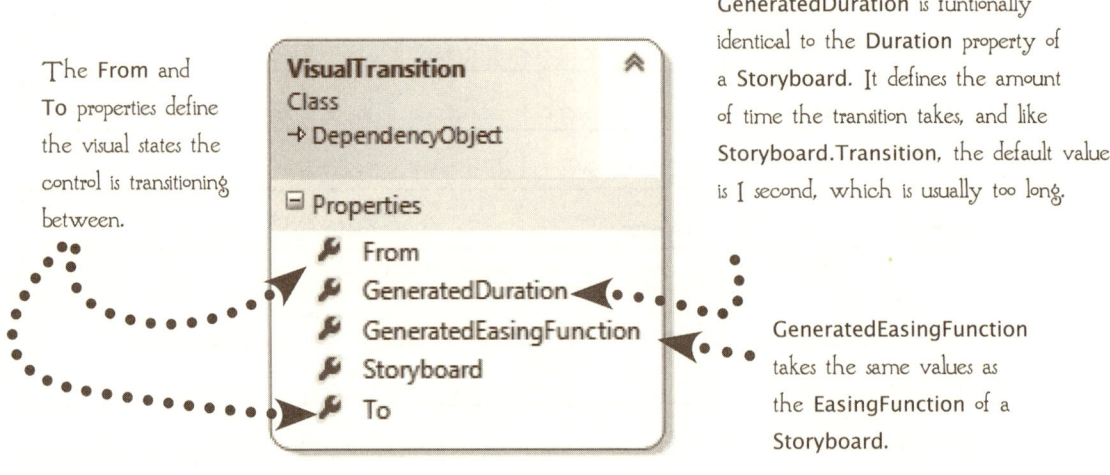

The `From` and `To` properties define the visual states the control is transitioning between.

GeneratedDuration is funtionally identical to the `Duration` property of a `Storyboard`. It defines the amount of time the transition takes, and like `Storyboard.Transition`, the default value is 1 second, which is usually too long.

GeneratedEasingFunction takes the same values as the `EasingFunction` of a `Storyboard`.

> **MAKE A NOTE:**
> When you explore the Windows.UI.Xaml.Media.Animations namespace, you'll see a lot of classes named `<Something>ThemeTransition`. These aren't visual transitions and can't be used inside the `VisualStateGroup.Transitions` class. For lack of a better term, I just call them theme transitions (although Microsoft doesn't use that term). You'll use them in the `Transitions` collection of the `UIElement`, and we'll talk about them in the next section.

424

PUT ON YOUR THINKING HAT

One last exercise before we're finished with animation and the VisualStateManager:

The properties of the VisualTransition behave like the comparable properties of the Storyboard, and like the Storyboard, the From and To properties are optional. Can you match up combinations of property settings with the result?

	From	To
1	Specified	Specified
2	Not Specified	Specified
3	Specified	Not Specified
4	Not Specified	Not Specified

From any state to the state specified

From the specified state to the specified state

From any state to any other state

From the specified state to any other state

Fix the problem with our button not returning to its default state?

Add a PointerDownThemeAnimation to the Pressed VisualState?

HOW'D YOU DO?

	From	To
1	Specified	Specified
2	Not Specified	Specified
3	Specified	Not Specified
4	Not Specified	Not Specified

② From any state to the state specified
① From the specified state to the specified state
④ From any state to any other state
③ From the specified state to any other state

```
<VisualStateManager.VisualStateGroups>
  <VisualStateGroup x:Name="CommonStates">
    <VisualState x:Name="Normal"/>
    <VisualState x:Name="Pressed">
      <Storyboard>
        <PointerDownThemeAnimation TargetName="ButtonBorder"/>
      </Storyboard>
    <VisualState x:Name="Disabled"/>
    <VisualState x:Name="PointerOver">
      <Storyboard StoryBoard.TargetName="ButtonBorder"
            StoryBoard.TargetProperty=(Button.BorderBrush).(SolidColorBrush.Color)">
        <ColorAnimation To="Red" Duration="0:0:1"/>
      </Storyboard>
    </VisualState>
    ...
</VisualStateManager.VisualStateGroups>
  ...
</Border>
```

TAKE A BREAK

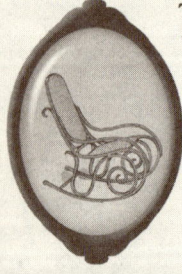

Whew, that sure got complicated, didn't it? Why don't you take a break before you complete the Review and we move on to the (nice and short) discussion of control transitions?

REVIEW

Can you answer the following questions based on what you've learned?

How many data types are supported by the Win8 XAML animation classes?

What does dot-down syntax allow you to do?

What's the difference between a Storyboard and a Timeline?

What's the difference between dependent and independent animations? Why should you be careful when you're using one of them?

Can an element be in more than one state in a VisualStateGroup at the same time?

What property of the VisualStateGroup controls how an element transitions from one state to another?

Theme Transitions

Don't confuse theme transitions with visual transitions. Although the two types of transitions provide very similar funcitonality—they animate some behavior of a control—they're not interchangeable. The `VisualTransition` class can only be used within a `VisualStateGroup`. The `Transition` class is exposed directly on an element by way of one of the `Transitions` collections, of which there are several:

Element Transitions

You can apply transitions to individual controls via the **Transitions** collection property of the **UIElement** class.

Content Transitions

The **ContentControl** and **ContentPresenter** classes expose a **ContentTransitions** collection property that will be applied to their content.

Container Transitions

The **ItemsControl** exposes an **ItemContainerTransitions** collection property that will be applied to the items in their containers. (Read that again. It's not quite the same as their children.)

Child Transitions

There are two different collection properties to use when you want to apply transitions to the children of a control: The Popup and Border classes expose a **ChildTransitions** collection, but in the Panel class, it's called **ChildrenTransitions**. (Just to confuse you.)

Theme transitions require that you explicitly declare the **TransitionCollection** property:

```xml
<TextBlock>
 <TextBlock.Transitions>
  <TransitionCollection>
   <EntranceThemeTransition />
  </TransitionCollection>
 </TextBlock.Transitions>
</TextBlock>
```

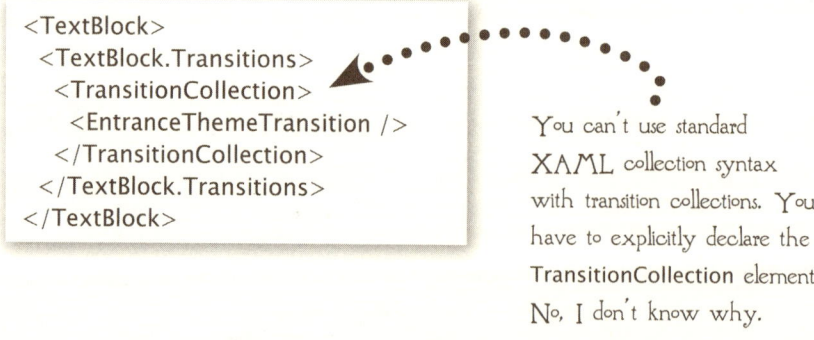

You can't use standard XAML collection syntax with transition collections. You have to explicitly declare the **TransitionCollection** element. No, I don't know why.

USING THEME TRANSITIONS

You don't have a lot of room to maneuver with theme transitions. Although the Transition base class is public, you can't write your own; you can only use the ones that are already defined as part of the XAML Framework. And the default styles for the existing controls already include transition declarations, so you don't need to use them very often. So the only thing you need to worry about is the slightly unusual syntax and the transitions that are available. Here's a list:

AddDeleteThemeTransition	Animates the addition and deletion of child controls within a panel
ContentThemeTransition	Animates changing a control's content
EdgeUIThemeTransition	Animates an edge UI transition
EntranceThemeTransition	Animates the initial appearance of a control
PaneThemeTransition	Animates panning UI
PopupThemeTransition	Animates the appearance of popup components like tooltips
ReorderThemeTransition	Animates the behavior of reordering controls
RepositionThemeTransition	Animates the repositioning of controls when one moves

ON YOUR OWN
Why don't you add an EntranceThemeTransition to our sample app? You'll need to decide whether you want to add it to the Button (probably in the template) or to the StackPanel that contains it.

REVIEW

When would you use BasedOn in a control style?

What themes are available in Windows 8.1?

Where can you declare a control template?

What's the difference between StaticResource and DynamicResource?

What do you have to do to load a ResourceDictionary into your app? What's the syntax? Where do you put it?

Congratulations! You've finished the chapter. Take a minute to think about what you've accomplished before you move on to the next one...

List three things you learned in this chapter:

①

②

③

Why do you think you need to know these things in order to develop Win8 apps?

Is there anything in this chapter that you think you need to understand in more detail? If so, what are you going to do about that?

XAML BINDING

12

If you were to ask me what sets XAML apart from other UI platforms, my answer would be templates and data binding. Of course, dependency properties and resources add useful functionality in their own right, but in my universe, they primarily exist to make templates and binding possible.

We explored control templates in the last chapter, and I hope you agree that they're a vast improvement over having to perform low-level graphic manipulations when you need to change the visual appearance and visual behavior—but not the basic functionality—of a control. We've also seen two examples of binding. We used the **TemplateBinding** in building our control templates, and I gave you an example of an element binding back in Chapter 10 when we were playing with colors.

In this chapter we'll look at XAML binding in its own right, starting with binding to simple, scalar values and then exploring binding to data collections in some detail.

Then, as an example of the ultimate interconnectedness of all things, we'll also see another kind of template, the **DataTemplate**, in this chapter. The **DataTemplate** provides the same kind of control over the visual tree of bound data that the **ControlTemplate** provides to XAML controls.

FITTING IT IN

The basic structure of a XAML binding is simple to use and understand. There are only three fundamental components: the BINDING SOURCE, a .NET object that provides the value; the BINDING TARGET, a dependency property that receives the value; and a Binding class that links the two.

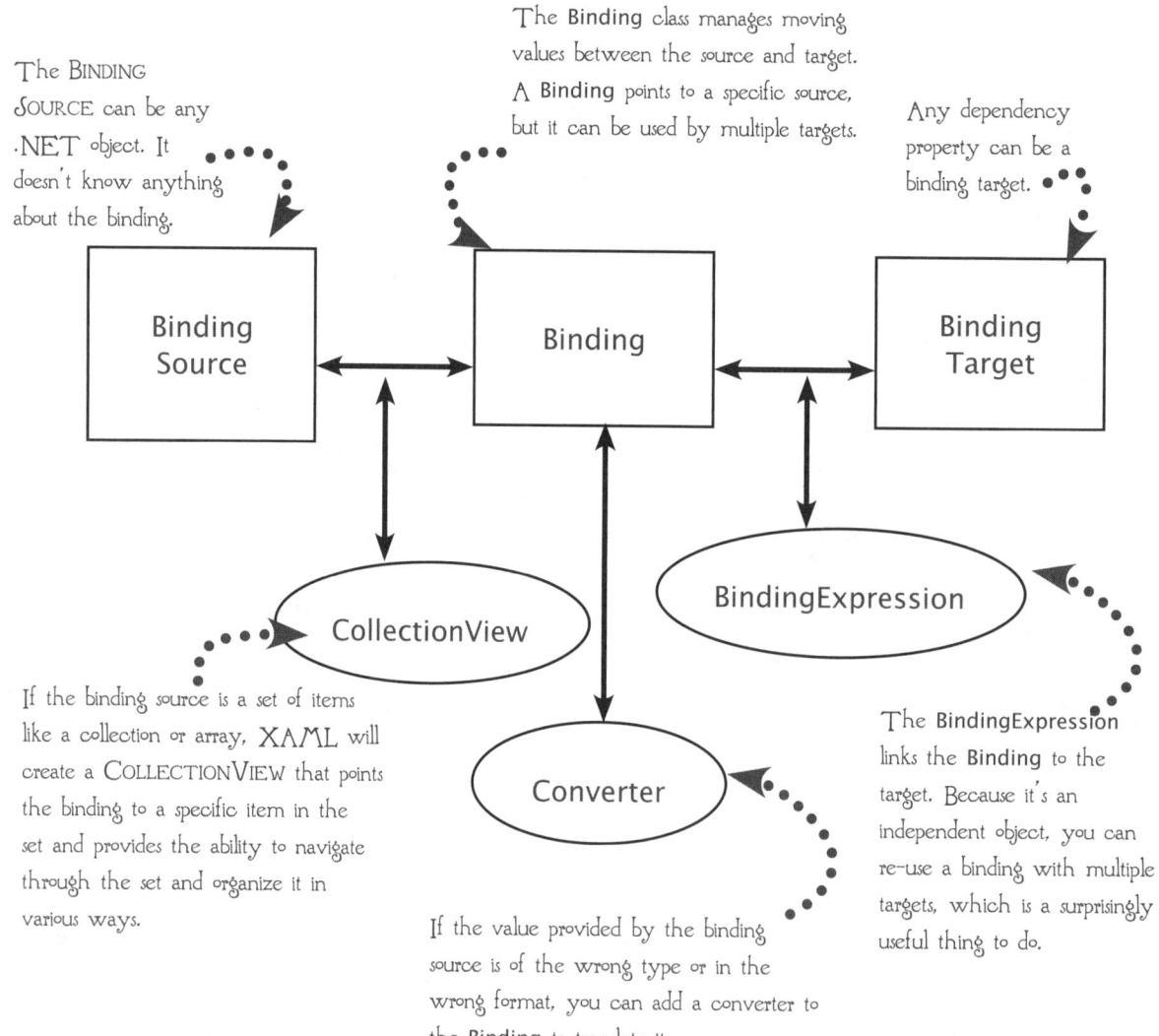

The BINDING SOURCE can be any .NET object. It doesn't know anything about the binding.

The Binding class manages moving values between the source and target. A Binding points to a specific source, but it can be used by multiple targets.

Any dependency property can be a binding target.

If the binding source is a set of items like a collection or array, XAML will create a COLLECTIONVIEW that points the binding to a specific item in the set and provides the ability to navigate through the set and organize it in various ways.

If the value provided by the binding source is of the wrong type or in the wrong format, you can add a converter to the Binding to translate it.

The BindingExpression links the Binding to the target. Because it's an independent object, you can re-use a binding with multiple targets, which is a surprisingly useful thing to do.

THE PROBLEM...

To get a sense of what the XAML binding mechanism does for you, let's look at a simple example. Here's a simple window that displays the actual width and height of the Border object in the top pane.

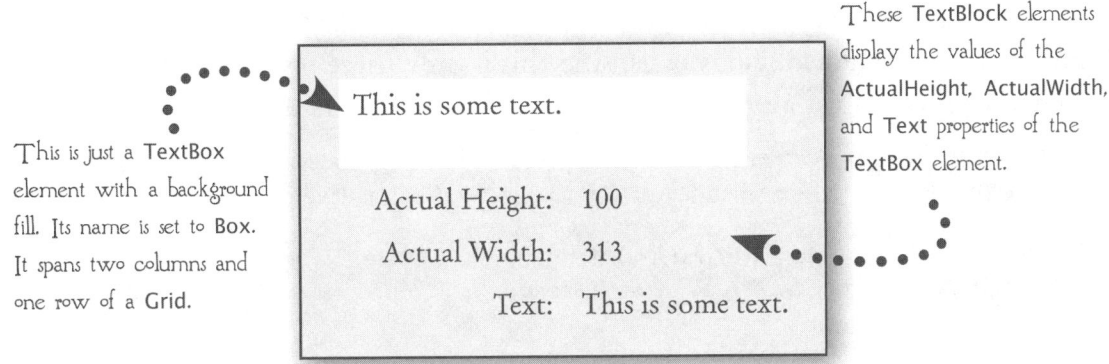

This is just a TextBox element with a background fill. Its name is set to Box. It spans two columns and one row of a Grid.

These TextBlock elements display the values of the ActualHeight, ActualWidth, and Text properties of the TextBox element.

Without binding, in order to change the values in the labels when the size of the window changes, you'll need to update them in code by responding to the Border.SizeChanged event. You'll need to convert the Double to a String, of course, but you can just call the ToString() method. (And if you're using Visual Basic, the compiler will take care of it for you.)

Now, that's not too tedious, but what about the TextLabel? Well, TextBox exposes a TextChanged event, and we can catch that to update the TextBlock. But there's a problem: As soon as the application runs, it generates a null reference exception because TextChanged gets called when the TextBox is created, which happens before the label is created. So you need to check that the Page is loaded first.

Starting to get a little complicated, isn't it? And what if you wanted to, say, bind a TextBlock to the background color of the TextBox? There's no event for that anywhere. And Color doesn't have a reasonable text representation. What do you do about that?

The solution, of course, is to let XAML handle all these ugly details for you. Keep reading...

THE SOLUTION...

Compare the increasingly complex set of event handlers on the previous page to the same functionality implemented with XAML binding. All we have to do is specify the element and property we want, and XAML handles all the rest. I know which version I'd rather write.

Here's the C# code for our original version. We had to find change events we could use and track down some non-obvious bugs. And this is only three properties. What if you had twenty, or fifty? What about binding to a collection? It gets ugly fast.

```csharp
private void Window_SizeChanged(object sender, SizeChangedEventArgs e)
{
    WidthLabel.Text = Box.ActualWidth.ToString();
    HeightLabel.Text= Box.ActualHeight.ToString();
}


private void Box_TextChanged(object sender, TextChangedEventArgs e)
{
    if (TextLabel != null)
        TextLabel.Text = Box.Text;
}
```

Here's a version that uses XAML binding. All we need to do is add a markup extension to the XAML. (We could also have done it in code, of course.) That's all we ever have to do. In every situation. No hunting for an event we can hook on to, no tracking down weird and wonderful unrelated problems...

```xml
<TextBox x:Name="Box" .../>
<TextBlock Text="{Binding ElementName=Box, Path=ActualWidth}" .../>
<TextBlock Text="{Binding ElementName=Box, Path=ActualHeight}" .../>
<TextBlock Text="{Binding ElementName=Box, Path=Text}" .../>
```

This syntax is correct, but the values won't change if, for example you snap the app. Keep reading to find out why.

TASK LIST

We'll start this chapter by exploring the basics of XAML binding. You've already done some basic binding in other contexts, so this might seem like old news, but then we'll move on to some more interesting stuff, including how to convert and format the data, and how to bind to and navigate entire sets of data.

CREATING BINDINGS

Before we get into the complexities of XAML bindings, we need to get the basics down, so we'll start by looking at the basic objects involved and how to use them.

BINDING TO COLLECTIONS

Next we'll explore binding entire sets of data to items controls like the **ListBox** and **ComboBox**. In order to use these controls effectively, you need to know how the data from the binding source is displayed, so we'll also examine data templates, which are just another form of the templates you learned how to build in the last chapter.

WORKING WITH COLLECTIONS

I'm going to go out on a limb here: Because Win8 doesn't have intrinsic support for local relational data—you don't have access to Entity Framework or the core ADO.NET classes—I don't think it's well-suited to applications whose primary purpose is the addition and editing of data (LOB apps doing CRUD, for those who do this kind of thing). It's possible, but you'll have to either use a third-party data library, write a whole lot of data manipulation code yourself, or do it all via a service, and any of those approaches is going to be a challenge.

But that doesn't mean Win8 isn't a wonderful platform for retrieving and displaying data that's maintained elsewhere. In the last section of this chapter we'll explore the functionality that you'll need in those kinds of apps: moving through a collection and grouping its items.

CREATING BINDINGS

You've already written one kind of binding expression when you used the `TemplateBinding` element in a control template, but the general binding syntax is a little different, so let's start with a simple little example.

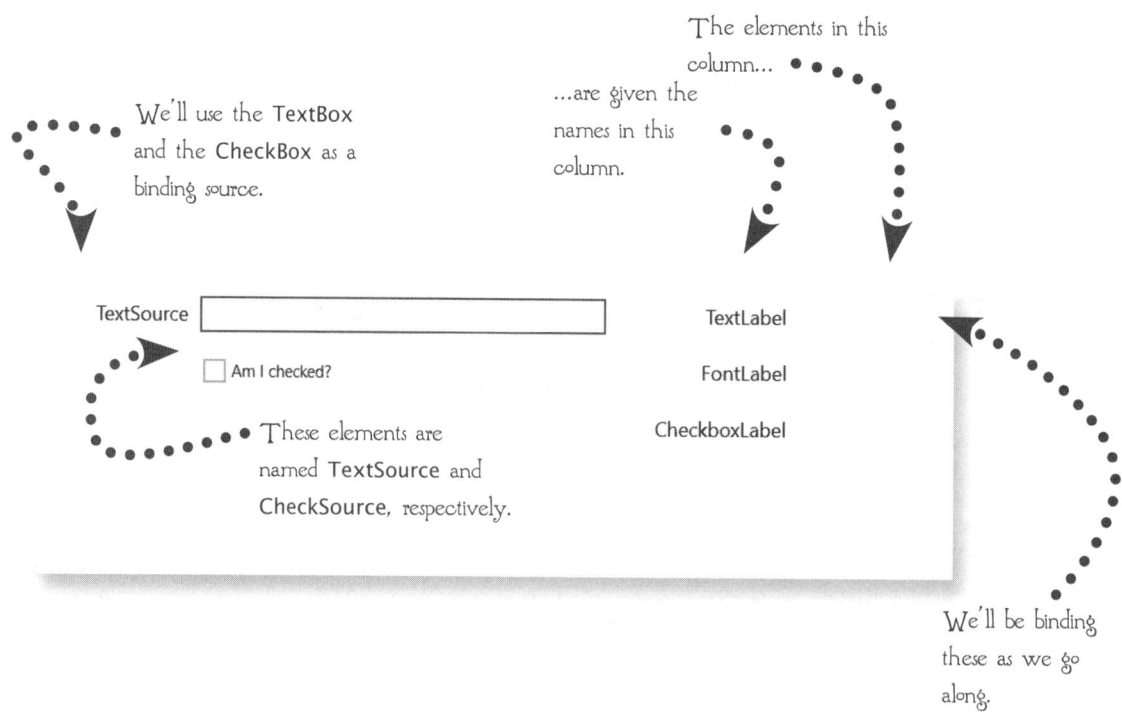

We'll use the TextBox and the CheckBox as a binding source.

These elements are named TextSource and CheckSource, respectively.

The elements in this column...

...are given the names in this column.

We'll be binding these as we go along.

TextSource
Am I checked?

TextLabel
FontLabel
CheckboxLabel

`{Binding ElementName="<name>", Path="<property>"}`

PUT ON YOUR THINKING HAT

Ready to get started? Here's a class diagram of the Binding object. Using it and the example from a couple of pages ago, can you do the following?

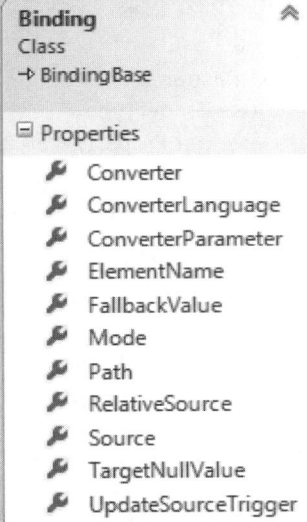

① Create a new project (I called mine BasicBindings) and build the basic **Page** shown on the previous page. Mine uses the default **Grid** as the root element, with four columns and three rows, but you don't need to organize it that way if you have a better idea. Make sure you give the **TextBox** and the **TextBlock** elements in the last column the names specified in the third column.

② Set the binding for the **TextBlock** named TextLabel so that it displays the contents of the TextBox.

③ Set the binding for the **TextBlock** named FontLabel so that it displays the FontFamily.Source property of TextLabel.

Ignore the CheckBoxLabel TextBlock for the time being. We'll add that later.

HOW'D YOU DO?

It's only fair to tell you that XAML binding can get pretty complicated—if you've ever written a data-bound application you know that—but most of the time, it's just this easy.

```xml
<Page ...>
   <Page.Resources>
      <Style TargetType="TextBlock">
         <Setter Property="FontSize" Value="18"/>
         <Setter Property="Margin" Value="10,15"/>
         <Setter Property="HorizontalAlignment" Value="Right" />
      </Style>
   </Page.Resources>

   <Grid ...>
      <Grid.ColumnDefinitions ... />
      <Grid.RowDefinitions ... />

      <TextBlock Grid.Column="0" Grid.Row="0">TextSource</TextBlock>
      <TextBox x:Name="TextSource" Grid.Column="1" Grid.Row="0"/>
      <CheckBox x:Name="CheckSource" Grid.Column="1" Grid.Row="1"
         Content="Am I Checked?"/>

      <TextBlock Grid.Column="2" Grid.Row="0">TextLabel</TextBlock>
      <TextBlock x:Name="TextLabel" Grid.Column="3" Grid.Row="0"
            HorizontalAlignment="Left"
            Text="{Binding ElementName=TextSource, Path=Text}"/>
      <TextBlock Grid.Column="2" Grid.Row="1">FontLabel</TextBlock>
      <TextBlock x:Name="FontLabel" Grid.Column="3" Grid.Row="1"
            HorizontalAlignment="Left"
            Text="{Binding ElementName=TextSource, Path=FontFamily.Source}"/>
      <TextBlock Grid.Column="2" Grid.Row="2">CheckBoxLabel</TextBlock>
      <TextBlock x:Name="CheckBoxLabel" Grid.Column="3" Grid.Row="2"
            HorizontalAlignment="Left" />
   </Grid>
</Page>
```

ElementName and Path (and that wierd quote-brace syntax) is all you need.

We'll create this binding in a minute.

We saw the "dot-down" syntax when we explored animations in the last chapter. It works with bindings, too.

VALUE CONVERTERS

If binding is as simple as I say it is, you might be wondering what all those other properties are doing there. The short answer is "They add functionality that you won't use often but will be very glad of when you do". The top of that list is probably the binding converters that provide the simplest mechanism around for translating values between the source and target.

It's a very common situation: You have a Boolean and you want to display "True" or "False". You have "Riordan, Rebecca M.", but you want to display "Rebecca M. Riordan". You have...well, you get the idea. Unfortunately, in most binding platforms, this very common thing is very tedious to do. (And ADO.Net is one of the worst offenders.) Not so in XAML, because the **Binding** exposes a **Converter** property that accepts an instance of the very sensible **IValueConverter** interface. All you need to do is create a class that implements the interface, declare it as a resource, and pass it to the **Binding** as a property.

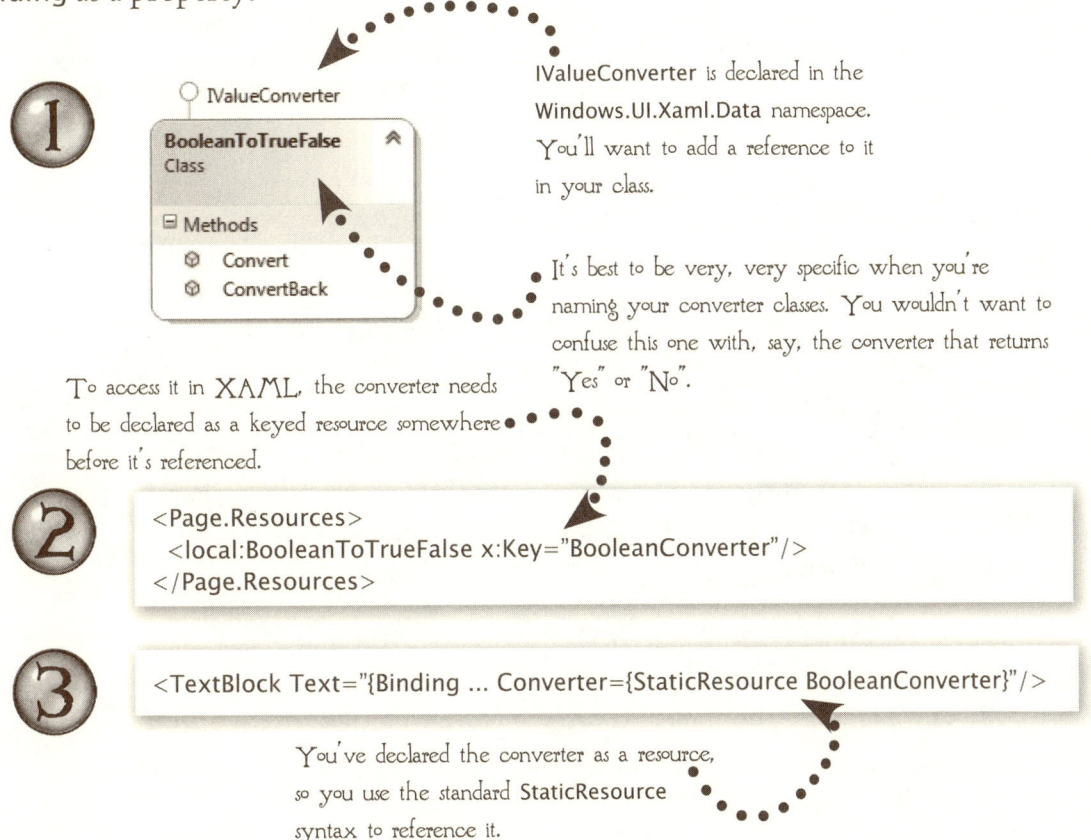

IValueConverter is declared in the Windows.UI.Xaml.Data namespace. You'll want to add a reference to it in your class.

It's best to be very, very specific when you're naming your converter classes. You wouldn't want to confuse this one with, say, the converter that returns "Yes" or "No".

To access it in XAML, the converter needs to be declared as a keyed resource somewhere before it's referenced.

②
```
<Page.Resources>
  <local:BooleanToTrueFalse x:Key="BooleanConverter"/>
</Page.Resources>
```

③
```
<TextBlock Text="{Binding ... Converter={StaticResource BooleanConverter}"/>
```

You've declared the converter as a resource, so you use the standard **StaticResource** syntax to reference it.

441

BUILDING CONVERTERS

The `IValueConverter` interface, declared in the `Windows.UI.Xaml.Data` namespace has only two methods: `Convert()` and `ConvertBack()`. The methods have rather a lot of parameters, but they're very simple to write and use, even though the actual code to do the conversions can get tricky sometimes.

IValueConverter Interface
- Methods
  - Convert
  - ConvertBack

The `value` parameter represents the original data that you need to convert.

The `targetType` parameter is the type the converter wants back.

```
object Convert(object value, Type targetType,
               object parameter, string language)
```
C#

```
Function Convert(value as Object, targetType as Type,
                 parameter As Object, language As String) As Object
```
VB

The `parameter` and `language` parameters will only be passed if you set them in the Binding.

MAKE A NOTE

There's no law that says you can't do anything else in the class that implements **IValueConverter**, but it's fairly unusual. (In fact, I've never done it or seen it done—these classes tend to be very lightweight.)

There's also no law that says you need to implement both methods. They must both be declared, of course, but if you're only ever going to need to convert in one direction, it's probably a good idea to leave the `NotImplementedException` that Visual Studio will add for you by default when you choose Implement Interface.

BINDING MODES

The next Binding property on our list is the BindingMode, which determines how the source and target interact. You have three options, declared in the BindingMode enumeration:

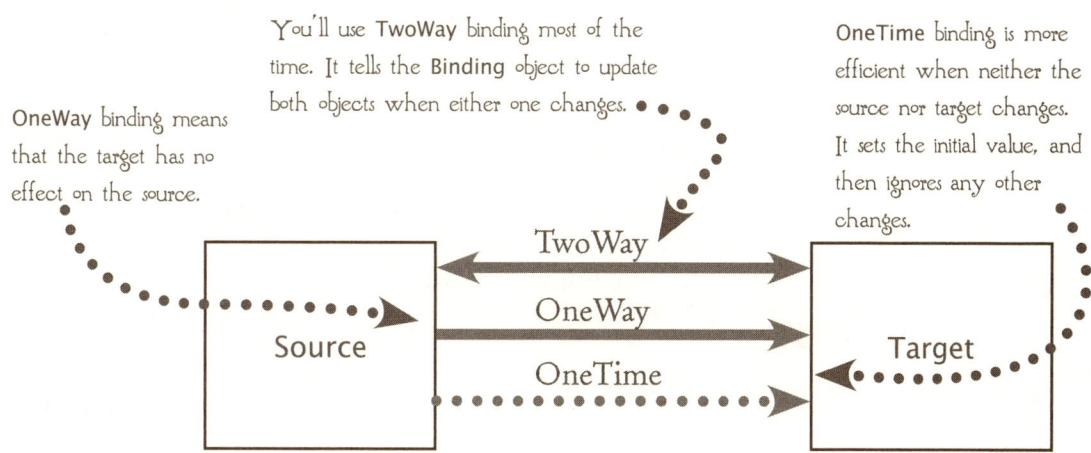

OneWay binding means that the target has no effect on the source.

You'll use TwoWay binding most of the time. It tells the Binding object to update both objects when either one changes.

OneTime binding is more efficient when neither the source nor target changes. It sets the initial value, and then ignores any other changes.

PUT ON YOUR THINKING HAT

Time to make our little application a bit more sophisticated and get some experience with the Binding properties:

Build a BooleanToTrueFalse converter class. You only need to implement one of the methods. Can you figure out which one?

Declare your class as a Page.Resource.

Bind the CheckBoxLabel TextBlock to the IsChecked property of the CheckBox using the converter.

All of the bindings on this page should use the same Mode. Can you figure out which one? Declare it.

PUT ON YOUR THINKING HAT
How'd you do?

```xml
<Page.Resources>
    <local:BooleanToTrueFalse x:Key="BooleanConverter"/>
<TextBlock x:Name="CheckboxLabel" Grid.Column="3" Grid.Row="2"
           HorizontalAlignment="Left"
           Text="{Binding ElementName=CheckSource, Path=IsChecked, Mode=OneWay,
                  Converter={StaticResource BooleanConverter}}"/>
```

```csharp
class BooleanToTrueFalse : IValueConverter
{
    object IValueConverter.Convert(object value, Type targetType, object parameter,
            string language)
    {
        return (bool)value ? "True" : "False";
    }

    object IValueConverter.ConvertBack(object value, Type targetType, object parameter,
            string language)
    {
        throw new NotImplementedException();
    }
}
```

```vb
Public Class BooleanToTrueFalse
    Implements IValueConverter

    Public Function Convert(value As Object, targetType As Type, parameter As Object, _
                    language As String) As Object Implements IValueConverter.Convert
        If value = True Then
            Return True
        Else
            Return False
        End If
    End Function

    Public Function ConvertBack(value As Object, targetType As Type, parameter As Object, _
                    language As String) As Object _
                        Implements IValueConverter.ConvertBack
        Throw New NotImplementedException
    End Function
End Class
```

UPDATE TRIGGERS

The other property that controls how the Binding behaves is the UpdateSourceTrigger that does exactly what the name implies: It defines when an update of the source is triggered.

UpdateSourceTrigger only applies when the source is actually being updated, which means the Mode must be TwoWay or OneWayToSource.

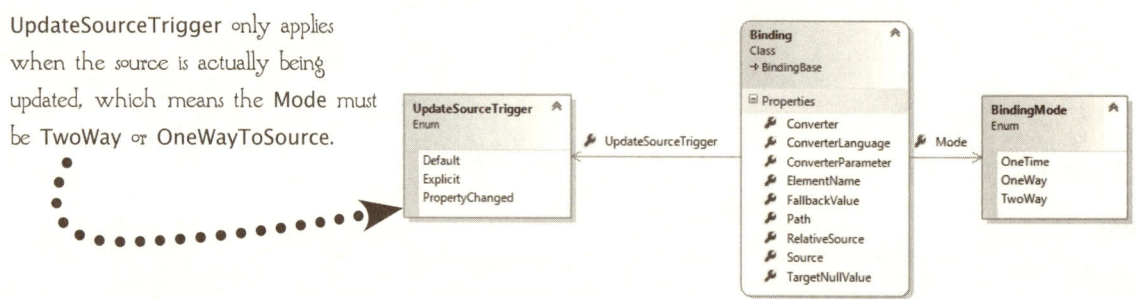

When the UpdateSourceTrigger is set to Explicit, you have to call UpdateSource() on the BindingExpression. (Remember that XAML creates a BindingExpression whenever you link a Binding object to a property on the binding source.) This allows you to re-use a Binding object for multiple source properties.

The GetBindingExpression() method returns an instance of the BindingExpression for you to work with in code.

Notice how the property is specified:
<Class>.<Property>Property

```
BindingExpression be = TextLabel.GetBindingExpression(Label.ContentProperty);
be.UpdateSource();
```

Once you have a reference to the BindingExpression, the UpdateSource() method tells the Binding to perform the deferred update.

```
BindingExpression be = TextLabel.GetBindingExpression(Label.ContentProperty)
be.UpdateSource()
```

BINDING SOURCES

All of our binding examples so far have used the ElementName property to specify the source of the bound data. But that's only one of three possible ways of specifying the source of the data; the others are RelativeSource, which uses the current element or its parent (we'll discuss RelativeSource in a moment), and Source, the most versatile of the three.

Almost anything you can access can be a binding source, but if the binding target is to be updated when the source changes, it must, of course, implement change notification. Here are your options:

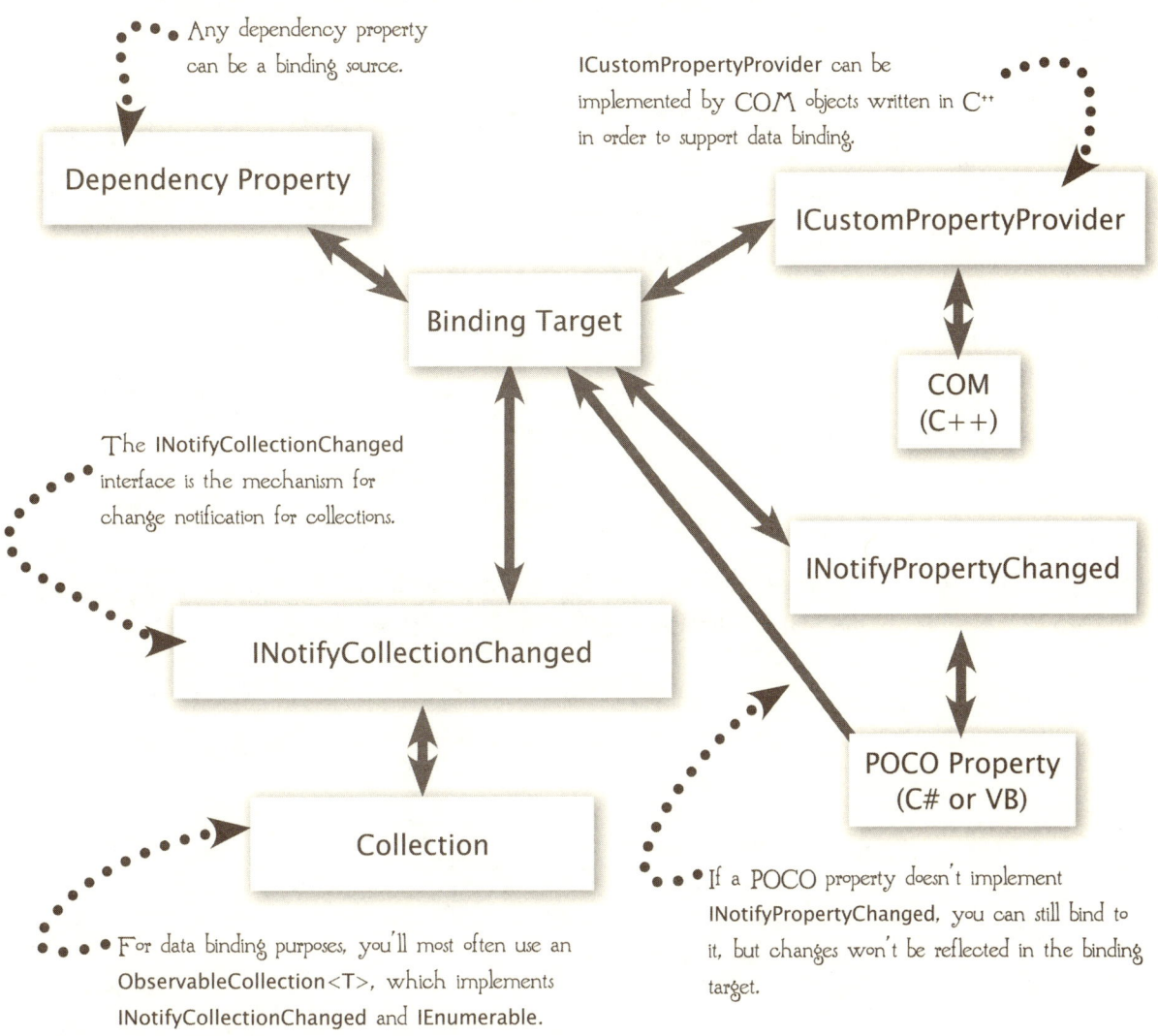

USING RELATIVESOURCE

The third alternative for specifying a binding source is the **RelativeSource** property, which lets you bind either to the current element or (inside a control template) to its parent. **RelativeSource** is actually a class in the XAML Framework with a single property, **Mode**, which you'll need to set to an instance of the **RelativeSourceMode** enumeration:

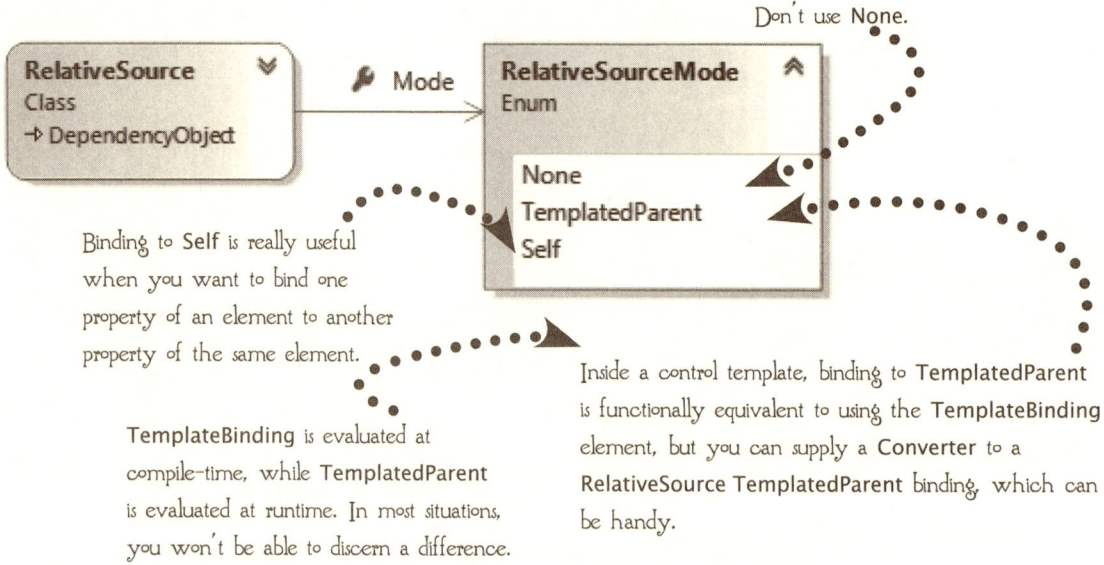

Binding to **Self** is really useful when you want to bind one property of an element to another property of the same element.

TemplateBinding is evaluated at compile-time, while **TemplatedParent** is evaluated at runtime. In most situations, you won't be able to discern a difference.

Inside a control template, binding to **TemplatedParent** is functionally equivalent to using the **TemplateBinding** element, but you can supply a **Converter** to a **RelativeSource TemplatedParent** binding, which can be handy.

When you use a **RelativeSource**, you need to instantiate the class. That's not a big deal in code, but the syntax in XAML is a little more complicated than we're used to:

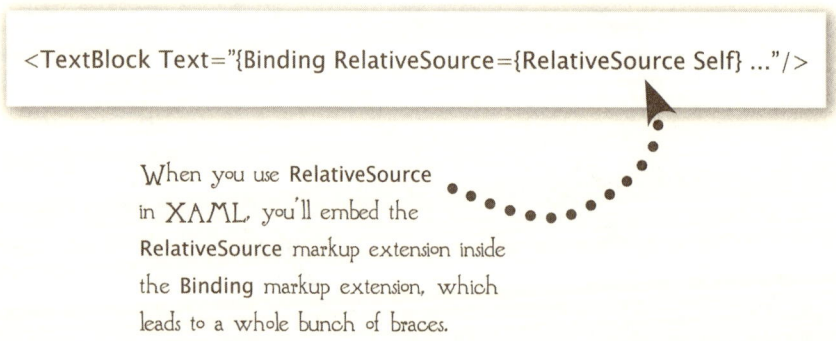

When you use **RelativeSource** in XAML, you'll embed the **RelativeSource** markup extension inside the **Binding** markup extension, which leads to a whole bunch of braces.

THE DATA CONTEXT

In addition to setting the binding source for a single `Binding`, the `FrameworkElement` class exposes a property named `DataContext` that you can use to set a binding source for multiple elements. Here's an example from the app we'll be building in the next section:

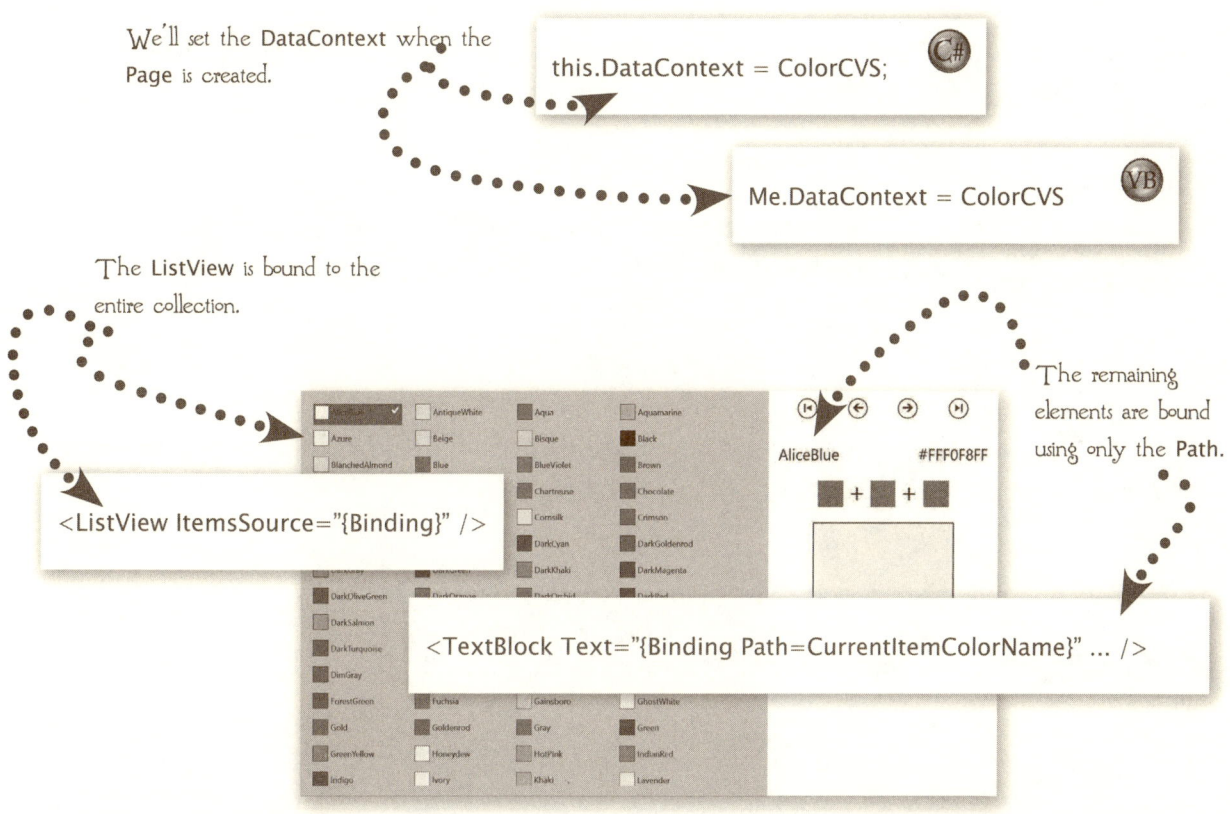

We'll set the `DataContext` when the `Page` is created.

`this.DataContext = ColorCVS;` C#

`Me.DataContext = ColorCVS` VB

The `ListView` is bound to the entire collection.

`<ListView ItemsSource="{Binding}" />`

The remaining elements are bound using only the `Path`.

`<TextBlock Text="{Binding Path=CurrentItemColorName}" ... />`

TAKE A BREAK

We'll see a lot more examples of bindings as we work through the book. The DataContext property is easy to use, and it's particularly useful when you're working with a collection of elements, as in our example. We'll get some more experience of it in the next section, so why don't you take a break now and we'll move on to binding to collections after the Review?

REVIEW

What advantage does RelativeSource TemplatedParent provide over a TemplateBinding?

Assuming that a FontStyleToString converter class exists, how would you write the binding to display the current FontStyle in the Text of a TextBlock?

There are two important interfaces for change notification: one for single properties and one for collections. What are they?

What binding mode should you use for a value that cannot be changed by the binding target?

What are the four ways of specifying the source of a binding?

BINDING TO COLLECTIONS

Back in Chapter 6 we examined items controls and the `Items` property that allows you to specify the items displayed by the control directly in XAML or code. Items controls also expose a second property, `ItemsSource`, that is bound to a collection.

The syntax for declaring a binding for the `ItemsSource` property is almost identical to the syntax for binding any other property, but because you're binding to the whole collection, not just a single value, you omit the `Path` property:

```
<ListBox ItemsSource="{Binding Source={x:StaticResource myCollection}}" />
```

There's another little wrinkle to binding the `ItemsSource`. I gave you an example of it a couple of pages ago. If you're binding to an inherited `DataContext`, which as I've said is very common, you can omit the `Source`, too. But you do have to specify that the value is bound, so you use what's known as an EMPTY BINDING:

```
<ListBox ItemsSource="{Binding}" />
```

Looks strange, doesn't it? But it's perfectly valid provided there's a `DataContext` somewhere in the logical tree that the `ListBox` (or any other items control) can find.

MAKE A NOTE
The `Items` and `ItemSource` properties of an items control are mutually exclusive! If you try to set both, your application won't compile.

BUILDING A COLLECTION

Before we can experiment with binding to collections, we need a collection to bind to. The Visual Studio Grid App and Split App both provide a sample data source, but it's difficult to extract and over-complicated for our purposes, so let's take a minute to roll our own. We'll pull the data from the static Colors class.

We'll need two classes: one to hold information about the color, and one to hold the collection. Here's the simple color information class.

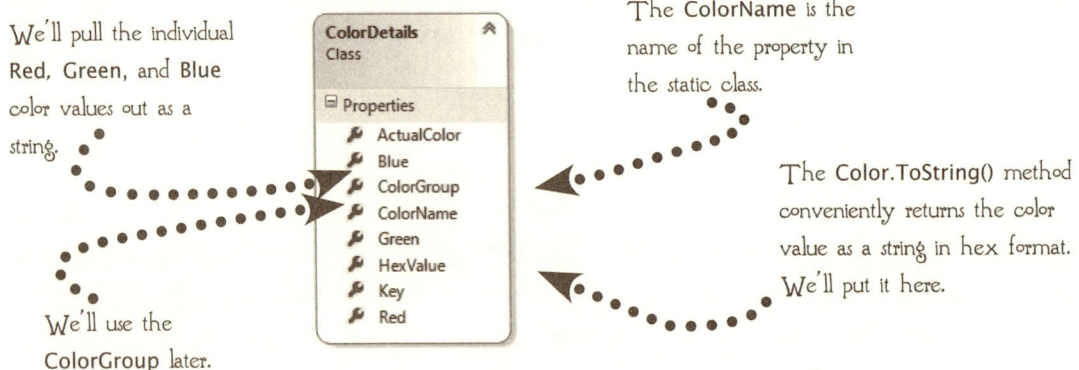

We'll pull the individual Red, Green, and Blue color values out as a string.

The ColorName is the name of the property in the static class.

The Color.ToString() method conveniently returns the color value as a string in hex format. We'll put it here.

We'll use the ColorGroup later.

The **ColorCollection** class should be an **ObservableCollection<ColorDetails>**. (We'll find out why in a page or two.)

```vb
Public Class ColorCollection
    Inherits ObservableCollection(Of ColorDetails)
    Public Sub New()
        LoadStandardColors()
    End Sub
    Public Sub LoadStandardColors()
        Dim t As Type = GetType(Colors)
        Dim pList As IEnumerable(Of PropertyInfo) = t.GetTypeInfo().DeclaredProperties
        For Each p As PropertyInfo In pList
            Dim cd As ColorDetails = New ColorDetails()
            Dim c As Color = DirectCast(p.GetValue(Nothing), Color)
            cd.ColorName = p.Name
            cd.ActualColor = c
            cd.Red = Color.FromArgb(255, c.R, 0, 0).ToString()
            cd.Green = Color.FromArgb(255, 0, c.G, 0).ToString()
            cd.Blue = Color.FromArgb(255, 0, 0, c.B).ToString()
            cd.HexValue = c.ToString()
            cd.Key = p.Name.Substring(0, 1)
            Add(cd)
        Next
    End Sub
End Class
```

All of the work happens in the ColorCollection.LoadStandardColors() method. Since this is just straight .NET programming (and reflection is outside our scope), I've given you the code:

```csharp
public class ColorCollection : ObservableCollection<ColorDetails>
{
    public ColorCollection()
    {
        LoadStandardColors();
    }
    public void LoadStandardColors()
    {
        Type t = typeof(Colors);
        IEnumerable<PropertyInfo> pList = t.GetTypeInfo().DeclaredProperties;

        foreach (PropertyInfo p in pList)
        {
            ColorDetails cd = new ColorDetails();
            Color c = (Color)p.GetValue(null);
            cd.ColorName = p.Name;
            cd.ActualColor = c;
            cd.Red = Color.FromArgb(255, c.R, 0, 0).ToString();
            cd.Green = Color.FromArgb(255, 0, c.G, 0).ToString();
            cd.Blue = Color.FromArgb(255, 0, 0, c.B).ToString();
            cd.HexValue = c.ToString();
            cd.Key = p.Name.Substring(0, 1);

            Add(cd);
        }
    }
}
```

ON YOUR OWN

Create a new blank app (I called mine ColorBrowser) and add the two class files.

You'll need to add a reference to the Windows.UI namespace to both files get access to the Color structure, and one to System.Collections.ObjectModel to have access to the ObservableCollection in the ColorCollection file and System.Reflection for PropertyInfo and GetTypeInfo().

Be sure to build your project so that the classes are available for the next step.

BUILDING BINDABLE COLLECTIONS

You already know that in order for binding to work the way you expect it to, the binding source needs to support change notification through the `INotifyPropertyChanged` and, for collections, the `INotifyCollectionChanged` interfaces. You can implement the interfaces yourself, of course, but you'll almost always use the `ObservableCollection<T>` class, since it handles all the messy details for you.

But when you're working with collections you need something else: currency. CURRENCY simply means that there's a pointer to one item in the collection. That item is considered the "current item". Not a difficult concept, but don't confuse it with CONCURRENCY, which is multiple processes operating at the same time. To achieve that, you'll wrap your collection in a `CollectionViewSource`, which will create an instance of `ICollectionView` for you. The `ICollectionView`, in turn, provides currency and support for grouping—very important in the world of `ISemanticZoom`. (We'll explore grouping later in this chapter.)

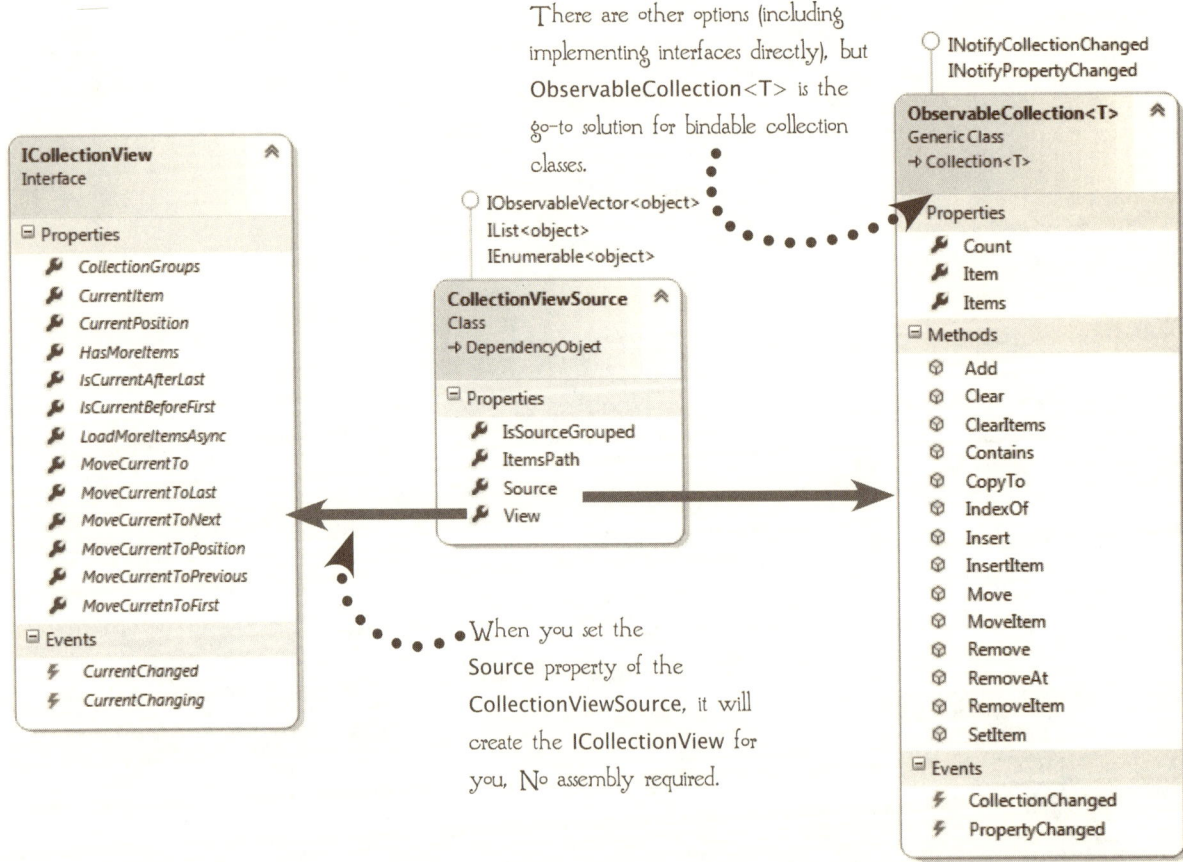

IN A NUTSHELL

Here are the basic steps for creating a bindable collection:

CREATE A COLLECTION

As I've said, you'll almost always derive from **ObservableCollection<T>**, as we did in our **ColorCollection** class.

INSTANTIATE THE COLLECTION

You could pass the collection in from a **ViewModel** or do something tricky with dependency injection, but we'll just add it as resource to our **Page**:

```
<Page.Resources>
    <local:ColorCollection x:Key="ColorList" x:Name="ColorList"/>
<Page.Resources>
```

Declaring the **x:Key** makes the collection easily available in your XAML as a resource.

Declaring the **x:Name** makes it available in code as well.

CREATE THE COLLECTIONVIEWSOURCE

You can bind directly to the collection, but you'll usually want to wrap it in a **CollectionViewSource**. (We'll find out why in the next section.) You can do this in code-behind or in XAML, which is more usual even if you create the collection itself in code:

```
<Page.Resources>
    <local:ColorCollection x:Key="ColorList" x:Name="ColorList"/>
    <CollectionViewSource x:Key="ColorCVS" x:Name="ColorCVS"
        Source="{StaticResource ColorList}"/>
<Page.Resources>
```

SET THE DATA CONTEXT

You want to set the data context fairly high up the visual tree. You can set it for the **Page** itself, but we'll set it for the root layout **Grid** because the syntax is a little simpler:

```
<Grid ... DataContext="{StaticResource ColorCVS}">
```

PUT ON YOUR THINKING HAT

Time to build the UI for our little app. It's more complex than most of our examples, but I think it's well within your capabilities if you take it one step at a time. (And you can always look at the next page if you get confused.)

The basic layout root is a two-column **Grid** with a **LightGray** background. The first column is given two-thirds of the available width.

This column contains a **Border** (to get the white background) that contains **StackPanel** that in turn contains other **StackPanel** and **Grid** elements (and one big **Rectangle**).

StackPanel

Grid

StackPanel

Rectangle

We'll have to do some work to get the **ListView** to display the colors like this, but don't worry about that yet.

 Declare the color collection resource and CollectionViewSource for the Page.

 Create the columns of the layout Grid, set its Background to LightGray, and set its DataContext to the CollectionViewSource.

 Put a ListView in the first column of the Grid and set its ItemsSource to an empty binding.

 The buttons are all AppBarButton elements with their Icon and Element properties set. Notice that our labels don't match the icon symbol names—the button labeled "First", for example, uses the Previous icon, while the button labeled "Previous" uses the Back icon.

 The second row of the StackPanel contains a Grid with two TextBlocks. The left-hand element is bound to the ColorName of the CurrentItem, and the right-hand element to the HexValue of the CurrentItem.

 The row of small Rectangles and TextBlocks (the "+" symbols) is also contained in a StackPanel. The Fill property of each of the Rectangle elements is bound to the Red, Green, or Blue values of the CurrentItem.

 The Fill property of the large Rectangle at the bottom is bound to the ColorName of the CurrentItem.

EXTRA CREDIT

Do you know why the large Rectangle is bound to the ColorName (a string) instead of ActualColor (a Color)? Is there another way to achieve the same result?

HOW'D YOU DO?

A lot of code, wasn't it? But like everything in programming, it's not so bad if you take it bit by bit.

```xml
<Page ...>
  <Page.Resources>
    <local:ColorCollection x:Key="Colors"/>
    <CollectionViewSource x:Key="ColorCVS" x:Name="ColorCVS" Source="{StaticResource Colors}"/>
  </Page.Resources>

  <Grid Background="LightGray" DataContext="{StaticResource ColorCVS}">
    <Grid.ColumnDefinitions>
      <ColumnDefinition Width="2*"/>
      <ColumnDefinition Width="1*"/>
    </Grid.ColumnDefinitions>
    <ListView x:Name="ListOfColors" Grid.Column="0" Margin="20" ItemsSource="{Binding}" />
    <Border Grid.Column="1" Background="White">
      <StackPanel>
        <StackPanel Orientation="Horizontal" HorizontalAlignment="Center" >
          <AppBarButton Icon="Previous" Label="First"/>
          <AppBarButton Icon="Back" Label="Previous"/>
          <AppBarButton Icon="Forward" Label="Next"/>
          <AppBarButton Icon="Next" Label="Last"/>
        </StackPanel>
        <Grid>
          <Grid.ColumnDefinitions>
            <ColumnDefinition Width="Auto"/>
            <ColumnDefinition/>
          </Grid.ColumnDefinitions>
          <TextBlock Foreground="Black" FontSize="30" Grid.Column="0"
                Margin="20" HorizontalAlignment="Left" Text="{Binding Path=CurrentItem.ColorName}"/>
          <TextBlock Foreground="Black" FontSize="30" Grid.Column="1"
                Margin="20" HorizontalAlignment="Right" TextAlignment="Right"
                Text="{Binding Path=CurrentItem.HexValue}"/>
        </Grid>
        <StackPanel x:Name="ComponentStack" Orientation="Horizontal" HorizontalAlignment="Center">
          <Rectangle Width="50" Height="50" Fill="{Binding Path= CurrentItem. Red}" Margin="10"/>
          <TextBlock Text="+" FontSize="50" Foreground="Black" VerticalAlignment="Center"/>
          <Rectangle Width="50" Height="50" Fill="{Binding Path= CurrentItem.Green}" Margin="10"/>
          <TextBlock Text="+" FontSize="50" Foreground="Black" VerticalAlignment="Center"/>
          <Rectangle Width="50" Height="50" Fill="{Binding Path= CurrentItem.Blue}" Margin="10"/>
        </StackPanel>
        <Rectangle Width="300" Height="300"
              Stroke="Black" StrokeThickness="2" Margin="0, 20"
              Fill="{Binding Path= CurrentItem.ColorName}" />
      </StackPanel>
    </Border>
  </Grid>
</Page>
```

MORE TEMPLATES

When you run our sample app, all of the bindings appear to be working, and you can even move around the collection by choosing items in the `ListView`. But the `ListView` is just displaying the class name, which is the default returned by the `ToString()` method. Well, remember in the last chapter I told you there were styles and templates all over the place in XAML? A bunch of them have to do with displaying data in list controls, and we'll need two of them to fix our `ListView` display. Here are the classes:

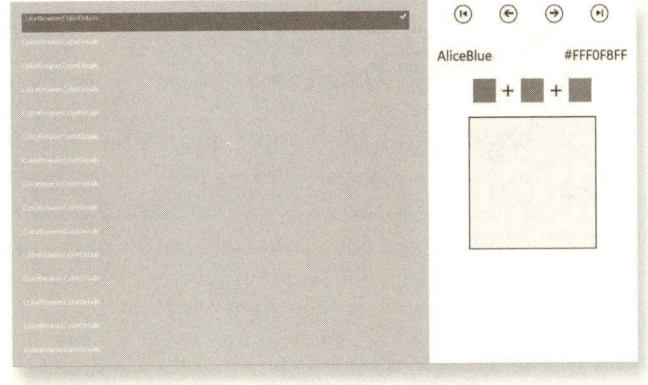

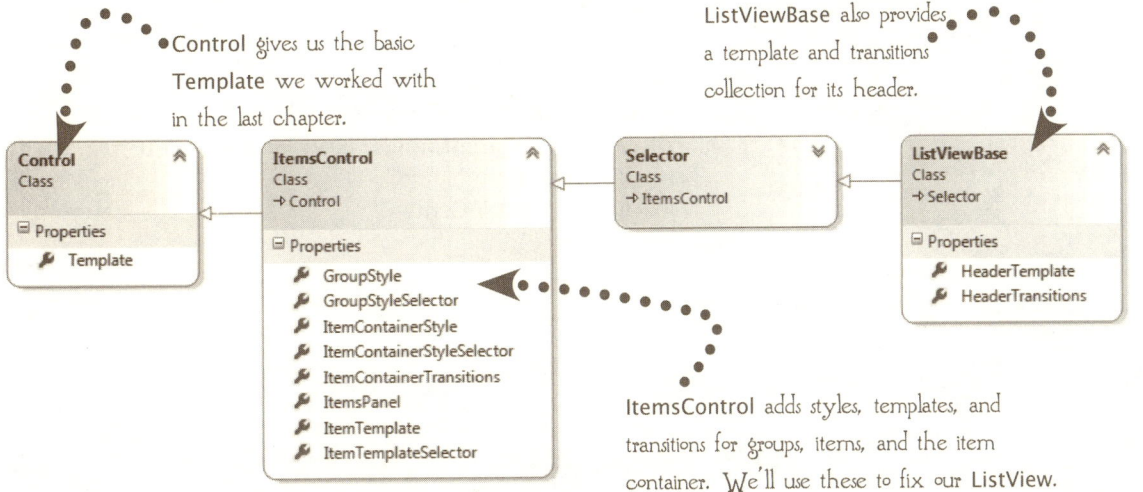

Control gives us the basic Template we worked with in the last chapter.

ListViewBase also provides a template and transitions collection for its header.

ItemsControl adds styles, templates, and transitions for groups, items, and the item container. We'll use these to fix our ListView.

PUT ON YOUR THINKING HAT

Let's start by fixing the ListView.ItemTemplate. The basic syntax is the same as we used for a ControlTemplate, but this time you'll need an instance of DataTemplate. Ours is a 30 pixel high StackPanel with a 30 x 30 Border and a TextBlock. The Background of the Border and the Text of the TextBlock are both bound to the ColorName.

Can you build it?

HOW'D YOU DO?

The only difference between declaring an **ItemTemplate** and the control templates we built in the last chapter is that it's a **DataTemplate**, not a **ControlTemplate**.

I added some additional formatting, did you?

```xml
<ListView x:Name="ListOfColors" Grid.Column="0" Margin="20"
          ItemsSource="{Binding}" >
    <ListView.ItemTemplate>
        <DataTemplate>
            <StackPanel Orientation="Horizontal"
                        HorizontalAlignment="Center"
                        Height="30">
                <Border Width="30" Height="30"
                    Background="{Binding ColorName}"
                    BorderBrush="Black" BorderThickness="1"/>
                <TextBlock FontSize="16" Foreground="Black" Margin="5,0"
                    Text="{Binding ColorName}"
                    VerticalAlignment="Center"/>
            </StackPanel>
        </DataTemplate>
    </ListView.ItemTemplate>
</ListView>
```

MAKE A NOTE

For simplicity, I'm specifying physical sizes for the elements in the app. As we'll see in the next chapter, this isn't really best practice, and it will come back and bite you. For now, we'll just go with it, but be aware there's a much better way (and you'll learn about it soon).

THE ITEMSPANEL

In designing the UX for our little app, I chose a `ListView` rather than a `GridView` because vertical scrolling felt more natural to me. (Feel free to disagree.) But just because the `ListView` scrolls vertically, it doesn't mean we can't have multiple columns. All we have to do is change the `ListView.ItemsPanel`, which defaults to a `StackPanel`, to a `WrapGrid`.

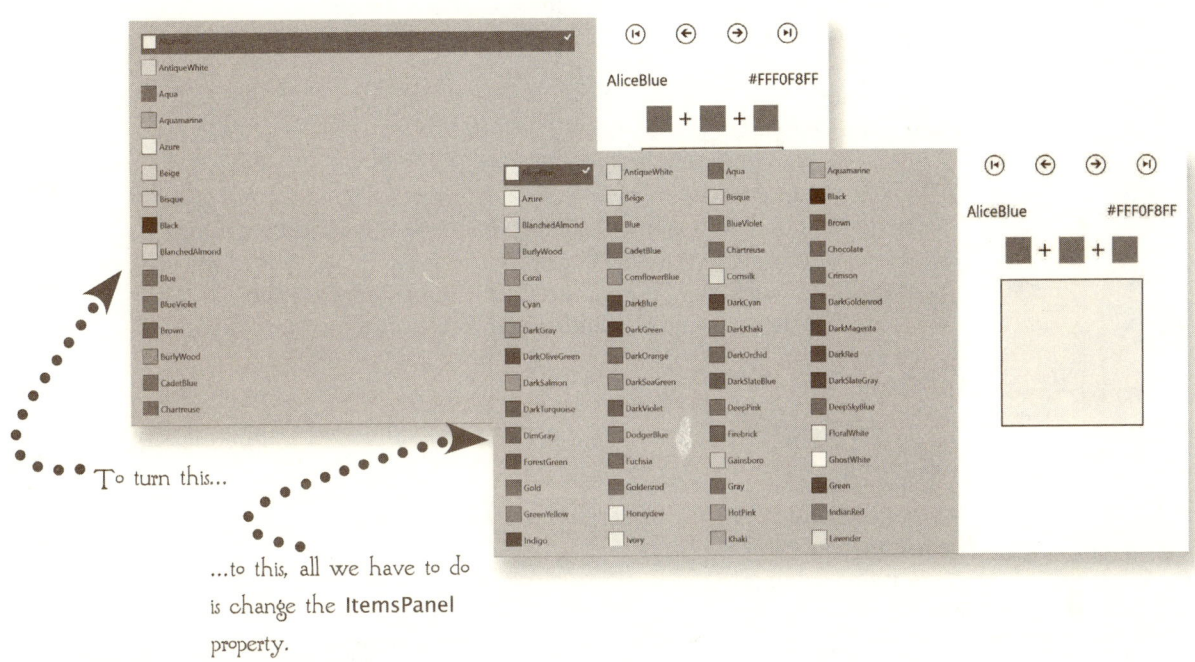

To turn this...

...to this, all we have to do is change the `ItemsPanel` property.

PUT ON YOUR THINKING HAT

Change the `ListView.ItemsPanel` to a `WrapGrid`. This time you'll need to use an `ItemsPanelTemplate`, but otherwise the syntax is the same.

The `WrapGrid` has a horizontal `Orientation`, and I set the `ItemWidth` to 200 to have room for (most) of the color names.

HOW'D YOU DO?

Here's my version of the final ListView element:

```xml
<ListView x:Name="ListOfColors" Grid.Column="0" Margin="20"
          ItemsSource="{Binding}" >
    <ListView.ItemTemplate>
        <DataTemplate>
            <StackPanel Orientation="Horizontal"
                        HorizontalAlignment="Center"
                        Height="30">
                <Border Width="30" Height="30" Background="{Binding ColorName}"
                        BorderBrush="Black" BorderThickness="1"/>
                <TextBlock FontSize="16" Foreground="Black" Margin="5,0"
                           Text="{Binding ColorName}" VerticalAlignment="Center"/>
            </StackPanel>
        </DataTemplate>
    </ListView.ItemTemplate>
    <ListView.ItemsPanel>
        <ItemsPanelTemplate>
            <WrapGrid Orientation="Horizontal" ItemWidth="200"/>
        </ItemsPanelTemplate>
    </ListView.ItemsPanel>
</ListView>
```

TAKE A BREAK

One of the things I really like about XAML is that once you know how one part of it works, you know a lot about how other parts of it work. That's certainly true of templates. Each type has little idiosyncrasies, but they have more in common than not.

So now that we have our ListBox working properly, why don't you take a break before we explore some of the other functionality XAML provides when you're working with collections?

REVIEW

Can you answer the following questions based on what you've learned?

What property do you set to control how individual items are displayed in an items control?

What kind of template does it take?

What class do you typically derive from when building bindable collections? Why?

When you wrap your bindable collection in a CollectionViewSource, it will create an instance of something else for you. What? What does that give you?

What is an empty binding? When do you use it?

WORKING WITH COLLECTIONS

As I've said, while it's possible to build a classic database application in Win8, the absence of ADO.NET makes it, well, tricky. But wherever our data lives or however it's created, you'll want to (at the very least) provide a means for your users to move around it, and you'll want to perform LINQ operations (sorting, filtering, and, most importantly, grouping) and reflect the results in your UI. We'll explore that kind of functionality in this section, beginning with moving through the data.

Although the master-detail structure of our sample app allows users to move through the data by selecting items in the ListView, not all pages use the master-detail pattern. The Move...() methods of the ICollectionView (which, you'll remember, is automatically created and accessed via the CollectionViewSource.View property) give you the functionality you need to build an alternate UI.

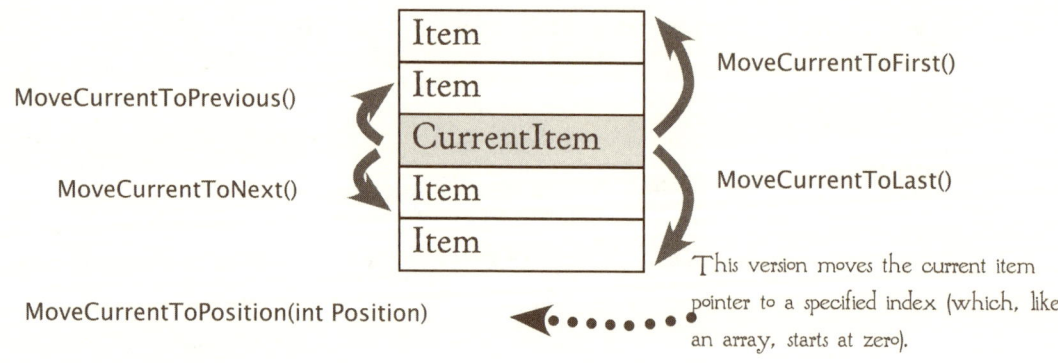

This version moves the current item pointer to a specified index (which, like an array, starts at zero).

The Move...() methods are pretty simple to work with, but there is one gotcha to pay attention to. MoveCurrentToPrevious() and MoveCurrentToNext() will quite happily move beyond the bounds of the collection, so when moving them, you'll need to check the IsCurrentAfterLast or IsCurrentAfterLast property and adjust the CurrentItem accordingly.

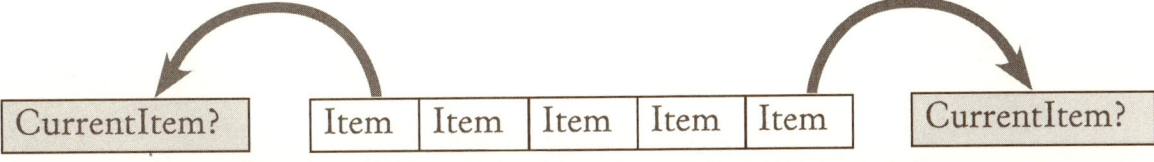

PUT ON YOUR THINKING HAT

Set up the buttons at the top of the details pane in our sample app so that they move through the ColorsCVS CollectionViewSource.

You'll probably want to assign each button an x:Name (the conventional names are MoveFirst, MovePrevious, MoveNext, and MoveLast), although it isn't absolutely necessary in this example.

Once you've got your buttons named, write a Click event handler using the methods of the ICollectionView. Remember to check whether MoveCurrentToPrevious() or MoveCurrentToNext() methods have moved outside the bounds of the collection.

ON YOUR OWN

If you find this exercise really easy (or you're just in the mood for a challenge), try adding a TextBox between the Previous and Next buttons that lets you type a position number. (Make sure you check the number entered against the Count property before you try to move!)

HOW'D YOU DO?

Here's my version. (I haven't shown the XAML for the Button elements because you know how to do that.) By the way, because of space constraints, I've only shown the C# code in its entirety. I know you Visual Basic programmers out there are more than smart enough to figure the rest out...

```csharp
private void MoveFirst_Click(object sender, RoutedEventArgs e)
{
   ColorCVS.View.MoveCurrentToFirst();
}

private void MovePrevious_Click(object sender, RoutedEventArgs e)
{
   ColorCVS.View.MoveCurrentToPrevious();
  if (ColorCVS.View.IsCurrentBeforeFirst)
       ColorCVS.View.MoveCurrentToFirst();
}

private void MoveNext_Click(object sender, RoutedEventArgs e)
{
   ColorCVS.View.MoveCurrentToNext();
  if (ColorCVS.View.IsCurrentAfterLast)
       ColorCVS.View.MoveCurrentToLast();
}

private void MoveLast_Click(object sender, RoutedEventArgs e)
{
   ColorCVS.View.MoveCurrentToLast();
}
```

```vb
Private Sub View_CurrentChanged(sender As Object, e As Object)
  ListOfColors.ScrollIntoView(ColorCVS.View.CurrentItem)
End Sub

Private Sub MovePrevious_Click(sender As Object, e As RoutedEventArgs)
  ColorCVS.View.MoveCurrentToPrevious()
  If ColorCVS.View.IsCurrentBeforeFirst Then
    ColorCVS.View.MoveCurrentToFirst()
  End If
End Sub
```

SYNCHRONIZING THE DISPLAY

In older XAML frameworks, you needed to set the IsSynchronizedWithCurrentItem property of an items control in order to achieve the kind of data synchronization we're seeing in the example app. The IsSynchronizedWithCurrent item is still present in Win8 XAML, but you only need it in unusual circumstances—if, for example you don't want something synchronized. But synchronizing the data and synchronizing what's displayed in your UI aren't exactly the same, and we need to fix that up in our app. (It's easy.)

If you click the MoveLast Button, the correct item becomes current, but you can't see it in the ListView.

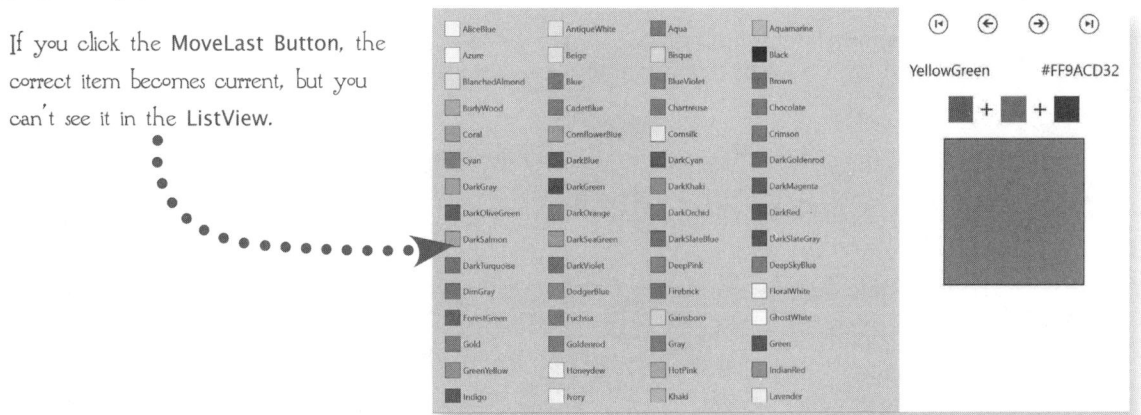

PUT ON YOUR THINKING HAT

The ICollectionView exposes a CurrentChanged event, and the ListViewBase (from which ListView derives, of course) exposes a ScrollIntoView(object) method.

To fix our app's display, all we need to do is connect them by registering a handler for the event that calls the method, passing in the CurrentItem.

Can you figure out how? Register the event in the MainPage constructor, after ColorList is instantiated.

467

HOW'D YOU DO?

```csharp
public MainPage()
{
  this.InitializeComponent();
  ColorCVS.View.CurrentChanged += View_CurrentChanged;
}

void View_CurrentChanged(object sender, object e)
{
  ListOfColors.ScrollIntoView(ColorCVS.View.CurrentItem);
}
```

You might have to go back and assign an x:Name to the ListView if you haven't done so already.

```vb
Public Sub New()
  InitializeComponent()
  AddHandler ColorCVS.View.CurrentChanged, AddressOf View_CurrentChanged
End Sub

Private Sub View_CurrentChanged(sender As Object, e As Object)
  ListOfColors.ScrollIntoView(ColorCVS.View.CurrentItem)
End Sub
```

ORGANIZING COLLECTIONS

So far we've seen that deriving your collection class from `ObservableCollection<T>` gives you change notification, and wrapping it in a `CollectionViewSource` creates an instance of `ICollectionView` that provides currency. But what about sorting, filtering, and grouping? The canonical way of providing that is by introducing (yet another) layer of indirection between the actual data and the UI, by binding to a LINQ query based on the collection rather than the collection itself:

We've been setting the **Source** property of the **CollectionViewSource** directly to the collection class. That gives us change notification and currency:

Instead of using the collection class directly, you can set the **CollectionViewSource.Source** to the results of a LINQ query that's based on the collection. (Or multiple collections, for that matter.) This pattern gives you all the power of LINQ for shaping and organizing data, but at the cost of change notification:

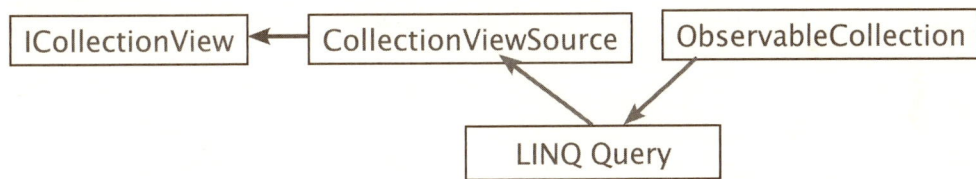

> ### MAKE A NOTE
> The collection type returned by a LINQ query varies, but to my knowledge, none of them support change notification. That may not be a problem in your app—it often isn't—but it's something to be aware of and think through. LINQ is the most common way to organize bound data and the one that's implicitly recommended by Microsoft, but it's not the only way.

GROUPING DATA WITH LINQ

You can use the results of any LINQ query as the `CollectionViewSource.Source` (although not all of them may make sense), but one query function that you'll probably use a lot is grouping. Grouping is, after all, fundamental to Semantic Zoom, which is one of the distinguishing capabilities of Win8. To get a sense of how grouping with LINQ works, let's group our color list alphabetically. The basic process is simple:

CREATE A LINQ QUERY

LINQ is part of C# and Visual Basic, so this has to be done in code. By a strange coincidence, the **ColorDetails** class contains a **Key** field that contains the first letter of the color name, so we can use that to simplify the LINQ (and the subsequent formatting):

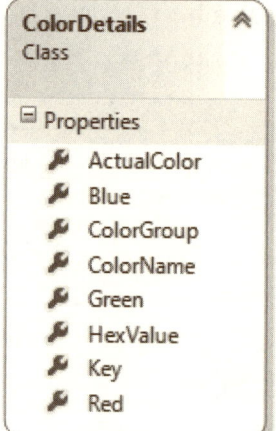

```csharp
var groupedColors = from c in ColorList
                    orderby c.ColorName
                    group c by c.Key into g
                    select g;
```

```vb
Dim GroupedColors = From c In ColorList
                    OrderBy c.ColorName
                    Group c by c.Key
                    Into Group
```

CONFIGURE THE COLLECTIONVIEWSOURCE

We need to do two things: set the new **Source**, and tell the **CollectionViewSource** that we're grouping by setting the **IsSourceGrouped** property. In our example, we'll set the source in code, but we'll set **IsSourceGrouped** in the XAML where **ColorCVS** is declared. You'll also want to remove the **Source** attribute there, so XAML doesn't get confused:

```xml
<CollectionViewSource x:Name="ColorCVS" IsSourceGrouped="True" />
```

470

 ### DECLARE THE GROUP HEADER DISPLAY

Yep, you guessed it. We need another template. But **ListViewBase** doesn't expose a **HeaderTemplate** property directly. Instead, it exposes a **GroupStyle** property, and the **GroupStyle** exposes the header template. So you'll wind up with a structure like this:

```xml
<ListView ... >
   ...
   <ListView.GroupStyle>
      <GroupStyle>
         <GroupStyle.HeaderTemplate>
            <DataTemplate>
               ...
            </DataTemplate>
         </GroupStyle.HeaderTemplate>
      </GroupStyle>
   </ListView.GroupStyle>
</ListView>
```

You'll define the template here.

In my example, I bound the **Text** property of a **TextBlock** to the **Key** and placed the **TextBlock** inside a **Border** with a white **Background**. (Of course, I also fiddled with the size and color of the font and the alignment of the elements. I'm like that.)

 ### PUT ON YOUR THINKING HAT
Update the sample application so that the colors are grouped.

HOW'D YOU DO?

Here's my version:

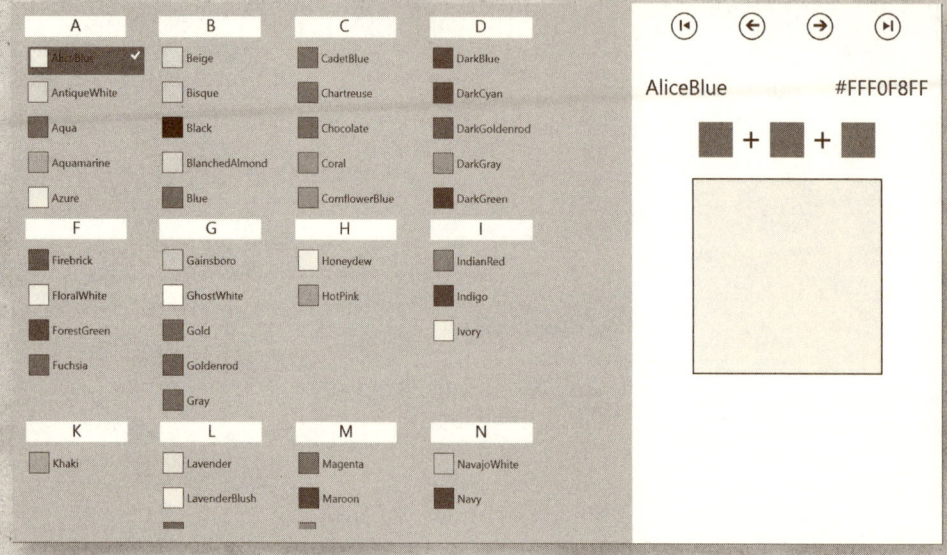

```
<Page.Resources>
    <!--<local:ColorCollection x:Key="Colors"/>-->
    <!--<CollectionViewSource x:Name="ColorCVS" Source="{StaticResource Colors}"/>-->
    <CollectionViewSource x:Name="ColorCVS" IsSourceGrouped="True" ItemsPath="Group"/>
</Page.Resources>
...
<ListView ... >
    ...
    <ListView.GroupStyle>
        <GroupStyle>
            <GroupStyle.HeaderTemplate>
                <DataTemplate>
                    <Border Background="White" Width="150" HorizontalAlignment="Center"
                            Margin="0,0,0,10">
                        <TextBlock Text="{Binding Key}"
                                   FontSize="24" Foreground="Black"
                                   HorizontalAlignment="Center"/>
                    </Border>
                </DataTemplate>
            </GroupStyle.HeaderTemplate>
        </GroupStyle>
    </ListView.GroupStyle>
</ListView>
```

```csharp
public MainPage()
{
    this.InitializeComponent();
    ColorCollection ColorList = new ColorCollection();
    var groupedColors = from c in ColorList
                        orderby c.Key
                        group c by c.Key into g
                        select g;
    ColorCVS.Source = groupedColors;

    ColorCVS.View.CurrentChanged += View_CurrentChanged;
}
```

```vb
Public Sub New()
  InitializeComponent()
  Dim ColorList As ColorCollection = New ColorCollection()
  Dim groupedColors = From c In ColorList
                      Order By c.Key
                      Group c By c.Key
                      Into g = Group
  ColorCVS.Source = groupedColors
  AddHandler ColorCVS.View.CurrentChanged, AddressOf View_CurrentChanged
End Sub
```

REVIEW

What interface do you implement to create a class that will convert values within a Binding?

What functionality does wrapping a collection in a CollectionViewSource give you?

What interface does a single property need to implement in order to be used as a binding source? How about a collection?

What's the syntax for binding an element to another element on the same Page?

Congratulations! You've finished the chapter. Take a minute to think about what you've accomplished before you move on to the next one...

List three things you learned in this chapter:

①

②

③

Why do you think you need to know these things in order to develop Win8 apps?

Is there anything in this chapter that you think you need to understand in more detail? If so, what are you going to do about that?

DISPLAYING YOUR APP 13

Because Win8 apps only ever have one primary app surface, managing the UI is in some ways easier than in a traditional Windows application—there aren't any child windows or dialogs to keep track of—but it can also be more complex. A well-designed Win8 app needs to adapt to a wide range of form factors in a variety of views. And even if we don't have multiple windows, we'll probably have multiple pages to keep track of. Then there's the UI you need to present when the user selects a charms like Settings or Search, and well, it can get interesting.

But like most things, if you just tackle one issue at a time, it's a complex problem, but not a difficult one, and both Visual Studio and WinRT provide a lot of support for the task.

We'll start the process in this chapter. First we'll explore the techniques you can use to adapt your application to multiple screen sizes and resolutions. You already know most of them, and the Visual Studio simulator makes it easy to test your application's performance. Then we'll look at the various views that Windows Store apps are required to support and how the `VisualStateManager` you learned about in Chapter 11 lets you respond to view changes declaratively.

Your application has very little control over changes in screen size or view, but if your application displays more than one page (and most will), it's up to you to design the navigation, and we'll look at the support WinRT provides for this process at the end of the chapter.

FITTING IT IN

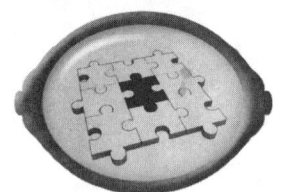

Here's how this chapter fits in to the book as a whole...

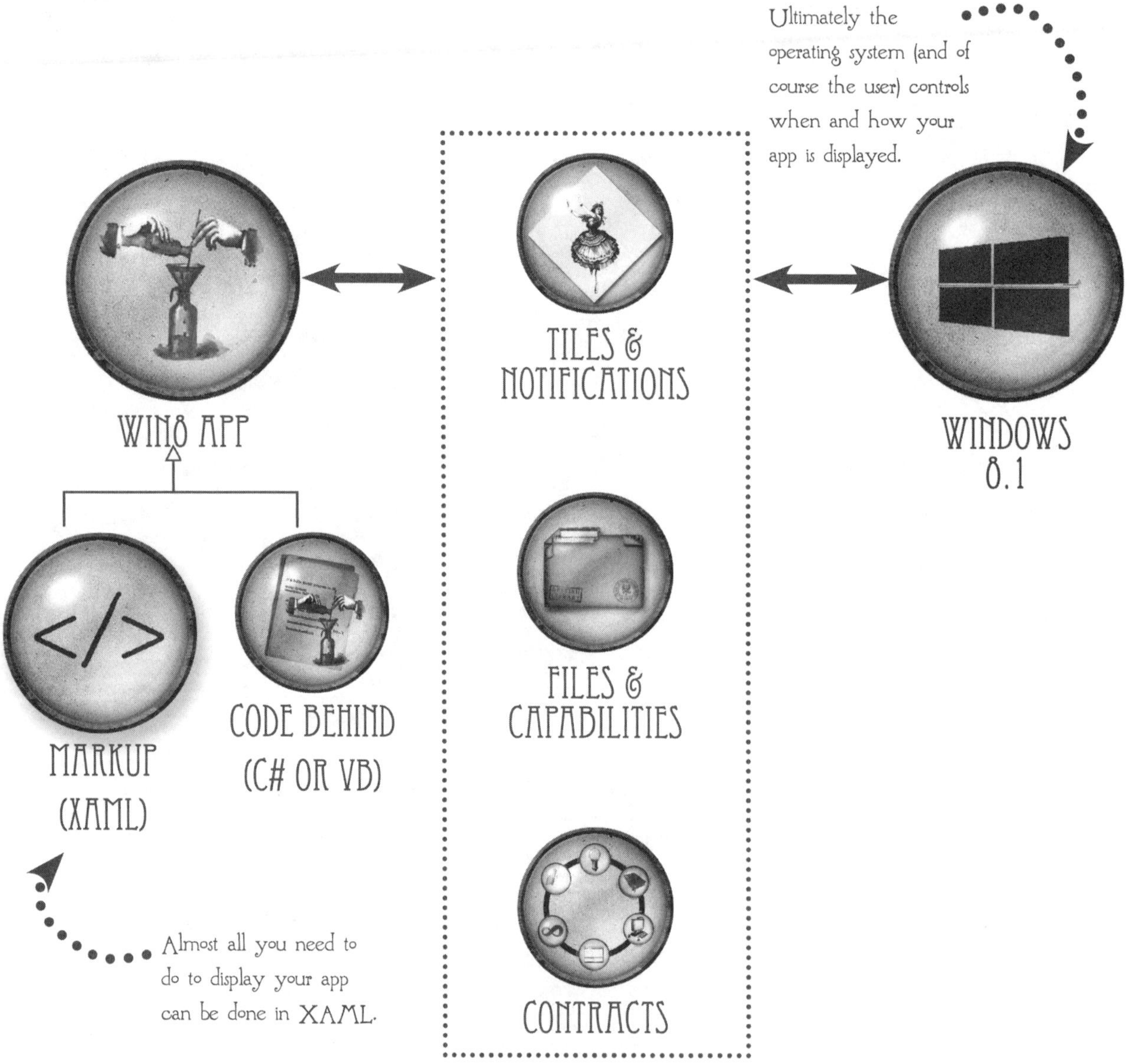

Ultimately the operating system (and of course the user) controls when and how your app is displayed.

WIN8 APP ↔ TILES & NOTIFICATIONS ↔ WINDOWS 8.1

FILES & CAPABILITIES

CONTRACTS

MARKUP (XAML)

CODE BEHIND (C# OR VB)

Almost all you need to do to display your app can be done in XAML.

TASK LIST

In this chapter we'll start exploring how your app interacts with the operating system.

LOADING SUPPORT CLASSES

We'll start off the chapter by convincing Visual Studio to load some support classes like the **SuspensionManager** and the **NavigationHelper**, which aren't added by default with a blank app but will be useful for the tasks that await us.

Once we have those basics in place, we'll re-build our color explorer from the last chapter using the capabilities the utility files give us.

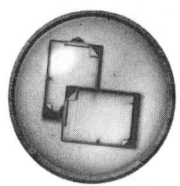

APPLICATION LAYOUT

In the next section, we'll start exploring the screen resolutions (from 1024×768 to 2560×1440), orientations (landscape and portrait), and window widths that your app needs to support, and the ways that Visual Studio and XAML make that much less difficult than it might be.

NAVIGATION

All of our sample apps have been one-page wonders. You can provide a surprising amount of functionality on a single **Page**, but you'll often need more than that, so in the last section we'll find out how to use the **Frame** and **Page** model to provide navigation.

LOADING SUPPORT CLASSES

I think of it as a Goldilocks syndrome: If you choose one of the "big" application templates like the Grid App, you get a lot of stuff that you may not need unless your final app architecture closely resembles the template. (Too much.) If you choose the Blank app template, all you get are some empty logo files and a single minimal page. (Too little.) But with a little bit of slight-of-hand, we can get Visual Studio to load some valuable support classes without overloading our project. (Just right).

 **CREATE A BLANK APP**

We'll start with the same blank application template we've been using throughout most of the book. Create one now, and name it **BasicPageItems**.

Visual Studio will add four dummy logo images to the Assets folder and a single **MainPage.xaml** that's based on the Blank Page template.

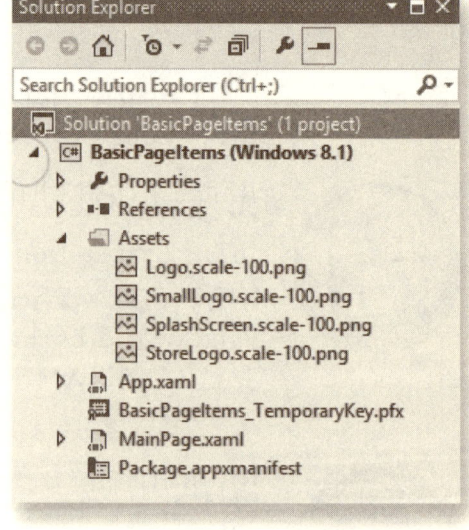

As we'll see later in the chapter, the **App.xaml.cs** or **App.xaml.vb** file contains the basic code to load and run a single **Page**, but there's no intrinsic support for navigation or saving and restoring the app's state. Let's fix that.

 REPLACE MAINPAGE.XAML

By default, the start-up code in **App.xaml.cs** expects to load a class named **MainPage**, which is what the Blank app template creates. We'll explore how the start-up code works and how to change the initial page type later in this chapter, but for now, let's just replace the existing **MainPage.xaml** file with a new one based on the Basic Page template instead of the Blank Page template. That'll prompt Visual Studio to load the support files we're looking for.

Ⓐ DELETE THE EXISTING MAINPAGE.XAML FILE

Nothing tricky here, just select it in the Solution Explorer and hit the Delete key.

Ⓑ ADD A NEW BASIC PAGE

Select Add New Item from the Project menu and choose Basic Page in the Add New Item dialog. (Make sure you choose Basic Page, not Blank Page. Basic Page is the second option.) Name the new page **MainPage.xaml** and click Add.

Visual Studio will display a dialog asking whether you want to add some needed support files automatically. Click Yes.

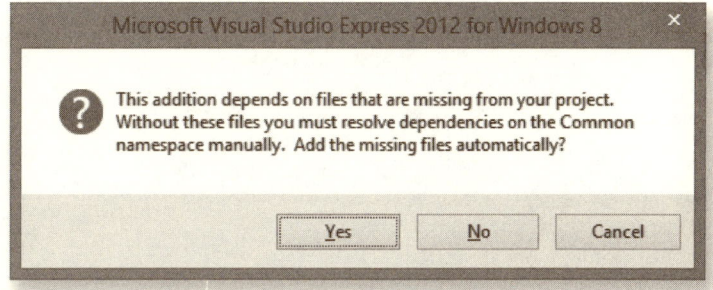

Ⓒ BUILD THE APP

Once Visual Studio adds the files, you'll need to build the app (just press F7) to compile the source files and display the new **MainPage** in the Designer.

COMMON FILES

Okay, let's see what that little exercise brought us:

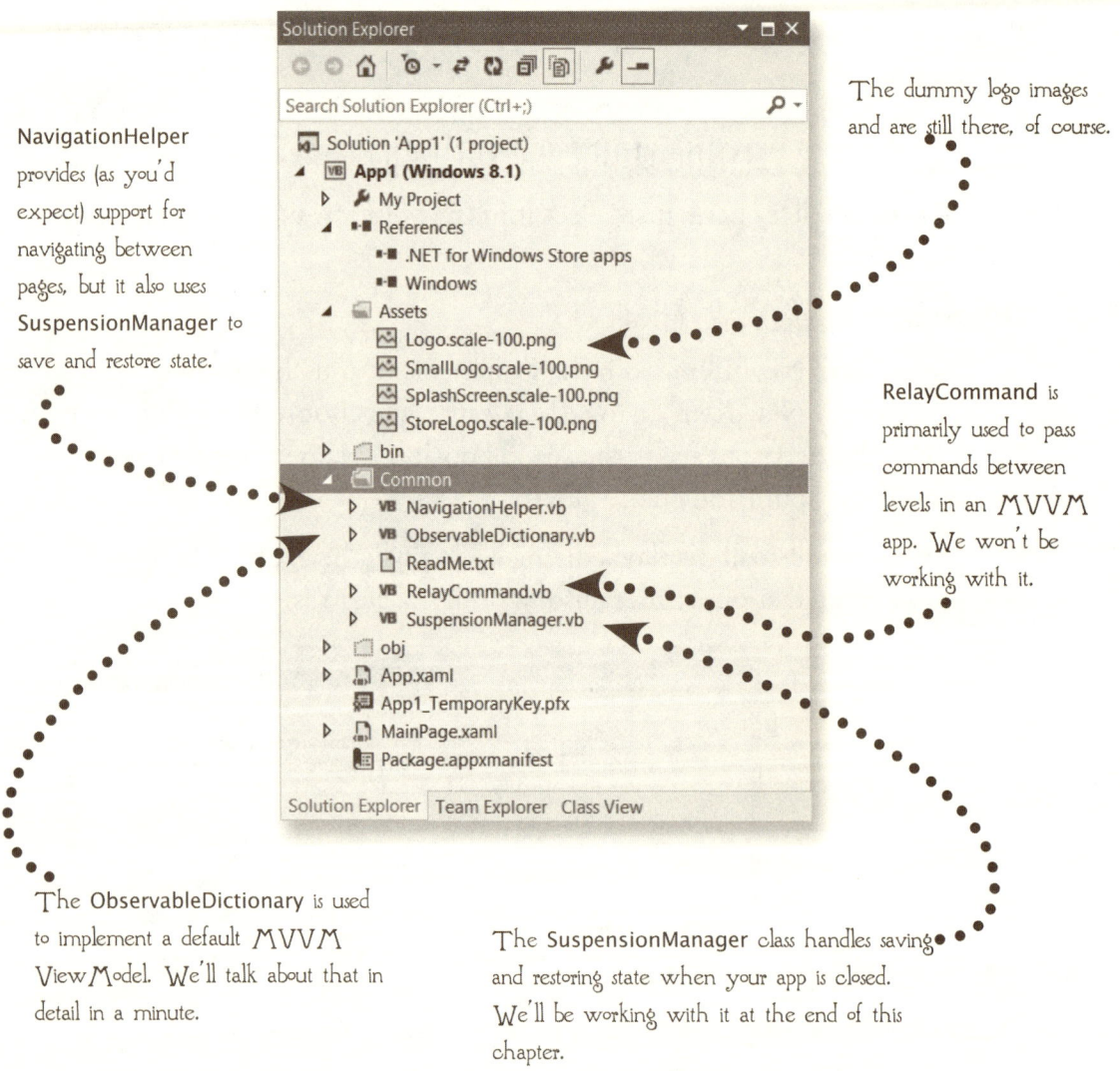

NavigationHelper provides (as you'd expect) support for navigating between pages, but it also uses **SuspensionManager** to save and restore state.

The dummy logo images and are still there, of course.

RelayCommand is primarily used to pass commands between levels in an MVVM app. We won't be working with it.

The **ObservableDictionary** is used to implement a default MVVM ViewModel. We'll talk about that in detail in a minute.

The **SuspensionManager** class handles saving and restoring state when your app is closed. We'll be working with it at the end of this chapter.

482

THE BASIC PAGE

I'm sure you've done enough work with the `MainPage.xaml` that's created when you choose a Blank app template to remember its structure: Some namespace declarations, and an empty `Grid`. In contrast, the Basic page that we've replaced it with is a lot more complicated. Some of the changes (like declaring an `AppName` resource) should be obvious, and we'll explore the rest in this chapter and the next.

The template gives it a Name.

It has a Resource, the AppName, declared. (You'll almost always want to move this to App.xaml, as the comment in the file suggests.)

The DefaultViewModel property is set as its DataContext. We'll see how this works in a minute.

The basic Grid has two rows, and a back Button and TextBlock showing the AppName defined in its first row.

```xml
<Page
    x:Name="pageRoot"
    DataContext="{Binding DefaultViewModel, RelativeSource={RelativeSource Self}}"
    ...>

    <Page.Resources>
        <x:String x:Key="AppName">My Application</x:String>
    </Page.Resources>

    <Grid ...>
        <Grid.ChildrenTransitions>
            <TransitionCollection>
                <EntranceThemeTransitions/>
            </TransitionCollection>
        </Grid.Children.Transitions>
        <Grid.RowDefinitions>
            <RowDefinition Height="140"/>
            <RowDefinition Height="*"/>
        </Grid.RowDefinitions>

        <Grid>
            <Grid.ColumnDefinitions>
                <ColumnDefinition Width="Auto"/>
                <ColumnDefinition Width="*"/>
            </Grid.ColumnDefinitions>
            <Button x:Name="backButton" .../>
            <TextBlock x:Name="pageTitle" Text="{StaticResource AppName}" .../>
        </Grid>
    </Grid>
</Page>
```

USING THE DEFAULTVIEWMODEL

We talked about XAML binding in the last chapter, but by way of proving that there's always more to learn and explore, let's take a look at the DefaultViewModel that the Basic page exposes. DefaultViewModel is very lightweight, but it will give you a taste of how binding works with the MVVM pattern.

The DefaultViewModel property is defined in the Page code behind as an instance of ObservableDictionary, one of the classes added to the Common folder of our solution. The ObservableDictionary class implements IObservableMap<K, V>. You can think of an ObservableDictionary as the dictionary version of an ObservableCollection.

DefaultViewModel	
Key	Value
Key	Value
Key	Value

You can add as many items as you need to the DefaultViewModel as long as you assign each one a unique Key value. Keys are always a string, but the Value is an object, and so they can be whatever you need.

In a real application, your ViewModel would probably include a lot more than just a single data collection. You might have multiple sets of data, and almost certainly some commands, as well.

The BasicPage template adds navigationHelper_LoadState() and navigationHelper_SaveState() methods to the code behind. We'll talk about exactly when they're called and how to use them later in this chapter, but for now you only know that you'll create the DefaultViewModel in the navigationHelper_LoadState() method:

```
protected override void navigationHelper_ LoadState(...)
{
    DefaultViewModel["Colors"] = new ColorCollection();
}
```
C#

```
protected override void navigationHelper_ LoadState(...)
{
    DefaultViewModel("Colors") = New ColorCollection()
}
```
VB

The Basic Page template sets the **DefaultViewModel** as the data context of the **Page** as a whole, so you don't need to do anything to make its contents available:

Notice the use of **RelativeSource Self** to set the **DataContext** to a property defined within the class.

```
<Page
  x:Name="pageRoot"
  ...
  DataContext="{Binding DefaultViewModel, RelativeSource={RelativeSource Self}}"
  ...>
```

But if you're binding to a collection, you'll still need to create a **CollectionViewSource**. You'll want to bind its **Source** property to the **Key** that you assigned to the collection in the **DefaultViewModel**:

The **AppName** resource is already in the template.

```
<Page.Resources>
   <x:String x:Key="AppName">My Application</x:String>
   <CollectionViewSource x:Name="ColorCVS" Source="{Binding Colors}" />
</Page.Resources>
```

Since the **DataContext** of the page is already set to the **DefaultViewModel**, you only need to specify the **Key**.

Once you have your **CollectionViewSource**, binding works just the way it did when we weren't using the indirection supplied by a **ViewModel**:

```
<TextBlock Text="{Binding Path=CurrentItem.ColorName}" ... />
```

485

RE-BUILD THE COLOR EXPLORER

So that we'll have something to work with in the rest of the chapter, let's rebuild the color explorer from the last chapter as a `Basic` page:

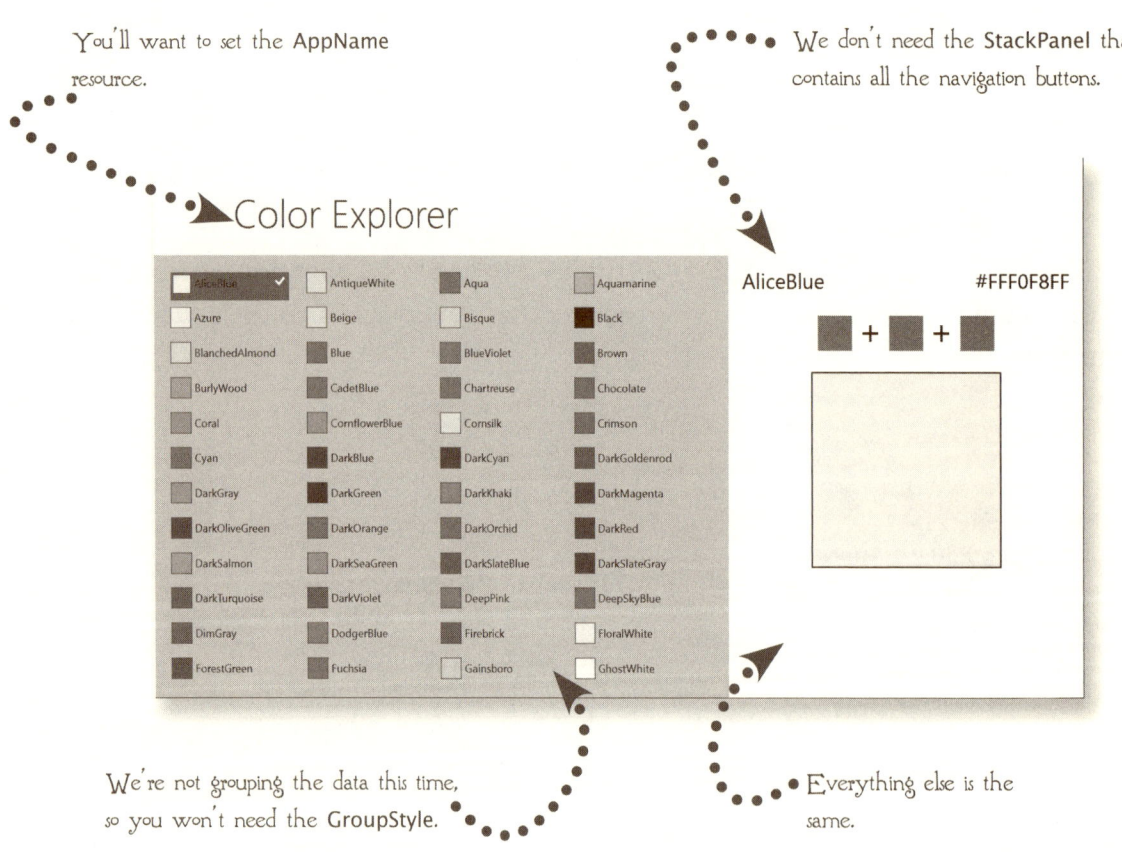

You'll want to set the `AppName` resource.

We don't need the `StackPanel` that contains all the navigation buttons.

We're not grouping the data this time, so you won't need the `GroupStyle`.

Everything else is the same.

PUT ON YOUR THINKING HAT
Build the basic app. Remember that cut and paste is your friend:

ADD THE COLORDETAILS AND COLORCOLLECTION CLASSES
Just choose Add Existing Item from the Project menu and Visual Studio will copy the class files into the new project for you. If you're working in C#, you'll need to change the namespace of the two classes to make them available.

CREATE THE COLORCOLLECTION
Inside the navigationHelper_ LoadState() method in the MainPage.xaml code-behind, create a new instance of a ColorCollection and add it to the DefaultViewModel using the key "Colors".

CREATE THE COLLECTIONVIEWSOURCE
Add a CollectionViewSource resource named ColorCVS to the Page.Resources element. Bind its Source to Colors.

COPY AND EDIT THE XAML
Of course, you can re-create the XAML from scratch if you really want to, but you can also just open the MainPage.xaml from Chapter 12 in Notepad and copy the layout grid into the new MainPage.xaml.

Make sure you add it after the Grid that contains the header items, and have it display in the content area of the basic page by setting the Grid.Row attached property to 1.

You'll want to delete the button StackPanel and the ListView.GroupStyle. Everything else is the same.

If all this seems like too much work, you can find the start-up version of the app as BasicPageItems-Startup of the sample code on the book's Web site.

HOW'D YOU DO?

I know that was rather a lot of setup, but it gives us a good foundation for the rest of the chapter. Here's the basic code showing the changes:

```xml
<Page ...>

  <Page.Resources>
    <x:String x:Key="AppName">Color Browser</x:String>
    <CollectionViewSource x:Name="ColorCVS" Source="{Binding Colors}"/>
  </Page.Resources>

  <Grid Style="{StaticResource LayoutRootStyle}">
    ...
    <!-- Back button and page title -->
    <Grid>...</Grid>

    <Grid x:Name="ContentGrid" Grid.Row="1" DataContext="{StaticResource ColorCVS}" ...>
      <Grid.ColumnDefinitions>...</Grid.ColumnDefinitions>

      <ListView x:Name="ListOfColors" Grid.Column="0" Margin="20"
          ItemsSource="{Binding}" >
        <ListView.ItemTemplate>
          ...
        </ListView.ItemTemplate>
        <ListView.ItemsPanel>
          ...
        </ListView.ItemsPanel>
      </ListView>

      <Border Grid.Column="1" Background="White">
        ...
      </Border>
    </Grid>
  </Grid>
</Page>
```

You needed to declare the CollectionViewSource.

The only thing that changed inside the original layout Grid is assigning it to Grid.Row 1, since it needs to display below the header items.

The GroupStyle isn't necessary any longer. (But it doesn't do any harm if you left it.)

If you forget to remove the button StackPanel inside the Border, you'll get compile errors because the event handlers are missing.

APPLICATION LAYOUT

Now that we have an app to work with, let's see how it stands up to the Win8 layout requirements. So far all of our sample applications have been built to display in landscape mode at a default resolution. But that's not really good enough for a Win8 app. It needs to support screen resolutions from a minimum of 1024×768 to 2560×1440, and it needs to support those resolutions in four different VIEW STATES:

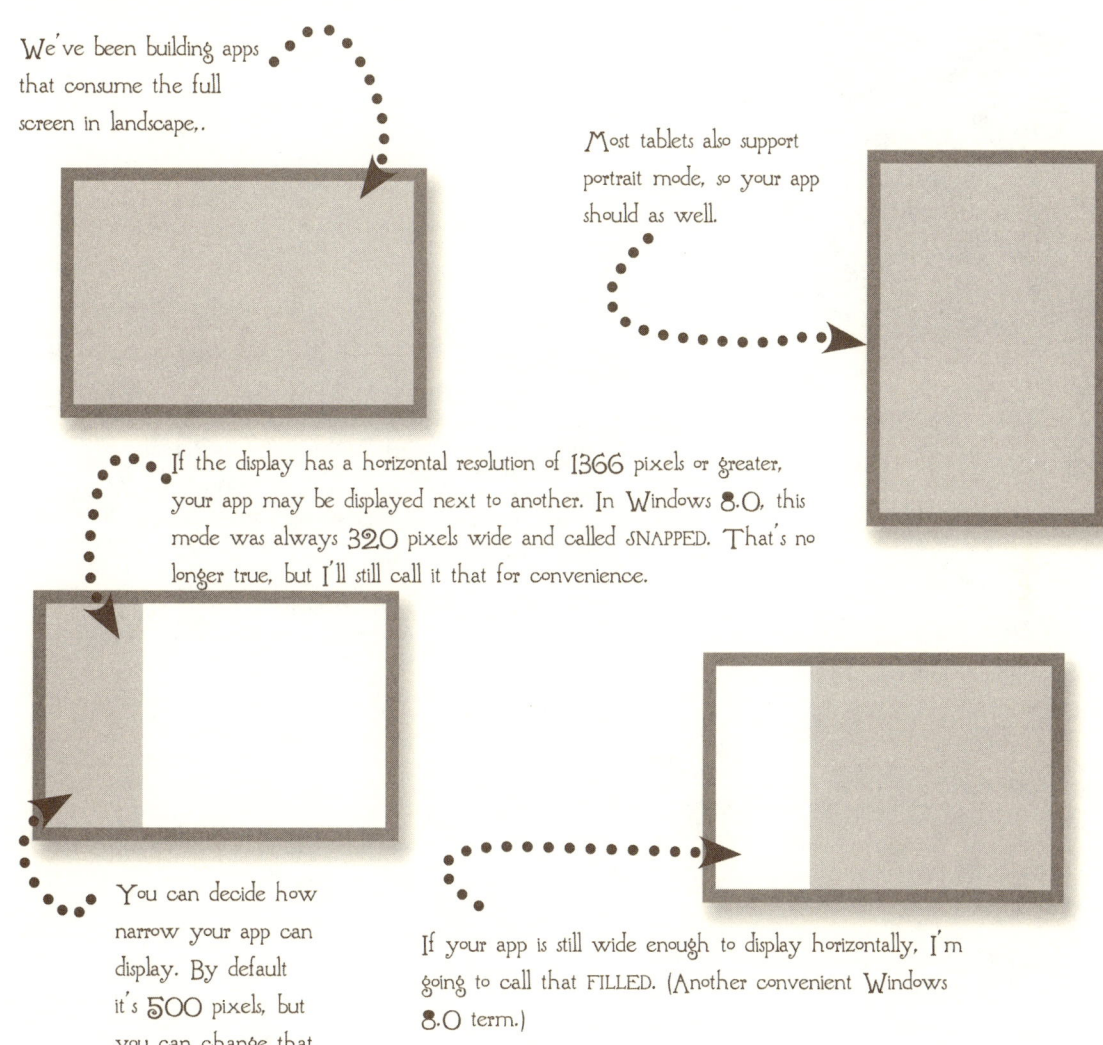

We've been building apps that consume the full screen in landscape,.

Most tablets also support portrait mode, so your app should as well.

If the display has a horizontal resolution of 1366 pixels or greater, your app may be displayed next to another. In Windows 8.0, this mode was always 320 pixels wide and called SNAPPED. That's no longer true, but I'll still call it that for convenience.

You can decide how narrow your app can display. By default it's 500 pixels, but you can change that to 320.

If your app is still wide enough to display horizontally, I'm going to call that FILLED. (Another convenient Windows 8.0 term.)

489

CHECKING RESOLUTIONS

Sounds like a nightmare, doesn't it? But it really just comes down to managing resolutions and horizontal/vertical orientations. The appearance of your app at different resolutions is the easiest aspect to check, and often to fix, so let's start with that. Just run your sample in the simulator and use the Change Resolution button to try it out:

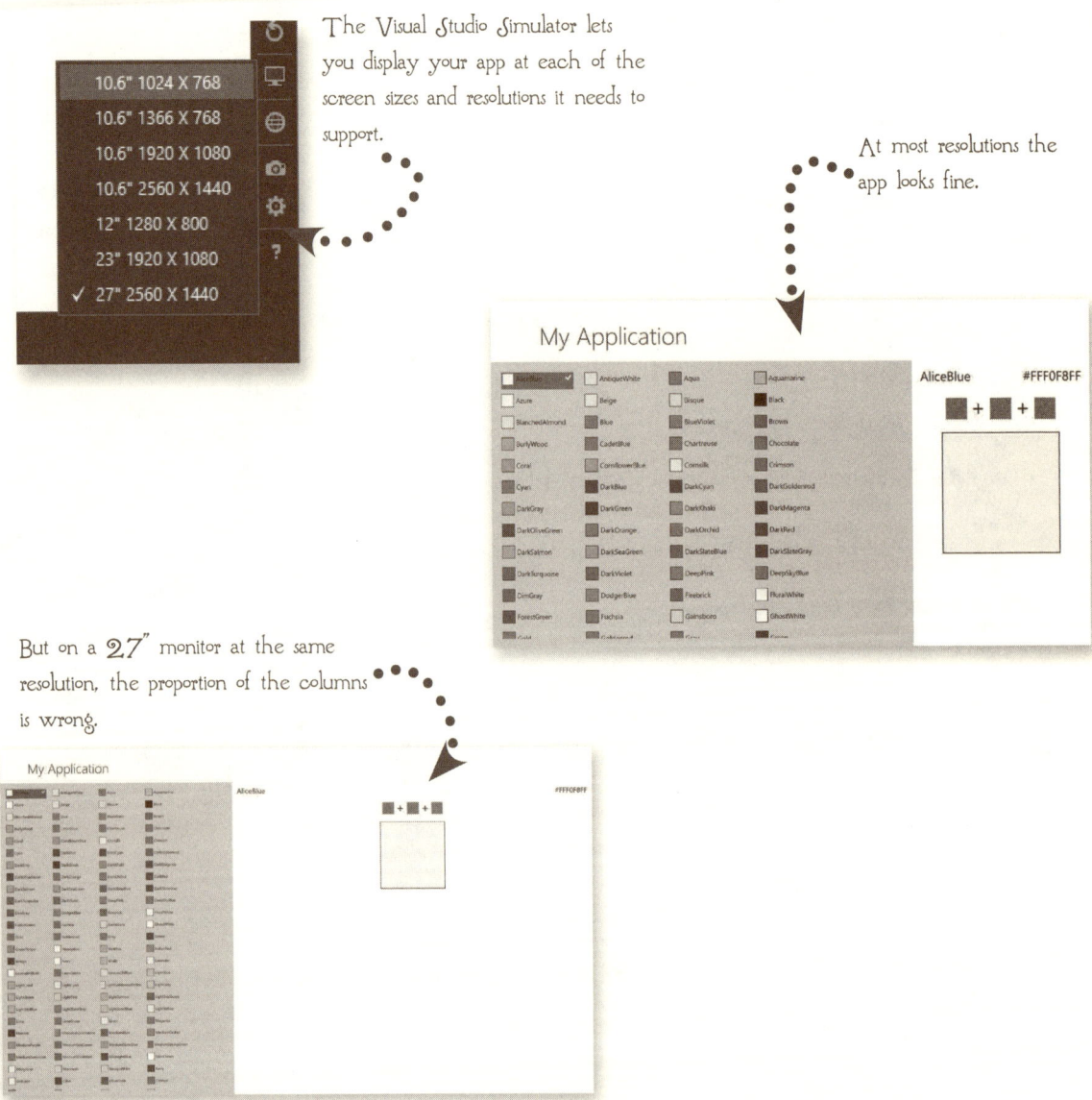

The Visual Studio Simulator lets you display your app at each of the screen sizes and resolutions it needs to support.

At most resolutions the app looks fine.

But on a 27" monitor at the same resolution, the proportion of the columns is wrong.

ADAPTIVE LAYOUT TECHNIQUES

Sometimes you can run into problems with getting your UI to look good in every situation, but those situations are fairly rare. Most of the time a few simple techniques will be all you need.

USE AUTOMATIC SIZING

Left to their own devices, most XAML elements will size themselves to fit their contents and resize to fit the available space. Leave the **Width** and **Height** properties of elements to "Auto" in XAML or the magic **Double.NaN** value in code whenever you can.

FAVOR MINIMUM AND MAXIMUM OVER EXPLICIT SIZING

Not every element will display correctly without some kind of size information. In this situation, adapting to different resolutions will be easier if you use the **MinWidth**, **MinHeight** and **MaxWidth**, **MaxHeight** properties instead of setting explicit **Width** and **Height** values.

USE PROPORTIONAL SIZING IN GRIDS

Unless a row or column of a Grid really does need to stay the same size at all resolutions (like the header row of the default Basic Page layout), assigning proportional values using the star notation will allow your layout to adapt automatically.

REMEMBER THE LAYOUT WIDGETS

When manipulating the size won't achieve what you need, try wrapping your content inside either a **ScrollViewer** or a **Viewbox**. (I consider the **ScrollViewer** a last resort. Scrolling is not friendly.)

PUT ON YOUR THINKING HAT

Using the techniques I've just described, can you fix the Color Browser so that it looks good at any resolution?

491

HOW'D YOU DO?

Here's what I did. You might have used different techniques to achieve slightly different results, and that's just fine as long as your Page looks good to you at every resolution. I only made two changes:

The ColumnDefinition Width properties already used proportional sizing, so that was a good start.

```
<Grid x:Name="ContentGrid" ...>
   <Grid.ColumnDefinitions>
      <ColumnDefinition Width="2*" />
      <ColumnDefinition Width="1*" />
   </Grid.ColumnDefinitions>
   ...
</Grid>
```

But at the largest resolution the right column seemed too wide to me, so I set a MaxWidth of 500 to that column:

```
<Grid x:Name="ContentGrid" ...>
   <Grid.ColumnDefinitions>
      <ColumnDefinition Width="2*" />
      <ColumnDefinition Width="1*" MaxWidth="500"/>
   </Grid.ColumnDefinitions>
   ...
</Grid>
```

This seemed too wide to me.

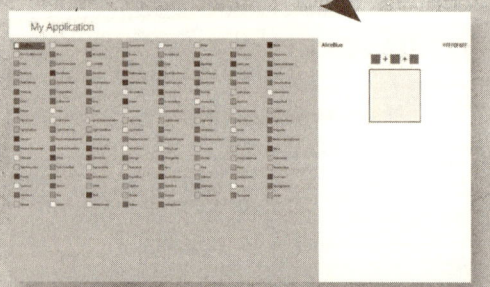

Setting MaxWidth kept the details pane a reasonable size.

492

CREATING A VERTICAL LAYOUT

We'll need to use the Device Panel, which we'll discuss in a minute, to do a thorough test of our layout, but we can use the Simulator to get a quick feel for what we'll need to do. Just click one of the two rotate buttons and the Simulator will re-display our app in portrait mode.

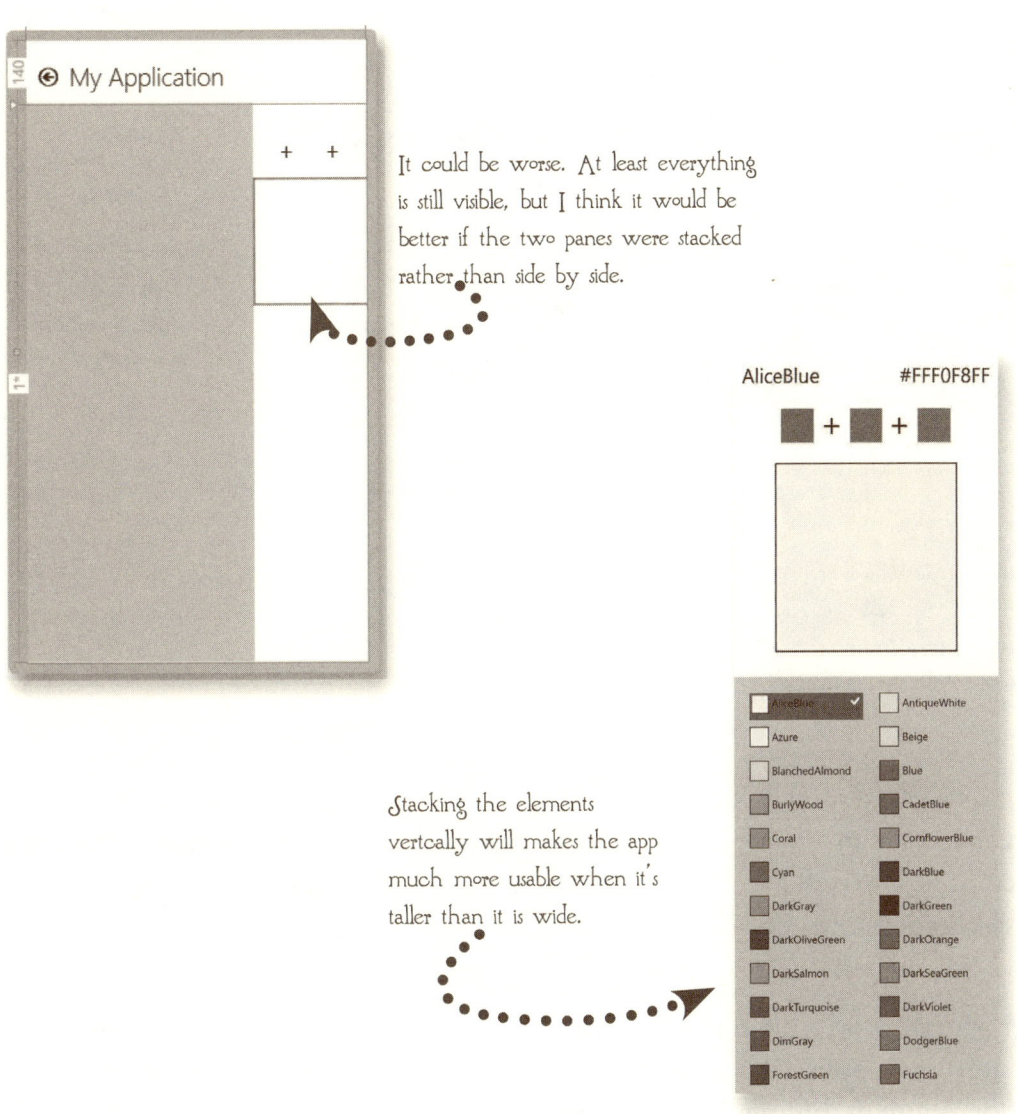

It could be worse. At least everything is still visible, but I think it would be better if the two panes were stacked rather than side by side.

Stacking the elements vertically will makes the app much more usable when it's taller than it is wide.

THE VISUALSTATEMANAGER

Portrait and landscape, horizontal and vertical (which, as we'll see, isn't quite the same thing), even different resolutions and screen sizes are represented in XAML as VISUAL STATES, and conveniently, there's a VisualStateManager class which, along with some related classes, makes it surprisingly simple to handle them.

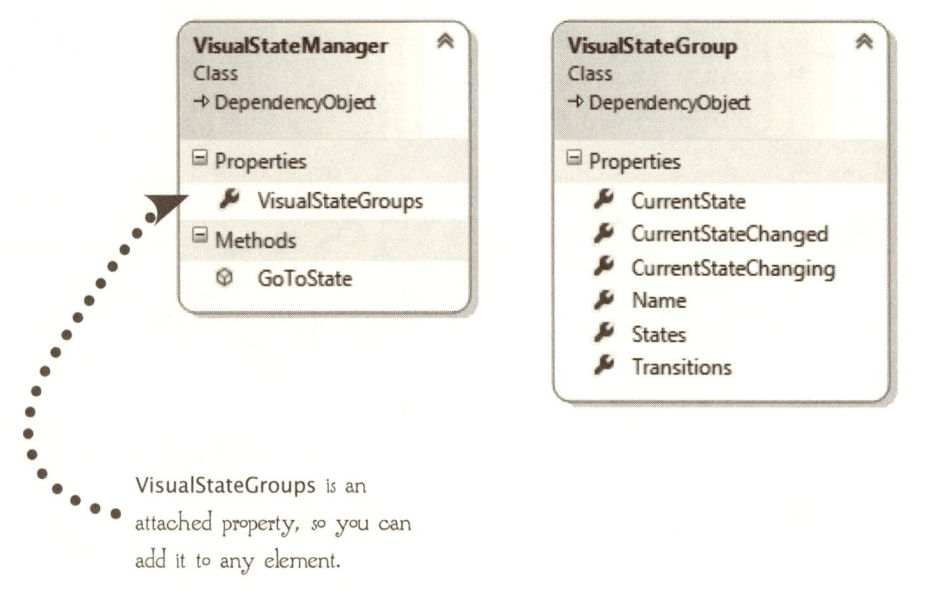

VisualStateGroups is an attached property, so you can add it to any element.

If the adaptive layout techniques we've been exploring work for your app in landscape mode, you can simply create a default state (conventionally given the name "Default") to represent it. You will need to create a visual state with a new layout for portrait mode, and possibly more than one if you need to change the layout based on the width of the window.

In order to transition from one state to another, you'll need to call VisualStateManager. GoToState() in response to a SizeChanged event. SizeChanged is defined on FrameworkElement, but you'll generally create the handler at the Page level.

BUILDING A VERTICAL LAYOUT

Let's stop and think about what we need to do to create a vertical layout. Structurally, the Basic Page contains a 2-row Grid. The first row contains the header information, and the second row contains your Page content. In our example, that content is contained in a second Grid. In order to support the vertical layout effectively, we'll need to build another content Grid, and swap the Visibility of the two elements as the view state changes:

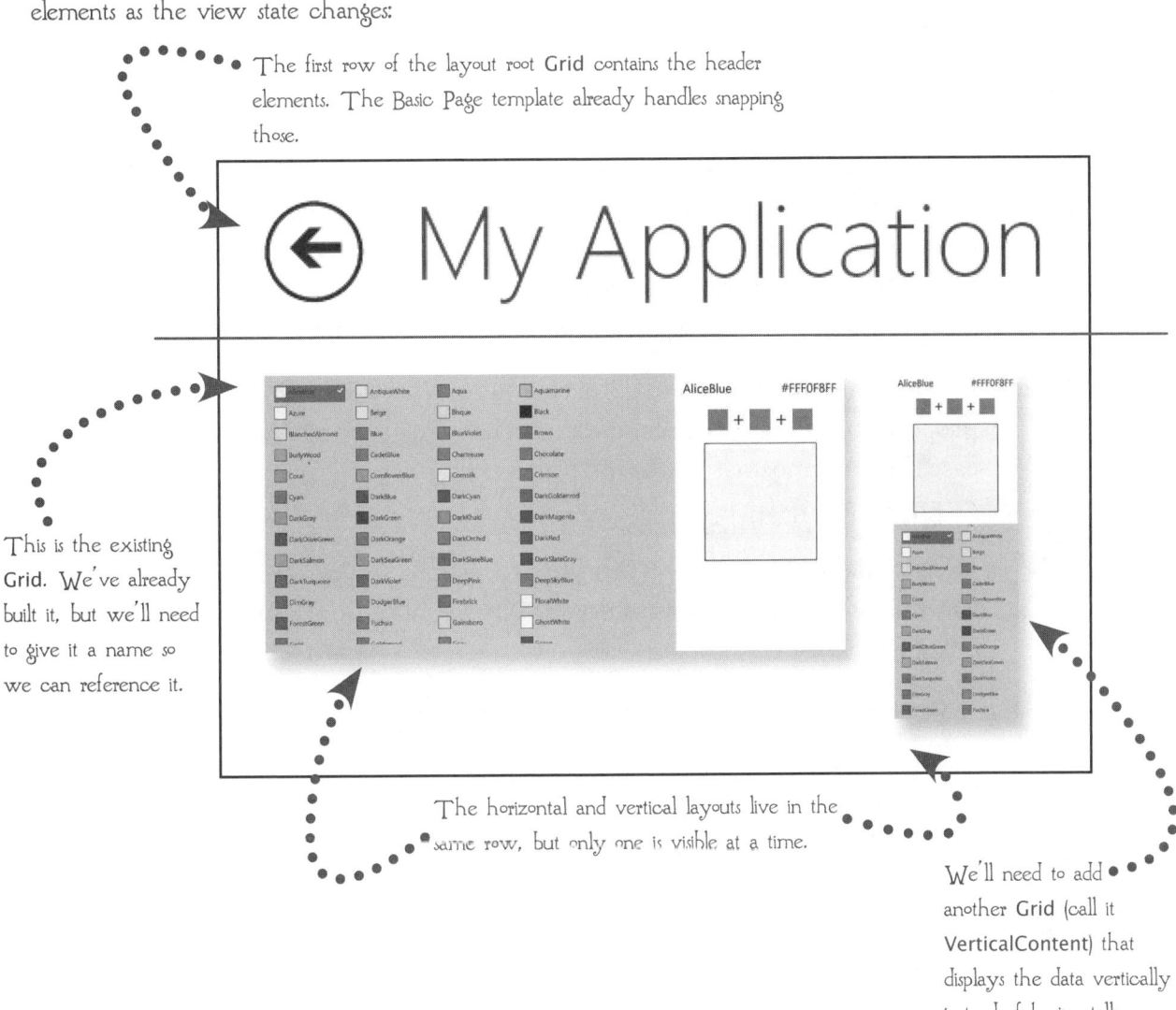

The first row of the layout root Grid contains the header elements. The Basic Page template already handles snapping those.

This is the existing Grid. We've already built it, but we'll need to give it a name so we can reference it.

The horizontal and vertical layouts live in the same row, but only one is visible at a time.

We'll need to add another Grid (call it VerticalContent) that displays the data vertically instead of horizontally.

CREATING THE PORTRAIT LAYOUT

The only trick to creating a separate layout for the portrait view—and it's a very simple one—is to use the `Visibility` property to ensure that only one of your content panes is displayed at a time. Just in case you've forgotten exactly what the `Visibility` property is, it's exposed by `UIElement` (so it will be available to pretty much any element you want to use as your root) and accepts two values: `Visible` and `Collapsed`. A collapsed element isn't visible (obviously), and it doesn't take up any room in the layout. It's like it isn't even there.

Here are the basic steps:

CREATE THE PORTRAIT WIDGETS

In our example, the portrait and landscape layouts contain the same elements; they're just arranged differently. That's pretty typical. Remember to set the initial `Visibility` property of the portrait layout to `Collapsed`.

CREATE THE VISUALSTATEMANAGER AND THE VISUALSTATEGROUPS

You'll want to add the `VisualStateManager.VisualStateGroups` attached property to the element that contains the widgets you're controlling, in this case the outermost `Grid`. (Again, that's pretty typical.)

CREATE THE VISUAL STATES

Each `VisualState` contains a `Storyboard`. When you're swapping layouts like this, you'll almost always use an `ObjectAnimationUsingKeyFrames` to change the property values:

```
<ObjectAnimationUsingKeyFrames Storyboaard.TargetProperty="{Element.Propedrty}"
                    Storyboard.TargetName="{ObjectName}">/
    <DiscreteObjectKeyFramed KeyTime="0">
        <Property>Value</Property>
    </DiscreteObjectKeyFramed">
</ ObjectAnimationUsingKeyFrames>
```

HANDLE THE PAGE.SIZECHANGED EVENT

Finally, you'll need to add a handler for the `Page.SizeChanged` event that calls `VisualStateManager.GoToState(this,"StateName",true)` based on the new size. (In our example, just compare the `e.NewSize.Height` and `e.NewSize.Width`).

PUT ON YOUR THINKING HAT

Let's try it out, shall we? Follow the steps outlined on the previous page to create the two layouts, and then try swapping between portrait and landscape in the simulator.

ON YOUR OWN

Our exerciser looks a whole lot like we made it up as we went along, which of course we did. But we've got duplicate code (those two sets of widgets), and the structure of the XAML at this point is probably less than self-explanatory. How would you re-factor the XAML to eliminate duplication and make maintenance simpler?

PUT ON YOUR THINKING HAT

That was a big exercise. Was that easier or more difficult than you expected? Either way, it gets easier with practice, I promise.

Here's the XAML. The event handler code is on the next page.

```xml
<Page ... SizeChanged="pageRoot_SizeChanged">
  ...
  <Grid ...>
    ...
    <!--Horizontal Contents-->
    <Grid x:Name="HorizontalContent" ... >
      ...
      <ListView x:Name="ListOfColors" Grid.Column="0" ... />
      <Border Grid.Column="1" ... />
    </Grid>

    <!--Vertical Contents-->
    <Grid x:Name="VerticalContent" Grid.Row="1" Grid.ColumnSpan="2"
        Visibility="Collapsed" ... >
      <Grid.RowDefinitions>
        <RowDefinition />
        <RowDefinition />
      </Grid.RowDefinitions>

      <Border Grid.Row="0" Background="White">
        <StackPanel>
          <Grid ... />
          <StackPanel x:Name="VComponentStack... />
        </StackPanel>
      </Border>
      <ListView x:Name="VListOfColors" Grid.Row="1" ... />
```

continued...

```xml
    </Grid>
    <VisualStateManager.VisualStateGroups>
      <VisualStateGroup>
        <VisualState x:Name="DefaultLayout">
          <Storyboard/>
        </VisualState>
        <VisualState x:Name="VerticalLayout">
          <Storyboard>
            <ObjectAnimationUsingKeyFrames Storyboard.TargetProperty="(Grid.Visibility)"
                      Storyboard.TargetName="HorizontalContent">
              <DiscreteObjectKeyFrame KeyTime="0">
                <DiscreteObjectKeyFrame.Value>
                  <Visibility>Collapsed</Visibility>
                </DiscreteObjectKeyFrame.Value>
              </DiscreteObjectKeyFrame>
            </ObjectAnimationUsingKeyFrames>
            <ObjectAnimationUsingKeyFrames Storyboard.TargetProperty="(Grid.Visibility)"
                      Storyboard.TargetName="VerticalContent">
              <DiscreteObjectKeyFrame KeyTime="0">
                <DiscreteObjectKeyFrame.Value>
                  <Visibility>Visible</Visibility>
                </DiscreteObjectKeyFrame.Value>
              </DiscreteObjectKeyFrame>
            </ObjectAnimationUsingKeyFrames>
          </Storyboard>
        </VisualState>
      </VisualStateGroup>
    </VisualStateManager.VisualStateGroups>
  </Grid>
</Page>
```

HOW'D YOU DO?

Here's what I did. You might have swapped the clauses or used a different calculation, and that's fine as long as it makes sense to you and it works.

```csharp
private void pageRoot_SizeChanged(object sender, SizeChangedEventArgs e)
{
    if (e.NewSize.Height > e.NewSize.Width)
    {
        VisualStateManager.GoToState(this, "VerticalLayout", true);
    }
    else
    {
        VisualStateManager.GoToState(this, "DefaultLayout", true);
    }
}
```

```vbnet
Private Sub pageRoot_SizeChanged(sender As Object, e As SizeChangedEventArgs)
    If e.NewSize.Height > e.NewSize.Width Then
        VisualStateManager.GoToState(Me, "VerticalLayout", True)
    Else
        VisualStateManager.GoToState(Me, "DefaultLayout", True)
    End If
End Sub
```

USING THE DEVICE PANEL

So far we've been using the Simulator to check your layout at different resolutions and orientations, but there is another option: the Visual Studio Device Panel, which by default is docked to the left side of the Designer window. The Device Panel provides an option the Simulator doesn't: showing your app docked to an edge of the screen.

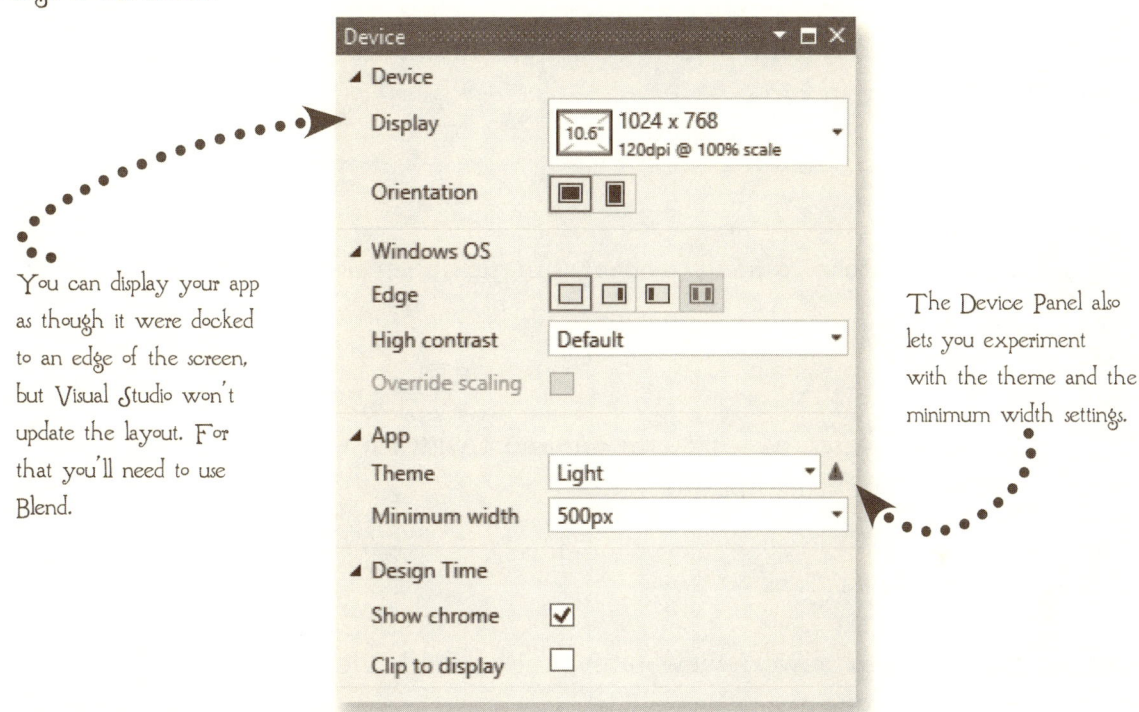

You can display your app as though it were docked to an edge of the screen, but Visual Studio won't update the layout. For that you'll need to use Blend.

The Device Panel also lets you experiment with the theme and the minimum width settings.

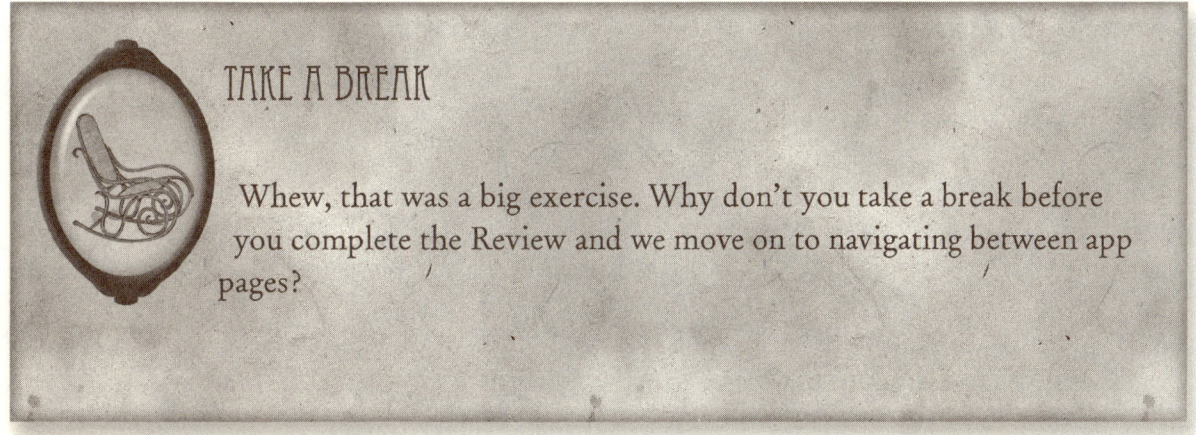

TAKE A BREAK

Whew, that was a big exercise. Why don't you take a break before you complete the Review and we move on to navigating between app pages?

REVIEW

Can you answer the following questions based on what you've learned?

Although there are lots of permutations of size and orientation, most apps only need to allow for two. What are they?

What object do you use to respond to changes in the screen area available to your **Page**?

Unless you specify differently, what's the minimum width at which an app can be displayed? What's your other option?

What's the relationship between **ViewStates** inside a single **ViewStateGroup**?

What's the relationship between **ViewStates** in differnt **ViewStateGroups**?

NAVIGATION

Of course, there are interesting and useful apps that only require a single **Page**, but many (including the apps based on the Grid, Split, and Hub App templates) require multiple **Pages** to display different information, or information at a different level of detail. Navigation is fairly simple to implement using the Win8 XAML Framework **Frame** and **Page** navigation model, but there are a few gotchas, which we'll explore in this section. Here's the basic structure:

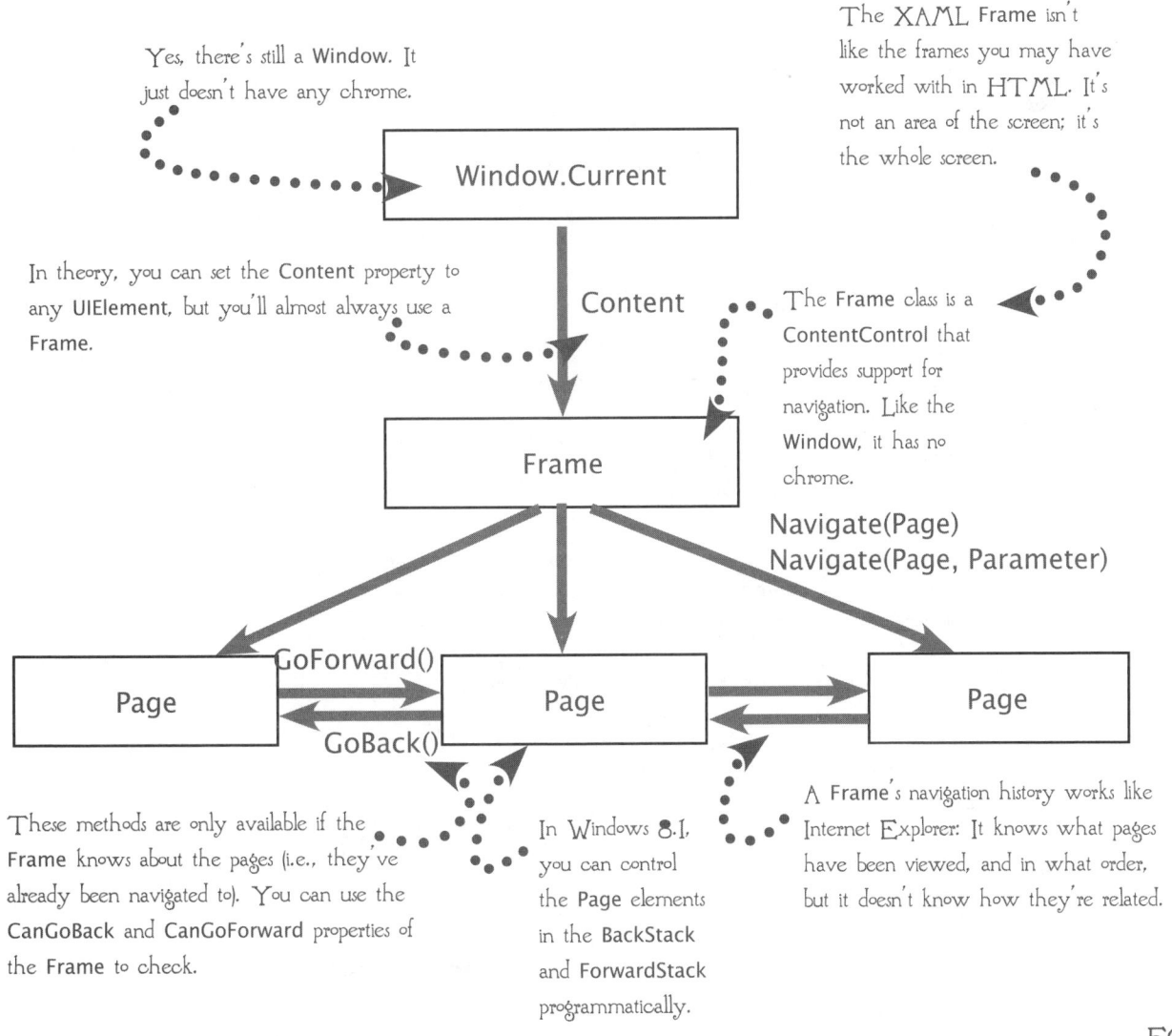

Yes, there's still a **Window**. It just doesn't have any chrome.

The XAML **Frame** isn't like the frames you may have worked with in HTML. It's not an area of the screen; it's the whole screen.

In theory, you can set the **Content** property to any **UIElement**, but you'll almost always use a **Frame**.

The **Frame** class is a **ContentControl** that provides support for navigation. Like the **Window**, it has no chrome.

These methods are only available if the **Frame** knows about the pages (i.e., they've already been navigated to). You can use the **CanGoBack** and **CanGoForward** properties of the **Frame** to check.

In Windows 8.1, you can control the **Page** elements in the **BackStack** and **ForwardStack** programmatically.

A **Frame**'s navigation history works like Internet Explorer: It knows what pages have been viewed, and in what order, but it doesn't know how they're related.

503

START-UP PROCESS

While we've been building our simple little apps to learn about different aspects of building Win8 apps, the Visual Studio template code has been doing quite a lot of work on our behalf. A lot of that work takes place in the `App.xaml.cs` or `App.xaml.vb` code behind file, where the app's `Frame` and `Page` are created.

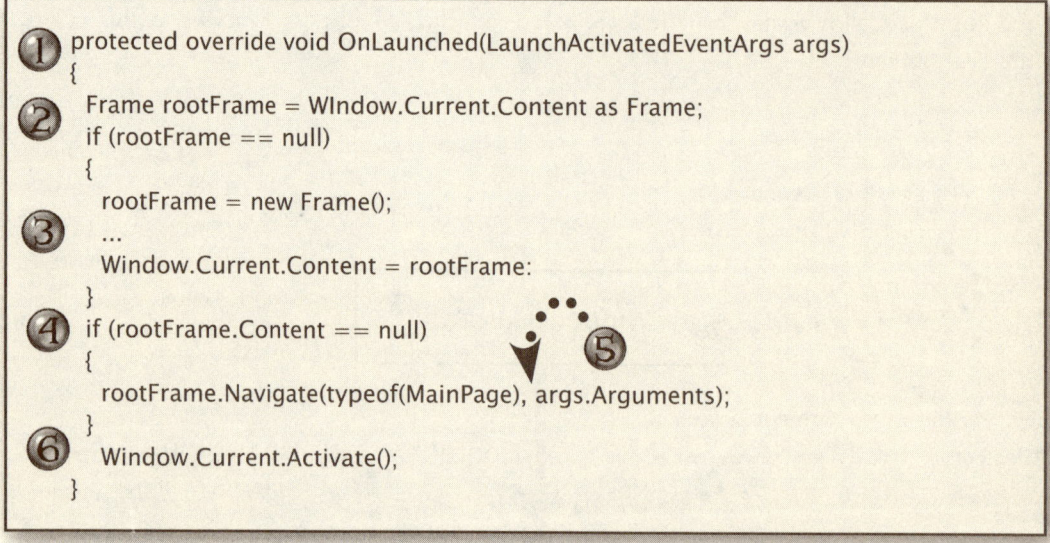

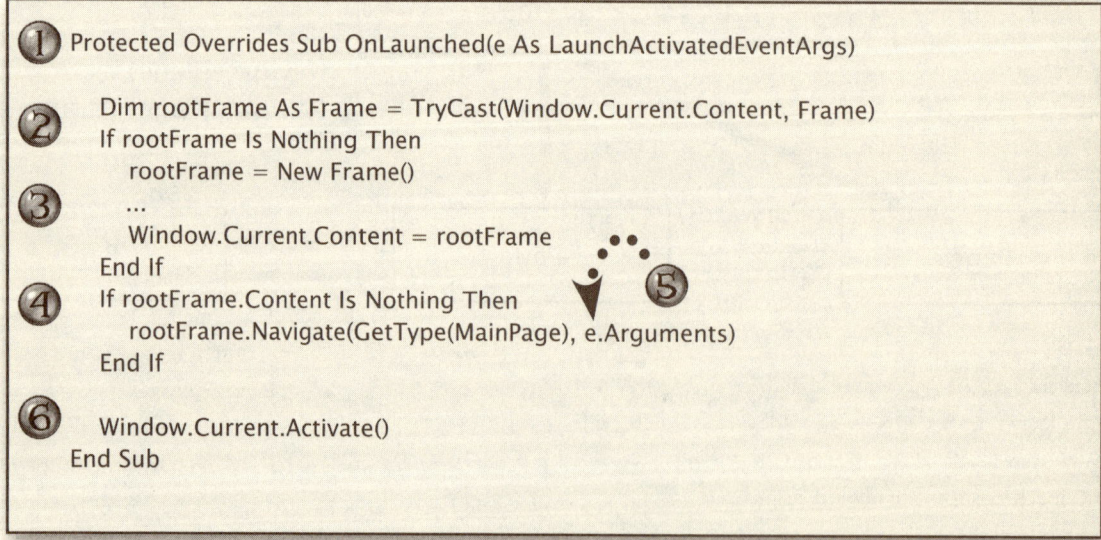

The Frame and start-up Page are initialized inside the Application.OnLaunched() method.

This is really the minimum functionality required. Most applications will need to do a little—or a lot—more than this in the OnLaunched() method, depending on how they're launched. We'll explore that, and the LaunchActivatedEventArgs, later in this chapter and revisit the issue in later chapters.

 Next the method checks to see if the content of the current window is already a Frame and creates and assigns a new one if it isn't.

 I've left out a bit of code here. It has to do with restoring state, and it's part of that "little or lot more" that we'll talk about later.

 If the rootFrame doesn't contain a page, the method calls the Frame.Navigate() method to assign it one. Notice that you don't need to instantiate the Page class before navigating to it.

 The start-up Page is specified here. It's MainPage by default (which is why I had you change the name of the new Basic Page we added to our app to MainPage), but you can change it to the name of any Page in the project that you want to be displayed whenever your app starts.

There's another version of the Navigate() method that doesn't require a parameter. We'll look at that in a minute. Also, since the Page has a Frame property, you can call Navigate() from the code-behind of a Page using similar syntax:

| this.Frame.Navigate(typeof(NewPage)) | Me.Frame.Navigate() |

 Once the Frame & Page are created and hooked up, the method calls Window.Current.Activate() to start the ball rolling.

PUT ON YOUR THINKING HAT

To get some experience with navigation, let's add some pages to our sample project. We'll add another Basic Page, and just for fun, we'll use a different **Page** template for the second new page.

This is another complicated exercise, but just follow the steps, and you'll be fine. (And you can always peek if you get confused.)

① CHANGE THE TITLE OF THE EXISTING PAGE

Right now, the **pageTitle** is bound to the **AppName** resource. You could change the resource, but that wouldn't be correct semantically, so just change the **TextBlock.Text** value to "Color Explorer". (I did that earlier, so if you've been looking at my examples closely, you may have already implemented this.)

② ADD A NEW START-UP PAGE

Add a new Basic **Page** named **HomePage** to the project. Change its **pageTitle** and add some elements to collect data and move between pages. The exact layout of your page doesn't matter, but you should have these elements:

Home Page

Please tell me your name: _____

Please pick your favorite color

[Color Picker]
[Color Browser]

The "Color Explorer" page is actually our original MainPage.

ADD AN ITEMS PAGE

Add a second new **Page** to the project, this time using the Items Page template. Call it **ColorBrowser**. At the very least, you should set the **pageTitle**, but it would be cool to make it actually work. In order to do that, you'll need to set up the **DefaultViewModel** the same way we did with the original page (except use the key "Items" instead of "Colors") and edit a copy of the Item Template to bind to the appropriate values. Here's the formatted version:

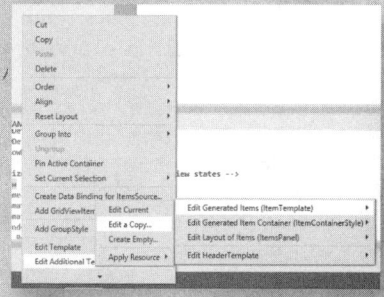

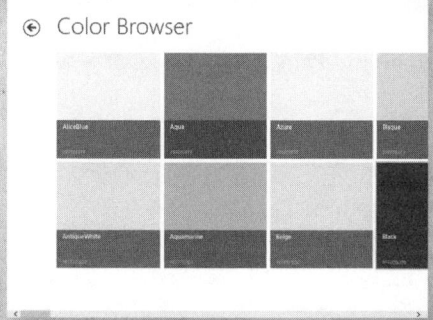

CONNECT THE BUTTONS

Add **Click** event handlers to the **Button** elements on the home page that call the **Frame.Navigate()** method.

SET THE START-UP PAGE

Change the **OnLaunched()** method in the **App.xaml.cs** or **App.xaml.vb** file so that the home page is loaded when the app is first launched.

When you run the app, the back buttons, which always display in the Designer, will display on the Color Browser and Color Picker pages, but not on the home page. Can you work out why, and how that functionality is implemented?

HOW'D YOU DO?

The pertinent parts of the files are shown here and on the next two pages. I've left out some of the formatting to save space.

HomePage.xaml

```xml
<Grid Style="{StaticResource LayoutRootStyle}">
  <Grid.RowDefinitions>
    <RowDefinition Height="140"/>
    <RowDefinition Height="*"/>
  </Grid.RowDefinitions>

  <!-- Back button and page title -->
  <Grid>
    <Grid.ColumnDefinitions>
      <ColumnDefinition Width="Auto"/>
      <ColumnDefinition Width="*"/>
    </Grid.ColumnDefinitions>
    <Button x:Name="backButton" .../>
    <TextBlock x:Name="pageTitle" Text="Home Page" .../>
  </Grid>

  <StackPanel Grid.Row="1" Orientation="Vertical" Margin="10" >
      <StackPanel Orientation="Horizontal">
        <TextBlock ...>Please tell me your name:</TextBlock>
        <TextBox x:Name="UserName" Width="500"/>
      </StackPanel>
      <Grid>
        <Grid.ColumnDefinitions>
          <ColumnDefinition Width="2*" MaxWidth="350" />
          <ColumnDefinition Width="1*" />
        </Grid.ColumnDefinitions>
        <StackPanel Margin="0,20">
          <TextBlock FontSize="18">Please pick your favorite color</TextBlock>
          <Rectangle x:Name="ColorRect" Margin="10" Width="300" Height="300" Fill="Gray" />
        </StackPanel>
        <StackPanel Margin="0,50" Grid.Column="1">
          <Button x:Name="ColorPickerButton" Margin="10,5,0,5"
              Click="ColorPickerButton_Click" Width="124">Color Picker</Button>
          <Button x:Name="ColorDetailsButton" Margin="10,5,0,5"
              Click="ColorDetailsButton_Click" >Color Browser</Button>
        </StackPanel>
      </Grid>
    </StackPanel>
</Grid>
```

```csharp
private void ColorPickerButton_Click(object sender, RoutedEventArgs e)
{
    this.Frame.Navigate(typeof(MainPage));
}

private void ColorDetailsButton_Click(object sender, RoutedEventArgs e)
{
    this.Frame.Navigate(typeof(ColorBrowser));
}
```
HomePage.xaml.cs

```vb
Private Sub ColorPickerButton_Click(sender as Object, e As RoutedEventArgs)
    Me.Frame.Navigate(GetType(MainPage))
End Sub

Private Sub ColorDetailsButton_Click(sender As Object, e As RoutedEventArgs)
    Me.Frame.Navigate(GetType(ColorBrowser))
End Sub
```
HomePage.xaml.vb

```csharp
protected override void LoadState(...)
{
    this.DefaultViewModel["Items"] = new ColorCollection();
}
```
ColorBrowser.xaml.cs

```vb
Protected Overrides Sub LoadState(...)
    Me.DefaultViewModel("Items") = New ColorCollection
End sub
```
ColorBrowser.xaml.vb

```csharp
rootFrame.Navigate(typeof(HomePage), args.Arguments))
```
App.xaml.cs

```vb
rootFrame.Navigate(GetType(HomePage), e.Arguments)
```
App.xaml.vb

HOW'D YOU DO?

Here's the final bit of the exercise: the Color Browser template:

```xml
<Page.Resources>
    <CollectionViewSource x:Name="itemsViewSource" Source="{Binding Items}"/>
    <x:String x:Key="AppName">My Application</x:String>
Bottom
    <DataTemplate x:Key="Customized250x250ItemTemplate">
        <Grid HorizontalAlignment="Left" Width="250" Height="250">
            <Border Background="{Binding ColorName}">
                <StackPanel VerticalAlignment="Bottom" HorizontalAlignment="Center">
                    <TextBlock Text="{Binding ColorName}" />
                    <TextBlock Text="{Binding HexValue}" FontFamily="Global User Interface" />
                </StackPanel>
            </Border>
        </Grid>
    </DataTemplate>
</Page.Resources>
...
<!-- Horizontal Scrolling Grid -->
<GridView ItemTemplate="{StaticResource Customized250x250ItemTemplate}" ... />
```

ColorBrowser.xaml

Were you able to work out what controlled the display of the back buttons? Two things work together. First, the **IsEnabled** property is bound to the **Frame.CanGoBack** property:

```xml
<Button IsEnabled="{Binding Frame.CanGoBack, ElementName=pageRoot}" ...>
```

and the Style is set to the **BackButtonStyle**, which is defined in the **StandardStyles.xaml** resource dictionary. The **VisualStateManager** for the **BackButtonStyle** collapses the element if it's in the **Disabled** state.

You could have achieved the same result in other ways, but that pattern really is best practice: The element declaration controls the state, the **VisualStateManager** changes the display based on the state, and there's no code involved. (That no-code rule isn't always completely possible, despite the fact that some MVVM people will insist on empty code-behind files.)

MANAGING STATE, PART 1

The combination of a bound `IsEnabled` state and the `VisualStateManager` handle the display of the back button. (I personally think that's moderately cool.) But other bits of state aren't being managed. Try this out:

ENTER A NAME
If you type something in the name text box, move to another page, and then return, the value you typed is gone. That's not friendly.

PICK A COLOR
If you navigate to the Color Explorer `Page` and choose a color, you'd expect that to be reflected in the home page, but it's not happening. Oops.

There are two things going on here: The state of the individual `Page` classes aren't being maintained, and we're not passing information between them.

The first problem, maintaining `Page` state between displays, is simple to fix by setting the `Page.NavigationCacheMode`.

The second problem, sharing information between pages, is really simple if you only need to pass a simple value—you can pass a parameter to the `Navigate()` method— but unfortunately, it can get a little tricky if you need more than that. We'll explore the issues in this section.

> ### ON YOUR OWN
> Let's start with the easy bit. NavigationCacheMode is a property of the Page. It accepts a member of the NavigationCacheMode enumeration, which has three members: Disabled, Required, and Enabled. Can you work out how to make home page remember your name?

NavigationCacheMode

The `Frame` class maintains two kinds of information about the pages it displays. In order to implement the `GoBack()` and `GoForward()` methods, it maintains the NAVIGATION STACK of the pages that have been displayed. Optionally, the `Frame` will also maintain the state of those pages in a NAVIGATION CACHE. (The number of pages the `Frame` will cache is (kinda sorta) controlled by the `Frame.CacheSize` property.) Whether or not a page is cached is controlled on the `Page` level by the `NavigationCacheMode` property, which defaults to `Disabled`.

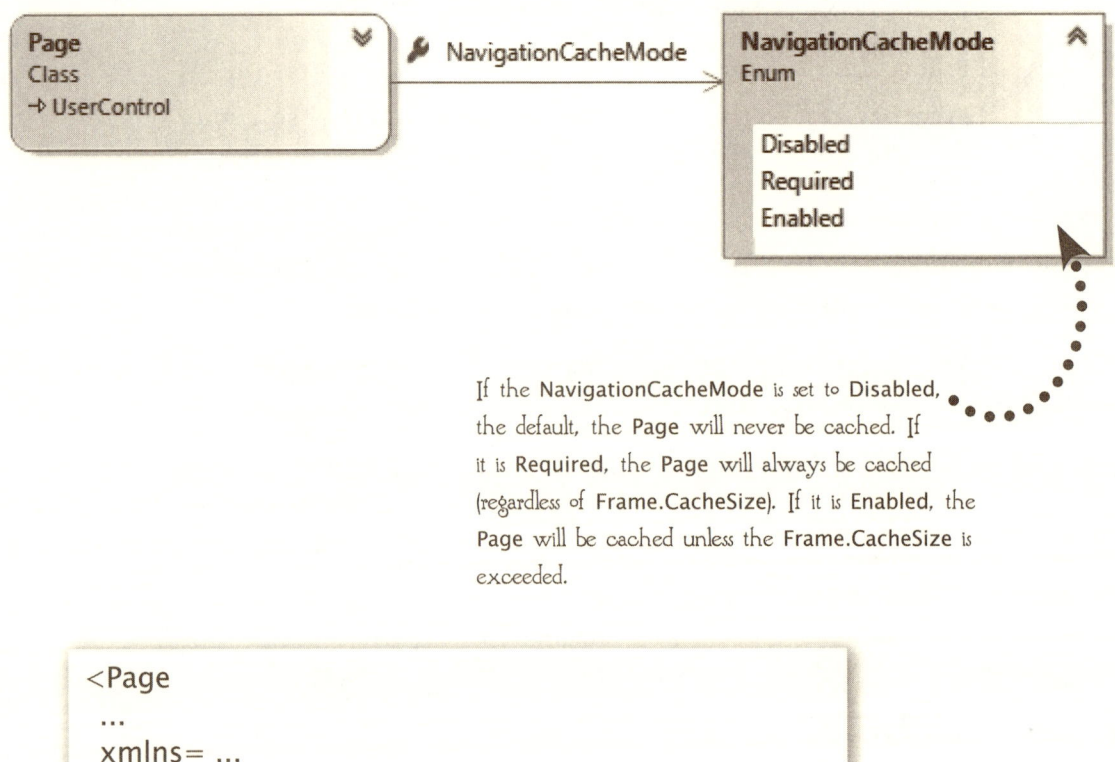

If the `NavigationCacheMode` is set to `Disabled`, the default, the `Page` will never be cached. If it is `Required`, the `Page` will always be cached (regardless of `Frame.CacheSize`). If it is `Enabled`, the `Page` will be cached unless the `Frame.CacheSize` is exceeded.

```
<Page
...
xmlns= ...
NavigationCacheMode="Enabled" />
```

SHARING DATA, PART 1

The back button that the Basic page template adds by default calls the NavigationHelper.GoBack() command method, which takes no parameters. (The NavigationHelper, which we'll talk about on the next page, also has a matching GoForward() method.) When we wrote the Click event handlers for the two buttons, we used the version of the Navigate() method that takes just the type of the Page. But if all we need is to send a simple value between pages, we can use the second version of Navigate, which accepts a single parameter:

The first parameter is the type of the Page. We've already used it.

 public bool Navigate(Type sourcePageType, object parameter)

 Public Function Navigate(sourcePageType as Type, parameter As Object) As Boolean

The second parameter is defined as an Object, but you should only use simple types like a string or an integer.

MAKE A NOTE

Despite the fact that the parameter you pass to the Navigate() method is defined as an Object, and despite the fact that you'll see people recommending that you create a custom class to pass multiple values, don't do it. Complex types cause problems for garbage collection and for saving and restoring state for the app. The NavigationHelper class, which we'll explore next, provides a simple solution.

513

THE NAVIGATIONHELPER

When we added the support files to our project, one of the classes Visual Studio added to the project was the declaration of the NavigationHelper class, which (as you'd expect) makes handling navigation simpler. Use of the NavigationHelper is wired into all the Page templates except the Blank Page (and of course, you can add it there). Here's what it looks like:

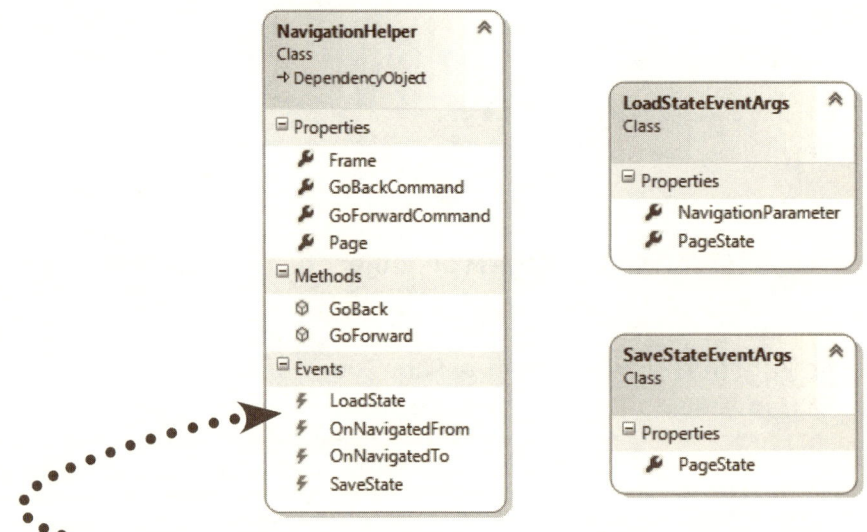

NavigationHelper replaces these core Page events with the much more convenient LoadState and SaveState events. You'll almost always want to respond to those instead.

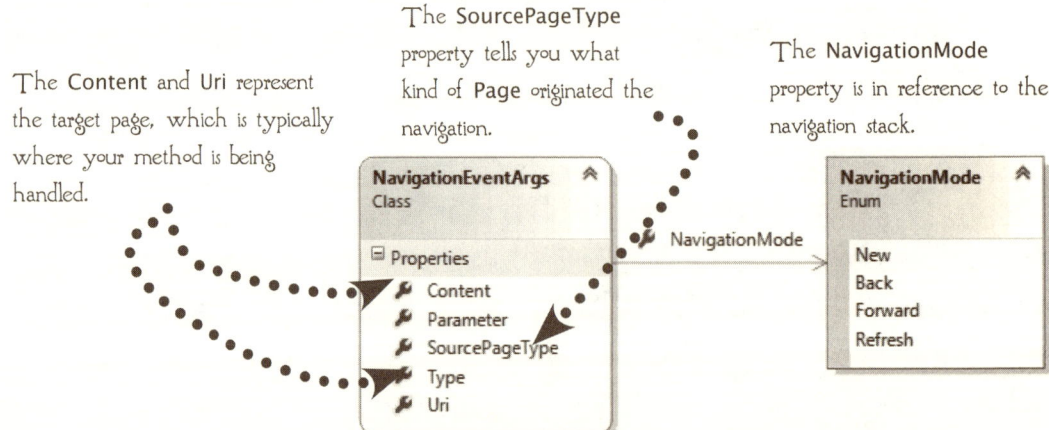

The Content and Uri represent the target page, which is typically where your method is being handled.

The SourcePageType property tells you what kind of Page originated the navigation.

The NavigationMode property is in reference to the navigation stack.

# PUT ON YOUR THINKING HAT

Let's try it out, shall we? We'll pass a Parameter back from the Color Picker Page to the home page, and display the user's favorite color.
HINT: You'll need to add references to Windows.UI and System.Reflection to the HomePage.xaml.cs or HomePage.xaml.vb file.

# CALL NAVIGATE WITH A PARAMETER

Of course, the exact mechanism for triggering the Navigate() method call will vary depending on your app and its UI, but for our purposes, we can just change the click event handler for the existing backButton on the color explorer Page. (Delete the existing Command property and add Click.)

You'll want to pass the ColorName property of the current item. (It would be easier to pass the ActualColor, but passing complex types like that is a no-no.) You'll need to cast CurrentItem to an instance of ColorDetails before you can get to the ColorName. See if you can figure out where all the parentheses go without peeking.

# OVERRIDE NAVIGATIONHELPER_LOADSTATE

For our example, we'll want to set the Fill property of the ColorRect on the home page. Turning the string into a property of the Colors class requires some fiddly reflection, so here's the code to plug into your method:

```csharp
TypeInfo ti = typeof(Colors).GetTypeInfo();
PropertyInfo pi = ti.GetDeclaredProperty((string)e.NavigationParameter);
Color c = (Color)pi.GetValue(null);

this.ColorRect.Fill = new SolidColorBrush(c);
```

```vb
Dim ti As TypeInfo = GetType(Colors).GetTypeInfo()
Dim pi As PropertyInfo = ti.GetDeclaredProperty(e.NavigationParameter)
Dim c As Color = CType(pi.GetValue(Nothing), Color)

Me.ColorRect.Fill = New SolidColorBrush(c)
```

HOW'D YOU DO?
Here are the two methods:

```csharp
private void backButton_Click(object sender, RoutedEventArgs e)
{
    this.Frame.Navigate(typeof(HomePage), ((ColorDetails)ColorCVS.View.CurrentItem).ColorName);
}
```
MainPage.xaml.cs

```csharp
private void navigationHelper_LoadState(object sender, LoadStateEventArgs e)
{
    if (e.NavigationParameter == null || (string)e.NavigationParameter = "")
    {
        return;
    }
    TypeInfo ti = typeof(Colors).GetTypeInfo();
    PropertyInfo pi = ti.GetDeclaredProperty((string)e.NavigationParameter);
    Color c = (Color)pi.GetValue(null);

    this.ColorRect.Fill = new SolidColorBrush(c);
}
```
HomePage.xaml.cs

```vb
Private Sub backButton_Click(sender As Object, e As RoutedEventArgs)
    Me.Frame.Navigate(GetType(HomePage), CType(itemsViewSource.View.CurrentItem, _
        ColorDetails).ColorName)
End Sub
```

MainPage.xaml.vb

```vb
Private Sub NavigationHelper_LoadState(sender As Object, e As Common.LoadStateEventArgs)
    If e.NavigationParameter Is Nothing Or CStr(e.NavigationParameter) = "" Then
        Return
    End If

    Dim ti As TypeInfo = GetType(Colors).GetTypeInfo()
    Dim pi As PropertyInfo = ti.GetDeclaredProperty(e.NavigationParameter)
    Dim c As Color = CType(pi.GetValue(Nothing), Color)

    Me.ColorRect.Fill = New SolidColorBrush(c)
End Sub
```

HomePage.xaml.vb

SHARING DATA, PART 2

Passing a parameter to the `Navigate()` method works just fine if all you need to do is pass a single piece of basic data, and we were able to make that work by passing the `ColorName` string that equates to one of the properties of the static `Colors` class. But that's a pretty artificial example. It's really much more likely that you'll need to pass multiple values, or, more accurately, share complex data structures between pages.

As it stands, each `Page` of our app has its own instance of the data, and it's shared only by manually passing a `Parameter` in the `Navigate()` method.

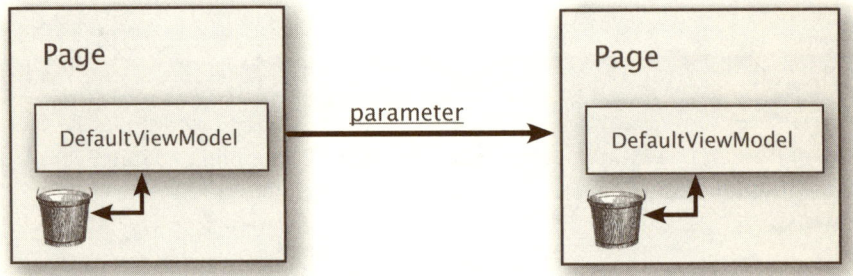

A better solution is to create a single instance of the data and share it wherever necessary. That way, we needn't worry about passing complex object to the `Navigate()` method or having multiple instances of large data structures using up memory.

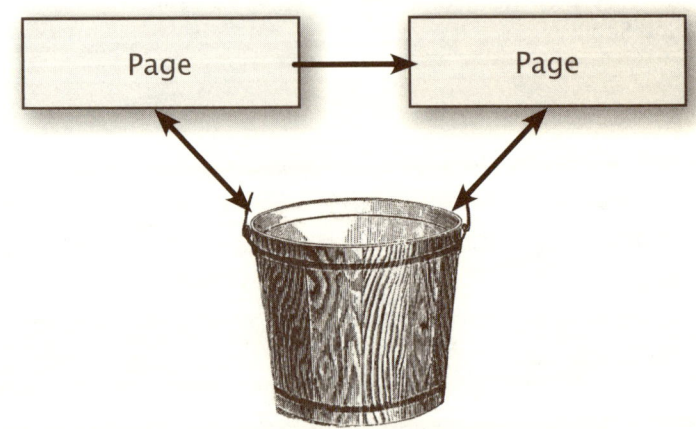

518

CREATING A DATA SOURCE

Let's get going. We'll start by building the data source that can be shared by all the pages in our app. We'll need two items: the same `ColorCollection` we've been using, and a single `ColorDetails` that represents the user's favorite color. Adding a `SolidColorBrush` that represents the favorite color will save some code elsewhere in the app, so let's do that as well.

Perhaps the cleanest way to do this (certainly one of the easiest) is to use the `PageState` dictionary that's passed around by the `NavigationHelper`. There's no need to duplicate that code, particularly not for a system as simple as this, but we will need to use an `ObservableDictionary` instead of a plain `Dictionary`.

ObservableDictionary is defined in the Common directory of all the Visual Studio Templates except the Blank App (which doesn't include a Common directory).

But you'll get it if you add the support files. (You knew that, right?)

PUT ON YOUR THINKING HAT

Let's get started. Create the data source in the App.xaml code-behind. You'll need to declare a **public static** (Shared in VB) property in the **App** class to store the data. (I called mine **ColorViewModel**.)

I put the code to initialize the property and add the items in a procedure called **CreateViewModel()**, which I call from the **OnLaunched** event. (You can embed the code if you'd rather.)

In CreateViewModel(), instantiate the ColorCollection (I called mine StaticColors) and then use a LINQ query to pick one query from the collection to assign to some value to FavoriteColor. (I chose Firebrick, because it's my favorite color. Pick one you like better.)

HOW'D YOU DO?

Did you figure out where to call CreateViewModel()?

```csharp
public static Common.ObservableDictionary StaticColors {get; set; }
...
protected override async void OnLaunched(...)
{
    ...
    if (rootFrame == null)
    {
        CreateViewModel();
        ...
    }
    ...
}

private void CreateViewModel()
{
    ColorViewModel = New Common.ObservableDictionary();

    ColorCollection colors = new ColorCollection;
    ColorDetails favorite
    favorite = (from cd in SystemColors
                    where cd.ColorName == "Firebrick"
                    select cd).First();
    SolidColorBrush favBrush = new SolidColorBrush(favorite.ActualColor);

    ColorViewModel = new Common.ObservableDictionary();
    ColorViewModel.Add("FavoriteColor", favorite);
    ColorViewModel.Add("FavoriteColorBrush", favBrush);
    ColorViewModel.Add("StaticColors", colors);
}
```

```vb
Private Shared _colorViewModel As Common.ObservableDictionary
Public Shared Property ColorViewModel() As Common.ObservableDictionary
    Get
        Return _colorViewModel
    End Get
    Set(ByVal value As Common.ObservableDictionary)
        _colorViewModel = value
    End Set
End Property
...
Protected Overrides Async Sub OnLaunched(...)
    ...
    If rootFrame Is Nothing Then
        CreateViewModel()
        ...
    End If
End Sub

Private Sub CreateViewModel()
    ColorViewModel = New Common.ObservableDictionary()

    Dim colors As New ColorCollection()
    Dim favorite As ColorDetails
    favorite = (From cd In colors
                Where cd.ColorName = "Firebrick"
                Select cd).First()
    Dim favBrush As New SolidColorBrush(favorite.ActualColor)

    ColorViewModel = New Common.ObservableDictionary()
    ColorViewModel.Add("FavoriteColor", favorite)
    ColorViewModel.Add("FavoriteColorBrush", favBrush)
    ColorViewModel.Add("StaticColors", colors)
End Sub
```

MAKING THE DATA AVAILABLE

Now that we've instantiated a `ColorCollection` in our `App` class, we don't actually have to do anything else to make it available to the pages of our app. We just have to set up a reference to it. The Visual Studio page templates (except for Blank Page) are already set up to use a view model, so all we have to do is change the code to return `App.ColorViewModel` instead of an empty dictionary.

```
public ObservableDictionary DefaultViewModel
{
    get { return App.ColorViewModel; }
}
```
C#

```
Public ReadOnly Property DefaultViewModel As
            Common.ObservableDictionary
    Get
        Return App.ColorViewModel
    End Get
End Property
```
VB

A HICCUP

Before we change the remaining pages to use the shared `ColorViewModel` we've created, I need to warn you about a bug. It may be fixed by the time you read this, but as I write, there's a problem with the `Selector` class and any of the classes, like `ListView`, that derive from it: It creates its contents before it implements its bindings. That means that for a brief moment in time while the `Page` is being created, the `SelectedItem` will be null and then it will be re-set to the first item in the element's `ItemsSource` collection. If you set up a binding for `SelectedItem` (we want to bind it to `FavoriteColor`), instead of pulling the existing value *from* the view model, it will push the first item *to* the view model.

The workaround is to use the `Loaded` event handler. (Everything's been created by the time it's triggered.) Because we want to set the current item to the favorite item, and that's a property of our view model, we can just call `MoveCurrentTo()` and pass the property.

If your view model doesn't have a convenient property like that, you'll need to capture the value before the call to `InitializeComponent()` in the constructor. It's easiest to just declare a class-level field to store the value.

By the way, you'll also want to call `ScrollIntoView()` after you set the value, because the `ListView` won't do that for you and it would be confusing if the selected item wasn't visible.

PUT ON YOUR THINKING HAT

Let's update the Color Explorer. You'll need to change all three pages, but the changes are mostly the same: set the DefaultViewModel to our shared data and deal with the Selector bug. We do need to make make one minor change to ColorBrowser.xaml, but no changes at all to MainPage.xaml.

MAINPAGE

- Update the DefaultViewModel property so that it returns the ColorViewModel we created in the App class.

- Create a method (I called mine DisplayFavorite) that sets the favorite color and scrolls it into view.

- Create a handler for the Loaded event that calls the method you just created from the page constructor.

- Change the backButton_Click() method so that it updates the shared ColorViewModel before it leaves the page.

COLORBROWSER

- Make the same changes to the code behind that you just made to MainPage. (Be aware, the instances of CollectionViewSource created in the XAML have different names in MainPage.xaml and ColorBrowser.xaml.)

- Out of the box, the itemGridView doesn't support selection. Change the SelectionMode property in the xaml file to Single.

PUT ON YOUR THINKING HAT

How'd you do? Has Microsoft fixed the bug yet? I've just given you one set of code, since it's the same for both pages.

```csharp
public ObservableDictionary DefaultViewModel
{
    get { return App.ColorViewModel; }
}
...
public ColorBrowser()
{
    ...
    this.Loaded += DisplayFavorite;
}
...
private void DisplayFavorite(Object sender, RoutedEventArgs e)
{
    itemsViewSource.View.MoveCurrentTo(App.ColorViewModel("FavoriteColor"));
    itemGridView.ScrollIntoView(App.ColorViewModel("FavoriteColor"));
}

private void backButton_Click(Object sender, RoutedEventArgs e)
{
    ColorDetails CurrentColor = (ColorDetails)itemsViewSource.View.CurrentItem;
    App.ColorViewModel("FavoriteColor") = CurrentColor;
    App.ColorViewModel("FavoriteColorBrush") = _
        new SolidColorBrush(CurrentColor.ActualColor);
    this.Frame.Navigate(typeof(HomePage));
}
```

```vb
Public ReadOnly Property DefaultViewModel As Common.ObservableDictionary
    Get
        Return App.ColorViewModel
    End Get
End Property
...
Public Sub New()
    ...
    AddHandler Me.Loaded, AddressOf DisplayFavorite
End Sub

Private Sub DisplayFavorite(sender As Object, e As RoutedEventArgs)
    itemsViewSource.View.MoveCurrentTo(App.ColorViewModel("FavoriteColor"))
    itemGridView.ScrollIntoView(App.ColorViewModel("FavoriteColor"))
End Sub
...
Private Sub backButton_Click(sender As Object, e As RoutedEventArgs)
    Dim CurrentColor As ColorDetails = CType(itemsViewSource.View.CurrentItem, _
        ColorDetails)
    App.ColorViewModel("FavoriteColor") = CurrentColor
    App.ColorViewModel("FavoriteColorBrush") = _
        New SolidColorBrush(CurrentColor.ActualColor)
    Me.Frame.Navigate(GetType(HomePage))
End Sub
```

TAKE A BREAK

As a review, why don't you update **HomePage** so that it displays the current favorite color. Change the **DefaultViewModel** property so that it returns the **ColorViewModel** we created in the App class. We're not using a navigation parameter any more, so comment out that code in the **NavigationHelper_LoadState()** method. Finally, bind the Rectangle to the **FavoriteColorBrush**.

Then take a break before you complete the review and we move on to the application life cycle in the next chapter.

REVIEW

What kind of values can you pass as a parameter to the **Navigate()** method?

The **Selector.SelectedItem** binding bug affects all the elements that descend from it. In addition to **ListView**, where else might you run into trouble?

What page template **doesn't** use the NavigationHelper? What about a default View Model?

How do you change the **Page** that is displayed when an app is launched via the **OnLaunched()** method?

The **Simulator** is great for checking how your app looks at various resolutions. What do you use to check it in different views?

Congratulations! You've finished the chapter. Take a minute to think about what you've accomplished before you move on to the next one...

List three things you learned in this chapter:

①

②

③

Why do you think you need to know these things in order to develop Win8 apps?

Is there anything in this chapter that you think you need to understand in more detail? If so, what are you going to do about that?

THE APPLICATION LIFECYCLE

Back in the days when Grandma was young, an application was either running or it wasn't. The most complicated thing you had to deal with was a command line argument or a file association. Your application stopped running either because the user closed it or because it (or some other application) crashed. Ah, the simplicity of bygone days.

In Windows 8.1, your app might start running because the user tapped its Start Menu tile, but they might have tapped a secondary file that they created or they might have chosen a charm like Search or Share. Or File Open. Or because they plugged in a device your app is registered to handle. Or because they've decided to print or update a file your app handles. Or because they've switched back to it after using another app for awhile. Or…

Your app might stop running because the user closed it or because they switched to a different app for more than about 10 seconds and Windows needed the memory. Or because your app took longer to load than Windows was prepared to give you. Or, of course, because it crashed. Or…

But however your app starts or stops, you need to maintain the state of the app and your user's operations.

Yep, life is a lot more complicated than it used to be. In this chapter we'll begin the process of managing all these possible activation and termination events by looking at the basic process of launching, suspending, and using the SuspensionManager to save and restore state. (We'll look at some of the issues involving Start Menu tiles in the next chapter, and we'll finish the discussion when we explore Windows 8 contracts in Chapter 17.)

FITTING IT IN

Here's the process we'll start exploring in this chapter.

We'll explore responding to contract and protocol activations in Chapter 17, and notifications in the next chapter.

Your app will be suspended about 10 seconds after the user closes it or opens another app.

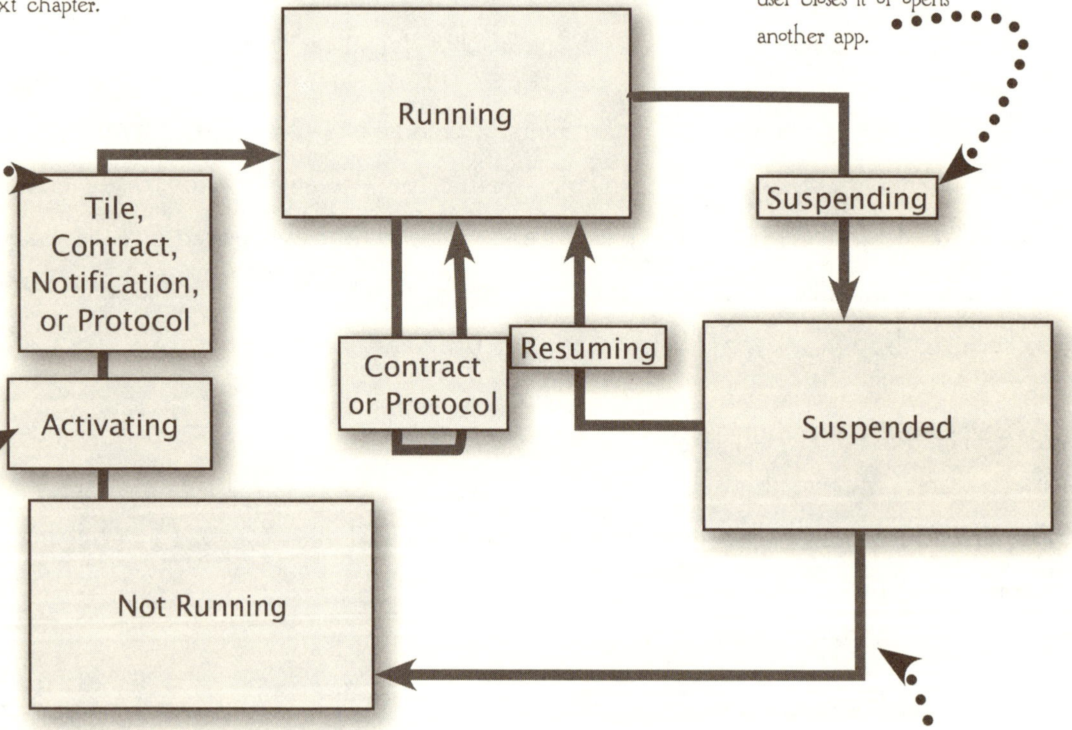

- Running
- Tile, Contract, Notification, or Protocol
- Activating
- Not Running
- Contract or Protocol
- Resuming
- Suspending
- Suspended

When your app is activated, Windows will display a splash screen. We'll see how to extend the default splash screen in this chapter.

Once your app has been suspended, it can be removed from memory without any further notice.

TASK LIST

In this chapter we'll explore the actions your app needs to take during a basic activation. We'll look at some of the special ways your app can be activated, like in response to the Search charm, in the next few chapters.

LAUNCHING AN APP
We'll start by taking another look at all the various ways to launch or activate an application (and the difference between launching and activating).

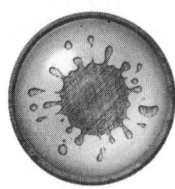

SPLASH SCREENS
Part of the launch process is the display of the app's splash screen. We'll see how to configure the splash screen that Windows creates for your app and also how to create an extended splash screen if your app needs more than two or three seconds to load.

THE SUSPENSION MANAGER
One of the things that a well-behaved Win8 app is required to do is maintain the user's state between activations. At the end of this chapter we'll explore the functionality the **SuspensionManager** provides for simply saving and restoring state.

LAUNCHING AN APP

Until you get it all sorted out, your app can go from "not running" to "running" in a bewildering number of ways, and there are a bewildering number of methods and events to support all those ways. But it's really not as complicated as it looks.

Apps can be launched or activated. They're LAUNCHED by tapping on a tile on the Start Menu when the app isn't already running. You override the OnLaunched() method to handle a launch. Apps are ACTIVATED if they're started in other way—by the Search charm, or by opening a file that's associated with the app, for example—and you override the appropriate On...Activated() method.

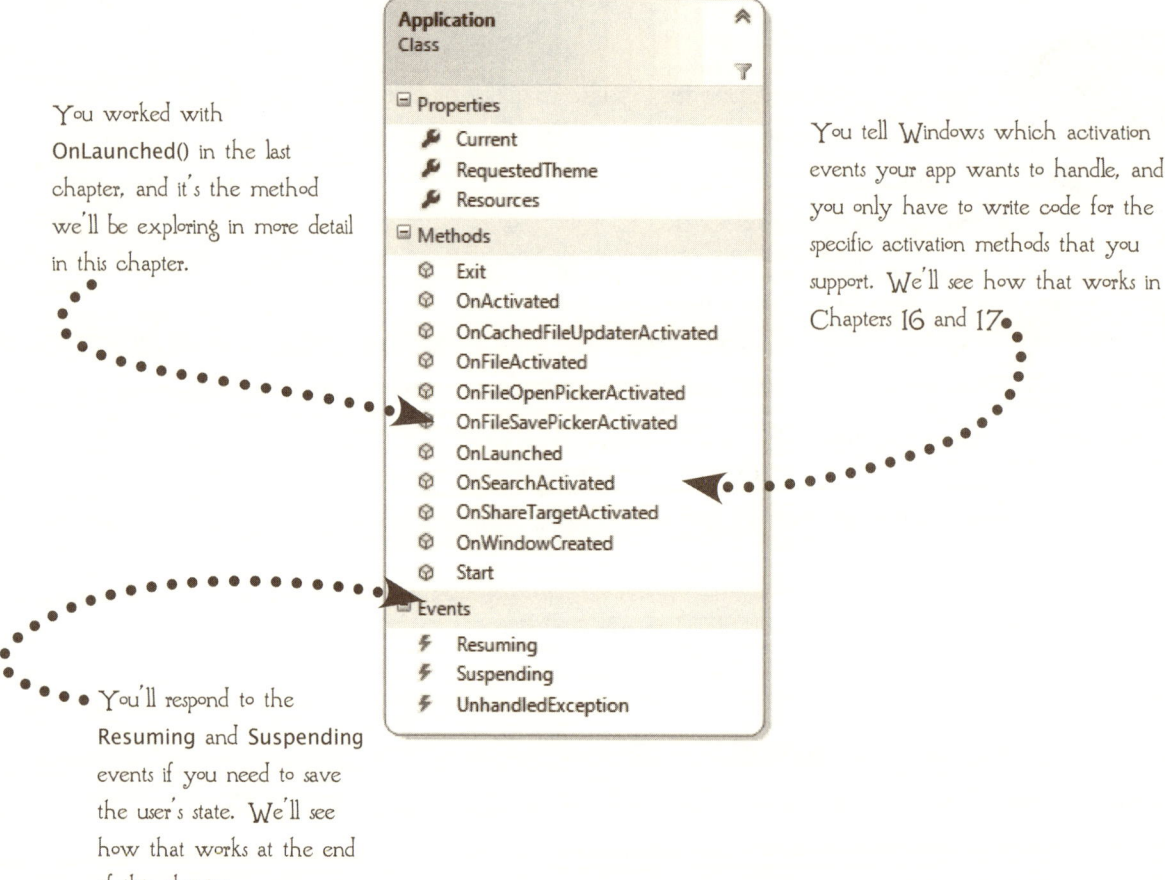

You worked with OnLaunched() in the last chapter, and it's the method we'll be exploring in more detail in this chapter.

You tell Windows which activation events your app wants to handle, and you only have to write code for the specific activation methods that you support. We'll see how that works in Chapters 16 and 17.

You'll respond to the Resuming and Suspending events if you need to save the user's state. We'll see how that works at the end of this chapter.

LAUNCH EVENT ARGS

As you'd expect, the OnLaunched() method receives an instance of an argument class, in this case the LaunchActivatedEventArgs, which provides some important information. Here's what it looks like:

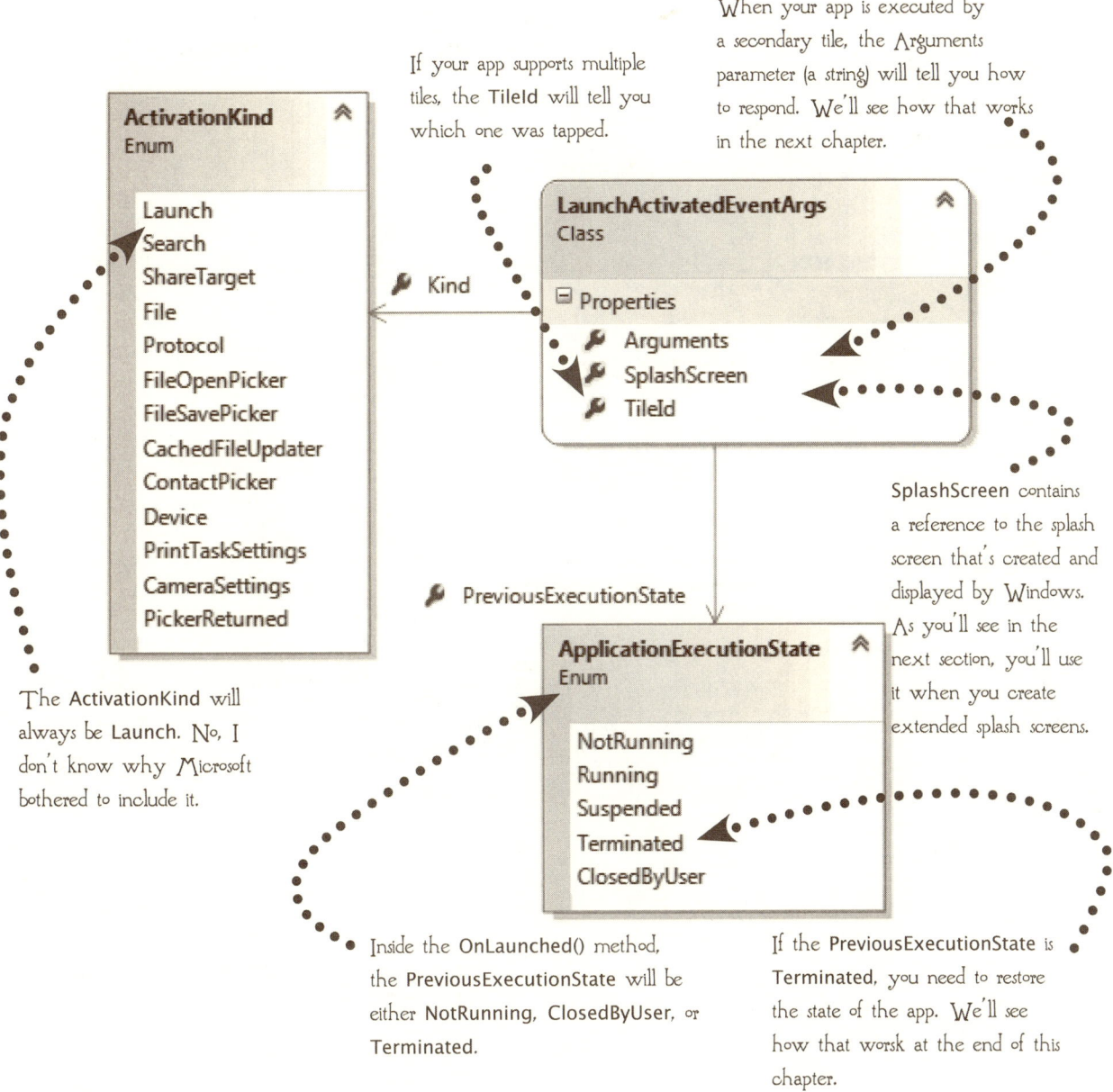

SPLASH SCREENS

You've probably noticed by now that Microsoft is pretty keen on maintaining a consistent look and feel for Win8 apps. One of the places they enforce that is in the application splash screen. You can control the splash screen and the image that's displayed. That's it. Even if you add an extended splash screen to your app (and we'll see how to do that in a few pages), it needs to closely resemble the one created by Windows. Let's see how it works:

To open the Manifest Designer, just double-click the **Package.appmanifest** file in the Solution Explorer.

Select the Visual Assets tab.

When you select the Splash Screen assets, the designer will give you the chance to specify the image and background color.

Your basic splash screen should be 620 x 300 pixels. At 140%, is should be 868 x 420, and at 180%, it should be 1116 x 540.

534

SCALING FOR PIXEL DENSITIES

In the last chapter we explored some techniques for making sure that your basic Page layout adapts to different screen resolutions, but those techniques won't prevent images from scaling (and looking ugly) at different pixel densities. (The world no longer consists solely of 72-dpi monitors.) When you're working with bitmapped images like pngs, Win8 expects you to provide three versions of these assets: 100%, 140%, and 180%.

Win8 uses one of two conventions for locating scaled assets. You can either append a scale tag (.scale-100, .scale-140, or .scale-180) to the file name before the usual extension, or you can maintain the different assets in folders with those names (Assets/Scale-100, for example). Either way works. I personally find it comforting to have the scale embedded in the file name, but that's just me.)

When you refer to one of the assets in code or in a Designer, you just use the plain file name:

    <Image Source="/Assets/SplashScreen.png" />

even though it may be named **SplashScreen.scale-100.png**. Win8 will sort it out at runtime.

PUT ON YOUR THINKING HAT

Let's get started. Create a new project, add the support files, and configure the splash screen:

Create a new blank project and replace the existing **MainPage.xaml** with one based on the Basic Page template in order to add the support files. (We don't need them now, but we will in a minute.)

Add three versions of a splash screen to the project's Assets folder. (If you name yours "SplashScreen..." you'll want to remove the version that Visual Studio adds by default.)

Change the background color and specify your image in the Manifest Designer. If you click the ellipsis below one of the image icons, you can choose the appropriate file, and Visual Studio will fill out the rest of the Designer for you.

HOW'D YOU DO?

Here's what my version of the Manifest Designer looks like when it's filled out. (You might have chosen to use your own images, and the file names might be different.)

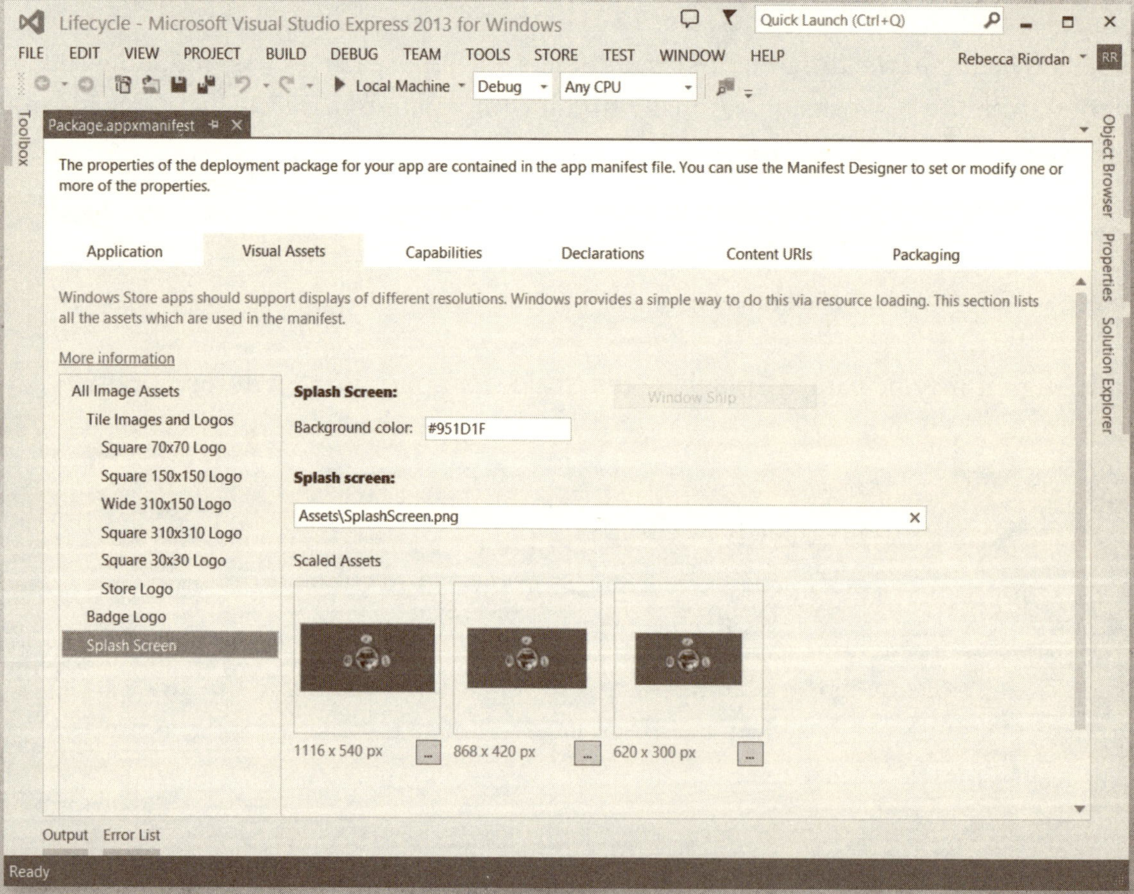

EXTENDED SPLASH SCREENS

Win8 only gives you a few seconds to get your app up and running and display the initial UI. During that time, it will display the default splash screen for you, but the operating system will assume your app has hung and terminate it if you take too long. So, what do you do if your app requires longer than that? Display an extended splash screen that acts as a kind of intermediate UI—it's enough to satisfy Windows, and it buys you the time you need to get everything ready to go. Here's the basic process:

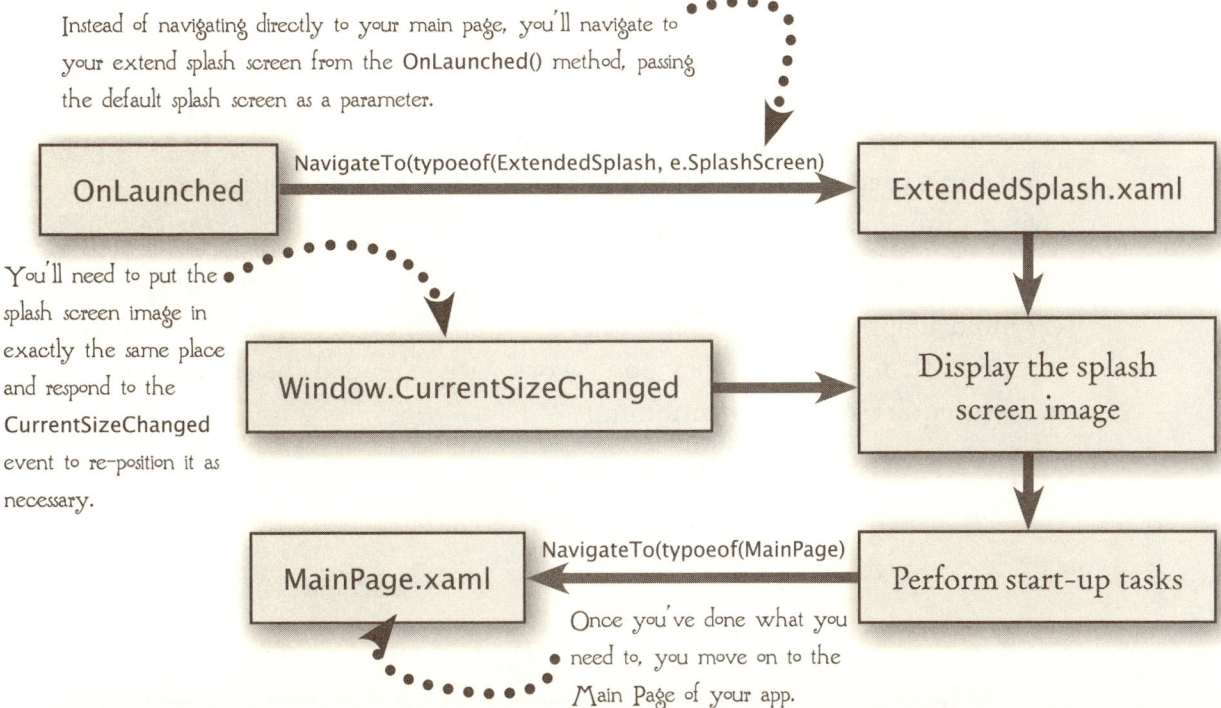

Instead of navigating directly to your main page, you'll navigate to your extend splash screen from the OnLaunched() method, passing the default splash screen as a parameter.

You'll need to put the splash screen image in exactly the same place and respond to the CurrentSizeChanged event to re-position it as necessary.

Once you've done what you need to, you move on to the Main Page of your app.

MY VIEW

Microsoft has written a splash screen sample; you can find it at code.microsoft.com. Unfortunately, like a lot of Microsoft sample code, I think it's over-complicated and under-explained. That makes it difficult to trace exactly what's happening, or more importantly, what needs to happen. Of course, you can argue that the example I'm presenting here is simplistic, and I'd agree with you. But my theory is to start as simple as possible and only add complexity as and when necessary...

Building an Extended Splash

There are quite a few steps to building an extended splash screen, but as always, if you concentrate on one thing at a time, each step is fairly simple. If you follow these steps, you'll see that for yourself.

Create the XAML

Of course, the first thing you'll need to do is add a XAML page to your app. You don't need the functionality of a Basic Page; the Blank Page template will do fine. I called mine **ExtendedSplash**, but feel free to be creative.

Now, we spent a lot of time in the last chapter learning how to use XAML to build adaptive layouts. (They're great, aren't they? They save so much tedious calculation.) But they don't work with extended splash screens, which require absolute positioning.

In the XAML of your extended splash screen, you must declare a Canvas and place all of your elements (including the splash screen image) inside it:

Specify the same background color that you used for the default splash screen.

```
<Grid Background="#d8cbbf">
    <Canvas>
        <Image x:Name="SplashImage" Source="Assets/SplashScreen.png"/>
        <ProgressRing x:Name="Ring" .../>
        <Button x:Name="CloseButton" .../>
    </Canvas>
</Grid>
```

Declare any other elements you want to display and set any properties except those relating to size and position.

You should keep your extended splash screen as simple as possible. We'll just add a ProgressBar and a Button.

538

ADD SOME FIELDS

You'll need to add references (using or imports) to the Windows.ApplicationModel.Activation, Windows.UI.Core and the Common folder of your project to the top of your code-behind file.

Then, because your extended splash screen class will receive an instance of the default splash screen when it's called by the OnLaunched() method, you'll need some place to store it. You'll also want a Rect structure to store the position of the splash screen image. (The Rect isn't strictly necessary, but it saves a lot of typing.) Add them to the top of the class declaration.

```csharp
private SplashScreen splash;
private Rect imageRect;
```

HANDLE ONNAVIGATEDTO

You'll need to handle the OnNavigatedTo() method, register for the SizeChanged event of the current window, set the values of your fields, and call the method that will position your elements:

```csharp
protected override void OnNavigatedTo(NavigationEventArgs e)
{
    base.OnNavigatedTo(e);
    Window.Current.SizeChanged += Current_SizeChanged;
    splash = (SplashScreen)(e.Parameter);
    imageRect = splash.ImageLocation;
    this.Loaded += (object s, RoutedEventArgs a) => {PositionImage();};
}
```

```vb
Protected Overrides Sub OnNavigatedTo(e As NavigationEventArgs)
    MyBase.OnNavigatedTo(e)
    AddHandler Window.Current.SizeChanged, AddressOf Current_SizeChanged
    splash = DirectCast(e.Parameter, SplashScreen)
    imageRect = splash.ImageLocation
    AddHandler Me.Loaded, Sub(s As Object, a As RoutedEventArgs)
                              PositionImage()
                          End Sub
End Sub
```

HANDLE THE SIZECHANGED EVENT

In **OnNavigatedTo()** you registered for the **Window.Current.SizeChanged** event. The handler just has to reassign the **imageRect Rect** and call PositionImage():

```csharp
void Current_SizeChanged(...)
{
    imageRect = splash.ImageLocation;
    PositionImage();
}
```

HANDLE THE CLICK EVENT

In a real application, you'd begin your start-up tasks in the OnNavigatedTo() method and navigate away from the extended splash screen when they're finished. We don't have any tasks to perform, so we'll navigate away when the user clicks the button:

```csharp
void CloseButton_Click(...)
{
    Frame rootFrame = (Frame)Window.Current.Content;
    rootFrame.Navigate(typeof(MainPage));
    Window.Current.Content = rootFrame;
}
```

```vb
Private Sub CloseButton_Click(sender As Object, e As RoutedEventArgs) _
   Handles CloseButton.Click

    Dim rootFrame As Frame = DirectCast(Window.Current.Content, Frame)
    rootFrame.Navigate(GetType(MainPage))
    Window.Current.Content = rootFrame
End Sub
```

6. POSITION THE ELEMENTS

Our last task is to position the elements on the **Page** based on the values supplied by the **SplashScreen.ImageLocation** property, which we've copied into **imageRect**:

```csharp
void PositionImage()
{
    this.SplashImage.SetValue(Canvas.LeftProperty, imageRect.Left);
    this.SplashImage.SetValue(Canvas.TopProperty, imageRect.Top);
    this.SplashImage.Height = imageRect.Height;
    this.SplashImage.Width = imageRect.Width;

    this.Ring.SetValue(Canvas.LeftProperty, imageRect.Left);
    this.Ring.SetValue(Canvas.TopProperty, imageRect.Top + SplashImage.Height + 20);
    this.Ring.Width = imageRect.Width;

    this.CloseButton.SetValue(Canvas.LeftProperty,
        imageRect.Left + (imageRect.Width/2) - CloseButton.ActualWidth/2);
    this.CloseButton.SetValue(Canvas.TopProperty, imageRect.Top + SplashImage.Height + 50);
}
```

MAKE A NOTE

You VB programmers out there will have noticed that I've only shown the VB version of the code when the syntax is substantially different. (Hey, paper costs money and trees!) If you have any trouble translating, you can check out the version of the project posted on the book's Website.

WIRE IT UP

Our extended splash screen is ready to go, so the last task is to wire it up to the OnLaunched method in App.xaml.cs. All you have to do is replace the name of the page in the Navigate() method call and pass the SplashScreen as the Parameter:

```csharp
rootFrame.Navigate(typeof(ExtendedSplash), e.SplashScreen);
```

```vb
rootFrame.Navigate(GetType(ExtendedSplash), e.SplashScreen)
```

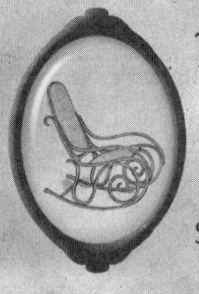 ## TAKE A BREAK

That's it for extended splash screens. If you haven't been following along, why don't you add one to your app now? Then you can take a break before you complete the Review and we move on to using the SuspensionManager to save and restore your application's state.

REVIEW

Can you answer the following questions based on what you've learned?

Where would you begin the start-up tasks inside an extended splash screen?

What's the difference between launching an app and activating one?

What Window event must an extended splash screen respond to?

What are the two options for specifying the scale of an image asset?

Why is it a good idea to put the code to position the elements on an extended splash screen into a separate method?

What parameter does an extended splash screen require when it is navigated to?

THE SUSPENSIONMANAGER

You know that users can suspend an app by switching away from it, and that once that happens, the app may be removed from memory without further notice. When that happens, and the user subsequently resumes the app, it will be launched with the `PreviousExecutionState` of `Terminated`. A well-behaved app will behave as though nothing had happened and return the user to exactly where they were before the suspension. In other words, it will first save its state (on suspension) and then restore it (on launch). The `SuspensionManager`, one of the goodies you get when you add the support classes to your app, makes this pretty painless, but you will need to wire it up. Here's how:

① REFERENCE THE NAMESPACE IN THE APP.XAML CODE-BEHIND

To save some typing, you'll want to add a **using** or **Imports** directive to the top of App.xaml.cs or App.xaml.vb that references the `<AppNamespace>.Common` directory where the `SuspensionManager` class lives:

```
using Lifecycle.Common;
```

```
Imports Lifecycle.Common
```

② REGISTER THE FRAME

In the `OnLaunched()` method, right after the `rootFrame` is created, you'll need to tell the `SuspensionManager` about the Frame by calling the `RegisterFrame()` method:

The string is a key that uniquely identifies the frame to the SuspensionManager.

```
SuspensionManager.RegisterFrame(rootFrame, "appFrame");
```

```
SuspensionManager.RegisterFrame(rootFrame, "appFrame")
```

544

TELL SUSPENSIONMANAGER ABOUT THE TYPES YOU'RE USING

The **SuspensionManager** knows about basic .NET types like strings and integers (the same types you can pass as the **Parameter** in a **Navigate()** method), but if you want to save and restore any complex types, you need to add them to the **SuspensionManager.KnownTypes** collection. We'll see how this works a little later.

RESTORE THE STATE

If your app was terminated, you need to restore the state in the **OnLaunched()** method. The basic code is there; all you need to do is call the **SuspensionManager.RestoreAsync()** method, but since the method is asynchronous, you'll also need to change the signature of the **OnLaunched()** method:

```csharp
protected async override void OnLaunched(...)
{
    if (args.PreviousExecutionState == ApplicationExecutionState.Terminated)
    {
        await SuspensionManager.RestoreAsync();
    }
    ...
}
```
C#

```vb
Protected Overrides Async Sub OnLaunched(...)
    ...
    If e.PreviousExecutionState = ApplicationExecutionState.Terminated Then
        Await SuspensionManager.RestoreAsync()
    End If
    ...
End Sub
```
VB

545

SAVE THE STATE

Of course, you can't restore the state of your app if you haven't saved it in the first place, so you'll also need to update the **OnSuspending()** method to call the **SuspensionManager.SaveAsync()** method. (I haven't shown it, but it's best to wrap this call in a **try...catch** because the **SuspensionManager** will fail if you haven't given it anything to save.) Again, you'll need to change the signature of the method:

```csharp
private async void OnSuspending(...)
{
    var deferral = e.SuspendingOperation.GetDeferral();
    await SuspensionManager.SaveAsync();
    deferral.Complete();
}
```
C#

```vb
Private Async Sub OnSuspending(...)
    Dim deferral As SuspendingDeferral = e.SuspendingOperation.GetDeferral()
    Await SuspensionManager.SaveAsync()
    deferral.Complete()
End Sub
```
VB

ON YOUR OWN

Go ahead and wire the **SuspensionManager** up to the **app.xaml** code-behind.

While you're at it, you might want to comment out the call to the extended splash screen while you're there. We won't be working with it again, and it will save some time in testing. Just navigate directly to the **MainPage**, passing **e.Arguments** as the **Parameter**.

PUT ON YOUR THINKING HAT

We worked with the `LoadState()` and `SaveState()` methods of the `NavigationManager` utility class in the last chapter. We'll use it again to wire up state for this project. Do you remember how?

My Application

Enter some text: [   ]

① Add a TextBlock and TextBox to the MainPage of your app. You'll need to refer to the TextBox in code, so give it a name. (I used "TitleText".)

② Add code to the NavigationState_SaveState() method to store the **Text** property of your TextBox in the **pageState** dictionary using the key "TBText".

③ Add code to the NavigationManager_LoadState() method to restore **TBText** and set it as the **Text** property of the TextBox. You'll always need to cast the values you retrieve, but in this case you can use ToString();

④ Run the app in the Simulator. Type something in the TextBox and then choose "Suspend and shutdown" from the Debug toolbar inside Visual Studio.

⑤ Run the app a second time to confirm that the process worked.

HOW'D YOU DO?

Did you find some errors in the App.xaml code-behind while you were working?

```csharp
protected override NavigationManager_LoadState(...)
{
    if (e.pageState != null && e.pageState.ContainsKey("TBText"))
    {
        this.TitleText.Text = e.pageState["TBText"].ToString();
    }
}
```

```csharp
protected override NavigationManager_SaveState(...)
{
    e.pageState["TBText"] = this.TitleText.Text;
}
```

```vb
Private Sub NavigationHelper_LoadState(...)
    If Not e.PageState Is Nothing AndAlso e.PageState.ContainsKey("TBText") Then
        Me.TitleText.Text = e.PageState("TBText").ToString()
    End If
End Sub
```

```vb
Private Sub NavigationHelper_SaveState(...)
    e.PageState("TBText") = Me.TitleText.Text
End Sub
```

IT ISN'T MAGIC

It may look like magic, but it really isn't. If you look at the code for `SuspensionManager`, you'll see that the `SaveAsync()` method is just serializing the objects you add to the `pageState` dictionary to a file in the `Application.Data.Current.LocalFolder`. We'll talk about file handling and the `LocalFolder` property in Chapter 16. For right now, you only need to know that it's the folder that Win8 provides for your application to store internal data (as opposed to user data, like pictures or documents that the user might create using your app).

To find the file the `SuspensionManager` created, you'll need the package name, which you'll find on the Packaging tab of the app manifest designer. Visual Studio will have assigned a GUID, but you can change it to something more reasonable. (But if you do, you'll need to uninstall the app on the Start Menu.)

Once you have the package name, you can find it in the Explorer. It will be in:

Users\<UserName>\AppData\Local\Packages\<Package>\LocalState

where <UserName> is your user name, and the <Package> will be something that resembles the package name in the manifest (but probably won't match exactly). If you open the _sessionState.xml file in Internet Explorer, you'll see a fairly simple structure:

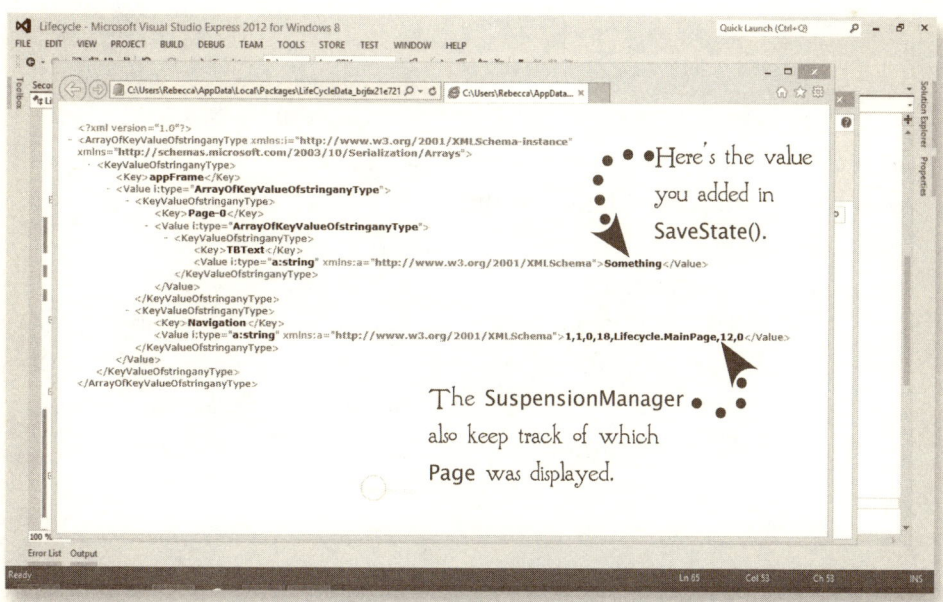

Here's the value you added in SaveState().

The SuspensionManager also keep track of which Page was displayed.

ON YOUR OWN

You shouldn't take my word for any of this. (Not that I'd lie to you, but you'll remember better if you test things out for yourself.)

○ Find the file that the `SuspensionManager` created in the package's `LocalState` directory and verify that the values are there.

○ Add a second page to the app and a `Button` to the first page that navigates to it. (And give yourself a gold star if you remember how to navigate without peeking.)

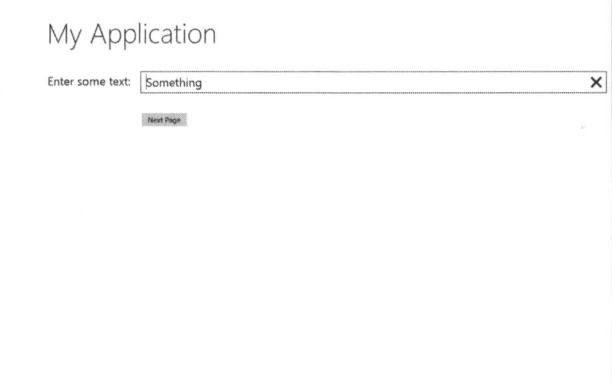

○ Run the app, navigate to the second page, and then choose "Suspend and shutdown" from the Debug toolbar.

○ Run the app a second time to confirm that the app goes directly to the second page. Pretty cool, huh? Can you figure out how the `OnLaunched()` method knows to do that? (HINT: What do you think the `Content` property of the `rootFrame` contains after the call to `RestoreAsync()`?

WORKING WITH CUSTOM TYPES

There is one more thing to know about the `SuspensionManager`. Out of the box, it only knows how to serialize basic data types, like the `string` we've been using. If you want it to serialize anything else, you have to warn it in advance by adding "whatever else" to the list of known types. You'll typically do this just after you register the root frame:

```
rootFrame = new Frame();
SuspensionManager.RegisterFrame(rootFrame, "appFrame");
SuspensionManager.KnownTypes.Add(typeof(MyType));
```

```
rootFrame = New Frame()
SuspensionManager.RegisterFrame(rootFrame, "appFrame")
SuspensonManager.KnownTypes.Add(GetType(MyType))
```

TAKE A BREAK

That's it for our exploration of the life cycle of a Win8 app. Feel free to test out storing and loading a complex type or two—the static **Colors** class gives you a nice, easy one to work with—and then why don't you take a break before you complete the chapter Review and we move on to tiles and notifications in the next chapter?

REVIEW

What size should the 140% splash screen be, in pixels?

What property of the LaunchActivatedEventArgs should you check to find out what your app was doing before it was launched?

Does the App.xaml.cs or App.xaml.vb page generated by Visual Studio register your root frame with the SuspensionManager?

Why should you try to keep your extended splash screen looking a lot like the one Windows displays for you?

What happens if you need to save and restore a custom class that you haven't warned the SuspensionManager about?

Congratulations! You've finished the chapter. Take a minute to think about what you've accomplished before you move on to the next one...

List three things you learned in this chapter:

Why do you think you need to know these things in order to develop Win8 apps?

Is there anything in this chapter that you think you need to understand in more detail? If so, what are you going to do about that?

Tiles & Notifications   15

So far we've been building Win8 bits and pieces (can't quite call them "applications") that are more or less independent of the Windows 8 operating system. Yes, of course, they run on Windows, and the WinRT components we've been using are native to that platform, but we haven't really interacted with the operating system, and the deep integration between Windows 8 and the Win8 App UI is one of the things that sets it apart from other XAML platforms. We'll begin in this chapter with the first thing your user will see about your application: the tile that represents it on the Windows 8 Start Screen.

I'm sure you've heard at least some of the same marketing pronouncements I heard when I started working with Windows 8, all about how it was "alive" and "connected" and "personal". Like me, you may have greeted them with some skepticism. "Yeah, fine. So the photo album tile swaps pictures of my cats. Big deal." But maybe like me, too, you found yourself choosing the news app that updated its tiles over the one that didn't. Hmmm. Maybe there's something to this...

We'll start this chapter by creating each of the types of tiles your app can display—the square tile that is required and the rectangular tile that you'll probably use if you're updating content. We'll also see how you can let users create secondary tiles that will take them to specific places in your application. Then we'll look at how to make your tiles "live": tile notifications and badges. Finally, we'll explore the other way your app can tell users what's going on: the toast notifications that you can use to display short messages.

FITTING IT IN

Here's how this chapter fits in to the book as a whole...

A lot of what we do in this chapter will happen in the Package.appmanifest.

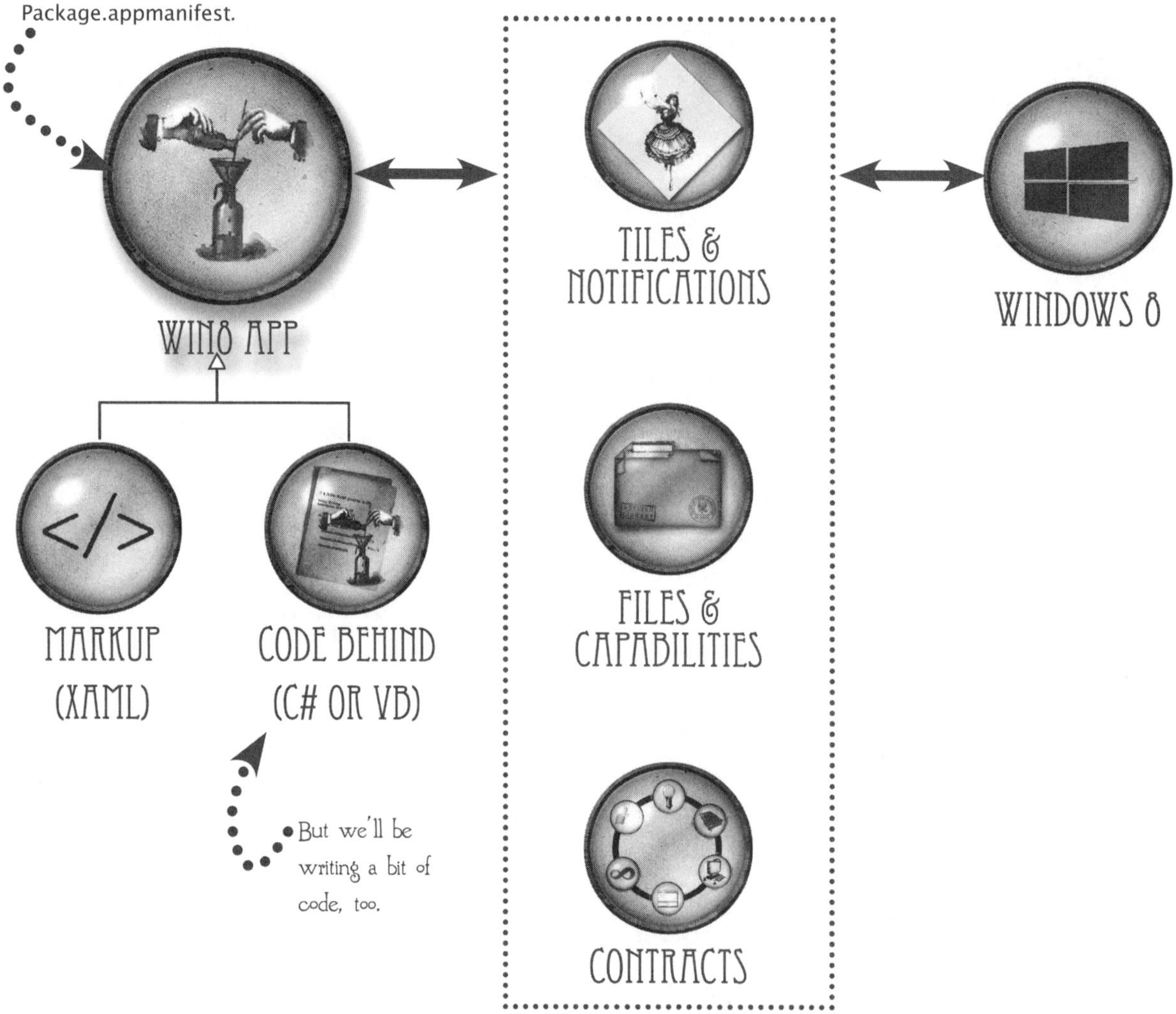

WIN8 APP

MARKUP (XAML)

CODE BEHIND (C# OR VB)

But we'll be writing a bit of code, too.

TILES & NOTIFICATIONS

FILES & CAPABILITIES

CONTRACTS

WINDOWS 8

TASK LIST

In this chapter we'll explore the ways your app can communicate with the user outside the app canvas, via tiles, toast notifications, and message dialogs.

PRIMARY TILES

We'll start by exploring the primary Start Menu tiles, the most iconic aspect of the Win8 interface. (And yes, *of course* the pun was intended.)

SECONDARY TILES

All apps have a primary tile, but it's up to you to decide whether it's appropriate for your app to also allow users to pin additional locations within your app to the Start Menu. If you do, you'll find out how in this section.

NOTIFICATIONS

Creating default tiles is all very well, but when you start updating them by sending them notifications, they start to get fun. We'll look at that process in this section, along with the Toast notifications that let you communicate whether or not your app is in the foreground.

PRIMARY TILES

Your app needs to have at least one tile: a square image that will represent it on the Start Menu. But tiles are an important part of Win8, or at least they can be, and Win8 gives you a lot of options beyond the default square tile:

Tiles come in either square or wide formats. (The square version comes in three sizes.) Your app is only required to provide the medium-sized square version, but if you provide multiple versions, the user gets to decide which one is displayed on the Start Menu. Primary tiles are static images.

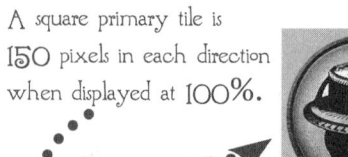

A square primary tile is 150 pixels in each direction when displayed at 100%.

The basic wide tile is 310 pixels wide and 150 pixels tall at 100%.

The basic primary tile is static. If you want it to come alive, you can send tile updates. We'll find out how to do that at the end of this chapter.

You choose a tile notification from a catalog. It can contain images, text and, optionally, the app logo.

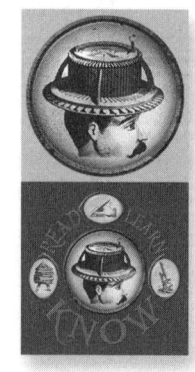

A notification can also contain a BADGE, which could be a number or a glyph.

IMAGE ASSETS

So...you've already created three different images for your splash screen, and now Win8 is asking for.... thirty-two more? Seriously? Yeah, seriously. But hey, you can always use that ugly little gray square that Visual Studio provides as a default, if you really want that to represent your app to users. (But it won't pass certification.)

		180%	140%	100%	80%
Square70x70Logo	Small Tile	126x126	98x98	70x70	56x56
Square150x150Logo	Medium Tile	270x270	210x210	150x150	120x120
Wide310x150Logo	Wide Tile	558x270	434x210	310x150	248x120
Square310x310Logo	Large Tile	558x558	434x434	310x310	248x248
Square30x30Logo	Small Logo—You'll also need to provide targeted assets for this one: 256x256, 48x48, 32x32, and 16x16	54x54	42x42	30x30	24x24
StoreLogo	Displayed in the app store	90x90	70x70	50x50	n/a
BadgeLogo	Displayed on the lock screen	43x43	33x33	24x24	n/a
SplashScreen	Displayed during activation	1116x540	868x420	620x300	n/a

The Visual Studio templates include blank assets for the Logo, Small Logo, Splash Screen, and Store Logo in the Assets folder. You'll want to replace those with actual images. I also recommend using core file names that match the specification in the Manifest Designer. It's just easier in the long run.

You have two options for naming your images: You can append a scale modifier (Square70x70Logo.scale-100.png, for example) to the file name and put them all in the Assets folder, or you can create subfolders and use the basic file type names (Assets\Scale-140\Logo.png, for example).

Note that the file association assets, which are specified along with Square30x30Logo assets in the Manifest Designer, use a different naming convention: They should have the same core name as the Square30x30Logo, but the extension targetsize-size. So, for example, the smallest would be SmallLogo.targetsize-16.png and be 16 pixels square. (We'll explore these in more detail in the next chapter.)

In a minute we'll look at how to specify the background color that your app will use. When you're creating your logo assets, it's generally best to make the background transparent so that it will display on that standard color. Saves you having to change a whole bunch of files if you want to tweak the background color.

THE VISUAL ASSETS TAB

You'll specify your images and other visual aspecst of your app on the Visual Assets tab of the Manifest Designer inside Visual Studio. (You can also specify them directly in the `Package.appxmanifest` file if you want to use a text editor like Notepad, but there's no particular reason to.)

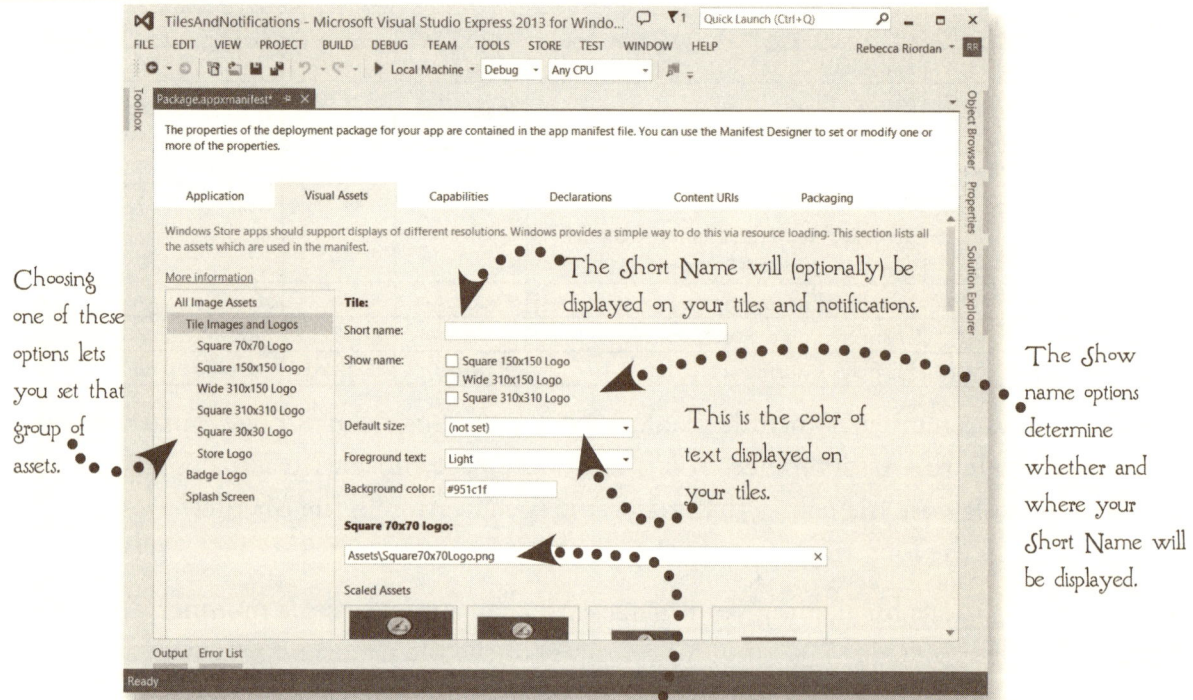

Choosing one of these options lets you set that group of assets.

The Short Name will (optionally) be displayed on your tiles and notifications.

The Show name options determine whether and where your Short Name will be displayed.

This is the color of text displayed on your tiles.

The easiest way to set your assets is to specify the folder and core name (without the scale extension) here.

MAKE A NOTE

In theory, you can specify any files you want for the image assets at various scales, and Visual Studio will rename them for you. In reality, while it does copy and rename your files, it doesn't work very well—it will only accept a single file at a time. I strongly recommend that you name your assets using the appropriate conventions from the beginning.

PUT ON YOUR THINKING HAT

Let's create an app with some custom image assets. There's an asset pack included in the sample code, or you can create your own (one for each tile size) if you like.

0. Create a new blank project (I called mine **TilesAndNotifications**), and replace **MainPage.xaml** with a new Basic page so that Visual Studio will add the support files. (You don't need the support files to work with tiles, but we'll use them later in the chapter.)

1. Delete the default images that the template provides, and add the assets from the sample project (or the ones that you've created yourself) to the project Assets folder.

2. In the Manifest Designer, tell Visual Studio not to show the app name.

3. Leave the default Light Background text color value, but set the Background color to **#951c1f**.

4. If you use the assets I've provided, or if you use the naming conventions I suggest, you'll need to specify the base file names in the Manifest Designer.

5. Run the app and check the Wide and Square logos. Are they correct? If you need to make changes, you'll need to uninstall the app to get the new images to display.

MAKE A NOTE

When you create your own assets, you may have to fiddle around with compression settings to avoid having files that exceed the maximum allowable by Visual Studio. A png-8 file will work in all cases, but a png-24 won't, for example.

HOW'D YOU DO?

Personally, I find creating the images kind of fun, but assigning them in the Manifest Designer is just a little tedious. Fortunately, you only have to do it once…

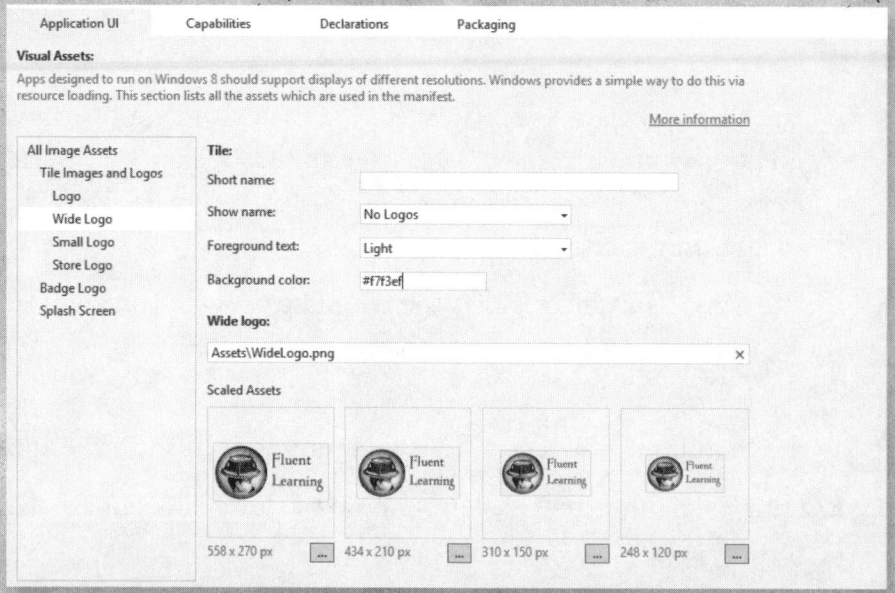

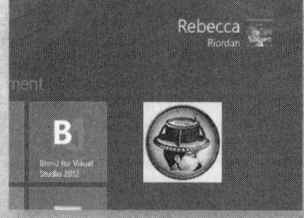

SECONDARY TILES

Your app must have a primary tile that leads users to the main page of your application. If it's appropriate for your app, you can also allow users to create secondary tiles that lead to other pages. Secondary tiles work pretty much the same as primary tiles—they have square and wide versions, and you can update them using the same techniques (only the method names are changed to protect the innocents)—but they're created (and removed) at the user's discretion, and you create them in code rather than via the manifest.

CREATE THE PINNING UI

Since it's up to the user to create a secondary tile, you need to expose some UI for them to make that happen. You'll almost always do that via an **AppBar** button (although we won't in our sample app), and if you're using the default styling, there are **AppBarButton** icons for both pinning and unpinning.

CREATE THE TILE

When the user initiates a pinning operation, you'll need to instantiate a **SecondaryTile** and assign its required properties.

REQUEST THE PIN

You must call one of the methods of **SecondaryTile** that allow the user to confirm that they want to create the tile.

RESPOND TO THE SECONDARY TILE

Of course, the whole point of a secondary tile is that it takes the user to someplace other than the main page, so you'll have to update the **OnLaunched()** method to respond to the arguments the secondary tile will pass to it.

THE SECONDARYTILE CLASS

After the work you've been doing with splash screens and tile updates, most of the properties and methods of the SecondaryTile class will probably seem familiar. Here's the class definition:

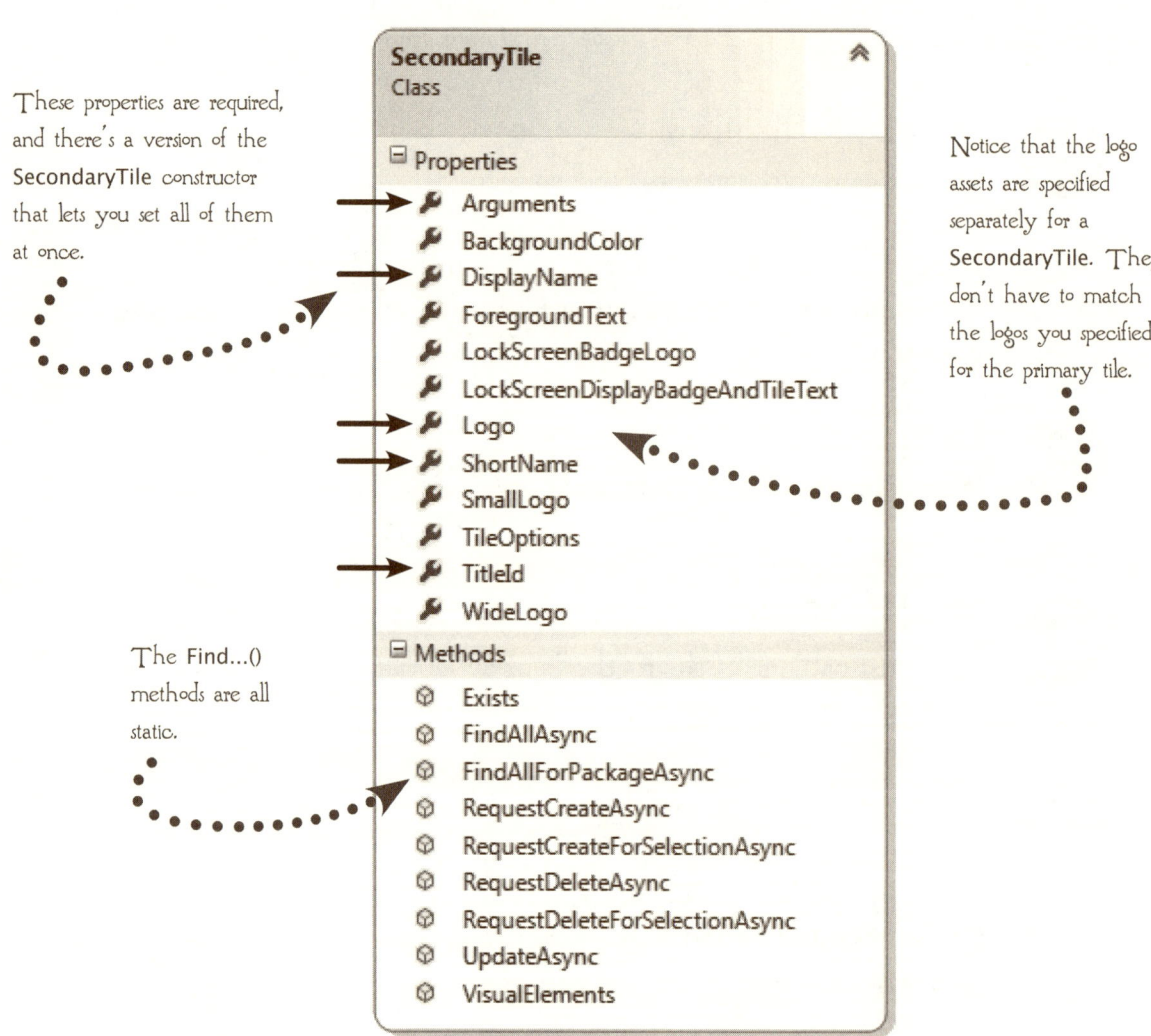

These properties are required, and there's a version of the SecondaryTile constructor that lets you set all of them at once.

Notice that the logo assets are specified separately for a SecondaryTile. They don't have to match the logos you specified for the primary tile.

The Find...() methods are all static.

PUT ON YOUR THINKING HAT

Based on what you already know about how tiles and notifications work, can you figure out the answers to these questions about the properties and methods of SecondaryTile? (Checking MSDN isn't cheating, exactly, but see what you can figure out on your own. It's okay if you guess wrong.)

Which property do you think uniquely identifies the tile?

Which property do you think represents the image that will be displayed on a square tile?

Which property represents the image on a wide tile?

The contents of the Arguments property are passed to the OnLaunched() method. How do you think you might use them?

Microsoft recommends that you enumerate all of an app's secondry tiles on start-up. What method do you think you'd use to do that? Why do you think they recommend that you do it?

What do you think the UpdateAsync() method does?

HOW'D YOU DO?

What matters is that you thought about the questions, not whether you got the "correct" answers. I asked you to guess here, and guesses can't really be right or wrong—they're just guesses.

Which property do you think uniquely identifies the tile?

> TileId uniquely identifies your app.

Which property do you think represents the image that will be displayed on a square tile?

> The Logo property contains a URI to the image for the square tile.

Which property represents the image on a wide tile?

> Well, if Logo represents the square tile, it stands to reason that WideLogo represents the wide tile, right? (Not that you can always trust that property name conventions will work that way.)

The contents of the Arguments property are passed to the OnLaunched() method. How do you think you might use them?

> Some secondary tiles, like the one we're about to create, just lead to a particular page. Others will lead to particular content on that page. You would typically use the tile's Arguments property to indicate which content to display.

Microsoft recommends that you enumerate all of an app's secondry tiles on start-up. What method do you think you'd use to do that? Why do you think they recommend that you do it?

> You won't be notified if a user unpins a tile from the Start Menu, even if your app is running. If your secondary tiles use any resources (custom images, or scheduled notifications, for example), you need to check that they're still needed.

What do you think the UpdateAsync() method does?

> You might have guessed that it sends a notification, like the Update() methods we've been working with, but in fact the SecondaryTile.Update() method is used to update all the properties of the SecondaryTile except the DisplayName, ShortName, and TileId.

ELEMENT RECTANGLES

The SecondaryTile class exposes two different creation methods, RequestCreateAsync() and RequestCreateForSelectionAsync(), but Microsoft recommends that you always use the second version, which allows you to specify the position of the confirmation dialog and, optionally, a relative placement. Before we start creating our tile, there's a little bit of housekeeping to take care of, in order to generate that placement information:

The **Rect** structure that you pass to the RequestCreateForSelectionAsync() method should be the bounding box of the element that triggers the pin request. In order to create it, you'll need to use some black box transformation code. Here it is:

```csharp
public static Rect GetElementRect(FrameworkElement element)
{
    GeneralTransform t = element.TransformToVisual(null);
    Point p = t.TransformPoint(new Point());
    return new Rect(p, new Size(element.ActualWidth, element.ActualHeight));
}
```

PUT ON YOUR THINKING HAT

Feeling brave? Do you think you have enough to go on? (I hope so.) Create a secondary tile. You'll need to:

- Add a second page to the sample app and a **Button** to the **MainPage** that navigates to it. (Any type of **Page** will do, but I used the Basic Page template.)
- Add a **Button** to the second page that pins a secondary tile. (You can build an **AppBar** if you want to, but it isn't necessary.) You *will* need to specify all of the required fields (use the name of your page as the **TileId**). You'll need to add a reference to **Windows.UI.StartScreen** to have access to the **SecondaryTile** class.

HOW'D YOU DO?

You should be proud of yourself if you got this working without peeking. I really didn't give you much to go on, so it's a measure of how much you've learned. (But don't feel bad if you did peek. Like I said, I didn't give you much to go on.)

```csharp
private async void PinButton_Click(...)
{
    SecondaryTile pageTile = new SecondaryTile("SecondaryPage");
    pageTile.DisplayName = "Secondary page";
    pageTile.Arguments = "SecondaryPage";
    pageTile.VisualElements.Square150x150Logo =
        new Uri("ms-appx:///Assets/Logo.png");
    pageTile.TileID = "Tiles&Notifications.SecondaryPage";

    Rect showRect = GetElementRect((FrameworkElement)(this.PinButton));
    bool Pinned = await pageTile.RequestCreateForSelectionAsync(showRect,
        Windows.UI.Popups.Placement.Right);
}
```

I set the properties separately for clarity, but you could have passed most of these to the constructor.

```vb
Private Async Sub Button_Click(...)
    Dim pageTile As SecondaryTile = New SecondaryTile("SecondaryPage")
    pageTile.DisplayName = "Secondary page"
    pageTile.Arguments = "Secondary page"
    pageTile.VisualElements.Square150x150Logo =
        New Uri("ms-appx:///Assets/Square150x150Logo.png")
    pageTile.TileId = "Tiles&Notifications.SecondaryPage"

    Dim showRect As Rect = GetElementRect(DirectCast(Me.PinButton, FrameworkElement))
    Dim Pinned As Boolean = Await pageTile.RequestCreateForSelectionAsync(showRect,
                                    Windows.UI.Popups.Placement.Right)
End Sub
```

RESPONDING TO ACTIVATION

The whole point of a secondary tile is to take the user directly to some point in your app other than the main page, so of course you'll need to handle the activation in the OnLaunched() method.

In a real app you'll need to think carefully about exactly how you set up your TileId and Arguments properties so that you can respond correctly to a secondary tile activation. (Both of these properties are available to OnLaunched() in the LaunchActivatedEventArgs that it receives.)

In our simple little exercise, we set the TileId to the name of the type (namespace. objectName). Since we're only loading the page, it's sufficient to pass the page name in the TileId, and we don't really need the Arguments (but they're required). In a more complex app, the user might want to pin a page multiple times showing different content, so you'd need a different way of creating a TileId and passing a content reference in the Arguments. It all depends on what your app does and what functionality you want to expose to your users.

PUT ON YOUR THINKING HAT

Update the OnLaunched() method to respond to activation via the secondary tile. You'll need to edit the bit of code that currently navigates to the MainPage.

In our case, you can use a fairly simple if statement—if the app is launched from the primary tile, the TileId will be "App"; anything else is a secondary tile.

HINT: You can get a type from a string by calling the static Type.GetType() method.

HOW'D YOU DO?

Here's my version. As always, it doesn't matter if you used a different technique, as long as it works.

```csharp
protected async override void OnLaunched(...)
{
   ...
   if (rootFrame.Content == null)
   {
      if (e.TileId == "App")
         rootFrame.Navigate(typeof(MainPage));
      else
      {
         Type pageType = Type.GetType(e.TileId);
         rootFrame.Navigate(pageType);
      }
      ...
   }
}
```

```vb
Protected Overrides Async Sub OnLaunched(...)
    ...
    If rootFrame.Content Is Nothing Then
        If e.TileId = "App" Then
            rootFrame.Navigate(GetType(MainPage), e.Arguments)
        Else
            Dim pageType As Type = Type.GetType(e.TileId)
            rootFrame.Navigate(pageType)
        End If
    End If
    ...
End Sub
```

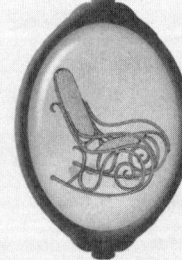

TAKE A BREAK

Why don't you take a break now before you complete the Review and we move on to sending notifications?

REVIEW

Can you answer the following questions based on what you've learned?

Where do you define the image assets for your apps default tile?

How is the app's small logo used by Windows?

Where do you typically put the UI for pinning a secondary tile?

What will the LaunchActivatedEventArgs.TileId property be if the app is launched via a primary or secondary tile?

What happens to the contents of the SecondaryTile.Arguments property when an app is launched via that tile?

Is there a standard pattern for responding to launching via a secondary tile?

NOTIFICATIONS

I'm sure that you've noticed by now that Windows 8 places a lot of constraints on how you interact with the user's system. You have (more or less) complete control over your app canvas, but any other kind of interactions need to follow some pretty strict rules. One set of rules controls how you send notifications to the user. There are only three ways:

You can send a TILE NOTIFICATION to change the contents of a tile.

You can send a BADGE NOTIFICATION to add a number or glyph to a tile.

You can send a TOAST NOTIFICATION to display a message at the top of the screen.

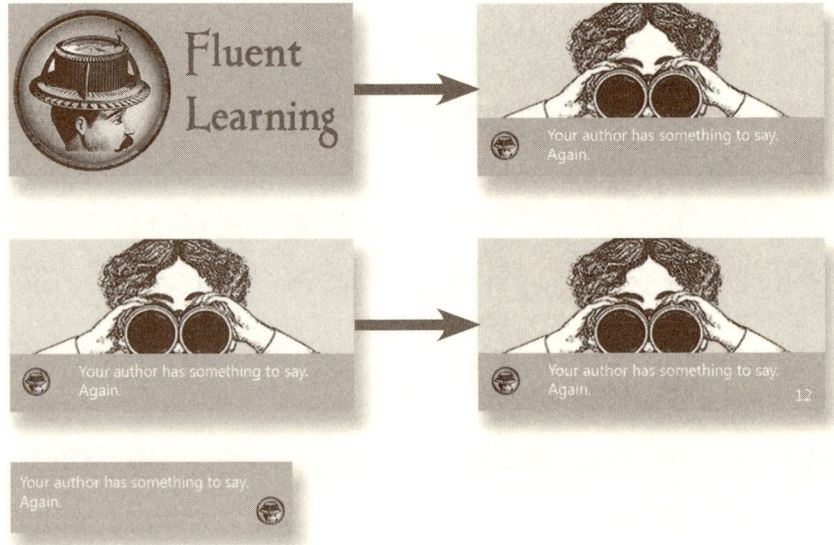

Win8 provides XML templates (XML, not XAML—this all happens in code) for each of these notification types that constrain both the layout and content. You can provide your own images and text to these notifications, choose a background and foreground color, but that's about it. Even the sound that Windows plays when a toast notification is displayed must come from a pre-defined list.

DELIVERY METHODS

There are only three types of notifications, but they can be delivered in four different ways:

LOCAL NOTIFICATIONS
Local notifications are sent by your application and delivered immediately. The APIs for all of the notifications are similar, but local notifications are logistically simplest (they don't require a server or waiting around for the notification to be delivered), so they're the ones we'll be working with.

SCHEDULED NOTIFICATIONS
Scheduled notifications are local notifications that are delivered by the operating system at the time specified, rather than immediately, and your app doesn't need to be running.

PERIODIC NOTIFICATIONS
As you might expect, periodic notifications are sent on a regular schedule by the operating system. Like scheduled notifications, your app doesn't need to be running for periodic notifications to be delivered.

PUSH NOTIFICATIONS
Push notifications are initiated outside your application by a cloud server using the Windows Push Notification Service (WNS).

MAKE A NOTE
Push notifications aren't dependent on the state of your application. The other methods are generally only available when your app is running, but you can launch a background task that can update a tile or send a notification when the app is terminated. There's nothing different about the way the notifications are generated, just the way they're triggered.

TILE NOTIFICATIONS

As with other areas where your app interacts with the operating system UI, Microsoft doesn't give you much freedom regarding the design of your tile updates. You can choose the text and images that are displayed, but you must display them using one of the pre-defined XML tile templates. The basic process looks like this:

RETRIEVE A TEMPLATE

The first step is to retrieve one of the pre-defined templates using the **TileUpdateManager.GetTemplateContent(<type>)** method, where <type> is one of the pre-defined templates. (You can see examples of each template on MSDN if you search for "tile catalog".)

By the way, the **TileUpdateManager**, like other notification classes, is defined in the **Windows.UI.Notifications** namespace, and you'll want to add a reference to it in your class file. You'll also need a reference to Windows.Data.Xml.Dom for the XML methods.

SET THE TEMPLATE CONTENTS

The **GetTemplateContent()** method returns an instance of **XmlDocument**. Once you have a reference to it, you can call the **GetElementsByTagName("tag")** method to retrieve an **XmlNodeList** of the type of contents specified.

Once you have the **XmlNodeList**, you use the methods of the **XmlElement** class to set the attributes of each element. (Don't panic if you're not an XML wiz. I'll show you examples of the kinds of things you'll need to do for tile notifications in a minute.)

The available tags are:

- tile—the base tile element
- binding—the template
- visual—the container for bindings
- text—one or more text elements to be displayed on the tile
- image—one or more image elements to be displayed on the tile

③ REPEAT FOR WIDE/SQUARE

Best practice is to include both a square and a wide tile in your notification. (Microsoft calls it a NOTIFICATION PAYLOAD.) So after you have your first template configured, you'll need to repeat the process with the other size. (It doesn't matter which size you start with.)

④ APPEND THE OTHER SIZE

Once you have the second tile configured, you'll import it into the XmlDocument that represents the original tile and then add it to the visual tag. (And I'll show you how to do this, too.)

⑤ CREATE A NEW TILE NOTIFICATION

Now that your tile is ready to go, your next step is to create an instance of either a TileNotification or a ScheduledTileNotification, passing the tile to the constructor and setting whatever properties are appropriate in your situation.

⑥ SEND THE NOTIFICATION

And finally, you'll send the notification using one of the methods in the TileUpdater class. (You'll need to choose the correct version of the StartPeriodicUpdate...() method for the size of tile you're using.)

NAVIGATING THE DOM

No matter your choice of development platform, if you've been developing for any length of time, the chances are very good that you've bumped up against XML. Probably more than once. But it doesn't follow that you know—or want to learn—the ins and outs of navigating the XML Document Object Model (DOM). So to save you some angst, here are somde examples (without a whole lot of explanation) of the tasks you'll need to perform in creating a tile.

TO RETRIEVE A TILE TEMPLATE

Use the static **TileUpdateManager.GetTemplateContent()** method, passing in the member of the **TileTemplateType** enumeration that corresponds to the template you want:

```C#
XmlDocument wideTile =
    TileUpdateManager.GetTemplateContent(TileTemplateType.TileWide310x150ImageAndText02);
```

TO SET A TEXT ATTRIBUTE

To set a text attribute, you first call **GetElementsByTagName("text")**, and then set the **InnerText** attribute of the element:

The tile schema docs talk about text (and image) attributes having ids, but from C# or VB you'll just index into the node list.

```C#
XmlNodeList textNodes = wideTile.GetElementsByTagName("text");
textNodes[0].InnerText = "this is my text";
```

TO SET AN IMAGE ATTRIBUTE

You should set two attributes for an image: the source ("src") and the alternate text ("alt"). You'll need to set the source to a Uri, so use http:// or https:// for a web-based image, ms-appx:/// for an image that's part of the app package (as ours are), or ms-appdata:///local/ for local storage:

```csharp
XmlNodeList imageNodes = wideTile.GetElementsByTagName("image");
((XmlElement)imageNodes[0]).SetAttribute("src", "ms-appx:///assets/WideTileImage.png");
((XmlElement)imageNodes[0]).SetAttribute("alt", "description of image");
```

TO TURN BRANDING ON AND OFF

One of the attributes of the binding element is branding, which controls whether Windows displays the logo or name of the app (or neither) on the tile. You control it using the SetAttribute() method:

```csharp
XmlNodeList binding = wideTile.GetElementsByTagName("binding");
((XmlElement)binding[0]).SetAttribute("branding", "none");
```

NAVIGATING THE DOM, CONT.

Just a few more operations, and only one of them actually uses the DOM.

APPENDING THE SECOND FORMAT

You'll use the examples on the previous couple of pages to retrieve and configure your tiles, but there's one last bit of syntax you'll need: adding the second tile format to your notification payload. Here it is:

```csharp
IXmlNode node = wideTile.ImportNode(binding[0], true);
wideTile.GetElementsByTagName("visual").Item(0).AppendChild(node);
```

CREATING THE NOTIFICATION OBJECT

The **Windows.UI.Notifications** namespace defines several types of notification objects. For creating tile updates, you'll need either a basic **TileNotification** or a **ScheduledTileNotification**. You'll need to pass your tile **XmlDocument** to both of them, and **ScheduledTileNotification** also requires a **DateTimeOffset** indicating when to deliver the update.

```csharp
TileNotification tn = new TileNotification(wideTile);
```

SEND THE UPDATE

And you're finally ready to actually update the tile, using the Update() method of the TileUpdater object returned by TileUpdateManager.CreateTileUpdaterForApplication() method for primary tiles or the CreateTileUpdaterForSecondaryTile() method for secondary tiles.

```csharp
TileUpdateManager.CreateTileUpdaterForApplication().Update(tn);
```

PUT ON YOUR THINKING HAT

Using the example syntax I've shown you in the last few pages as boilerplate, can you add square and wide tile updates to your app?

Add a Button to the MainPage.xaml to trigger the update, and configure the tiles and send the notification from the Click event handler.

I used the TileWide310x150ImageAndText04 and TileSquare150x150PeekImageAndText04 template, but you can choose any templates you like—the process of configuring them is the same.

HOW'D YOU DO?

Here's my version:

```csharp
private void Button_Click(object sender, RoutedEventArgs e)
{
    XmlDocument wideTile =
        TileUpdateManager.GetTemplateContent(TileTemplateType.TileWide310x150ImageAndText02);
    XmlNodeList textNodes = wideTile.GetElementsByTagName("text");
    textNodes[0].InnerText = "Your author has something to say.";
    textNodes[1].InnerText = "Again.";
    XmlNodeList imageNodes = wideTile.GetElementsByTagName("image");
    ((XmlElement)imageNodes[0]).SetAttribute("src", "ms-appx:///assets/WideTileImage.png");
    ((XmlElement)imageNodes[0]).SetAttribute("alt", "your author");
    XmlNodeList binding = wideTile.GetElementsByTagName("binding");
    ((XmlElement)binding[0]).SetAttribute("branding", "logo");

    XmlDocument squareTile =
        TileUpdateManager.GetTemplateContent(TileTemplateType.TileSquare150x150PeekImageAndText04);
    textNodes = squareTile.GetElementsByTagName("text");
    textNodes[0].InnerText = "Your author has something to say. Again.";
    imageNodes = squareTile.GetElementsByTagName("image");
    ((XmlElement)imageNodes[0]).SetAttribute("src", "ms-appx:///assets/SquareTileImage.png");
    ((XmlElement)imageNodes[0]).SetAttribute("alt", "your author");
    binding = squareTile.GetElementsByTagName("binding");
    ((XmlElement)binding[0]).SetAttribute("branding", "none");

    IXmlNode node = wideTile.ImportNode(binding[0], true);
    wideTile.GetElementsByTagName("visual").Item(0).AppendChild(node);

    TileNotification tn = new TileNotification(wideTile);
    TileUpdateManager.CreateTileUpdaterForApplication().Update(tn);
}
```

```vb
Private Sub Button_Click_1(sender As Object, e As RoutedEventArgs)
    Dim wideTile As XmlDocument =
        TileUpdateManager.GetTemplateContent(TileTemplateType.TileWide310x150ImageAndText02)
    Dim textNodes As XmlNodeList = wideTile.GetElementsByTagName("text")
    textNodes(0).InnerText = "Your author has something to say"
    textNodes(1).InnerText = "Again"
    Dim imageNodes As XmlNodeList = wideTile.GetElementsByTagName("image")
    Dim node As XmlElement = DirectCast(imageNodes(0), XmlElement)
    node.SetAttribute("src", "ms-appx:///Assets/Wide310x150Logo.png")
    node.SetAttribute("alt", "your author")
    Dim binding As XmlNodeList = wideTile.GetElementsByTagName("binding")
    node = DirectCast(binding(0), XmlElement)
    node.SetAttribute("branding", "logo")

    Dim squareTile As XmlDocument =
        TileUpdateManager.GetTemplateContent(TileTemplateType.TileWide310x150ImageAndText02)
    textNodes = squareTile.GetElementsByTagName("text")
    textNodes(0).InnerText = "Your author has something to say. Again."
    imageNodes = squareTile.GetElementsByTagName("image")
    node = DirectCast(imageNodes(0), XmlElement)
    node.SetAttribute("src", "ms-appx:///Assets/Square30x30Logo.png")
    node.SetAttribute("alt", "your author")
    binding = squareTile.GetElementsByTagName("binding")
    node = DirectCast(binding(0), XmlElement)
    node.SetAttribute("branding", "none")

    Dim bindingNode As IXmlNode = wideTile.ImportNode(binding(0), True)
    wideTile.GetElementsByTagName("visual").Item(0).AppendChild(bindingNode)

    Dim tn As TileNotification = New TileNotification(wideTile)
    TileUpdateManager.CreateTileUpdaterForApplication().Update(tn)
End Sub
```

BADGE NOTIFICATIONS

In Win8 terms, badges are actually a special kind of tile update that lets you place a glyph or a number in the lower-right corner of a tile (lower-left corner if the operating system reads right-to-left). The process for creating badges is almost identical to that for creating tile updates; only the names are changed to protect the innocent:

RETRIEVE THE TEMPLATE

Again, you'll want to add references to the **Windows.UI.Notifications** and **Windows.Data.Xml.Dom**, and then you'll call the **BadgeUpdateManager.GetTemplateContent()** method which, like the corresponding **TileUpdateManager**, accepts an instance of an enum, in this case the **BadgeTemplateType**. The enum only supports two possible values: **BadgeNumber** and **BadgeGlyph**.

SET THE BADGE VALUE

Badges are simpler animals than tile updates, and the templates only contain a single instance of a single node type, so you can use the **SetSingleNode** method instead of the **GetElementsByTagName()** method:

```
XmlElement badgeElement = (XmlElement)badgeXml.SelectSingleNode("/badge");
badgeElement.SetAttribute("value", "paused");
```

CREATE AND SEND THE UPDATE

Again, only the names have changed: You'll create a **BadgeNotification** and call the **CreateBadgeUpdaterForApplication()** method of the **BadgeUpdateManger**, but otherwise the syntax is identical to the corresponding **TileNotification** objects and methods.

AVAILABLE GLYPHS

As with tile updates, Microsoft keeps a pretty tight reign on badge updates, and your options for glyphs are limited: you can display a number or one of the glyphs provided by the operating system. Here are the glyph values that are available to your template if you choose a `BadgeGlyph` template:

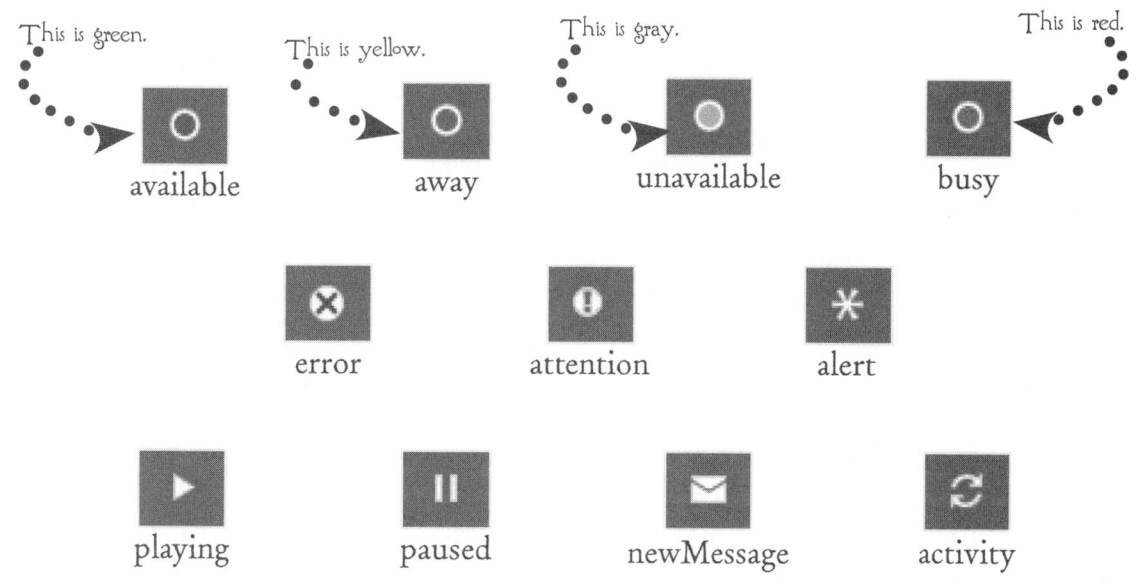

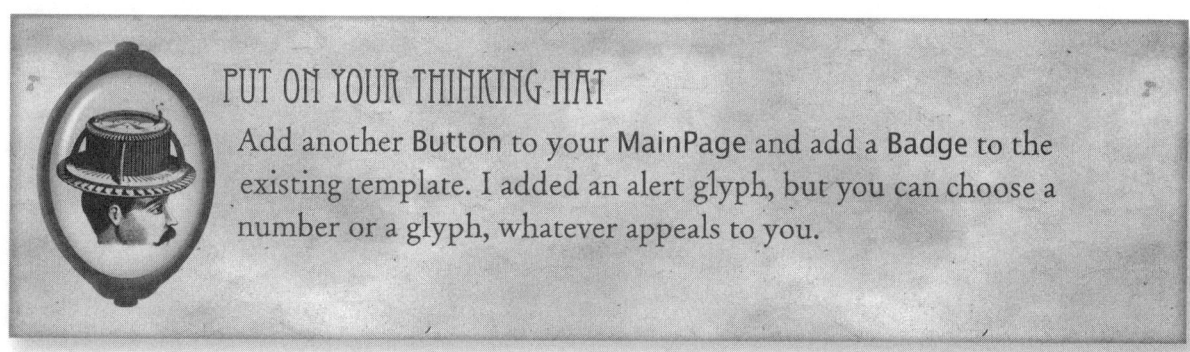

PUT ON YOUR THINKING HAT

Add another **Button** to your **MainPage** and add a **Badge** to the existing template. I added an alert glyph, but you can choose a number or a glyph, whatever appeals to you.

PUT ON YOUR THINKING HAT
How'd you do?

```csharp
private void BadgeButton_Click(object sender, RoutedEventArgs e)
{
    XmlDocument badgeXml =
        BadgeUpdateManager.GetTemplateContent(BadgeTemplateType.BadgeGlyph);
    XmlElement badgeElement = (XmlElement)badgeXml.SelectSingleNode("/badge");
    badgeElement.SetAttribute("value", "alert");

    BadgeNotification bn = new BadgeNotification(badgeXml);
    BadgeUpdateManager.CreateBadgeUpdaterForApplication().Update(bn);
}
```

```vb
Private Sub BadgeButton_Click(sender As Object, e As RoutedEventArgs)
    Dim badgeXML As XmlDocument =
        BadgeUpdateManager.GetTemplateContent(BadgeTemplateType.BadgeGlyph)
    Dim badgeElement As XmlElement =
        DirectCast(badgeXML.SelectSingleNode("/badge"), XmlElement)
    badgeElement.SetAttribute("value", "alert")

    Dim bn As BadgeNotification = New BadgeNotification(badgeXML)
    BadgeUpdateManager.CreateBadgeUpdaterForApplication().Update(bn)
End Sub
```

Toast Notifications

One of the nice things about working with a well-designed framework—and even though it drives me to destraction on occasion, .NET is well designed—is that once you learn a pattern, you'll find it applied in similar situations throughout the framework. It's theme and variations, of course, and every implementation of the pattern will have minor variations, but it still makes the learning curve just a little less steep. By way of review, here's the pattern we're working with:

Use a Manager to Retrieve a Template

You'll use the manager class that matches the kind of notification you want to send, and you'll pass a member of the appropriate enumeration to the GetTemplateContent() method.

Configure the Template

The GetTemplateContent() method returns an XmlDocument, and you'll use the methods declared in the Windows.Data.Xml.Dom namespace to configure its attributes.

Create a Notification

Create an instance of the type of notification you need to send.

Create an Updater and Send the Notification

Again, using the correct classes for the type of notification, you'll create an updater and call its Update() method, passing in the notification you created in Step 3.

TOAST CAPABILITIES

Did I mention theme and variations? The first difference between toast notifications and the updates we've been exploring is that you need to tell Windows that your application is going to be issuing toast notifications. We've used the Manifest designer to specify tile and splash screen images, and we'll talk about declaring capabilities in the next chapter, but here's your first taste:

By default, the toast notifications property in the Application tab will be "(not set)". You need to set it to "Yes" before your notifications will be displayed.

CREATING TOAST NOTIFICATIONS

You've probably already figured out that when you create a toast notification you'll need to use the objects that are specific to toast notifications: `ToastNotificationManager`, for example, instead of `TileNotificationManager`. And, of course, you'll need one of the toast templates (you can find the catalog on MSDN if you search for "toast catalog". But there's one other minor difference: Instead of using a `TileUpdater` or `BadgeUpdater`, you use a `ToastNotifier` that exposes a `Show()` method instead of an `Update()` method:

You're not updating anything, so it makes sense that you're working with a "notifier" rather than an "updater".

```
ToastNotificationManager.CreateToastNotifier().Show(toastNotification)
```

Since it's not an update, you just want to Show() a toast.

PUT ON YOUR THINKING HAT

I bet you know what I'm going to ask you do do next: Add (yet another) `Button` to the `MainPage` of our sample app and display a toast notification when it's clicked.

You can pick out a template from the toast template catalog or just use `ToastText01` like I did. `ToastText01` has a single text attribute, and you'll use the `InnerText` syntax you used with tile notifications to update it.

Remember to update the package manifest, or you'll spend a lot of time debugging something that isn't broken. (Yes, I made that mistake, but only once.)

Oh, one more thing: Toast notifications don't work inside the simulator. You'll need to test your app on the local machine.

HOW'D YOU DO?

Here's my version. Did you pick a different template?

```csharp
private void ToastButton_Click(...)
{
    XmlDocument toastXml =
        ToastNotificationManager.GetTemplateContent(ToastTemplateType.ToastText01);
    XmlNodeList textNodes = toastXml.GetElementsByTagName("text");
    textNodes[0].InnerText = "Your author has something to say. Again.";

    ToastNotification tn = new ToastNotification(toastXML);
    ToastNotificationManager.CreateToastNotifier().Show(tn);
}
```

```vb
Private Sub ToastButton_Click(sender As Object, e As RoutedEventArgs)
    Dim toastXml As XmlDocument =
        ToastNotificationManager.GetTemplateContent(ToastTemplateType.ToastText01)
    Dim textNodes As XmlNodeList = toastXml.GetElementsByTagName("text")
    textNodes(0).InnerText = "Your author has something to say. Again."

    Dim tn As ToastNotification = New ToastNotification(toastXml)
    ToastNotificationManager.CreateToastNotifier().Show(tn)
End Sub
```

TOAST AUDIO

When you displayed your toast notification, Windows played a default notification sound. You can change the default sound to one of the others in the audio catalog (search for "toast audio"), but in order to do so you must create and add an audio node explicitly:

The audio node has two attributes: src and loop.

You need to preface the sound you pick from the catalog with "ms-winsoundevent:" It's kinda sorta like specifying a URI.

```
IXmlNode toastNode = toastXml.SelectSingleNode("/toast");

XmlElement audio = toastXml.CreateElement("audio");
audio.SetAttribute("src", "ms-winsoundevent:Notification.IM");
audio.SetAttribute("loop", "false");
toastNode.AppendChild(audio);
```

You must set the loop attribute to the value specified in the catalog. (It doesn't actually change behavior.)

MAKE A NOTE:
Beware of the documentation for the audio attribute! As of this writing, well over a year after the problem was brought to Microsoft's attention, much of the documentation is still incorrect.

Although included in the schema documentation, the audio element does not exist in the toast template. Despite the fact that the audio catalog shows (Javascript) examples of GetElementsByTagName("audio"), these will not work. You must use the CreateElement() and AppendChild() methods shown here to control the sound your toast notification makes when it is displayed.

589

OTHER TOAST ATTRIBUTES

In order to control the sound that Windows plays when it displays your toast notification, you needed to get a reference to the **toast** node using the `SelectSingleNode()` method. Once you have that reference, there are two other attributes that you can set: `duration` and `launch`.

SETTING DURATION

The **duration** attribute controls how long the toast notification is displayed. By default, its value is **short**, which displays the notification for seven seconds. Setting the value to **long** displays the notification for 25 seconds and allows for looping audio. (You should only use long notifications if there's a person waiting for a response to the toast, like an IM or a phone call.)

```
IXmlNode toastNode = toastXml.SelectSingleNode("/toast");
...
((XmlElement)toastNode).SetAttribute("duration", "long")
```

SETTING LAUNCH ARGUMENTS

You may not have noticed, but toast notifications are clickable. It's a nice UX feature that makes it simple for users to respond to the notification. Of course, you need to respond appropriately in your OnLaunched() method, just as you do when your app is launched from a secondary tile.

When the user clicks a toast notification, the TileId will be "App", just as it is when the app is launched from its primary tile. So you'll need to rely on the LaunchActivateEventArgs.Arguments property, which you set in the launch attribute of the toast notification:

```
IXmlNode toastNode = toastXml.SelectSingleNode("/toast");
…
((XmlElement)toastNode).SetAttribute("launch", "launch arguments")
```

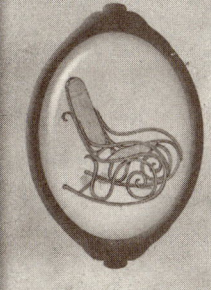

TAKE A BREAK

That's it for tiles and notifications. Why don't you take a break before you complete the Review and we move on to our exploration of files and capabilities?

REVIEW

Are secondary tiles represented by a class or an XML schema?

In what method should your app decide how to respond when it's launched from a secondary tile or toast notification?

What are the four canonical steps for creating and sending a notification?

A notification requires three classes: one to represent the notification itself, one to manage the notifications, and one to represent a single update. What are the names of these classes when you're working with badge notifications?

What are the names of these classes when you're working with toast notifications?

Can you use the GetElementsByTagType() method to configure the sound Windows plays when a toast notification is displayed?

Congratulations! You've finished the chapter. Take a minute to think about what you've accomplished before you move on to the next one...

List three things you learned in this chapter:

Why do you think you need to know these things in order to develop Win8 apps?

Is there anything in this chapter that you think you need to understand in more detail? If so, what are you going to do about that?

Files & Capabilities

16

In the last chapter we talked about interacting with the operating system to present the very top level of your app: its Start Screen tiles. In this chapter, we'll move to the very bottom, and explore how a Win8 app interacts with the operating system to access files and folders.

Before your app can access the **resources on the user's system**, you must explicitly declare your intention to do so in the app manifest. We've already worked with the manifest a little bit, and we'll explore it in more detail in this chapter; it's a simple matter of setting some checkboxes. And then, once the user installs your application, they're presented with a message asking them for permission the first time your app accesses a privileged resource. (No more worries about a game that secretly captures your laptop camera and broadcasts your bedroom to the Internet.) The app manifest is also how you **register file extensions** and **auto-play** capabilities, and we'll explore that here as well. Again, it's pretty simple, and the operating system makes it easy for the user to understand and control. We'll also explore the **FilePicker** and the **Windows Storage API** that gives you access to file data and metadata.

In addition to files that represent user data, Win8 provides powerful and easy-to-use mechanisms for storing data that is unique to your app—the kind of thing you might store in the Registry or the application folder in other platforms—and we'll spend most of this chapter exploring the application data API that allows you to store data as key/value pairs. It can be used to easily **store settings on the user's local machine**, and can also be used to automatically roam them so that your app can **maintain the user's context** wherever and whenever they log in. There's a limit to the amount of data you can store this way, but the operating system handles all the synchronization on your behalf. How cool is that?

FITTING IT IN

Here's how this chapter fits in to the book as a whole...

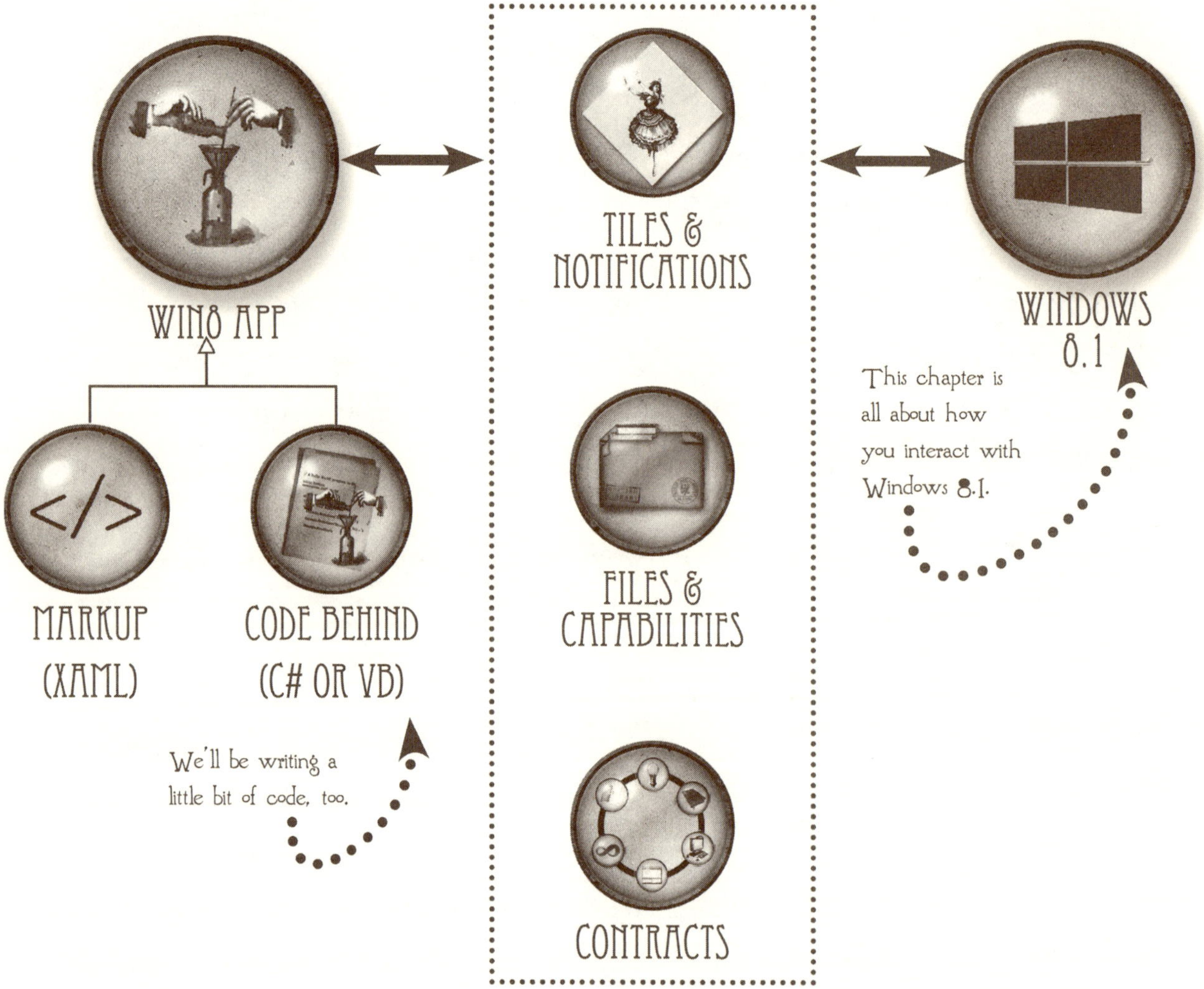

- **WIN8 APP**
  - **MARKUP (XAML)**
  - **CODE BEHIND (C# OR VB)**

We'll be writing a little bit of code, too.

- **TILES & NOTIFICATIONS**
- **FILES & CAPABILITIES**
- **CONTRACTS**

- **WINDOWS 8.1**

This chapter is all about how you interact with Windows 8.1.

TASK LIST

In this chapter we'll explore the objects and methods that Windows 8.1 provides for working with files and folders.

CAPABILITIES & DECLARATIONS

We'll start by taking another look at the package manifest that tells Windows what system resources (including files and folders) your app wants to use. Along the way, we'll see an example of opening a file in code.

FILE PICKERS

Once we've got our declarations sorted out, we'll look at the Picker classes that provide a UI for users to choose files and folders for your app to work with.

FILE ASSOCIATIONS

Next we'll look at the very simple mechanism for establishing a default file association so that your app will be loaded when a file is selected in the Explorer or Search Pane.

APPLICATION DATA

In addition to the user files that we worked with in the beginning of the chapter, your app might need to maintain data that belongs to it. We'll explore one way of storing that data, through the ApplicationDataContainer, next.

THE STORAGE API

Finally, we'll look at the Storage API and the classes and functions for working with files and folders that are unique to Windows 8.1. After all, you'll want to do something with those files once you have references to them, right?

Capabilities & Declarations

In order to increase the security of the operating system, Windows 8.1 limits your app's access to system resources, including storage locations. You must declare what you want to use, and before you can use them, you must obtain the user's permission.

By default, your app has access to files in the directory where it's installed, to the folder Windows creates for application data (we'll see how that works later in this chapter), and to the Downloads folder.

For programmatic access to any other resource or location, you must declare your app's intention to use the resource, and the user must grant permission to your app when it's first installed (and for some locations, every time the app runs):

The first time your app tries to use a restricted resource, Windows will display a prompt to the user requesting permission

Your app needs to deal with permission denied, even if that means displaying a message that says "Sorry, can't run."

WALK-THROUGH

Declaring your app capabilities is pretty straightforward, so to make things interesting, let's start by creating a little app that breaks the rules.

CREATE A PROJECT

Create a new Blank project, replace **MainPage.xaml** with a Basic page to get the support files (and the basic Page formatting), and build the core XAML.

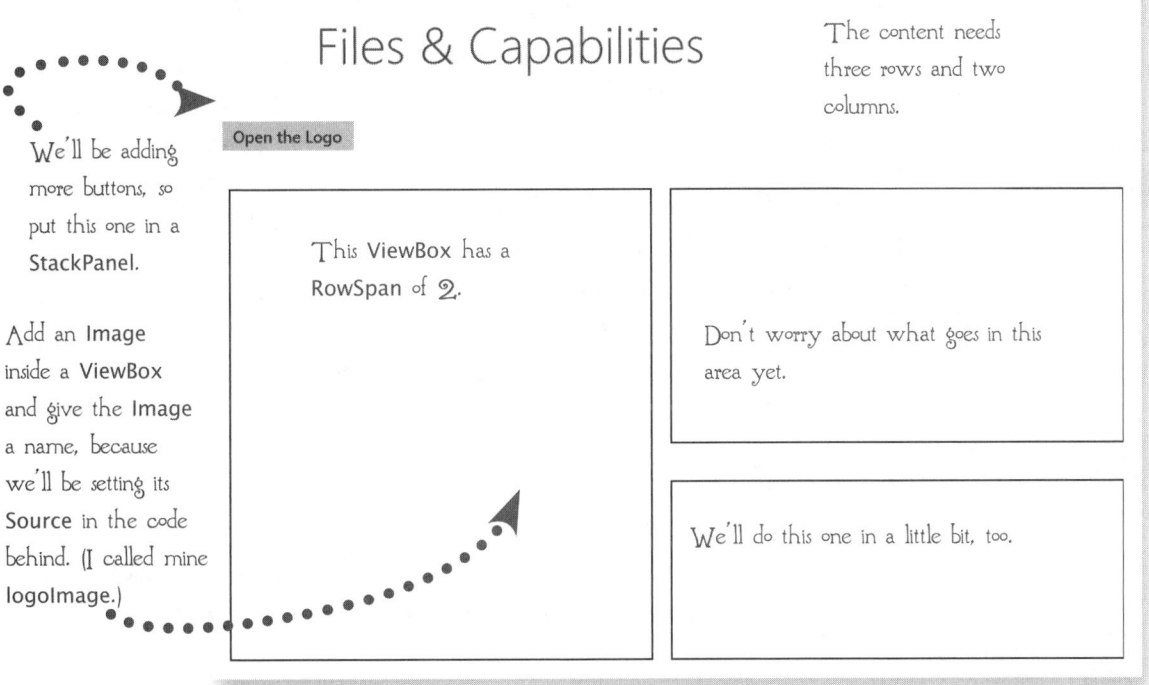

Files & Capabilities

We'll be adding more buttons, so put this one in a **StackPanel**.

Add an **Image** inside a **ViewBox** and give the **Image** a name, because we'll be setting its **Source** in the code behind. (I called mine **logoImage**.)

The content needs three rows and two columns.

This **ViewBox** has a RowSpan of 2.

Don't worry about what goes in this area yet.

We'll do this one in a little bit, too.

ADD REFERENCES

You'll need to add some references to the code-behind. Add using (C#) or **Imports** (VB) statements for:

- Windows.Storage
- Windows.Storage.Search
- Windows.Storage.Pickers
- Windows.Storage.Streams
- Windows.UI.Xaml.Media.Imaging

599

LOAD AN IMAGE

Next we'll open a file in the `Click` event handler for the `Button` you created in the XAML. We'll swing back around and talk about most of these objects and methods later in the chapter, but here are the basic steps:

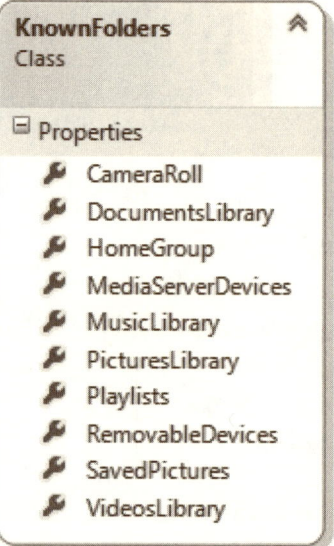

① GET A FOLDER REFERENCE

Folders are represented by the `StorageFolder` class. We'll talk about the `StorageFolder` and `StorageFile` in some detail at the end of the chapter.) You get a reference to a folder through the `KnownFolders` enumeration.

② OBTAIN THE FILE

We'll use the `StorageFolder.GetFileAsync()` method which takes the file name as a `String`. The `FluentLogo.png` file is included in the sample code. You'll either need to copy it to the Pictures folder or change the string to the name of an existing file on your hard drive.

③ CREATE A METHOD TO LOAD THE FILE

Because we'll be setting the `Source` property of the `Image` element from several different `Click` event handlers, we'll create a method that we can call rather than repeating the code.

④ OPEN THE FILE

The `StorageFile` is an abstraction. In order to set the `Source` of the `Image` element, we'll need to use the `SetSourceAsync()` method of a `BitmapImage`, which takes an instance of `IRandomAccessStream`. Conveniently, the `StorageFile.OpenAsync()` method returns just that.

⑤ SET THE BITMAPSOURCE

Once we have a reference to the stream, we can call `SetSourceAsync()` to set the `BitmapImage.Source` and then set the `Source` of the `Image` element.

① ② ③ ④ ⑤

```csharp
private async void OpenButton_Click(...)
{
    StorageFolder picFolder = KnownFolders.PicturesLibrary;
    StorageFile logoFile = await picFolder.GetFileAsync("FluentLogo.png");
    await SetSource(logoFile);
}

private async Task SetSource(StorageFile file)
{
    if (file != null)
    {
        BitmapImage bitmap = new BitmapImage();
        using (IRandomAccessStream fileSteam =
                await file.OpenAsync(FileAccessMode.Read))
        {
            await bitmap.SetSourceAsync(fileStream);
            logoImage.Source = bitmap;
        }
    }
}
```

Be sure you reference a file you've added to your project.

```vb
Private Async Sub OpenButton_Click(...) Handles OpenLogoButton.Click
    Dim picFolder As StorageFolder = KnownFolders.PicturesLibrary
    Dim logoFile As StorageFile = Await picFolder.GetFileAsync("FluentLogo.png")
    Await SetSource(logoFile)
End Sub

Private Async Function SetSource(file As StorageFile) As Task
    If Not file Is Nothing Then
        Dim bitmap As BitmapImage = New BitmapImage()
        Using fileStream As IRandomAccessStream =
            Await file.OpenAsync(FileAccessMode.Read)

            Await bitmap.SetSourceAsync(fileStream)
            logoImage.Source = bitmap
        End Using
    End If
End Function
```

Be sure you reference a file you've added to your project.

NOT QUITE...

When you try to run the code after creating the Click event handler and the SetSource() method, you'll receive an UnauthorizedAccessException:

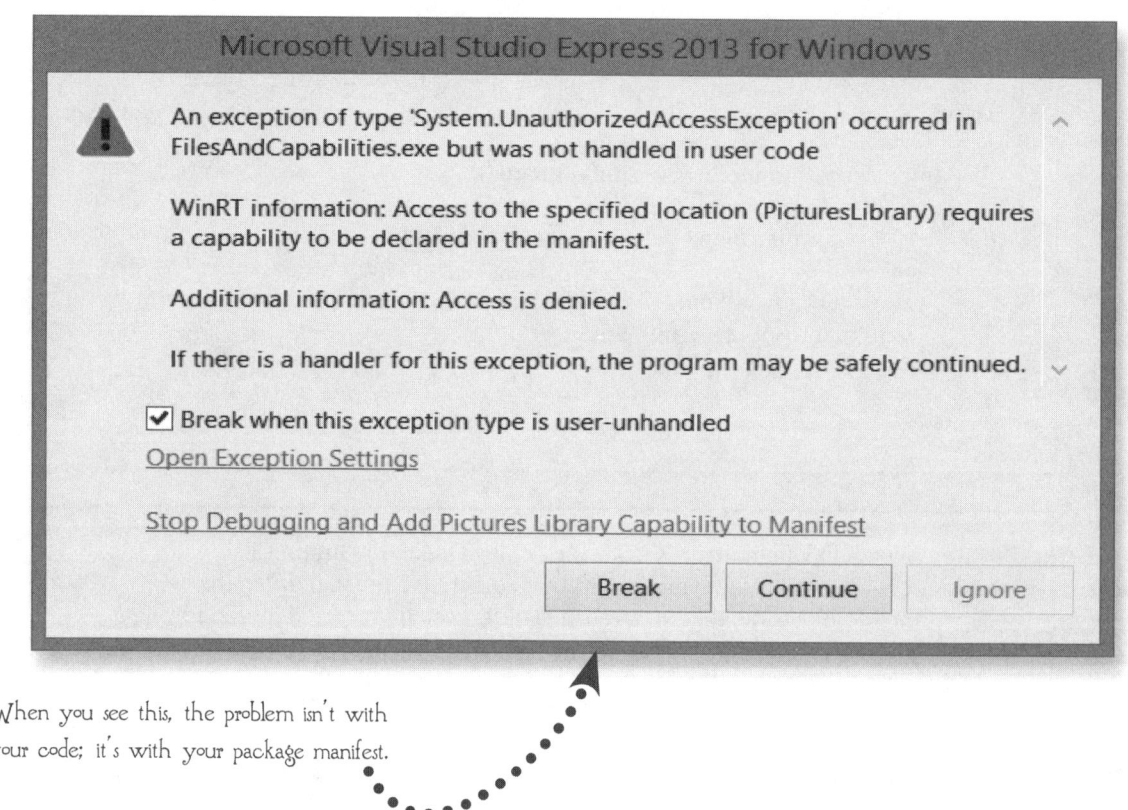

When you see this, the problem isn't with your code; it's with your package manifest.

Without adding any declarations, your app has access to the directory where your application is installed via the Windows.ApplicationModel.Package.Current.InstalledLocation property, the isolated storage for the application via ApplicationData.Current.LocalFolder (we'll explore this one more in the next section), and the user's Downloads directory via the static DownloadsFolder class. Attempting to access anything else will trigger the exception.

The problem is easy to fix: Just open the Manifest Designer and select the libraries or resources your app needs to access on the Capabilities tab. Notice that by default Visual Studio has added client Internet access, which tells you something about the kinds of apps Microsoft expects us to be developing, doesn't it?

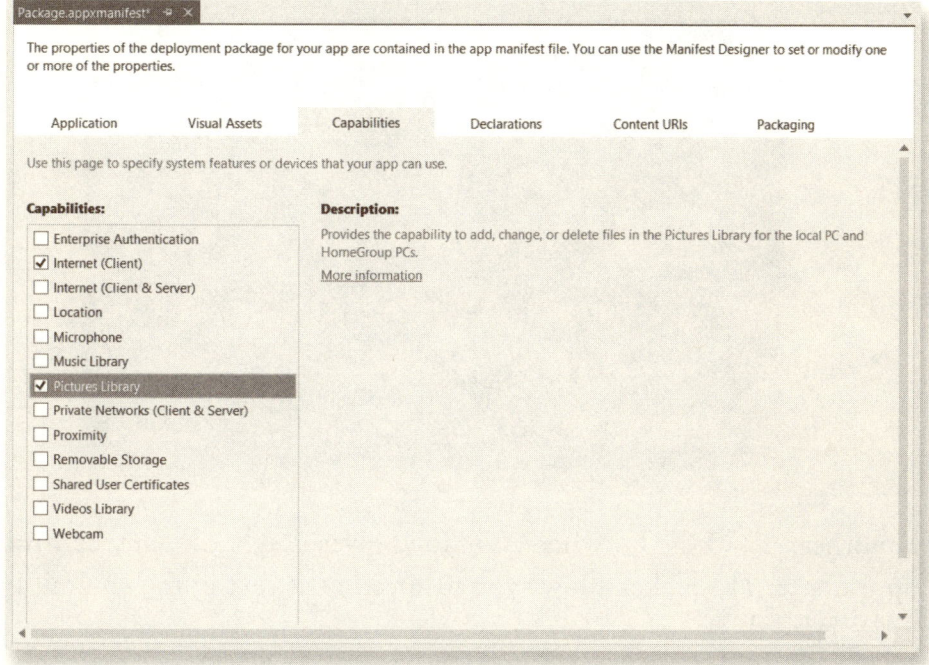

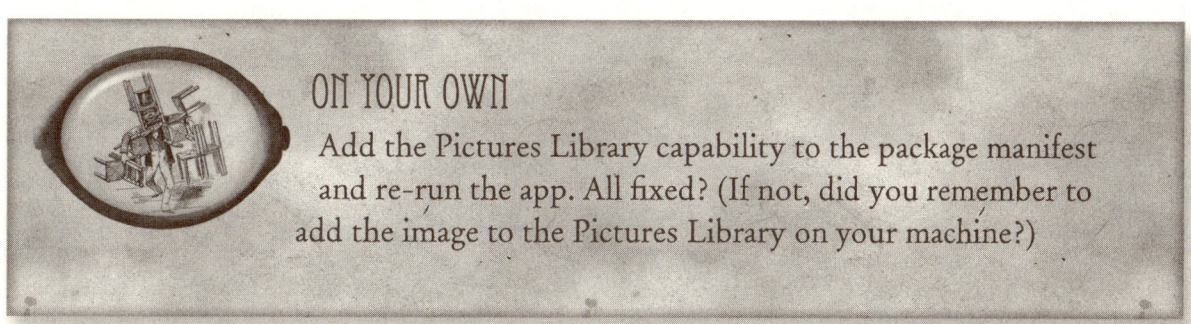

ON YOUR OWN

Add the Pictures Library capability to the package manifest and re-run the app. All fixed? (If not, did you remember to add the image to the Pictures Library on your machine?)

FILE PICKERS

You must warn Windows before you can access a folder directly in your code, but there is another way to obtain access to the user's files. The file picker classes, of which there are three, `FileOpenPicker`, `FileSavePicker`, and `FolderPicker`, don't require a capability declaration because access to the files and folders via a picker is under the user's control.

Pickers are another area of the UI where Windows gives you hardly any control over the visual appearance. The picker allows you to specify the text in the commit button. Everything else is fixed.

MAKE A NOTE

There are two other pickers available in WinRT: the CredentialPicker defined in Windows.Security.Credentials, and the ContactPicker defined in Windows.ApplicationModel.Contacts.Provider. They're fairly specialized objects, and so we won't be talking about them, but they work the same way as the file and folder pickers we'll explore in this section.

PICKER CLASSES

There's very little to configure with a picker, so the classes are fairly simple:

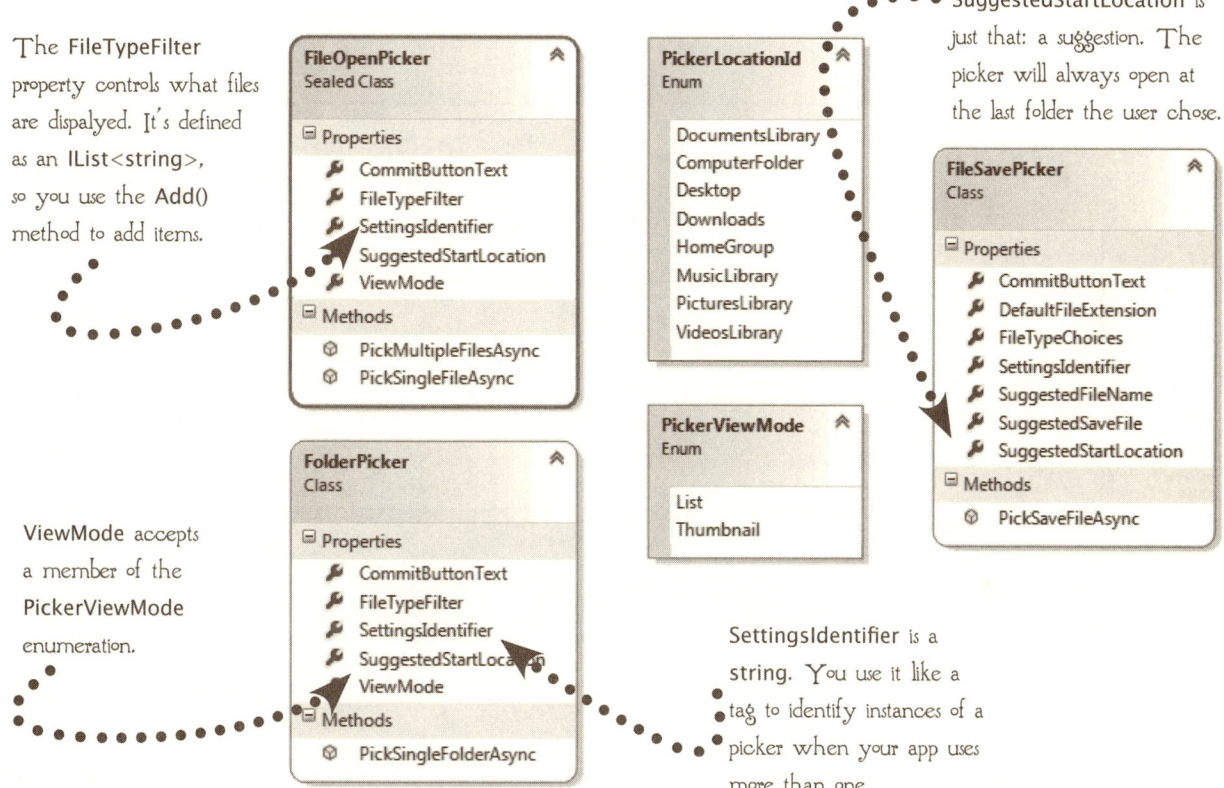

The **FileTypeFilter** property controls what files are displayed. It's defined as an **IList<string>**, so you use the **Add()** method to add items.

ViewMode accepts a member of the **PickerViewMode** enumeration.

SuggestedStartLocation is just that: a suggestion. The picker will always open at the last folder the user chose.

SettingsIdentifier is a string. You use it like a tag to identify instances of a picker when your app uses more than one.

PUT ON YOUR THINKING HAT

Add another button to the sample app. In the Click event handler, use a **FileOpenPicker** to allow the user to select an image file, and then call the **SetSource()** method to display the image. The **SuggestedStartLocation** should be the **PicturesLibrary**, and the **FileTypeFilter** should include (at a minimum) .png and .jpg file types.

HOW'D YOU DO?

Did you figure out which method to call to display the picker?

```csharp
private async void PickButton_Click(...)
{
    FileOpenPicker picker = new FileOpenPicker();
    picker.ViewMode = PickerViewMode.Thumbnail;
    picker.SuggestedStartLocation = PickerLocationId.PicturesLibrary;
    picker.FileTypeFilter.Add(".png");
    picker.FileTypeFilter.Add(".jpg");

    StorageFile file = await picker.PickSingleFileAsync();
    await SetSource(file);
}
```

```vb
Private Async Sub OpenPickerButton_Click(...)
    Handles OpenPickerButton.Click

    Dim picker As FileOpenPicker = New FileOpenPicker()
    picker.ViewMode = PickerViewMode.Thumbnail
    picker.SuggestedStartLocation = PickerLocationId.PicturesLibrary
    picker.FileTypeFilter.Add(".png")
    picker.FileTypeFilter.Add(".jpg")

    Dim file As StorageFile = Await picker.PickSingleFileAsync()
    Await SetSource(file)
End Sub
```

FILE ASSOCIATIONS

A third way to obtain a reference to a file is by setting up a file association in the Declarations tab of the Manifest Designer so that your app will be launched when the user opens a file of that type.

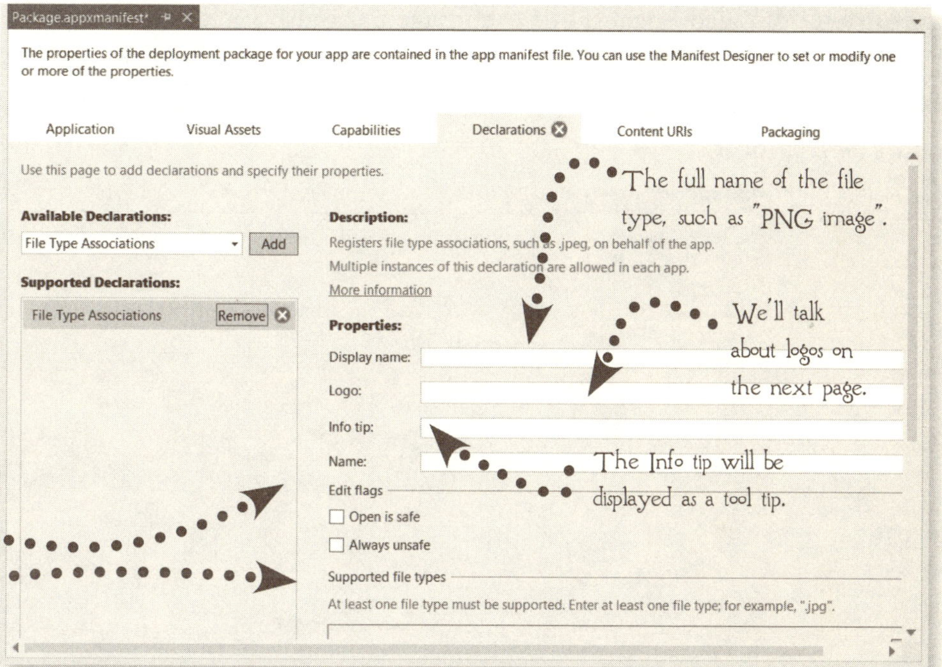

The full name of the file type, such as "PNG image".

We'll talk about logos on the next page.

*The name used internally to identify the group of files defined by this declaration. **Name** must be all lowercase.*

The Info tip will be displayed as a tool tip.

*This is the MIME type of the content, such as **application/pdf** or **image/png**.*

MAKE A NOTE

There are certain types, such as **application/force-download**, and extension types, such as .bat, .ttf, .dll, and .exe, that are either reserved or forbidden. You can find the complete list in the topic "How to handle file activation" on MSDN.

(YET) MORE IMAGE ASSETS

And you thought the umpteen-bazillion images and scales you'd already created were enough and more than enough...nope. There's more. You should include a set of images at precise pixel sizes.

When we added `Square30x30Logo` images to the Application UI tab in the last chapter, we only used scaled images, but the image pack also included another set of icon images. (MSDN calls them "icons", but they need to be standard png or jpg image files, not ico files.) They're used to represent files that are associated with your app in the File Picker and File Explorer.

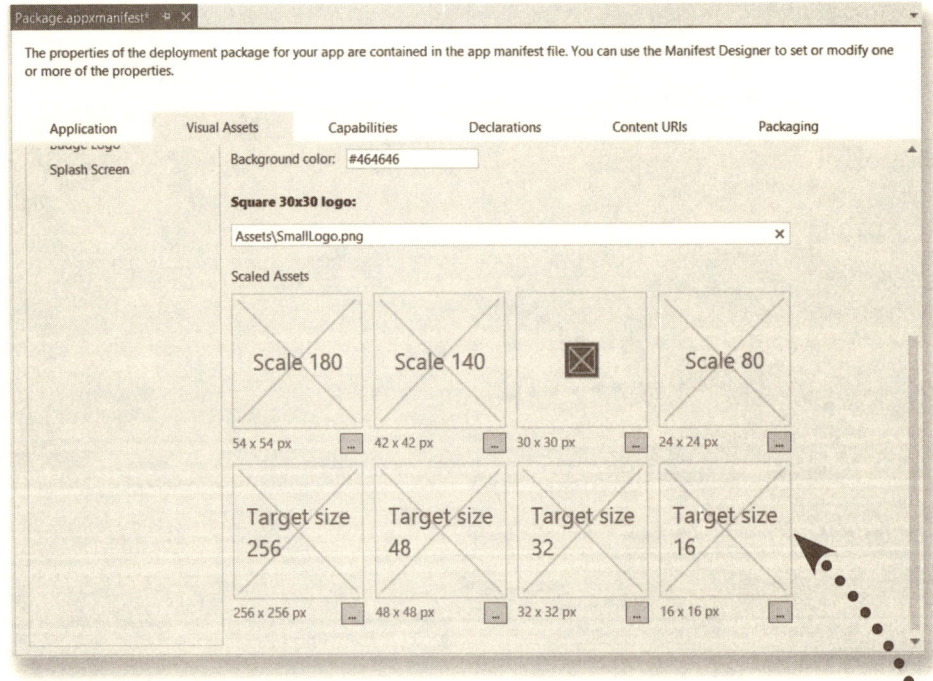

You can create another set of images to use for the file association, or if you leave that part of the Declaration blank, the Small Logo images will be used.

You can specify four square images for your small logo: 16 pixel, 32 pixel, 48 pixel, and 256 pixel.

There are two differences between the fixed pixel size "icon" images and the other logo and splash screen images we've been using:

"ICON" IMAGES SHOULD NOT BE TRANSPARENT
You should place your images on the application background color, rather than leaving them transparent and allowing Windows to do that for you.

"ICON" IMAGES SHOULD USE THE TARGET-SIZE
Rather than the scale qualifier we used for the other app images, these images should use a **targetsize** qualifier: **SmallLogo.targetsize-32.png** rather than **SmallLogo.scale-100.png**.

PUT ON YOUR THINKING HAT

Let's set up our app to handle png files:

Add a set of "icon" images to the sample app. There are a set of Logo images included in the sample application, or of course you can create your own. If you use the provided images, or if you create your own and include a set of scaled logos as well, you'll need to delete the default **SmallLogo.png** that was included in the template. Otherwise you'll get an error about both a targeted and untargeted image being ignored.

Complete the Declarations section so that our app can become the default for png files.

HOW'D YOU DO?

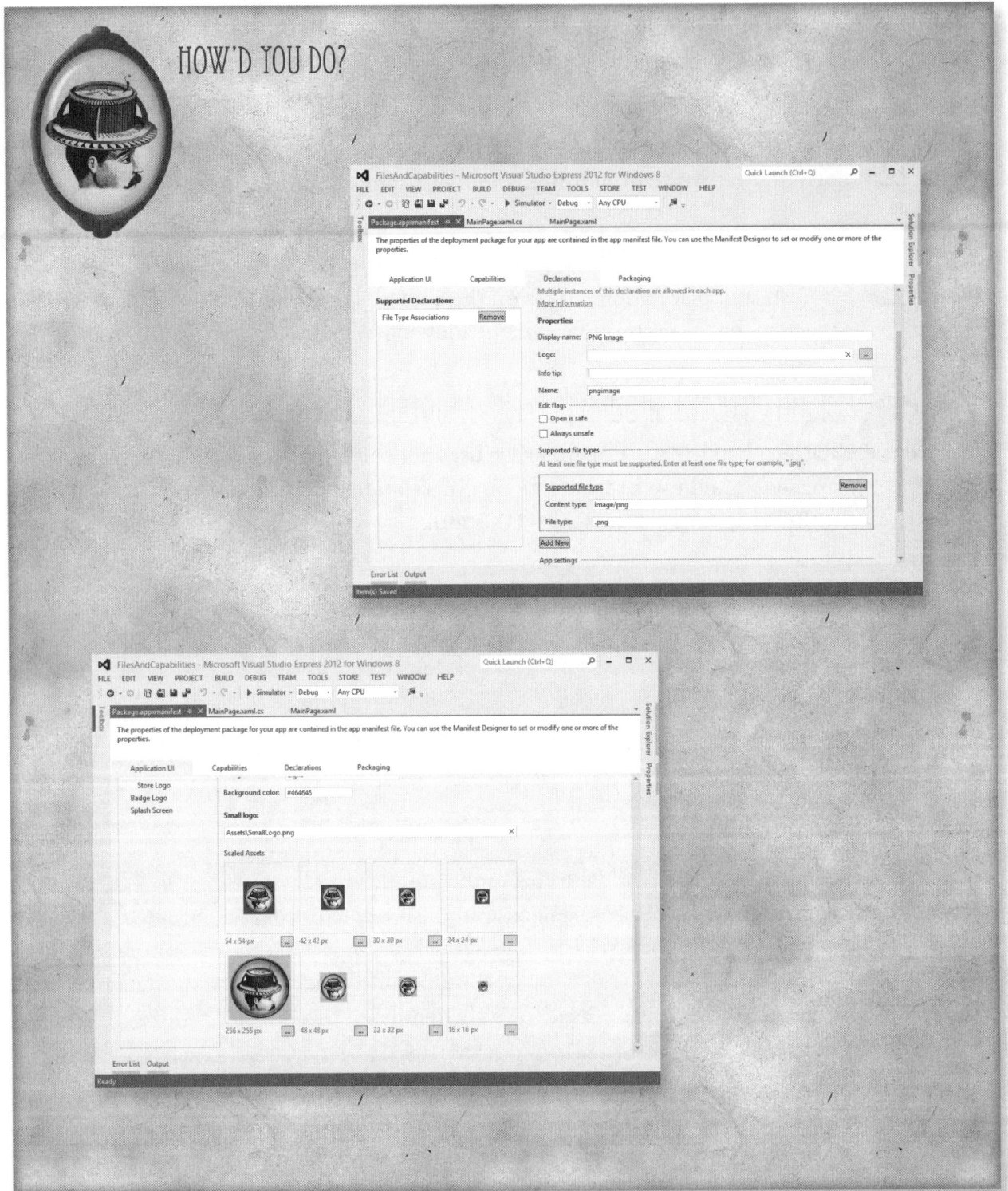

RESPONDING TO FILE ACTIVATION

We've worked a lot with the `OnLaunched()` method to handle various launch and activation situations. File associations are somewhat different (and rather simpler).

Rather than handling a file activation in the `OnLaunched()` method, you'll respond to the `Application.OnFileActivated()` method, which receives an instance of `FileActivatedEventArgs`:

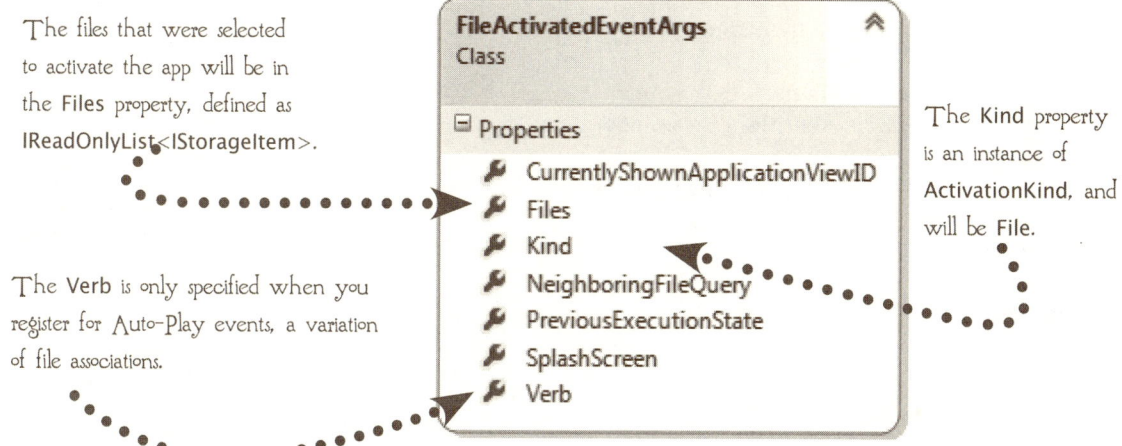

The files that were selected to activate the app will be in the Files property, defined as `IReadOnlyList<IStorageItem>`.

The Kind property is an instance of ActivationKind, and will be File.

The Verb is only specified when you register for Auto-Play events, a variation of file associations.

Inside the `OnFileActivated()` method you create a root frame, navigate to a page using the same techniques you used in `OnLaunched()`, and then activate the current Window. You'll typically pass the files to be opened as the Parameter of the Navigate() method.

> ### PUT ON YOUR THINKING HAT
>
> Add an `OnFileActivated()` method to app.xaml.cs or app.xaml.vb, and add code to the `OnNavigatedTo()` method of the MainPage to load the first selected file into the Image element.
>
> Since our app can only handle a single file, you can pass `args.Files[0]` to the Navigate() method, but be sure you check the type in `NavigationHelper_LoadState` before you try to open it.

HOW'D YOU DO?
Here's my version.

```csharp
protected override void OnFileActivated(...)
{
    base.OnFileActivated(args);

    Frame rootFrame = new Frame();
    Window.Current.Content = rootFrame;

    rootFrame.Navigate(typeof(MainPage), args.Files[0]);
    Window.Current.Activate();
}
```

```csharp
private async void navigationHelper_LoadState(...)
{
    StorageFile imageFile = e.Parameter as StorageFile;
    if (imageFile != null)
        SetSource(imageFile);
}
```

```vb
Protected Overrides Sub OnFileActivated(...)
    MyBase.OnFileActivated(args)

    Dim rootFrame As Frame = New Frame()
    Window.Current.Content = rootFrame

    rootFrame.Navigate(GetType(MainPage), args.Files(0))
    Window.Current.Activate()
End Sub
```

```vb
Private Async Sub navigationHelper_LoadState(...)
    Dim imageFile As StorageFile = TryCast(e.Parameter, StorageFile)
    If Not ImageFile Is Nothing Then
        Await SetSource(imageFile)
    End If
End Sub
```

BUT IT'S NOT YOUR DECISION...

Not any more, anyway. Earlier versions of Windows allowed applications to take over as the default app for file types, even if the type was already associated with another application. It's rude, but some applications did it anyway. (Ask me why I uninstalled Picasa.) That's no longer true with Windows 8.1. So before you can test that your app is working, you have to install it and then tell Windows that you want to use it as the default app for png files.

You specify the default program for a file type in the Set Default Programs pane of the Control Panel. (The easiest way to get to it is by using the Search charm—just search for "Default Programs".

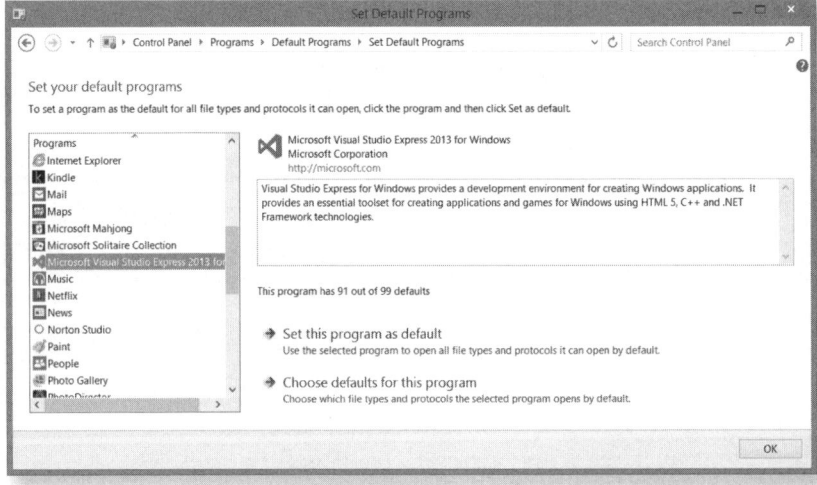

TAKE A BREAK

Go ahead and set your app as the default for png files and test that it works correctly. You'll probably want to remove the setting when you're through, either via the Control Panel or by simply uninstalling the app. Then take a break before you complete the Review and we move on to application data.

REVIEW

Can you answer the following questions based on what you've learned?

Looking at the capabilities list, which option would you choose to access the Documents Library? A USB drive? The camera?

What classes represent folders and files in WinRT?

What locations can you access programmatically without declaring them?

What qualifier do you use on fixed-sized image assets?

What images will Windows use if you don't specify a Logo for a file association?

What method do you use to respond to a file activation?

APPLICATION DATA

When we were exploring navigation in Chapter 13, we worked with the `SuspensionManager` class in order to maintain the state of an app. The `SuspensionManager` works extremely well for that purpose, but you do have another option: the `ApplicationData` class that provides access to an app-specific data store (and that `SuspensionManager` actually uses under the covers).

You should use locations like the Pictures or Documents folders for files that belong to the user, not the app. (A good way to think about the difference is to ask yourself whether the user would expect the file to still be present if the app were to be uninstalled.) But your app will probably want to store some data that the user doesn't care about (except in so far as it helps your app run). That's what the **ApplicationData** data store is for.

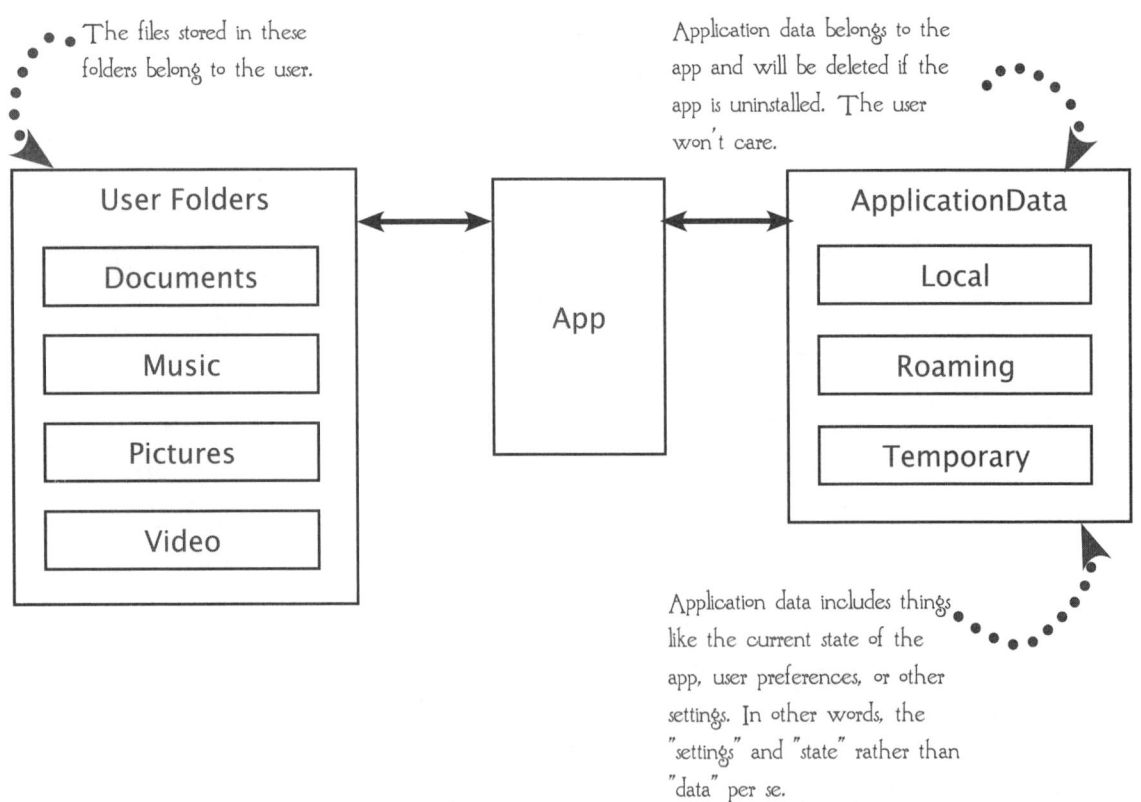

The files stored in these folders belong to the user.

Application data belongs to the app and will be deleted if the app is uninstalled. The user won't care.

Application data includes things like the current state of the app, user preferences, or other settings. In other words, the "settings" and "state" rather than "data" per se.

You can retrieve a reference to the ApplicationData object for the current app using the static ApplicationData.Current property. ApplicationData, in turn, contains properties that give you access to StorageFolder and ApplicationDataContainer objects:

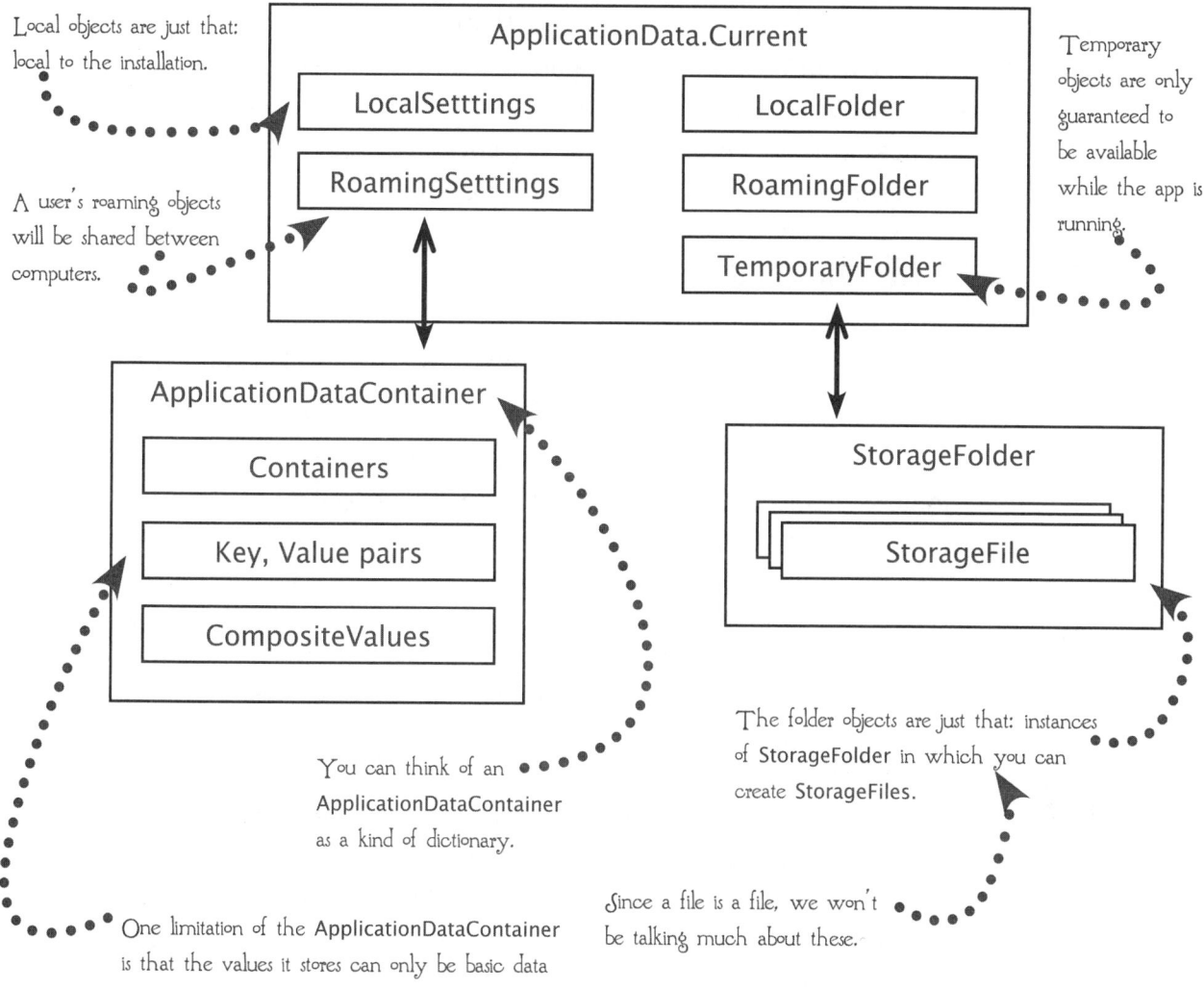

USING A DATA CONTAINER

Using the ApplicationDataContainer class to store the state and settings of your app is almost as simple as using the SuspensionManager. Here are the steps:

TO SAVE A SETTING:

RETRIEVE THE APPLICATIONDATACONTAINER

The **ApplicationData.Current** property is static, so you only need a reference to **Windows.Storage** to reference it. Once you have the reference to **ApplicationData**, you can choose the **LocalSettings** or **RoamingSettings** to access the appropriate **ApplicationDataContainer**.

CREATE SETTINGS

The **ApplicationDataContainer** can store two kinds of values: simple key/value pairs and composite values that consist of multiple key/value pairs treated as a single setting (we'll talk about those in a bit).

You create settings using the same syntax you'd use for any **Dictionary<string,object>** (including the **SuspensionManager**).

TO RETRIEVE A SETTING:

RETRIEVE THE APPLICATIONDATACONTAINER

First you need the reference, just as if you were creating settings.

RETRIEVE VALUES

The **Values** property is defined as an instance of **IPropertySet**, which in turn implements **IObservableMap<string, object>**, **IDictionary<string, object>**, and **IEnumerable<KeyValuePair>**, so you can use any of the methods defined on those interfaces to retrieve your values. The simplest, of course, is just to reference the key:

ApplicationData.Current.LocalSettings.Values["myValue"]

WHEN AND WHERE

One thing you need to consider when using `ApplicationData` is when and where you want to update the values. The `SuspensionManager` uses a fairly complex method of tracking frames in order to catch suspending events, but even then, it only stores local values, and it always stores them in a file. (It does, however, support complex types, which the `ApplicationDataContainer` doesn't.)

You can build an infrastructure like the one used by SuspensionManager, but in most cases it isn't necessary. Even though settings are saved on the UI thread, the operation is fast, so as a general rule, keep it simple. (You may have noticed, that's my general rule for most things.)

CREATE OR UPDATE THE SETTING AS SOON AS IT CHANGES
That usually means you'll create the setting in an **Updated** or **Changed** event handler, but (as in our example) it could be via a **Button.Click**.

RESTORE THE SETTINGS IN THE LOADSTATE EVENT HANDLER
There are a few rare situations in which you'll need to restore the settings when the page is loaded or created, but you'll almost always be able to use the navigationHelper_LoadState() method to load your settings.

PUT ON YOUR THINKING HAT
Give it a try.

In the code-behind for the **MainPage**, add the code to save the **Path** of the current image to the SetSource() method and to restore the stored image to the navigationHelper_LoadState() method.

You need to store just the **Path** property (a string) because ApplicationDataContainer doesn't support complex types like **BitmapImage** or **StorageFile**.

To restore the file from the path, you can use the static **StorageFile.GetFileFromPathAsync()** method. You'll need to put that functionality as an **else** clause in the existing code, which is handling file associations.

HOW'D YOU DO?

```csharp
private async void navigationHelper_LoadState(...)
{
    StorageFile imageFile = e.NavigationParameter as StorageFile;

    if (imageFile != null)
        await SetSource(imageFile);
    else
    {
        ApplicationDataContainer localSettings =
            ApplicationData.Current.LocalSettings;
        if (localSettings.Values["imageSource"] != null)
        {
            string filePath = (string)localSettings.Values["imageSource"];
            imageFile = await StorageFolder.GetFileFromPathAsync(filePath);
            SetSource(imageFile);
        }
    }
}
```

```csharp
private async void SetSource(StorageFile file)
{
    if (file != null)
    {
        ...
        ApplicationDataContainer localSettings =
            ApplicationData.Current.LocalSettings;
        localSettings.Values["imageSource"] = file.Path;
    }
}
```

```
Private Async Sub navigationHelper_LoadState(...)
    Dim imageFile As StorageFile = e.NavigationParameter as StorageFile;

    If Not imageFile Is Nothing Then
        Await SetSource(imageFile)
    Else
        Dim localSettings As ApplicationDataContainer =
            ApplicationData.Current.LocalSettings
        If Not localSettings.Values("imageSource" Is Nothing Then
            Dim filePath As String =
                DirectCast(localSettings.Values("imageSource"), String)
            imageFile = Await StorageFolder.GetFileFromPathAsync(filePath)
            SetSource(imageFile)
        End If
    End If
End Sub
```

```
Private Async Sub SetSource(StorageFile file)
    If Not file Is Nothing Then
        ...
        ApplicationDataContainer localSettings =
            ApplicationData.Current.LocalSettings
        localSettings.Values("imageSource") = file.Path
    End If
End Sub
```

ORGANIZING SETTINGS

Most of the time the simple dictionary structure of the **ApplicationDataContainer** will do what you want, but if you have a lot of settings, or settings that have to be treated as a single group, there are two other options that you should be aware of.

ADDITIONAL CONTAINERS

If you have a lot of settings and start to run into name collisions, or if you simply like to keep your code super-organized, you can nest **ApplicationDataContainer** settings containers using the **CreateContainer()** method and reference them via the **Containers** dictionary property:

```csharp
ApplicationDataContainer container =
    localSettings.CreateContainer("MainPage", ApplicationDataCreateDisposition.Always);

ApplicationDataContainer container = localSettings.Containers["MainPage"];
container.Values["myKey"] = myValue;
```

COMPOSITE VALUES

The **ApplicationDataCompositeValue** class is a dictionary of settings that can be added to an ApplicationDataContainer as a single entity. It's useful when you need to store more than one property of a complex class or when you have values that need to be treated as a transaction.

```csharp
ApplicationDataCompositeValue composite = new ApplicationDataCompositeValue();
composite["firstValue"] = 1;
composite["secondValue"] = "hello";

roamingSettings.Values["MyComposite"] = composite;
```

ROAMING SETTINGS

Microsoft allots cloud storage to every Win8 app, and Windows8 handles synchronizing the data across multiple devices. The `RoamingSettings ApplicationDataContainer` and `RoamingFolder StorageFolder` behave in precisely the same way as their local siblings. Nothing you need to worry about there except that there is a non-deterministic latency in the syncing—it will happen, but it can take quite a long time to do so. But roaming data does have a few more requirements, simply because it's being synchronized across the cloud.

STORAGE QUOTA

Microsoft hosts roaming storage, but there is a limit. You can use the **ApplicationData. RoamingStorageQuota** property to determine the current maximum amount of roaming storage (it's subject to change). Unfortunately, there's no way to find out how much of the quota you've used—you'll have to calculate that yourself—and you won't get an error if you exceed it; Windows will simply cease synchronizing the data. The lesson here is to be extremely stingy about what you roam.

THE DATACHANGED EVENT

Roaming data could be synchronized at any time, including when your application is running. The **DataChanged** event will be triggered if it does, so you should register an event handler for the event that refreshes your data. Like **StorageQuota**, the **DataChanged** event is exposed on **ApplicationData** itself. The event receives an instance of **ApplicationData** as the sender and an argument defined as an object that will be null. (In other words, there's a parameter, but no actual argument.)

PUT ON YOUR THINKING HAT

Change our application to use roaming storage rather than local storage for the image Path. There's no reason to check the storage quota, but be sure to add a handler for the DataChanged event.

HOW'D YOU DO?

The only changes to **navigationHelper_LoadState()** and **SetSource()** are referencing ApplicationData.Current.RoamingSettings instead of ApplicationData.Current.LocalSettings, and I haven't shown those two procedures.

For simplicity, I've repeated the code to load the image path in the event handler. Give yourself a gold star if you refactored it into a separate procedure.

```csharp
public MainPage()
{
    InitializeComponent();
    ApplicationData.Current.DataChanged += Current_DataChanged;
    ...
}
```

```csharp
async void Current_DataChanged(ApplicationData sender, object args)
{
    ApplicationDataContainer roamingSettings =
        ApplicationData.Current.RoamingSettings;
    if (roamingSettings.Values["imageSource"] != null)
    {
        string filePath = (string)roamingSettings.Values["imageSource"];
        StorageFile imageFile = await StorageFile.GetFileFromPathAsync(filePath);
        await SetSource(imageFile);
    }
}
```

```vb
Public Sub New()
    InitializeComponent()
    AddHandler Me.ApplicationData.Current.DataChanged,
        AddressOf Current_DataChanged
    ...
End Sub
```

```vb
Async Sub Current_DataChanged(ApplicationData sender, object args)
    Dim roasmingSettings As ApplicationDataContainer =
        ApplicationData.Current.RoamingSettings
    If Not roamingSettings.Values["imageSource"] Is Nothing Then
        Dim filePath As AString =
            DirectCast(roamingSettings.Values("imageSource"), String)
        Dim imageFile As StorageFile = Await StorageFile.GetFileFromPathAsync(filePath)
        Await SetSource(imageFile)
    End If
End Sub
```

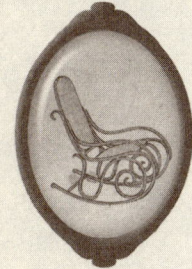

TAKE A BREAK

Before we move on to the storage API and explore the **StorageFolder** and **StorageFile** objects in more detail, why don't you take a break?

REVIEW

Can you answer the following questions based on what you've learned?

What class of object does ApplicationData.Current.TemporaryFolder return?

How about ApplicationData.Current.LocalSettings?

How can you tell how much roaming storage space is still available?

What kind of data can you store as a value in an ApplicationDataContainer? How would you compare the application data API to the SuspensionManager? Would you ever expect to use both?

Do you need to register for a DataChanged event if you're using local data?

THE STORAGE API

To work with the contents of files, you'll use streams and buffers that are equivalent to those in standard .NET, and we won't be talking much about that. But the abstractions, `StorageFolder` and `StorageFile`, are quite different from their `File` and `Directory` .NET equivalents.

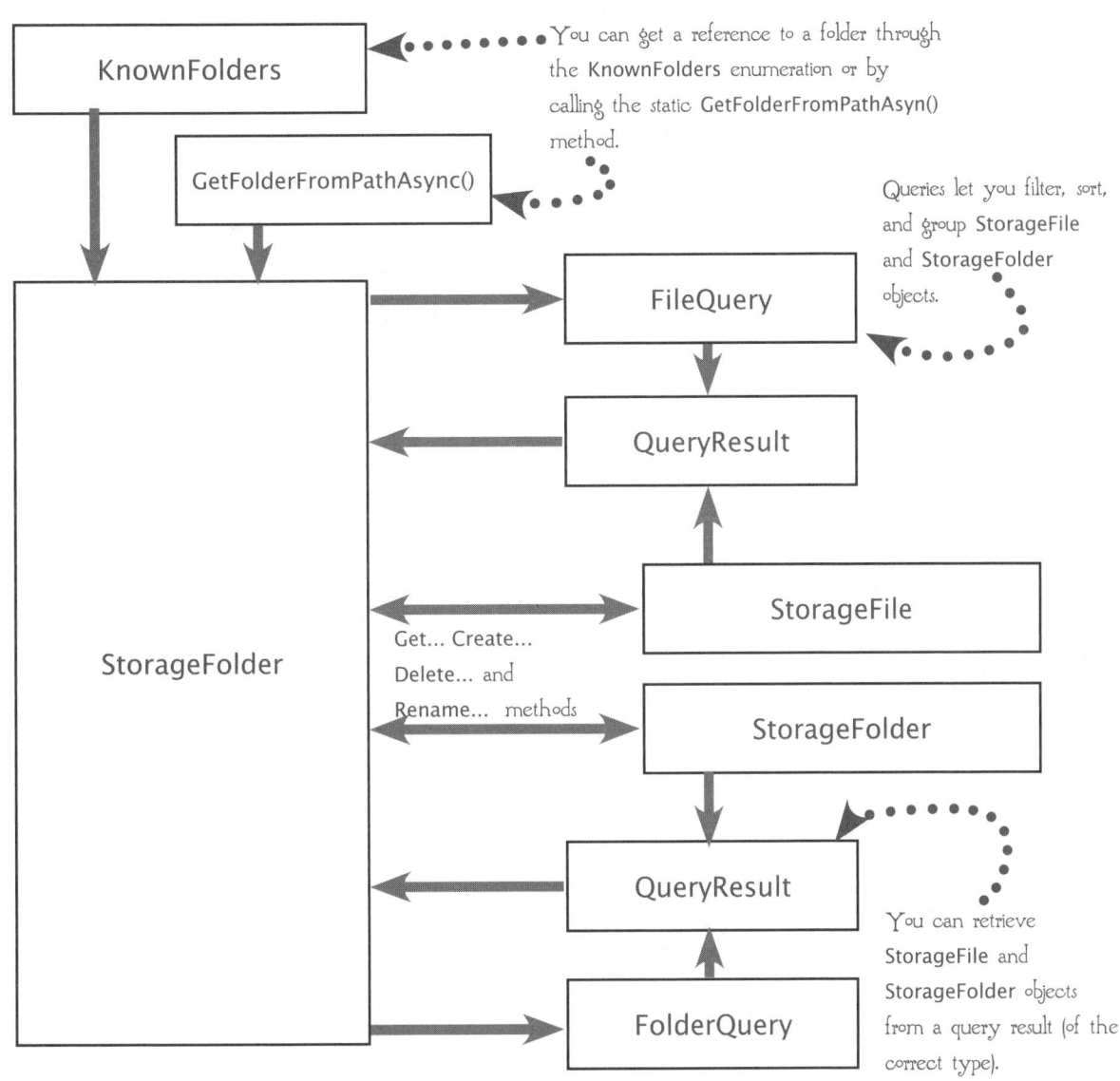

You can get a reference to a folder through the KnownFolders enumeration or by calling the static GetFolderFromPathAsyn() method.

Queries let you filter, sort, and group StorageFile and StorageFolder objects.

You can retrieve StorageFile and StorageFolder objects from a query result (of the correct type).

STORAGE CLASSES

The two primary classes in the Win8 Storage API are, of course, the `StorageFile`, which provides an abstraction over physical files, and `StorageFolder`, which does the same for folders. There aren't any real surprises in the objects—they provide the functionality you expect them to—except for the query capability of `StorageFolder` which isn't easily availble in the standard `.NET Directory` class.

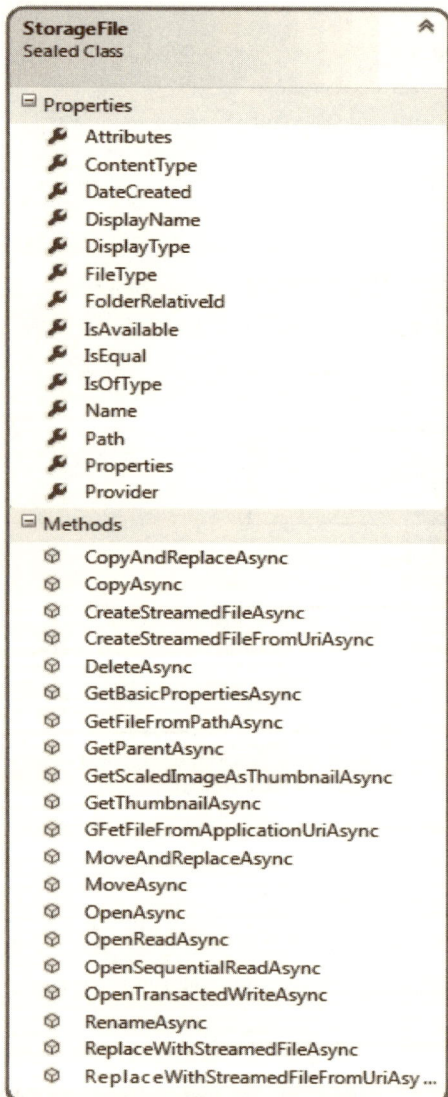
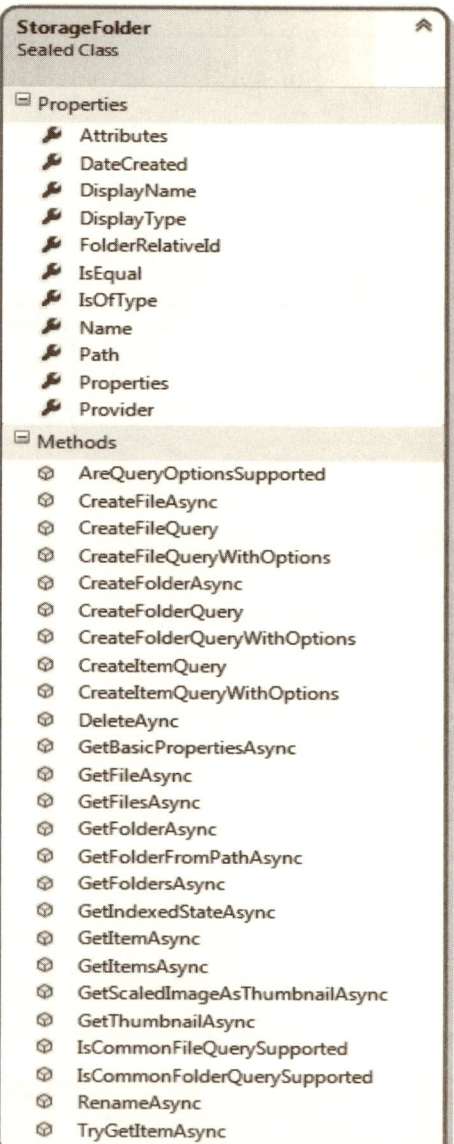

PUT ON YOUR THINKING HAT

Working with basic StorageFile and StorageFolder properties and methods is pretty straightforward, so to make it interesting, let's use this exercise to do that, and review some other techniques.

Add another button to the MainPage that opens a FolderPicker and calls PickSingleFolderAsync(). Once the picker returns, add the chosen StorageFolder to the DefaultViewModel.

Add a Grid next to the image element that displays labels and StorageFolder properties in TextBlock elements. Bind the property elements to the DefaultViewModel.

HOW'D YOU DO?

Here's my version.

```xml
<Grid Style="{StaticResource LayoutRootStyle}">
  ...
  <Grid Grid.Row="1" >
    <Grid.RowDefinitions>
      <RowDefinition Height="76"/>
      <RowDefinition />
    </Grid.RowDefinitions>
    <StackPanel Grid.Row="0" Orientation="Horizontal">
      <Button x:Name="OpenButton" .../>
      <Button x:Name="PickButton".../>
      <Button x:Name="FolderButton" Content="Pick a Folder"
              FontSize="18" Margin="10"
              Click="FolderButton_Click"/>
    </StackPanel>
    <Grid Grid.Row="1">
      <Grid.ColumnDefinitions>
        <ColumnDefinition />
        <ColumnDefinition />
      </Grid.ColumnDefinitions>
      <Border ... />
      <Grid Grid.Column="1">
        ...
        <TextBlock Grid.Row="0" Grid.Column="0" Text="Name:" .../>
        <TextBlock Grid.Row="0" Grid.Column="1"
            Text="{Binding Path=folder.Name}" .../>

        ...
      </Grid>
    </Grid>
  </Grid>
</Grid>
```

These elements are repeated for each property displayed.

```csharp
private async void FolderButton_Click(object sender, RoutedEventArgs e)
{
    FolderPicker picker = new FolderPicker();
    picker.ViewMode = PickerViewMode.Thumbnail;
    picker.SuggestedStartLocation = PickerLocationId.PicturesLibrary;
    picker.FileTypeFilter.Add(".jpg");
    picker.FileTypeFilter.Add(".png");

    StorageFolder folder = await picker.PickSingleFolderAsync();

    DefaultViewModel["folder"] = folder;
}
```

```vb
Private Async Sub FolderButton_Click(object sender, RoutedEventArgs e)
    Dim picker As FolderPicker = new FolderPicker()
    picker.ViewMode = PickerViewMode.Thumbnail
    picker.SuggestedStartLocation = PickerLocationId.PicturesLibrary
    picker.FileTypeFilter.Add(".jpg")
    picker.FileTypeFilter.Add(".png")

    Dim folder As StorageFolder = Await picker.PickSingleFolderAsync()

    DefaultViewModel("folder") = folder
End Sub
```

FILE & FOLDER QUERIES

The `StorageFolder` class exposes a set of methods that return a set (actually an `IStorageQueryResultBase`) of sorted `StorageFile` objects or grouped `StorageFolder` objects, based on either a pre-defined query enumeration or a more complex set of options. Here are the classes involved when you use a pre-defined query:

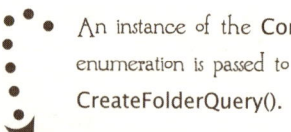
An instance of the `CommonFolderQuery` enumeration is passed to `CreateFolderQuery()`.

Not every file or folder supports every possible query. The `Is...Supported` methods let you check before you issue one.

An instance of the `CommonFileQuery` enumeration is passed to `CreateFileQuery()`.

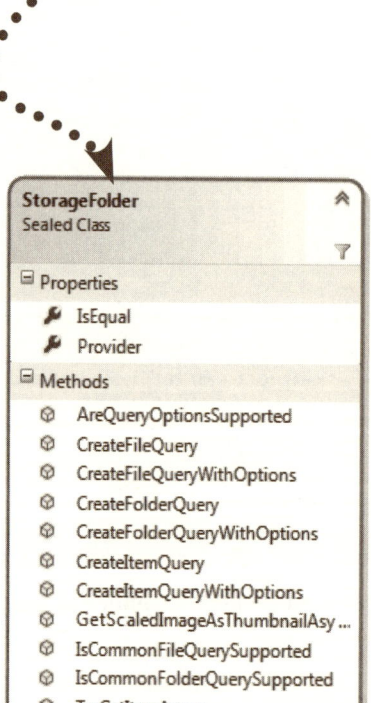

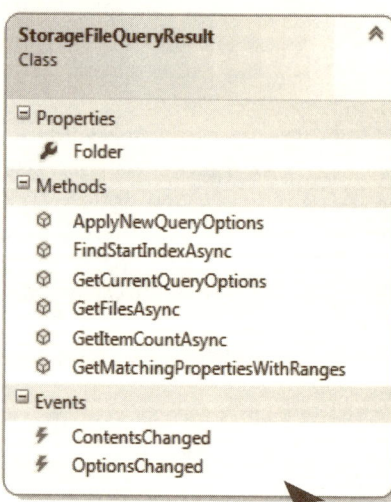

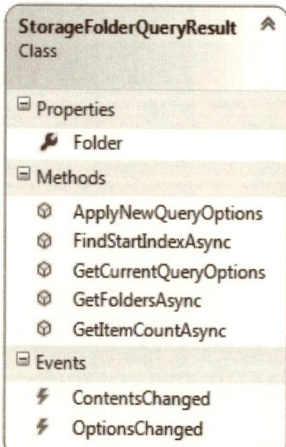

The `ContentsChanged` event notifies you of additions, deletions, and modifications of the files or folders returned by the query result.

QUERY OPTIONS

If a `CommonFileQuery` or `CommonFolderQuery` won't return the results you need, you can use the `Create...QueryWithOptions()` methods to access more advanced functionality. (You can also set additional options once you issue a common query.) These two methods return an "empty" query result, and then you set the `QueryOptions` that define the results you require.

There are a lot of classes involved in this scenario, and they actually look more complicated than they are, simply because there are so many enumerations involved. Here's a sampling:

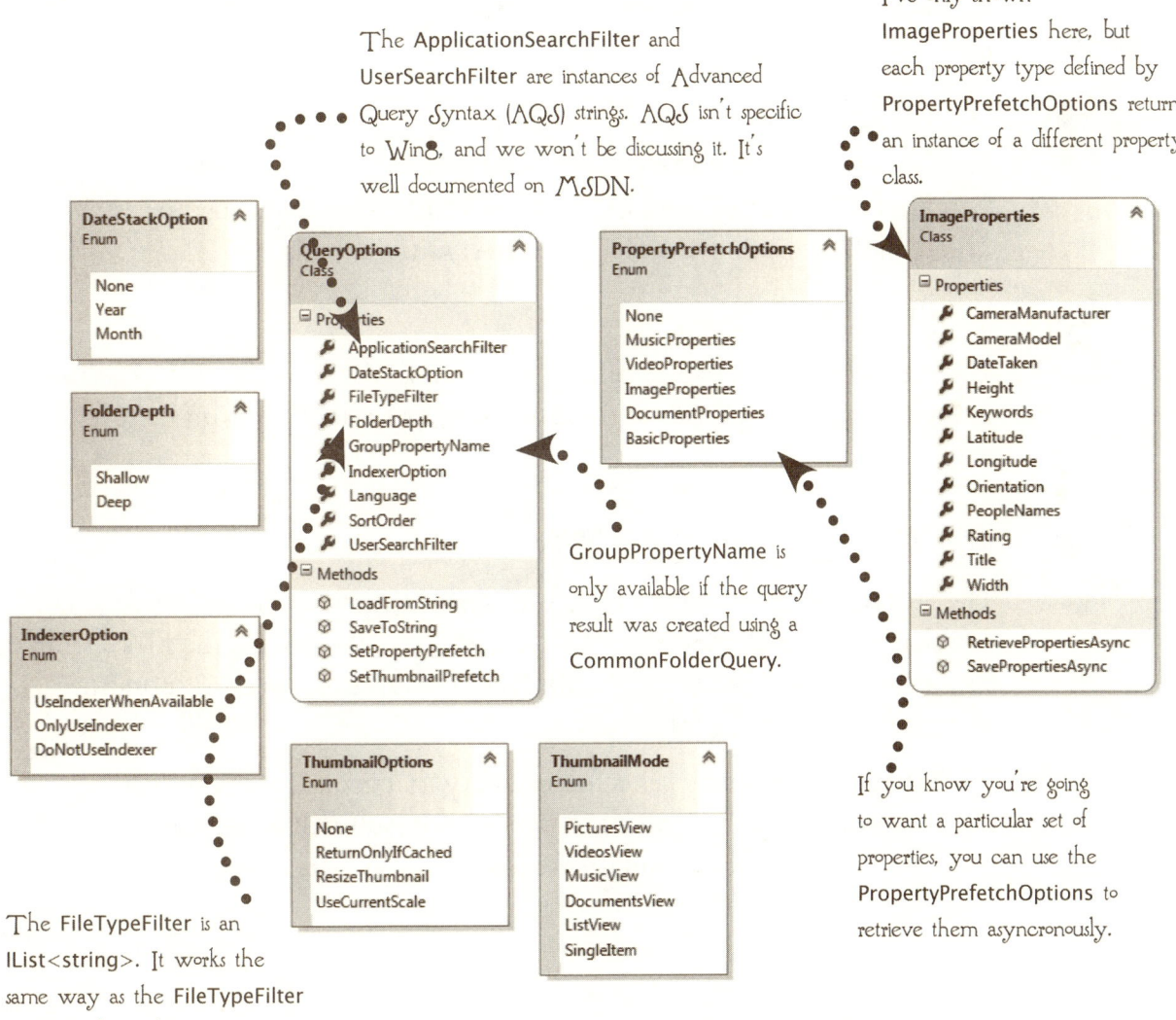

The `ApplicationSearchFilter` and `UserSearchFilter` are instances of Advanced Query Syntax (AQS) strings. AQS isn't specific to Win8, and we won't be discussing it. It's well documented on MSDN.

I've only shown `ImageProperties` here, but each property type defined by `PropertyPrefetchOptions` returns an instance of a different property class.

`GroupPropertyName` is only available if the query result was created using a `CommonFolderQuery`.

The `FileTypeFilter` is an `IList<string>`. It works the same way as the `FileTypeFilter` property of a picker.

If you know you're going to want a particular set of properties, you can use the `PropertyPrefetchOptions` to retrieve them asynchronously.

EXECUTING QUERIES

Whether you use one of the pre-defined common queries or the query option syntax, the basic process of executing queries is straightforward.

OBTAIN A FOLDER REFERENCE

You can either use the **KnownFolders** enumeration or the **GetFolderFromPathAsync()** method. Remember that whenever you're accessing files and folders programmatically, you'll have to declare the folder in the manifest.

CREATE THE QUERY

Next you'll create an instance of an appropriate query result class (**StorageFolderQueryResult** or **StorageFileQueryResult**) using one of the **CreateFileQuery...()** or **CreateFolderQuery...()** methods.

SET THE QUERY OPTIONS

You can optionally set additional query options to refine the results of the query using the properties of the **QueryOptions** class shown on the previous page.

RETRIEVE THE FILES AND FOLDERS

The **StorageFileQueryResult** class exposes two versions of **GetFilesAsync()**: one that retrieves all files in the folder and one that retrieves the files within a specified range. The **StorageFolderQueryResult** exposes corresponding methods for retrieving folders.

Note that if you have chosen a folder query that groups the results, the folders returned by the **StorageFolderQueryResult** will be virtual folders that don't correspond to a physical directory anywhere.

PUT ON YOUR THINKING HAT

Okay, let's issue a query. We'll use a **CommonFolderQuery** to display the number of files of each type in your Pictures Library:

Add another **Button** element to the **MainPage**. In the event handler for the **Button**, create a **CommonFolderQuery.GroupByType** query to retrieve the files in the **KnownFolders.PicturesLibrary**.

Retrieve the folders using the **GetFoldersAsync()** method.

Since you can't bind directly to a query result (and I just made you do some binding in the last exercise), we'll just create some text: Create an instance of **StringBuilder()** and loop through each folder. Call **StorageFolder.GetFilesAsync()** for each folder to retrieve the files, and then append the folder **Name** and file list **Count** to the **StringBuilder**.

Finally, call the **StringBuilder.ToString()** method to set the **Text** property of the **TextBlock** and display the results on the **Page**.

HOW'D YOU DO?

Notice that in the last line of the event handler I named my TextBlock QueryText. If you named it something else, of course that line will look different. Don't let that confuse you.

```csharp
private async void QueryButton_Click(object sender, RoutedEventArgs e)
{
    StorageFolder folder = KnownFolders.PicturesLibrary;
    StorageFolderQueryResult result =
        folder.CreateFolderQuery(CommonFolderQuery.GroupByType);
    IReadOnlyList<StorageFolder> folderList = await result.GetFoldersAsync();

    System.Text.StringBuilder sb = new System.Text.StringBuilder();

    foreach (StorageFolder f in folderList)
    {
        IReadOnlyList<StorageFile> fileList = await f.GetFilesAsync();
        sb.AppendLine(f.Name + "s: " + fileList.Count.ToString());
    }

    QueryText.Text = sb.ToString();
}
```

```
Private Async Sub QueryButton_Click(object sender, RoutedEventArgs e)
    Dim folder As StorageFolder = KnownFolders.PicturesLibrary
    Dim result As StorageFolderQueryResult =
        folder.CreateFolderQuery(CommonFolderQuery.GroupByType)
    Dim folderList As IReadOnlyList(Of StorageFolder) = Await result.GetFoldersAsync()
    Dim sb As System.Text.StringBuilder = New System.Text.StringBuilder()

    For Each f As StorageFolder in FolderList
        Dim fileList As IReadOnlyList(Of StorageFile) = Await f.GetFilesAsync()
        sb.AppendLine(f.Name + "s: " + fileList.Count.ToString())
    Next

    QueryText.Text = sb.ToString()
End Sub
```

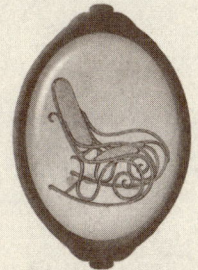

TAKE A BREAK

That's it for our exploration of files and capabilities. Why don't you take a break before you complete the Review and we move on to our last subject, Windows 8.1 contracts?

REVIEW

What class of object does ApplicationData.Current.TemporaryFolder return?

What happens if you try to programmatically access a restricted location without declaring it in the package manifest?

What kind of data can you store as a value in an ApplicationDataContainer?

Do you need to add a declaration to the package manifest in order to use a picker?

What method do you use to respond to a file activation?

When might you want to use an ApplicationDataCompositeValue?

Can you set additional query options if you use a CommonFileQuery or CommonFolderQuery?

Congratulations!
You've finished the chapter. Take a minute to think about what you've accomplished before you move on to the next one...

List three things you learned in this chapter:

Why do you think you need to know these things in order to develop Win8 apps?

Is there anything in this chapter that you think you need to understand in more detail? If so, what are you going to do about that?

App Contracts

Next up: app contracts. An app contract is an abstraction that allows apps to interact without knowing about one another.

There's a lot about Windows 8 that's pretty cool, but I think contracts might just be the coolest. Contracts power the charms that make Windows 8 apps consistent and discoverable (and allow them to function effectively without chrome). They also provide the infrastructure that allows Win8 apps to collaborate without prior knowledge.

Windows 8 defines seven contracts, although as we'll see in the next chapter, only six are really available to your app. In this chapter, we'll be exploring at the two most important in detail, because they'll give you the basic techniques you need to use the others.

We'll start by extending the work you've been doing with file handling by exploring the Share contract that allows you to make the files (and, actually, any other information that you choose) available to other applications. Share uses a lot of the techniques that are common to all contracts, so it seems a good place to start.

We'll build on that knowledge by exploring the Settings contract and see how simple it is to extend a Windows 8 charm with application-specific UI.

Fitting it in

Here's how this chapter fits in to the book as a whole...

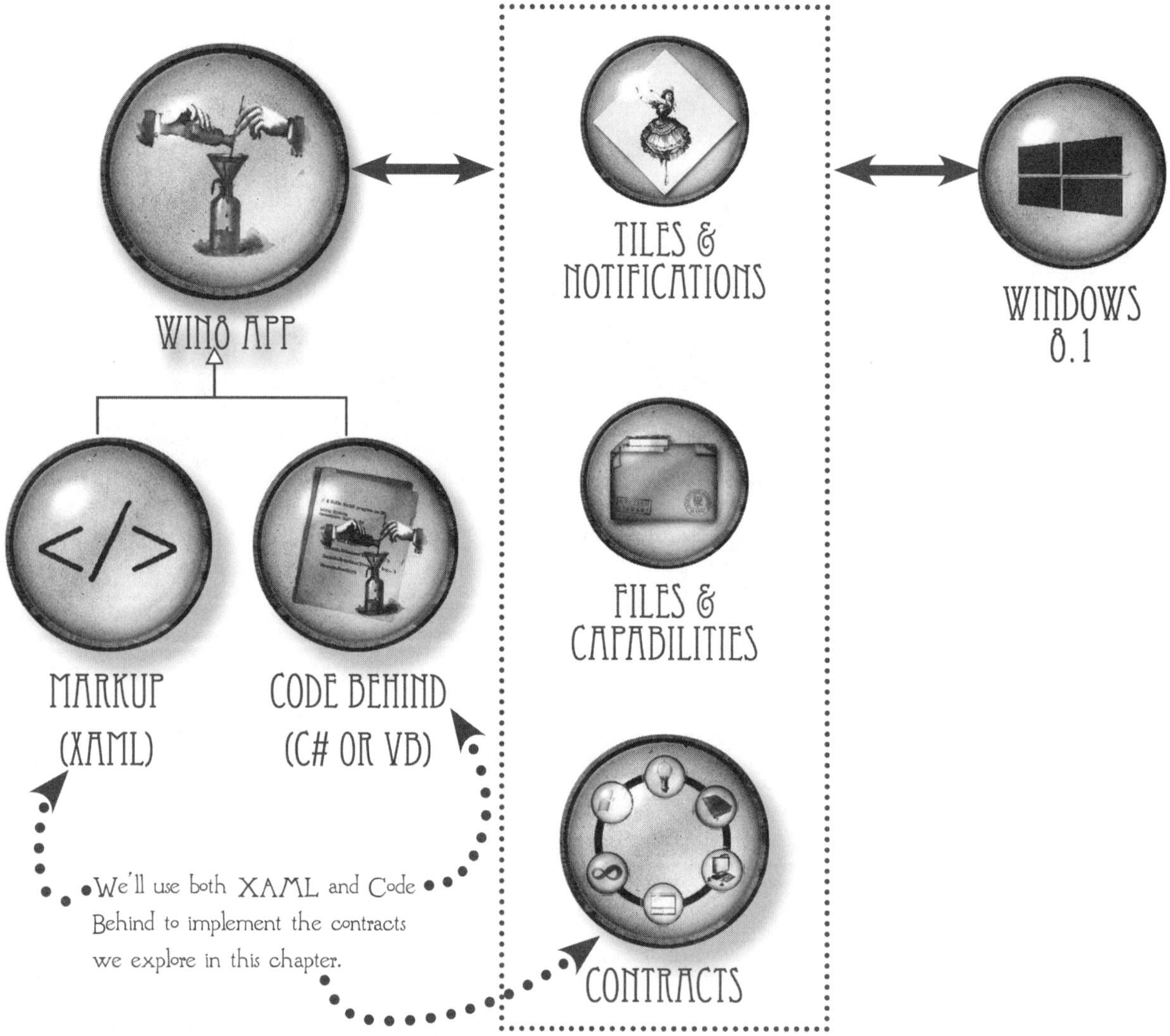

WinRT App

- MARKUP (XAML)
- CODE BEHIND (C# OR VB)

We'll use both XAML and Code Behind to implement the contracts we explore in this chapter.

- TILES & NOTIFICATIONS
- FILES & CAPABILITIES
- CONTRACTS

Windows 8.1

TASK LIST

In this chapter we'll explore the two most important and most commonly used of the app contracts that allow your app to interact with Windows 8 and other applications.

THE SHARE CONTRACT

There are actually two Share contracts in Win8. Your app can either provide data to other apps, receive data from other apps, or both. Since the Share contract is in many ways the simplest to implement, we'll start the chapter by building basic implementations of both providing and receiving shared data.

THE SETTINGS CONTRACT

The Settings contract is slightly unusual because it's not so much a way for apps to interact, as a common way for all apps to perform a particular set of tasks. It's a good example of how your app can interact with the UI displayed by the Win8 charm, and we'll explore it next.

THE SHARE CONTRACT

The Share contract includes two quite distinct operations—providing and receiving share data—that are implemented in very different ways. Here are the basic objects and processes involved in both:

SHARING DATA SYNCHRONOUSLY

Sharing data is much simpler than receiving it. (I'm sure there's a deep philosophical lesson there, but let's just move on, shall we?) In order to provide data to other apps, all you need to do is respond to the **DataRequested** event by returning a **DataRequest** object:

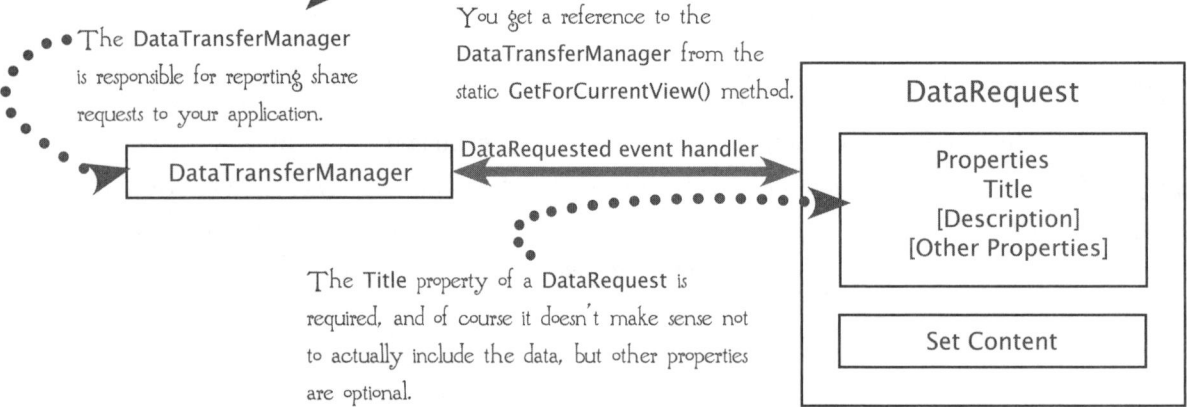

SHARING DATA ASYNCHRONOUSLY

If it might take a while for your app to provide the data being shared, you can use the **SetDataProvider** method to specify an asynchronous method instead of providing it directly:

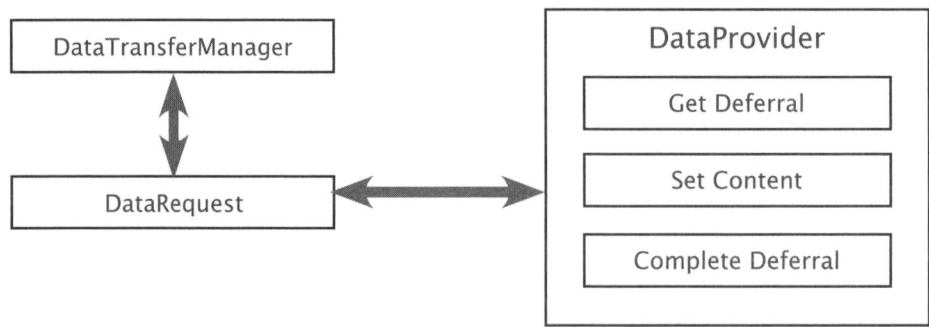

RECEIVING SHARED DATA

The process of receiving data from another application has a few more moving parts: You need to declare your intention to participate in the App Manifest, provide some UI to be displayed by the Share charm, and, of course, process the data you receive:

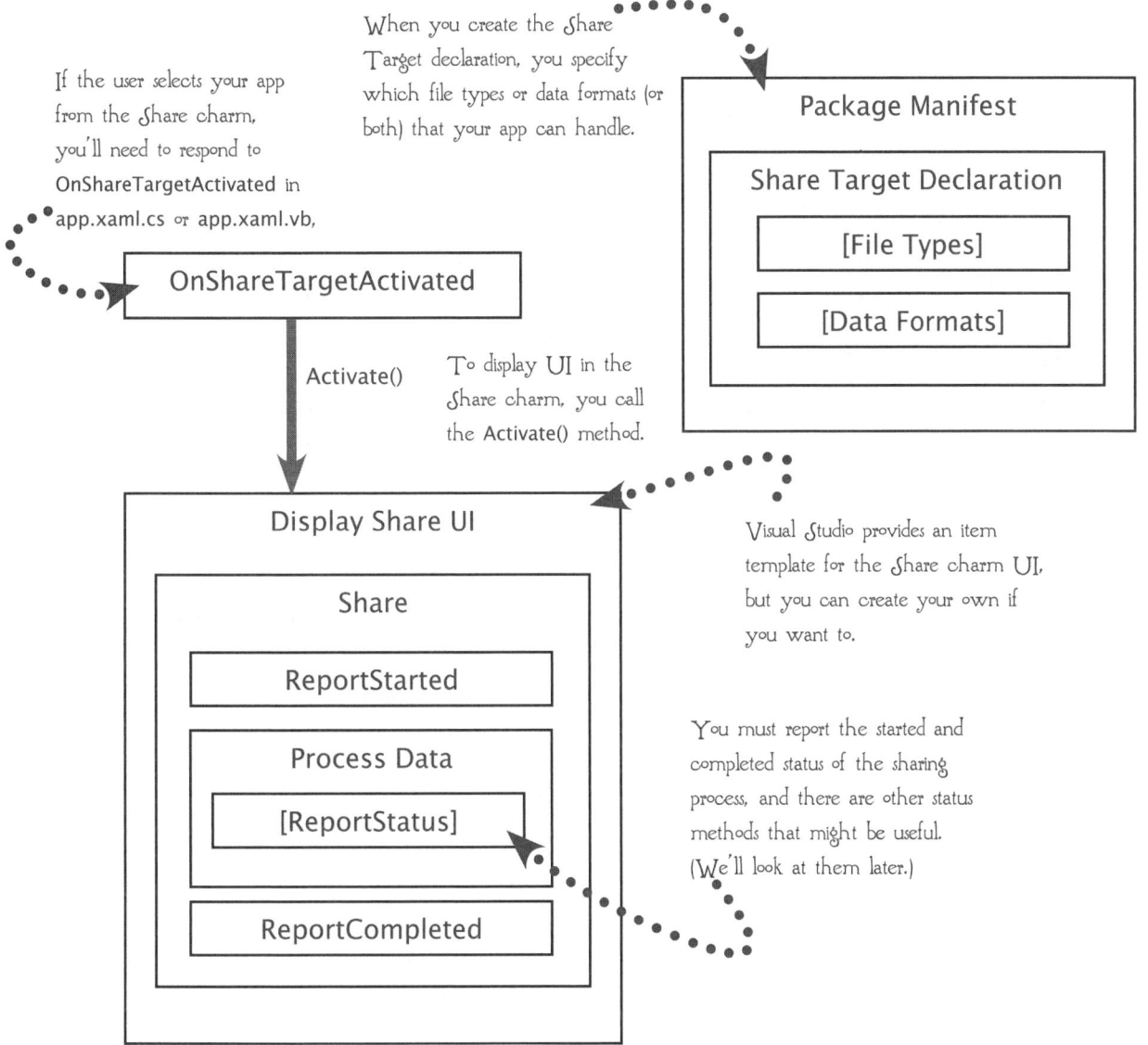

THE DATA REQUEST

In order to provide data to other apps via the Share contract, you only need to do a single thing: handle the DataRequested event. (But you do need to do it on each Page that can share data; it's not an App function.) The DataRequested event handler receives an instance of the DataRequestedEventArgs, which contains a single property, Request, and an instance of the DataPackage. In order to provide the data, all you need to do is set the properties of that object.

REGISTER FOR THE EVENT
You'll need to add a reference to the Windows.ApplicationModel.DataTransfer namespace and then call static the GetForCurrentView() method to retrieve a reference to the DataTransferManager:

```
DataTransferManager dtm = DataTransferManager.GetForCurrentView();
dtm.DataRequested += OnShareDataRequested;
```

COMPLETE THE REQUEST
In the event handler, you must provide the Title property (Description is strongly recommended, but not required) and call one of the Set...() methods to provide the data.

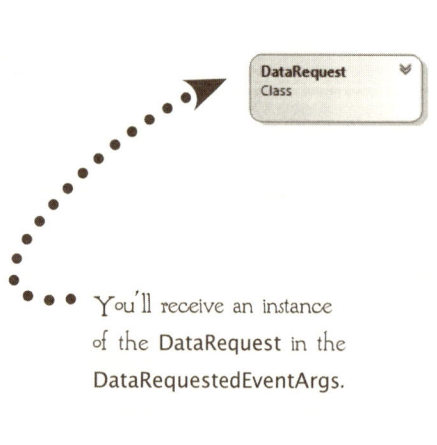

You'll receive an instance of the DataRequest in the DataRequestedEventArgs.

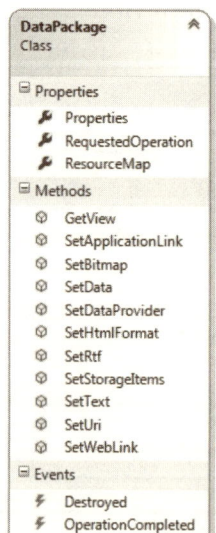

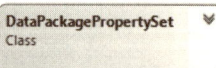

PUT ON YOUR THINKING HAT

Let's get started. Create a new project, and add the ability to share data:

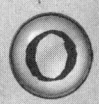

CREATE THE PROJECT

Create a new Blank project (I called mine **Sharing**), and replace the blank **MainPage.xaml** with one based on the Basic template.

DEFINE THE UI

We won't do anything tricky in this example, just share the contents of a **TextBox**, so define your app UI so that it has at least one **TextBox** with an x:Name property. Here's my version:

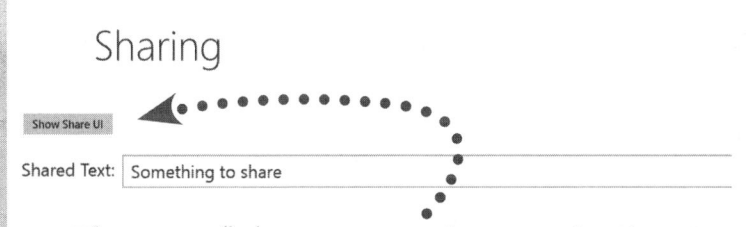

This **Button** calls the static **DataTransferManager.ShowShareUI()** method in its **Click** event handler. It's not necessary. In fact you'll hardly ever have a reason to do this. But I find it difficult to call up the Charms pane from inside the Simulator, and this does it for me.

REGISTER FOR AND RESPOND TO THE SHAREDATAREQUESTED EVENT

You'll need to set a reference to the **Windows.ApplicationModel.DataTransfer** namespace at the top of your file.

Inside the event handler, you'll need to set the **request.Data.Properties.Title** and **request.Data.Properties.Description** properties, and then call **request.Data.SetText()**.

HOW'D YOU DO?

Here's my version.

```csharp
public MainPage()
{
    ...
    DataTransferManager dtm = DataTransferManager.GetForCurrentView();
    dtm.DataRequested += ShareDataRequested;
}
```

```csharp
void ShareDataRequested(DataTransferManager sender,
        DataRequestedEventArgs args)
{
    DataRequest request = args.Request;
    request.Data.Properties.Title = "Sharing Newbie";
    request.Data.Properties.Description = "Our first example.";
    request.Data.SetText(this.SharedText.Text);
}
```

I called my TextBox SharedText. You could have named it something different.

```csharp
private void ShowShare_Click(object sender, RoutedEventArgs e)
{
    DataTransferManager.ShowShareUI();
}
```

```vb
Imorts Windows.ApplicationModel.DataTransfer
...
Public Sub New()
    ...
    Dim dtm As DataTransferManager = DataTransferManager.GetForCurrentView()
    AddHandler dtm.DataRequested, AddressOf ShareDataRequested
End Sub
```

```vb
Sub ShareDataRequested(sender As DataTransferManager,
            args As DataRequestedEventArgs)
    Dim request As DataRequest = args.Request
    request.Data.Properties.Title = "Sharing Newbie"
    request.Data.Properties.Description = "Our first example."
    request.Data.SetText(this.SharedText.Text)
End Sub
```

I called my TextBox SharedText. You could have named it something different.

```vb
Private Sub ShowShare_Click(sender As Object, e As RoutedEventArgs)
    DataTransferManager.ShowShareUI()
End Sub
```

DELAYED SHARING

Most of the time, returning the data immediately in the **DataRequested** event handler works just fine. If it's going to take your app some time (more than 200 milliseconds) to prepare the data, however, you can use the delayed sharing pattern. To use delayed sharing (sometimes called a **pull operation**), you call **SetDataProvider()** inside your event handler to reference an asynchronous method, and then use the deferral pattern to provide the data. Here are the basic steps:

SET THE DATA PROVIDER

Inside your **DataRequested** event handler, you'll call the **SetDataProvider()** method (instead of, for example, **SetText()**) and provide the format of data your handler handles, and a reference to the handler itself:

```
request.Data.SetDataProvider(StandardDataFormats.StorageItems,
    new DataProviderHandler(this.OnDeferredData));
```

The first parameter passed to the SetDataProver() method is actually defined as a string. You can use either one of the formats defined in the static **StandardDataFormats** class (which correspond to the Set...() methods of the request) or an actual string if you're providing a custom data type.

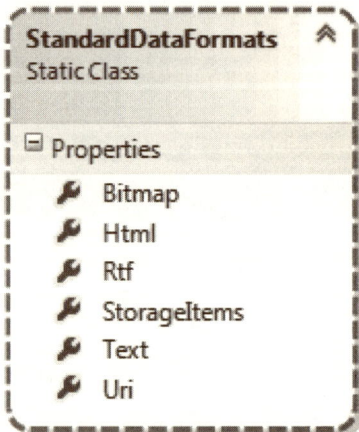

REQUEST A DEFERRAL

Inside your **DataProviderHandler**, you use the **DataRequest.GetDeferral()** to tell the **DataPackage** that you're going to be returning results asynchronously:

```csharp
DataProviderDeferral deferral = request.GetDeferral();
```

GENERATE THE DATA

After you have the **DataProviderDeferral**, you generate your data and call the appropriate **Set…()** method to provide it to the **DataPackage**. You don't need to do anything special here, just whatever needs to be done to create the data, which may or may not include making asyncronous calls like **LoadFileAsync()**.

SIGNAL COMPLETION

Once your **DataPackage** is complete, just call the **Complete()** method on the **DataProviderDeferral** to tell the **DataTransferManager** that everything's ready to go:

```csharp
deferral.Complete();
```

SHARE TARGETS

Providing data via the Share charm only requires interacting with an object that's available to your application without any special action on your part. It's not really a "contract" at all. Receiving shared data, however, is a different issue. It requires a declaration in the package manifest, the provision of UI to the Share charm, and (of course) interaction with an object, this time a `ShareOperation` instead of a `DataRequest`.

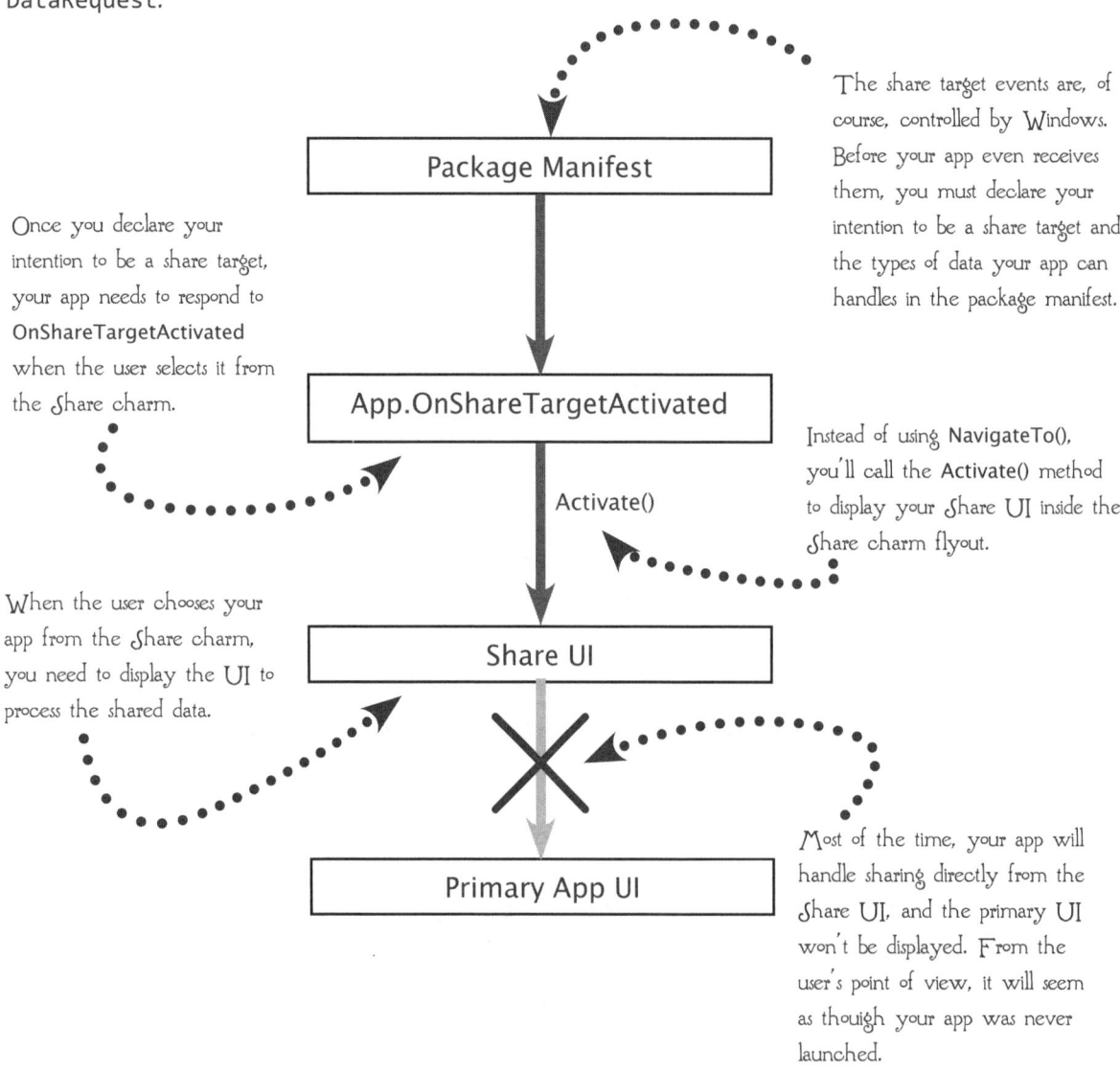

The share target events are, of course, controlled by Windows. Before your app even receives them, you must declare your intention to be a share target and the types of data your app can handles in the package manifest.

Once you declare your intention to be a share target, your app needs to respond to OnShareTargetActivated when the user selects it from the Share charm.

Instead of using NavigateTo(), you'll call the Activate() method to display your Share UI inside the Share charm flyout.

When the user chooses your app from the Share charm, you need to display the UI to process the shared data.

Most of the time, your app will handle sharing directly from the Share UI, and the primary UI won't be displayed. From the user's point of view, it will seem as though your app was never launched.

BUILDING A SHARE TARGET

Despite the number of moving parts involved in being a Share target, at least when compared to being a share data provider, there are really only four steps required:

DECLARE THE SHARE CONTRACT
Your app's participation in the Share contract is defined on the Declarations tab of the Manifest Designer. Once you select the declaration, you also need to tell Windows what types of data your app can display. We'll see how that works on the next page.

CREATE A SHARE UI
When the user selects your app from the Share charm, it needs to display some metadata about the shared data based on the **ShareTargetActivatedEventArgs** and a confirmation widget (typically a Button) to activate the sharing. You can create the UI from scratch or use the Share Contract Visual Studio item to give you a jump start, which is what we'll be doing in this chapter.

RESPOND TO ONSHARETARGETACTIVATED
Once you've registered for the Share target contract, your app will need to respond to **OnShareTargetActivated** within the **app.xaml.cs** or **app.xaml.vb** file. Typically, all you'll need to do is create an instance of the Share UI that you've created and then call its **Activate()** method.

HANDLE THE SHARED DATA
When the user activates the confirmation widget on your Share UI, your app needs to do...something....with the data being shared. What that "something" is will, of course, depend on the nature of your app. In our example, we'll just add it to the **LocalSettings** store and display in on the **MainPage** when the app is next launched.

SHARE TARGET CONTRACT

The first step to becoming a share target is to register a Share target declaration in the App Manifest. When you add the declaration, you must specify either a data format or a file extension, or select Supports any file type. You can add both data formats and extensions, but you must choose at least one.

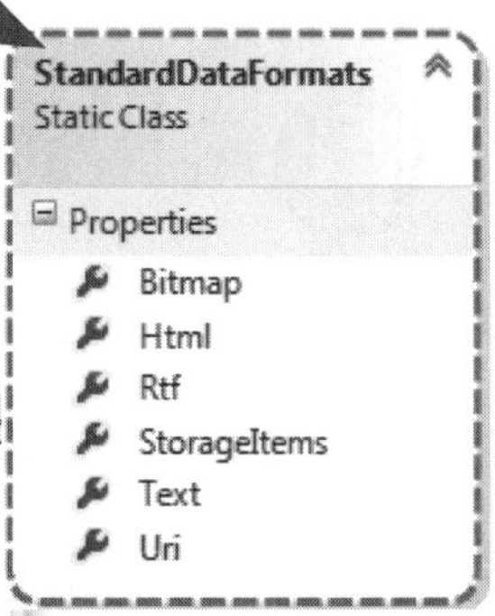

To add the declaration, just select it from the dropdown.

The specified data formats can be one of those defined by the StandardDataFormats enumeration, or a custom format.

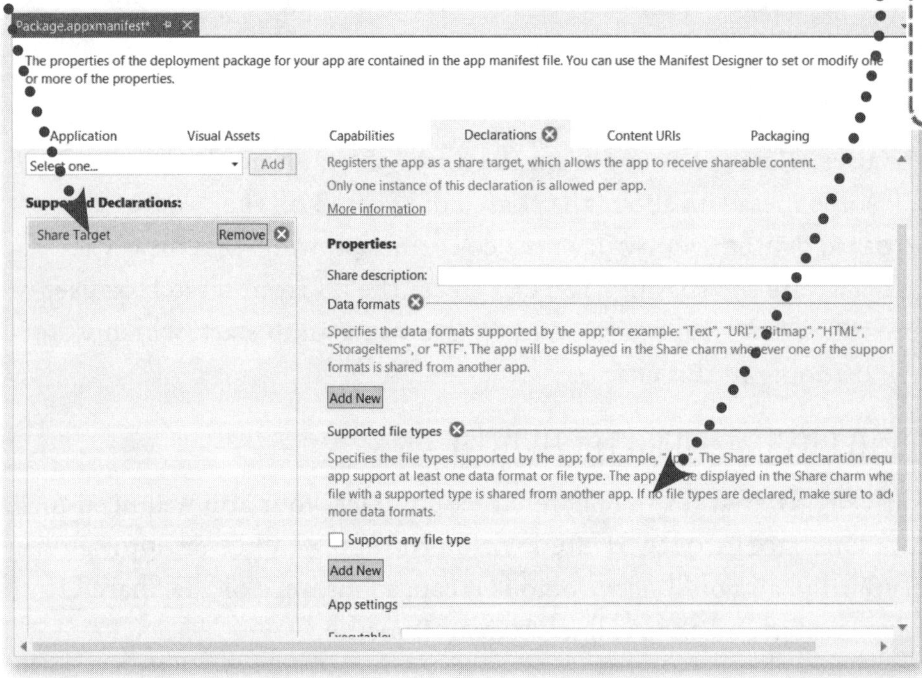

StandardDataFormats
Static Class

Properties
- Bitmap
- Html
- Rtf
- StorageItems
- Text
- Uri

> ## ON YOUR OWN
>
> Add the declaration to our sample project. Choose Text as the data format.

THE SHARE UI

When the user chooses your app from the Share charm, you need to display some content that replaces the original Share flyout. A standard Page will work, but Visual Studio contains an item template that gives you a jump-start on the process. (But your page won't look like this when we start. Trust me, we'll get there.

This heading will be added by Windows. The background color will be set to the background specified for your app, but otherwise you have no control over its content.

This TextBlock is bound to the Title of the shared data.

If the Thumbnail property of the DataRequest was set, it will be displayed here.

This TextBox allows the user to add a comment. If your app supports comments, you'll probably want to add some default text here.

I added a thumbnail to the sample. You won't see this in your example unless you do the same.

This TextBlock displays the Description.

You'll actually retrieve and process the data in the event handler for this Button.

There's plenty of room to add app-specific elements here.

ON YOUR OWN

Add the Share Target Contract item to our sample project.

Once you've added it, take a look at the code-behind. Where does the Share UI Page get the data it displays? How is it wired up?

THE CODE-BEHIND

The elements on the Page created by the Share Target Contract item are bound to entries in the DefaultViewModel of the Page which, in turn, are set to values in the ShareOperation passed to the ShareTargetActivatedEventArgs.

The ShareTargetActivatedEventArgs class includes a ShareOperation property. You'll need to access this later, so the item template stores it in a field called _shareOperation.

```csharp
public async void Activate(ShareTargetActivatedEventArgs e)
{
    this._shareOperation = e.ShareOperation;

    // Communicate metadata about the shared content through the view model
    var shareProperties = this._shareOperation.Data.Properties;
    var thumbnailImage = new BitmapImage();
    this.DefaultViewModel["Title"] = shareProperties.Title;
    this.DefaultViewModel["Description"] = shareProperties.Description;
    this.DefaultViewModel["Image"] = thumbnailImage;
    this.DefaultViewModel["Sharing"] = false;
    this.DefaultViewModel["ShowImage"] = false;
    this.DefaultViewModel["Comment"] = String.Empty;
    this.DefaultViewModel["Placeholder"] = "Add a comment";
    this.DefaultViewModel["SupportsComment"] = true;
    Window.Current.Content = this;
    Window.Current.Activate();

    // Update the shared content's thumbnail image in the background
    if (shareProperties.Thumbnail != null)
    {
        var stream = await shareProperties.Thumbnail.OpenReadAsync();
        thumbnailImage.SetSource(stream);
        this.DefaultViewModel["ShowImage"] = true;
    }
}
```

```vb
Public Async Sub Activate(e As ShareTargetActivatedEventArgs)
    Me._shareOperation = e.ShareOperation

    Dim shareProperties = Me._shareOperation.Data.Properties;
    Dim thumbnailImage = new BitmapImage()
    Me.DefaultViewModel["Title"] = shareProperties.Title
    Me.DefaultViewModel["Description"] = shareProperties.Description
    Me.DefaultViewModel["Image"] = thumbnailImage
    Me.DefaultViewModel["Sharing"] = false
    Me.DefaultViewModel["ShowImage"] = false
    Me.DefaultViewModel["Comment"] = String.Empty
    Me.DefaultViewModel["Placeholder"] = "Add a comment"
    Me.DefaultViewModel["SupportsComment"] = true
    Window.Current.Content = Me
    Window.Current.Activate()

    // Update the shared content's thumbnail image in the background
    If No tshareProperties.Thumbnail Is Nothing
        Dim stream = await shareProperties.Thumbnail.OpenReadAsync()
        thumbnailImage.SetSource(stream)
        Me.DefaultViewModel["ShowImage"] = true
    End If
End Sub
```

The ShareOperation and its associated classes replace the DataRequest but provides similar functionality.

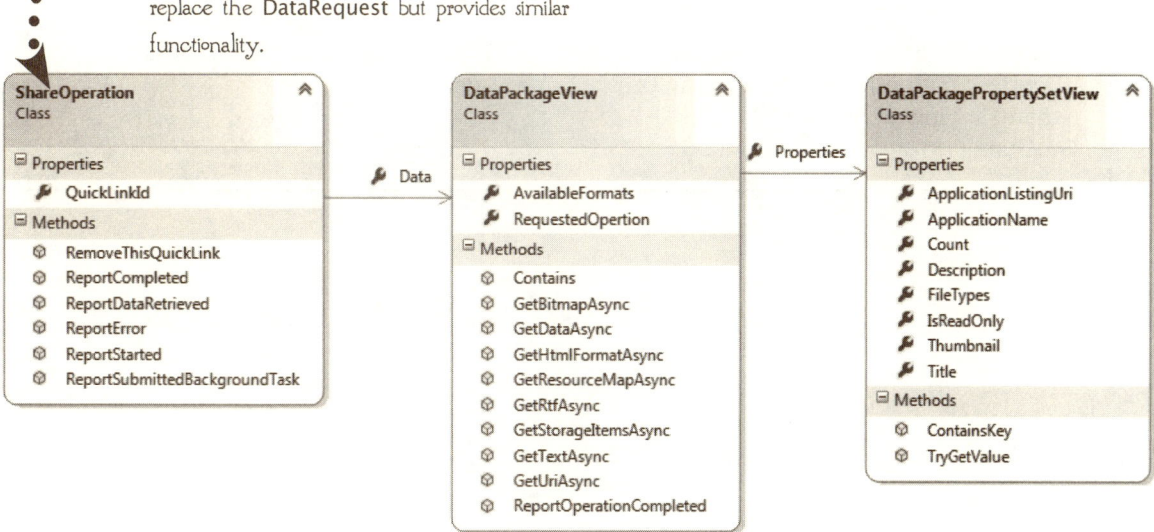

ACTIVATING AND RESPONDING

Just two steps left: Your app must display the Share page in response in the `OnShareTargetActivated` method in `app.xaml.cs` or `app.xaml.vb`, and it must do something with the data it receives. The first step, activation, is simple:

TO RESPOND TO ACTIVATION

As I've said, once you declare your intention to be a share target, your app will begin to receive share activation methods. You respond to them by instantiating your Share UI class and passing the **ShareTargetActivatedEventArgs** to it in the **Activate()** method. The code is actually added when you add the template:

```csharp
private override void OnShareTargetActivated(ShareTargetActivatedEventArgs e)
{
    var shareTargetPage = new Sharing.ShareTargetPage();
    shareTargetPage.Activate(e);
}
```

```vb
Private Overrides Sub OnShareTargetActivated(e As ShareTargetActivatedEventArgs)
    Dim shareTargetPage = New Sharing.ShareTargetPage()
    shareTargetPage.Activate(e)
End Sub
```

The Page created by the Share Target Contract item provides the basic UI infrastructure for responding to the share activation, but of course you can replace it with a UI that better suits the function of your app. Either way, the basic steps you'll need to use inside your "do it" widget, whether it's the Button provided by the item template or something you've built yourself, are pretty straightforward.

TELL WINDOWS YOU'RE STARTING

You should call the ShareOperation.ReportStarted() method to let Windows know that you're starting to process the data. If you're using the template infrastructure, you should also set the Sharing item in the DefaultViewModel. The template contains code to do both of these things for you.

PROCESS THE DATA

In this step you do whatever it is your app is going to do with the data. The ShareOperation includes a couple more methods you can call to keep Windows up to date during this process: ReportDataRetrieved(), ReportSubmittedBackgroundTask(), and ReportError().

TELL WINDOWS YOU'RE DONE

The last step is just to call ShareOperation.ReportCompleted() to tell Windows that you're finished.

> ### PUT ON YOUR THINKING HAT
>
> In the ShareButton_Click event handler, add the received data to the LocalSettings collection (you'll need to add a reference to the Windows.Storage namespace), and then call ApplicationData.Current.SignalDataChanged() to let the rest of your app know that it's happened.

HOW'D YOU DO?

Here's my version. Notice that in order to call **GetTextAsync()** you'll need to update the method signature.

```csharp
private async void ShareButton_Click(object sender, RoutedEventArgs e)
{
    this.DefaultViewModel["Sharing"] = true;
    this._shareOperation.ReportStarted();
    ApplicationData.Current.LocalSettings.Values["receivedText"] =
        await this._shareOperation.Data.GetTextAsync();
    ApplicationData.Current.SignalDataChanged();
    this._shareOperation.ReportCompleted();
}
```

```vb
Imports Windows.Storage
...
Private Async Sub ShareButton_Click(sender As Object, e As RoutedEventArgs)
    Me.DefaultViewModel("Sharing") = True
    Me._shareOperation.ReportStarted()
    ApplicationData.Current.LocalSettings.Values("receivedText") =
        await this._shareOperation.Data.GetTextAsync()
    ApplicationData.Current.SignalDataChanged()
    Me._shareOperation.ReportCompleted()
End Sub
```

PUT ON YOUR THINKING HAT

One last task: Update MainPage.xaml to display the received data. You'll need to register for the ApplicationData.Current.DataChanged event in the class constructor and write a couple of methods to update the display.

Sharing

Show Share UI

Shared Text: Something to share

Received Text: Something shared

There's nothing particularly tricky about registering for the DataChanged event, but updating the display does present a problem: the event occurs on a background thread, not the UI thread, so you have to use the Dispatcher to re-allocate it:

```csharp
async void OnDataChanged(ApplicationData sender, object args)
{
    await this.Dispatcher.RunAsync(Windows.UI.Core.CoreDispatcherPriority.Normal,
        UpdateDisplay);
}
```

```vb
Async Sub OnDataChanged(sender As ApplicationData, args As Object)
    Await Me.Dispatcher.RunAsync(Windows.UI.Core.CoreDispatcherPriority.Normal,
        UpdateDisplay)
End Sub
```

Test the app. You can share directly from the app to the app, which is a strange thing to do, but works, or you can share from another app.

HOW'D YOU DO?
Here's my version.

```csharp
public MainPage()
{
    ...
    ApplicationData.Current.DataChanged += OnDataChanged;
}

async void OnDataChanged(ApplicationData sender, object args)
{
    await this.Dispatcher.RunAsync(Windows.Ui.Core.CoreDispatcherPriority.Normal,
        UpdateDisplay);
}

void UpdateDisplay()
{
    ApplicationDataContainer settings = ApplicationData.Current.LocalSettings;

    if (settings.Values.ContainsKey("receivedText"))
        this.ReceivedText.Text = (string)settings.Values["receivedText"];
}
```

```vb
Public New()
    ...
    AddHandler ApplicationData.Current.DataChanged, AddressOf OnDataChanged
End Sub

Async Sub OnDataChanged(sender As ApplicationData, args As Object)
    Await Me.Dispatcher.RunAsync(Windows.Ui.Core.CoreDispatcherPriority.Normal,
        AddressOf UpdateDisplay)
End Sub

Sub UpdateDisplay()
    Dim settings As ApplicationDataContainer = ApplicationData.Current.LocalSettings

    If settings.Values.ContainsKey("receivedText") Then
        Me.ReceivedText.Text = TryCast(settings.Values("receivedText"), String)
    End If
End Sub
```

REVIEW

Can you answer the following questions based on what you've learned?

Your app can both share data and receive shared data. Which operation requires a declaration?

What method do you call inside the OnShareRequested() method in order to provide data asynchronously?

Do you need to provide both a data format and a file type in a Share target declaration?

What two properties are required in a DataRequest?

What two methods must you call when you're processing received data to keep Windows up to date with what's going on?

Why do you need to use the Dispatcher when you update the display in response to a DataChanged event?

THE SETTINGS CONTRACT

In complexity, participating in the Settings contract lives somewhere between providing and receiving shared data. You don't need to add a declaration, but you do need to provide a UI (there's a template). Like both sharing functions, you'll interact with an object (the SettingsPane in this case) and respond to an event (CommandsRequested) in your app.xaml code-behind.

The documentation calls these ENTRY POINTS. The class library calls them COMMANDS. Either way, you shouldn't have more than about four of them.

We're only adding options, but your app would typically also include Privacy Policy (required) and Help entry points.

The header must contain a back button, the name of the entry point, and the app logo.

The Settings UI must be either 346 or 646 pixels wide. (The template is 346.)

Windows will add a Permissions and possibly a Rate and Review entry point.

When a user selects an entry point, your app displays the appropriate UI.

The header background should be the same as your app background, the border should be 20% darker, and the content pane background should be white.

665

CREATING COMMANDS

The `SettingsPane` class, declared in the `Windows.UI.ApplicationSettings` namespace, is responsible for handling the interaction between the Settings charm and your app. Unlike the Share charm, you won't receive app-level events for the Settings charm; you need to register for the `SettingsPane.CommandRequested` event instead, typically in the `OnWindowCreated()` method of the App class.

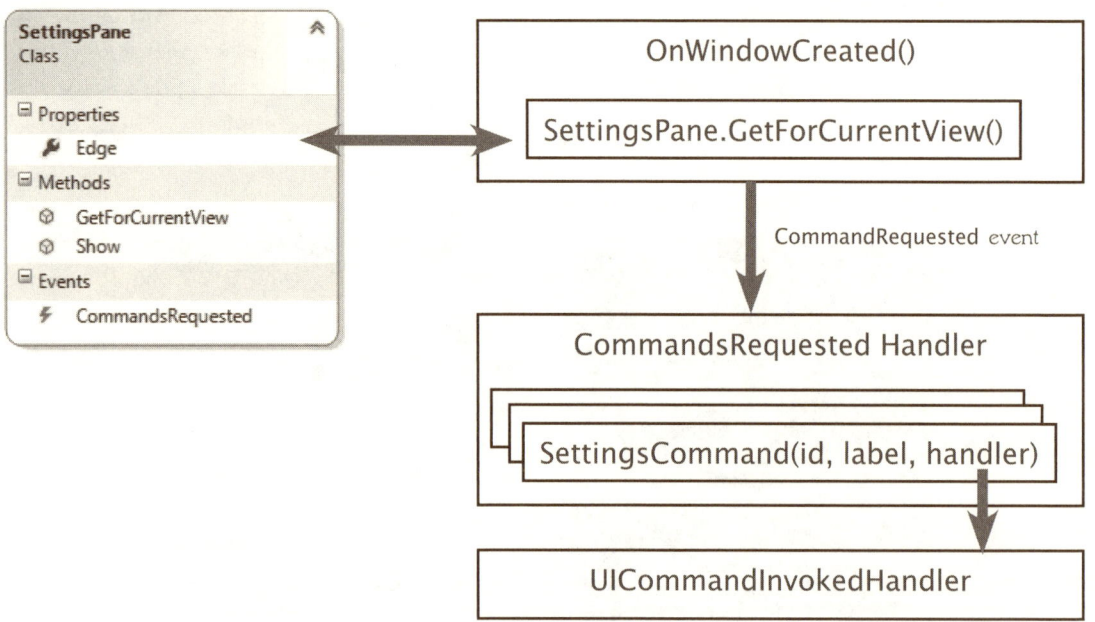

MAKE A NOTE

There was no intrinsic support for the Settings contract in the Windows 8.0 XAML platform. (Yes, there was in JavaScript. Lucky sods.) Windows 8.1 has changed that with the introduction of the `SettingsFlyout` control. There's even an item template that gives you a pretty good head start on layout. All this is good stuff, but be careful when you're poking around MSDN—as I write this, there's still a lot of guidance that pertains to 8.0. If what you're reading doesn't talk about the `SettingsFlyout`, it's probably obsolete.

DISPLAYING SETTINGS

You actually did this back in Chapter 2 (but I'll forgive you if you don't remember). Here's the process in a nutshell.

CREATE A SETTINGS FLYOUT
You'll almost always start with the Settings Flyout item template.

REGISTER FOR THE COMMANDSREQUESTED EVENT
The **SettingsPane** class exposes a static **GetForCurrentView()** method that you can use to register for the event. You'll typically do this in an **OnWindowCreated()** method in the **App.xaml** code-behind. (You'll need to add a reference to the **Windows.UI.ApplicationSettings** namespace.)

CREATE THE ENTRY POINT
Inside the **CommandsRequested** event, you'll need to create an instance of a SettingsCommand and add it to the **args.Request.ApplicationCommands** collection for each entry point that you want to add to the Settings charm.

CREATE THE EVENT HANDLER
Finally, you'll need to create the body of the event handler that will be called whenever the user selects one of your entry points on the Settings charm. It just needs to instantiate and show your flyout.

PUT ON YOUR THINKING HAT

Think you can do it? Add a Settings Flyout item to your project (I called mine **CustomSettings**) using the template and wire it up using the steps above to guide you.

If you can get everything working without help, be very proud of yourself. But don't feel bad if you need to check some syntax here and there. After all, checking syntax is pretty much standard operating procedure, right?

HOW'D YOU DO?
Here's my version.

```csharp
protected override void OnWindowCreated(WindowCreatedEventArgs args)
{
    base.OnWindowCreated(args);
    SettingsPane.GetForCurrentView().CommandsRequested += App_CommandsRequested;
}

void App_CommandsRequested(SettingsPane sender, SettingsPaneCommandsRequestedEventArgs args)
{
    args.Request.ApplicationCommands.Add(new SettingsCommand(
        "Custom Setting", "Custom Setting", (handler) => ShowCustomSettingsFlyout()));
}

public void ShowCustomSettingsFlyout()
{
    CustomSettings settingsFlyout = new CustomSettings();
    settingsFlyout.Show();
}
```

```vb
Imports Windows.UI.ApplicationSettings
Imports Windows.UI.Popups
...
Protected Overrides Sub OnWindowCreated(args As WindowCreatedEventArgs)
    MyBase.OnWindowCreated(args)
    AddHandler SettingsPane.GetForCurrentView().CommandsRequested,
        AddressOf App_CommandsRequested
End Sub

Sub App_CommandsRequested(sender As SettingsPane, args As
        SettingsPaneCommandsRequestedEventArgs)
    Dim handler as New UICommandInvokedHandler(AddressOf ShowCustomSettingsFlyout)
    args.Request.ApplicationCommands.Add(new SettingsCommand(
        "Custom Setting", "Custom Setting", handler))
End Sub

Public Sub ShowCustomSettingsFlyout()
    CustomSettings settingsFlyout = New CustomSettings()
    settingsFlyout.Show()
End Sub
```

SETTINGS UI

As I've said, a `UserControl` works well for defining the content of your Settings UI. The working content can contain whatever you want, but the guidelines have some specific requirements for the heading.

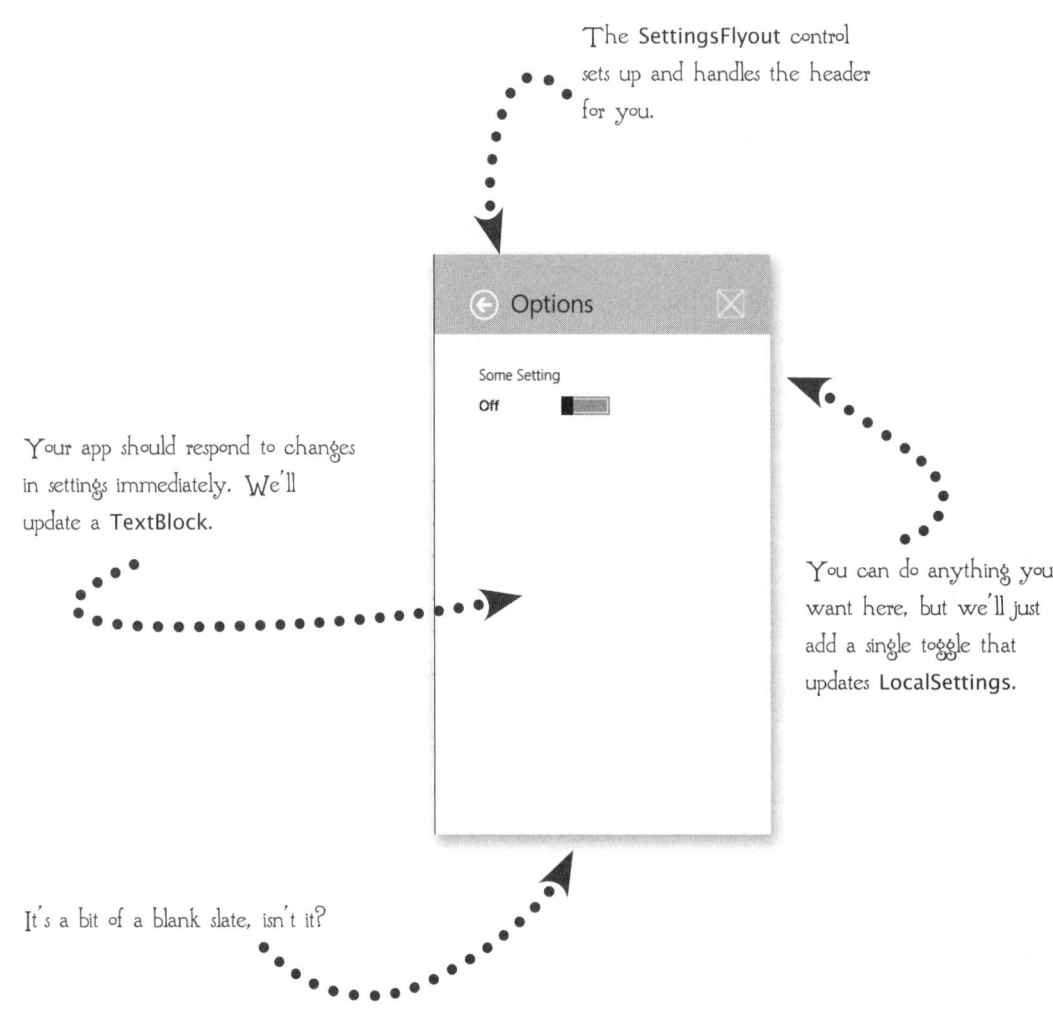

PUT ON YOUR THINKING HAT

Well, are you sitting down? You already know everything you need to know to implement the settings toggle. Shouldn't come as too much of a surprise, after all, you've almost finished the book. But everything you need to do at this point, you've already done:

CREATE THE TOGGLESWITCH

This is just standard XAML. You'll want to give it a name so you can refer to it in code, and add a Toggled event handler.

SET THE INITIAL TOGGLE VALUE

We'll use ApplicationData.Current.LocalSettings to store the value of the setting. You'll need to read that in the Page constructor. I created a class property to store the ApplicationDataContainer, but that isn't strictly necessary.

HANDLE THE TOGGLED EVENT

You'll need to update LocalSettings and call the SignalDataChanged event to make sure any Page that's displayed updates its value.

DISPLAY THE SETTING

Add a simple TextBlock to MainPage.xaml and give it a name so you can refer to it in code.

UPDATE THE PAGE

Because the MainPage.xaml in our sample app is based on the Basic page template, most of the plumbing we need—registering for the DataChanged event and updating the display—is already there. (You'd have to add it if we were working with a Blank page.)

All you need to do is add the code to update the TextBlock to the UpdateDisplay() method, and add a call to UpdateDisplay() at the end of the constructor to set up the Page up when it first loads.

HOW'D YOU DO?
Here's my version. (The VB code is on the next page.)

```csharp
using Windows.Storage;

namespace Sharing
{
    public sealed partial class CustomSettings : SettingsFlyout
    {
        private ApplicationDataContainer settingsData;

        public CustomSettings()
        {
            this.InitializeComponent();
            settingsData = ApplicationData.Current.LocalSettings;
            if (settingsData.Values.ContainsKey("setting"))
            {
                this.SettingToggle.IsOn = ((string)settingsData.Values["setting"] == "On" ? true : false);
            }
            else
            {
                settingsData.Values["setting"] = "Off";
                this.SettingToggle.IsOn = false;
            }
        }

        private void SettingToggle_Toggled(object sender, RoutedEventArgs e)
        {

            settingsData.Values["setting"] = (this.SettingToggle.IsOn ? "On" : "Off");
            ApplicationData.Current.SignalDataChanged();
        }
    }
}
```

```csharp
namespace Sharing
{
    ...
    public sealed partial class MainPage : Page
    {
        ...
        public MainPage()
        {
            ...
            ApplicationData.Current.DataChanged += OnDataChanged;
            UpdateDisplay();
        }

        ...
        void UpdateDisplay()
        {
            ApplicationDataContainer settingsData = ApplicationData.Current.LocalSettings;
            if (settingsData.Values.ContainsKey("receivedText"))
                this.ReceivedText.Text = (string)settingsData.Values["receivedText"];
            if (settingsData.Values.ContainsKey("setting"))
            {
                this.SettingText.Text = "The custom setting is " + (string)settingsData.Values["setting"];
            }
            else
            {
                this.SettingText.Text = "The custom setting is off";
            }
        }
    }
}
```

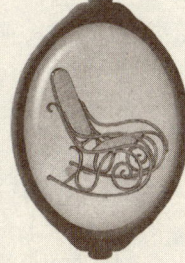

TAKE A BREAK

That's it for our exploration of contracts. We didn't look at all of them, but we did use all the techniques you'll need to implement the others. Why don't you take a break now before you complete the Review and we move on to searching in the next chapter?

REVIEW

Can you think of any reason not to use a SettingsFlyout in an app?

There are actually two Share contracts. What are they? Can your app subscribe to just one?

Why do you need to use the Displatcher when you respond to a DataChanged event? Do you think that might apply to other contracts?

What entry points are required in the Settings pane for Windows Store certification?

In our example, we used LocalSettings to store our data. We could have used RoamingSettings instead. Why would you use one over the other?

Congratulations! You've finished the chapter. Take a minute to think about what you've accomplished before you move on to the next one...

List three things you learned in this chapter:

Why do you think you need to know these things in order to develop Win8 apps?

Is there anything in this chapter that you think you need to understand in more detail? If so, what are you going to do about that?

Search

One of the biggest, and certainly one of the most confusing, changes between Windows 8.0 and Windows 8.1 is in the handling of search functionality. This book isn't really about the platform differences, but in this case the change is so fundamental, and because of concerns about backward compatability, the documentation is so confusing, that I want to start by explaining exactly what's going on.

In Windows 8.0, Search was a contract, just like the Share and Settings contracts we looked at in the last chapter. The Search guidance was that "find on page" functionality should be implemented inside your app (typically via the `AppBar`), but more general "find information my app manages" functionality should be accessed through the charm.

In Windows 8.1, the Search contract is effectively a front end to the Bing search engine (although it does provide the option of searching local files and settings). A new XAML control, the `SearchBox`, has been added to the platform to provide rich in-app searching using essentially the same techniques that were used to support the Search charm in 8.0.

Now Microsoft, for all their faults (and they do suffer from enthusiasms, don't they?), are pretty good about maintaining backward compatibility, and they haven't broken the 8.0 apps that rely on Search charm integration. All that functionality is still there, and there's even an app sample demonstrating Search charm integration in 8.1.

So far, so good. But this is where it gets confusing. The 8.0 functionality isn't broken, exactly, the apps still run, but the functionality is, well, let's call it "bent". If an app implements the Search contract using the techniques you learned in the last chapter, it might appear that it is participating in system-wide search, but it isn't. **The Search charm is just how your users will get to in-app search.** The app will only be listed on the "Search Where" dropdown when it's open and has focus.

So the take-away here is that **Windows 8.1 has a very powerful application search mechanism** that includes search history and several different kinds of suggestions. The XAML platform now has a control to surface that functionality in your apps. These are all very good things. But you no longer have access to system-wide search. The Microsoft documentation that implies (and occasionally states outright) that you do is essentially incorrect. Sigh. They meant well.

FITTING IT IN

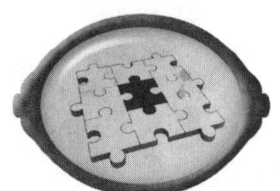

Here's how this chapter fits in to the book as a whole...

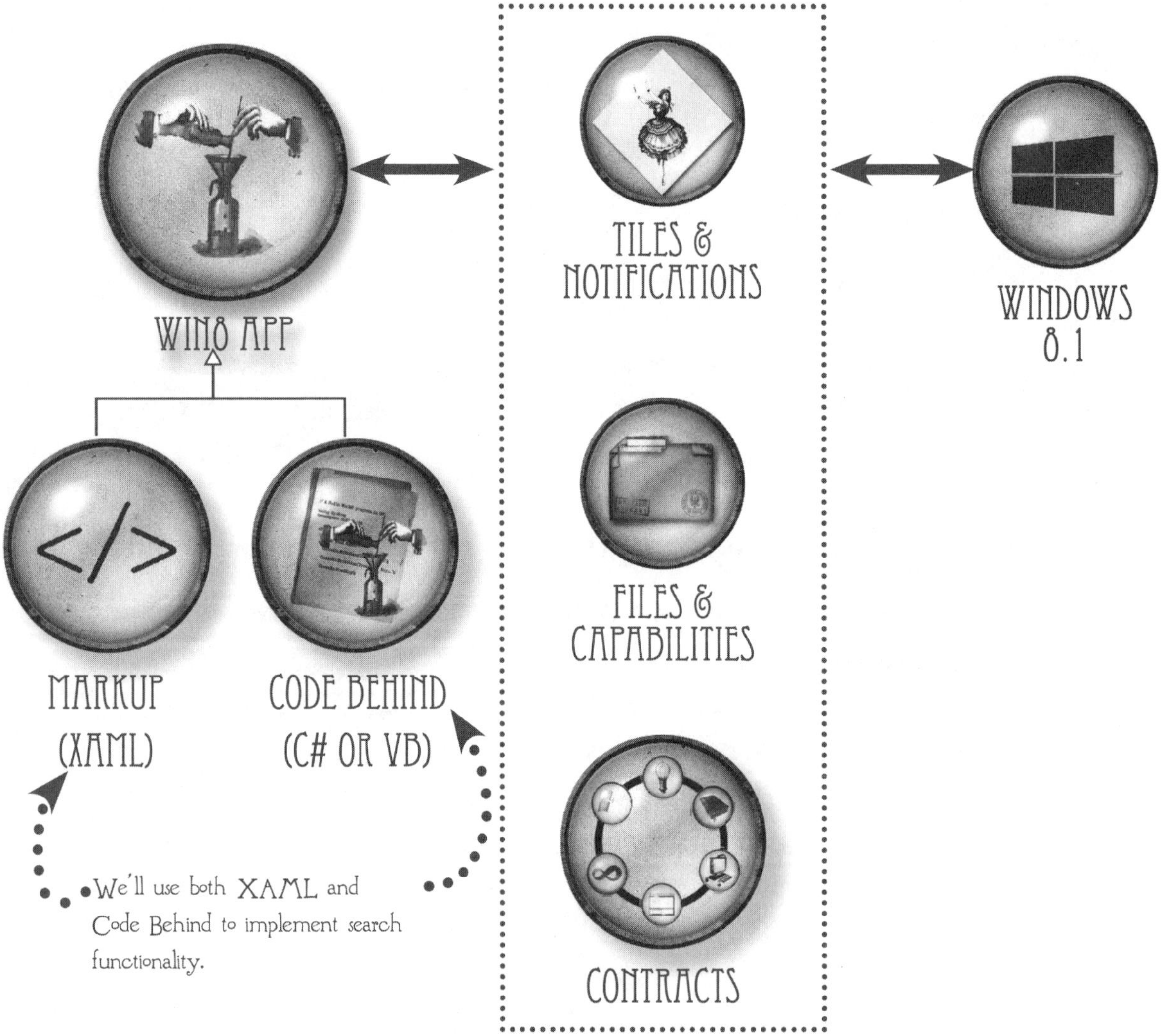

WIN8 APP

MARKUP (XAML)

CODE BEHIND (C# OR VB)

• We'll use both XAML and Code Behind to implement search functionality.

TILES & NOTIFICATIONS

FILES & CAPABILITIES

CONTRACTS

WINDOWS 8.1

TASK LIST

In this chapter we'll explore the last of the important app contracts that allow your app to interact with Windows 8.1 and other applications: Search.

SEARCH BASICS

We'll start off by looking at how search functionality works in Windows 8.1 and exploring the properties and methods of the **SearchBox** control.

QUERY SUGGESTIONS

Once we have a simple app to work with, we'll explore the two types of query suggestions that you can provide your users and how you'll generate and submit each.

QUERY RESULTS

Finally, we'll look at handling the **QuerySubmitted** event. In doing so, we'll explore (and modify) the Query Results page template that provides a lot of the basic functionality but doesn't quite get things right.

SEARCH BASICS

There are two essential "bits" to implementing search in your app: some way for the user to enter a search term, and a page to display the results. You'll almost always use the SearchBox as the input mechanism, and Visual Studio provides a Search Results item template that will give you a head start on the results page.

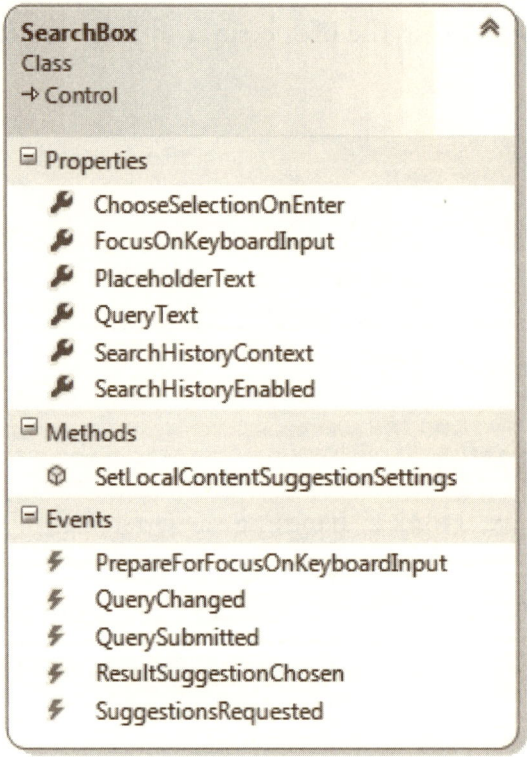

ON YOUR OWN

In order to have something to search, let's create a new project and import the color classes we created in Chapter 12.

⓪ CREATE THE PROJECT

Create a new project (I called mine **Search**) and replace the MainPage.xaml with one based on the Basic Page template.

① IMPORT THE CLASSES

Import the **ColorDetails** and **ColorCollection** classes from the project you created in Chapter 12 (or the sample code). You'll need to update the namespace declarations.

② ADD A SEARCHBOX

For our purposes, we can just put the widget directly on the app canvas. Be sure to give it a name. (I called mine **ColorSearch**.)

③ ADD A SEARCH RESULTS ITEM

We'll be modifying this later, but go ahead and add a new **Page** now. (I called mine **ColorSearchResults**.)

SEARCH EVENTS

Like the Settings contract, Search is an application-level function, so the methods for responding to it should live in the **App.xaml** code-behind. Here are the ones you'll need to think about:

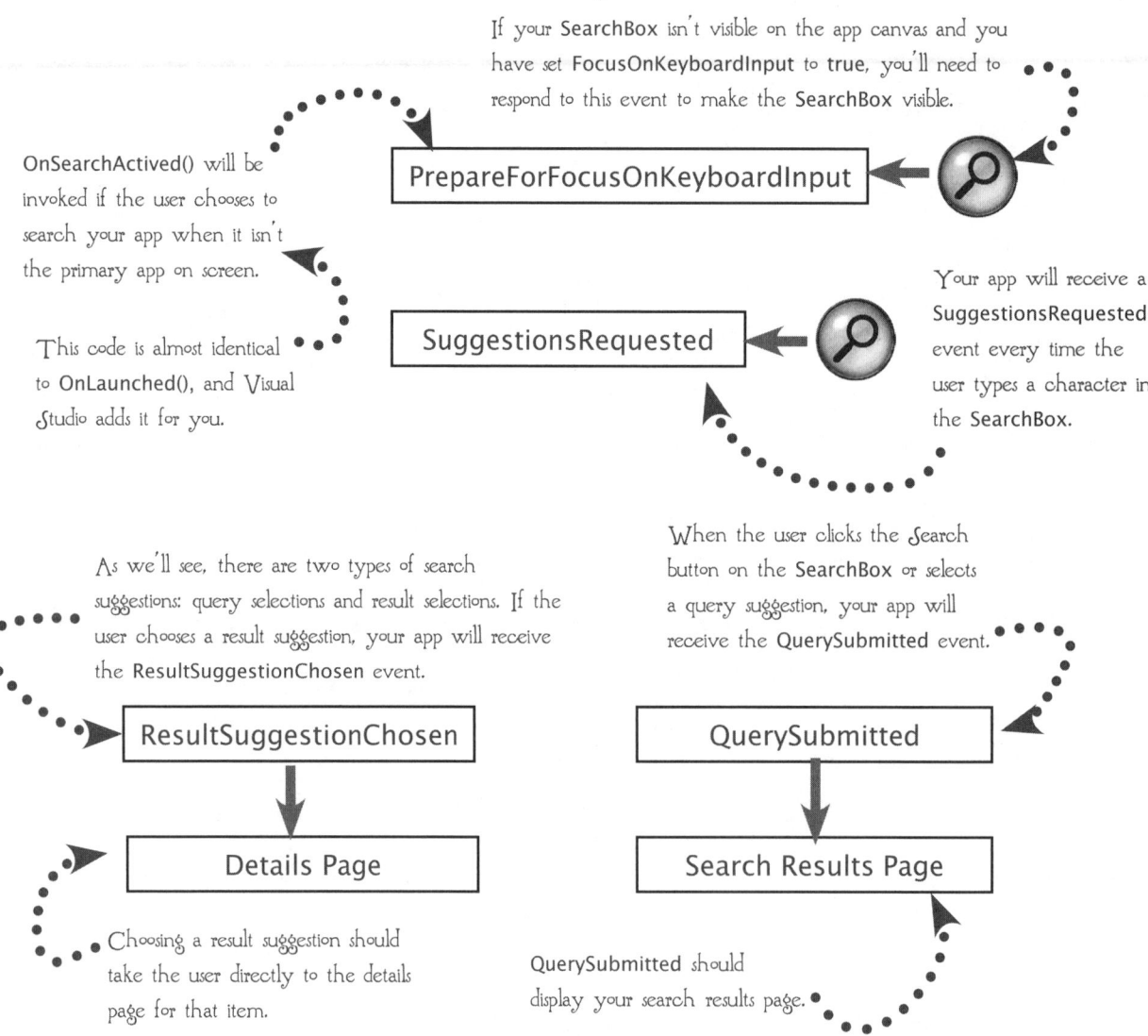

PUT ON YOUR THINKING HAT

There's one last thing we need to do to get the basic search plumbing in place: display the search results in response to the QuerySubmitted event.

The QuerySubmitted event receives an instance of the SearchBoxQuerySubmittedEventArgs. The class exposes some properties that are useful in multi-lingual apps, but the only one we need to worry about is the QueryText, which you should pass to the Frame.Navigate() method.

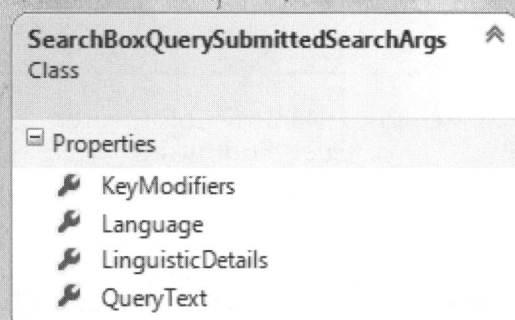

① Add a QuerySubmitted event handler to the SearchBox on MainPage that displays your search results page, passing it the QueryText from event args.

② Run the app and enter a search term. Everything work okay? (If not, fix it!) Now run it a second time. What happens? Do you know why?

MAKE A NOTE

The UX guidelines for search dictate that if you implement it, you should implement it on every page (in the same place, in the same way). We'll only have a single page to worry about in our little example, so we'll put the code directly in the code-behind file. But in a real application, you don't want to be duplicating code all over the place, so you'll almost certainly want to create a custom control based on the SearchBox to wrap up your app-specific search code.

HOW'D YOU DO?
Here's my version.

```
<SearchBox x:Name="ColorSearch" ...
           QuerySubmitted="ColorSearch_QuerySubmitted" />
```

```csharp
private void ColorSearch_QuerySubmitted(SearchBox sender,
                    SearchBoxQuerySubmittedArgs args)
{
   this.Frame.Navigate(typeof(ColorSearchResults), args.QueryText)
}
```

```vb
Private Sub ColorSearch_QuerySubmitted(sender As SearchBox,
                    args As SearchBoxQuerySubmittedArgs)
   Me.Frame.Navigate(GetType(ColorSearchResults), args.QueryText)
End Sub
```

When you run the app a second time, the query term you entered the first time will show up below the **SearchBox**. This happens because the **SearchBox** is the only thing on our page, so it automatically has focus, and because the control's **SearchHistoryEnabled** property is **true**, which it is by default.

QUERY SUGGESTIONS

It isn't strictly necessary, but it's only polite to provide suggestions to users when they start typing in the **SearchBox**. There are two types of suggestions your app can provide: QUERY SUGGESTIONS and RESULT SUGGESTIONS. A query suggestion is just that: a suggested query that, if selected, will lead the user to the search results page for that query. Think of it as a kind of autocomplete. A result suggestion is an actual result and takes the user directly to the details page for that item, bypassing the search results pane altogether.

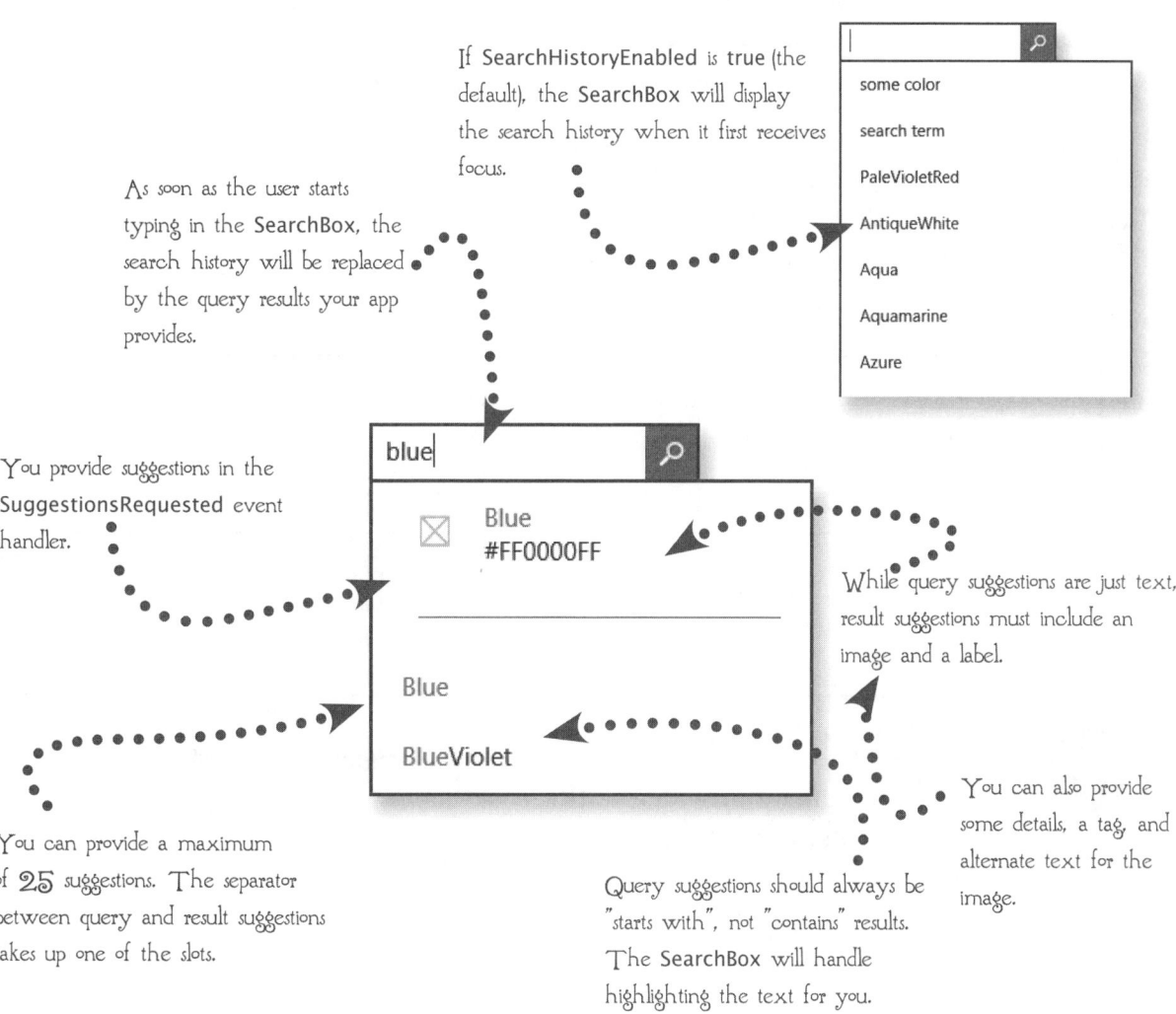

If **SearchHistoryEnabled** is true (the default), the **SearchBox** will display the search history when it first receives focus.

As soon as the user starts typing in the **SearchBox**, the search history will be replaced by the query results your app provides.

You provide suggestions in the **SuggestionsRequested** event handler.

You can provide a maximum of **25** suggestions. The separator between query and result suggestions takes up one of the slots.

Query suggestions should always be "starts with", not "contains" results. The **SearchBox** will handle highlighting the text for you.

While query suggestions are just text, result suggestions must include an image and a label.

You can also provide some details, a tag, and alternate text for the image.

PROVIDING SUGGESTIONS

The SearchBox will display a maximum of 25 query suggestions. (But beware: some of the docs still say 5, which was true of the 8.0 Search contract.) The guidelines specify that result suggestions should be "strong" matches (which I tend to interpret to mean "exact", but it really depends on context). They should be listed first, followed by a separator and the more general query suggestions.

REGISTER FOR THE EVENT
Just as you did for the QuerySubmitted event, you'll need to register your handler for the SuggestionsRequested method. You'll generally do this in the XAML SearchBox declaration, but of course you can do it in code-behind if you prefer.

CREATE THE HANDLER
Visual Studio will stub out the event handler for you when you register for the event.

```csharp
void ColorSearch_SuggestionsRequested(SearchBox sender,
        SearchBoxSuggestionsRequestedEventArgs args)
{ ... }
```

```vb
Sub ColorSearch_SuggestionsRequested(sender As SearchBox,
        args As SearchBoxSuggestionsRequestedEventArgs)
    ...
End Sub
```

GENERATE THE SUGGESTIONS
The event argument provided to the SuggestionsRequested event handler provides the text the user typed. You can search your app data for items that start with the provided text to generate query suggestions, and for close or exact matches to generate result suggestions.

SearchBoxSuggestionsRequestedEventArgs
Class

Properties
- Language
- LinguisticDetails
- QueryText
- Request

 ## ADD THE SUGGESTIONS TO THE REQUEST

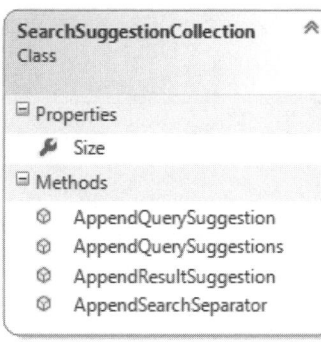

As you generate the suggestions, you'll use one of the **Append...()** methods to append them to the **SearchSuggestionCollection** that's provided in the **Request** property of the event args.

Remember, you only get 25. You can use the **SearchSuggestionCollection.Size** property to keep track.

 ### PUT ON YOUR THINKING HAT

Although result suggestions are listed first, let's start with adding some query suggestions, because they're a little easier to handle—you only need to provide the text to be displayed. (Although there is a version of the method that lets you provide a list.)

① In order to have something to search, create an instance of **ColorCollection** in the Page constructor. I called mine `AllColors`.

② Add a handler for the **SuggestionsRequested** event to the **SearchBox** declaration.

③ Inside the event handler, add no more than 25 query suggestions, using the **StartsWith()** extension method to compare the **QueryText** to the **ColorName**:

   `c.ColorName(StartsWith(args.QueryText, StringComparison.CurrentCultureIgnoreCase))`

④ Be sure to run the app and check your results at this point.

HOW'D YOU DO?

It doesn't matter if you used a different algorithm for generating the search suggestions, as long as you get the results you should.

```csharp
public sealed partial class MainPage : Page
{
    private ColorCollection AllColors;
    ...

    public MainPage()
    {
        ...
        AllColors = new ColorCollection();
    }

    ...

    private void ColorSearch_SuggestionsRequested(SearchBox sender,
            SearchBoxSuggestionsRequestedEventArgs args)
    {
        var suggestions = args.Request.SearchSuggestionsCollection;

        foreach (ColorDetails c in AllColors)
        {
            if (c.ColorName.StartsWith(args.QueryText,
                    StringComparison.CurrentCultureIgnoreCase))
                suggestions.AppendQuerySuggestion(c.ColorName);
            if (suggestions.Size == 25)
                break;
        }
    }
}
```

```vb
Public Sealed Partial Class MainPage
    Inherits Page

    Private AllColors As ColorCollection
    ...

    Public New()
        ...
        AllColors = New ColorCollection()
    End Sub

    ...

    Private Sub ColorSearch_SuggestionsRequested(sender As SearchBox,
        args As SearchBoxSuggestionsRequestedEventArgs)

        Dim suggestions = args.Request.SearchSuggestionsCollection

        For Each  c As ColorDetails In AllColors
            If c.ColorName.StartsWith(args.QueryText,
                StringComparison.CurrentCultureIgnoreCase) Then
                suggestions.AppendQuerySuggestion(c.ColorName)
            If suggestions.Size = 25 Then
                Exit For
            End If
        Next
    End Sub
End Class
```

RESULT SUGGESTIONS

Of course, you'll use different, more stringent, criteria for selecting result suggestions, but the big difference is the process of adding them. The `AppendResultSuggestions()` method has a lot of required parameters and passing the image is, well, fiddly, because for reasons known only to the architects at Microsoft, it's declared as an `IRandomAccessStreamReference`.

`public void AppendResultSuggestion(text, detailText, tag, image, imageAlternateText)`

Although the paramter name is "image", this is actually an IRandomAccessStreamReference.

The tag is all your event handler will receive when a user choses a result suggestion, so be sure it's meaningful to your app.

I'm sure there are other, more esoteric methods of obtaining an **IRandomAccessStreamReference**, but in most situations you can use one of the static **Create…()** methods of the **RandomAccessStreamReference** class (which, of course, implements the **IRandomAccessStreamReference** interface).

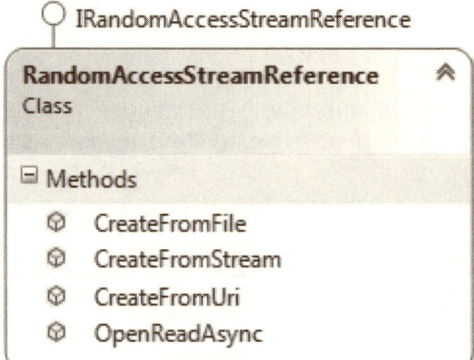

MAKE A NOTE

The image displayed by the SearchBox is 40 pixels square. Windows will scale for you, but you'll probably get better results if you DIY.

PUT ON YOUR THINKING HAT

Okay, let's finish our suggestions by adding a result suggestion when the user types an exact match into the SearchBox. This exercise is a little trickier than you'd expect, so here are some hints:

Result suggestions should come before query suggestions, so add this loop to the top of your SuggestionsRequested handler.

You could use a standard comparison operator, but because we don't want to worry about case sensitivity, it's probably easier to use the Equals() method that takes a StringComparison, just like we did for the query suggestions.

Remember that the image parameter can't be null. You could create individual image files for each color (but really, wouldn't you rather get a life?) or do something tricky with DirectX to generate an image on the fly, but since image creation isn't the point of the exercise, you can just use the default Logo.scale-100.png from the Assets folder.

You'll need to add a reference to the Windows.Storage.Streams namespace to get (easy) access to the RandomAccessStreamReference class. Then you can create a URI, passing it the image file name using the "ms-appx:///" syntax, and call CreateFromUri() to get the IRandomAccessStreamReference.

Remember to add a separator using AppendSearchSeparator() after the result suggestion. (Since we're looking for an exact match, there should only ever be one.)

HOW'D YOU DO?

It doesn't matter if you used a different algorithm for generating the search suggestions, as long as you get the results you should.

```csharp
using Windows.Storage.Streams;
...

public sealed partial class MainPage : Page
{
    ...
    private void ColorSearch_SuggestionsRequested(SearchBox sender,
        SearchBoxSuggestionsRequestedEventArgs args)
    {
        var suggestions = args.Request.SearchSuggestionsCollection;

        foreach (ColorDetails c in AllColors)
        {
            if (c.ColorName.Equals(args.QueryText,
                StringComparison.CurrentCultureIgnoreCase))
            {
                Uri imageUri = new Uri("ms-appx:///Assets/Logo.scale-100.png");
                var imageSource = RandomAccessStreamReference.CreateFromUri(imageUri);
                suggestions.AppendResultSuggestion(c.ColorName, c.HexValue, c.ColorName,
                    imageSource, "");
                suggestions.AppendSearchSeparator("");
                break;
            }
        }

        foreach (ColorDetails d in AllColors)
        {
            if (d.ColorName.StartsWith(args.QueryText,
                StringComparison.CurrentCultureIgnoreCase))
                suggestions.AppendQuerySuggestion(c.ColorName);
            if (suggestions.Size == 25)
                break;
        }
    }
}
```

```vb
Imports Windows.Storage.Streams
...

Public Sealed Partial Class MainPage
    Inherits Page

    ...
    Private Sub ColorSearch_SuggestionsRequested(sender As SearchBox,
        args As SearchBoxSuggestionsRequestedEventArgs)

        Dim suggestions = args.Request.SearchSuggestionsCollection
        For Each (c As ColorDetails In AllColors
            If (c.ColorName.Equals(args.QueryText,
                    StringComparison.CurrentCultureIgnoreCase)) Then
                Dim imageUri As Uri = New Uri("ms-appx:///Assets/Logo.scale-100.png")
                Dim imageSource = RandomAccessStreamReference.CreateFromUri(imageUri)
                suggestions.AppendResultSuggestion(c.ColorName, c.HexValue, c.ColorName,
                    imageSource, "")
                suggestions.AppendSearchSeparator("")
                Break
            End If
        Next

        For Each d As ColorDetails in AllColors
            If d.ColorName.StartsWith(args.QueryText,
                    StringComparison.CurrentCultureIgnoreCase)) Then

                suggestions.AppendQuerySuggestion(c.ColorName)
                If suggestions.Size = 25 Then
                    Break
            End If
        Next
    End Sub
End Class
```

REVIEW

Can you answer the following questions based on what you've learned?

Why should you care about the differences between the Search contract in Windows 8 and the SearchBox control in Windows 8.1?

What are the two types of query suggestions, and how is each used?

Whar event should you respond to if your SearchBox isn't on the app canvas and you've set FocusOnKeyboardInput to true?

How many query suggestions can you provide in response to a SearchBox.SuggestionsRequested event?

QUERY NAVIGATION

I'm sure you've noticed that there's one big chunk missing from our app: We need to respond when a user enters a query term or chooses one of the suggestions. There are several ways that the user can submit a query, and two possible events to respond to.

USER ENTERS SOME TEXT AND PRESSES ENTER

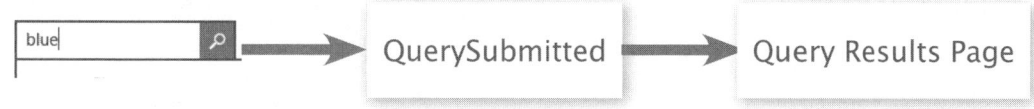

USER SELECTS A QUERY SUGGESTION

USER SELECTS A RESULT SUGGESTION

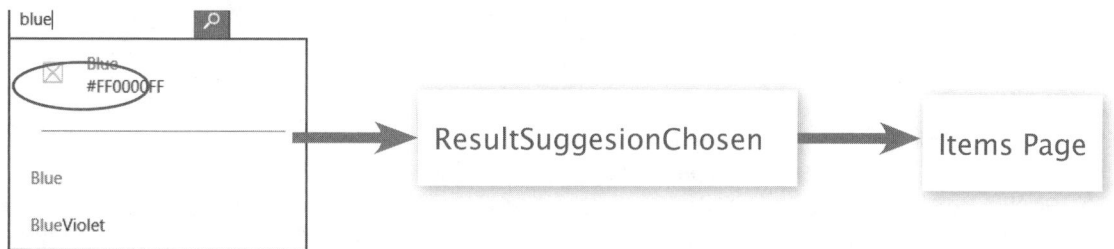

> ### THINKING HAT
> We've aleady built the basic **QuerySubmitted** event handler, and we'll tackle the search results page in a minute, but before we do, can you work out how to handle **ResultSuggesionChosen**? You'll need to add an items page to your app. You can make it as complicated as you like, but just displaying the name of the chosen color will do.

HOW'D YOU DO?
Here's my version. I haven't included the XAML for the results page (because it's pretty boring at this point).

```xml
<SearchBox x:Name="ColorSearch" ...
        QuerySubmitted="ColorSearch_QuerySubmitted"
        SuggestionsRequested="ColorSearch_SuggestionsRequested"
        ResultSuggesionChosen="ColorSearch_ResultSuggestionChosen" />
```

```csharp
private void ColorSearch_ResultSuggestionChosen(SearchBox sender,
            SearchBoxResultSuggestionChosenEventArgs args)
{
    this.Frame.Navigate(typeof(ColorItem), args.Tag));
}
```

```vb
Private Sub ColorSearch_ResultSuggestionChosen(sender As SearchBox,
            args As SearchBoxResultSuggestionChosenEventArgs)
    Me.Frame.Navigate(GetType(ColorItem), args.Tag))
End Sub
```

```csharp
private void navigationHelper_LoadState(object sender, LoadStateEventArgs e)
{
    ChosenColor.Text = e.NavigationParameter as string;
}
```
C#

```vb
Private Sub navigationHelper_LoadState(sender as Object, e As LoadStateEventArgs)
    ChosenColor.Text = TryCast(e.NavigationParameter, String)
End Sub
```
VB

SOME HOUSEKEEPING

Before we start exploring the search results page, we need to do a little housekeeping on our sample app. This stuff isn't pertinent to the subject of the chapter, so I'm just going to give you the code:

ADD A COLOR GROUP

In order to be able to filter our search results, we need to have some way of grouping them. Let's create an enumeration called **ColorGroup** and change the existing **ColorGroup** property in the **ColorDetails** class. We'll also need to calculate the **ColorGroup** inside the property accessor. Here's the code:

```csharp
public enum ColorGroup
{
    Red, Green, Blue, Neutral
}

public class ColorDetails
{
    ...
    public ColorGroup ColorGroup
    {
        get
        {
            Color c = ActualColor;
            if (c.R > c.G && c.R > c.B)
                return Search.ColorGroup.Red;
            else if (c.G > c.R && c.G > c.B)
                return Search.ColorGroup.Green;
            else if (c.B > c.R && c.B > c.G)
                return Search.ColorGroup.Blue;
            else
                return Search.ColorGroup.Neutral;
        }
    }
}
```

```vb
Public Enum ColorGroup
    Red
    Green
    Blue
    Neutral
End Enum

Public Class ColorDetails
    ...
    Public Property ColorGroup As ColorGroup
        Get
            Color c = ActualColor
            If c.R > c.G And  c.R > c.B Then
                Return Search.ColorGroup.Red
            ElseIf c.G > c.R And c.G > c.B Then
                Return Search.ColorGroup.Green
            Elseif (c.B > c.R && c.B > c.G)
                Return Search.ColorGroup.Blue
            Else
                Return Search.ColorGroup.Neutral
            End If
        End Get
    End Property
End Class
```

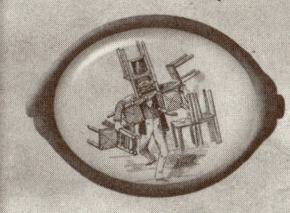

ON YOUR OWN

Add the ColorGroup enumeration and update the property in the ColorDetails class file.

THE SEARCH RESULTS TEMPLATE

The Search Results Page we added to our project provides the basic structure and functionality that you'll need to respond to your users' queries. But it makes a lot of assumptions about the structure of your data, and of course, they're hardly every going to match how your data is actually structured. In order to figure out what we'll need to do, let's start by figuring out what the template does out of the box.

THE DEFAULTVIEWMODEL

As you might expect, the data model for the template uses a DefaultViewModel that's declared as a simple ObservableDictionary. The XAML binding assumes that the dictionary has the following structure:

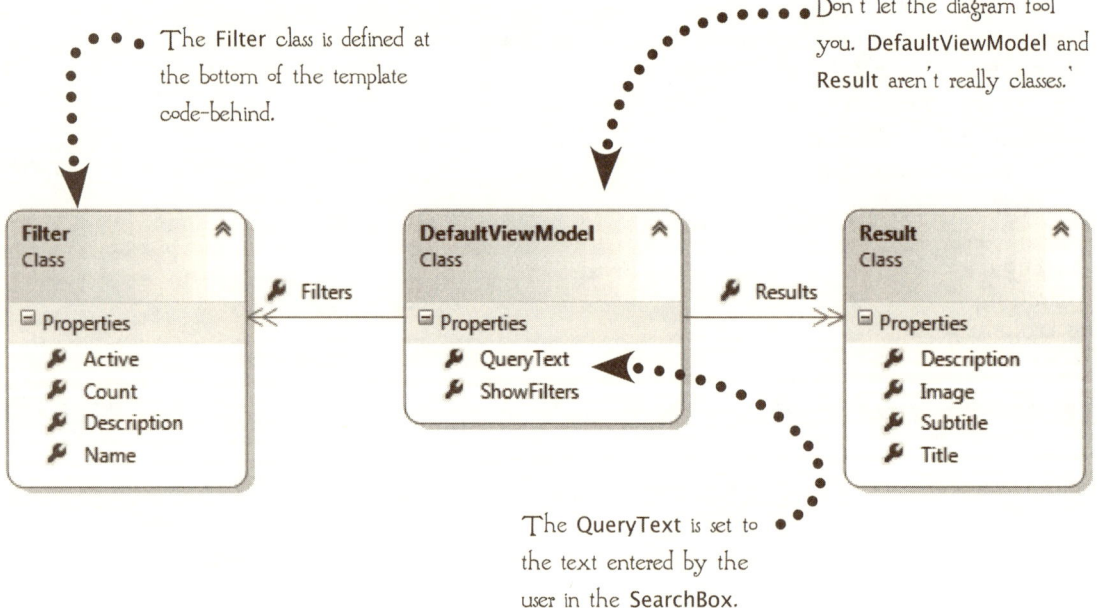

The Filter class is defined at the bottom of the template code-behind.

Don't let the diagram fool you. DefaultViewModel and Result aren't really classes.

The QueryText is set to the text entered by the user in the SearchBox.

The (unnamed) **Grid** layout root is divided into two rows. The top one contains the **Page** header; the bottom one contains a second **Grid** (resultsPane).

This row contains the page header.

This row contains an **ItemsControl** (filtersItemsControl) that displays each of the filters as a **RadioButton**. Changing a selection triggers the **Filter_ Checked** event handler in the code-behind.

This row contains a **GridView** (resultsGridView) that's bound to the **Results** collection. It uses a **DataTemplate** to display each of the "properties" of the **Result** collection.

ON YOUR OWN

We're going to use the page to display instances of the **ColorClass**, which doesn't have the same properties as the **Result** collection. What two changes do you think we'll need to make (one to the XAML, one to the code-behind) to accomodate our different data model?

701

CHANGING THE DATA MODEL

We'll talk about filtering results in a minute, but first let's update the XAML to display ColorCollection items instead of the default Results created by the template.

CHANGE THE DATA TEMPLATE

Since the basic structure of the Page suits us, all we need to do is update the DataTemplate that's used to display the individual items. Here's the XAML:

```xml
<GridView.ItemTemplate>
  <DataTemplate>
    <Grid Width="150" Margin="6">
      <Grid.ColumnDefinitions>
        <ColumnDefinition Width="Auto"/>
        <ColumnDefinition Width="*"/>
      </Grid.ColumnDefinitions>
      <Border Background="{Binding ColorName}" Margin="0,0,0,10"
              Width="40" Height="40"/>
      <StackPanel Grid.Column="1" Margin="10,-10,0,0">
        <TextBlock Text="{Binding ColorName}" .../>
        <TextBlock Text="{Binding HexValue}" ... />
      </StackPanel>
    </Grid>
  </DataTemplate>
</GridView.ItemTemplate>
```

ON YOUR OWN
Update the XAML with the new DataTemplate. The only changes are the Grid.Width, the Border.Background, and other bindings, and deleting a couple of items.

PUT ON YOUR THINKING HAT

Two things you've probably worked out on your own: Microsoft isn't always right, and I'm a bit of a heretic. I think this is a good example.

Here's how the template manages the results and filters. What's wrong with this picture? Can you work out where the problems are?

NavigationHelper_LoadState()

- Creates the list of filters
- Adds the query text, filters, and a showFilter state toggle to the DefaultViewModel

---

Filter_SelectionChanged()

- Creates a results collection based on the query text
- Suggests you filter the results, but doesn't include any code to do so
- Adds results to DefaultViewModel
- Sets the VisualStateManager state based on whether results exist

---

Why don't you have all the information you need to generate the filter list before the results are generated? (HINT: It isn't just the name of the filter that should be shown. Take a look at the Filter constructor; it's in the same code file.)

Why is creating the result collection every time the filter is changed a bad idea?

HOW'D YOU DO?

Did you find the problems? Do you agree with me that they are problems?

Why don't you have all the information you need to generate the filter list before the results are generated? (HINT: It isn't just the name of the filter that should be shown. Take a look at the **Filter** constructor; it's in the same code file.)

The UI guidelines specify that you shouldn't just list the possible filters; you should include how many results qualify for each one. The constructor for the **Filter** class defined inside the template code-behind supports this:

> public Filter(String name, int count, bool active = false)

> Public New(name as String, count as Integer, active as Boolean = false)

But until the results are calculated, you can't know how many results qualify for each filter.

Why is creating the result collection every time the filter is changed a bad idea?

The query text doesn't change when the filter does. There's no need to go back to the original data and recalculate the qualifying items.

What you should do (that isn't shown in the sample code) is to filter the original results. Not the same thing at all. Even if your result sets aren't large, it's always going to be more efficient to filter a smaller set—only the items that match the query string.

MY WAY

I think the key to handling the search results page (assuming you use a page that's based on the template, which you aren't required to do) is to create two sets of results: a core set that includes all of the core data that matches the query string, and a filtered set that is shown to the user, based on the initial result set and the currently active filter. Here's the way to set it up:

> Navigation_LoadState()
>
> - Create the basic result set based on the query string.
> - Create the list of filters, calculating how many items in the basic result set match the specified filter value.
> - Add the query text, filters, and a showFilter state toggle to the DefaultViewModel (as per the template).

> Filter_SelectionChanged()
>
> - Create a filtered result set from the basic results and the selected filter.
> - Add the filtered results to DefaultViewModel.
> - Sets the VisualStateManager state based on whether results exist (as per the template).

PUT ON YOUR THINKING HAT

Add the DataTemplate if you haven't already done so, and then set up the results display. You'll want to declare an IList<ColorDetails> at the class level (I called mine currentColors) to represent the data that matches the query string. Allow users to filter by ColorGroup.

HOW'D YOU DO?

Here's my version. It's fine if you used different techniques, as long as you got the result you want. The VB code is on the next page.

```csharp
public sealed partial class ColorSearchResults : Page
   private IList<ColorDetails> currentColors;
   ...
   private void Navigation_LoadState(...)
   {
      var queryText = e.navigationParameter as String;
      IList<ColorDetails> allColors = (new ColorCollection()).ToList();

      if (String.IsNullOrEmpty(queryText))
         currentColors = allColors;
      else
      {
        var results = from c in allColors
                      where c.ColorName.StartsWith(queryText,
                               StringComparison.CurrentCultureIgnoreCase)
                      select c;
        currentColors = results.ToList();
      }
      this.DefaultViewModel["Results"] = currentColors;

      var filterList = new List<Filter>();
      filterList.Add(new Filter("All", currentColors.Count, true));

      int RedCount = (from c in currentColors
                      where c.ColorGroup == ColorGroup.Red
                      select c).Count();
      filterList.Add(new Filter("Red", RedCount, false));

      ....
}
```

Repeat this for each ColorGroup.

```
void Filter_Checked(...)
{
    var filter = (sender as FrameworkElement).DataContext;
    var selectedFilter = filter as Filter;

    if (selectedFilter != null)
    {
        selectedFilter.Active = true;
        if (selectedFilter.Name == "All")
            this.DefaultViewModel["Results"] = currentColors;
        else
        {
            var filteredResults = from c in currentColors
                                  where c.ColorGroup.ToString() == selectedFilter.Name
                                  select c;
            this.DefaultViewModel["Results"] = filteredResults.ToList();
        }

        object results;
        ICollection resultsCollection;
        if (this.DefaultViewModel.TryGetValue("Results", out results) &&
            (resultsCollection = results as ICollection) != null &&
            resultsCollection.Count != 0)
        {
            VisualStateManager.GoToState(this, "ResultsFound", true);
            return;
        }
    }
    VisualStateManager.GoToState(this, "NoResultsFound", true);
}
```

This block of code hasn't changed.

NAVIGATING TO RESULTS

Searching is, of course, just a way for users to quickly find a particular bit of information in your app. It follows that the Search Results page should provide a mechanism for them to get to that data quickly. If you use the Search Results Page template, you just need to navigate to the appropriate page in the **ItemClick** event handler for the **resultsGridView**. (If you build your own page, you'll use a similar mechanism—just navigate when an item is selected.)

REGISTER FOR THE SELECTION EVENT
This will usually be an **ItemClick** event, but it depends on what element you're using to display your results.

```
<GridView x:Name="resultsGridView" ...
    ItemClick="resultsGridView_ItemClick">
```

RETRIEVE THE SELECTED ITEM
If you're responding to an **ItemClick**, the **ItemClickEventArgs.ClickedItem** will contain the relevant item; you just need to cast it to the type you need.

```
ColorDetails color = (ColorDetails)e.ClickedItem;
```

NAVIGATE TO THE APPROPRIATE PAGE
Depending on how your app is structured, you'll need to pass the selected item, either directly in the **Navigate()** method, or by way of a local data setting.

```
this.frame.Navigate(typeof(ColorItem), color.ColorName)
```

ON YOUR OWN

You've done enough navigating by now that you don't need my help, so go ahead and add the **ItemClick** event handler and then test to make sure your search functionality works the way it needs to.

Some things to check:

What happens if you press Enter in the **SearchBox** without selecting anything?

Do choosing a query or result suggestion take you where they should?

TAKE A BREAK

That's it for the search functionality in Windows 8.1, and in fact that's it for our exploration of 8.1 functionality in general. (Well done!) Why don't you take a break now before you complete the Review and we walk through building a soup to nuts app in the next chapter?

REVIEW

Can you think of any reason you'd use the Search charm instead of, or in addition to, a `SearchBox` in a new app?

Do you agree with me about the way filtering is handled in the default Search Results template? Why or why not?

When do you need to respond to the `PrepareForFocusOnKeyboardInput` event?

Assuming that you use the Search Results page template, what section of the XAML will you need to update if your results don't match the model provided by the `DefaultViewModel` it provides?

Congratulations! You've finished the chapter. Take a minute to think about what you've accomplished before you move on to the next one...

List three things you learned in this chapter:

①

②

③

Why do you think you need to know these things in order to develop Win8 apps?

Is there anything in this chapter that you think you need to understand in more detail? If so, what are you going to do about that?

ON YOUR OWN

So we've reached the end of the book. I hope you feel a lot more comfortable about developing Win8 apps in XAML than you were eighteen chapters ago.

This chapter is a little different. Well, okay, it's a whole lot different. In this chapter I won't be presenting any new information. Instead, I'll walk you through building a little piece of the color application we've been playing with. Not a full-blown app, of course (nothing that would make it through Store certification), but the beginnings of one. Enough, I think, to give you a sense of how the process works in the real world and to help you consolidate what you've learned in the last 700-odd pages.

And I won't be giving you any answers. Instead, I'll present you with some requirements and ask you some questions, but all the design and coding decisions are yours to make. In fact, if you're tired of colors, you can substitute a completely different application domain. Would you rather work with one of your apps from the list you made when you started? Or if those all seem a bit too complex, how about a browser for all those standard styles Visual Studio defines for you? Something else entirely? Whatever you'd like to tackle, now's your chance, because in this chapter, you're (almost) on your own.

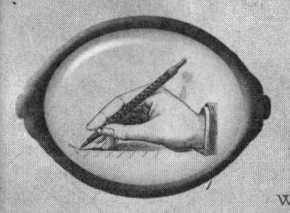

MAKE A NOTE

Throughout this chapter I talk about what decisions I'd make. They're only opinions, so please don't take them as recommendations. Just because I happen to know a bit more about Windows 8.1 than you do, it doesn't follow that you can't run rings around me in other areas of application design and development.

FITTING IT IN

In this chapter we'll work will all the bits and pieces we've learned about from the very beginning...

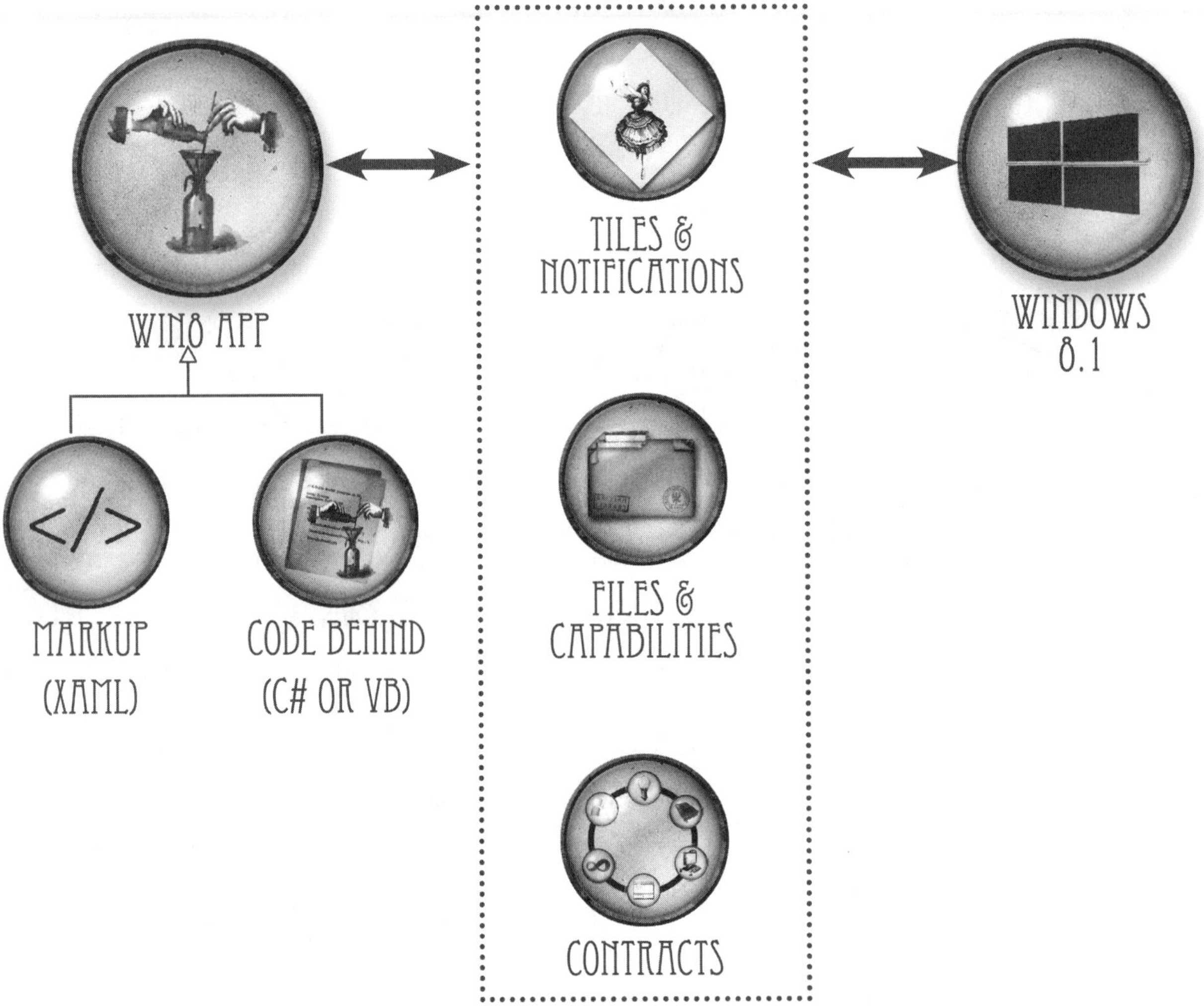

- WIN8 APP
  - MARKUP (XAML)
  - CODE BEHIND (C# OR VB)

- TILES & NOTIFICATIONS
- FILES & CAPABILITIES
- CONTRACTS

- WINDOWS 8.1

TASK LIST

You can think of this chapter as an extended walk-through. The steps I outline are things you'll need to do in almost any Win8 application, but they don't represent a development methodology. In a real project, you'd have additional steps (um, testing, anyone?) and you probably wouldn't do things in precisely this order. But they'll do for our little system.

DETERMINE THE REQUIREMENTS
Any project has to start with figuring out what you're trying to achieve, even a little ad hoc system like this one.

DESIGN THE UX
Once we know what tasks your app is going to help users perform, we'll start to work out what pages they'll need and how we're going to get from one place to another.

DESIGN THE DATA STRUCTURES
Many apps involve manipulating data of some kind. Even if your actual storage is on the Cloud somewhere, you'll need to give some thought to how you're going to access and represent it in your application.

CREATE THE GRAPHIC ASSETS
You already know that a Win8 app has a lot of logo assets. I've included some basic assets for you to use if you decide to build the color tool, but if you're feeling adventurous, let loose your inner artist!

IMPLEMENT THE SYSTEM
The last thing we'll do is build our pages. For this app, we'll adapt a couple of pages we've already used. We'll also look at implementing contracts and adding a tile update.

A Determine the Requirements

Let's pretend: You've spent some time looking at the apps available on the Windows Store and noticed a lack of color tools. You've decided that would be a good little project to get your feet wet. After doing some brainstorming, you've decided that because the release cycle for a Win8 app resembles a Web app, it makes sense to release what is essentially a MINIMUM VIABLE PRODUCT. You've decided to include three core functions, which by a strange coincidence look a lot like some of the screens we've built for our exercisers:

Display Standard .NET Colors

Nobody worries too much about Web-safe colors any more, but you think it might still be useful for .NET developers to be able to pick and choose among the standard colors defined in the **Colors** class.

Create Colors

Of course, users don't want to be limited to choosing from the colors .NET defines; they'll want to create their own colors.

Display Favorite Colors

Having created the perfect shade of blue, a user is going to want to save it, and having saved it, find it later (which, of course, implies a **SearchBox** somewhere). You'll need to display the colors they've saved.

> ### Words for the Wise
>
> MINIMUM VIABLE PRODUCT is a concept popularized by Eric Ries. The basic concept (at least as I understand it; I refer you to the books of Eirc Reis and Steven Blank for a fuller explanation) is that you release an absolute minimum subset of functionality to test the waters and then allow commited users to help define the needed features.

ON YOUR OWN

I've identified the "big 3" functions for you, but our requirements specification isn't finished. This is a Win8 app, so we want to leverage the special functions that operating in that environment provides. Since we're using the minimum viable product development approach, we want to be able to solicit opinions and suggestions from our users. How would you handle these things?

WIN8 CONTRACTS

Which of the contracts, if any, should your app integrate with? Do you think users would want to pick a color and share it with another app? What about picking a color in another app and adding it to their favorites? What format or formats would be best?

You'll need a Settings page for the privacy policy because that's required for the Store, but is there anything else you think people would want to configure?

CUSTOMER FEEDBACK

A big part of the MVP process is to solicit customer feedback on what works well, what doesn't, and what other functionality people need or want. How will you incorporate that in the app? At a minimum, you could put a link to your website on the Settings pane, but is there another way?

COLOR FUTURES

"Minimum viable" implies that additional functionality will be added to the product in the future. (Which isn't at all the same as having "coming soon" pages in your app. That's unlikely to pass certification.)

How will you make this available? Store updates? In-app purchases? Some combination of the two?

B DESIGN THE UX

Let's start with the basic structure of the app. I think the core functionality we've defined lends itself to a very simple hierarchical navigation system. Can you think of a better way? Should it be possible for users to move between secondary pages? If so, how should that work?

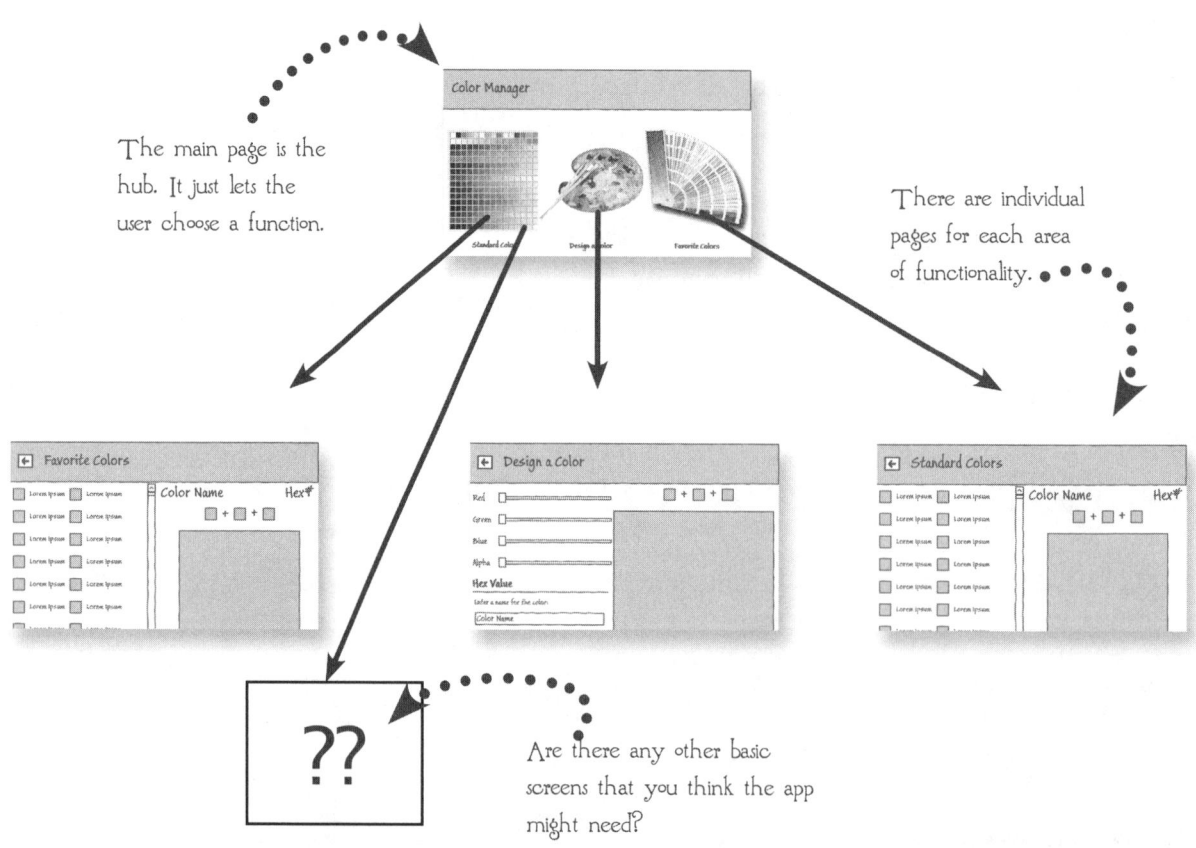

The main page is the hub. It just lets the user choose a function.

There are individual pages for each area of functionality.

Are there any other basic screens that you think the app might need?

MAKE A NOTE

I'm only showing the example pages in a single resolution in full screen view. Remember that your app needs to support multiple resolutions in landscape and portrait and at various widths.

THE LANDING PAGE

Here's a sketch of the landing page that I created in Expression Blend Sketchflow. Like all the sketches we're going to look at in this section, it shows the absolute minimum functionality and out-of-the-box control styles.

How can you make it work and look better? Do you think I've chosen good images to represent the core functionality? What would you use instead? Do you need images at all, or just a big friendly button?

Clicking on an image or the label takes the user to the relevant Page.

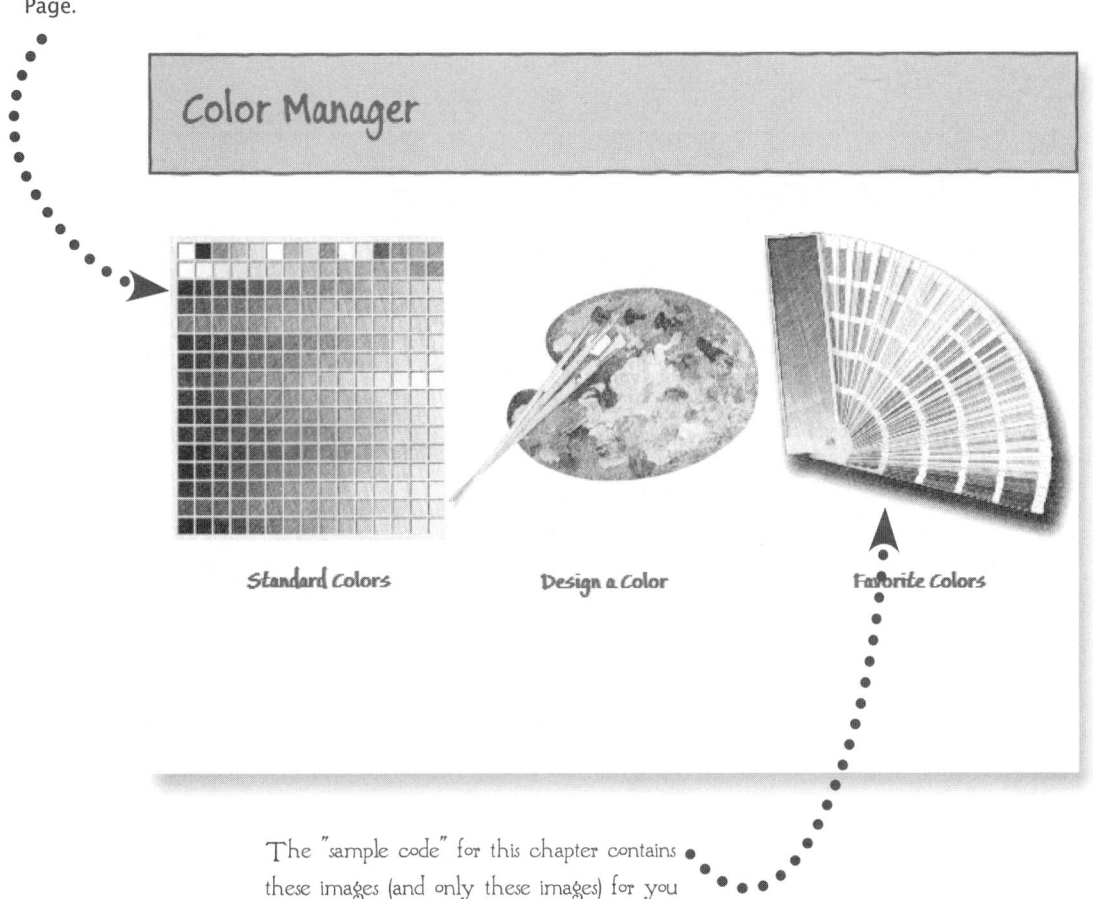

The "sample code" for this chapter contains these images (and only these images) for you to play with.

THE STANDARD COLORS PAGE

I'm sure you recognize this **Page** design. You might say that it's a minimum version of minimum functionality. How could you improve it?

The colors aren't grouped because I think the grouping we used in our Binding example wasn't particularly useful. Should they be? How? Should users be able to create groups?

What about SemanticZoom? Would that be useful here?

Is there any other information or functionality you think should be included? What about being able to add a selected color to a Favorites list? Should users be able to rate colors?

This sketch doesn't show an **AppBar**. Should the **Page** have one? If so, what functionality should it provide?

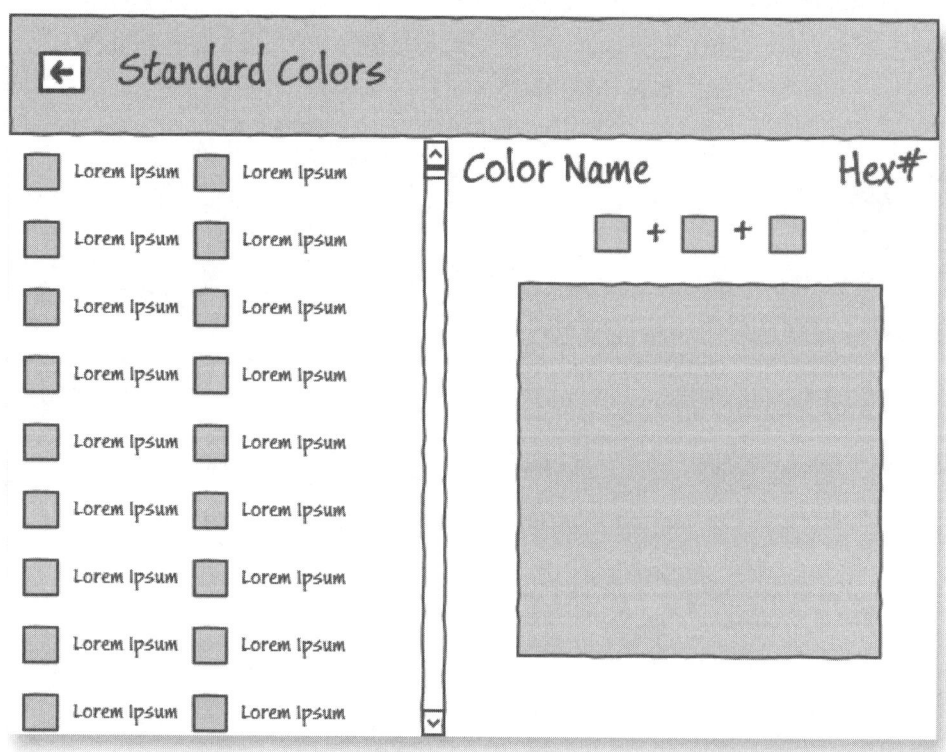

THE COLOR DESIGNER

This sketch probably looks pretty familiar, too. I've rearranged it a little from the version in Chapter 10, removed the Gradients, and added the ability to add the color to Favorites.

Do you think Gradients should be included? What about other functions, like changing the value or saturation of a color?

What about that button on the bottom. Is that the right place for it do you think, or should it be in an AppBar?

Using four sliders for ARGB is really boring. Given that XAML controls are lookless, can you think of a better way of picking a color? If you hunt around on the Web, you'll see some very cool examples of color pickers. Maybe you could adapt one of those graphics to the XAML environment.

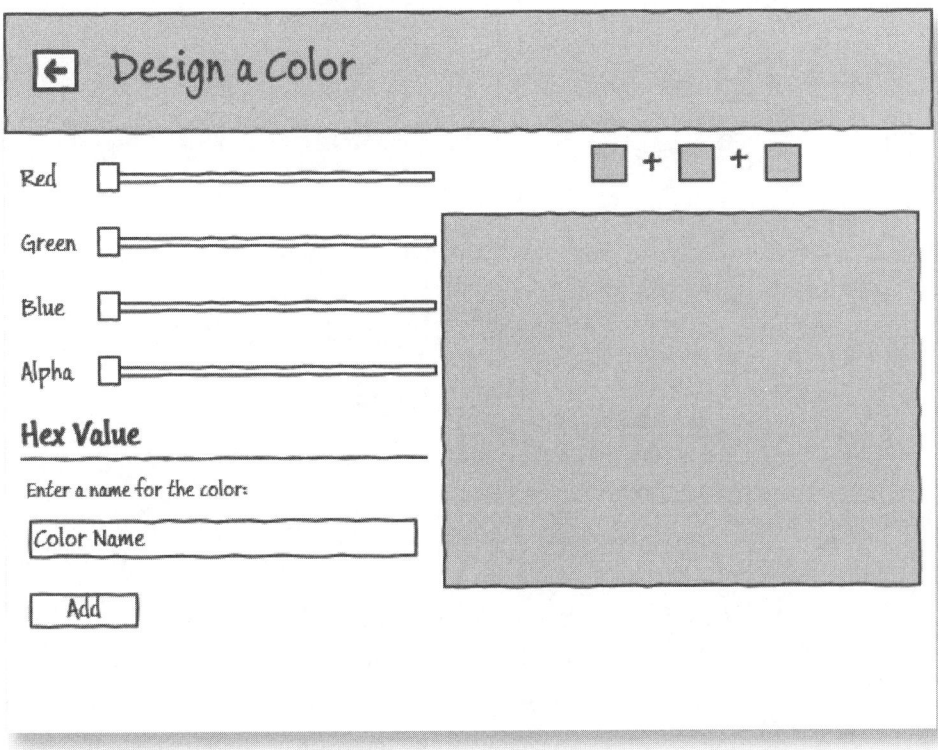

THE FAVORITE COLORS PAGE

This is basically a duplicate of the Standard Colors page, with just the ability to remove a color. Should it be? Can you think of a more attractive or useful way to present this information?

What about that **Remove** button? Should that, like the Add functionality on the previous screen, be moved to an **AppBar**? Do you think users should be able to edit the color or its name here?

ON YOUR OWN

If you're using the color app as your project, review the page sketches I've given you and make any changes you think would improve the app. If you're building your own app, prepare some sketches (scribbly hand-written ones are just fine), taking into consideration the same kinds of questions I've asked about my examples.

Design the Data Structures

Now that you've made some decisions about functionality, it's time to figure out how you're going to represent the data. There are (at least) three parts to this: how the data will be represented in code, what you need to persist, and how it will be persisted.

Let's start with how we're going to represent the data in code. Here's a class diagram of the color classes we've been using in the book. How do they need to change to support the functionality of this app?

We know we're going to need at least two different collections: the **StandardColors** and the **FavoriteColors**. Does that require an additional class? ······▶

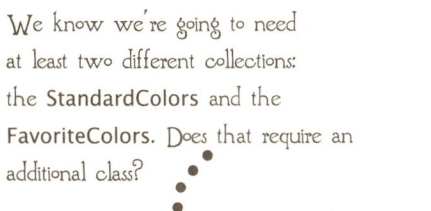

If you've decided your app should include support for gradients, how does the ColorDetails class need to change? ·······▶

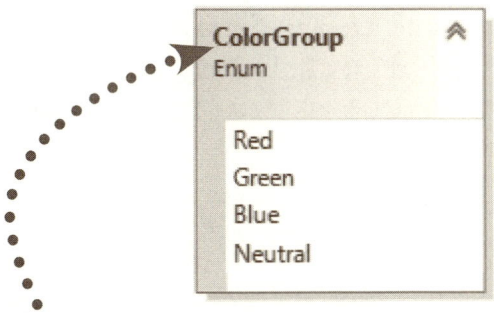

Depending on the decision you made about grouping colors, this Enum and its corresponding property may no longer be necessary or may need to change.

723

DATA PERSISTENCE

The next issue is how you're going to persist the data. In our little examples in this book, we've used `ApplicationDataContainer.LocalSettings`. Is that still a good idea? Here are some options to consider:

APPLICATIONDATACONTAINER

As we've seen, the **LocalSettings** and **RoamingSettings** properties of the **ApplicationDataContainer** are very simple to use, but they only accept simple data types. That doesn't mean they're not an option. You could store the hex value of the color and then re-create the actual objects as needed.

LOCAL FILE

We haven't explored the creation of files because there's not much in Win8 that differs from .NET. Storing your app data in XML or JSON (or a custom format) is certainly an option and might simplify runtime processing.

WEB STORAGE

I have the sense that this is the option Microsoft would like us to take—storing the application data on the Cloud somewhere, and making it available via a web service. Does this make sense for your vision of the app?

LOCAL RELATIONAL DATA

Although Win8 doesn't provide intrinsic support for local relational data, there are several third-party tools available. Do you think this app requires that option, given that relational data always adds a certain level of complexity?

ON YOUR OWN

Pick one. Or pick another option I haven't listed. (The options are really only limited by your creativity, skill, and budget.)

 CREATE THE GRAPHIC ASSETS

In reality, creating the application's "pretties" can, and probably will, happen at various points in the development cycle. I've included three graphics for you to play with, but you'll need to adapt them and re-size them. (And, of course, you're free to replace them.) You can refer back to the chart on page 559 to figure out what sizes you'll need.

 ON YOUR OWN
Fire up your favorite graphics program and create the assets you'll need for logos, buttons, and any other UI widgets you want to use.

Implement the System

Finally. The good stuff. Or the tedious stuff, depending on your point of view. Now, in a "proper" development project, or even a little project if you're working in a team, you'll no doubt have adopted a development methodology. But this is a little application and you're working alone, so for what it's worth here's how I'd tackle development:

CREATE THE SOLUTION

I'd start by creating the basic Visual Studio solution. It might be one project, or perhaps more if you've decided to use a formal MVVM architecture. Since you have the assets you need, I'd go ahead and add them to the manifest at this point and declare any capabilities that you'll be using.

BUILD THE NAVIGATION WITH DUMMY SCREENS

Next, I'd add dummy screens to the project and build the basic navigation (which is trivially simple). I'd probably add the splash screen at this point, if it's necessary, and think through (if not yet implement) any tile updates, secondary tiles, or notifications.

CREATE THE DATA STRUCTURES AND SAMPLE DATA

Since the content pages are all data bound, you'll need to have something to bind them to before you can really start building them, so I'd do that next. First create the data structures, and then (if you're feeling rigorous) build some sample data.

Of course, exactly what you do in this step depends on how you've decided to represent and persist the data in your app. Will you use a simple resource like we did in earlier chapters, or will you build a proper Model project to support an MVVM architecture? Are you using a third-party relational database that needs methods for storing and loading?

The details of your data structure might change as you tweak the individual pages, but you'll want to make some basic decisions and implement and test the required functionality at this point.

BUILD THE PAGES
Next I'd build the basic structure of each of the screens, concentrating on the layout and data binding of the widgets, and any custom templates (like the lists or the color picker).

DEFINING APP-WIDE STYLES AND TEMPLATES
In reality, defining the styles and templates that apply throughout your application really needs to happen in conjunction with building the pages—you won't know how to lay out a **TextBox** until you know what your **TextBlock** labels look like—but I find I usually wind up doing some tweaking after the basic screen layouts are finished.

FINALIZE THE DATA STRUCTURES AND PAGES
You may find that you want to make some adjustments to the data structures as you refine your screens, and unless you're working with an existing web service or legacy database, I don't think there's anything wrong with that. But at some point, you will want to nail it. That point is just about now.

You'll also want to finalize your pages and make sure that they work correctly at all the resolutions and form factors you need to support.

IMPLEMENT THE CONTRACTS
You might have implemented support for Settings and Share (or whatever contracts you've decided would be useful) as you defined the pages, and that's just fine. I generally don't, since I want the pages to be relatively stable before I add that functionality.

TEST THE NAVIGATION AND LIFE CYCLE
I assume you've been testing core functionality as you implemented it, but you'll also want to make sure that your app handles suspend and resume events correctly, and that all of the navigation works. I do that last, once everything else is stable.

BE PROUD OF YOURSELF

Don't be misled—just because I presented this project in a few pages, it would take the most experienced Win8 programmer several days (at least) to develop. But if you've made it this far, take a minute to think about what you've accomplished.

- You've gone from knowing very little about Windows 8.1 to building a working application with very little assistance.

- Based on a very rough sketch of the UI, you've made informed decisions about the design and implementation of a real app.

- You've designed and built a non-trivial data structure and implemented data storage.

- You've built a functional Win8 app, complete with support for some basic contracts.

AND PERHAPS MOST IMPORTANTLY...

- You've made it to the end of this book!

MOVING ON

I won't blame you at all if you've had all you want of me, colors, and this <insert your favorite swear word here> application that turned out to be a whole lot more trouble to implement than you expected. But if you want to keep playing with it, there are a lot of ways it could be expanded. Go for it. Submit it to the store if you want to. (And please let me know if you do.)

If you're ready to move on, here are a few resources that you might find helpful:

Programming Windows: Writing Windows 8 Apps with C# and XAML by Charles Petzold

Charles Petzold has been teaching us Windows programming since the first version of the operating system. In my opinion, he's still the best person to turn to if you want low-level nuts and bolts advice.

The Microsoft Dev Center for Windows Store apps

Located (at the time of this writing) at msdn.microsoft.com/en-us/windows/apps, this is Microsoft's portal for all things Win8 development-related.

The Windows Store apps Forums

When you get stuck, ask a question on the Microsoft forums. You'll find them by clicking the Community tab on the Dev Center page, and then choosing Developer Forums.

CodePlex

If you don't already know about Microsoft's open source project site, you really should check it out at www.codeplex.com. You'll find tools, templates, and previews of things to come on this incredibly useful site.

INDEX

A

abstraction, command, 318
accessing
    binding sources, 447
    contracts, 11
    UnauthorizedAccessException, 601–602
actions, 23, 175
activating
    contracts, 658–663
    files, 611–613
    responding to, 569–570
adaptive layout techniques, 491–492
AddHandler() method, 292–293
adding
    colors
        functionality, 722
        groups, 698
    columns, 129
    contracts, 55
    data sources, 519–521
    DateTemplate, 705
    dictionaries, 393
    fields, 539
    items
        controls, 218–220
        pages, 507
        runtime, 135
    live tiles, 63–64
    resources to dictionaries, 397
    searchboxes, 681
    Settings Flyout item, 55
    snippets to dependency properties, 253
    startup pages, 506
    suggestions to requests, 687
    Toggled event handlers, 671
Add() method, 218
alignment, 147
alive (Win8 apps), 32–33
animation
    dependent, 419
    dot-down syntax, 421–422
    elements, 416
    independent, 419
    pre-defined, 423

    properties, 421
    storyboards, 417
    themes, 423
    timelines, 420
    transitions, 424–426
    XAML, 415
APIs (application programming interfaces)
    input, 299–301
    keyboards, 304
    manipulation, 305
    .NET Framework, 116–118
    Storage, 627
    UICommand, 318–319
AppBars, 320–323
    widgets, 324–325
Application class, 70
ApplicationDataContainer object, 617, 619, 724
Application.OnLaunched() method, 505
application programming interfaces. *See* APIs
applications (apps)
    basic pages, 483
    building, 49
    closing, 51
    collaboration with Win8 apps, 34–35
    color explorers, re-building, 486–488
    common files, 482
    configuring, 19
    contracts, 642. *See also* contracts
    custom types, applying, 551
    data, 616–617
        making available, 522–525
        sharing, 513, 518
        sources, adding, 519–521
    DefaultViewModel, 484–485
    desktop, 12
    Device Panels, applying, 501
    displaying, 477, 480–481
    extended splash screens, 537–543
    extensible, building, 116
    interpolation, 11
    LaunchActivatedEventArgs, 533
    layouts, 489
        adaptive techniques, 491–492
        building vertical, 496

creating vertical, 493
formatting portrait, 496–500
lifecycles, 529
navigating, 503
NavigationCacheMode property, 512
NavigationHelper, 514–517
pixel densities, scaling for, 535–536
planning, 12
resolutions, checking, 490
running, 62
splash screens, 534
starting, 504–510, 532
state, managing, 511
surfaces, 20
SuspensionManager class, 544–548
VisualStateManager, 494
Win8 apps, 12. *See also* Win8 apps
applying
collections, 464
commands, 316–317
custom types, 551
Device Panels, 501
Property window, 54
ScrollViewer control, 208–210
Semantic Zoom control, 232–235
Simulator, 74–76
styles, 401
theme transitions, 428–429
transforms, 378–380
XAML Designer, 77–78
arguments, launching
configuring, 591
events, 533
arranging. *See* managing; moving
assets
graphics, formatting, 725
images, 559, 608–610
Visual Assets tab, 560–562
Assets folder, 70
assigning resources to properties, 397
associations
files, 607
images, formatting, 608
asynchronous data sharing, 644
attached properties, 124–127
dependency properties, 263–266
ToolTips, 331
attributes
images, configuring, 578
syntax, 146
text, configuring, 576
XAML, 89, 98–99
audio, toast notifications, 589
authentically digital phrase, 27
automatic sizing, 491
Auto sizing, 141-142
availability
data, 522–525
glyphs, 583–584
axes, gradients, 370

B

Back Stacks, 24
badges
notifications, 582
values, configuring, 582
base values, 245
basic pages, 483
BasicPage template, 484
basic wide tiles, 558. *See also* tiles
behavior
runtime, testing, 74
visual, defining, 414
BindingMode property, 443
bindings, 100
empty, 451
templates, 409–410
XAML
building converters, 442
collections, 451–458, 464–466
data context, 449
formatting, 438–441
grouping data with LINQ queries, 470–473
ItemsPanel, 461–462
managing collections, 469
modes, 443–445
RelativeSource property, 448
sources, 447
synchronizing displays, 467
templates, 459–460
update triggers, 446
value converters, 441
BitmapImage.Source, 600
blend integration, 79
blocks, building
alignment, 147
attached properties, 124–127
class libraries, 116–118

    Grid panel, 128–130
    layout properties, 139–140
    lengths, Grid panel, 142–144
    Margin/Padding properties, 146
    nesting panels, 137–138
    panels, 123
    relative positioning, 145
    sizing properties, 141
    StackPanel, 135–136
    VariableSizedWrapGrid panel, 131–134
    WinRT namespaces, 119
    XAML class hierarchies, 120–122
bold, 381
books, 727
bounding boxes, drawing, 351
branding
    starting, 578
    stopping, 578
brushes, 361
    gradient, 370–376
bubbling events, 284
building
    applications (apps), 49
    blocks, 116–147
        alignment, 147
        attached properties, 124–127
        class libraries, 116–118
        Grid panel, 128–130
        layout properties, 139–140
        lengths, Grid panel, 142–144
        Margin/Padding properties, 146
        nesting panels, 137–138
        panels, 123
        relative positioning, 145
        sizing properties, 141
        StackPanel, 135–136
        VariableSizedWrapGrid panel, 131–134
        WinRT namespaces, 119
        XAML class hierarchies, 120–122
    converters, 442
    extended splash screens, 537–543
    extensible applications, 116
    progress display rules, 166–168
    templates, 406–408
    vertical layouts, 496
Button element, 291
buttons, 175. *See also* controls
    Change Resolution, 490
    clicks, 287
    connecting, 507
    formatting, 400
    MoveLast, 467
    pressing, 287. *See also* events
    styles, formatting, 400

C

C#
    commands, 318-319
    events, 286
calculating values, 243
    dependency properties, 244
callbacks
    CreateDefaultValueCallback, 269
    dependency properties, 267–275
    formatting, 252
    PropertyChangedCallback, 268
    registering, 272
CanExecute() method, 316-317
CanGoBack property, 503
CanGoForward property, 503
Canvas panel, 123, 125, 128
Canvas widget, 20
capabilities of toast notifications, 586
certifying Win8 apps, 65–68
Change Resolution button, 490
change tracking, 243
ChangeView() method, 212
characteristics of Win8 apps, 13, 26–33
Charm Bar, 11, 19
charms
    devices, 19
    Settings, 19
        hooking Settings Flyout items, 56–62
        opening, 62
    Share, 24, 652
children
    disconnecting, 109
    formatting, 132
    transitions, 428
choice controls, 175
chromeless, 28
classes
    Application, 70
    ColorCollection, 452
    Colors, 365
    CompositeTransform, 378
    ContentControl, 176
    Control, 154–157, 405

DependencyObject, 120–121
dependency properties, 250–251
DependencyProperty, 250–251
Ellipse, 347
FileOpenPicker, 604
file pickers, 605–606
FileSavePicker, 604
FillRule, 355
FocusManager, 163–164
FolderPicker, 604
FrameworkElement, 139, 154–157
GestureRecognizer, 303
importing, 681
ItemsControl, 218
libraries, 116–118, 120
Line, 347
ListViewBase, 221–227
NavigationHelper, 482, 515
owner, specifying, 256
PointerRoutedEventArgs, 300
Polyline, 347
PropertyMetadata, 250–251, 272
Rectangle, 347
RelayCommand, 482
ResourceDictionary, 396
RoutedEventArgs, 292
SecondaryTile, 564–566
Selector, 229
Semantic Zoom control, 235
SettingsPane, 665
Shape, 348
storage, 628–631
StorageFile, 600, 628
StorageFolder, 600, 628
support, loading, 480–481
SuspensionManager, 71, 482, 544–548, 616
timeline animation, 420
transform, 378
UIElement, 122
    events, 296
    routed events, 296
    shapes, 348
VisualTransition, 424
XAML hierarchies, 120–122
Click event handler, 600
clicks
    buttons, 287
    events, handling, 540
    items, 224

closing applications (apps), 51
CLR (Common Language Runtime), 116, 243
CMYK (Cyan, Magenta, Yellow, Black), 362. *See also* colors
code
    resources in, 396–397
    targets, sharing, 656
CodePlex, 729
collaboration (Win8 apps), 34–35
collections
    applying, 464
    bindings, 451–458, 464–466
    formatting, 455
    managing, 469
    point, 357–358
    XAML, 94–95
CollectionViewSource
    configuring, 470
    formatting, 455
ColorCollection class, 452
Color Designer, 721
Color Explorer, updating, 522
colors
    explorers, re-building, 486–488
    favorite colors page, 722
    formatting, 716
    functionality, adding, 722
    futures, 717
    gradients, 370
    groups, adding, 698
    models, 362
    .NET Framework, 716
    selecting, 511
    specifying, 365–369
    standard colors page, 720
    structures, 363–364
    text, modifying, 49, 54
    viewing, 716
Colors class, 365
columns
    adding, 129
    Grid panel, 128. *See also* Grid panel
    VariableSizedWrapGrid panel, 131
ColumnSpan property, 131
CommandBars, 320–323, 327–328
commands, 10, 309–339, 315
    abstraction, 318
    applying, 316–317
    flyouts, 333–334

formatting, 666
MenuFlyouts, 335
message dialog boxes, 336–339
objects, connecting, 317
Relay, 71
surfaces, 312–314, 330
   AppBars, 320–325
   CommandBars, 320–323, 327–328
ToolTips, 331–332
UICommand API, 318–319
WinRT, 315
XAML, 315
CommonFileQuery enumeration, 632
common files, 71–72
applications (apps), 482
Common folder, 70
Common Language Runtime. *See* CLR
complex shapes, 355
components, navigating, 44
CompositeTransform class, 378
composite values, 622
Composition namespace, 116
concrete geometries, 356. *See also* geometries
concurrency, 454
configuring
   applications (apps), 19
   arguments, launching, 591
   attributes
      images, 578
      text, 576
   badge values, 582
   BitmapImage.Source, 600
   CollectionViewSource, 470
   data context, 455
   data providers, 650
   development environments, 49
   duration of toast notifications, 590
   pickers, 605–606
   startup pages, 507
   template content, 574
   TileId, 569
   XAML properties, 51–52
connecting
   buttons, 507
   commands to objects, 317
constructors, PropertyMetadata class, 272
containers, 622
   ApplicationDataContainer, 617, 619, 724
   data, 618

transitions, 428
content
   controls, 176–179
   properties, 90–92
   syntax, 176
   templates
      configuring, 574
      presenting, 411–412
   transitions, 428
ContentControl class, 176
Content property, 156, 410
ContentsChanged event, 632
context
   bindings, 449
   configuring, 455
contracts, 11
   activating, 658–663
   adding, 55
   commands, formatting, 666
   data requests, 646–649
   delayed sharing, 650–651
   implementing, 727
   responding, 658–663
   Settings, 665, 670–673
   settings, viewing, 667–669
   Share UIs, 655
   targets
      code, 656
      sharing, 652–654
   Win8 apps, 717
Control class, 154–157, 405
controlling default values, 267
controls, 39
   actions, 175
   choice, 175
   content, 176–179
   DatePicker, 193
   dates, 185, 192
   focus, 158–162
   FocusManager class, 163–164
   items, 217
      adding, 218–220
      ListViewBase class, 221–227
      selection properties, 228–230
   overview of, 154–157
   panels, 123
   primitive, 156
   progress display, 165
   properties, 169–172

rules, 166–168
ScrollViewer, 202, 206–210
    optical zoom, 212–214
    snap points, 215–216
Semantic Zoom, 17–18, 232–235
Slider, 181–184
StrokeDashCap, 352
StrokeEndLineCap, 352
StrokeStartLineCap, 352
templates, 122
text, 185
TextBox, 187, 189
time, 192
TimePicker, 193
ToggleSwitch, 180
transitions, 429
UX guidelines, 173–174
Viewbox, 202
XAML, 151. *See also* widgets
ControlTemplates, 405
ConvertBack() method, 442
converters
    building, 442
    values, 441
Convert() method, 442
copying
    files, 600
    XAML, 487
CreateContainer() method, 622
CreateDefaultValueCallback, 269
Create() methods, 272
CreateViewModel() method, 519
creating. *See* formatting
Ctrl-key combinations, 304
customer feedback, 717
customizing types, 551
custom namespaces (XAML), 101
CustomResource extension, 100
Custom Settings, selecting, 62
Cyan, Magenta, Yellow, Black. *See* CMYK

D

data
    applications, 616–617
    containers, 618
    context
        bindings, 449
        configuring, 455
    generating, 651

    local relational, 724
    making available, 522–525
    models, modifying, 702–704
    persistence, 724
    providers, configuring, 650
    sample, 726
    sharing, 513, 518, 653
    sources, adding, 519–521
    structures, 723, 726
    synchronization, 623, 644
    templates, modifying, 702
DataChanged event, 623
DataContext property, 449
DataModel folder, 70
DatePicker control, 193
dates
    controls, 185, 192
    formatting, 193–195
DateTemplate, adding, 705
debugging, 49, 116
declaring
    group header displays, 471
    share contracts, 653
default programs, specifying, 614
default scrollbars, 211
default values
    controlling, 267
    modifying, 257
DefaultViewModel property, 484–485, 700
deferrals, requests, 651
defining
    resources, 393
    styles, 727
    templates, 727
    UIs (user interfaces), 647
    visual behavior, 414
    XAML schemas, 97
delayed sharing, 650–651
deleting focus from elements, 162
delivery methods, notifications, 573
densities of pixels, scaling, 535–536
DependencyObject class, 120–121
dependency properties, 120, 124, 243
    attached properties, 124–127, 263–266
    callbacks, 267–275
    classes, 250–251
    examples, 246–249
    formatting, 252–262
    snippets, adding, 253

values
    calculating, 244
    determining base, 245
DependencyProperty class, 250–251
dependent animation, 419
design
    Color Designer, 721
    data structures, 723
    MVVM, 72
    UX, 718
    XAML, 77–78
desktop applications, 12
Determinate mode, 165
determining requirements, 716–717
development
    environments, configuring, 49
    processes, 46, 69
Device Panels, applying, 501
devices
    charms, 19
    synchronization, 16
Diagnostic namespace, 116
dialog boxes
    messages, 336–339
    New Item, 55
dictionaries, 392
    ObservableDictionary, 519
    resources, adding, 397
disconnecting children, 109
displaying. *See also* viewing
    applications (apps), 477
        adaptive layout techniques, 491–492
        adding data sources, 519–521
        applying Device Panels, 501
        basic pages, 483
        building vertical layouts, 496
        checking resolutions, 490
        common files, 482
        creating vertical layouts, 493
        DefaultViewModel, 484–485
        formatting portrait layouts, 496–500
        layouts, 489
        loading support classes, 480–481
        making data available, 522–525
        managing state, 511
        navigating, 503
        NavigationCacheMode property, 512
        NavigationHelper, 514–517
        re-building color explorers, 486–488

        sharing data, 513, 518
        starting, 504–510
        VisualStateManager, 494
    progress, 165
        properties, 169–172
        rules, 166–168
    synchronizing, 467
Document Object Models. *See* DOMs
Document Outline pane, 52
DOMs (Document Object Models), 576–581. *See also*
  models; objects
dot-down syntax, 421–422
drawing
    bounding boxes, 351
    brushes, 361
    colors
        models, 362
        specifying, 365–369
        structures, 363–364
    complex shapes, 355
    geometries, 356
    gradient brushes, 370–376
    objects, transforming, 377
    path geometries, 359–360
    Pen properties, 352–354
    point collections, 357–358
    shapes, 348–350
    transforms, applying, 378–380
    XAML, 347
dummy screens, formatting, 726
duration of toast notifications, 590
Duration property, 424
Dynamic namespace, 116

E

editing XAML, 487
editors, Manifest Editor, 64
elements
    animation, 416
    Button, 291
    focus, deleting, 162
    by location, searching, 109
    PathFigure, 359
    positioning, 541
    rectangles, 567–568
    rendering, 139
    sizing, 145
    transitions, 428
    XAML objects, 89

Ellipse class, 347
embedding scaling, 535
empty bindings, 451
enabling rails, 206
entry points, creating, 667
environments, development, 49
events
    arguments, launching, 533
    bubbling, 284
    clicks, handling, 540
    ContentsChanged, 632
    DataChanged, 623
    handlers
        formatting, 667
        QuerySubmitted, 683, 695
        registering, 57, 60, 293
        routed, 285–286
    handling, 58, 61, 292
    input, 295
    ItemClick, 708
    LoadState, 514
    PointerPoint property, 303
    Pointer property, 302
    registering, 646
    routed, 282–283
    SaveState, 514
    searching, 682–684
    SizeChanged, 494, 539–540
    sorting, 297–298
    SuggestionsRequested, 682
    testing, 288–289
    troubleshooting, 291
    UIElement class, 296
examples of dependency properties, 246–249
exceptions, UnauthorizedAccessException, 601
Execute() method, 316–317
executing queries, 634–637
exercises, progress displays, 166–168
explicit sizing, 491
Expression Blend, 79, 347
Express version, 73
extended splash screens, 537–543
eXtensible Application Markup Language. *See* XAML
extensible applications, building, 116
extensions
    StaticResource, 100, 395, 399
    TemplateBinding, 409, 438
    XAML markup, 100
external files, 392–393

F

favorite colors page, 722
feedback, customer, 717
fields, adding, 539
FileOpenPicker class, 604
files
    activating, 611–613
    associations, 607
    common, 71–72, 482
    copying, 600
    data
        applications, 616–617
        containers, 618
    default programs, specifying, 614
    exceptions, 601
    external, 392–393
    images
        assets, 608–610
        formatting, 608
        loading, 600–601
    local, 724
    pickers, 604–606
    queries, 632
        executing, 634–637
        options, 633
    settings
        managing, 622
        roaming, 623–625
    specifying, 569
    Storage APIs, 627
    storage classes, 628–631
    values, updating, 619–621
    Win8 apps, saving, 67
    XAML, 96. *See also* XAML
FileSavePicker class, 604
FileTypeFilter property, 605
filled windows, 30
FillRule class, 355
Filter_SelectionChanged() method, 705
flyouts
    commands, 333–334
    Settings Flyout, formatting, 667
focus, 158–161
    elements, deleting, 162
    state, 162
FocusManager class, 163–164
Focus() method, 162, 164
FocusState property, 162
FolderPicker class, 604

folders
- Assets, 70
- Common, 70
- DataModel, 70
- queries, 632

fonts, 381
- modifying, 53

formatting
- bounding boxes, 351
- buttons, 400
- callbacks, 252
- children, 132
- collections, 455
- CollectionViewSource, 455
- Color Designer, 721
- colors, 716
- commands, 666
- dates, 193–195
- dependency properties, 252–262
- dummy screens, 726
- entry points, 667
- event handlers, 667
- graphic assets, 725
- images, 608
- landing pages, 719
- LINQ queries, 470
- metadata, 252
- object notification, 578
- portrait layouts, 496–500
- projects (Win8 apps), 48
- Search Results template, 700–701
- Settings Flyout, 667
- Share UIs, 653
- styles, 400
- text, 381
- tiles, 558, 563. *See also* tiles
- titles, 506
- toast notifications, 587
- updates, 582
- vertical layouts, 493
- XAML bindings, 438–441

forums, Windows Store apps, 729
Frame.Navigate() method, 505
frames
- navigating, 503
- registering, 544

FrameworkElement class, 139, 154–157
free stuff, 13, 38–39
FromArgb() method, 363, 365

full screen view, 21
functionality, 15, 722
fundamentals, XAML, 87–88
futures, colors, 717

G

generating
- data, 651
- query suggestions, 686

geometries, 356
- paths, 359–360

GestureRecognizer class, 303
gestures, 295
- events, 297–298
- log in screens, 16
- touch languages, 22–23

GetChild() method, 106
GetChildrenCount() method, 106
GetCurrentPoint() method, 303
GetFilesAsync() method, 632
GetFocusedElement() method, 163
GetFocus() method, 292
GetFoldersAsync() method, 632
GetForCurrentView() method, 667
GetIntermediatePoint() method, 303
GetParent() method, 106
GetValue() method, 263
glyphs, 382
- availability, 583–584

GoBack() method, 512
GoForward() method, 512
gradient brushes, 370–376
GradientButtonTemplate template, 409
gradient stops, 370
graphics
- assets, formatting, 725
- bounding boxes. drawing, 351
- brushes, 361
- colors
  - models, 362
  - specifying, 365–369
  - structures, 363–364
- complex shapes, 355
- geometries, 356
- gradient brushes, 370–376
- objects, transforming, 377
- path geometries, 359–360
- Pen properties, 352–354
- point collections, 357–358

shapes, drawing, 348–350
transforms, applying, 378–380
XAML, drawing, 347
GridApp, 39
Grid panel, 123, 128–130
  lengths, 142–144
grids, sizing, 491
GridView, 132
grouping data, LINQ queries, 470–473
groups, 39
  colors, adding, 698
  headers, declaring displays, 471
  item controls, 225
guidelines, UX, 173–174
Gutenberg, Johannes, 382

H

handlers
  Click event, 600
  events
    formatting, 667
    QuerySubmitted, 683, 695
    registering, 293
    routed, 285–286
  registering, 286
Handles keyword, 286
handling
  events, 58, 61, 292, 540
  results, 705–707
  shared data, 653
Header property, 180
headers, 471
Height property, 129, 139
hierarchies
  classes, 120–122
  styles, 399
HighContrast theme, 402
high contrast themes, 403–404
HorizontalAlignment property, 147
HSV (hue, saturation, value), 362
hue, saturation, value. *See* HSV

I

ICommand interface, 315
icons, 609. *See also* images
IDictionary interface, 396
IEnumerable interface, 396
images
  assets, 559, 608–610

attributes, configuring, 578
loading, 600–601
log in screens, 16
scaling, 535
sizing, 609
specifying, 64
splash screens, 568
transparency, 609
immersive (Win8 apps), 28–29
implementing
  contracts, 727
  Semantic Zoom control, 233
  systems, 726–727
implicit styles, 398. *See also* styles
importing classes, 681
independent animation, 419
Indeterminate mode, 165
indexes, Tab key, 158
InitializeComponent() method, 522
input, 28
  APIs, 299–301
  events, 282, 295. *See also* events
InputScope property, 188
integers, modifying properties, 260
integration, blend, 79
IntelliSense, 254
interaction
  events, 297–298
  ListViewBase class, 221
  ScrollViewer control, 206
interfaces. *See also* screens; surfaces
  ICommand, 315
  IDictionary, 396
  IEnumerable, 396
  IValueConverter, 442
  navigating, 10–39
  Settings UI, 670–673
  Share UIs, 655
  widgets, 154–157
interpolating apps, 11
IsEnabled state, 511
IsInContact property, 302
IsOn property, 180
IsSynchronizedWithCurrent item, 467
italics, 381
ItemClick event, 708
items
  clicks, 224
  controls, 217

adding, 218–220
  ListViewBase class, 221–227
  selection properties, 228–230
IsSynchronizedWithCurrent, 467
pages, adding, 507
reordering, 224
retrieving, 708
runtime, adding, 135
search, 681. *See also* searching
Settings Flyout
  hooking to Settings charm, 56–62
  Settings charm, hooking to, 56–62
ItemsControl class, 218
ItemsPanel, 461–462
ItemsSource property, 451
IValueConverter interface, 442

K

KeyboardNavigationMode, 158
keyboards, 28
  APIs, 304
  navigating, 23, 158, 295
  touch, 39
KeyDown() method, 304
key frame animation, 420. *See also* animation
keys, navigating Tab, 158–161
KeyUp() method, 304
keywords, Handles, 286

L

landing pages, formatting, 719
languages
  touch, 22–23
  XAML, 85. *See also* XAML
LaunchActivatedEventArgs, 533
launching. *See also* starting
  applications (apps), 532
  arguments, configuring, 591
  event arguments, 533
layouts
  applications (apps), 489
    adaptive techniques, 491–492
    building vertical, 496
    creating vertical, 493
    formatting portrait, 496–500
  properties, 139–140
  testing, 493
  visibility, 495
  widgets, 202–210, 491

lengths, Grid panel, 142–144
libraries
  classes, 116–118
  navigating, 120
lifecycles
  applications (apps), 529
    applying custom types, 551
    extended splash screens, 537–543
    LaunchActivatedEventArgs, 533
    scaling for pixel densities, 535–536
    splash screens, 534
    starting, 532
    SuspensionManager class, 544–548
  testing, 727
linear animation, 420. *See also* animation
Line class, 347
LINQ queries, grouping data with, 470–473
ListViewBase class, 221–227
live tiles, 17, 32, 63–64
live updates, 16
loading
  images, 600–601
  support classes, 480–481
LoadState event, 514
LoadState() method, 547
local files, 724
local notifications, 573
local relational data, 724
location, searching elements by, 109
Lock Screen, 16
logical trees, 103–104
log in screens. *See* Lock Screen
logos, 561. *See also* images; tiles

M

maintenance, searching, 698–699
managing
  children, 132
  collections, 469
  file settings, 622
  panes, 51
  state, 511
Manifest Designer
  opening, 534
  viewing, 536
Manifest Editor, 64
manipulation
  APIs, 305
  events, 297–298

Margin property, 146
margins, 145
markup extensions, 100
Maximum property, 169
MaxZoomFactor property, 212
members, selection properties, 228
MenuFlyouts, 335
menus
   Start (Windows 7), 15, 17
   viewing, 10
MessageDialog, 315, 336–339
messages, dialog boxes, 336–339
metadata, formatting, 252
methods
   Add(), 218
   AddHandler(), 292–293
   Application.OnLaunched(), 505
   CanExecute(), 316–317
   ChangeView(), 212
   Convert(), 442
   ConvertBack(), 442
   Create(), 272
   CreateContainer(), 622
   CreateViewModel(), 519
   delivery notifications, 573
   Execute(), 316–317
   files, loading, 600
   Filter_SelectionChanged(), 705
   Focus(), 162, 164
   Frame.Navigate(), 505
   FromArgb(), 363, 365
   GetChild(), 106
   GetChildrenCount(), 106
   GetCurrentPoint(), 303
   GetFilesAsync(), 632
   GetFocus(), 292
   GetFocusedElement(), 163
   GetFoldersAsync(), 632
   GetForCurrentView(), 667
   GetIntermediatePoint(), 303
   GetParent(), 106
   GetValue(), 263
   GoBack(), 512
   GoForward(), 512
   InitializeComponent(), 522
   KeyDown(), 304
   KeyUp(), 304
   LoadState(), 547
   Move(), 464
   MoveCurrentTo(), 522
   Navigate(), 505, 518, 611
   Navigation_LoadState(), 705
   OnFileActivated(), 611
   OnLaunched(), 532–533, 611
   OnNavigatedTo(), 539, 611
   OnSearchActivated(), 682
   OnWindowCreated(), 666
   Register(), 257
   ReportStarted(), 659
   SaveAsync(), 549
   SaveState(), 547
   ScrollIntoView(), 522
   SetDataProver(), 650
   SetSource(), 601
   SetSourceAsync(), 600
   SetValue(), 254, 263
   UpdateAsync(), 566
   UpdateSource(), 446
Microsoft Dev Center for Windows Store apps, 729
Minimum property, 169
MinZoomFactor property, 212
MiterLimit property, 352
models
   colors, 362
   data, modifying, 702–704
   DefaultViewModel, 484–485
   ScRGB, 365
Model-View-ViewModel. *See* MVVM
modes
   bindings, 443–445
   Determinate, 165
   Indeterminate, 165
   ScrollViewer control, 211
modifying
   data models, 702–704
   data templates, 702
   default values, 257
   fonts, 53
   properties
      integers, 260
      strings, 254
   text, 49, 54, 381
   value properties, 267
   width, 21, 501
   XAML, 53
mouse movements, 23, 28, 295
MoveCurrentTo() method, 522
MoveLast button, 467

movement, naturalness of, 415
Move() methods, 464
moving. *See also* managing
   elements, 541
   panes, 51
   tans, 51
multiple menus, viewing, 10
multi-touch support, 38
MVVM (Model-View-ViewModel) design pattern, 72

N

namespaces
   class libraries, 116–118
   referencing, 544
   WinRT, 119
   XAML, 96
      custom, 101
      standard, 97
naming
   images, 568
   properties, 255
Navigate() method, 505, 518, 611
navigating
   applications (apps), 503
   class libraries, 120
   DOMs, 576–581
   frames, 503
   interfaces, 10–39
   keyboards, 23, 158, 295
   object trees (XAML), 105
   pages, 503, 708
   parameters, 515
   queries, 695–697
   to results, 708–709
   Tab key, 158–161
   testing, 727
   Visual Assets tab, 560–562
   visual trees (XAML), 106–108
   Win8 apps
      components, 44
      development process, 46
   XAML, 52
NavigationCacheMode property, 512
NavigationHelper, 71, 514–517
NavigationHelper class, 482
   overriding, 515
Navigation_LoadState() method, 705
nesting panels, 137–138
.NET Framework
   APIs, 116–118
   colors, 716
New Item dialog box, 55
notifications, 555, 572
   badges, 582
   delivery methods, 573
   DOMs, 576–581
   local, 573
   objects, formatting, 578
   periodic, 573
   push, 573
   scheduled, 573
   sending, 575
   sizing, 575
   tiles, 574–575
   toast, 585–591
   viewing, 32

O

objects
   ApplicationDataContainer, 617, 619, 724
   commands, connecting, 317
   notification, formatting, 578
   transforming, 377
   XAML
      elements, 89
      trees, 105
ObservableDictionary, 71, 519
OneWay binding, 443
OnFileActivated() method, 611
OnLaunched() method, 532–533, 611
OnNavigatedTo() method, 539, 611
OnSearchActivated() method, 682
OnShareTargetActivated, responding, 653
OnWindowCreated() method, 666
opening
   Manifest Designer, 534
   Settings charm, 62
optical zoom, 207, 212–214
options, queries, 633
Orientation property, 131
OriginalSource property, 285
overriding NavigationHelper class, 515
owner classes, specifying, 256

P

Padding property, 145–146, 156
pages
   applications (apps), 483

favorite colors, 722
items, adding, 507
landing, formatting, 719
navigating, 503, 708
standard colors, 720
startup
adding, 506
configuring, 507
panels, 123
dependency properties, 124–127
nesting, 137–138
panes
Document Outline, 52
managing, 51
XAML, 77
parameters
navigating, 515
passing, 518
passing parameters, 518
passwords, log in screens, 16
PathFigure elements, 359
paths, 347
geometries, 359–360
patterns, MVVM, 72
PenLineCap enumeration, 352
Pen properties, 352–354
periodic notifications, 573
persistence, data, 724
Petzold, Charles, 729
pickers
date and time, 192
files, 604, 604–606
pinning, 563
pixels, 141–142. See also resolutions
densities, scaling for, 535–536
planning applications (apps), 12
POCO property, 252
point collections, 357–358
PointerDeviceType enumeration, 301
PointerPoint property, events, 303
PointerPressed event, 292, 299
Pointer property, events, 302
PointerReleased event, 292
PointerRoutedEventArgs class, 300
pointers, 287
polygons, 347
Polyline class, 347
Popup widgets, 330
portrait layouts, formatting, 496–500

positioning
elements, 541
relative, 145
pre-defined animation, 423
predicting text, 188–189
preferences, 616. See also configuring
presenters, 411
presenting content, templates, 411–412
pressing buttons, 287. See also events
PrimaryCommands property, 327
primary tiles, 558
primitive controls, 156
processes, development, 46, 69
programming animation, 415
Programming Windows: Writing Windows 8 Apps With C# and XAML, 729
programs, specifying default, 614
ProgressBar, 165
progress display, 165
properties, 169–172
rules, 166–168
ProgressRing, 165
projects
events, 288
Settings Flyout item, adding, 55
Win8 apps, creating, 48
properties
animation, 421
attached, 124–127
BindingMode, 443
CanGoBack, 503
CanGoForward, 503
CLR, 243
ColumnSpan, 131
Content, 156, 410
Control class, 157
DataContext, 449
default scrollbars, 211
DefaultViewModel, 484–485, 700
dependency, 120, 124, 243
adding snippets, 253
attached properties, 124–127, 263
calculating values, 244
callbacks, 267–275
classes, 250–251
determining base values, 245
examples, 246–249
formatting, 252–262
Duration, 424

FileTypeFilter, 605
FocusState, 162
Header, 180
Height, 129, 139
HorizontalAlignment, 147
InputScope, 188
integers, modifying, 260
IsInContact, 302
IsOn, 180
ItemsSource, 451
layouts, 139–140
Margin, 146
Maximum, 169
MaxZoomFactor, 212
Minimum, 169
MinZoomFactor, 212
MiterLimit, 352
naming, 255
NavigationCacheMode, 512
Orientation, 131
OriginalSource, 285
Padding, 145–146, 156
Pen, 352–354
POCO, 252
Pointer events, 302
PointerPoint events, 303
PrimaryCommands, 327
progress display, 169–172
registering, 252
RelativeSource, 448
RenderTransform, 379
RequestedTheme, 402
resources, assigning, 397
RowSpan, 131
SecondaryCommands, 327
selection, 228–230
SelectionBoxItem, 229
sizing, 141
strings, modifying, 254
StrokeLineJoin, 352
syntax, 146
TabNavigation, 158–161
values, modifying, 267
VerticalAlignment, 147
Visibility, 158, 496
Width, 139
Win8 apps, 188–191
XAML, 51–52, 89–92
ZoomMode, 212

ZoomSnapPoints, 213
ZoomSnapPointsType, 213
Properties window, 127
PropertyChangedCallback, 268
PropertyMetadata class, 250–251, 272
Property window, applying, 54
providers, data, 650
punctuation marks, 382
push notifications, 573

Q

queries
   files, 632
      executing, 634–637
      options, 633
   folders, 632
   LINQ, grouping data with, 470–473
   navigating, 695–697
   suggestions, 685–694
QuerySubmitted event handler, 683, 695
quick tours, 13–15
quotas, storage, 623

R

rails, ScrollViewer control, 206
re-building color explorers, 486–488
receiving shared dates, 645
Rectangle class, 347
rectangles, elements, 567–568
red, green, blue. *See* RGB
referencing
   namespaces, 544
   resources, 395
registering
   callbacks, 272
   event handlers, 57, 60, 293
   events, 646
   frames, 544
   handlers, 286
   properties, 252
Register() method, 257
relative positioning, 145
RelativeSource property, 100, 448
RelayCommand class, 482
Relay commands, 71
renaming files, 569. *See also* naming
rendering elements, 139
RenderTransform property, 379
reordering items, 224

reports, Win8 app certification, 67
ReportStarted() method, 659
RequestedTheme property, 402
requesting pins, 563
requests, 646
   data, 646–649
   deferrals, 651
requirements, Win8 apps, 489, 716–717
resolutions
   applications (apps), checking, 490
   screens, 30, 489
ResourceDictionary class, 396
resources, 392–394, 727
   in code, 396–397
   defining, 393
   dictionaries, adding, 397
   properties, assigning, 397
   referencing, 395
   styles, 398
      hierarchies, 399
      in Visual Studio, 400–401
   themes, 398
responding
   to activation, 569–570
   contracts, 658–663
   OnShareTargetActivated, 653
responsive (Win8 apps), 30–31
restoring states, 545
results
   handling, 705–707
   navigating to, 708–709
   Search Results template, 700–701
retrieving
   items, 708
   templates, 574, 582
   tile templates, 576
RGB (red, green, blue), 362. *See also* colors
roaming settings, 623–625
RotateTransform, 377
RoutedEventArgs class, 292
routed events, 282–286
rows
   Grid panel, 128. *See also* Grid panel
   VariableSizedWrapGrid panel, 131
RowSpan property, 131
rules, progress display, 166–168
running
   applications (apps), 62
   Simulator, 49–50

runtime, 116
   behavior, testing, 74
   items, adding, 135
Runtime namespace, 116

S

sample apps, selecting, 66
sample data, 726
SaveAsync() method, 549
SaveState event, 514
SaveState() method, 547
saving
   files, 67
   states, 546
ScaleTransform, 377
scaling
   images, 609
   for pixel densities, 535–536
scheduled notifications, 573
schemas (XAML), 97
screens. *See also* views
   dummy, formatting, 726
   Lock Screen, 16
   resolutions, 30, 489
   splash, 534, 537–543
   Start Screen, 11, 15, 17
ScRGB model, 365
scrollbars, defaults, 211
ScrollIntoView() method, 522
ScrollViewer control, 202, 206–210
   modes, 211
   optical zoom, 212–214
   snap points, 215–216
searchboxes, adding, 681
searching
   data models, modifying, 702–704
   elements by location, 109
   events, 682–684
   maintenance, 698–699
   overview of, 680–681
   queries, 685. *See also* queries
      navigating, 695–697
      suggestions, 685–694
   results
      handling, 705–707
      navigating to, 708–709
      Search Results template, 700–701
Search Results template, 700–701
SecondaryCommands property, 327

SecondaryTile class, 564–566
secondary tiles, 563
selecting
   colors, 511
      Custom Settings, 62
      sample apps, 66
SelectionBoxItem property, 229
selection properties, 228–230
Selector class, 229
semantic events, 297–298
Semantic Zoom control, 17–18, 232–235
sending
   notifications, 575
   updates, 579, 582
SetDataProver() method, 650
SetSourceAsync() method, 600
SetSource() method, 601
settings
   files
      managing, 622
      roaming, 623–625
   viewing, 667–669
Settings charm, 19
   opening, 62
   Settings Flyout items, 56–62
Settings contract, 665, 670–673
Settings Flyout
   adding, 55
   formatting, 667
   Settings charm, hooking to, 56–62
SettingsPane class, 665
SetValue() method, 254, 263
Shape class, 348
shapes
   complex, 355
   drawing, 348–350
   geometries, 356
Share charm, 24, 652
Share UIs, 655
sharing
   data, 513, 518
      handling, 653
      synchronization, 644
   delayed, 650–651
   targets, 652–654, 656
signal completion, 651
Simulator
   applying, 74–76
   layouts, testing, 493

running, 49–50
SizeChanged event, 494, 539–540
sizing
   Auto, 141–142
   automatic, 491
   elements, 145
   explicit, 491
   grids, 491
   images, 609
   notifications, 575
   properties, 141
   star, 142
SkewTransform, 377
Slider control, 181–184
snapped windows, 30
snap points, ScrollViewer control, 207, 215–216
snippets, dependency properties, 253
sorting events, 297–298
sources, bindings, 447
sparse storage, 243
specifying
   colors, 365–369
   default programs, 614
   files, 569
   images, 64
   owner classes, 256
spell checking systems, 188–189
   system-wide, 38
splash screens, 534
   extended, 537–543
Split App (XAML) template, 48
square primary tiles, 558. *See also* tiles
StackPanel, 123, 135–136
stacks, Back Stacks, 24
standard colors page, 720
standard hexadecimal color code, 365
standard namespaces, 97
star sizing, 142
starting
   applications (apps), 504–510, 532
   branding, 578
   debugging, 49
Start menus, 15
   Windows 7, 17
Start Screen, 11, 15, 17
startup pages
   adding, 506
   configuring, 507
states

application data, 616
focus, 162
IsEnabled, 511
managing, 511
push notifications, 573
restoring, 545
saving, 546
templates, 405
views, 21, 489
visual, creating, 496
StaticResource extension, 100, 395, 399
static tiles, 32
stopping branding, 578. *See also* closing
stops, 370
storage
   APIs, 627
   classes, 628–631
   roaming, 623
   sparse, 243
   web, 724
StorageFile class, 600, 628
StorageFolder class, 600, 628
storyboards, animation, 417
strings, modifying properties, 254
StrokeDashCap control, 352
StrokeEndLineCap control, 352
StrokeLineJoin property, 352
StrokeStartLineCap control, 352
structures
   colors, 363–364
   data, 723, 726
styles. *See also* formatting; text
   applying, 401
   buttons, formatting, 400
   defining, 727
   hierarchies, 399
   implicit, 398. *See also* styles
   resources, 398
   text, 381
   in Visual Studio, 400–401
stylus, 28, 295
suggestions, queries, 685–694
SuggestionsRequested event, 682
support
   classes, loading, 480–481
   multi-touch, 38
   screen resolutions, 489
surfaces
   applications (apps), 20

commands, 312–314, 330
   AppBars, 320–325
   CommandBars, 320–325
SuspensionManager class, 71, 482, 544–548, 616
synchronization, 16
   data, 623
   displays, 467
   sharing, 644
syntax
   attributes, 146
   binding, 438
   content, 176
   dot-down, 421–422
   properties, 146
   transitions, 429
   XAML, 89
System.Collections, 118
system commands, 10. *See also* commands
System.Deployment namespace, 117–118
System.Reosurces, 116
systems, implementing, 726–727
system-wide spellchecking, 38

T

Tab key, navigating, 158–161
TabNavigation property, 158–161
tabs
   managing, 51
   Visual Assets, 560–562
targets, sharing, 652–654
   code, 656
TemplateBinding extension, 100, 409, 438
templates, 405
   BasicPage, 484
   bindings, 409–410, 459–460
   building, 406–408
   content
      configuring, 574
      presenting, 411–412
   Control class, 405
   controls, 122
   data, modifying, 702
   DateTemplate, adding, 705
   defining, 727
   GradientButtonTemplate, 409
   retrieving, 574, 582
   Search Results, 700–701
   splash screens, 568
   Split App (XAML), 48

tiles, retrieving, 576
VisualStateManager, 414
Visual Studio, 17, 39, 49–50, 70
terminology, XAML, 382–383
testing
    events, 288–289
    layouts, 493
    lifecycles, 727
    navigating, 727
    runtime behavior, 74
    Win8 apps, 66
text. *See also* content
    attributes, configuring, 576
    bounding boxes, 351
    colors, modifying, 49, 54
    controls, 185
    fonts, modifying, 53
    formatting, 381
    prediction, 188–189
TextBox control, 187-189
themes. *See also* styles
    animation, 423
    high contrast, 402–404
    resources, 398
    transitions, 428–429
    Win8 apps, 402
TickPlacement, 181
TileId, configuring, 569
tiles, 555
    DOMs, 576–581
    formatting, 563
    live, 17, 32, 63–64
    notifications, 574–575
    primary, 558
    secondary, 563
    static, 32
    templates, retrieving, 576
time controls, 192
timelines, animation, 420
TimePicker control, 193
titles, formatting, 506
toast notifications, 585–591
ToggleButton, 179
Toggled event handlers, adding, 671
ToggleSwitch control, 180
ToolTip commands, 331–332
touches, 23, 295
    keyboards, 39
    languages, 22–23

ScrollViewer control, 206
touch-first, 28
tracking change, 243
transforms
    applying, 378–380
    objects, 377
transitions
    animation, 424–426
    children, 428
    containers, 428
    content, 428
    controls, 429
    elements, 428
    themes, 428–429
TranslateTransform, 377
transparency, images, 609
trees (XAML), 103–108
    objects, 105
    visual, 106–108
triggers, updating, 446
troubleshooting
    events, 291
    exceptions, 601. *See also* exceptions
    routed events, 283
    UnauthorizedAccessException, 601–602
TwoWay binding, 443
types
    .NET Framework Class library, 117
    of notifications, 573
    of panels, 123
typography (XAML), 381

U

UICommand API, 318–319
UIElement class, 122
    events, 296
    routed events, 296
    shapes, 348
UIs (user interfaces). *See also* interfaces
    defining, 647
    Settings, 670–673
    Share, 655
    widgets, 154–157
UnauthorizedAccessException, 601
unpinning, 564
UpdateAsync() method, 566
UpdateSource() method, 446
updating
    Color Explorer, 522

sending, 579, 582
triggers, 446
values, 619–621
UserControl, 670
user interfaces. *See* UIs
user preferences, 616. *See also* configuring
UX
    design, 718
    guidelines, 173–174

V

validating Win8 app certifications, 65
values
    badges, configuring, 582
    calculating, 243
    composite, 622
    converters, 441
    default
        controlling, 267
        modifying, 257
    dependency properties
        calculating, 244
        determining base, 245
    properties, modifying, 267
    updating, 619–621
VariableSizedWrapGrid panel, 123, 131
VerticalAlignment property, 147
vertical layouts. *See also* layouts
    building, 496
    formatting, 493
Viewbox control, 202
viewing. *See also* displaying
    certification kits, 68
    Charm Bar, 19
    colors, 716
    Manifest Designer, 536
    multiple menus, 10
    notifications, 32
    Semantic Zoom control, 17–18
    settings, 667–669
    updates, 16
views
    GridView, 132
    states, 21, 489
VirtualizingPanel class, 132
visibility, 415
    layouts, 495
Visibility property, 158, 496
Visual Assets tab, 560–562

Visual Basic
    binding, 445
    commands, 318, 319
    events, 286
visual behavior, defining, 414
VisualStateManager, 496
    applications (apps), 494
    templates, 414
Visual Studio
    2013 express, 73
    projects, creating, 48
    Simulator. *See* Simulator
    styles in, 400
    templates, 17, 39, 49–50, 70
VisualTransition class, 424
visual trees, 103–104, 106–108

W

web storage, 724
widgets
    actions, 175
    AppBars, 324–325
    Canvas, 20
    choice, 175
    focus, 158–161, 162
    FocusManager class, 163–164
    layouts, 202–205, 491
    overview of, 154–157
    Popup, 330
    portrait layouts, 496
    progress display, 165
        properties, 169–172
        rules, 166–168
    ScrollViewer control, 206–210
    UX guidelines, 173–174
width, modifying, 21, 501
Width property, 139
Win8 apps, 12. *See also* applications
    certifying, 65–68
    characteristics of, 13, 26–33
    class libraries, 116–118
    collaboration, 34–35
    common files, 71–72
    components, navigating, 44
    contracts, 55, 642, 717
    development process, 69
    Expression Blend, 79
    files, saving, 67
    live tiles, adding, 63–64

projects, creating, 48
properties, 188–191
Property window, applying, 54
requirements, 489, 716–717
Settings Flyout item, 56–62
Simulator
    applying, 74–76
    running, 49–50
testing, 66
themes, 402
Visual Studio
    2013 express, 73
    templates, 70
XAML
    designer, 77–78
    modifying, 53
    properties, 51–52
windows
    Properties, 127
    Property, applying, 54
Windows 7
    Start menus, 15, 17
Windows App Certification Kit, 65. *See also* certifying
Windows.Data namespace, 118
Windows Store apps forums, 729
Windows.UI.ApplicationSettings namespaces, 59
Windows.UI.Popups namespaces, 59
WinRT
    commands, 315
    input handling, 299
WinRT namespaces, 119
workflows (XAML), 88

X

XAML (eXtensible Application Markup Language), 85, 89
    animation, 415
    attributes, 98–99
    bindings
        building converters, 442
        collections, 451–458, 464–466
        data context, 449
        formatting, 438–441
        grouping data, LINQ queries, 470
        ItemsPanel, 461–462
        managing collections, 469
        modes, 443–445
        RelativeSource property, 448
        sources, 447
        synchronizing displays, 467
        templates, 459–460
        update triggers, 446
        value converters, 441
    bounding boxes, drawing, 351
    brushes, 361
    class hierarchies, 120–122
    collections, 94–95
    colors
        models, 362
        specifying, 365–369
        structures, 363–364
    commands, 315
    complex shapes, 355
    content properties, 90–92
    controls, 151
    copying, 487
    designer, 77–78
    editing, 487
    events, 286
    fundamentals, 87–88
    geometries, 356
    gradient brushes, 370–376
    graphics, drawing, 347
    markup extensions, 100
    modifying, 53
    namespaces, 96
        custom, 101
        standard, 97
    navigating, 52
    objects, transforming, 377
    path geometries, 359–360
    Pen properties, 352–354
    point collections, 357–358
    properties, 51–52
    splash screens, 534
    syntax, 89
    terminology, 382–383
    transforms, applying, 378–380
    trees, 103–108
        objects, 105
        visual, 106–108
    typography, 381
    workflows, 88
x:Boolean attribute, 99
x:Class attribute, 98
x:Double attribute, 99
x:Int32 attribute, 99
x:Key attribute, 98, 392

x:Name attribute, 98
x:Null attribute, 99
x:String attribute, 99

Z

zoom
- ScrollViewer control, 207, 212–214
- Semantic Zoom control, 17–18, 232

ZoomMode property, 212
ZoomSnapPoints property, 213
ZoomSnapPointsType property, 213

The Fluent Learning Series

We Don't Want to Teach You Things. We Want to Help You Learn

Visit **informit.com/fluent** for a complete list of available publications.

Titles in **The Fluent Learning Series** are based on the principles of cognitive science and instructional design and are true tutorials that will help you build effective working models for understanding a large and complex subject.

Most introductory books just talk at you and give you "exercises" that have more to do with taking dictation than actually learning. **The Fluent Learning Series** is different. These books guide you through learning the way your mind likes to learn: by solving puzzles, making connections, and building genuine understanding instead of just memorizing random facts.

Make sure to connect with us!
informit.com/socialconnect

ALWAYS LEARNING   PEARSON

FREE Online Edition

Your purchase of **Fluent Windows® 8.1 App Development** includes access to a free online edition for 45 days through the **Safari Books Online** subscription service. Nearly every Sams book is available online through **Safari Books Online**, along with thousands of books and videos from publishers such as Addison-Wesley Professional, Cisco Press, Exam Cram, IBM Press, O'Reilly Media, Prentice Hall, Que, and VMware Press.

Safari Books Online is a digital library providing searchable, on-demand access to thousands of technology, digital media, and professional development books and videos from leading publishers. With one monthly or yearly subscription price, you get unlimited access to learning tools and information on topics including mobile app and software development, tips and tricks on using your favorite gadgets, networking, project management, graphic design, and much more.

Activate your FREE Online Edition at informit.com/safarifree

STEP 1: Enter the coupon code: LZRTREH.

STEP 2: New Safari users, complete the brief registration form. Safari subscribers, just log in.

If you have difficulty registering on Safari or accessing the online edition, please e-mail customer-service@safaribooksonline.com